Research Anthology on Racial Equity, Identity, and Privilege

Information Resources Management Association
USA

Volume II

Published in the United States of America by
IGI Global
Information Science Reference (an imprint of IGI Global)
701 E. Chocolate Avenue
Hershey PA, USA 17033
Tel: 717-533-8845
Fax: 717-533-8661
E-mail: cust@igi-global.com
Web site: http://www.igi-global.com

Copyright © 2022 by IGI Global. All rights reserved. No part of this publication may be reproduced, stored or distributed in any form or by any means, electronic or mechanical, including photocopying, without written permission from the publisher. Product or company names used in this set are for identification purposes only. Inclusion of the names of the products or companies does not indicate a claim of ownership by IGI Global of the trademark or registered trademark.

Library of Congress Cataloging-in-Publication Data

Names: Information Resources Management Association, editor.
Title: Research anthology on racial equity, identity, and privilege /
   Information Resources Management Association, editor.
Description: Hershey, PA : Information Science Reference, [2022] | Includes
   bibliographical references and index. | Summary: "This 3-volume
   reference book analyzes the impact that past racial inequality has on
   society today and discusses the barriers that were created throughout
   history and the ways to overcome them and heal as a community,
   iincluding topics such as critical race theory, transformative change,
   and intergenerational trauma"-- Provided by publisher.
Identifiers: LCCN 2021056171 (print) | LCCN 2021056172 (ebook) | ISBN
   9781668445075 (hardcover) | ISBN 9781668445082 (ebook)
Subjects: LCSH: Racism. | Race. | Ethnicity. | Discrimination. | Equality.
   | Social structure.
Classification: LCC HT1521 .R4568 2022 (print) | LCC HT1521 (ebook) | DDC
   305.8--dc23/eng/20211119
LC record available at https://lccn.loc.gov/2021056171
LC ebook record available at https://lccn.loc.gov/2021056172

British Cataloguing in Publication Data
A Cataloguing in Publication record for this book is available from the British Library.

The views expressed in this book are those of the authors, but not necessarily of the publisher.

For electronic access to this publication, please contact: eresources@igi-global.com.

Editor-in-Chief

Mehdi Khosrow-Pour, DBA
Information Resources Management Association, USA

Associate Editors

Steve Clarke, *University of Hull, UK*
Murray E. Jennex, *San Diego State University, USA*
Ari-Veikko Anttiroiko, *University of Tampere, Finland*

Editorial Advisory Board

Sherif Kamel, *American University in Cairo, Egypt*
In Lee, *Western Illinois University, USA*
Jerzy Kisielnicki, *Warsaw University, Poland*
Amar Gupta, *Arizona University, USA*
Craig van Slyke, *University of Central Florida, USA*
John Wang, *Montclair State University, USA*
Vishanth Weerakkody, *Brunel University, UK*

List of Contributors

Abu Rabia, Hazza / *University of Hartford, USA* 1155
Adams, David A. / *Urban Assembly, USA* 241
Ahluwalia, Muninder K. / *Montclair State University, USA* 398
Akinro, Ngozi / *Texas Wesleyan University, USA* 1025
Amponsah, Samual / *University of Ghana, Ghana* 1132
Atkins, Celeste / *University of Arizona, USA & Cochise College, USA* 488
Audley, Shannon / *Smith College, USA* 538
Awokoya, Janet / *California Lutheran University, USA* 946
Ba', Stefano / *Leeds Trinity University, UK* 522
Bailey, Ronald William / *University of Illinois at Urbana-Champaign, USA* 921
Barrón, Daisy Indira / *Missouri State University, USA* 1321
Billups, Christie / *Lewis University, USA* 41
Bledsoe, T. Scott / *Azusa Pacific University, USA* 122
Brant-Rajahn, Sarah N. / *Messiah University, USA* 1365
Brookfield, Stephen D. / *University of St. Thomas, USA* 1173
Brown, Karen H. / *Independent Researcher, USA* 90
Browning, Thomas / *Wayne State College, USA* 985
Bryant, Jordan J. / *Lamar University, USA* 271
Campbell, Danella May / *Manchester Metropolitan University, UK* 325
Carbone, Valeria / *University of Buenos Aires, Argentina* 768
Carlson, Bronwyn / *Macquarie University, Australia* 142
Carrim, Nasima Mohamed Hoosen / *University of Pretoria, South Africa* 1186
Chang, Eunjung / *Francis Marion University, USA* 709
Christensen, Jeffrey K. / *Lewis and Clark College, USA* 25
Collier, Crystal S. / *Argosy University, USA* 398
Conwill, William Louis / *University of Illinois at Urbana-Champaign, USA* 921
Curry, Lauren C. / *Black Lesbian Literary Collective, USA* 601
Dahle-Huff, Kari / *Montana State University, Billings, USA* 228
Dallman, Laura L. / *George Mason University, USA* 1
Dar, Sadhvi / *Queen Mary University of London, UK* 585
DeMulder, Elizabeth K. / *George Mason University, USA* 1
Destine, Shaina V. / *University of Tennessee, Knoxville, USA* 1096
Destine, Shaneda L. / *University of Tennessee, Knoxville, USA* 1096
Dogbey, James / *Texas A&M University – Corpus Christi, USA* 1132
Dominguez, Maggie / *University of Phoenix, USA* 1254

Dopwell, Donna M. / *Middle Tennessee State University, USA* 601
Dorn-Medeiros, Cort M. / *Lewis and Clark College, USA* 25
Duru, Adaobi Vivian / *University of Louisiana at Monroe, USA* 1025
Eakins, Sheldon Lewis / *Shoshone-Bannock School District, USA* 241
Engebretson, Kathryn E. / *Indiana University – Bloomington, USA* 985
Ezikwelu, Evelyn / *University of Utah, USA* 689
Falaise, Josue B. / *GOMO Educational Services, USA* 241
Farooqui, Jannat Fatima / *University of Delhi, India* 430
Frolow, Miriam L. / *University of Phoenix, USA* 1254
Fuentes, Milton A. / *Montclair State University, USA* 398
Gibson, Eva M. / *Austin Peay State University, USA* 1365
Ginsburg, Julia L. / *Smith College, USA* 538
Grant, Marquis C. / *Grand Canyon University, USA* 157
Grant, Marquis Carter / *Grand Canyon University, USA* 1224
Griffen, Aaron J. / *DSST Public Schools, USA* 847
Griffen, Karen D. / *Creighton University, USA* 847
Hargrave, Constance P. / *Iowa State University, USA* 1043
Harushimana, Immaculee / *Lehman College (CUNY), USA* 946
Herridge, Andrew S. / *Texas Tech University, USA* 1069
Hobley Jr., Montelleo DeLeon / *Mississippi State University, USA* 1069
Howell, Crystal D. / *Indiana University – Bloomington, USA* 985
Hur, Jung Won / *Auburn University, USA* 751
Jackson, Helen C. / *African Scientific Institute, USA* 810
Johnson, Natasha N. / *Georgia State University, USA* 105
Johnson, Thaddeus L. / *Georgia State University, USA* 105
Johnson, Tonya / *Bronx Community College, City University of New York, USA* 1206
Jones, V. Nikki / *Middle Tennessee State University, USA* 601
Karkouti, Ibrahim M. / *The American University in Cairo, Egypt* 1155
Kaushik, Archana / *University of Delhi, India* 430
Kavanagh, Kara Maura / *James Madison University, USA* 375
Kemp, Roxanne Elliott / *Elliott Kemp, USA* 970
King, Victorene L. / *Divergent Consulting, USA* 886
Koenig, Kirsten A. / *Northcentral University, USA* 62
Kumi-Yeboah, Alex / *University at Albany (SUNY), USA* 1132
Lavette Williams, Tanishia / *The New School, USA* 1281
Lawrence, Salika A. / *The College of New Jersey, USA* 1299
Lehner, Edward / *Bronx Community College, City University of New York, USA* 1206
Lertora, Ian / *Texas Tech University, USA* 25
Lisbon, April J. / *Spotsylvania County Public Schools, USA* 907
López, Minda Morren / *Texas State University, San Marcos, USA* 623
Maätita, Florence / *Southern Illinois University Edwardsville, USA* 1346
Madondo, Silas Memory / *CeDRE International Africa, Zimbabwe* 522
Maultsby, Michelle Lee / *South Carolina State University, USA* 729
McCray, Carissa / *The Harley-Jackson Foundation, USA* 1330
Miles, Annette Deborah / *University of the District of Columbia, USA* 451
Moahi, Kgomotso H. / *University of Botswana, Botswana* 1387

Monroe, Calvin / *Saint Mary's College of California, USA* 1116

Mootoo, Alexis Nicole / *University of South Florida, USA* 933

Nkosinkulu, Zingisa / *University of South Africa, South Africa* 567

Nussli, Natalie / *University of Applied Sciences and Arts Northwestern Switzerland, Switzerland* . 350

Oh, Kevin / *University of San Francisco, USA* 350

Organista, Joél-Léhi / *Columbia University, USA* 505

Padía, Lilly B. / *New York University, USA* 791

Pickett Miller, Niya / *Samford University, USA* 257

Price-Williams, Shelley / *Southern Illinois University Edwardsville, USA* 1346

R'boul, Hamza / *Public University of Navarre, Spain* 466

Reed, Thomas / *University of San Diego, USA* 1005

Rudge, Lucila T. / *University of Montana, USA* 867

Sandifer, Mariama Cook / *Columbus State University, USA* 1365

Saunders, Jane M. / *Texas State University, San Marcos, USA* 623

Schneider, Jennifer / *Community College of Philadelphia, USA* 212

Senne, Yvonne / *Tshwane University of Technology, South Africa* 1186

Setterlund, Kimberly A. / *Azusa Pacific University, USA* 122

Shange, Xolani Mathews / *University of South Africa, South Africa* 283

Shannon, Casey R. / *Yeshiva University, USA* 398

Sharp, Sacha / *Indiana University, USA* 191

Shockley, Ebony Terrell / *University of Maryland – College Park, USA* 451

Simpson Jr., Artha L. / *Lamar University, USA* 271

Simpson, Teresa E. / *Lamar University, USA* 271

Small, Dwayne / *DePaul University, USA* 680

Spencer, Kalina G. / *John Carroll University, USA* 833

Stribling, Stacia M. / *George Mason University, USA* 1

Thomas, Tammara Petrill / *Winston-Salem State University, USA* 729

Thorsos, Nilsa J. / *National University, USA* 415

Travers, Christopher S. / *North Carolina State University, USA* 1079

Tshabangu, Icarbord / *Leeds Trinity University, UK)* 522

View, Jenice L. / *George Mason University, USA)* 1

Weiss, Alexandra M. / *Indiana University – Bloomington, USA* 985

Williams, Richard D. / *American University, USA* 907

Williams, York / *West Chester University, USA* 310, 644

Wilson, Donna L. / *Equity Options Consulting, LLC, USA* 660

Wilson, Scot / *Indiana University – Bloomington, USA* 985

Yuan, Guangji / *University at Albany (SUNY), USA* 1132

Table of Contents

Preface xvii

Volume I

Section 1
Fundamental Concepts and Theories

Chapter 1
Identity Work 1
Jenice L. View, George Mason University, USA)
Elizabeth K. DeMulder, George Mason University, USA
Stacia M. Stribling, George Mason University, USA
Laura L. Dallman, George Mason University, USA

Chapter 2
Mondays With Mac: An Interpersonal Journey of Cultural Humility 25
Cort M. Dorn-Medeiros, Lewis and Clark College, USA
Jeffrey K. Christensen, Lewis and Clark College, USA
Ian Lertora, Texas Tech University, USA

Chapter 3
Dismantling Cultural Walls: Peace Through Stories, Ritual, Community, and Action 41
Christie Billups, Lewis University, USA

Chapter 4
Struggles With Historical Trauma: Cognitive Awareness and Native American Culture 62
Kirsten A. Koenig, Northcentral University, USA

Chapter 5
From PWI to HBCU: When the Oppressed Takes on the Characteristics of the Oppressor 90
Karen H. Brown, Independent Researcher, USA

Chapter 6
Microaggressions: An Introduction 105
Natasha N. Johnson, Georgia State University, USA
Thaddeus L. Johnson, Georgia State University, USA

Chapter 7
Let's Talk About Cultural Identity 122
    T. Scott Bledsoe, Azusa Pacific University, USA
    Kimberly A. Setterlund, Azusa Pacific University, USA

Chapter 8
Indigenous Killjoys Negotiating the Labyrinth of Dis/Mistrust 142
    Bronwyn Carlson, Macquarie University, Australia

Chapter 9
Revisiting Equity, Equality, and Reform in Contemporary Public Education 157
    Marquis C. Grant, Grand Canyon University, USA

Section 2
Development and Design Methodologies

Chapter 10
Applying Critical Theories to Social Media Mining and Analysis: #WokeAcademy 191
    Sacha Sharp, Indiana University, USA

Chapter 11
Impacting and Influencing the System to Support Student Career Readiness, Voice, and Efficacy:
Development of an Experiential Service-Learning Course 212
    Jennifer Schneider, Community College of Philadelphia, USA

Chapter 12
Making Room for Race in Your Classroom Discourse: A Journey of Identity and Homecoming..... 228
    Kari Dahle-Huff, Montana State University, Billings, USA

Chapter 13
Building Resilient Voices: A Conceptual Framework for Culturally Responsive SEL 241
    Sheldon Lewis Eakins, Shoshone-Bannock School District, USA
    David A. Adams, Urban Assembly, USA
    Josue B. Falaise, GOMO Educational Services, USA

Chapter 14
Narrative Theory as a Pedagogical Strategy for Culturally Responsive Teaching at HBCUs............ 257
    Niya Pickett Miller, Samford University, USA

Chapter 15
Together We S.O.A.R. A Theoretical Framework for the Underrepresented Student Leader............ 271
    Teresa E. Simpson, Lamar University, USA
    Artha L. Simpson Jr., Lamar University, USA
    Jordan J. Bryant, Lamar University, USA

Chapter 16
The Ambit of Ethics in the South African Academic Institutions: Experience of Coloniality 283
  Xolani Mathews Shange, University of South Africa, South Africa

Chapter 17
Building a Conceptual Framework for Culturally Inclusive Collaboration for Urban
Practitioners 310
  York Williams, West Chester University, USA

Chapter 18
Black Lives Matter vs. All Lives Matter in the Generation of "Hashtivism": Constructing the
Paradigms of Cyber-Race 325
  Danella May Campbell, Manchester Metropolitan University, UK

Chapter 19
Culturally Responsive Pedagogy, Universal Design for Learning, Ubiquitous Learning, and
Seamless Learning: How These Paradigms Inform the Intentional Design of Learner-Centered
Online Learning Environments... 350
  Natalie Nussli, University of Applied Sciences and Arts Northwestern Switzerland, Switzerland
  Kevin Oh, University of San Francisco, USA

Chapter 20
Bridging Social Justice-Oriented Theories to Practice in Teacher Education Utilizing Ethical
Reasoning in Action and Case-Based Teaching 375
  Kara Maura Kavanagh, James Madison University, USA

Chapter 21
Transgressions on Students and Faculty of Color in Higher Education: A Consideration of
Potential Strategies.. 398
  Milton A. Fuentes, Montclair State University, USA
  Casey R. Shannon, Yeshiva University, USA
  Muninder K. Ahluwalia, Montclair State University, USA
  Crystal S. Collier, Argosy University, USA

Chapter 22
Language Loss: Implications for Latinx Cultural Identity... 415
  Nilsa J. Thorsos, National University, USA

Chapter 23
Situational Analysis of Muslim Children in the Face of Islamophobia: Theoretical Frameworks,
Experiences, and School Social Work Interventions 430
  Jannat Fatima Farooqui, University of Delhi, India
  Archana Kaushik, University of Delhi, India

Chapter 24
Project EXCEL: A Teacher Education Partnership for Culturally and Linguistically Diverse
Communities 451
    Annette Deborah Miles, University of the District of Columbia, USA
    Ebony Terrell Shockley, University of Maryland – College Park, USA

Volume II

Chapter 25
Interculturally Relevant Pedagogy: Developing Contemporary Approach 466
    Hamza R'boul, Public University of Navarre, Spain

Section 3
Tools and Technologies

Chapter 26
Teaching Up: Female Sociologists Teaching About Privilege 488
    Celeste Atkins, University of Arizona, USA & Cochise College, USA

Chapter 27
Machitia: An Educator-Focused Liberation Platform for Education 505
    Joél-Léhi Organista, Columbia University, USA

Chapter 28
Critical Theory in Research 522
    Icarbord Tshabangu, Leeds Trinity University, UK)
    Stefano Ba', Leeds Trinity University, UK
    Silas Memory Madondo, CeDRE International Africa, Zimbabwe

Chapter 29
Caring as an Authoritative Act: Re-Thinking Respect for Students and Teachers 538
    Shannon Audley, Smith College, USA
    Julia L. Ginsburg, Smith College, USA

Chapter 30
A Decolonial Curriculum Is Everything: An Afrocentric Approach 567
    Zingisa Nkosinkulu, University of South Africa, South Africa

Chapter 31
Facebook Aesthetics: White World-Making, Digital Imaginary, and "The War on Terror" 585
    Sadhvi Dar, Queen Mary University of London, UK

Section 4
Utilization and Applications

Chapter 32
Silenced, Shamed, and Scatted: Black Feminist Perspective on Sexual Trauma and Treatment
With African American Female Survivors 601
V. Nikki Jones, Middle Tennessee State University, USA
Donna M. Dopwell, Middle Tennessee State University, USA
Lauren C. Curry, Black Lesbian Literary Collective, USA

Chapter 33
Where Our Paths Crossed: Latina Teachers, Professional Development, and Funds of Identity 623
Minda Morren López, Texas State University, San Marcos, USA
Jane M. Saunders, Texas State University, San Marcos, USA

Chapter 34
Culturally Responsive Teaching and Inclusion for Online Students With Exceptionalities and
Other Needs 644
York Williams, West Chester University, USA

Chapter 35
More Than the Sum of Their Struggles: Success Factors of First-Generation African American
Women With Doctorates 660
Donna L. Wilson, Equity Options Consulting, LLC, USA

Chapter 36
Public School Education: Minority Students at a Disadvantage 680
Dwayne Small, DePaul University, USA

Chapter 37
Race, Class, and Community Cultural Wealth: Impacts on Parental Involvement Among Black
Families in K-12 Public Schools 689
Evelyn Ezikwelu, University of Utah, USA

Chapter 38
Building a Racial Identity: African American Students' Learning Experiences at the Florence
County Museum 709
Eunjung Chang, Francis Marion University, USA

Chapter 39
Mentoring African American Women at Historically Black Colleges/Universities: Beyond the
Misconceptions of Our Identity 729
Tammara Petrill Thomas, Winston-Salem State University, USA
Michelle Lee Maultsby, South Carolina State University, USA

Chapter 40
Minority Students in Computer Science: Barriers to Access and Strategies to Promote
Participation 751
Jung Won Hur, Auburn University, USA

Chapter 41
"Just Listen to What the Panthers Are Saying": A History of the Black Panther Party From Its
Vision and Perspective 768
Valeria Carbone, University of Buenos Aires, Argentina

Chapter 42
Teaching Safety, Compliance, and Critical Thinking in Special Education Classrooms 791
Lilly B. Padía, New York University, USA

Chapter 43
Overcoming the Layers of Obstacles: The Journey of a Female African American Physicist to
Achieve Equity, Diversity, and Inclusiveness 810
Helen C. Jackson, African Scientific Institute, USA

Section 5
Organizational and Social Implications

Chapter 44
Men and Women Against the Other.. 833
Kalina G. Spencer, John Carroll University, USA

Chapter 45
Sustaining Our Diminishing Teachers of Color in Urban and Suburban Schools: A Crisis of an
Othered Identity 847
Karen D. Griffen, Creighton University, USA
Aaron J. Griffen, DSST Public Schools, USA

Chapter 46
What Is It Like to Be a Minority Student at a Predominantly White Institution? 867
Lucila T. Rudge, University of Montana, USA

Chapter 47
Agnotology and Ideology: The Threat of Ignorance and Whiteness Ideology to Transformative
Change 886
Victorene L. King, Divergent Consulting, USA

Chapter 48
I Can't Breathe: The African American Male With Emotional Disabilities in Education 907
Richard D. Williams, American University, USA
April J. Lisbon, Spotsylvania County Public Schools, USA

Chapter 49
Action Research, Design Thinking: Consulting at a Trauma-Informed Community School 921
    William Louis Conwill, University of Illinois at Urbana-Champaign, USA
    Ronald William Bailey, University of Illinois at Urbana-Champaign, USA

Volume III

Chapter 50
Students of Color and Anecdotal Pedagogy: A Success Story 933
    Alexis Nicole Mootoo, University of South Florida, USA

Chapter 51
The Threat of Downward Assimilation Among Young African Immigrants in U.S. Schools............ 946
    Immaculee Harushimana, Lehman College (CUNY), USA
    Janet Awokoya, California Lutheran University, USA

Chapter 52
Perceived Discrimination Among African-American Faculty and the Elliott Kemp Organizational
Change Model 970
    Roxanne Elliott Kemp, Elliott Kemp, USA

Chapter 53
"I Didn't Believe Privilege Existed Before This": Service-Learning in a Multicultural Education
Course 985
    Thomas Browning, Wayne State College, USA
    Scot Wilson, Indiana University – Bloomington, USA
    Crystal D. Howell, Indiana University – Bloomington, USA
    Alexandra M. Weiss, Indiana University – Bloomington, USA
    Kathryn E. Engebretson, Indiana University – Bloomington, USA

Chapter 54
Intergenerational Trauma and Other Unique Challenges as Barriers to Native American
Educational Success.. 1005
    Thomas Reed, University of San Diego, USA

Chapter 55
Navigating Academia Away From Home: Exploring the Challenges of African-Born
Academics.. 1025
    Adaobi Vivian Duru, University of Louisiana at Monroe, USA
    Ngozi Akinro, Texas Wesleyan University, USA

Chapter 56
Analyzing University Exploitation of Diversity to Legitimize Hiring Discrimination: A Black
Woman Professor's Narrative.. 1043
    Constance P. Hargrave, Iowa State University, USA

Chapter 57

Impact of Mentoring and Support Programs on Academic Performance of African American
Males: Analysis Through a Critical Race Theory Lens 1069
Andrew S. Herridge, Texas Tech University, USA
Montelleo DeLeon Hobley Jr., Mississippi State University, USA

Chapter 58

Mapping Mindset and Academic Success Among Black Men at a Predominantly White
Institution 1079
Christopher S. Travers, North Carolina State University, USA

Chapter 59

Black Joy as Emotional Resistance: A Collaborative Auto-Ethnography of Two Black Queer
Married Academics as Contingent Labor 1096
Shaneda L. Destine, University of Tennessee, Knoxville, USA
Shaina V. Destine, University of Tennessee, Knoxville, USA

Chapter 60

Race, Imposter Thoughts, and Healing: A Black Man's Journey in Self-Discovery While Working
at a PWI 1116
Calvin Monroe, Saint Mary's College of California, USA

Chapter 61

Cultural Diversity in Online Learning: Perceptions of Minority Graduate Students 1132
Alex Kumi-Yeboah, University at Albany (SUNY), USA
James Dogbey, Texas A&M University – Corpus Christi, USA
Guangji Yuan, University at Albany (SUNY), USA
Samual Amponsah, University of Ghana, Ghana

Section 6
Managerial Impact

Chapter 62

Promoting the Representation of Historically Disadvantaged Students: What Educational Leaders
Need to Know 1155
Ibrahim M. Karkouti, The American University in Cairo, Egypt
Hazza Abu Rabia, University of Hartford, USA

Chapter 63

Repressive Tolerance and the "Management" of Diversity 1173
Stephen D. Brookfield, University of St. Thomas, USA

Chapter 64

Life Context Model, Intersectionality, and Black Feminist Epistemology: Women Managers in
Africa 1186
Nasima Mohamed Hoosen Carrim, University of Pretoria, South Africa
Yvonne Senne, Tshwane University of Technology, South Africa

Chapter 65
Understanding the Attrition Rates of Diverse Teacher Candidates: A Study Examining the
Consequences of Social Reproduction... 1206
Tonya Johnson, Bronx Community College, City University of New York, USA
Edward Lehner, Bronx Community College, City University of New York, USA

Chapter 66
Equity, Equality, and Reform in Contemporary Public Education: Equity, Equality, and Reform... 1224
Marquis Carter Grant, Grand Canyon University, USA

Section 7
Critical Issues and Social Implications

Chapter 67
DACA-Mexico Origin Students in the United States-Mexican Borderlands: Persistence,
Belonging, and College Climate 1254
Maggie Dominguez, University of Phoenix, USA
Miriam L. Frolow, University of Phoenix, USA

Chapter 68
Liberty Needs Glasses: A Critical Race Theory Analysis of a Culture of Miseducation in the
Intersection of Power, Privilege, and Positionality 1281
Tanishia Lavette Williams, The New School, USA

Chapter 69
"I Will Never Look at This Movie the Same Again": Using Critical Literacy to Examine Popular
Culture Texts Helps Adolescents Critique Social Issues 1299
Salika A. Lawrence, The College of New Jersey, USA

Chapter 70
My Skin Color Is Not Mi Pecado.. 1321
Daisy Indira Barrón, Missouri State University, USA

Chapter 71
Multicultural Literature as Critical Literature: Redefine the Trajectory for Black Students 1330
Carissa McCray, The Harley-Jackson Foundation, USA

Chapter 72
Critical Examination of Tokenism and Demands of Organizational Citizenship Behavior Among
Faculty Women of Color.. 1346
Shelley Price-Williams, Southern Illinois University Edwardsville, USA
Florence Maätita, Southern Illinois University Edwardsville, USA

Chapter 73
WOKE: Advocacy for African American Students 1365
  Mariama Cook Sandifer, Columbus State University, USA
  Eva M. Gibson, Austin Peay State University, USA
  Sarah N. Brant-Rajahn, Messiah University, USA

Chapter 74
The Research Process and Indigenous Epistemologies 1387
  Kgomotso H. Moahi, University of Botswana, Botswana

Index xx

Preface

Past injustice against racial groups rings out throughout history and negatively affects today's society. Not only do people hold onto negative perceptions, but government processes and laws have remnants of these past ideas that impact people today. To enact change and promote justice, it is essential to recognize the generational trauma experienced by these groups.

Staying informed of the most up-to-date research trends and findings is of the utmost importance. That is why IGI Global is pleased to offer this three-volume reference collection of reprinted IGI Global book chapters and journal articles that have been handpicked by senior editorial staff. This collection will shed light on critical issues related to the trends, techniques, and uses of various applications by providing both broad and detailed perspectives on cutting-edge theories and developments. This collection is designed to act as a single reference source on conceptual, methodological, technical, and managerial issues, as well as to provide insight into emerging trends and future opportunities within the field.

The *Research Anthology on Racial Equity, Identity, and Privilege* is organized into seven distinct sections that provide comprehensive coverage of important topics. The sections are:

1. Fundamental Concepts and Theories;
2. Development and Design Methodologies;
3. Tools and Technologies;
4. Utilization and Applications;
5. Organizational and Social Implications;
6. Managerial Impact; and
7. Critical Issues and Social Implications.

The following paragraphs provide a summary of what to expect from this invaluable reference tool.

Section 1, "Fundamental Concepts and Theories," serves as a foundation for this extensive reference tool by addressing crucial theories essential to understanding racial equity. The first chapter of this section, "Identity Work," by Profs. Jenice L. View, Elizabeth K. DeMulder, Stacia M. Stribling, and Laura L. Dallman of George Mason University, USA, describes the first crucial step in antiracist teacher professional development – developing a deep understanding of one's identity. The last chapter of this section, "Revisiting Equity, Equality, and Reform in Contemporary Public Education," by Prof. Marquis C. Grant of Grand Canyon University, USA, revisits equity, equality, and reform in public education.

Section 2, "Development and Design Methodologies," presents in-depth coverage of the design and development of critical theories on racial identity. The first chapter of this section, "Applying Critical Theories to Social Media Mining and Analysis: #WokeAcademy," by Prof. Sacha Sharp of Indiana University, USA, provides an example for how to use social media mining in combination with critical theories as an exploratory tool. This study is designed to apply critical theories to social media mining techniques in order to examine how membership organizations have engaged in discourse around racial issues and social inequities in higher education. The last chapter of this section, "Interculturally Relevant Pedagogy: Developing Contemporary Approach," by Prof. Hamza R'boul of Public University of Navarre, Spain, makes a case for interculturally relevant pedagogy as an educational approach that recognizes the importance of considering students' cultures while emphasizing intercultural communication in K-12 classrooms procedures with the aim of simultaneously attaining social justice and scholastic achievement.

Section 3, "Tools and Technologies," explores the various tools and technologies used in educating and advocating for racial equity. The first chapter of this section, "Teaching Up: Female Sociologists Teaching About Privilege," by Prof. Celeste Atkins of University of Arizona, USA & Cochise College, USA, explores how female faculty (who also identify as working-class, queer, or as racial minorities) experience teaching about privilege. It builds an understanding of issues surrounding teaching about inequity from an intersectional perspective and moves the focus beyond tenure-track faculty. The last chapter of this section, "Facebook Aesthetics: White World-Making, Digital Imaginary, and 'The War on Terror'," by Prof. Sadhvi Dar of Queen Mary University of London, UK, seeks to provide a critique of imagery posted on Facebook in the aftermath of "terror attacks" in Paris 2015. The author renders these images as structured by deep forms of white world-making, ways of thinking and feeling that reproduce whiteness as ethically superior, innocent, and in need of preserving at the cost of non-white knowledges and peoples. In this chapter, the author argues that the internet provides yet another site for whiteness to engage in white world-making by extending the white gaze to digital platforms in the service of transforming the violence of Paris into a racialised attack on white innocence.

Section 4, "Utilization and Applications," describes how race theory is applied for racial equity advocacy. The first chapter of this section, "Silenced, Shamed, and Scatted: Black Feminist Perspective on Sexual Trauma and Treatment With African American Female Survivors," by Profs. V. Nikki Jones and Donna M. Dopwell of Middle Tennessee State University, USA and Prof. Lauren C. Curry of Black Lesbian Literary Collective, USA, offers perspective on how religiously-motivated heterocentric-patriarchy marginalizes Black female sexual trauma survivors. Recommendations are informed by Black feminisms in order to support culturally congruent practice. The last chapter of this section, "Overcoming the Layers of Obstacles: The Journey of a Female African American Physicist to Achieve Equity, Diversity, and Inclusiveness," by Prof. Helen C. Jackson of African Scientific Institute, USA, documents the experiences in the journey of an African American female physicist. They correspond to those in documented studies of other African Americans and females in both the specific field of physics as well as the broader area of all STEM.

Section 5, "Organizational and Social Implications," includes chapters discussing the impact of advocacy and race theory in society and various organizations. The first chapter of this section, "Men and Women Against the Other," by Prof. Kalina G. Spencer of John Carroll University, USA, discerns the oppressive and prejudicial treatment inflicted on Black students at John Carroll University, a private white institution. This chapter outlines instances of oppression, culturally and racially insensitive behavior, and lack of solidarity that one student of color in particular experienced throughout her four years of attendance. The last chapter of this section, "Cultural Diversity in Online Learning: Perceptions of Minority Graduate Students," by Profs. Alex Kumi-Yeboah and Guangji Yuan of University at Albany (SUNY), USA; Prof. James Dogbey of Texas A&M University – Corpus Christi, USA; and Prof. Samual Amponsah of University of Ghana, Ghana, explores the perceptions of minority graduate students about cultural diversity and the challenges they face in online learning environments.

Preface

Section 6, "Managerial Impact," discusses the impact of race theories and racial equity. The first chapter of this section, "Promoting the Representation of Historically Disadvantaged Students: What Educational Leaders Need to Know," by Prof. Ibrahim M. Karkouti of The American University in Cairo, Egypt and Prof. Hazza Abu Rabia of University of Hartford, USA, highlights the importance of diversity, provides an overview of the historical plight that minorities suffered during the formation of the American history, describes the policies that aim at expanding educational opportunities for socially and economically disadvantaged groups, and presents a conceptual framework that guides educational leaders towards creating inclusive campuses. The last chapter of this section, "Equity, Equality, and Reform in Contemporary Public Education: Equity, Equality, and Reform," by Prof. Marquis Carter Grant of Grand Canyon University, USA, considers both equity and equality to advocate for creating indivualized pathways to learning environments for the academic benefit of all students.

Section 7, "Critical Issues and Social Implications," presents coverage of academic and research perspectives and implications to using race theory. The first chapter of this section, "DACA-Mexico Origin Students in the United States-Mexican Borderlands: Persistence, Belonging, and College Climate," by Profs. Maggie Dominguez and Miriam L. Frolow of University of Phoenix, USA, confirms the need for higher education faculty and staff to provide services and resources and to build trust with this vulnerable student population. The last chapter of this section, "The Research Process and Indigenous Epistemologies," by Prof. Kgomotso H. Moahi of University of Botswana, Botswana, discusses the research process and indigenous epistemologies, specifically, what is involved in conducting research using indigenous epistemology.

Although the primary organization of the contents in this multi-volume work is based on its seven sections, offering a progression of coverage of the important concepts, methodologies, technologies, applications, social issues, and emerging trends, the reader can also identify specific contents by utilizing the extensive indexing system listed at the end of each volume. As a comprehensive collection of research on the latest findings related to racial equity, the *Research Anthology on Racial Equity, Identity, and Privilege* provides sociologists, community leaders, government officials, policymakers, education administration, preservice teachers, students and professors of higher education, justice advocates, researchers, and academicians with a complete understanding of the applications and impacts of racial equity. Given the vast number of issues concerning impacts of racial equity in modern practices and institutions, the *Research Anthology on Racial Equity, Identity, and Privilege* encompasses the most pertinent research on the applications, impacts, uses, and development of racial equity.

Chapter 25
Interculturally Relevant Pedagogy:
Developing Contemporary Approach

Hamza R'boul

ⓘD https://orcid.org/0000-0003-4398-7573
Public University of Navarre, Spain

ABSTRACT

Although culturally responsive pedagogy has been geared towards students' cultures, interests, and needs, it does not meaningfully consider intercultural communication dynamics that are always existing in almost all classrooms, especially highly multicultural ones. This assumption is problematized by the current academic discussion on individuals' tendency to oscillate between different identities/cultures and the significance of intersubjectivity in the epistemological complexity of interculturality. This chapter makes a case for interculturally relevant pedagogy as an educational approach that recognizes the importance of considering students' cultures while emphasizing intercultural communication in K-12 classrooms procedures with the aim of simultaneously attaining social justice and scholastic achievement. It argues for the plausible need of integrating popular culture in order to present sociopolitical realities and accordingly enable students, along with teachers' guidance, to critically question the current power imbalances and the cultural hegemony of dominant group.

INTRODUCTION

Most scholars interested in the intersections of culture and education have corroborated the assumption that culture is central to learning as it contributes not only to the processes of communicating, receiving and interpreting 'culturally coded' information but also to the shaping of the thinking process of groups and individuals. Increasing student identification with the course content across all levels would necessarily entail encouraging a pedagogy that acknowledges, responds to, and celebrates fundamental cultures and offers full, equitable access to education for students from all cultures (Gloria Ladson-

DOI: 10.4018/978-1-6684-4507-5.ch025

Copyright © 2022, IGI Global. Copying or distributing in print or electronic forms without written permission of IGI Global is prohibited.

Billings, 1994). Culturally relevant pedagogy helps to realize a meaningful relationship between students as cultural beings and the objective of scholastic retention and learning. It is constructed to establish active engagement, enrichment, and academic achievement of all students by promoting an appreciation of diversity, recognizing and valuing students' cultural strengths, and meaningfully considering students' lived experiences and their place in the world (Villegas & Lucas, 2007). Implementing culturally responsive/relevant teaching/pedagogy across content areas and grade levels involves "using the cultural knowledge, prior experiences, frames of reference, and performance styles of ethnically diverse students to make learning encounters more relevant to and effective for [students]" (Gay, 2010, p. 31). This type of content delivery contributes to the development of students' involvement through "knowing their opinions will be valued, and expressing themselves in multiple ways" (Edwards & Edwick, 2013, p. 10).

Culturally relevant pedagogy's (CRP) pedagogical realization/ applicability is anchored in empowering "students intellectually, socially, emotionally, and politically [because it uses] cultural referents to impart knowledge, skills, and attitudes" (Ladson-Billings, 2009, p. 20). Moreover, culturally responsive teaching primarily focuses on the consideration of the students' native culture (as a counterpart to intercultural-oriented education) and embracing it as a standard for the selection and design of instructional activities and contents. It is, therefore, made distinctive by teachers who aim at developing the cultural competence, determining high expectations, and rendering their task as both facilitators and learners.

Irrespective of epistemological orientations underpinning any educational framework, culture is often presented as an indispensable aspect in the delivery of appropriate learning experience. Particularly, popular culture with its defining feature of enjoying currency and contemporary topics enables constructing teaching elements that reflect students' interests and concerns as they tend to imitate/re-live what they have been exposed to in movies, music, etc... Popular culture is succinctly described as the cultural texts, practices and artifacts that are attractive to large numbers of youth (Marsh, 2005). Many researchers have confirmed the usefulness of embracing culturally responsive instruction, materials and curriculum in K-12 schools (Aronson & Laughter, 2016; Ladson-Billings, 2014; Milner, 2011; Paris, 2012;; Warren, 2018). Scholars interested in literacy have reported that integrating popular culture can propel students' critical thinking and writing abilities about "the media they produce and consume both in and outside of school "(Schmier, 2014, p. 39).

Promoting youth engagement in critical media pedagogy using popular culture can concurrently empower youth as media consumers and develop their academic literacy skills (Morrell and Duncan-Andrade, 2006). By using popular culture, literacy educators are provided with opportunities to develop culturally sustaining pedagogies (Paris, 2012) that will assist in creating pedagogical third spaces (Gutierrez, 2008). This, in turn, situates literacy curricula in the lives of "students and repurpose traditional literacy curricula to be more useful and pertinent for the complex literate lives of today's K-12 students" (Petrone, 2013, p. 5). It seems, therefore, clear that implementing culturally responsive pedagogy while using popular culture is rather more promising especially in the case of youth who are constantly exposed to media with all its means. Bringing different forms of popular culture serves the need for contextualizing learning and catering to students' needs/interests by meaningfully taking their daily lives/routines into account while designing courses. Yet, it is important to emphasize that these objectives are only met when teachers are keen on using popular culture which is unfiltered and wisely selected under the rubrics of supporting the objective of learning. In other words, through these media avenues including whether in TV, media, music, articles, or books, people are learning. The daily pedagogical onslaught of information that people are experiencing through popular media can either "create conflict within [themselves] or elicit great insights for change and acceptance "(CohenMillar, 2019, p. 1).

In contemporary societies, cultural plurality/diversity is increasingly submitted as an accurate characterization of the multiple realities entailed in our current times. This situation renders constructing culturally relevant pedagogies quite problematic and incomprehensive due to (a) the students' variety of cultures that have been brought to the classroom; (b) students' multiple identities/cultures that recent theories of intercultural communication and intersubjectivity emphasize as individuals cannot be assumed to be influenced by/manifest a sole particular culture/identity. The aim is to provide a range of pedagogical suggestions with practical recommendations in order to address classrooms' cultural complexity. Another argument is that establishing culturally relevant pedagogy in K-12 settings is rather more complex due to cultural globalization, convergence, glocalization and cross-cultural pollination among various societies. Also, accounting for the cultural dynamics requires a certain level of cognitive development on the part of students which might be an issue while dealing with younger students (Byram & Wagner, 2018). This may lead to questioning the accuracy of generalizing a particular approach to all grades since any representation/consideration of culture would necessitate taking into account students' age and their ability to engage in the self-reflective process. That is why culturally relevant pedagogy cannot be assumed to reflect the current complexities/challenges that characterize our societies (especially highly multicultural ones). It is important to consider an interculturally relevant pedagogy that makes the case for not only one's culture but also considers students as individuals who are incessantly involved in intercultural encounters (with teachers and students). This type of education is bound up with multiple pragmatic, societal and cultural conditions which stipulate a pedagogical framework informed with the overall contextual and situational factors. The content delivery has to be resilient and continuously updated according to context-sensitivity, the socio-cultural milieu and cultural makeup of the students and teachers, and grades.

This chapter argues for the importance of considering the intersections of culturally responsive teaching-learning and intercultural communication within the call for multicultural education (Gay, 2012), multicultural instruction (Banks, 2002, 2010), intercultural responsiveness (Jones & Mixon, 2020; Jones et al., 2017), culturally sustaining pedagogy (Paris & Alim, 2014) and studying interculturality within intersubjectivity (Holliday & Macdonald, 2019). These assumptions are delivered in relation to popular culture in order to clarify its significance in realizing interculturally-imbued teaching that is responsive to students' daily lives and interests. One objective is to elaborate on how interculturally-relevant pedagogy can be conceptually thought of and its range of theoretical underpinnings in terms of the teaching-learning philosophy. All arguments presented consider that treatments of culture, that are based on nation-wide understandings, solid and hyper-essentialist lenses, have been inaccurate in delivering what would be considered to be highly culturally relevant instruction. A first step in interculturally responsive/relevant teaching is to embrace liquidity and non-linearity of interculturality (Dervin, 2016).

LITERATURE REVIEW

The current debate around diversity is a "salient and permanent aspect of educational discourse, as learning and teaching in multicultural classrooms have brought major challenges to both teachers and students" (Abacioglu et al., 2020, p.1). Therefore, the significance of CRT is perceived in its endeavor to offer broad guidelines for managing classrooms' cultural diversity. A wide number of studies have documented CRE's positive impact on student outcomes across content areas (Caballero, 2010; Wah & Nasri, 2019), especially students coming from underrepresented ethnicities (Credit, 2020; Hill, 2012).

Interculturally Relevant Pedagogy

Cooperative learning opportunities among culturally different students who exhibited varying achievement levels fosters positive social relationship including friendship, sympathy, acceptance of differences, and support for peers' learning (Harriott & Martin, 2016).

Although there is an extensive body of research on how to ameliorate CRT, the implementation of its principles in the classrooms has not been proven to be optimal (Lim et al., 2019; Sleeter, 2012). Scholars believe that, before practicing CRT, there is a need to emphasize teacher education that supports culturally relevant pedagogy (Hramiak, 2015; Jackson & Boutte, 2018); parents, teachers, and education leaders have to be educated about "what culturally responsive pedagogy means and looks like in the classroom" (Sleeter, 2012, p. 578). One explanation of teachers' inability to putt CRT into practice is that certain teacher characteristics (Rychly & Graves, 2012) are necessary for culturally responsive pedagogy/teaching to serve as change-makers and leaders (Atwater et al., 2014; ; Kaysar et al., 2020; Kumashiro, 2012). By taking this assumption into account, recent research has largely aimed at investigating teachers' perceptions and implementation of multicultural education (Abacioglu et al., 2020; Agirdag et al., 2016; Samuels, 2018).

As a response to Sleeter's (2012) call for research that is comprehensive and usable, Aronson and Laughter (2016) indicated in their synthesis of research that "recent work describes how standardized curricula and testing have marginalized CRE in educational reform discourses" (p. 1). Researchers noted that principles of CRT have been either not implemented at all (Kim & Pulido, 2015; Ladson-Billings, 2014) or were made as an additional factor as they were implemented at a superficial level; for example, teachers may present elements of surface/material culture that are often stereotypical or overgeneralizable such as the celebration of ethnic foods (Sleeter & McLaren, 2009).

Current themes in the scholarship go beyond theorizing and presenting practical applications of CRT. Recent research has engaged with related issues that include linking literacy and CRP (Wearmouth, 2017), situating education within sociocultural approach and connecting intercultural education and social justice (Choi, 2013; Dimick, 2012; Dover, 2013). However, the majority of research has only examined the cultural diversity of student, and, thus, did not place the same emphasis on the concomitant aspects of multiculturalism especially the linguistic dimension including multilingualism, linguistic diversity and translanguaging (Garcia & Lin, 2017; Lewis et al., 2012). There is a need to incorporate linguistically and culturally responsive teaching in concurrently multicultural and multilingual classrooms (Wernicke, 2019).

INTERCULTURALISM IN MULTICULTURAL SOCIETIES: PROMOTING EQUAL PROCESS OF INTERCULTURALITY

Interculturalism delivers a sense of emphasis on respect, interaction, reciprocation, empathy, and cultural exchange while working towards empowering minorities by challenging power relations (Hajisoteriou & Angelides, 2013). It is relatively opposed to multiculturalism which "is an attempt to allow for a measure of cultural diversity by making certain exceptions for minorities while limiting the effect of changes on the majority" (Bleich, 1998, p. 83). Interculturalism entails embracing critical sociocultural study within the educational experience through encouraging teachers to construct and implement an emancipatory curriculum (Hickling-Hudson, 2003). It particularly argues for individuals' capacity for establishing rapport with a culturally different other on the basis of mutual compromise and effort to socialize. Its aim is promoting intercultural understanding which is built on undermining power differentialism and imbalanced sociopolitical realities. While "the challenge for educators in contemporary multicultural classrooms is twofold: to sustain collective identities and to facilitate individual academic success" (Valiandes et al., 2018, p. 1), teachers are required to imbue their instructional practices with a consideration of the students' needs with diverse cultural backgrounds.

Interculturalism-oriented strategies involve integrating effective intercultural communication methods and managing the multicultural capital in today's' classroom through collectively-inclusive materials. Interculturalism serves an emancipatory and transforming purpose. It does not "restrict itself to corrective interventions within the curriculum, but rather aims at the radical transformation of the educational system (curricula, school manuals, teaching strategies, teacher training) with the perspective of societal change"(Maniatis, 2012, p. 157). It, therefore, (a) confronts any educational rituals that continue to emphasize the cultural hegemony of particular dominant group and (b) concurrently reveal and transform the 'hidden' educational processes that perpetuate discrimination (Leclercq, 2002). Interculturalism not only impeaches "the politics of equal dignity, which is grounded on all students' undifferentiated treatment" but also " draws upon the politics of recognition by challenging power relations in order to promote social change" (Valiandes et al., 2018, p. 4). Therefore, promoting an equal process of interculturality is built on the active participation of all students by dismantling power imbalances and the inability to confirm the validity of both northern and southern ontologies. Interculturalism's principles are structured within an educational framework as 'intercultural education' which is often presented as a contemporary approach that is sensitive to cultural differences. It places more emphasis on intersubjectivity by considering students' subjective needs, interests, and sociocultural conditions. Its major feature resides in realizing an actional application towards social justice with the necessity of questioning personal, institutional and education ready-made assumptions.

Intercultural education, as an educational realization of interculturalism, derives its principles from multicultural instruction (Banks, 2002) which proposes five key elements that multicultural teaching should be based on: content integration, knowledge construction process, equity pedagogy, prejudice reduction, and empowering school culture and social structure. (a) Content Integration entails integrating materials, content and examples from different cultures to deliver information about particular principles, concepts and theories in the studies subject or discipline (Banks & Banks 2010). This ensures that all students' cultural affiliations are presented regardless of the cultural hegemony of a specific group; (b) Knowledge Construction Process aims at helping students to explore and critically examine how ontologies, cultural assumptions and perspectives tend to shape knowledge production in different disciplines(marginalized perspectives are often disregarded). This involves how authors from different contexts are represented in curriculum/textbook and if they have equal value in terms of the knowledge they have produced; (c) Equity Pedagogy refers to "teaching strategies and environments that help diverse students attain necessary knowledge, skills, and attitudes for functioning effectively within a just, democratic society" (Banks & Banks, 1995, p. 152). It includes all strategies that seek to ensure the academic achievement of all students simultaneously through group work, collaboration and role-playing; (d) Prejudice Reduction tries to develop students' positive attitudes towards the culturally different other by suspending stereotypes and any feeling of cultural superiority. Teachers are encouraged to present materials that encourage students to respect differences; (e) Empowering School Culture and Social Structure relates to the organization of school by involving students and their families in school-related decisions and promotes equality between all students in the classroom.

While culturally responsive pedagogy (CRP) is founded on the assumption that our cognition, thinking, and behaviors are directly dictated by one's culture (Gay, 2010); an argument which can be fairly perceived as "essentialist" (Ferry, 2018; MacDonald, 2019), culturally sustaining pedagogy (CSP) seeks to "perpetuate and foster linguistic, literate, and cultural pluralism as part of the democratic project of schooling and as a needed response to demographic and social change" (Paris and Alim 2014, p. 85). CSP argues for transcending CRP by accommodating the current discussion on fluid interculturality (Dervin, 2016) and intersubjectivity (Holliday and Macdonald, 2019). CRP is closely related to constructivism in the sense that students are asked to value multiple cultural viewpoints while critically criticizing the offered input (popular culture is emblematic here) instead of absentmindedly absorbing what they are taught/exposed to (Kea et al., 2006). CSP's epistemological stance is further clarified in (a) questioning widespread socio-cultural inequities, (b) advancing the counter-hegemonic character of culture and (c) structuring the pluriform and evolving character of cultural identity (Paris and Alim 2014). Since culture influences how people think, what they believe and how they behave, CRP considers failure to attain desirable school/learning outcomes among particular student populations to be "due to the lack of consideration of their cultural capital in the overall educational design. CRP contends that education should "become culturally relevant" (Valiandes et al., 2018 p. 10) so as to ameliorate the scope of scholastic achievement across all grades and content fields. To account for the limitations of the approaches above, Valiandes et al. (2018) suggested blending intercultural education and differentiated instruction in practice to construct interculturally differentiated teaching.

INTERCULTURALLY-RELEVANT TEACHING: EMPHASIZING POPULAR CULTURE

Since "in the cosmopolitanization era as diversity is defined on the basis of interconnectivity" (Arvanitis, 2016, p. 1), interculturally-responsive teaching (IRT) entails the accommodation of culturally responsive teaching in the conditions of intercultural communication. Considering how cultures do not exist in isolation but rather co-exist/interact and continuously evolve in constant cross-cultural pollination, it primarily seeks to reinforce the students' ability to maintain their cultural integrity while concurrently achieving academic excellence at the same time (Zhang & Wang, 2016, p. 55).In other words, it offers the potential of finding ways to meaningfully consider and address the specificities/needs of students and families from diverse cultures and life-experiences (Gonzalez, 2016, p. 213). Due to the increasingly widespread feeling of hyper-nationalism, ethnocentricity, and radicalization of the modern world, IRT precisely perceives popular culture to be a manifestation of non-strict conformity to sociopolitical realities and a reflection of everyday life with representations of a variety of classes and cultures. Using wisely selected instantiations of popular cultures offers the possibility of mediating between cultures. This can contribute to unconsciously inculcating in students a sense of questioning the current sociopolitical realities that are often imbued with an aura of westernization and marginalizing other underrepresented cultures.

IRT makes use of popular culture as "the everyday social experiences of marginalized students as they confront, make sense of, and contend against social institutions such as schools, the mass media, corporations and governments" (Morrell, 2002, p. 7). Although culturally responsive pedagogy presents "...a solid pattern of interaction, accommodation and ownership so that students feel comfortable working together" (Edwards & Edwick, 2013, p. 10), it fails to account for the complexity of interculturality which is constantly taking place in today's' highly multicultural classrooms. IRT understands identity and culture in the plural connotation in keeping with current intercultural communication scholarship that emphasizes plurality/fluidity of culture/ identity and intersubjectivity (Dervin; 2016, Holliday & Macdonald; 2019). The necessity of meaningfully addressing the dynamics/processes entails when students bring their various cultures/identities to the classroom is underpinned by the plausible need to (a) reinforce the humanistic concern of education in fulfilling social justice and (b) to ascertain the smooth functioning of intercultural interactions among students and teachers while supporting their scholastic achievements.

Interculturally responsive teaching is anchored in interculturalism and its objective is to ensure not only an equally valid education but also a proportionate appreciation of all cultures regardless of the widespread moralistic value-laden judgments (West vs East). While culturally responsive education "has the potential to make some worthy contributions to these social dynamics by teaching students how to engage positively with their own and others' racial, social, cultural, experiential, linguistic, and ancestral origins" (Gay, 2015, p. 131), it does not have well-delineated principles that are accurately responsive to the liquidity of interculturality. It indeed caters to students' cultures through implementing teaching materials and instructional designs that are inspired by cultures brought to the classroom, but the interaction aspect is not efficiently considered. Culturally responsive pedagogy may entail that culturally diverse groups are required to reject/give up their 'inherited' cultural characteristics and embrace the national culture so as to blend in and smoothly integrate. Classrooms in multicultural societies are the site of unprecedented cultural diversity which may result, due to power imbalance, either in bullying, cultural contestation or assimilation; these realities further problematize communication dynamics among students since more issues may arise as a result of reinforcing those power hierarchies in classrooms. Another aspect which renders accounting for cultural variety in classrooms a complex task is that students have not fully developed the cognitive capacities that may enable them to foster a sense of meta-awareness and thus question cross-cultural normativities. Some notions may be too abstract for younger students to digest. Concepts of 'injustice' and 'power relations' are not simple; therefore, teachers are required to tackle interculturality in simple terms and procedures by focusing on showing rather than describing or imagining.

Interculturally relevant pedagogy concurrently considers the importance of making use of insights from intercultural education and intercultural communication education. Because our perceptions of multicultural society have evolved, this endeavor allows for a profound understanding of how modern nations are "neither a mosaic where cultures are placed side-by-side without any effect on each other not is it a melting pot where everything is reduced to the lowest common denominator" (Brander et al., 2004, p. 41). This paradigm shift entails a research-based development of the Response to Cultures Continuum (Jones & Mixon, 2015) by moving along the cultural continuum until the goal of being interculturally responsive is obtained: starting by Monocultural to Cross-cultural to multicultural to finally intercultural. The importance of interculturally relevant education is further emphasized considering how cultural diversity makes teaching practices more influential in the sense of managing the plurality of perspectives and ontologies. Teachers are tasked with the process of making choices and instructional practices that smoothly manage cultural diversity. Several questions are pertaining to this discussion including: To what extent cultural differences can entail problems that inhibit the overall flow of classroom dynamics? Is it more meaningful and efficient to exercise different or the same treatment towards all students? Is intercultural communication effectively considered and integrated? How can teachers ascertain that different expectations are met with equal efficiency? How can teachers construct classroom teaching materials and practices that acknowledge and celebrate diversity?

The rationale for embracing intercultural-oriented and focused teaching resides in the fact that "…as the student population becomes increasingly diverse in terms of race, ethnicity, language, socio-economic level, teachers are challenged to meet the academic, cultural and community needs of tomorrow's citi-

Interculturally Relevant Pedagogy

zens" (Edwards & Edick, 2013, p. 1). This condition necessitates, therefore, considering that "effective teaching and learning occur in a culturally supported, learner-centered context, whereby the strengths students bring to school are identified, nurtured, and utilized to promote student achievement" (Richards et al., 2007, p. 64). Since the term 'intercultural' necessarily implies exchange, interaction and reciprocity, interculturalists accentuate the dynamic/liquid nature of cultures/identities, which are an "unstable mixture of sameness and otherness" (Leclercq, 2002, p. 6). This orientation is specifically sensitive to the potential consequences of any particular model/approach in addressing cultural and religious diversity in education for both the majority and the minority (or immigrant) student populations. It is mindful of the current academic debate between interculturalism which implies interaction that is imbued with justice and equality between cultures and multiculturalism that presents political orientation which recognizes the plurality of cultures but without clear approach is ascertaining equality and justice (Hajisoteriou & Angelides, 2016). Different countries adopt a variety of approaches to handle cultural and religious diversity in education (Faas et al., 2014). It is necessary to consider that (a) the academic success of students from diverse backgrounds is contingent on "attention to biased instructional materials, and awareness of differences between students' lived experiences and the curricular mandates and societal norms" (Williams et al., 2019, p.4); and (b) applying intercultural development/understanding theories to students' development is important, but this endeavor stipulates teachers' prior intercultural reflection and critical assessment of each classroom' nature of interculturality with the attendant problematics.

Jones and Mixon's approach of 'intercultural responsive' (IR) is important here since some elements of IRT are inspired by IR, and, thus, it can contribute to addressing the limitations and ameliorating the scope of culturally responsive pedagogy. Intercultural Responsiveness (IR) refers to "the blending of multicultural awareness, intercultural sensitivity, and cultural responsiveness bound by self-reflection" (Jones & Mixon, 2020). It was accordingly differentiated from CRP as a "merging of multicultural awareness, intercultural sensitivity while cultural responsiveness is overlapping both along a cultural awareness continuum "(Jones &Mixon, 2017, p. 253). The major key in achieving IR is perceived in emphasizing positive dispositions, being culturally aware, and responding by incorporating cultural differences; thus, IR self- actualization is the culminating professional and personal experience that enhances relationships between all cultures (Jones et al., 2017, p.1). Therefore, principles of interculturally responsive teaching (IRT) include (a) avoiding 'methodological nationalism' as well as reflect on and adapt their teaching philosophy using learners' cultural and linguistic backgrounds as a valuable resource." (Arvanitis, 2016, p. 1), (b) taking into account the dynamics of intercultural communication which are to be delineated/discussed by the teachers according to the specific contextual and situational factors, (c) developing learning outcomes, assessments, and learning activities to emphasize intercultural learning for all students that reinforce social justice and questioning the biased sociopolitical realities, (d) promoting politics of equal recognition that support the active participation of all students with their cultures. This is essentially coupled with reconsidering educational objective to include not only scholastic achievements but also intercultural understanding and co-negotiation of intersubjectivities, and (e) using popular culture as a means of presenting social acts of underrepresented cultures and ontologies. Integrating some interculturally-oriented media outlets is expected to provide access to all students' cultures and identities while accentuating cultural co-existence and positive attitudes. Importantly, IRT has to be actualized/implemented at all levels of the institutional (administration and its policies and values), personal- the cognitive and emotional processes) and instructional dimensions (the materials, strategies and activities) (Taylor, 2010).

By considering sociopolitical conditions that precipitate unequal treatment of different cultures (western ontologies are favored), the major practical aims of IRT are to (a) consider strategies for facilitating multicultural group work that are inspired by the dialectics of intercultural communication and (b) taking into account that the critical teaching of popular culture can play "an integral role in helping these teachers to help their students to acquire and develop the academic and critical literacies needed to succeed in new century schools"(Morrell, 2002, p. 2). Multicultural group work would also build collaborative learning which assists in promoting the intellectual and personal development of all students by considering them as active influential agents and encouraging them to occupy significant roles in the teaching/learning process (Hajisoteriou, 2012); however, to ascertain the effectiveness of such practice (collaborative learning), sociocultural justice is essential in classrooms. The curricular knowledge delivered in the school should represent and come from all groups (dominant, subordinate, or minority). The aim is to reconceptualize the normative educational norms that may fail to consider how power differentials can strongly impact classroom learning and interactive dynamics (Gundara & Sharma, 2013).

Since interculturality is often presented as a matter of co-construction of identity/culture, intersubjectivity and sense-making processes, classroom discussions, dialogue, and negotiation are all considered to be indispensable tools in developing intercultural awareness (Radstake & Leeman, 2010). Culturally responsive teaching takes multi-cultural competencies as an equally important definitional dimension. It refers to the practice of "helping students learn more about their own and others' cultures, as part of their personal development and preparation for community membership, civic engagement, and social transformation" (Gay, 2015, p. 124). Nonetheless, teachers nowadays have a complex task of catering for the cultural needs and interests of all students in the highly multicultural and mixed-ability classroom. It is rather more plausible to address this challenge by two key elements: (a) adopting "an intercultural education framework" in addition to (b) introducing " high-quality teaching that will provide equal opportunity for learning to all students, regardless of their ethnic origin or other characteristics" (Valiandes et al., 2018, p. 1).

POPULAR CULTURE AND INTERCULTURALLY RELEVANT PEDAGOGY: SENSITIVE/CRITICAL TO SOCIOPOLITICAL REALITIES

Culturally responsive teaching has always been underpinned by the deliberate attempt to rebalance power differentialisms and to dissuade instructors from reinforcing/reacting unequal social realities (Western vs. Non-western; Natives vs. Immigrant/refugees…). This orientation is clarified by the fact that CRT is "an approach that originated in the context of African American educational disadvantage, has shown promising outcomes among marginalized student populations internationally "(Morrison et al., 2019, p. 5). It was initially designed to redress "academic failures within Native American and other marginalized groups in the United States" (Zhang & Wang, 2016, p. 55). Because relevant themes of culturally responsive pedagogy include instructional engagement, culture, language, racial identity, multicultural awareness, high expectations, critical thinking and social justice (Aceves & Orosco, 2014), proposing IRT is rather an extension of CRP's traditions while acknowledging the need to establish an intercultural meta-awareness of intercultural communication and daily cultural cross-pollination. Since current times are characterized by sheer cultural plurality, it is not any more conceivable to solely emphasize culturally responsive pedagogy in the contexts of highly multicultural classrooms. Instead of focusing on some cultures and try to reorient teaching processes and dynamics towards their specificities, it seems more

Interculturally Relevant Pedagogy

feasible to capitalize on cultural diversity and establish a teaching philosophy that is built of linking cultures and encouraging intercultural communication.

While cultural responsive is about harmony between teaching practices and students' cultures, intercultural relevant pedagogy stems its critical validity from the assumptions that "intercultural learning is necessary for critique" (Young, 1996, p. 209). There is a need to consider how k-12 classrooms can bring about social changes and attune students towards criticizing inequalities, power imbalances between cultures (Western vs Non-western) and "hierarchized spaces" (Makoni, 2019). Instead of absentmindedly taking any type of input for granted, students can be guided towards critically examining the range of attitudes, stereotypes, and ideas they are exposed to. Individuals, especially younger ones, end up absorbing everything that is routinely presented as 'valid' and 'true'. Particularly, many normative rituals continue to benchmark western cultures/societies as having 'cultural ascendency' while non-western cultures remain underrepresented and characterized by powerlessness. If students are influenced by these hierarchical processes, they may tend to reflect western-centric and hegemonic assumptions. This, in turn, results in unequal treatment of the cultures brought to the classroom and lack of appreciation of southern/now-western ones. Therefore, education has to serve a counter-hegemonic purpose and seeks to re-balance how students' perceive cultures by suspending any western-centric attitudes on the part of both teachers and students. IRT recognizes that pedagogical practices have to move from constructing instructional procedures in alignment with students' cultures to reflect the state of interaction between cultures in the classroom and the outside world. Intercultural communication scholarship confirms that power conditions between cultures are imbalanced; that's why IRT calls from taking into account these conditions and then try to undermine their reproduction in the classroom.

Considering all the ideas above, it is necessary to (a) consider frames of references that pave the way " to a more reflective professional practice presupposing teachers' strong intercultural awareness, competence, and responsiveness" (Arvanitis, 2016, p. 1), (b) delineate the salient features of contemporary discussions of social justice and their implementations/contextualizations in K-12 education; and (c) explore the relevancies between the conceptual objectives of intercultural education/intercultural communication education and those of teaching for social justice. Setting out the rationale for embracing an intercultural perspective in aligning K-12 pedagogy with students' various cultural identities is a precursor to support the significance of questioning current sociopolitical realities and how they are often reflected in classroom interaction dynamics. Intercultural education is conceptualized here under the rubrics of culturally relevant pedagogy along with its concomitant principles of freedom, equality, and social justice (Bassey, 2016). It is, thus, perceived as a project for social transformation and interculturally-building strategy which is sensitive/critical to social realities in the broader context of K-12 learning spaces. Intercultural education as a philosophy of socio-educational change bears the possibility of empowering and transforming school culture and social attitudes. With these assumptions in mind interculturally relevant pedagogy places prominent emphasis on relational justice and accentuates its value in multicultural societies where "collective identities, interdependencies, mutual respect, and equal participations are to be advocated among racially, ethnically, socially, and culturally different individuals and groups" (Cho, 2017, p. 4).

Interculturally responsive pedagogy entails an inclusive intercultural perspective on education that aims at making the case for rights, equal educational opportunities, cultural understanding and social justice. While these themes appear desirable, they can be only achieved by questioning/relativizing sociopolitical realities that represent sheer inequalities. For these reasons, IRT advances that "the discourses between teaching for social justice and multicultural education be mutually associated with one another

475

so that they can more effectively serve as a vehicle for promoting social justice" (Cho, 2017, p. 3). By accentuating "the practical dangers of disengaging social justice from multicultural education"(Lawyer, 2018, p. 1) and establishing feasible connections between North's (2009) social justice literacies and Gay's (2012) goals of multicultural education, interculturally relevant pedagogy serves an educational function while endeavoring to reimage the fundamental constructs of classroom dynamics. The aim here is to build upon the principles of other educational philosophies including education for human rights, anti-racist education and development education. To attain this objective, i is necessary to pay equal attention to both micro and macro factors. We need to develop an understanding of (a) the influence of culture, gender, ability, and socioeconomic status on students' communication; (b) patterns of learning; and (c) classroom behavior as well as teachers' expectations and interactions (Bloom, 2009). IRT encourages instructors to develop strategies/ processes that "enable the discovery of mutual relationships and the dismantling of barriers" (Brander et al., 2004, p. 41). Achieving these objectives is by no means an easy task, but teachers can actively work towards promoting positive learning experiences.

Cultural diversity does not necessarily imply justice in the sense that all students' cultures are equally appreciated and recognized. Although the teachers' beliefs about cultural diversity management may serve an equalitarian objective (Agirdag et al., 2016), it remains questionable to what extent students are not deliberately trying to perpetuate the world' s social realities and power imbalances in their classrooms. Children are often educated to reflect normativity and associate themselves with what is common and popular. Transitioning from culturally- focused education to interculturally-sensitive teaching can address this issue as it stipulates first reflecting current realities and then constructing a critical appraisal of the world' circumstances. Instead of drawing on multicultural education and its concomitant objectives, it is rather more rational to conceptualize interculturality and smooth functioning of student-student/ students-instructors' intercultural encounters as the next aim in establishing social justice and equality.

An important proposition is to bring the outside world with a real-life sense to the classroom by using popular culture since it allows educators to capitalize on what is current and appealing to students' interests. Contemporary scholarship is investigating youth engagement with popular culture within three conceptions." (a) popular culture as a site of identity formation for youth, (b) popular culture as a context for youth literacy development, and (c) popular culture as a vehicle for youth sociopolitical critique and action"(Petrone, 2013, p. 241). Popular culture can be contributive to the critique of sociopolitical realities since using media texts and popular culture can provide "relevant examples for entry into abstract concepts that are often politically and emotionally charged, and sometimes too sensitive or too distant to begin discussing on a personal level" (Share et al., 2019, p. 15).

Although the Centre for Contemporary Culture Studies at the University of Birmingham initially accentuated "issues of class politics and conflicts in their examination and theorizing about popular culture", subsequent scholars have marked a focus shift in the study of popular culture. The current scholarship shows that researchers have started to emphasize macro-level dynamics and include issues of "race, gender, sexuality, meaning, pleasure, and other sociocultural factors" (Petrone, 2013, p. 244). Advancing the consideration of cultural constructs and identity categories in K-12 is rather promising in the sense of embracing a critical approach to interculturality, cultural and identity dynamics in intercultural interpersonal communication. While self-reflection seems bit overambitious in the case of children since they have not had reached yet that particular level of cognitive development to question sensitive matters including manifestations of power imbalances and western/northern cultural ascendency (Acevedo, 2019), using popular culture materials seems more appropriate in these situational circumstances (Tuzel & Hobbs, 2017). For example, introducing movies that depict scenarios of recon-

Interculturally Relevant Pedagogy

sideration of sociopolitical realities and realizing social justice among all cultural ontologies can even reorient students towards not only respecting/valuing their culturally different classmates but also seek change outside the classroom space.

Teachers can be encouraged to select popular culture materials that exhibit (a) cross-cultural pollination, (b) equal appreciation of all culture and (c) suspending attitudes and beliefs that assume the inherent superiority of some individuals coming from particular societies/cultures. This can specifically help in avoiding any patronizing and condescending attitude among students. Emphasizing social justice and reimaging sociopolitical realities are necessary for successful intercultural communication not only at the level of interaction but also ontological existence. Popular culture offers an interesting opportunity to contextualize major issues relating to education and cultural diversity and place them within the current conditions. It indeed represents "important sites of meaning-making, identity formation, and political activity" (Petrone, 2013, p. 244): While young people may find issues of identity and politics to be problematic and difficult to fathom, popular culture serves a both exploratory and explanatory function by providing some understandings of these issues from different perspectives. That way, young people can bridge a number of problematics and manage to develop particular perception of these issues If principles of IRT are implemented suitably, classrooms can go beyond the state of only reflecting current circumstances; they can serve a participatory and transforming purpose by challenging imbalanced sociopolitical realities and reinforcing social justice.

IMPLEMENTING INTERCULTURALLY RELEVANT TEACHING

Interculturality is highly contextual with different situational factors and its defining parameters can vary greatly from one place to another. Interculturally relevant teaching provides 'general' educational guidelines for managing classrooms' cultural diversity. Implementing IRT has to be aligned with the particularities of each classroom (students' age, achievement level, etc…). Teachers are expected to have a deep understanding of their students and the cultural capital that they teach. In other words, the element of responsiveness is important in order not to generate fitting-all teaching that misreads the specificity of each learning space and fails to practice appropriate instructional procedures. It is also up to the teachers to design activities as long as the materials and instructional activities are following the elements constituting IRT.

Teaching about interculturality with the aim of undermining the hegemony of some cultures cannot be realized by focusing on delivering verbal messages or information. Instead of teaching about interculturality, there is a need to teach interculturality as it takes place in real life. For the optimal implementation of IRT, the teaching-learning process has to facilitate new ways of knowing-through-being for students. IRT emphasizes bounding knowing and being; a process that supports relating epistemology and ontology. Therefore, teachers need to aim at presenting materials that either depict interculturality as it unfolds in a wide array of context or use real-life content that reifies intercultural interactions between individuals from different cultural backgrounds. In the case of K-12 education, some students would not be able to fathom a wide range of complex ideas if they are not being exemplified and more importantly embodied as visual content.

Particularly, popular culture representations, as visual content, can be ingeniously used in not only informing about interculturality but also developing intercultural awareness that is accompanied by interculturally critical teaching. Teachers are encouraged to selectively use popular culture materials that embody interculturality in current times. They can make use of movies and documentaries that present intercultural experiences of different individuals, but they should be used with caution since they may contain inappropriate scenes, e.g., Babies (2010), Save the Last Dance (2001), Yasmin (2004), and Bread and Roses (2000). Teachers need to ascertain that their discourse and the materials used are always characterized by positive attitudes towards other individuals, their multiple personal identities and cultures.

Implementing IRT entails two aspects that relate to students and teachers: (a) teaching interculturality to students and fostering their willingness to co-exist with other individuals; and (b) encouraging teachers to manage their classrooms' cultural diversity by considering intercultural interactions within a critical understanding of current power relations and sociopolitical conditions.

The broad practical guidelines for teaching interculturality to students include:

1. Soliciting students in an indirect way in order to to talk about how they feel about other individuals (explicitly requesting them to talk about attitudes may prompt students to deliver favorable answers) and then identify any negative attitudes and try to change them.
2. Making use of materials and texts that explain imbalanced power relations and how they can impact our behaviors towards others.
3. Presenting activities that showcase differences, similarities and intersections between individuals from multiple cultures in order to exemplify that understanding and co-existence can be achieved.
4. Presenting popular culture that depicts intercultural interactions (preferably in the video) in different contexts with interlocutors from different social positions, educational level, backgrounds... and draw students' attention to the context and particularities of the interaction at hand and how individuals manage all these factors to reach intercultural understanding and respect.
5. A teacher can develop an activity where they act as an intercultural speaker and thus adopt different identities and cultures in a particular context (preferably out of the home country or classroom). Then, each student is instructed to communicate with the teachers (intercultural speaker) in a cross-cultural context.
6. Providing students with different instances of unfair treatment of culturally different other (contextualizing the instances and providing comprehensive information about interlocutors is necessary). Then, each student is asked to offer what kind of procedures can be followed to overcome those issues depicted.

Importantly, the following practical recommendations are proposed for teachers to manage interculturality that emanates from their classrooms' cultural capital. These illustrations of IRT are not restrictive and can be enriched with other suggestions and practical ideas depending on the context (the type of interculturality in classrooms, prior intercultural conflicts in classroom or school):

1. Focusing on students coming from underrepresented cultures by trying to provide equal treatment of all students regardless of their cultural backgrounds.
2. Avoiding the reinforcement of power hierarchies in the classroom. Students might be inclined to re-exercise the type of perspective they have been exposed to.
3. Bearing in mind that interculturality is not at the level of communication only. Solid representations of cultures have to be avoided including stereotypes and normative expectations.
4. Paying attention to the fact that besides cultures, any race/gender-based discrimination is also an issue. A lot of students are exposed to bullying based on some identity-defining categories.

Interculturally Relevant Pedagogy

5. Taking into account that Students oscillate between different identities and cultures. They may exhibit their affiliation to the same nation-wide culture in varying degrees. Interculturality is liquid, unstable and unpredictable.
6. Managing cultural diversity might involve being responsive to all cultures at the same time. It is important to develop students' understanding that cultures are perspectives and not necessarily a source of conflicts.
7. Considering how not all classrooms are characterized by the same level of interculturality. Some learning spaces would need more work and attention on the part of instructors. Teachers are encouraged to examine cross-cultural pollination and cultural hybridity; especially in highly multicultural societies (US and Canada are emblematic).

CONCLUSION

The discussion above has been introduced primarily to support the epistemological foundations of interculturally relevant pedagogy as it seeks to reconcile students' various cultural/social realities with the aim of scholastic achievement in learning spaces. This chapter' main argument resides in arguing for the plausible need, as dictated by the contemporary circumstances, to move from focusing on cultural realities that students manifest in the classroom to meaningfully considering the ontological intercultural communication. This chapter makes the case for the importance of taking into account interculturality that takes place daily and from which multiple issues may arise accordingly if it is not properly accounted for in multicultural classrooms. Therefore, introducing interculturally responsive pedagogy appears as a logically required extension of the additional conditions emanating from the necessities of (a) managing cultural diversity, (b) taking into account students' multiple cultures and identities (Liquid interculturality) and (c) considering how cultures never exist in isolation but rather they are constantly in processes of reshaping and cultural cross-pollination with other cultures.

Interculturally responsive pedagogy offers a potential answer to the issue of simultaneously supporting students' critical engagement with course content and developing their intercultural awareness. It builds on the assumptions that (a) people are not any more cultural beings but rather intercultural individuals that oscillate between different cultures/identities and (b) today's societies are highly multicultural, a fact which entails that individuals have to connect, communicate and establish close relationships with culturally different others; all society members have to engage in intercultural negotiation and sense-making. K-12 education, as a preparatory program for real-life conditions, is required to reflect and respond to these new circumstances. It is no more valid to focus on singular culture; students can be trained for future challenges by considering multiculturalism as a site of cultural communication, tolerance rather than contestation, nationalism and assimilation. Instructional decisions and materials, across all content areas and grades, can be specifically constructed to encourage/mirror intercultural communication and willingness to appreciate the other and value oneself since we never exist in isolation but always in co-existence with other cultures and individuals. Popular culture provides the possibility of reinforcing these assumptions both at as a site of intercultural activity and educational material. It is not only something that youth people are constantly exposed to, but also a source of different perspectives and attitudes. Therefore, it can be used to simultaneously address the development of intercultural understanding and academic achievement.

Culturally responsive teaching focalizes using culture to enhance the academic and social achievement of students (Bassey, 2016; Ladson-Billings, 2009). That is why the argument here is that using popular culture while implementing interculturally responsive pedagogy serves a complementary orientation. Media outlets can be highly contributive in the sense of reflecting and questioning current sociopolitical realities that are heavily imbued with western-centric orientation and cultural ascendency of northern spaces. Students have grown up in a world pervaded by "the electronic, symbolic, commodity, and ideological signification system of popular culture," teachers are required to engage in "teaching with and about media and popular culture" (Luke, 1997, p. 45); an idea that was delivered more than 20 years ago and which shows the criticality of using popular culture in an era that is characterized by even more sheer digitalization and unprecedented technological advancement. That's why, interculturally relevant pedagogy places particular emphasis on popular culture as a way of drawing shared links between culturally different individuals as it is usually the conversation starter at different contexts including school, work and social occasions. Nowadays, youth tend to situate themselves within the popular by reflecting popular culture that is desirable and establish connections between individuals who share similar interest (Petrone, 2013). Friendships often start and solidify "around a shared love for a particular band, music video, or television show, and being outside of the currents of the popular can lead to social isolation" (Dolby, 2003, p. 258). Popular culture could be, therefore, an opportunity of linking those who are culturally different as it often functions as social "glue" and a social divider Accentuating the relevance of using popular culture in K-12 in the pursuit of (a) developing students' intercultural existence and awareness and (b) questioning current sociopolitical conditions is further substantiated by current literature. Popular culture positions students as "community activists who designed and published texts that gave voice to inequities in their community" (Schmier, 2014, p. 39).

REFERENCES

Abacioglu, C. S., Volman, M., & Fischer, A. H. (2020). Teachers' multicultural attitudes and perspective-taking abilities as factors in culturally responsive teaching. *The British Journal of Educational Psychology*. Advance online publication. doi:10.1111/bjep.12328

Acevedo, M. V. (2019). Young children playing their way into intercultural understanding. *Journal of Early Childhood Literacy*, *19*(3), 375–398. doi:10.1177/1468798417727134

Aceves, T. C., & Orosco, M. J. (2014). *Culturally responsive teaching (Document No. IC-2)*. Retrieved from University of Florida, Collaboration for Effective Educator, Development, Accountability, and Reform Center website: https://ceedar.education.ufl.edu/tools/innovation-configurations/

Agirdag, O., Merry, M. S., & Van Houtte, M. (2016). Teachers' understanding of multicultural education and the correlates of multicultural content integration in Flanders. *Education and Urban Society*, *48*(6), 556–582. doi:10.1177/0013124514536610

Aronson, B., & Laughter, J. (2016). The Theory and Practice of Culturally Relevant Education: A Synthesis of Research Across Content Areas. *Review of Educational Research*, *86*(1), 163–206. doi:10.3102/0034654315582066

Arvanitis, E. (2016). Culturally Responsive Pedagogy: Modeling Teachers' Professional Learning to Advance Plurilingualism. In Handbook of Research and Practice in Heritage Language Education. Springer International Handbooks of Education. Springer.

Atwater, M. M., Russell, M., & Butler, M. B. (2014). *Multicultural science education: Preparing teachers for equity and social justice.* Springer. doi:10.1007/978-94-007-7651-7

Banks, J. A. (2002). *An Introduction to Multicultural Education.* Allyn & Bacon.

Banks, J. A., & Banks, C. A. M. (2010). *Multicultural Education: Issues and Perspectives.* John Wiley & Sons.

Bassey, M. O. (2016). Culturally responsive teaching: Implications for educational justice. *Education Sciences*, *6*(35). doi:10,3390/educsci6040035

Bleich, E. (1998). From International Ideas to Domestic Policies: Educational Multiculturalism in England and France. *Comparative Politics*, *31*(1), 81–100. doi:10.2307/422107

Bloom, L. A. (2009). *Classroom management: Creating positive outcomes for all students.* Pearson Education.

Brander, P., Cardenas, C., Gomes, R., Taylor, M., & de Vincente Abad, J. (2004). *All equal all different. Education pack: Ideas, resources, methods and activities for informal intercultural education with young people and adults* (2nd ed.). Council of Europe.

Byram, M., & Wagner, M. (2018). Making a difference: Language teaching for intercultural and international dialogue. *Foreign Language Annals*, *51*(1), 140–151. doi:10.1111/flan.12319

Caballero, J. A. R. (2010). *The effects of the teacher-student relationship, teacher expectancy, and culturally-relevant pedagogy on student academic achievement* (Doctoral dissertation). Available from Proquest Dissertations and Theses database. (UMI No. 3474274)

Cho, H. (2017). Navigating the meanings of social justice, teaching for social justice, and multicultural education. *International Journal of Multicultural Education*, *19*(2), 1–19. doi:10.18251/ijme.v19i2.1307

Choi, Y. (2013). Teaching social studies for newcomer English language learners: Toward culturally relevant pedagogy. *Multicultural Perspectives*, *15*, 12–18. doi:10 .1080/15210960.2013.754640

CohenMiller, A. S. (2019). From the news to zombies: Teaching and learning about Otherness in popular culture. Dialogue: *The Interdisciplinary Journal of Popular Culture and Pedagogy*, *6*(3). http://journaldialogue.org/issues/v6-issue-3/from-the-news-to-zombies-teaching-and-learning-about-otherness-in-popular-culture/

Credit, A. L. (2020). *Perceptions of High School Principals about Improving African American Male Academic Outcomes* (Doctoral dissertation). Walden University. Available from the Walden Dissertations and Doctoral Studies Collection at ScholarWorks. https://scholarworks.waldenu.edu/dissertations

Dervin, F. (2016). *Interculturality in education: A theoretical and methodological toolbox.* London: Palgrave Macmillan.

Dimick, A. S. (2012). Students' empowerment in an environmental science classroom: Toward a framework for social justice science education. *Science Education*, *96*(6), 990–1012. doi:10.1002ce.21035

Dolby, N. (2003). Popular culture and democratic practice. *Harvard Educational Review*, *73*(3), 258–284. doi:10.17763/haer.73.3.l225466l06204076

Dover, A. G. (2013). Teaching for social justice: From conceptual frameworks to classroom practices. *Multicultural Perspectives*, *15*, 3–11. doi:.754285 doi:10.1080/15210960.2013

Edwards, S., & Edwick, N. (2013). Culturally responsive teaching for significant relationships. *Journal of Praxis in Multicultural Education*, *7*(1). Advance online publication. doi:10.9741/2161-2978.1058

Faas, D., Hajisoteriou, C., & Angelides, P. (2014). Intercultural Education in Europe: Policies, Practices and Trends. *British Educational Research Journal*, *40*(2), 300–318. doi:10.1002/berj.3080

Ferri, G. (2018). *Intercultural Communication: Critical Approaches and Future Challenges*. Palgrave Pivot. doi:10.1007/978-3-319-73918-2

García, O., & Lin, A. M. (2017). Translanguaging in bilingual education. *Bilingual and Multilingual Education*, 117–130.

Gay, G. (2010). *Culturally responsive teaching: Theory, research, & practice*. Teachers College Press.

Gay, G. (2012). Multicultural education, purposes, and goals. In J. A. Banks (Ed.), *Encyclopedia of diversity in education* (pp. 1548–1553). Sage. doi:10.4135/9781452218533.n495

Gay, G. (2013). Teaching to and through cultural diversity. *Curriculum Inquiry*, *43*(1), 48–70. doi:10.1111/curi.12002

Gay, G. (2015). The what, why, and how of culturally responsive teaching: International mandates, challenges, and opportunities. *Multicultural Education Review*, *7*(3), 123–139. doi:10.1080/200561 5X.2015.1072079

González, K. (2016). Culturally Responsive Pedagogy in Early Childhood Classrooms. In A. G. Welch & S. Areepattamannil (Eds.), *Dispositions in Teacher Education*. Sense Publishers., doi:10.1007/978-94-6300-552-4_11

Gundara, J. S., & Sharma, N. (2013). Some Issues for Cooperative Learning and Intercultural Education. *Intercultural Education*, *24*(3), 237–250. doi:10.1080/14675986.2013.797202

Gutierrez, K. (2008). Developing a sociocritical literacy in the third space. *Reading Research Quarterly*, *43*(2), 148–164. doi:10.1598/RRQ.43.2.3

Hajisoteriou, C. (2012). Intercultural Education Set Forward: Operational Strategies and Procedures in Cypriot Classrooms. *Intercultural Education*, *23*(2), 133–146. doi:10.1080/14675986.2012.686022

Hajisoteriou, C., & Angelides, P. (2013). The Politics of Intercultural Education in Cyprus: PolicyMaking and Challenges. *Education Inquiry*, *4*(1), 103–123. doi:10.3402/edui.v4i1.22064

Hajisoteriou, C., & Angelides, P. (2016). Intercultural Education in Situ: Examining Intercultural Policy in Cyprus in the Context of European Integration. *Journal for Multicultural Education*, *10*(1), 33–52. doi:10.1108/JME-03-2015-0006

Harriott, W. A., & Martin, S. S. (2016). Using culturally responsive activities to promote social competence and classroom community. *Teaching Exceptional Children, 37*(1), 48–54. doi:10.1177/004005990403700106

Hickling-Hudson, A. (2003). Multicultural Education and the Postcolonial Turn. *Policy Futures in Education, 1*(2), 381–401. doi:10.2304/pfie.2003.1.2.13

Hill, A. L. (2012). *Culturally responsive teaching: An investigation of effective practices for African American learners* (Doctoral dissertation). Available from Proquest Dissertations and Theses Database. (UMI No. 3549438)

Holliday, A. R., & MacDonald, L. N. (2019). Researching the intercultural: Intersubjectivity and the problem with postpositivism. *Applied Linguistics*, 1–20. doi:10.1093/alin/amz006

Hramiak, A. (2015). Applying the framework for culturally responsive teaching to explore the adaptations that teach first beginning teachers use to meet the needs of their pupils in school. *Cogent Education, 2*(1). DOI: 10.1080/2331186X.2015.1108950

Jackson, T. O., & Boutte, G. S. (2018). Exploring Culturally Relevant/Responsive Pedagogy as Praxis in Teacher Education. *New Educator, 14*(2), 87–90. doi:10.1080/1547688X.2018.1426320

Jones, K., & Mixon, J. R. (2015). Six easy and beneficial strategies for an inter-culturally responsive classroom. *Journal of English Language Teaching, 5*(2), 1–6.

Jones, K., & Mixon, J. R. (Eds.). (2017). *Intercultural Responsiveness in the Second Language Learning Classroom*. IGI Global. doi:10.4018/978-1-5225-2069-6

Jones, K., & Mixon, J. R. (2020). How to Be Interculturally Responsive to Your English Language Learners' Writing Needs. In A. Slapac & S. A. Coppersmith (Eds.), *Beyond Language Learning Instruction: Transformative Supports for Emergent Bilinguals and Educators*. IGI Global. doi:10.4018/978-1-7998-1962-2.ch003

Jones, K., Mixon, J. R., Henry, L., & Butcher, J. (2017). Response to Cultures Continuum and the Development of Intercultural Responsiveness (IR). *Education Leadership Review of Doctoral Research, 4*, 1–16.

Kayser, A. A., Nash, A. M., & Kayser, B. (2020). Change-Makers: A Grassroots Approach to Culturally Responsive Leadership and Teaching. *Journal of Education Human Resources, 38*(1), 35–56. doi:10.3138/jehr.2019-0009

Kea, C., Campbell-Whatley, G., & Richards, H. (2006). *Becoming Culturally Responsive Educators: Rethinking Teacher Education Pedagogy*. National Center for Culturally Responsive Educational Systems. http://www.niusileadscape.org/docs

Kim, J., & Pulido, I. (2015). Examining hip-hop as culturally relevant pedagogy. *Journal of Curriculum and Pedagogy, 12*(1), 17–35. doi:10.1080/15505170.2015.1008077

Kumashiro, K. (2012). *Bad teacher: How blaming teachers distorts the bigger picture*. Teachers College Press.

Ladson-Billings, G. (1994). *The dreamkeepers*. Jossey-Bass Publishing Co.

Ladson-Billings, G. (2009). *The dreamkeepers: Successful teachers of African American children (2nd ed.).* Jossey-Bass.

Ladson-Billings, G. (2014). Culturally relevant pedagogy 2.0: Aka the remix. *Harvard Educational Review, 84*(1), 74–84. doi:10.17763/haer.84.1.p2rj131485484751

Lawyer, G. (2018). The dangers of separating social justice from multicultural education: Applications in higher education. *International Journal of Multicultural Education, 20*(1), 86–101. doi:10.18251/ijme.v20i1.1538

Leclercq, J. M. (2002). *The Lessons of Thirty Years of European Co-Operation for Intercultural Education.* Steering Committee for Education.

Lewis, G., Jones, B., & Baker, C. (2012). Translanguaging: Developing its conceptualisation and contextualisation. *Educational Research and Evaluation, 18*(7), 655–670. doi:10.1080/13803611.2012.718490

Lim, L., Tan, M., & Saito, E. (2019). Culturally relevant pedagogy: Developing principles of description and analysis. *Teaching and Teacher Education, 77*(1), 43–52. 1016/j.tate.2018.09.011

Luke, C. (1997). Media Literacy and cultural studies. In S. Muspratt, A. Luke, & P. Freebody (Eds.), *Constructing critical literacies: Teaching and learning textual practice* (pp. 19–49). Hampton Press.

MacDonald, M. (2019). The discourse of 'thirdness' in intercultural studies. *Language and Intercultural Communication, 19*(1), 93–109. doi:10.1080/14708477.2019.1544788

Makoni, S. (2019). Conflicting reactions to chi'ixnakax utxiwa. *Language. Cultura e Scuola, 1*(1), 147–151. doi:10.1075/lcs.00011.mak

Maniatis, P. (2012). Critical Intercultural Education: Necessities and Prerequisites for Its Development in Greece. *The Journal for Critical Education Policy Studies, 10*(1), 156–167.

Marsh, J. (2005). *Popular Culture, New Media and Digital Literacy in Early Childhood.* Routledge Falmer.

McGee Banks, C. A., & Banks, J. A. (1995). Equity Pedagogy: An Essential Component of Multicultural Education. *Theory into Practice, 34*(3), 152–158. doi:10.1080/00405849509543674

Milner, H. R. IV. (2011). Culturally relevant pedagogy in a diverse urban classroom. *The Urban Review, 43*(1), 66–89. doi:10.100711256-009-0143-0

Morrell, E. (2002). Teaching Popular Culture to Diverse Students in Secondary English Classrooms: Implications for Literacy Development. *Language Arts Journal of Michigan, 18*(1), 9–12. doi:10.9707/2168-149X.1299

Morrell, E., & Duncan-Andrade, J. (2006). Popular culture and critical media pedagogy in secondary literacy classrooms. *International Journal of Learning, 12*(9), 273–280. doi:10.18848/1447-9494/CGP/v12i09/48068

Morrison, A., Rigney, L., Hattam, R., & Diplock, A. (2019). *Toward an Australian culturally responsive pedagogy: a narrative review of the literature.* Retrieved from Analysis and Policy Observatory Website: https://apo.org.au/node/262951

North, C. E. (2009). *Teaching for social justice? Voices from the front lines*. Paradigm Publishers.

Paris, D. (2012). Culturally sustaining pedagogy: A needed change in stance, terminology, and practice. *Educational Researcher, 41*, 93–97. doi:89X12441244 doi:10.3102/00131

Paris, D., & Alim, H. S. (2014). What Are We Seeking to Sustain through Culturally Sustaining Pedagogy? A Loving Critique Forward. *Harvard Educational Review, 84*(1), 85–100. doi:10.17763/haer.84.1.982l873k2ht16m77

Petrone, R. (2013). Linking contemporary research on youth, literacy, and popular culture with literacy teacher education. *Journal of Literacy Research, 45*(3), 240–266. doi:10.1177/1086296X13492981

Radstake, H., & Leeman, Y. (2010). Guiding Discussions in the Class about Ethnic Diversity. *Intercultural Education, 21*(5), 429–442. doi:10.1080/14675986.2010.521378

Richards, H. V., Brown, A. F., & Forde, T. B. (2007). Addressing Diversity in Schools: Culturally Responsive Pedagogy. *Teaching Exceptional Children, 39*(3), 64–68. doi:10.1177/004005990703900310

Rychly, L., & Graves, E. (2012). Teacher Characteristics for Culturally Responsive Pedagogy. *Multicultural Perspectives, 14*(1), 44–49. doi:10.1080/15210960.2012.646853

Samuels, A. J. (2018). Exploring culturally responsive pedagogy: Teachers' perspectives on fostering equitable and inclusive classrooms. *SRATE Journal, 27*(1), 22–30.

Schmier, S. (2014). Popular culture in a digital media studies classroom. *Literacy, 48*(1), 39–46. doi:10.1111/lit.12025

Share, J., Mamikonyan, T., & Lopez, E. (2019). *Critical Media Literacy in Teacher Education, Theory, and Practice*. Oxford Research Encyclopedia of Education. doi:10.1093/acrefore/9780190264093.013.1404

Sleeter, C. (2012). Confronting the marginalization of culturally responsive pedagogy. *Urban Education, 47*(3), 562–584. doi:10.1177/0042085911431472

Sleeter, C. E., & McLaren, P. (2009). Origins of multiculturalism. In W. Au (Ed.), *Rethinking multicultural education: Teaching for racial and cultural justice* (pp. 17–19). Rethinking Schools.

Taylor, R. (2010). The role of teacher education programs in creating culturally competent teachers: A moral imperative for ensuring the academic success of diverse student populations. *Multicultural Education, 17*(3), 24–28.

Tuzel, S., & Hobbs, R. (2017). The use of social media and popular culture to advance cross-cultural understanding. *Comunicar, 51*(51), 63–72. doi:10.3916/C51-2017-06

Valiandes, S., Neophytou, L., & Hajisoteriou, C. (2018). Establishing a framework for blending intercultural education with differentiated instruction. *Intercultural Education, 29*(3), 379–398. Advance online publication. doi:10.1080/14675986.2018.1441706

Villegas, A. M., & Lucas, T. (2007). The culturally responsive teacher. *Educational Leadership, 64*(6), 28–33.

Wah, Y. L., & Nasri, N. B. M. (2019). A Systematic Review: The Effect of Culturally Responsive Pedagogy on Student Learning and Achievement. *International Journal of Academic Research in Business and Social Sciences*, *9*(5), 588–596. doi:10.6007/IJARBSS/v9-i5/5907

Warren, C. A. (2018). Empathy, Teacher Dispositions, and Preparation for Culturally Responsive Pedagogy. *Journal of Teacher Education*, *69*(2), 169–183. doi:10.1177/0022487117712487

Wearmouth, J. (2017). Employing culturally responsive pedagogy to foster literacy learning in schools. *Cogent Education*, *4*(1). Advance online publication. doi:10.1080/2331186X.2017.1295824

Wernicke, M. (2019). Toward Linguistically and Culturally Responsive Teaching in the French as a Second Language Classroom. *TESL Canada Journal*, *36*(1), 134–146. doi:10.18806/tesl.v36i1.1306

Williams, N. N., Williams, B. K., Jones-Fosu, S., & Carter, T. (2019). An examination of cross-cultural experiences on developing culturally responsive teacher candidates. *Emerald Open Res*, *1*, 13. doi:10.12688/emeraldopenres.12852.1

Young, M. (1996). *Intercultural communication: pragmatics, genealogy, deconstruction*. Multilingual Matters.

Zhang, L., & Wang, Y. (2016). Culturally responsive teaching in China: Instructional strategy and teachers' attitudes. *Intercultural Education*, *27*(1), 54–69. doi:10.1080/14675986.2016.1144632

KEY TERMS AND DEFINITIONS

Culturally Responsive Pedagogy: Is an approach that caters for students' cultures and tries to construct materials and practices informed by students' needs, interests.

Intercultural Education: Is an approach that seeks to overcome society' power imbalances from being reproduced in classrooms by ensuring social justice and active participation of all students.

Interculturalism: Is a political orientation that supports equality among cultures and promotes active participation of all society's cultures.

Interculturality: Refers to dynamics and processes involved in the co-construction and negotiation of meanings, attitudes, and perspectives during intercultural interactions.

Interculturally Relevant Pedagogy: Is an orientation that seeks to concurrently accommodate for students' multiple cultures/identities (liquid interculturality), intercultural communication dynamics and question unequal power imbalances.

Multicultural Education: Is an educational approach that recognizes multiculturality in today's classroom and proposes five elements that make teaching multicultural: Content Integration, Knowledge Construction Process, Equity Pedagogy, Prejudice Reduction, and Empowering School Culture and Social Structure.

Social Justice: Is the outcome of achieving equal treatment and value of all individuals in society dynamics regardless of their identity features (e.g., race, culture, etc.).

This research was previously published in Disciplinary Literacy Connections to Popular Culture in K-12 Settings; pages 252-272, copyright year 2021 by Information Science Reference (an imprint of IGI Global).

Section 3
Tools and Technologies

Chapter 26
Teaching Up:
Female Sociologists Teaching About Privilege

Celeste Atkins
University of Arizona, USA & Cochise College, USA

ABSTRACT

In the current political climate, racial, gender, and sexual differences are controversial topics, particularly on college campuses. This illuminates the need for increased focus on these issues in college classes. Although the literature on teaching about privilege is small, it is dominated by the voices of White faculty and almost completely focuses on racial issues. Marginalized faculty are rarely heard in this literature for our intersectional understanding of teaching about oppression and inequality. This chapter explores how female faculty (who also identify as working-class, queer, or as racial minorities) experience teaching about privilege. It builds an understanding of issues surrounding teaching about inequity from an intersectional perspective and moves the focus beyond tenure-track faculty. It expands an understanding of the experiences of faculty within the classroom and provides ways to support marginalized faculty in their teaching. Although the faculty interviewed here are sociologists, there are broad implications for teaching across disciplines.

INTRODUCTION

The lack of diversity within the professoriate is an acknowledged problem (Moody, 2004; Ndandala, 2016). As the student body becomes increasingly more diverse, these changes are not reflected in the faculty. Data from the Integrated Postsecondary Education Data System (IPEDS) shows that 77% of full-time faculty are White, with only 8% identifying as Asian or Pacific Islander, 5% identifying as Black, 4% identifying as Latinx/Hispanic, 4% as nonresidential, 2% as unknown and less than 1% (.5%) as Native American. The picture is similarly bleak when exploring full-time faculty with tenure. A full 83% are White, 7% are Asian or Pacific Islander, 5% Black, 3% Latinx/Hispanic, 1% nonresidential, less than 1% unknown, and less than half a percent Native American.

DOI: 10.4018/978-1-6684-4507-5.ch026

Copyright © 2022, IGI Global. Copying or distributing in print or electronic forms without written permission of IGI Global is prohibited.

Teaching Up

Furthermore, according to IPEDS, in fall of 2007 women were 42% of full-time faculty and only 34% of full-time faculty with tenure. Women who identify as racial minorities are underrepresented in academia across all institutions (Kelly & McCann, 2014). In order to create institutions that attract a diverse student population and more importantly, to facilitate a learning environment that is inclusive, welcoming, and engaging for those students, the author argues that a diverse faculty is needed.

Empirical evidence illustrates that, particularly on predominantly White campuses, minority students experience a sense of isolation (Harpalani, 2017). While diversifying faculty is not the single solution to increasing diversity and inclusion, it is a vital step. Moreover, Ferber, Herrera, and Samuels (2007) posit "If racism, sexism, and homophobia are the result of a process of socialization, then mounting a public argument for equality and social justice from a forum such as the classroom can theoretically challenge students' racist, sexist, and homophobic attitudes, and potentially evoke individual transformation and effect social and political change" (p. 521). The respondents from the study presented in this chapter utilize their classrooms to evoke social change and advocate for social justice and their successes create more space for diversity and inclusion in the campuses where they work.

The literature on challenges faced by women faculty discusses sexist environments, gender inequity, having higher teaching and service loads than male counterparts due to the perception of women being more nurturing, and lack of mentoring (Kelly & McCann, 2014). The literature on faculty of color primarily focuses on issues of isolation, tokenism, and tenure (Pittman, 2010; Stanley, 2006; Turner, Gonzalez, & Wood, 2008). As teaching is central to faculty experiences in higher education, similar attention should be focused upon faculty experiences within the classroom.

It is clear that women and faculty of color are more harshly criticized by their students in relation to their male White counterparts (Bavashi, Hebl, & Madera, 2010), but how does that play out in the learning environment? To explore this question, this chapter focuses on how women sociologists teach about privilege in their classes. Messner (1996) introduces the idea of "studying up" which "in sociology . . . refers to studying 'up' in the power structure" (p. 222). This concept led the author to the reframing of marginalized faculty, including women, teaching about privilege as "teaching up." Although Tomlinson (2012) outlines how to "Teach Up for Excellence," that concept focuses on how to help underserved students. In contrast, the focus here is on the experiences of teaching as a minority to the dominant group in line with Messner's idea. The scholarly knowledge regarding teaching about privilege is incomplete. Most has been published by those in the dominant group. Much less has been written by those from marginalized statuses and most of the research focuses exclusively on issues surrounding race. There is a dearth of research on teaching about privilege beyond race, and there exists an intersectional understanding of teaching about oppression and inequality.

This chapter explores how women sociology faculty's position in social groups relates to their students' perceptions of them and how this may affect their teaching strategies. Sociology faculty were chosen because of the pervasive focus on privilege and inequality in sociology classes. Data was drawn from a subset of semi-structured in-depth interviews with twenty-five faculty from a variety of social groups and diverse institutions who occupy a range of professional statuses from adjunct to tenured. The data in this chapter focuses only on those who identified as women (n= 15) to address the research questions:

1. What is the experience of women sociologists as they teach about privilege?
2. How does the meaning-making of their experience vary across different intersecting social identities?
3. How are these experiences and meanings reflected in their teaching practice?
4. What implications do these findings have for retention and support of marginalized faculty?

BACKGROUND

Issues of diversity and inclusion are at the forefront on many college campuses in the current political climate. This priority illustrates the need for a more diverse faculty but also the need for classes that address and explore issues of social inequality. In the literature, much has been written about women faculty (Amey, 1996; Gardner, 2013; Greene et al., 2010; Kelly & Fetridge, 2012; Tierney & Bensimon, 1996), but this research tends to focus primarily on job satisfaction and barriers to success. In contrast, Kelly and Fetridge (2012) explored how student interactions affected job satisfaction for tenure track women. They found that for many women students were a source of joy; however, some reported that their biggest drawback to teaching was pushback from students and challenges to their authority in the classroom, mainly by male students. The literature about faculty of color (Pittman, 2010; Stanley, 2006; Turner, Gonzalez, & Wood, 2008) highlights issues of isolation, tokenism, and tenure, rarely focusing on experiences in the classroom.

The research literature about privilege centers on White faculty, with its main focus on the role race plays. With only two exceptions (Brooms & Brice, 2017; Sue, Rivera, Watkins, Kim, Kim, & Williams 2011), research on teaching about privilege features the experiences of White faculty (e.g., Davis, Mirick, & McQueen, 2015; Lawrence & Bunche, 1996; Messner, 2011). Messner (2011) has written about how he "as a white, male, heterosexual, tenured professor [can] teach in a critical and self-reflexive way about privilege," and acknowledges the ability to reflect on that is a privilege in itself (p. 4). Speaking about how privilege works to extend him even more privilege in his act of teaching about privilege, he uses Peretz's (2010) idea of "the pedestal effect" which is "when men openly support feminism, [they] benefit" (p. 10). Messner (2011) finds "…I reinforce my own white male heterosexual tenured professor privilege in the very act of being so 'open minded'" (p. 10), asserting that this is another way that structural privilege works in his favor.

Lawrence and Bunche (1996) studied the effect of a one semester multicultural education class on five White future teachers using Janet Helm's (1990) model of racial identity development. They posited that White persons must "alter their color-blind perspective and work through the feelings of guilt and shame" (p. 532) in order to teach effectively in a multicultural setting. These researchers found that while all five students made progress along the racial identity model, none reached the final stage and two were still unable "to abandon their racist personas" (p. 540). The current emphasis in the literature on how Whites should teach about privilege abandons faculty of color and faculty from other traditionally marginalized groups to traverse the rocky terrain of facilitating student understanding of their own privilege and structured systems of privilege without any sort of road map.

In studies about faculty of color, the discussion centers again on race, such as Brooms and Brice's (2017) case study of their own experiences of teaching about race and white privilege as Black men. Brooms and Brice introduce the conceptual framework of "noise" and argue "Whiteness is like a ubiquitous force that influences or is the standard by which all racial identities are framed" (2017, p. 151). They contend that as faculty of color, they too are immersed within that force, while trying to introduce students to concepts such as White privilege. Sue et al. (2011) interviewed faculty of color about their experiences discussing racially charged issues that emerged in the classroom. They found that "(a) faculty of color experience unique teaching challenges that make their classroom experiences less than positive, (b) they have learned to develop valuable teaching strategies to facilitate difficult dialogues on race, and (c) the impact of the professor's race on students is an important factor that influences racial

Teaching Up

dialogues" (p. 32). It is unclear whether these faculty of color teach directly about privilege and oppression as sociology faculty do.

WOMEN SOCIOLOGISTS: AN INTERSECTIONAL EXPLORATION

The main focus of this chapter is an exploration of the experiences of fifteen sociology faculty gleaned through semi-structured in-depth interviews. They identify as women and come from a variety of backgrounds. Two of the women were at the beginning of tenure-track positions, although they did possess prior teaching experience, while two others were nearing the end of their teaching careers with over twenty-five- and thirty-five-years teaching, respectively. One woman identified as Asian, one as mixed-race Asian/Pacific Islander and White, eight identified as Black/African-American, and five identified as White. Two women identified as disabled and one identified as gay. Eleven of the women were tenured/tenure-track, two were contingent faculty, and three taught at the community college level. From these diverse voices, some profound similarities and some interesting differences surfaced.

The intersectional nature and purposefully diverse sampling in this chapter makes it unique and fills a clear gap in the scholarship. While race is arguably one of the major areas of social oppression in the United States, it is by no means the only area of oppression. Furthermore, many theorists argue that one cannot explore issues of race without paying attention to how race intersects with other social identities such as gender, sexual orientation, ability status, and age, among others, to shape the experiences of an individual. (Collins, 2015; Ferber et. al, 2007). This chapter centers on the experiences of faculty who identify as women and who also have marginalized identities such as working class, queer, disabled, and/or racial minority.

Qualitative methodology is particularly appropriate in a project that focuses on traditionally marginalized individuals, as the "goal of qualitative research is to examine how things look from different vantage points" (Taylor, Bodgan & DeVault, 2016, p. 10). Interviewing as the primary means of data collection was a deliberate choice. Seidman (2013) asserts, "stories are a way of knowing...Telling stories is essentially a meaning-making process" (p. 7). He goes on to explain that, "At the root of in-depth interviewing is an interest in understanding the lived experience of other people and the meaning they make of that experience" (2013, p. 9).

Deterding and Waters (2018, p. 14) offer a novel approach to coding which allows researchers to "communicate the logical steps underpinning their argument and report these as they write up their study findings." Their flexible coding begins with indexing the transcripts (connecting content to the interview questions). As researchers work through this process, they start to develop an idea of how concepts may be related through memoing (Deterding & Waters, 2018, p. 15). In the second stage analytic codes are applied only to applicable sections of interview transcripts (as indicted in the indexing) and in the third stage, computer software is used "for conceptual validation, model building, and the testing and refinement of the data-based theory" (Deterding & Waters, 2018, p. 15).

In the research that follows, the author uses a variation of this method by indexing the transcripts, including notating attributes, or "the salient personal characteristics of the interviewees" (Deterding & Waters, 2018, p. 17), to illustrate themes and patterns across and among institution types, and social groups incorporating intersectional analysis. Coding then focused only on the relevant sections of transcript, as indicated by the indexing, which discuss respondents' experiences teaching about privilege, how they make meaning of these experiences, how those meanings are reflected in their teaching practices, and any implications for support and job satisfaction. This approach allows for reanalysis or secondary analysis focused on different themes in the transcripts.

Three main questions from the interviews are considered here. The first question explored how central issues of privilege and inequality were to their curriculum. This question was central to the research as the assumption of the author was that in some way, all sociology classes focused on these issues. The second question asked faculty how they expected students to address them. The final question explored classroom management and their approach to teaching and it is here that differences emerge along racial lines. The section ends with the respondents' advice to graduate students getting ready to embark on a teaching career.

Central Role of Teaching About Privilege and Inequality

"No Matter What I'm Teaching, You Have to Always be Talking About Privilege"

An overwhelming number of respondents felt that teaching about privilege was a major part of their teaching. Patty, a White heterosexual contingent faculty member, explains: "I feel like it's so woven into my orientation to the discipline . . . my definition of sociology is the causes and consequences of socially patterned inequality . . . that entails being able to talk about privilege." Eleanor, a Black heterosexual tenured faculty member, concurs: "Well, it's really got to be central to what I do, because I'm, you know, working against social injustice and oppression. And obviously, that means they have to understand, you know, how these systems are relational, and that privilege is created through oppression." Angie, a Black heterosexual tenure-track faculty member explains further:

as a sociologist, I feel like privilege and discrimination are two sides of the same coin . . . only talking about discrimination . . . you're missing a whole other side of the way the world is working. A more insidious side of the way the world is working because it's super easy to tell people to quit beating that person over there, but it's much harder to quit hiring Becky with the bad grades . . .

This statement supports the underlying assumption that issues of privilege and inequality are embedded within sociology classes and within most instructors' approaches to teaching sociology.

"Indirectly, It's About Privilege"

Among the minority who felt that privilege was not a core element of their teaching, explanations varied. Katherine Rose, a White disabled tenure-track sociologist, stated:

Well, it's probably implicit in everything I do. I could do a better job of teaching it explicitly. . . because I worry about coming across as too liberal . . . so I want to get them to the idea of privilege via the structural idea.

In contrast, Marie, a Black Community College sociologist, asserts, "I would say power is what I teach most about . . . sometimes they go hand in hand, I talk about power and privilege." She further explains that this is partly due to the student demographics as she teaches at a campus where Latinx and

Teaching Up

African American students are a majority: "and it's also partly due to me, my kind of philosophy . . . how fundamental I think power dynamics are."

Mbali, a Black tenured sociologist at a predominantly White institution, feels that "it's somewhere in the middle. And I say that, because everything I teach tends to have some Marxism in there." Finally, Rebecca, a tenure-track White woman with many years of teaching experience who teaches mainly graduate students, shares:

I do teach a lot about inequality. So indirectly, it's about privilege. . .. Explicitly, you know, that's like, not on the agenda, so to speak, as a topic, privilege for me, but it comes up all the time.

These findings show that issues of privilege, inequality, and power are addressed broadly--both directly and indirectly in a variety of sociology classes that span institutions and class levels.

Faculty Expectations on How Students Address Them

"After I Got That Sheet of Paper, Everyone's Calling Me Doctor"

For many of the women in this study, titles are important and necessary as a way to combat sexism. Eleanor, a Black woman, states, "Oh I make them call me professor or doctor . . . and I refuse to let them call me by any kind of marital designation…We do not do that to the other gender." She shared that she used to let students call her by her first name, "But I found that only the White students were doing this…And the students of color were respectfully using my title." Once that happened, she decided to use her title because "I'm going to be that for the students of color." Similarly, Angie who is also Black, "asked the White man, 'Do you ever get called by your first name? Or Mr. So and So instead of Dr?'" When he responded that 100% of his students called him Dr., she "integrated into my class how women, in particular women of color, are not given that title because it . . . jars their stereotypes" and decided "everyone's calling me doctor." Mbali stated:

Oh, they have to address me as doctor or professor. Seriously, I put that out there the first day… I understand that there are people who have no problem with students calling them by their first names. I also find very interesting that a lot of people start doing that [when] there's an increase of folks of color who become professors. So I'm not having it.

Willie and Tina, both Black faculty members, started by "wanting to be cool" and having students call them by their first names, but they "got rid of that real quick." Willie shared, "Honey, the first time somebody called me [Willie], I was like, I'm gonna have to put something in front of that . . . that thing hit deep. I was like, I ain't that cool."

"I Am No One's Mrs."

For others it is less about what they are called and more about what they do not want to be addressed as. Lori, who is mixed race, states, "I do not want to be addressed as Mrs., Period." She explains "I have students . . . that I've had, you know, consistently every semester, and I do have some students who by their senior year are calling me by my first name." She reiterates, "I would actually rather be called by

493

my first name then Mrs." Patty, who is White, shared, "I have never required my student to refer to me by anything…I am no one's Mrs. So I am not Mrs. my last name. But aside from that, I really don't care." She goes on to say, "it is not what they refer to me as but rather how they interact with me that matters."

Wendy, who is White and disabled agrees, "It's not super important to me at this point . . . like all female faculty just avoid Mrs. or Miss." She shares, "it usually doesn't come up. My students are unfailingly polite." Katherine Rose, a White woman who just earned her doctorate stated that her students call her by her first name. When asked why she stated, "Um, I don't know? It's my name. I don't feel like it diminishes the respect they have for me." However, once she starts her tenure-track position in the fall, "apparently the convention is doctor or professor last name. So I will apparently be changing that."

"If You Don't Know If They Have a PhD, Call Them Professor."

An interesting phenomenon appears when one looks more closely at who is giving which answers. For the Black faculty, they are overwhelmingly adamant about being called by their proper title. As stated above, for Angie once she found out that her White male colleagues did not have to address the issue at all, she drew the line in the sand. Tina also stated, "I think if I was not a Black woman, I would not feel compelled to say that on the first day of school."

Tutsy and Marie, who have taught twenty-five and fifteen years respectively and are nearing retirement, do not find it necessary to tell students how to address them. Marie states, "so most of them will say, Doctor." The only time she corrects students is when they address her by her first name. "Yeah that seemed to come from a couple of students that probably are not Black on my online classes." Tutsy has had "I would say, maybe half a dozen students over the past twenty-five years call me by my first name and other students kind of look at them." For her, "that's not where I get my respect from . . . students have been very respectful in the way they address me." It seems that Black women, particularly at the beginning of their careers, feel the need to establish that respect through the title, although once they are established in other ways that may lessen.

In contrast, the focus for the White women was more about not being designated by marital status. Patty jokes with her students "my mother was Mrs. my last name, as well as her mother-in-law before her. But I am no one's Mrs. so I am not Mrs. my last name." For Wendy, Mrs. comes up but she realizes that the students are attempting to be polite. "We usually more address it in a group… Remember, you want to address your female professors as doctor or professor, if you don't know if they have a PhD, call them professor."

Teaching as a Woman Sociologist: Divergent Views by Race

"I Don't Believe in the Feminist Classroom for Women of Color"

White feminists such as Maryellen Weimer, Ada Sinacore, and Karyn Boatwright argue for a shift in power in the classroom as part of a feminist, learner-centered approach to teaching. For example, Sinacore and Boatwright (2005) assert, "Principles and activities that define a unified feminist pedagogy include (a) addressing power and authority [and] (b) establishing equality" among others (pp. 109-110). Weimer (2013) believes:

494

Teaching Up

When students share power in the classroom, when they are entrusted with some decision making and feel a sense of control, there is less disruptive behavior. When they don't feel powerless, they have fewer reasons to challenge authority. Power sharing redefines the teacher-student relationship, making it less adversarial (p. 97).

Several of the white women in this study discussed being fairly informal or casual in their classrooms. Katherine Rose describes her teaching style as "very discussion based . . . for two reasons. One, I want them to take ownership of the knowledge. And, second, I think the discoveries are more powerful if they make them themselves." Patty believes, "You can get A's in my classes, even if you haven't passed exams. But you've got to keep doing the rewrites and gotta bring it too, you gotta do that."

In contrast, Tutsy, a Black sociologist with twenty-five years' experience, argues that this brand of White feminism will not work for Black women.

White women . . . this is a gross generalization, but they come across as just wanting you to be nice, you know, the feminist classroom . . . which is bullshit!. . . I don't believe in the feminist classroom for women of color because women of color are treated differently in the classroom. So you've got to come across as confident and assertive. And you know, I'm not taking any bullshit. If I tell you to put your phones away, that's exactly what I mean.

This belief is echoed in Kavita, who offers an Asian woman's perspective: "I think it's more about establishing my authority and experience and getting respect at first…I realized it matters to students . . . that gives me . . . some legitimacy in their eyes." Angie, a tenure-track Black woman, finds her administration unsupportive when it comes to her policies. She is accused of being too rigid and inflexible. Angie retorts,

[Administrators] don't understand that they're trying to get over on me because I'm a Black woman . . . students are skipping [my tests] and thinking I should just come in any time of day and let them have a makeup. They're not doing that to the White man over there. I know because I asked him.

For the Black women it seems to be an issue of respect that has cultural roots. Angie states, "You know why I'm so inflexible? The reason is that I'm constantly barraged with students who are being disrespectful . . . it's not me being inflexible, not being a doormat is different." Marie shares, "I feel very comfortable keeping control in a classroom . . . I had to make sure everyone understood…this is my class."

Tutsy remembers discussions with her White feminist colleagues: "They know I'm a feminist, but I'm just not the kind of feminist they are." She believes that her colleagues' brand of feminism will not work for her because "there is less respect for Black women in the classroom. And unless you plant your feet and assert that yeah, I have a PhD. So don't ask me what my sources are . . . That's disrespectful, disrespectful."

She goes on to say, "You've always got to prove yourself." This finding leads to the conclusion that perhaps the multiracial feminist classroom, or the Black feminist classroom, may look very different from the feminist classroom advanced in the literature.

SOLUTIONS AND RECOMMENDATIONS

It is clear from the literature that women and faculty of color, as well as those who embody both identities, face specific challenges from their students based on their membership in a traditionally marginalized group(s). How does one face those issues and become an effective instructor? The advice from the faculty interviewed in this study forms a set of solutions and recommendations that primarily falls into five categories: 1) be confident and true to oneself; 2) reflect on your privilege and/or lack thereof and share that with your students; 3) be mindful of the context; 4) be prepared for pushback; and 5) make sure you find ways to get support.

Confidence and Authenticity

"Look, You Belong Here"

For Kavita, one challenge she faced was "just addressing that imposter syndrome or inferiority complex" and she encourages faculty to remember "You've put in the years of work and study and blood, sweat and tears to be here you have something to teach them." Marie feels that "comfort and being true to yourself is important. So, make sure...even if you're in institutions that are oppressive . . . you have to still be true to what you teach, who you are, and how you interact with folks." Stella states, "To me, it's important to be visible as a queer woman." Her philosophy is "you should try as hard as you can to own who you are." However, she warns, "at the same time, you don't owe that to people, you don't have to share any parts of yourself." She reminds us that:

people who have less privilege shouldn't be the ones who have to be a prop for learning . . . maybe a guide . . . maybe a co-learner. But it should never be tell your sad story to make other people understand.

Stella also wants her students to know she came from a working-class background "to make it a little less scary for them." Tina reiterates trusting one's expertise and asserts "teaching is not . . . something that you just learn how to do and you do it, it's something that's developed over time."

Another issue with being a marginalized individual is advocating for oneself. Marie talked about her experiences in this regard:

I think you have to keep it real. What I dread all the time . . . that means that, you know, there's some issues that sometimes you feel like, 'Oh I don't really want to be that voice again.' But you know, I got to be that voice because maybe other people aren't wiling...You have to own your own strength and own what you believe and feel. . . Where there aren't spaces create them.

Mbali agrees, saying that one needs to hold others accountable and gives the advice, "don't be afraid to actually be contrary." Willie concurs, encouraging new faculty to be sincere and honest about their experiences.

I did not do that. . . And in some ways, I really wish that I would have been a little bit more vocal about my experiences . . . because if not, you might feel like you sold your soul.

Teaching Up

For faculty from marginalized groups who are often isolated or tokenized it may seem easier to assimilate in order to fit in. However, these faculty members argue for keeping one's sense of self and finding ways to fit in without being inauthentic or losing oneself. This may mean calling out sexist and racist behaviors and microaggression when they occur.

Privilege and Self-Reflection

"Tell Your Story"

Several respondents discussed the importance of being reflexive in their teaching, particularly about privilege. For Tutsy, "I would say start with where you are, tell your story." She believes the students need to see you, not a mystique. She advises, "Talk about what your privilege is. I'm Black, but I speak English, I speak Standard English. I'm light skinned. I'm thin. . . these are my privileges." Lori asserts that it is important to "know who you are first . . . reflect on your own privilege, and those spaces where you have it or don't have it." Lori believes "the more you can insert yourself as a real person into the story and, you know, give real world examples, I think it makes it that much more accessible for the students."

Patty exhorts new faculty to "be firm in what your comfort zone is and knowing that you've examined it." She further explains "don't be afraid about speaking about things you know to be real." What works for Shamari is to "talk about how I have privilege in which ways and how that works . . . Because I find when I put the privilege within myself and how it functions in different ways, I also always teach privileged intersections."

Finally, Katherine Rose speaks specifically about being disabled:

As a group with disabilities, we can deploy disability as a way to identify in ourselves as an example, an identity that is less privileged. . . We can show our students sort of that vulnerability and open up the invitation to them.

The consensus is that effective teaching often includes sharing one's own experiences and vulnerability in order to help students see how it affects them.

Mind the Context

"Base Your Pedagogy on Who Is in That Classroom"

Another important issue in teaching, particularly teaching about privilege and inequality, is the social context. For Eleanor:

I think you really have to base your pedagogy on who is in that classroom. If I've got a classroom full of very privileged people, I'm going to have them reading some novels or autobiographies to bring them inside the experience.

Mbali agrees, stating "I would actually say, you know, learn your audience, get to know your audience. Don't assume one size fits all . . . Try to understand the environment that you find yourself in."

She argues, "That matters on how you learn to teach your subject matter, because you need to know who your students are." Rebecca reminds faculty:

not to assume that the starting point of students is the same as their own . . . There's, you know, a huge distance between the two. And that's a really challenging thing to break through that and get people to see what's going on.

What worked for Marie at a school that is primarily students of color did not work for her at a predominantly White institution. Patty admits:

If I were teaching at a more diverse school, I would have to learn all of this all over again, I'm only able to do a lot of what I do so relatively comfortably because I've been in this environment now, I've put down my roots for twenty years. But pick me up and put me some place in a city put me in a place that is, you know, more diverse, put me in a place that has different types of populations that I hadn't worked with. And I'd have to learn it all over again.

Be Prepared for Pushback

"I've Got Receipts"

The reality of teaching about privilege and inequality in today's social context is that one must be prepared for students to challenge and pushback. Patty states:

Be real and expect that you may get pushback. But if you come from a place where you're genuine and you have your facts on your side, any challenge that you may get, you will be able to more easily withstand.

Tina asserts that one "not be intimidated to talk about it and to challenge the students to think about their own privilege." Tutsy encourages faculty to "be real, be concrete, be data driven." She goes on to say, "You have to think about how people are much more interested in stories, but you can tell stories in lots of different ways." For Tutsy:

I think in sociology, it's really critical to sort of show that link between the personal lived experience and that larger data . . . both how it's working in a social structural way and also here's how it's impacting the lived experiences of individuals in ways that are profound and impactful.

Angie gives more practical advice, urging faculty:

Document everything! I mean, I document everything because that way I've got receipts when people make complaints. Because know that they will make complaints either in your class or behind your back to your chair or on rate my professor.

In sum, teaching about privilege and inequality is never easy. According to the respondents, one should expect a measure of disbelief and challenge, particularly from students who claim to not see or experience privilege. However, by using a combination of reflexive teaching, personal storytelling, sharing one's

Teaching Up

own privilege, and connecting large scale data to individual experiences one can effectively introduce these concepts in a meaningful way. At the same time, one should also make sure to keep good records in case a student does lodge a complaint.

Finding Support Inside and Outside of Academia

"Your Institution Isn't Your End All Be All"

The final recommendation from respondents is less about teaching and more about work/life balance. Stella would tell new faculty "to find mentors, and to find their teaching family, their comrades, their support network." She advises:

You need people that you can talk to about work and they know it and they get it . . . they've been there. And it's ideal if there's some folks who are just like you and some folks who are less so that there are different conversations you can have when you need them.

Stella shares that she feels:

super lucky. I've got amazing colleagues. . . It's a very supportive campus. . .. My department is full of people who have a similar approach to teaching and want to talk about it.

For Shamari:

I am with my dream people . . . I came home to my academic home with the people who like raised me . . . I'm not sure how well I would have done amongst a bunch of strangers with no support that I trust.

In any career, it is important to find a good fit with your organization. However, this may be more vital for marginalized women teaching about privilege. There are expected challenges teaching about inequality so having a supportive department, division, or institution becomes more pertinent.

While finding a good fit within an institution is important, Mbali reminds faculty to "make sure that you have people that are your support system away from your institution, so that your institution isn't your end all be all." One way she does so is by participating in a women of color writing group. Stella also encourages faculty to "find some people outside of academia who will be the counterpart to that . . . people that they trust and feel good with, who don't have any stakes in that academic game." She goes on to explain:

I keep thinking about sanity . . . I don't mean to throw the word around lightly, but I think that we get tired and we get ground down. . . We love teaching about this stuff . . . It's so exciting and it's so fulfilling, and it's so satisfying, and it will wear you down.

It is often easy to base one's whole life around career goals, finding a job, earning tenure, publishing in the right journals, but it is also important to have a life outside of work.

FUTURE RESEARCH DIRECTIONS

This research expands the understanding of women faculty, particularly when it comes to teaching about privilege; however, more research is needed. Future research should explore further the intersection of race and gender by including Latina and Indigenous women as well as more Asian and mixed-race women. Another area for further exploration is the experience of men of color. Issues of sexual orientation and disability are touched upon in this study; however, more research is needed that is specifically focused in these areas. Moreover, research that moves into the classroom to observe student-teacher dynamics would provide information that interviews cannot.

As this research is based on a snowball sample, the results are not generalizable to the larger sociology faculty population in the United States. Efforts were made to find respondents from different areas of the country, from a variety of institutions including Research 1 institutions and with diverse backgrounds, but the small sample size indicates that important variations may be missed. However, while not generalizable, this research points to challenges women sociologists face in teaching about issues of privilege, inequality, and oppression.

CONCLUSION

In conclusion, it is clear from this study that, for these women sociologists at least, issues of power, privilege, and inequality are important if not central to their teaching and student outcomes. It is also clear that for most, what students call them matters. While some are not bothered by the use of a first name, most are emphatically against gendered terms such as Miss and Mrs. which, in the words of Shamari, have "all kinds of gendered layered patriarchal shit on top of it." At the same time, there were clear racial differences in that White women were less likely to demand they be addressed by their title, while all but one of the women of color insisted they be referred to as Doctor or Professor. This may be due to different cultural measures of respect. For example, Katherine Rose (who is White) felt that using her first name did not diminish the respect she received from students, while Marie (who is Black) was not particular about what her students called her as long as it was not her first name. It seemed that for White women, the issue was the sexism inherent in the use of Mrs. which defines them through a man, while for Black women it was more about establishing respect.

In terms of classroom environment, a clear racial divide also exists with women of color, particularly the Black women, needing to immediately assert their dominance and take control of the classroom. More research is needed to understand the subtleties of differences in definitions of "respect" in the classroom. From this study, it is clear that Black women prefer a classroom in which they have primary control and they see student misconduct and requests for special treatment as disrespect. One example would be Marie who encourages open dialogue, "but I'm definitely much more one who sets the tone early." Another would be Tutsy, for whom "the subtext is privilege, but the outward is just disrespect, you know, talking and laughing in the classroom . . . I interpret that as total disrespect."

In terms of supporting marginalized faculty, this research suggests that building their confidence, encouraging them to find a teaching style that suits their own personality and cultural background, can make a difference. It is important as well to create institutional environments which support faculty and allow them safe places within which to debrief, process, and vent their frustrations. Moreover, instead of a nose-to-the-grindstone approach, a focus on work/life balance will help them to better cope with the challenges of teaching. It seems that in terms of retention, institutional climate and culture is key. Several of the respondents who have found ways to be successful still feel unhappy and unsupported in their work environment, such as Willie who mentioned feeling like she "sold [her] soul." Moving beyond diversity as tokenism to creating an institutional culture that encourages diversity of thought, dress, and action that allows faculty to bring their individual strengths and passions to their work may prove an important step in retention.

Overall, according to these respondents, when it comes to teaching about issues such as power, inequality and privilege, it is important to be reflective about one's self and one's own power and oppression as well as the experiences one brings to the table. Faculty should be encouraged to share their own experiences with oppression as well as with privilege and to find videos or books that immerse students in experiences different from their own. However, faculty should also be realistic that some students will not react well when faced with their own privilege.

ACKNOWLEDGMENT

The author wishes to thank the sociologists who shared their time and experiences in this study as well as Dr. Regina Deil-Amen, Dr. Z Nicolazzo, and Dr. Kevin Henry Jr. at the University of Arizona's Education Policy and Practice Department, Melody Allan, retired educator, the editors, and peer reviewers for their feedback on drafts of this paper. This research received no specific grant from any funding agency in the public, commercial, or not-for-profit sectors.

REFERENCES

Amey, M. J. (1996). The institutional marketplace and faculty attrition. *Thought & Action, XII,* 23–36.

Bavishi, A., Hebl, M. R., & Madera, J. M. (2010). The effect of professor ethnicity and gender on student evaluations: Judged before met. *Journal of Diversity in Higher Education, 4*(3), 245–256. doi:10.1037/a0020763

Collins, P. H. (2015). Intersectionality's definitional dilemmas. *Annual Review of Sociology, 41*(1), 1–20. doi:10.1146/annurev-soc-073014-112142

Ferber, A. L., Herrera, A. O., & Samuels, D. R. (2007). The matrix of oppression and privilege: Theory and practice for the new millennium. *The American Behavioral Scientist, 51*(4), 516–531. doi:10.1177/0002764207307740

Gardner, S. K. (2013). Women faculty departures from a striving institution: Between a rock and a hard place. *The Review of Higher Education, 36*(3), 349–370. doi:10.1353/rhe.2013.0025

Greene, J., Stockard, J., Lewis, P., & Richmond, G. (2010). Is the academic climate chilly? The view of women academic chemists. *Journal of Chemical Education, 87*(4), 381–385. doi:10.1021/ed800042z

Harparlini, V. (2017). "Safe spaces" and the educational benefits of diversity. *Duke Journal of Constitutional Law & Public Policy, 13*(1), 117.

Kelly, B. T., & Fetridge, J. S. (2012). The role of students in the experience of women faculty on the tenure track. *NASPA Journal About Women in Higher Education, 5*(1), 22–45. doi:10.1515/1940-7890.1095

Kelly, B. T., & McCann, K. I. (2014). Women faculty of color: Stories behind the statistics. *The Urban Review, 46*(4), 681–702. doi:10.100711256-014-0275-8

Lawrence, S. M., & Bunche, T. (1996). Feeling and dealing: Teaching white students about racial privilege. *Teaching and Teacher Education, 12*(5), 531–542. doi:10.1016/0742-051X(95)00054-N

Messner, M. A. (1996). Studying up on sex. *Sociology of Sport Journal, 13*(3), 221–237. doi:10.1123sj.13.3.221

Messner, M. A. (2011). The privilege of teaching about privilege. *Sociological Perspectives, 54*(1), 3–14. doi:10.1525op.2011.54.1.3

Moody, J. (2004). *Faculty Diversity: Problems and Solutions.* New York, NY: Taylor & Francis. doi:10.4324/9780203463741

National Center for Education Statistics. (n.d.). Retrieved from https://nces.ed.gov/ipeds/Search/ViewTable?tableId=4555&returnUrl=/ipeds/Search/View?resultType=all&sortBy=relevance&query=faculty+diversity&query2=faculty+diversity&query=faculty diversity

Ndandala, S. (2016). A portrait of faculty diversity at selected elite universities. *International Journal of Higher Education Management, 3*(1). Retrieved from http://ezproxy.library.arizona.edu/login?url=https://search-proquest-com.ezproxy3.library.arizona.edu/docview/1874715417?accountid=8360

Peretz, T. (2010, Winter). No more Mr. Good Guy? Stepping off the pedestal of male privilege. *Voice-Male: Changing Men in Changing Times,* 10–13.

Pittman, C. T. (2010). Race and gender oppression in the classroom: The experiences of women faculty of color with white male students. *Teaching Sociology, 38*(3), 183–196. doi:10.1177/0092055X10370120

Stanley, C. A. (2006). Coloring the academic landscape: Faculty of color breaking the silence in predominantly white colleges and universities. *American Educational Research Journal, 43*(4), 701–736. doi:10.3102/00028312043004701

Taylor, S. J., Bogdan, R., & DeVault, M. L. (2016). *Introduction to qualitative research methods: A guidebook and resource* (4th ed.). Hoboken, NJ: John Wiley & Sons, Inc.

Tomlinson, C. A., & Javius, E. L. (2012). Teach up for excellence. *Educational Leadership, 69*(5), 28–33.

Turner, C. S. V., Gonzalez, J. C., & Wood, J. L. (2008). Faculty of color in academe: What 20 years of literature tells us. *Journal of Diversity in Higher Education, 1*(3), 139–168. doi:10.1037/a0012837

ADDITIONAL READING

Harris, J. C. (2017). Multiracial women students and racial stereotypes on the college campus. *Journal of College Student Development, 58*(4), 475–491. doi:10.1353/csd.2017.0038

Teaching Up

Ladson-Billings, G. (1995). But that's just good teaching! The case for culturally relevant pedagogy. *Theory into Practice, 34*(3), 159–165. doi:10.1080/00405849509543675

Ladson-Billings, G. (2014). Culturally relevant pedagogy 2.0: A.k.a. the remix. *Harvard Educational Review, 84*(1), 74–84. doi:10.17763/haer.84.1.p2rj131485484751

Levin, J. S., Haberler, Z., Walker, L., & Jackson-Boothby, A. (2014). Community college culture and faculty of color. *Community College Review, 42*(1), 55–74. doi:10.1177/0091552113512864

Levin, J. S., Jackson-Boothby, A., Haberler, Z., & Walker, L. (2015). "Dangerous work": Improving conditions for faculty of color in the community college. *Community College Journal of Research and Practice, 39*(9), 852–864. doi:10.1080/10668926.2014.917596

Lewis, M. (2012). Pedagogy and the sista' professor: Teaching Black queer feminism through the self. In E. R. Meiners & T. Quinn (Eds.), Counterpoints: Vol. 367. *Sexualities in Education: A Reader* (pp. 33–40). New York, NY: Peter Lang Publishing.

Narui, M. (2014). Hidden populations and intersectionality: When race and sexual orientation collide. In D. Mitchell, C. Simmons, & L. Greyerbiehl (Eds.), *Intersectionality & Higher Education: Theory, Research, & Praxis* (pp. 185–200). New York, NY: Peter Lang Publishing.

Osei-Kofi, N., Shahjahan, R. A., & Patton, L. D. (2010). Centering social justice in the study of higher education: The challenges and possibilities for institutional change. *Equity & Excellence in Education, 43*(3), 326–340. doi:10.1080/10665684.2010.483639

Penner, A., & Saperstein, A. (2013). Engendering racial perceptions: An intersectional analysis of how social status shapes race. *Gender & Society, 27*(3), 319–344. doi:10.1177/0891243213480262

Stanley, C. A. (2006). Coloring the academic landscape: Faculty of color breaking the silence in predominantly white colleges and universities. *American Educational Research Journal, 43*(4), 701–736. doi:10.3102/00028312043004701

KEY TERMS AND DEFINITIONS

Disability: A socially constructed social identity based upon differences in physical or intellectual ability.

Diversity: The idea that a community or environment will benefit from the inclusion of a wide variety of individuals from various gender, racial, ethnic, religious, age, and ability statuses.

Feminist Classroom: An approach to teaching that encourages reducing the power differential between faculty and students.

Gender: A socially constructed social identity based on an individual's sex, outward expression and internal identification as male, female, genderqueer, genderfluid, gender nonconforming, etc.

Inclusion: The idea that for diversity to be successful various individuals need to not only be represented in a space, but welcomed and made to feel heard and respected.

Intersectionality: The idea that an individual's experiences are not based solely on one social identity such as race, but on the interactions of multiple social identities such as race, gender, sexual orientation, age, class, and ability status among others.

Oppression: The denying of resources and privileges to a particular social group based on their membership in that group.

Pedagogy: An individual teacher's approach to teaching and learning including their teaching philosophy.

Race: A socially constructed social identity loosely connected to biological factors such as skin color, eye shape, and hair texture.

Sexual Orientation: A socially constructed social identity based on an individual's attraction to or interaction with others of similar and different genders.

Sociology: A social science that studies social groups and human interactions and focuses on social context.

This research was previously published in Accessibility and Diversity in the 21st Century University; pages 140-156, copyright year 2020 by Information Science Reference (an imprint of IGI Global).

Chapter 27
Machitia:
An Educator–Focused Liberation Platform for Education

Joél-Léhi Organista
Columbia University, USA

ABSTRACT

Machitia is an educator-focused mobile app prototype where educators create, collaborate, and share lesson plans. These lesson plans embed the following liberating and transformative theoretical frameworks and pedagogies called in this chapter "circles of liberation": (1) Dis/ability critical race theory (DisCrit), (2) biliteracy, (3) culturally sustaining pedagogy, (4) radical healing, (5) critical pedagogy, (6) proficiency-based learning, (7) queer theory, and (8) decolonizing theory. After introducing those frameworks, a mapping of currently existing educator-focused platforms prelude the review of mobile technology theoretical frameworks Machitia's design incorporates. Then, the discussion turns to how all the circles of liberation and mobile technology theoretical frameworks manifest as features within Machitia. By the end of the chapter, learners and educators will have a sense of the various possibilities of, and the need for, an education-focused liberation platform.

INTRODUCTION

The word "machitia" in the Mexican indigenous Nahuatl language means, "to teach someone something". By starting with centering an indigenous language and word, this chapter seeks to decolonize the intersectionality and possibilities of lesson plans, pedagogies, mobile technology, transformation, as well as liberation. At the core of Machitia is focus on an education for liberation platform, where educators create, collaborate, and share lesson plans. Through this core task, educators are empowered and enabled to further their own lifelong learning, facilitate peer to peer constructive criticism, labor alongside each other in the education justice movements, and, most importantly, build community among the various intersectionalities that are found within the community of educators dedicated to the emancipatory potential in teaching and learning.

DOI: 10.4018/978-1-6684-4507-5.ch027

Copyright © 2022, IGI Global. Copying or distributing in print or electronic forms without written permission of IGI Global is prohibited.

The aim of this chapter is to consider that transformative and liberating theoretical frameworks and pedagogies are neither static or monolithic, but fluid and directly connected to each other. Such frameworks and pedagogies must manifest themselves beyond the classroom and actualize within the lifelong learning, teaching of an educator through their lesson plans on mobile technologies, and community building. Just as knowledge is constructed and deconstructed, an educator focused mobile application (app) prototype has been constructed as a platform, in order to invite, engage, and lead how education for liberation is a constant process of transformation of learning and unlearning. The chapter will offer reports from the user testing in addition to the usability testing conducted by using the interactive mobile app prototype.

OVERVIEW OF CIRCLES OF LIBERATION

Prior to any discussion on the specific mobile technology theoretical frameworks informing Machitia's design, it is vital to understand what liberating, transformative theoretical frameworks and pedagogies the author will draw from, as well as how technology can facilitate the process of education for liberation. Since the purpose of Machitia focuses on liberating and transformative lesson plans, it is important to articulate what that means. There are eight theoretical frameworks and pedagogies that have been identified that collectively make up what a liberating and transformative lesson plan has the potential to be. We call these within Machitia, "circles of liberation": (1) Dis/ability Critical Race Theory (DisCrit), (2) Biliteracy (3) Culturally Sustaining Pedagogy, (4) Radical Healing, (5) Critical Pedagogy, (6) Proficiency Based Learning, (7) Queer Theory, and (8) Decolonizing Theory.

Dis/ability Critical Race Theory

DisCrit combines aspects of Critical Race Theory (CRT) and Disability Studies to propose a new theoretical framework that incorporates a dual analysis of race and ability. CRT has at least five tenets that "inform theory, research, pedagogy, curriculum, and policy: (1) the intercentricity of race and racism; (2) the challenge to dominant ideology; (3) the commitment to social justice; (4) the centrality of experiential knowledge; and (5) the utilization of interdisciplinary approaches" (Yosso, 2005, p. 73). While there are different ethnicities, the word racism is used here as it has been purveyed as a trope in society, even though scientific fact indicates that there is only one race. The word racism in this chapter is used to refer to forms of bias and discrimination experienced by people because of their ethnicity.

While there are seven tenets of DisCrit:

1. DisCrit focuses on ways that the forces of racism and ableism circulate interdependently, often in neutralized and invisible ways, to uphold notions of normalcy (Annamma, Connor, & Ferri, 2016, p. 11);
2. DisCrit values multidimensional identities and troubles singular notions of identity such as race or dis/ability or class or gender or sexuality, and so on (ibid, p. 11);
3. DisCrit emphasizes the social constructions of race and ability yet recognizes the material as well as the psychological impacts of being labeled as raced or dis/abled, which sets one outside of the western cultural norms (ibid, p. 11);

4. DisCrit privileges voices of marginalized populations, traditionally not acknowledged within research (ibid, p. 11);
5. DisCrit considers legal and historical aspects of dis/ability and race, additionally how both have been used separately and together to deny the rights of some [individuals] (ibid, p. 11);
6. DisCrit recognizes whiteness and Ability as Property and that gains for people labeled with dis/abilities have largely been made as the result of interest convergence of white, middle-class citizens (ibid, p. 11);
7. DisCrit requires activism and supports all forms of resistance (ibid, 2016, p. 11).

Biliteracy

Biliterate, bilingual, and bicultural lessons focus on using two-dimensional practices when teaching language. The language experience approach can be one of many approaches to reading, writing, listening, and speaking naturally. Biliterate education should be incorporated within any and all lesson plans to aid knowledge construction and deconstruction of tropes. Machitia will provide the starting place of resources to help educators use "evidence-based strategies for fostering biliteracy in any classroom" (Delbridge & Helman, 2015) which will aid sustaining culturally sensitive pedagogy.

Culturally Sustaining Pedagogy

Culturally Sustaining Pedagogy (CSP) builds on the literature of culturally relevant teaching and culturally responsive pedagogy. Culturally relevant teaching has three components: (a) the teachers' conceptions of themselves and others, (b) the way classroom social interactions are structured, and (c) teachers' conception of knowledge (Thompson, 2014). Then, culturally responsive pedagogy describes educators who: (1) are socio-culturally conscious, (2) are favorably disposed to diversity, (3) see themselves as cultural brokers in educational institutions, (4) understand and embrace constructivist as well as deconstructivist views of knowledge, teaching, and learning, (5) know about the lives of their students, (6) design instruction to draw on students' strengths and to address their needs (Thompson, 2014).

All these foundations come together and are expanded to become CSP which "seeks to perpetuate and foster—to sustain—linguistic, literate, and cultural pluralism as part of the democratic project of schooling" (Paris, 2012, p. 93). Shifting from culturally responsive to culturally sustaining, allows the focus to not be on the "translation of schooling into culturally responsive materials for the purpose of achievement, but positions education as the vehicle for cultivating, celebrating and sustaining cultural knowledges that have otherwise been targeted for extinction" (Smith, Tuck, & Yang, 2019. p. 16) which could also lead to radical healing.

Radical Healing

Radical Healing is a lens that is critical and liberating in addressing both ourselves as educators/learners, and those we are experiencing a formal educational lesson. While Social Emotional Learning (SEL) has become a foundational theory that has been established with educators, SEL is still in the process of providing all children and adolescents with the opportunities to learn, acquire and practice the social-emotional competencies needed to succeed in life. Its components are: 1) Self-awareness, 2) Self-management, 3) Social awareness, 4) Relationship skills, 5) Responsible decision-making skills (Oberle,

Domitrovich, Meyers, Weissberg, 2016). Radical Healing Framework (RHF) challenges both SEL and Trauma-sensitive practices in a critical lens through a five framework: Culture, Agency, Relationships, Meaning, and Achievement, referred to as "CARMA" (Ginwright, 2016). CARMA also includes identity exploration, action, social connectedness, understanding positionality and power. Students experience trauma within and outside of school, for which trauma sensitive awareness and practices could help.

Trauma-sensitive practices and learning environment are about a classroom, school, or any other teaching location in which each student is healthy, safe, engaged, supported, and challenged. The trauma-sensitive strategies toward practice are organized around four primary themes: self-awareness, relationship, belief, and "live, laugh, love" (Morgan, Pendergast, Brown, Heck, 2015). All of the aforementioned, in many school contexts, still require a social transformation as the schools act as a microcosm of following social structures that can be traumatic.

Critical Pedagogy

Critical Pedagogy is both the theory and practice of social transformation that connects education to social justice. Critical pedagogy became popular because of Paulo Freire's book, Pedagogy of the Oppressed (1970). His book calls for problem-posing education which is education for freedom, and it emphasizes that both teachers/educators and students/learners must see each other in a partnership "in the fight for their own liberation" (p. 53). He identifies five stages in the process that leads to action and reflection on that action: (1) Identify a problem, (2) Analyze the problem, (3) Create a plan of action to address the problem, (4) Implement the plan of action, (5) Analyze and evaluate the action. Liberatory pedagogy roots in understanding that knowledge is not a product, but a process that can be utilized to build proficiencies. Proficiency based learning counters the deficit and dehumanizing manner lesson plans as well as pedagogies can be operationalized if they focus solely on memorization, performance, and evaluations. Sometimes termed as competency or mastery-based learning, proficiency on a content and the application of knowledge should be aligned with the rest of the liberation and transformation pedagogies. Once this happens the learner is being empowered to take what they are learning outside the classroom and into their lives.

Queer Theory

Queer Theory centers around "anyone who self-identifies as a member of the LGBTQAI+ community. That includes but is not limited to lesbian, gays, bisexual, transgender, agender, asexual, pansexual, intersex, genderqueer, aromantic, androgynous, bigender, bicurious, androsexual, gynosexual, demisexual, polyamorous, genderfluid, and questioning individuals" (Berila, 2016, p. 6). It challenges heteropatriarchy and gendernormativity.

It is important to keep in mind how one learns about oppression and its role towards deconstructing and dismantling systems of oppression. Anti-oppressive pedagogies like all the circle of liberation recognize knowledge production as a political practice where power dynamics are always in play. There is an intersectionality between other anti-oppressive pedagogies, including contemplative pedagogy and a feminist queer pedagogy, where they recognize "that knowledge is contextual, a focus on the generative nature of teaching practices, an embrace of multiple perspectives, and a recognition that the 'life of the mind' is inevitably connected to our bodies" (Berila, 2016, p. 8). Queer theory should intersect with

Machitia

other circles of liberation. An example of this is how queer anti-oppressive pedagogy and mindfulness practices within radical healing allow for liberatory and transformative experiences (Berila, 2016).

Decolonizing Theory

Decolonizing Theory is "informed by Indigenous theory, history, epistemology, and futurity…[it] emphasize[s] the ways that colonization and decolonization are time-specific and land-specific" (Smith, Tuck, & Yang, 2019. p. 12). Decolonizing the mind reminds us that "coloniality shapes and severs human and non-human relationships across land, nation-state, water and time" and intersects with social justice education that contributes to "broad implications for pedagogy, curriculum, schooling, education policy, and social movements" (p. 13). Three demonstrations of decolonizing theory include (1) Red Pedagogy, (2) Decolonial Participatory Action Research, and (3) Culturally Sustaining Pedagogy for Indigenous Students.

Red pedagogy draws upon critical pedagogy becoming a pedagogy "that attends to decolonization in its material politics in order to recognize and nurture Indigenous practices of present and future changes" (Smith, Tuck, & Yang, 2019. p. 15). Decolonial participatory action research attempts to accomplish ground- and grassroots-knowledge production and most importantly, "draws limits to this territory by refusing to hand over anything and everything to the academic enterprise, by drawing attention to power's code of ethics" (ibid., p. 16). Culturally sustaining pedagogy for Indigenous students can manifest in endless ways. Some examples of this and how intersectionality with the other circles of liberation include: "literacies of Land" (p. 39), "paddling as pedagogy" (ibid., p. 40), place-based knowledges engaging "Xicanx epistemology that engages Indigenous as well as attempting to decolonizing pasts, presents, futures" (p. 40). Additionally the "fluidity of oceanic boundaries and movements to unsettle the naturalization of land-as-territory with stable landscapes readily available for cartographic borders" (ibid.,p. 41), "Indigenous educational institution-building beyond the parameters of nation-state" (ibid., p. 41), "Queering Indigenous Education" that clarifies the "inseparability of land sovereignty and body sovereignty" and "restoring traditional understanding of bodies to land, fluidity and tradition become complementary" (ibid., p. 42), "community ideologies of disability" (ibid., p. 44) and reshaping them, "incorporating elder input, science input, and policy input into climate change problem-solving" (ibid., p. 44), and "remembering of language as a restorative practice to counter the dismemberment or disembodiment enacted by residential schools and the reserve system…pedagogies of land-based language education that triangulate stories, ontologies, and place with Indigenous language" (ibid., p. 44).

Practicing decolonizing theory in our teaching and learning should naturally be intersectional with the other circles of liberation as figure 1 shows. Decolonizing is the:

acknowledgment that lands and waters are polluted everywhere, and so to treat water as 'pure' and sacred and others as impure is against Indigenous callings for defending the water. Likewise, to treat normative bodies as capable and pure enough to be defenders of the waters, and others as too ill, to contaminated, too disconnected, is a form of ableism and queer-phobia. To meet lands and peoples where they're at is to engage with waters/bodies as they are…these practices may not be free of colonial contamination, but they are practices of harm reduction, of healing (Smith, Tuck, & Yang, 2019. p. 45).

Figure 1. A Diagrammatic representation of Intersectionalities showing decolonizing theory and the other seven circles of liberation

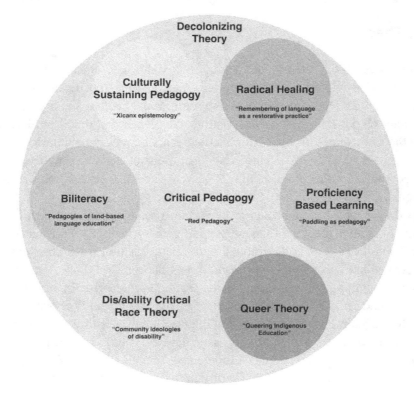

MAPPING EDUCATORS FOCUSED PLATFORMS

Imagine an educator named Terry. Terry creates amazing lesson plans, but does not have any easy, simple, and practical way or space to share and collaborate on lesson plans they create. Sharing and collaborating on lesson plans should not be so frustrating. Educators use various platforms available to fulfill their need of finding, sharing, and collaborating on lesson plans. In figure 2, the horizontal axis ranges from "hard to collaborate" to "easy to collaborate", and the vertical axis ranges from "student focus" to "educator focus".

Student Focused and Collaborative

Surveying the landscape of educator focused apps, highlights the greater need for the Machitia app.

The bottom right quadrant includes various collaborative platforms educators use in their teaching, but are student focused. They are collaborative platforms we could call "whiteboard and screencasting apps," which allow anyone in that live space to insert different multimedia documents such as PowerPoints, PDF, pictures, audio, video files, and drawings. The only platform in that bottom right quadrant that is not that type of app is Nearpod, which is a "ready-to-teach K-12 lessons" interactive learning platform that requires technology like iPads and other tablets for every student, in order to work. The lessons are "slideshows" that are interactive, and capture data on student's learning. It is easy to create and share "ready-to-teach" lessons, but they are not lesson plans and it is not focused on educators' collaboration.

Figure 2. Graph of educator focused platforms

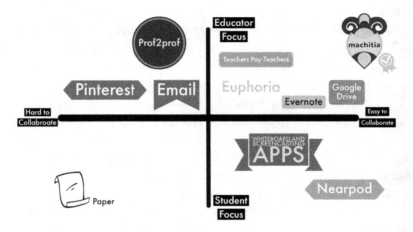

Student Focused and Not Collaborative

The bottom left quadrant is paper, which is not a digital platform, but important to put into perspective what educators use for both themselves and youth learning. Paper is used for creating lesson plans and is sometimes easy to share, however it is never ideal for collaboration.

Educator Focused and Not Collaborative

The top left quadrant includes platforms that millions of educators use to share lesson plans and resources, but sharing is not collaboration. Emailing someone your lesson plan is not a collaborative act, but is nonetheless a real interaction that happens often between educators seeking to help other educators and educators seeking to learn from other educators. Prof2Prof is a "professor-centric" platform where mainly higher education educators share syllabus and reading recommendations. Again, the focus here is sharing and not collaborating.

Pinterest is the last major platform in top left quadrant focused on educators sharing, over educators collaborating. In an article published in 2015 titled "There's a big hole in how teachers build skills, and Pinterest is helping fill it", the author quotes educators stating "often, in-person [professional development] does not offer strategies we can immediately use in our classroom… Pinterest does" (Cummings). The article positions Pinterest as the main platform educators have adopted for sharing images of lesson plans. Pinterest usage has risen steadily over the years, yet educators have become a vital group for the platform to the point that Pinterest gave educators their own "hub" on the site (Cummings, 2015). That hub includes over 30 boards and more than 163,000 followers. Educators do not need to be following that hub or boards to engage in their own created boards. Cummings shares that "education pins per day climbed from 500,000 to about 1.3 million in [2015]…popular lesson plans on Pinterest can be posted and reposted thousands of times" (2015). Posting and reposting pins are all behaviors of sharing, but not collaborating.

Educator Focused and Collaborative

The last quadrant in the figure 2 is the top right one, which includes platforms that vary in how educators focus on educator collaboration. Eduphoria is the most comprehensive tool in this quadrant. It has three integrated apps that allow for lesson planning, monitoring student progress in assessments, and provides a collaborative platform for educators and administrators. "Forethought" is the main app within Eduphoria that allows for adaptable, responsive, intertwined, team focused lesson plan creation, sharing, and collaboration. The only very real drawback of this comprehensive platform is that it is expensive, only school/district wide licensing, and the collaboration can only happen within that paying school/district, which excludes everyone without the licensing of a school/district.

Teachers Pay Teachers (TpT) is popular and known educator focused platform. Just as the name suggests, educators create lesson plans, materials, and resources available for free or for sell. TpT claims that more than 2 out of 3 educators in the US have used a resource, that over 5 million educators used TpT in the last year, and that over 1 billion resources have been downloaded from TpT (About us, 2019). Content for sell range from zero dollars to hundreds of dollars depending on the amount of resources provided within a bundle. It is common practice for new educators to spend their own money in buying resources not only from TpT, but wherever they can find what they need. The main reason TpT is on the quadrant for collaboration is because educators can rank and post comments on the quality of the resources. The majority of the comments are constructive and positive, but they are still limited because educators cannot truly collaborate with the created lesson plan on sale. They would either need to buy it, adapt it, and make it clear what they improved on by themselves, and post it on TpT again. The thread of the original lesson plan will not be officially or easily correlated to the new lesson plan posted. Therefore TpT is closely on the border leading to "hard to collaborate".

The two other platforms in this educator focused collaborative quadrant are well known platforms for non-educators as well. Evernote and Google Drive use a cloud space for documents that can be easily created, shared, and collaborated on. It is simple to control who has access to view, comment, and edit a document created within those two platforms. The documents allow for live collaboration across devices and users. Both are not initially educator focused, but educators have adopted these and other "cloud spaces" or "virtual flash drives" to share and collaborate on lesson plans.

Educators in the ethnic studies movement use Google Drive, but have come across the stress of how this tool has no frameworks specific to enhancing, reminding, and reinforcing liberating, and transformative pedagogies. It is a great tool, but it was neither built by educators for educators. Organizations have also come across the lack of organizing their resources they produce and communicating within their own members how their creation of resources, in this circumstance that being lesson plans, should have certain baselines of frameworks and pedagogies. A great example of this are summer camps that create lesson plans for their activities, but sometimes forget to keep in mind how they can use a platform for sustainability. They reinvent the wheel every year because they forgot to create a digital copy in a platform that allows for easy sharing and collaborating. Additionally, educational consultants currently only have cloud spaces and email as a place for providing specific and constructive feedback to their clients like individual teachers and sometimes whole school districts. There is not an exclusive platform that is specific to educators supporting their continual growth, which is necessarily accessible, affordable, and more importantly, rooted in applying transformative and liberating frameworks.

Machitia

Machitia is on the furthest top right corner of figure 2 because it strives to be educator focused and streamline collaboration to be an experience that is not only easy, but a practice of transformation and liberation. This is possible by understanding and designing the platform from theoretical frameworks that solve the gaps the platforms mapped lack and enhance the nature of the circles of liberation.

Figure 3. Intersectionalities of mobile technology theoretical frameworks and features in Machitia

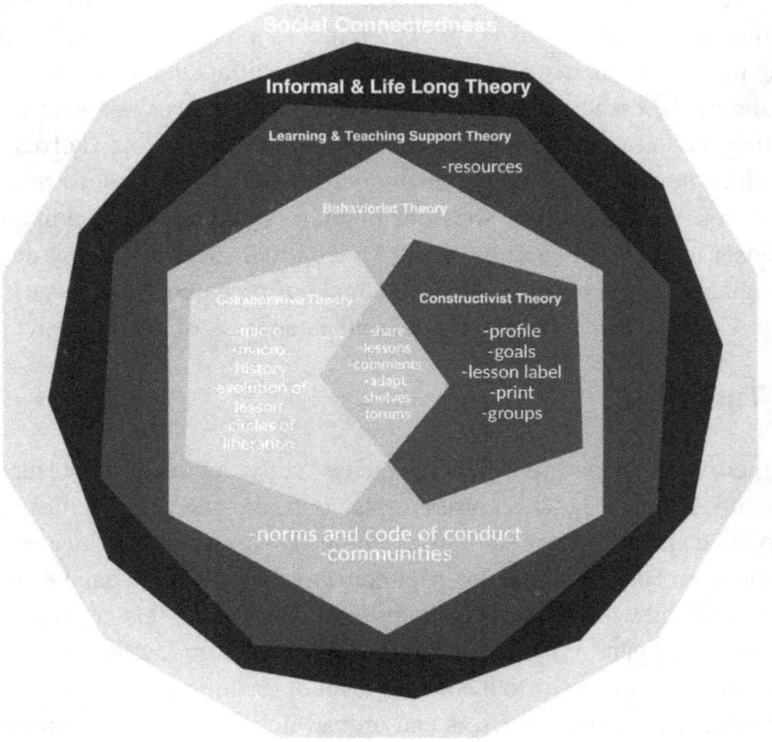

MOBILE FRAMEWORK

There are six broad mobile technology theoretical frameworks informing Machitia's design. Those frameworks are: (1) Constructivist Theory, (2) Collaborative Theory, (3) Social Connectedness Theory, (4) Behaviorist Theory, (5) Learning and Teaching Support Theory, and (6) Informal and Lifelong Theory. When describing the following theories, the "learner" in this context is the users, usually k-12 educators because they are the ones that would use the app and are "learners" engaging in activities within the app like creating lesson plans.

Constructivist Theory

The first theory is the Constructivist theory that centers on "activities in which learners actively construct new ideas or concepts based on both their previous and current knowledge" (Naismith, 2006, p. 2). This happens through the core task of educators applying their own knowledge on constructing a lesson plan in their private space in the app from "scratch" or building off previous lessons. Constructing lessons is the core task in the app and is the center of where the rest of the interactions, activities, engagement, and learning stem branch out from.

In figure 4 you can see constructivist theory with units or clusters of lesson plans the educator creates having a space to articulate the narrative of how the lesson plans come together and build upon each other. The circles of liberation will also be visible on both the label area of the lesson plans and the units. Similarly, to video playlists or music playlists on other platforms; Machitia allows the user to create shelves within their library of any combination of lesson plans they create, and others create that are available to the public. No matter what is created in Machitia, the credit goes to the creator.

In figure 5 it shows the creator can easily choose which options they want to allow for viewing, sharing, commenting, and collaborating for their lesson plans, units, and shelves. Comparable to the Snapchat feature which notifies the user if someone screenshot a picture they sent or uploaded on their story; Machitia will notify users anytime someone duplicates your lesson plan in order to adapt it. This is of course if the user allows it to be duplicated. An icon will show up on any duplicated lesson plan linking it to the original. Lesson plans will have a couple of prepared templates users can choose from or create their own. Constructing theory is central to the core task of creating anything in Machitia.

Collaborative Theory

The second board theory is Collaborative theory, which is "activities that promote learning through social interaction" (Naismith, 2006, p. 3). This comes to play once the educator decides to change the private setting of the lesson to a shared and collaborative setting. This settings of who can view, comment, and edit the lesson, in order to enable the peer-to-peer educator collaboration can be adjusted at anytime.

Figure 6 demonstrates how the platform is unique and like nothing that is out there, because it allows that the collaboration to happen in the micro and macro level. From the micro level of commenting on any element of the lesson specifically, to the macro level of creating groups, and communities working on whole units, lessons, and curricula. Users can upload images and videos on any aspect of the lesson plan, including at the end where you can showcase final products of what happened in the lesson after it was taught. This allows for a collage of examples of possible outcomes in result to teaching that lesson. Through any level of collaboration, it is easy to see the history and evolution of a lesson plan updating its content because of the positively constructive feedback. The unique element of Machitia compared to the other platforms that have been mapped out is the way collaborative theory is designed in the mobile technology.

Social Connectedness Theory

The collaborative practice also creates a community of practice with elements of social connectedness highly present (Mentor, 2016). The sense of affiliation as educators share lessons went beyond just saving time and effort, but created virtual communities of practice who share the same work requirements. Additionally, educators can now also experience social connectedness through the app's various virtual engagement media, such as from the online social networking channel and instant messaging options in the app. Similarly, as with online social media, the app provides the user with a connected presence in addition to on-the-go accessibility (Mentor, 2018).

Figure 4. Menu screen, My Lessons screen, and Home screen in Machitia

The mobile phone affords quick virtual check-ins with family and friends. In short, the consequences of using and interacting with, and on the app, offers a new, professional, interpersonal means to stay in contact (Mentor, 2016) while feeling socio-emotionally supported in a job that can feel devoid of community support. The previous examples provided hinge on the tacit existence of the cultivation of intended and unintended social connectedness. the latter signify the production and value of the successful maintenance of reciprocal professional relationships and support. In short, the app offers a means to relate to networks of like-minded contacts, thus enhancing feelings of socio-emotional support, especially important in an educational environment.

Behaviorist Theory

Behaviorist theory is the fourth framework, which is "activities that promote learning as a change in learners' observable actions" (Naismith, 2006, p. 2). This is manifested when the creator of the lesson plan is engaging with the comments and feedback on their lesson plan which "provides the reinforcement" needed to update the lesson plan. Likewise, the educator can comment on any public lesson plans to provide the same "stimulus" for the creator of that lesson plan, in turn promoting that behavior of changing content, pedagogy, and approaches possible in future implementation of a lesson plan.

Machitia has ways the educator can articulate tips of applying the circles of liberation to the specific lesson plan being constructed built into the lesson plan structure as seen in figure 6. This is another activity that promotes learning for observable actions, which in this audience is the pedagogy of educators in the classroom and outside the app. Within the terms and conditions of Machitia, it includes norms and a code of conduct that brings together all the circles of liberation. Users must follow that in order to be allowed on the platform. Users can be reported by other users on specific norms that have been violated. If found that the report is true, the reported user will have restorative practices as options to continue their learning and be permitted back to the space they have been removed from.

Figure 5. My Library screen, lesson label features, create lesson screen in Machitia

Learning and Teaching Support Theory

As seen in figure 3 the fifth theory builds off the past three, because it highlights the way Machitia is the first platform to provide a space for educators to apply within the app what they learn from resources shared within the community. Learning and Teaching Support theory is understood as "activities that assist in the coordination of learners as well as resources for learning activities" (Naismith, 2006, p. 4). This comes in the form of both the collaborative direct feedback as comments within the public lessons plans, as well as the peer led creation of spaces, communities and forums. Additionally outside the lesson plans, the provision of resources on anything educators want to coordinate around. Examples of topics of resources educators can collaborate around are the eight circles of liberation, classroom decor, wellness, parent engagement, trainings, events, and activism.

One feature that educators as user testers have requested is having a one-click printing feature, which allows them to have all their lesson plans to be easily accessible on paper, digitally, and offline. Like in other mobile technologies, there will be bi-monthly challenges to grow and learn, which is mainly to expose users to content, frameworks, pedagogies, resources, and practices they might otherwise not come across.

Informal and Lifelong Theory

The last broad mobile technology theory brings together all of the theories previously mentioned as demonstrated in figure 3. The Informal and Lifelong theory are "activities that support learning outside a dedicated learning environment as well as formal curriculum" (Naismith, 2006, p. 4). As mentioned in the brief review, through the core task of creating, sharing, and collaborating on lesson plans, educators are empowered then enabled to further their own lifelong learning. While facilitating peer to peer constructive criticism, and most importantly build community among the various intersectionalities that are found within the community of educators dedicated to the emancipatory potential in learning.

Machitia

Figure 6. Circles of Liberation, comment section, and create lesson sections in Machitia

Since the platform is targeted and catered to educators who are on there to improve the own teaching, which requires being a lifelong learner themselves; Machitia, has endless opportunities and potential for an educator to become both empowered and a learner as well. Within the user's profile they create, they have the option to articulate the level they know, understand, and can apply all the circles of liberation within their pedagogy and interactions. This allows for others to engage in empathic ways to any comments, feedback, questions, and engagement of a user because others can actually see where the user is coming from and wanting to go in terms of their own learning.

USER EXPERIENCE

Imagine Terry again, who is now using Machitia for the first time. They create their profile articulating that they are gender non-conforming, high school health teacher, Latinx, polyglot fluent in Spanish, English, Japanese, Portuguese, Nahuatl, and American Sign Language (ASL). Terry is well versed in the following circles of liberation: DisCrit, Biliteracy, Culturally Sustaining Pedagogy, Critical Pedagogy, Proficiency Based Learning, Queer Theory, and Decolonizing Theory. However, Terry is not proficient in Radical Healing Framework. Terry can make that known on their profile page and say that they are still new to radical healing framework, but is available as a resource and support for the other circles of liberation.

The first thing Terry does is create a lesson plan on Machitia after creating a profile. The lesson plan is titled "Sleep", which is a lesson in the unit of physical health. On the third image in figure 5, it shows the layout where Terry can start to fill out the label of the lesson plan with information on the grade, subject, and length. Additionally, Terry fills out the quick summary of the lesson and tags, so others can find the lesson once Terry makes the lesson public or shares it to groups and individuals. Afterwards, Terry adds what the objectives are and any preparation needed for the lesson.

The third image in figure 6 shows how Terry can break down the lesson plan with a beginning part titled "Getting Started", middle part called "During Lesson", and ending titled "Wrapping Up". Terry adds in the Getting Started section an activity that lasts 5 minutes long titled "Warm Up". At the beginning of every lesson Terry always has a warm up ready on the whiteboard for students to complete, in order to get them started in thinking about the topic or reviewing what was taught before. Terry can continue to add as many activities in the Getting Started section and add attachments, go into detail about what the educator does, the learner does, and any tips to applying any of the circles of liberation. The During Lesson section is the core of the lesson plan. Similar to the beginning section, Terry can be as detailed as they want on how the plan is written up. The Wrapping Up section is where Terry can articulate how the lesson plan can end.

Once Terry has finished everything, they want to create by themselves, they can invite specific individuals and groups to collaborate in viewing, commenting, and editing the lesson plan. Terry has an educator friend named Joshua that also teaches health, but in another state. Terry adds Joshua as a collaborator who can edit and comment on the lesson plan. Joshua starts by commenting on the lesson plan on sections he really likes. He notices that the worksheet Terry uploaded to an activity is outdated and he recently created a new worksheet for that exact activity. Joshua comments that information and uploads the more worksheet he created. Once Terry allows the lesson plan to be public to either the whole Machitia platform or just to certain groups, educators can see all the comments, updates, and history of the lesson plan. This includes seeing the options of the original worksheet Terry uploaded and the newer version by Joshua.

Terry decides that both have created the lesson plan to a level they feel comfortable to share with a group of health teachers they are a part of. Terry makes the lesson plan public with that group. Farima is part of that group and is able to comment on the lesson plan. She starts with providing feedback on potential new tags that can be added, in order to make it easier for other educators to find this lesson plan. Farima is also well versed in Radical Healing Framework and noticed in Terry's profile that he is seeking to learn how to apply this in their pedagogy. Farima's comments focus on suggestions as to how Terry can apply Radical Healing in the lesson plan. Terry then changes Farima from a view and comment only collaborator to now also be able to edit the lesson plan. Farima is now free to directly add the tips to the lesson plan, rather than just comment about them in the comment sections.

Throughout the school year, Terry receives notifications on comments from educators all over the country on how great the lesson plan is, how they have implemented it, and images of results from the activities in the lesson plan educators upload. Terry allowed the lesson to be duplicated. This means when an educator like Farima who now teaches pre-school, can duplicate Terry's original lesson plan and adapt it. Farima does this because she feels lots of the content already there can just be adapted for younger kids and does not want to type everything again. There is an icon on this duplicated lesson plan that links it to the original lesson plan. The same collaborating process happens with this new lesson plan. The creators and owners of a lesson plan can turn off the features for others to view, comment, edit, share, and duplicate a lesson plan. Every user can also control the amount, pace, and type of notifications they receive on a lesson plan, comment section, direct message, group message, and page. Terry, Joshua, and Farima are just examples of creators, community, users, and educators that can be on Machitia. There are endless opportunities and ways to create, share, and collaborate on Machitia.

CONCLUSION

Reflecting on the mapping of educator focused platforms and their degree of allowing accessible collaboration, it becomes clear that there is a need for Machitia. There is an urgency for a space where

Machitia

knowledge, resources, best practices, and ideas rooted within transformative and liberating frameworks and pedagogies can be created, collaborated on, and shared. Machitia embodies the circles of liberation in the space it constructs. It goes beyond lesson plans, but into the actualization of how community building happens in a liberating and transformative manner. Machitia is truly the only educator focused platform that provides the space for organic and constructive collaboration. By centering educators, the circles of liberation, and the mobile technology theoretical frameworks, Machitia is a unique platform that enables education for liberation and transformative learning for educators and learners.

FUTURE RESEARCH

The future and possibilities of Machitia are endless. The more diversity there is of educators on Machitia that have different intersectionalities of identities, lived experiences, subject matter expertises, and age group focus, the more empowering the platform becomes. All of which requires various research approaches as well as short and long term research foci. Machitia enables both informal and lifelong theory and learning and teaching support theory to the educator, focused through a new central space and platform for educator empowerment and learning.

Through user feedback and engagement, Machitia will improve as constructivist, collaborative, social connectedness, behaviorist, learning and teaching support, as well as informal and lifelong theories manifest in the platform. This includes, but is not limited to templates of lesson plans, showcasing new circles of liberation, moderating comment sections, communities, and forums. Furthermore, what is highlighted in your profile, new ways to collaborate, and using restorative practices in addressing any harm caused between users will also be addressed. In the future it will be important to explore how to take advantage of in-person gatherings of platform users, in order to bridge the gap between the digital space and the physical plane to support and enhance teaching, learning and transformative experiences happening through Machitia. Every educational space should facilitate as many circles of liberation no matter if it is a mobile platform, an actual in person space, as well as the digital world we traverse.

Future research on how the platforms mapped in figure 2 can be enhanced by bringing both the circles of liberation and mobile theoretical frameworks even closer, is another possible important step, since the educators using Machitia might use those platforms as well. In this regard, Machitia will explore the Learning Tools Interoperability (LTI) framework to provide users the ability to seamlessly connect between those platforms and Machitia. The research, theoretical frameworks, and practices in Machitia are applicable to the application of teaching and learning spaces, opening up additional spaces for future research. For example, using the data analytics from the app, a quantitative approach could help the developers of the app, as well as the platform users if shared responsibly while respecting FERPA, PIP, and individuals' privacy. While a qualitative approach could also help gather feedback for enhancements of the app, or input or sharing from platform users in specific districts or distally located, regarding specific lesson plans, projects or subjects. A mixed method approach of various research tools, could obviously also add a means of triangulating or crystalizing the data. There is both an invitation and challenge to implement what this chapter shares in such both physical and digital spaces and platforms, with much more research to track, monitor and evaluate the success of the app as well as the goals and objectives of what it sets out to achieve.

REFERENCES

About Us. (2019). Retrieved March 5, 2019, from https://www.teacherspayteachers.com/About-Us

Annamma, S. A., Connor, D. J., & Ferri, B. A. (2016). Disability critical race studies (DisCrit): Theorizing at the intersections of race and dis/ability. In J. D. Connor, B. A. Ferri, & S. A. Annamma (Eds.), *DisCrit: Disability studies and critical race theory in education*. New York: Teachers College Press.

Berila, B. (2016). Mindfulness as a healing, liberatory practice in queer anti-oppression pedagogy. *Social Alternatives*, *35*, 5–10.

Cummings, M. (2015, April 2). *There's a big hole in how teachers build skills, and Pinterest is helping fill it*. Retrieved from https://slate.com/human-interest/2015/04/pinterest-and-teachers-how-the-site-is-filling-a-gap-in-teacher-training.html

Delbridge, A., & Helman, L. (2015). *Evidence-Based Strategies for Fostering Biliteracy in Any Classroom*. New York: Springer Science & Business Media.

Freire, P. (1970). *Pedagogy of the Oppressed*. Academic Press.

Ginwright, S. (2016). *Hope and Healing in Urban Education: How Urban Activist and Teachers are Reclaiming Matters of the Heart*. New York, NY: Routledge.

Mentor, D. (2016). EMxC3=e&mLearning Cultivating Connected Communities: Sustainable Workforce Talent Development. In *Handbook of Research on Mobile Learning in Contemporary Classrooms* (pp. 240–259). IGI Global. doi:10.4018/978-1-5225-0251-7.ch012

Mentor, D. (2018). Micro to macro social connectedness through mobile phone engagement. In *Encyclopedia of Information Science and Technology* (4th ed.; pp. 6184–6194). IGI Global. doi:10.4018/978-1-5225-2255-3.ch537

Morgan, A., Pendergast, D., Brown, R., & Heck, D. (2015). Relational ways of being an educator: Trauma-informed practice supporting disenfranchised young people. *International Journal of Inclusive Education*, *19*(10), 1037–1051. doi:10.1080/13603116.2015.1035344

Naismith, L. Lonsadale, P., Vavoula, G., & Sharples, M. (2006). *Literature Review in Mobile Technologies and Learning*. Academic Press.

Oberle, E., Domitrovich, C., Meyers, D., & Weissberg, R. (2016). Establishing systemic social and emotional learning approaches in schools: A framework for schoolwide implementation. *Cambridge Journal of Education*, *46*(3), 277–297. doi:10.1080/0305764X.2015.1125450

Paris, D. (2012). Culturally sustaining pedagogy: A needed change in stance, terminology, and practice. *Educational Researcher*, *41*(3), 93–97. doi:10.3102/0013189X12441244

Smith, L. T., Tuck, E., & Yang, K. W. (2019). Indigenous and decolonizing studies in education: Mapping the long view. New York, NY: Routledge, an imprint of the Taylor & Francis Group.

Thompson, S. (2014). Encyclopedia of Diversity and Social Justice. Academic Press.

Machitia

Yosso, T. (2005). Whose culture has capital? A critical race theory discussion of community cultural wealth. *Race, Ethnicity and Education, 8*(1), 69–91. doi:10.1080/1361332052000341006

Zembylas, M., & Keet, A. (2018). *Critical human rights, citizenship, and democracy education: Entanglements and regenerations.* London: Bloomsbury Academic.

KEY TERMS AND DEFINITIONS

Behaviorist Theory: Activities that promote learning as a change in learners' observable actions.

Biliterate: Strengthening bridges between languages in their reading, writing, listening, and oracy.

Collaborative Theory: Activities that promote learning through social interaction.

Constructivist Theory: Activities in which learners actively construct new ideas or concepts based on both their previous and current knowledge.

Critical Pedagogy: A collective process that utilizes dialogical learning approaches which are critical of the underlying systems and structures of oppression, systemic in their inquiry into both theory and practice, participatory in involving communities in transformation, and creative in bringing into play cultural productions to re-read society.

Culturally Sustaining Pedagogy: Teaching that perpetuates and fosters linguistic, literate, and cultural pluralism as part of schooling for positive social transformation.

Decolonizing Theory: Indigenous theory, history, cosmologies, axiologies, epistemology, and futurity that is people-specific, time-specific, land-specific, in critiques of settler colonialism, borders, conceptualizations of antiblackness, heteropatriarchy, gendernormativity, and ableism.

Disability Critical Race Theory: Critical race theory and disability studies intersecting in a new theoretical framework that incorporates a dual analysis of race and ability.

Informal and Lifelong Theory: Activities that support learning outside a dedicated learning environment and formal curriculum.

Learning and Teaching Support Theory: Activities that assist in the coordination of learners and resources for learning activities.

Machitia: In the Nahuatl language it means to "teach someone something" and in this chapter refers to the mobile app showcased.

Pedagogy: The art of teaching.

Proficiency-Based Learning: The focus on mastery and being proficient over the deficit and dehumanizing focus on solely memorization, performance, and evaluations.

Queer Theory: A fluid framework of challenging heteropatriarchy, and gendernormativity, and its relation to intersectionalities.

Radical Healing: Interdisciplinary approach to healing bringing in psychological trauma, civic engagement, cultural sustainability, and social justice frameworks.

Social Connectedness: Concept often been used to characterize degrees of interpersonal trust, attachment security, social competency, and a sense of belonging, online and in the real world.

This research was previously published in Advancing Mobile Learning in Contemporary Educational Spaces; pages 243-264, copyright year 2019 by Information Science Reference (an imprint of IGI Global).

Chapter 28
Critical Theory in Research

Icarbord Tshabangu
Leeds Trinity University, UK)

Stefano Ba'
Leeds Trinity University, UK

Silas Memory Madondo
CeDRE International Africa, Zimbabwe

ABSTRACT

Based on critical theory, this chapter focuses on the first generation of Frankfurt School (mainly to authors such as T.W. Adorno, M. Horkheimer, and W. Benjamin). For discussing methodology in research, these authors are considered more representative than the younger generation (e.g., Habermas and Honneth) mainly because of the renewed interest in the direct critique of society and because of the failure of the younger generation to produce empirical research. The proponents of critical theory establish connections between theory and practice, in the sense that the social content of research must have human dignity at its centre. The difference between method-led and content-led research is discussed and considered central for this kind of approach to empirical research. Feminist research methodologies and critical race methodology are considered as closely associated with critical theory. These different approaches have developed autonomously from critical theory and are not directly related to it. However, feminist research methodologies and critical race methodology are expounded here because of their similarities to the critical theory of the Frankfurt School aimed at providing an emancipatory approach to empirical research.

INTRODUCTION

The 'first generation' of Frankfurt School, mainly authors such as T.W. Adorno, M. Horkheimer, H. Marcuse and W. Benjamin, have a bad reputation concerning empirical research, in the sense that their critique of social injustices, and modernity more in general, was accused of having paralysing effects on the impulse of researching the circumstances of specific social conditions and social actors. However, recent scholarly studies on Adorno's Critical Theory (Benzer, 2011; Holloway, Matamoros & Tischler,

DOI: 10.4018/978-1-6684-4507-5.ch028

Critical Theory in Research

2009; Holloway, 2010) and the influence of broader critical approaches (Bonefeld, 2014; Best, Bonefeld & O'Kane, 2018) are making the overall critical enterprise of the early Frankfurt School appealing to several fronts. Not least to those who are not satisfied with the mainstream methods of social sciences, still influenced by positivism (and indeed this term will be used to refer to mainstream social science).

This chapter then explores some fundamentals of Critical Theory's social philosophy and social criticism considering their potentials for social research. This chapter will provide a broad induction to the approach of Critical Theory and other critical methodologies, such as Feminist Methodologies and Critical Race Methodology, insofar as these approaches have developed methodologies very close to the principles of Critical Theory.

This chapter is targeting undergraduate students, but also post-graduate students and early career researchers who are disappointed in mainstream research methods and their apparent disregard for the emancipatory potentials of social sciences. This chapter aims at explaining as simply as possible the tenets of Critical Theory and how these principles have been applied to empirical research. This chapter may be appealing to postgraduates and early career researchers who are cut out from big research grants, because Critical Theory offers effective tools to pursue an objective social inquiry that is content-led, rather than method-led. In this examination, Critical Theory is considered that of the 'first generation' of the Frankfurt School of Critical Theory, to be precise: Theodor W. Adorno (1903-1969), Max Hork-heimer (1895-1973), Walter Benjamin (1892-1940), Herbert Marcuse (1898-1979), Friedrich Pollock (1894-1970), Leo Lowenthal (1900-1993) and Eric Fromm (1900-1980). The reason for privileging the first generation is double: firstly Habermas' linguistic turn has lost its initial impulse and (*contra* Mar-row, 1994) never really produced empirically-informed critical research (Best, Bonefeld, & O'Kane, 2018); secondly, several scholars are now referring to the 'negative turn' of Adorno as one of the main theoretical sources for critical projects and for renewing social analysis (Dinerstein et al., 2020; Hol-loway, Matamoros & Tischler, 2009).

To our knowledge, there is no systematic presentation of Critical Theory's approach to empirical research. Marrow's *Critical Theory and methodology* (1994) has Habermas' as a reference point, rather than the 'first generation' of the Frankfurt School. The only systematic approach of this kind is in Ben-zer's *The Sociology of Theodor Adorno* (2011), where there are two chapters on Adorno's empirical studies and methodology. However, these represent philological studies, rather than an exposition of the kind attempted here.

The chapter explores the general approach to Critical Theory paying attention to the type of critique to mainstream social research that its proponents developed during a long period. Furthermore, connec-tions between theory and practice are explored, in the sense that for the proponents of this approach the social content of research must have human dignity at its centre. In this section, the difference between method-led and content-led research will be discussed. Feminist Research Methodologies and Critical Race Methodology can be taken as instances of Critical Theory applied to empirical research; in that sense, these will be briefly presented. Examples of research carried out by proponents of these two ap-proaches will be illustrated. Lastly, this chapter will examine how best to do critical research and will illustrate this with an in-depth example of Critical Theory's empirical research.

By the end of this chapter, the reader should be able to understand the difference between Criti-cal Theory and traditional theory and show knowledge of specific approaches, such as Critical Race Methodology or Feminist Research Methodologies, their positions within social science and their main principles. Furthermore, the reader will be able to demonstrate how a research project deals with the criteria of 'objectivity' in a critical way that develops a rigorous research project even though constrained by lack of material resources (such as money). Though examples and tasks, the reader should be able to use their own subjective experience as a source of 'cultural intuition' and 'theoretical sensitivity'.

BACKGROUND

Before further making the case for Critical Theory, it is important to put forward two clarifications: with Critical Theory, some different approaches are often confused, most notably the post-structuralist approach to social sciences. While Max Horkheimer (2002) used this term in the 1930s to develop a research programme about the social, political and economic transformation of capitalism, later on in the 1970s and 1980s authors associated to post-structuralism and post-modernism appropriated this label to describe their work in a broad sense and to dissociate themselves from mainstream social science. This has created a certain level of confusion because Critical Theory (as defined above) would be critical of post-structuralism (e.g. Bonnet, 2009; Holloway, 2010). As pointed above, here Critical Theory is strongly associated with the 'first generation' of Frankfurt School, again authors such as T.W. Adorno, M. Horkheimer and W. Benjamin. The term Critical Theory is now very much linked to the intellectual enterprise if Habermas and Honneth, and this again may create confusion as to what constitutes the main focus of the critical approach, as Habermas shifted the conceptual terrain from existing social relations to linguistic and normative rationality. However, on the back of very recent scholarly work (e.g. Best, Bonefeld & O'Kane, 2018; Dinerstein et al., 2020) it is possible and defensible to maintain that an exclusive focus on Adorno's (but again also on Horkheimer's, Benjamin's and Marcuse's) Critical Theory.

Why Critical Theory?

The specific approach of Critical Theory maintains that social science research should find out the important and vital issues for us and that personal experience of social issues (especially in the case of the experience of disadvantage) is not just 'personal' but can be the basis for reflection and inquiry. This should be taken as a very interesting perspective because it is neither linked to methodological purity nor accept a purely deductive approach, that would dispense us from talking to people and assessing their experiences and circumstances. It is an approach that sides with those at the margin of society as much as those who are at the margin of official, well-funded administrative research, representing the 'cunny' of the reason for developing a critique of social reality.

Social Science and Empirical Research

Max Horkheimer (2002) distinguishes Critical Theory from traditional theory in the terrain of practice: influenced by Marx's critique of capitalism, the main aim for theory is changing the social conditions of exploitation and injustice. This concept of practice does not rest on normative assumptions, that is, on ideals formulated in abstract by the theorists themselves. Rather, the theory's task for practice is to find out social trends that inherently challenge the conditions of exploitation and injustice. Social research is about finding out if, how and when social actors can transform their conditions to achieve greater freedom and equality. Critical Theory aims to find what are the main struggles, hopes, desires that are coming out of social practices and how these practices can be understood as values; moral and political values understood not in the abstract, but the concrete sense.

Critical Theory in Research

Stop and Reflect

Is Critical Theory's aim to simply going out there and collecting data? No, Critical Theory approach does not start from 'zero', or a blank sheet. It always assumes a human interest in the research and assume that existing social conditions are far from ideal and need a change to obtain a greater amount of social justice

From these premises, the methodology inspired by Critical Theory needs to be attuned not simply to facts, but the potentiality of human action. Adorno (Bobka & Braunstein, 2018) maintain that 'dialectics is the ontology of the wrong state of things', which means that in the everyday social practice there is already the potentiality to resist injustice. But this potentiality is hard to be revealed by standard methodologies. Hence the continuous polemic of Adorno (and more recent social science researchers) with positivist and main-stream approaches. In a few texts on methodology and Critical Theory, it is stressed that the Frankfurt School resisted the quantifying aspects of positivist sociology to privilege a more subjective approach to the data of social science. In other words, there is a common understanding that Adorno, Marcuse and others, in criticising the 'objectivity' of economic and social science, aligned themselves with an interpretive approach to the analysis of society. If it is true that interpretation of data, in the sense of the understanding of social phenomena, belongs to Critical Theory, it is also true that they rejected the label 'subjective', which to be sure they reserved for the positivistic approach. Indeed, Adorno talked about objective tendencies of society, about general trends of objectification and reification. Let's see this more in details.

Horkheimer and Adorno (Jay, 2020), but also Benjamin (Kaufmann, 2018; Loewy, 2016; Vedda 2013), maintained that mainstream social science, influenced by the positivistic paradigm, was 'subjective' even when using quantitative data: this because the starting point of this science is a subject which is completely severed from social relations, and observes social reality as if it is something separated from the subjects and their social relations. These social relations are constituted by subjects, even if these relations tend to assume an automatic, independent form. The positivist and mainstream social science tend to understand the object of research as something external from the mind of the researcher, and for that reason, it tends to be unreachable. On the contrary, the objective approach implies a social subject constructing the social object, in other words, it is 'us' that constitute social reality. The 'object' of the research is always constituted through history and collective action, but the researcher is part of that history and that collective action. It is then possible to know this process of constitution of the object, as it is done by human beings. Yes, it is not a transparent process, it happens at the back of individuals': the social relations tend to assume an independent character from the people that perform these relations, however, social groups are involved in this complex process of social creativity and the substance of the social object so created is part of a shared, social substance.

Stop and Reflect

Is it possible to do qualitative research, starting from a very particular point of view (in terms of 'human interests') and still claim objectivity? Given that objectivity should mean a social process in which all the members of a social group are involved and broadly aware of, then yes, it is acceptable for the research process to start from 'human interests. For Critical Theory (Reitz, 2018) there is no external reality completely independent from the human mind and human interest. The point is to know more about this reality to address issues of inequality.

The Critique of Mainstream Social Research

The fundamental objection to the mainstream social science research procedure is that it does not account for the concept of 'totality', the totality of society (Adorno, 2019), that is: society is a whole that influences all of us, on all the parts of society itself and it is not possible to fully understand a part of it (let's say education or childhood) without having a general idea of the whole. Critical theorists denounce as improbable the project of researching society in an atomistic fashion, in the sense that even a large number of empirical studies on a segment of society (let's say family) cannot produce full knowledge of it, but only a series of discrete and evermore analytical reports on part of that segment itself. One just needs to browse a handbook of Sociology of Family to see that this concept (family) is taken from several different points of view and segmented through many different substantive issues which are not possible to be reconducted into a unifying view.

To obtain the sense of totality above mentioned, empirical research methods have serious limitations and simply cannot achieve that. The research paradigm influenced by positivism is so concerned about establishing 'facts' and so focused in making the research procedure 'objective' that necessarily produce a major split between the need for logical clarity and actual empirical material. On one hand, the need for logical clarity requires ever more clear categories and the 'operationalisation' of concepts, which becomes ever more an abstract procedure. On the other hand, the obvious 'scientific' need for empirical material is ever more entrapped in the need for basic observable facts, which tend to become divorced by any social relations experienced by subjects. From these two 'prongs' (Adorno, 2019), there comes the difficulty for mainstream science to say anything that has a precise foundation in clear concepts and at the same time strictly grounded on empirical material.

It is through reflection on the concepts to be used for research that Critical Theory tries to solve the problem. The object to be researched should not be thought of as something completely separated by the subject who is researching. Furthermore, social 'objects' and social issues should be thought as something in between facts and possibilities, or better: something that has an existence and something that has the potentiality of being something else (Adorno, 2019). This is not an idealist as it looks: Raymond Aron (2019) analysed how even one of the founding fathers of sociology, the positivist Emile Durkheim, had to postulate something similar for his total concept of social constraints and social force. Aron shows how in Durkheim's work of the basic elements of religion (in his sociology of religion and culture), society needs to be taken as it is and as an 'ideal focal point'. But let's make another example of this point.

Example 1: What Is Work?

Work has been framed as part of industrial sociology and always connected with employer-employee wage relationships. However feminist sociologists discovered housework as work, even if it is unpaid, simply shifting the perspective from what is usual to what is not usual. In this case, the unusual perspective was always linked to the possibility that housework may be recognised as work and valued, whether monetarily or not. In this example, the social fact of housework had to be conceptualised against a state of things which saw women exploited in the household. It had to be conceptualised against a practical idea of equality. Only after these theoretical and practical moments, housework was 'discovered'

Critical Theory in Research

empirically. We also must add that there was not simply a theoretical discovery: housework had to 'traverse' women's social experience. This example tells us how 'social objects' are never something that is completely severed from us and from social practices that we (in very different degrees, as the historical experience of women may prove) are involved in. Moreover, in this example, we see how positivist science had to narrowly define 'work' and missed the gendered experience of work. Positivist approaches to work had to atomise the concept of work and isolate, or even sanitise the experience of work to research it empirically. We can say that through reflection, feminist scholars managed to achieve a more accomplished sense of totality which made justice to the experience of women whilst generating concepts that were dealing with society.

As a further difficulty of the positivist approach, Adorno (Bobka & Braunstein, 2018) highlights how the rationality of the method cannot be separated from the rationality that produces categories in the social world, categories that have an administrative use, in the sense of maintaining social order and social control over subjects. The mainstream methods often tend to fix states of facts as natural, rather than historical, to give these facts a semblance of relations between things, rather than human arrangements that can be changed. At that regards Horkheimer and Adorno (Jay, 2020) mention the specific phenomenon of 'reification', a social tendency of transforming social relations in natural things: through this phenomenon human activity is valued not for the relations it establishes but only for the visible and measurable effects it produces.

Example 2: An Example of Reification

As an example of reification, we can assume how a teacher is not valued for the type of relationships she establishes with pupils, but only for the measurable side of the tests her pupils produce and for the wage (in terms of the amount of money) she is accountable for. So, reification turns everything social in almost natural quantities in the same way the categories of positivist empirical research tend to fix as data social issues that are continuously constituted and shaped by social practices.

Human Dignity in Researching Society

It is not a coincidence that Critical Theory and other critical methodologies strive to save the 'dignity' of the social object under examination: first, because these social objects are the products of social relations. Even in the case of a social object like 'traditional values', for mainstream social sciences, the standard procedure would be to carry out a survey whereby standardised questions would have standardised answers, with a numerical value associated to them (Adorno, 2019). These standardised questions, and the numerical value associated to the answers, may have in the end little to do with the historical reconstruction of the traditions and values of a given community, their experience and their collective endeavour. In any case, the standard survey would posit its objectivity in the mere sum of subjective answers, subjective opinions given to the rigidly standardised questions. Critical Theory would strive to recuperate the sense of dignity of the given community first, in the same way Critical Race Methodology's counter-narratives give voice to oppressed ethnic minorities.

However, the appeal to human dignity should not make us think that this would be the only reason whereby Critical Theory is suspicious of quantitative methods. Adorno (2019) thinks that human dignity

527

cannot represent a guarantee for emancipation. On that basis, quantitative empirical material can serve critical purposes, exactly because it may show that in some social circumstances human dignity is denied.

Illustration 1: The 'Cycle of Poverty

To illustrate how certain types of quantitative research can be used to (and interpreted in the sense of providing evidence in) support to human dignity let's take the case of research on the 'cycle of poverty'. The hypothesis of 'cycle of poverty' would maintain that children who are born from disadvantaged families and experience lack of resources (and even care) from an early age, are then very likely to fall into poverty in later life, and indeed to reproduce the very same conditions of this material disadvantage for their offspring. Thus, this type of research would predict that, given certain circumstances, poverty cannot be escaped, as if free will does not exist. Usually, progressive social science tends to reject the 'cycle of poverty' explanations on the ground that these explanations rely on the psychological concept of 'aspiration' (and thus can be used to blame the victims) and that these explanations usually disregard more general structural reasons, linked to the redistribution of wealth. However, Critical Theory would observe that the unfreedom of the methods serves freedom as it implicitly testifies of the general un-freedom (Adorno, 2019), that is: the implicit determinism of the methods pointing at the cycle of poverty, its fate-like course of events, would also reflect the social determinism that the lack of material resources imposes on disadvantaged part of the population.

Method-Led and Content-Led Research

The last example helps us to introduce the difference between method-led and content-led research (Benzer, 2011). That example tells us that the approach to methodology must be critical and not dogmatic: Critical Theory favours research driven by the content rather by the method and it would reject the identity of empirical research with method-led research. So, as in the case above, a quantitative approach can be preferred to a qualitative method. In the example above, assumptions based on the understanding of human and social action as in itself coherent and meaningful would not lead us very far. Critical Theory would rather observe that social action can be systematically distorted by powerful material interests (Adorno, 2019; Horkheimer, 2002). Empirical research is needed exactly for this reason.

Thus, content-led research is about empirical research informing concepts that may be already established, whilst developing them in comparison with concrete social reality. It allows the content of social reality (e.g. poverty) to appear in the form of social relations between individuals and groups (for example, exclusion from the production of wealth, the organisation of employment which excludes part of the population etc.). Method-led research is about abstract methodological concerns which are privileged over human interest. The assumption of this approach is the separation between the researcher and social reality. In this case (e.g. poverty) the researcher is not interested in the content of the social issue, he/she just need to report it in a value-free manner.

Thus, Critical Theory invites to content-led research, rather to method-led research (Benzer, 2011).

It is important to emphasise that these critical approaches do not assume that research starts from zero knowledge about the social issue to be researched. As explained above, the mind of the subject is always involved in the dynamics of the object: from a practical point of view, this also means that the researcher should not forget about her subjectivity. This wider principle is, for instance, taking place in the "co-research methodology" developed in Italy (e.g. Armano, 2020), following the collective enterprise

Critical Theory in Research

of collective movements. Feminist Research Methodologies and Critical Race Methodology developed principles that overlap the ones above discussed.

Critical Thinking Challenge 1

What are the methodological implications of this theoretical approach?

The split between the subject (the knowledge-seeking subject) and object (the content of knowledge to be discovered and determined) has been mentioned. This is an epistemological point that has methodological implications because if there is a clear split between the subject and the object, rather than a dialectic and interactive movement between these two poles, then social knowledge is simply about replicating the object in the mind of the subject. Critical Theory accuses mainstream methodology of aiming at that: simply reproducing the superficial appearance of social reality, of 'duplicating' reality without understanding its inner connections (Reitz, 2018). With inner connections, critical theorists mean the active part that subjects (we, the people, collectively or individually) play in the construction of social reality, as much as they are constituted by these social forces (we are not indeterminably free). This dialectic is not symmetrical and social research can determine from issue to issue what is the position and the power of the subjects concerning their environment. Importantly, this is also where qualitative and quantitative research may converge, as the dialectics between subjective creative moments, and their quantitative manifestations need to be explored at each successive step and through the overall picture.

Adorno (2019) would add that the overall picture may not necessarily appear harmonically: contradictions and disharmonies exist at the very heart of modern society and the way it is constituted (Bobka and Braunstein, 2018). On the other hand, mainstream methodology tends to present social reality coherently, eliminating the contradictions that characterise most of the social relations. This critical engagement with the methodology is what set Critical Theory aside from standard methodologies (Jay, 2020). Quantitative data may be used to describe standard, general trends, but critical social research would try to find counter-stories about individuals and groups that do not conform to social pressure, because through this resistance a different idea of social order and justice may emerge. The next section will illustrate exactly two examples of that.

Instances and Practices of Critical Theory

Critical Theory approach to research has similarities with many approaches to empirical research, this section focuses on two: Feminist Research Methodologies because according to their principles, all those involved in the research process are considered active agents in constructing knowledge (e.g. Kelly & Gurr, 2020; Leavy & Harris, 2019) and Critical Race Methodology (e.g. Acevedo-Gil et al., 2019; Solórzano & Yosso, 2002) because of its rigorous focus on counter-story telling and its aim to articulate the voice of the oppressed and the exploited.

Feminist Research Methodologies

There are, of course, a variety of feminist approaches to knowledge and thus research. This section does not want to provide a review of these approaches, but simply to highlight similarities with Critical Theory's understanding of social research. First of all, Feminism emphasizes the empowerment of women and transformation of patriarchal social institutions through research and research results, in the same way, that Critical Theory criticises traditional theory and stresses the importance of a theory linked to emancipatory practice (Reitz, 2018). The other important overlap concerns the challenge to the norm of objectivity of positivism, that assumes that the subject and object of research can be separated from each other and that personal and/or grounded experiences are unscientific (Leavy & Harris, 2019).

Feminism is critical of the main-stream social science approach assumption about the unproblematic nature of "evidence" and data and would reject the statement that "data exist in a one-to-one relationship with the social reality that is being studied" (Fonow & Cook, 2005: 2211; see also: Kelly & Gurr, 2020). However, Critical Theory would differ from post-structuralist feminists who consider observations about social reality a construction, in the sense that the description of social reality in form of a text, produced by the researcher, has its meaning, disjointed from the meanings of the social reality. The critical view of Adorno would maintain social relations of oppression and exploitation are materially real and these can be documented.

The other major point of overlap is about researching developing issues with participants in a way that allows them to oversee the research process (Leavy & Harris, 2019). All those involved in the research process are considered active agents in constructing knowledge, for example in the decolonising methodologies of Darder (2019) and Acevedo et al. (2019). Again, Critical Theory's scholars would be sceptical about turning social science research into a political project, especially if it is done in an unmediated fashion. But they are also critical of the neutrality of the researcher and would have welcomed a renewed conceptuality around agency, whereby the subject of the research is also collective subjects. Dignity represents a key concept in Critical Theory's understanding of social research. Feminist Methodologies move in the same direction insofar as the social conditions of women are concerned.

Feminist Geography and 'Fixity Constraint'

Despite a preference for voicing directly the experience of women, feminist research shows how the conceptualisation of gender relations can be linked to quantitative research which advances the understanding of specific issues without sacrificing the focus on injustices. So, concepts such as 'fixity constraint' is used in Feminist research (Mei-Po Kwan, 2018): 'fixity constraint' the need to perform activities at a fixed location or time, such as child-care drop-off, and 'time budget constraint', which represents limitations on the amount of time available for daily activities, such as time for housework before or after one's job. This type of research allowed a better understanding of women's everyday lives through measurable data obtained through quantitative research and this is done to highlight gendered differences and inequality (see also: Caretta & Riaño 2016).

To conclude the review of Feminist Research Methodologies and its overlap with Critical Theory's principles, there is the need to highlight a similarity on their discrimination between content-led research and method-led research: it seems clear that Feminist Research Methodologies does not advance a single specific approach to methodology, nor it advocates specific methods, but it is committed to the substantive area of gender (Leavy & Harris, 2019; Kelly & Gurr, 2020). Like Critical Theory, feminism tries to avoid being sucked in abstract methodological formulations by centring the content of their research project around gender and gender inequality.

Critical Theory in Research

Critical Race Methodology

Critical Race Methodology (CRM), as the feminist approach to research, is similar to Critical Theory in focussing not on mainstream approaches, accused of simply providing a 'master-narrative', but on the practice side of theory, and focus on a 'liberatory or transformative solution to racial, gender, and class subordination' (Solórzano & Yosso, 2002: 22; see also Darder 2019). Research must have content from the outset: a methodology that out of principles excludes content, cannot be included in this overarching research project. This fundamental project of CRM begins by defining race and racism – in the same way as Critical Theory focuses on a theory that is linked with practice, geared in identifying oppression, exploitation and the way out of these (Allen, 2017; Darder 2019). Like the project of classical German Idealism, CRM would happily cease to exist once humanity is freed from racial oppression and discrimination: it is a finite project.

As with feminism and Critical Theory, CRM also rejects notions of 'neutral' research or 'objective' researchers (Darder 2019). One of its main tasks is negative, in the sense that it aims at exposing and criticising research that silences and distorts the voice and the social realities of 'minoritised' communities based on skin colour, accent, religion and other cultural markers: "Critical Race Theory recognizes that the experiential knowledge of people of colour is legitimate, appropriate, and critical to understanding, analysing, and teaching about racial subordination" (Solórzano & Yosso, 2002: 26)

It is though important to discuss CRM here because of a particular method that has been devised by their researchers: counter-story telling (Allen, 2017).

What is counter storytelling? Solórzano and Yosso (2002: 32) give us a simple definition: 'We define the counter-story as a method of telling the stories of those people whose experiences are not often told (i.e., those on the margins of society).' This method has been used in education research, it is similar to narrative-interviews, but it includes the critique of bias representations of reality from the outset: it assumes the pervasive presence of a 'master narrative' produced by powerful elites which hide privilege and frame people from the different ethnic background as non-subjects (Haywood, 2017).

Example 3: What Is a Good Neighbourhood?

An example of this matter narrative is when US American white middle-class people fall victim to violence in their neighbourhoods and their schools, the shock comes from the standard story: 'How could this happen? This is a good neighbourhood' or 'We never thought this could happen here. This is a good school.' Whereby, if the same happens in the 'minoritised' neighbourhood, then the master narrative would frame these communities as violence-ridden communities, it would ascribe lawlessness and lack of civility as part of their nature (Solórzano and Yosso, 2002: 29).

There is a double function of this approach: on the one hand, it challenges the dominant ideology in the sense that develops a research programme that is explicitly in opposition with the master-narrative. On the other hand, bear witness of the traditions and the experiences and struggles of 'minoritised' classes. This referring back to 'minoritised' and neglected traditions is a fundamental contribution of CRM, which develops further feminist accounts of 'silenced' voices and provide a positive turn to the critique of ideology (Darder, 2019).

This approach is further articulated by the methodological approach devised by Delgado Bernal (2016). As a way to be open and receptive to counter-story telling, Bernal assumes and encourage 'cultural intuition', which is about using one's personal experience as well as a collective experience and community memory in formulating the research issues. Cultural intuition is like the concept of 'theoretical sensitivity' used by Grounded Theory Methodology (see chapter 9 in this book). Postulating collective memory in devising and practising the research process opens the possibility for members of the oppressed group to engage with the research process (Acevedo-Gil et al., 2019).

Thus, as in Critical Theory, there is no *tabula rasa* at the beginning of the research process. The counter-story telling can then assume a precise form, which can make use of four sources: '(a) the data gathered from the research process itself, (b) the existing literature on the topic(s), (c) our own [the researchers] professional experiences, and (d) our own [the researchers as minoritized people] personal experiences.' (Solórzano & Yosso, 2002: 34). The sources (b) and (c) can be translated in Critical Theory's tenet that the theoretical material always precedes and accompanies the research process and that the subject is always involved in the research of the social issue.

This last point may well be exemplified by the concept of 'racialisation': racialisation is a social process of domination through which powerful elites frame a certain group of people as racially different through the arbitrary use of markers (e.g. skin colour, accent). Thus, researchers and subjects who have been through the process of racialisation can use (c) and (d) above to make sense of that social process, capture the master narrative which underpins it and collect counter stories from other people who have been 'racialised' (Darder, 2019).

Example 4: Counter-Story Telling in the Education Field

Solórzano and Yosso (2002: 35) offer examples of counter-story telling. They refer to their research in the education field and their multi-method approach: ethnographic fieldwork, observation and discussions with participants of specific groups and narrative interviews, but also the reflexive position of the researchers and the members of the minoritised groups were mobilised to produce a theoretically grounded explanation. Moreover, previous studies, secondary data, critical views and even cultural production of that specific group (like poetry!) also came in aiding of their articulation of counter-stories. The outcome of this research process was the creation of counter-stories which assumed the form of storylines and narratives which would reflect the complexity of marginalisation in mainstream education.

In sum, counter-story telling can either take a literary or even fiction-form (it can even be the use of poetry) or can take a 'standard' form of qualitative data in form of text which are then interpreted and systematised by the researcher, who, through personal or collective experience has become part of a tradition which stands against oppression.

Methods Used in Critical Theory Research

Following the previous sections, it is important to state again that Critical Theory in methodology and methods does not follow a mainstream approach to empirical research. Indeed, Critical Theory resists and some cases subvert standard quantitative and qualitative research. It is also the case to mention that critical social research represents the struggle of critical social scientists who are plighted from lack of resources (that is money) for doing research. It is not a secret for anyone that money for research is preserved for researchers aligned to mainstream academia and approved research programmes. On that,

Critical Theory in Research

Critical Theory offers a dialectical way out of institutional marginalisation for research programmes that are committed to unmasking injustice and exploitation.

Thus, following the need to say *something* about the conditions of exploited people, Critical Theory is and must be eclectic concerning techniques and methods of data collection. The main point is that methodology cannot silence critical research and critical reflection on an unjust state of social issues. So, empirical studies can "include the whole gamut of research tools: observations, semi-structured, unstructured and in-depth interviewing; key informants testimonies, analysis of personal and institutional documents; mass-media analysis; archive searching; official statistics and reviews of published literature, ethnography and auto-ethnography, historical reconstruction, action research and semiological analysis" (Harvey, 1990: 196 – see also Jay, 2020). All of the above could be part of the critical research approach to data collection and data analysis.

Critical Theory, and the other independently connected strands in social critical research, would then encourage the researcher a bold attitude in fashioning her/his project, making full use of the 'sociological imagination', and not being afraid to challenge dominant paradigms. At the same time, Critical Theory and others (Feminist Methodologies and CRM) maintain that this challenge should be carried forward rigorously, revaluing the concept of 'objectivity' as seen above, as a dialectical relationship between the mind of the researcher and the social issues researched. This is the main reason why sometimes these approaches (CRM, feminist and critical approaches to research) are not considered 'scientific'. However, scientific neutrality and pure knowledge of facts are simply epistemologically impossible (Bobka & Braunstein, 2018).

Rather than describing a series of prescriptions about how to do Critical Theory-inspired empirical research, underneath a case study is discussed, as a way of illustrating some of the features of content-led research.

Case Study: Mario Payeras, Writer and Leader of a Revolutionary Guerrilla Group

Sergio Tischler's monograph (2009) on the political sociology of Guatemala represents a good example of Critical Theory research in action. As methods of inquiry, Tischler used: the semiotic analysis of novels of Mario Payeras, a Guatemalan writer who was also a leader of a revolutionary guerrilla group; the analysis of documents publicly available for the period in question (from the 1960s to the 1980s); his own experience of being born and raised in Guatemala (so, auto-ethnography).

The monograph is about the internal contradictions of this revolutionary guerrilla group, the feeling and the reflections of Mario Pareyas, as a novelist and as a political leader, and the different social context of the political struggle: in the countryside and the city. Tischler shows how the guerrilla movement failed, and the reasons why it failed. Through the novels and memoirs of Pareyas, he also shows how the subjectivities of people involved in the struggle change over time. Finally, Tischler shows how Guatemalan society is still moving towards changes through the organisation of ordinary people, rather than professional revolutionary militias.

Tischler is not interested in studying that part of Guatemalan society and history from a neutral standpoint, he does not seek to come up with an impartial account of class inequalities in his country (see also: Acevedo-Gil et al., 2019). As a critical theorist, Tischler (2009) wanted to depict social objectivity as antagonism and possibility of transformation (p. 29). So, Critical Theory argues for a very different concept of objectivity.

Critical Theory never starts from zero, from a blank sheet, it always starts from concrete situations of struggle and injustice. This approach is very evident in the case study reported above. In his study, Tischler (2009) goes as far as posting the theoretical concept of value-form at the beginning of his study (p. 25) and postulating the rupture of time itself for the understanding of revolutionary activities of Mario Payeras and his group. Let's unpack these points: without going into its technicality, the use of the concept of value-form (which is taken from Critical Theory studies) signifies taking a position in what it is important for a society in a given moment: the production of useful things, the production of our livelihood. What it counts here is that the critical theorist, in her or his research project, can start from an established concept that would make sense of her or his 'cultural intuition' – as in CRM (Allen, 2017). Similar, and linked to this acquired theoretical sensitivity, the 'concept of time' is positioned in a way to make sense of the 'experience of time' which is changing during intense phases of social struggles. This conception is both a product of the research itself and its presupposition.

So, in this case, study, the above-mentioned concepts (value-form and the different experience of time) are both acquired from previous studies (Vedda, 2013) and the intellectual experience of the researcher. What is important to take from this case study is that the researcher who intends to practice critical empirical research can continuously refer back to theories that make sense subjectively and also make sense in the light of the data collected during the period of research (see also Acevedo-Gil et al., 2019).

This qualitative research offers the possibility of collecting 'images' that capture the 'objectivity' confronting the subjects of this history. The 'images' he captures are the counter-narratives, as in CRM. Images that make possible to understand the social antagonism of Guatemala in that period, the political struggle of the Mario Payeras' revolutionary group, why they failed and why this failure is not the last word for a struggle for a more just society.

CONCLUSION

One of the main reasons for suggesting Critical Theory as a methodological approach to social science is that it offers sophisticated tools for those who are cut out from 'resources' and large research grants. On that, Critical Theory represents the 'cunny' of the reason for developing a critique of social reality for and with those who are less privileged. This does not mean that 'anything goes', in terms of methods used to gather data. Rather, Critical Theory would oppose any orthodoxy in the methodology where a supposed lack of correct research methods would not allow the less privileged to 'speak'.

The preference for content-led research means that critical researchers are free to design the most appropriate research method to conduct an enquiry appropriate to the object or the issue that is vital to be explored. This procedure may be subjective, but the preoccupation of Critical Theory is about devising a theory which is embedded in empirical material (Adorno, 2019). The insistence on the primacy of the issue itself (Cook, 2011) aims at using all the methods at the researcher's disposal to collect data and then reflect *through* the data, rather than *on* the data.

The strength of critical approach (in the sense delineated in this chapter) for empirical research is that allows the individual researcher to take advantage of her/his own intellectual experience: it is not just about a body of literature, from the Frankfurt School to Feminist Methodologies and to CRM, that

Critical Theory in Research

has developed critical categories and set ways of confronting social issues. It is about a live approach which is determined to resist 'the wrong state of things' (Bobka & Braunstein, 2018) and needs to be articulated in the concrete intellectual actions of the researchers.

REFERENCES

Acevedo-Gil, N., Cannella, G. S., & Huerta, M. E. (2019). Toward a Critical Race Nepantlera Methodology: Embracing Liminality in Anti-Colonial Research. *Cultural Studies, Critical Methodologies, 19*(3), 231–239. doi:10.1177/1532708618819625

Adorno, T. W. (2000). *Introduction to Sociology*. Polity Press.

Adorno, T. W. (2019). *Philosophical Elements of a Theory of Society*. Polity Press.

Allen, M. (2017). Critical Race Methodology. In M. Allen (Ed.), *The SAGE Encyclopaedia of Communication Research Methods*. Sage Publisher.

Armano, E. (Ed.). (2020). *Pratiche di inchiesta e conricerca oggi*. Ombre Corte.

Aron, R. (2019). *Main Currents in Sociological Thought: Volume two*. Routledge.

Benzer, M. (2011). *The Sociology of Theodor Adorno*. Cambridge University Press. doi:10.1017/CBO9780511686894

Best, B., Bonefeld, W., & O'Kane, C. (2018). The SAGE Handbook of Frankfurt School Critical Theory (vol. 3). Sage Publisher.

Bobka, N., & Braunstein, D. (2018). Theodor W. Adorno and Negative Dialectics. In B. Best, W. Bonefeld, & C. O'Kane (Eds.), The SAGE Handbook of Frankfurt School Critical Theory (Vol. 1). Sage Publisher.

Bonefeld, W. (2014). *Critical Theory and the critique of political economy*. Bloomsbury.

Bonnet, A. (2009). Antagonism and difference: negative dialectics and post-structuralism in view of the critique of modern capitalism. In J. Holloway, F. Matamoros, & S. Tischler (Eds.), *Negativity and revolution, Adorno and political activism* (pp. 41–78). Pluto Press.

Caretta, M. A., & Riaño, Y. (2016). Feminist participatory methodologies in geography: Creating spaces of inclusion. *Qualitative Research, 16*(3), 258–266. doi:10.1177/1468794116629575

Cook, D. (2011). *Adorno on Nature*. Routledge.

Darder, A. (2019). *Decolonizing interpretive research: a subaltern methodology for social change*. Routledge. doi:10.4324/9781351045070

Delgado Bernal, D. (2016). Cultural intuition: then, now and into the future. *Centre for Critical Race Studies at UCLA – Research Brief*, 1. Available at: https://issuu.com/almaiflores/docs/ddb_research_brief_final_version/3

Dinerstein, A. C., Vela, A. G., González, E., & Holloway, J. (Eds.). (2020). *Open Marxism 4. Against a Closing World*. Pluto Press.

Harvey, L. (1990). *Critical Social Research*. Unwin Hyman.

Haywood, J. (2017). 'Latino spaces have always been the most violent': Afro-Latino collegians' perceptions of colorism and Latino intragroup marginalization. *International Journal of Qualitative Studies in Education: QSE, 30*(8), 759–782. doi:10.1080/09518398.2017.1350298

Holloway, J. (2010). *Crack Capitalism*. Pluto Press.

Holloway, J., Matamoros, F., & Tischler, S. (Eds.). (2009). *Negativity and revolution, Adorno and political activism*. Pluto Press.

Horkheimer, M. (2002). *Critical Theory: Selected Essays*. The Continuum Publishing Company.

Jay, M. (2020). *The splinter in your eye. Frankfurt School provocations*. Verso.

Kaufmann, D. (2018). The Image of Benjamin. In B. Best, W. Bonefeld, & C. O'Kane (Eds.), The SAGE Handbook of Frankfurt School Critical Theory (Vol. 1). Sage Publisher. doi:10.4135/9781526436122.n8

Kelly, M., & Gurr, B. (Eds.). (2020). *Feminist Research in Practice*. Rowman & Littlefield.

Kwan, M-P., & Schwanen, T. (Eds.) (2018). *Geographies of Mobility: Recent Advances in Theory and Method*. Routledge.

Leavy, P., & Harris, A. (2019). *Contemporary Feminist Research from Theory to Practice*. Guilford Press.

Loewy, M. (2016). *Fire Alarm. Reading Walter Benjamin's 'on the concept of history*. Verso.

Marrow, R. A. (1994). *Critical Theory and methodology*. Sage Publisher.

Reitz, C. (2018). Herbert Marcuse: Critical Theory as Radical Socialism. In The SAGE Handbook of Frankfurt School Critical Theory (Vol. 1). Sage Publisher.

Tischler, S. (2009). *Imagen y dialéctica. Mario Payeras y los interiores de una constelación revolucionaria*. Guatemala F&G Editores.

Vedda, M. (2013). *Constelaciones dialécticas. Tentativas sobre Walter Benjamin*. Herramienta.

KEY TERMS AND DEFINITIONS

Content-Led Research: It happens when empirical research informs concepts that are already established, and the researcher develops them in comparison with concrete social reality. It allows the theory to be specific and to further articulate its concepts. It allows the content of social reality to appear in the form of social relations between individuals and groups.

Critique: The faculty of our mind to resist the appearance of reality. Research should not simply duplicate reality, it should be able to find out how this reality rests on social relations that are exploitative or unjust.

Method-Led Research: It happens when methodological concerns take over the human interest regarding the content of a specific social issue. With this approach, the fundamental thing is to have a method that is a neutral vis-à-vis social reality and that it may be capable to duplicate reality, rather than show its internal contradictions and its spaces for struggle.

Positivism: An approach to the study of social science which privilege facts, narrowly defined empirical evidence and systematically defined methodology. It tends to isolate social facts, disregarding their connections, at the expenses of social relations.

Reification: A social tendency transforming social relations in relations between things; through this phenomenon, human activity is valued not for the relations it establishes but only for the visible and measurable effects it produces.

Theory: Here 'theory' means something different from the traditional concept and usage of theory: it is not about a set of abstract concepts. The theory is connected to practice and concepts are derived from a state of things that need to be 'put right'.

This research was previously published in Approaches and Processes of Social Science Research; pages 67-88, copyright year 2021 by Information Science Reference (an imprint of IGI Global).

Chapter 29
Caring as an Authoritative Act:
Re-Thinking Respect for Students and Teachers

Shannon Audley
Smith College, USA

Julia L. Ginsburg
(iD) https://orcid.org/0000-0003-2432-3026
Smith College, USA

ABSTRACT

This chapter serves to discuss common perspectives of respect in the classroom and highlight ways to re-conceptualize authority in student-teacher relationships so that respect can be grounded in both authority and caring. The authors believe that through the framework of critical race theory, teachers can learn how to express caring respect in ways that will be validating to their students. Furthermore, because of this reframing of authority, teachers will be able to accept non-authority-based respect. Finally, this chapter encourages teachers to experience and understand respect in the ways that validate their students as people and honor their own abilities as teachers. Rather than using ideas of respect to exhibit and reinforce institutional authority, teachers can instead promote caring respect in their classrooms by highlighting students' voices and reflecting on their own roles as both an educator and a person.

INTRODUCTION

Respect is like boundaries. And some boundaries are not meant to be crossed. (Black Female High School Student)

I think [students] show respect by doing what's supposed to be done, even when others are not. (White Female Middle School Teacher)

DOI: 10.4018/978-1-6684-4507-5.ch029

Caring as an Authoritative Act

I think teachers, when they raise their voice they try to make like the…make it clear like they're in charge. So um, that's why they raise their voice, 'cause they're scared of like losing that control. (Latino Male High School Student)

What makes a teacher effective? When pre-service teachers are asked to write about an effective teacher they remember from their years in school, often they do not recall the teacher whose lesson plans were well organized and engaged their previous knowledge. They do not discuss assignments that required deep learning, nor critical thinking, nor their former teachers' carefully facilitated discussions and activities. Most (if not all) pre-service teachers write about a teacher who *cared*. This perception of effective teaching extends beyond those engaged in the teaching profession to students themselves; research suggests that students are successful – academically and personally – when they perceive their teachers as caring (Wentzel, 1997; Woolley, Kol, & Bowen, 2009). Not surprisingly, many who enter the field of education enter because they care about children and their learning. Once in the classroom, however, teachers often put caring aside and instead focus on creating an orderly and efficient classroom (Weinstein, 1998). Why does caring cease to be a pedagogical tool when a teacher first enters the classroom?

One possible explanation for overlooking the necessity of care is that novice teachers find it difficult to navigate their dual roles as both caring and authority figures (Aultman, Williams-Johnson, & Schultz, 2009). Novice teachers describe caring as important (Laletas & Reupert, 2016) but antithetical to authority (McLaughlin, 1991). Thus, novice teachers often conclude that they can either be a caring figure or an authority figure, but not both (Aultman, Williams-Johnson, & Schutz, 2009; Weinstein, 1998). As teacher education programs and professional development modules promote authority-based classroom techniques, such as SLANT (*S*it up, *L*ean Forward, *A*sk and *A*nswer questions, *N*od your head, and *T*rack the speaker), it becomes professionally risky for teachers to care, as best practices in pedagogy do not include caring. Yet, teachers can integrate, rather than oscillate between, caring and authority by engaging in *caring respect*.

Respect is a fundamental, but understudied, component of positive and healthy interpersonal relationships (Frei & Shaver, 2002). Although respect relies on the given, recognized, and accepted power differential among persons (Piaget, 1932/1952), people do not have to express respect in this manner; respect can also be a caring response to the unique attributes of personhood (Dillion, 1992). That is, respect can be conceptualized and practiced as the integration of caring and authority.

The focus of this chapter is three-fold. First, it introduces pre-service and novice teachers to thinking about classroom interactions through a Critical Race Theory (CRT) framework and highlights the importance of teachers' understanding the impact of their social location on classroom interactions. As the US teaching population is primarily White, middle class, and female, expressions of respect to and from students may go unrecognized in diverse classrooms and schools. Given the structural racism that exists within the power structure of the school system, students may not feel comfortable explicitly respecting the authority of the teacher. Thus, teachers may miss opportunities of experiencing respect from their students if they expect authoritative respect behaviors such as obedience.

Second, this chapter serves to discuss common perspectives of respect in the classroom and highlights ways to re-conceptualize authority in student-teacher relationships so that respect can be grounded in both authority and caring. The authors believe that through the framework of Critical Race Theory, teachers can learn how to express caring respect in ways that will be validating to their students. Furthermore, through this reframing of authority, teachers will be able to accept non-authority based respect.

Finally, this chapter encourages teachers to experience and understand respect in ways that validate their students as people and honor their own abilities as teachers. Rather than using ideas of respect to exhibit and reinforce institutional authority, teachers can instead promote caring respect in their classrooms by highlighting students' voices and reflecting on their roles as both educator and person.

CRITICAL RACE THEORY AND SOCIAL JUSTICE FRAMEWORK

Critical Race Theory (CRT) and social justice frameworks are imperative in shifting notions of authoritative respect towards caring respect in the classroom. Because the systematic oppression of marginalized populations is the basis on which both western society and the Euro-centric education system are built (Delgado & Stefancic, 2001), respect built upon the principle of authority can easily exacerbate existing power imbalances. Approaching respect in terms of care and self-evaluation, on the other hand, will allow teachers to: (a) begin to address structural inequality in school systems and; (b) celebrate and recognize individual differences in students' backgrounds while building relationships with students and other members of the school community. By situating respect within CRT, educators can critically examine their interactions with students, and problematize the power dynamics that necessarily come with those interactions. In doing the above, educators can shift their notions of respect from a sign of obedience to authority, and towards an ethic of care in each student-teacher interaction. Further, it is imperative, especially in Euro-American culture, for teachers not to position themselves on the side of the colonizing mentality (hooks, 2004) – that of the mentality of the White, cis-gender, able-bodied, and upper-middle-class majority.

Beyond thinking about respect within the framework of CRT, it is also important that educators consider their social locations, which are fundamentally structured by relations of power (Hartsock, 2004). Social statuses influence educators' expectations about respect. As teachers are paid comparatively little, respect is often a replacement for monetary value and to some degree is the cultural currency of teachers. However, the manner in which people show respect and expect others to show respect is based on one's own identity and experience. Because respect is culturally situated (Li & Fischer, 2007; Mann Mitsui, Beswick, & Harmoni, 1994), it is important for novice and pre-service teachers to contemplate who they are, with specific consideration to their social location, how this influences why they think they should be respected, and whether or not there are limitations or red flags for this respect. When teachers begin to situate respect within CRT, they will be able to identify education's commonly accepted notions of respect as problematic.

What Is Critical Race Theory?

Critical Race Theory (CRT) is a framework of seeing the world that centralizes race through a critical lens and highlights concerns of racial privilege and inequalities (Delgado & Stefancic, 2001; Roithmayr, 1999). It recognizes that race has social implications while also highlighting the need for intersectionality. Intersectionality, as originally coined by Dr. Kimberlé Crenshaw (1991), is the idea that different types of oppression based on categorization, such as race and gender, exist simultaneously and create more powerful systems of oppression for groups and individuals than if a single type of oppression were to exist singularly. This interconnectedness means that parts of one's identity intersect to highlight and exacerbate different experiences of oppression. For example, a Black female teacher will have different experiences

Caring as an Authoritative Act

of oppression and different needs than a Latina female teacher and a White female teacher, although all of these teachers identify as female. These –isms, such as racism, sexism, and ableism, to name a few, have the effect of treating dominated groups, such as people of color, females, gender non-conforming or trans persons, and disabled individuals, as the 'other,' and as lacking in humanity (Collins, 2004).

It is important to note that different aspects of a person's identity, such as, but not limited to, race, ethnicity, class, gender, ability, sexual orientation, and religion, combine to form a person's social location (Case, 2013). These identity-based –isms also reinforce a hierarchal view of society, giving some persons, based on their social locations, 'automatic authority' (Crenshaw, 1991). For this reason, and because the systematic oppression of marginalized peoples is the foundation of both western society and the dominant education system, deference towards White authority by students of color, in particular, cannot be assumed (Ladson-Billings, 1996) and should not be encouraged. Thus, a Critical Race Theory framework can aid in a shift away from viewing society, and notions of respect, in such a hierarchal light.

The CRT approach arose in the 1980's as a response to the unmet promises of the Civil Rights movement to end racism (Delgado & Stefancic, 2001). Pre-dating CRT, the desegregation of schools in 1954 informed a need for continued awareness and revision of policies around race and differential treatment of students. The desegregation of schools did not necessarily mean equal opportunity for students of color (Abrams & Moio, 2009; Delgado & Stefanic, 2001; Ladson-Billings & Tate, 1995). This lack of equal opportunity is but one of the manifestations of the fact that American culture is founded on accepted notions of racism and the fact that such racist ideals are engrained in the fabric of society. Whether intentional or unintentional, privilege and social inclusion were the foundation of early American education. For example, women were largely excluded from equal education, as separate public schools were designed to teach girls domestic skills until the early 19th century (Sadker & Sadker, 1994). Slavery and then de-jure segregation during the Jim Crow era kept African-Americans and others from accessing equal education until as late as the 1960s in some parts of the country (Johnston, 2011). Even Jews, who generally experienced less anti-Semitism in the United States than they had in Europe, were subject to strict quotas that limited their ability to participate in American higher education for the better part of the 20th century (Kolko, 2003).

To this day, differentials in income, political influence, and social capital create a situation where some racial groups are privileged over others. From the perspective of CRT, racism – the social system that perpetuates these racial hierarchies in Euro-American society – is embedded in the very structure of the United States' education system. CRT and intersectionality take into consideration this structural inequality. Contemporary Western society is rampant with institutional racism, and though that fact is unavoidable, teachers' recognition of this fact is necessary for the betterment of society. Through recognizing that institutional racism is inherent in Euro-American society, teachers can use a CRT lens to affect change regarding how they currently view and enact respect in the classroom.

Critical Race Theory, which was introduced to the education field in 1995 (see Ladson-Billings & Tate, 1995), is a necessary framework for caring because it takes into consideration both the social locations from all persons involved and the creation of caring human relationships. Respect should not be based on the inherent authority of the teacher, but rather, on the unique value that each student brings to the classroom. It is up to the teacher to understand their/her/his[1] assumptions about behavior expectations from students, the role of a teacher, and deference to authority. By first understanding one's social location and the limitations of that vantage point, teachers can then reconsider student behavior expectations, the role of a teacher, and deference to authority from different social locations. In this way, teachers can begin to see the limitations for considering respect from a single approach.

What Are Social Locations?

When people think of diversity, many use an analogy of a big box of crayons, with many different colors. However people are not all the same except for color (Miller, 2010); people are more like writing instruments, such as crayons, pencils, pens, chalk, and markers. Not all writing instruments are the same, and not all humans are the same (Case, 2013). Intersectionality takes into consideration the myriad aspects of personhood that play on one another and affect someone's entire experience of personhood. People have different dimensions and identities that are given meaning through social construction. In society, identities are both given value, and de-valued, depending on one's social location. Identities include, but are not limited to, race, ethnicity, gender, class, ability, sexual orientation and religious background.

A person's social location – the unique combination of their identities – is relational and, not surprisingly, complex. Personal identities that may superficially seem similar, such as two persons with the same ethnic identity, actually render different experiences and outcomes because of intersectionality. Take the example of two black students, who differ in sexual orientation. The heterosexual black male student will belong to a privileged group in relation to women and gender non-conforming people because of his gender, and sexual orientation, while simultaneously belonging to an oppressed racial group. The gay black male student, although having gender privilege, experiences oppression because of his blackness and his sexual orientation, and perhaps, depending on whether he is "out" or not, may also experience oppression from his racial group. Probing further, and complicating our stereotypes of these two students, what if the first student was Muslim, upper class, and identified as a trans-male? What if the second student was from Ethiopia, identified as a cis-male and was from a working-class family? Only seeing them as "black students" or "black male students" and categorizing them as such, limits understanding of students' needs and experiences within classrooms.

Privilege is intertwined with the American educational system in numerous ways. Generally speaking, teachers do not take into consideration their social location when approaching their students on a day-to-day basis, especially when considering respect. For example, a White male is automatically granted authority in society; therefore, as a teacher, he is also granted authority, which may be interpreted as respect. Simultaneously, a White female teacher may desire that same automatic authority, but may not be automatically granted it because of her gender. To earn her students' respect, she may demand authority by requiring complete student obedience. White students may challenge a Black teacher's authority, as authority is often associated with White privilege, society does not grant this same respect to members of other racial groups. In most cases, when respect is tied to authority, it furthers oppression for students and teachers who are already oppressed by society because of their social location. Respect based authority grants respect to a person because of their social position, not despite it, and demands for students to recognize and privilege social locations that are oppressive to their own. In essence, how teachers and others think about respect, how it is given, and how it is earned is tied to social locations. Before re-conceptualizing respect, teachers must first identify their social locations and question how this relates to their expectations about respect.

How to Identify Social Location

To understand students' social locations, teachers first have to identify their own social location, as these identities shape their experiences, beliefs, and expectations of others. In other words, teachers need to consider where they are coming from, how they got to where they are, and because of their social loca-

Caring as an Authoritative Act

tions, what their limitations are before they can truly recognize the complexity of interacting with their students. As authors, we want to acknowledge our social locations, as it has shaped our writing of this chapter. Shannon identifies as a White, able-bodied, middle class, heterosexual, cis-gender woman. She offers the perspective of a former high school biology teacher with experience in both diverse and non-diverse school environments, and of a teacher educator, who focuses on understanding how children and adolescents experience and respond to injustice within their schools. Julia identifies as a White, middle class, cis-gender, queer, able-bodied, Jewish, woman. She has basic formal teaching experience in mostly non-diverse environments and offers the perspective of the novice early childhood and elementary school teacher, and pre-service teacher. The authors acknowledge that we have experienced both privilege and oppression and that our experiences have shaped how we view and enact respect.

Teachers' Social Locations

To help you identify and think about your social location as a teacher, please answer the following questions. We will start with simple questions, such as your identity, before asking you to reflect on your social location in conjunction with privilege, oppression, and your students' social locations:

- What is your social location? That is, how do you identify in terms of:
  ○ Race and ethnicity
  ○ Gender
  ○ Class
  ○ Ability
  ○ Religion
  ○ Sexual Orientation
  ○ Nationality
  ○ Other (see the questions below to help guide your thinking)
- Where are you from? What was your own upbringing like, and how does that affect who you are today, and more specifically, who you are as an educator?
- In what ways, or through what aspects of your social location, do you experience privilege? In what ways could this experience of privilege impact your role as a teacher? In what ways could it impact how your students respond to you?
- In what ways, or through what aspects of your social location, do you experience oppression? In what ways could these experiences impact your role as a teacher? In what ways could they impact how your students respond to you?
- In what ways, or through what aspects of your social location, do you experience respect? How is this respect shown to you? Why do you believe that it is shown to you in this way?
- In what ways are you expected to give deference to, or respect to others based on your social location? How are you expected to, or how do you show respect to others? Why do you believe that you show it in this way? What is this belief based on?
- In what ways do you experience disrespect based on your social location? How is this disrespect shown to you? Why do you believe that it is shown to you this way? What is this belief based on?

Students' Social Locations

To help you identify and think about your students' social locations, please answer the following questions:

- What is your social location relative to the students that you teach?
  - This includes aspects of identity such as socio-economic status, race, religious affiliation, sexual orientation, ability, and so on.
- Based on your social location, in what ways are you able, and unable, to relate to the experience of the students in your class?
- Based on your perception of your students' social locations, in what ways are they privileged? In what ways are they oppressed? How do they relate to authority?
- In what ways do you show your students respect? Based on your perception of your students' social locations, which students receive this respect? In what ways do you think this respect could be or has been misunderstood?
- In what ways do your students show you respect? Based on your perception of your students' social locations, are your students exhibiting behaviors that you are misinterpreting as respect? Are they enacting respect behaviors that you are not identifying as such?
- If you demand respect from your students in the form of authority, which of your identities are you unknowingly privileging (e.g., which privileged identities would your students be responding to)? In what ways may your students, given their social locations, feel oppressed by giving your privileged identity automatic authority?

Social Locations in the Teaching Process

To help you identify and think about your students' social locations in relation to your teaching and their learning, please answer the following questions:

- Think back to your most recent unit or lesson. First, identify the writer, character, or person whose ideas your lesson was based on. What was their social location? What identities were not included (excluded) in the unit or lesson plan? What was the reason for their exclusion? If this exclusion was not purposeful, what was it based on?
- Think back to a lesson or a unit that you taught recently. Is there a way to include a character, person, idea, that is based on non-privileged identities? Is there a way to make this a core unit and not an "extra" lesson?
- During class discussion, question and answer sessions, or group activities, which students speak the most and/or for the longest period of time? Which students speak the least? Do you know why this might be?
- Are there certain students whose opinions are expressed or reflected more often than others?
- As the teacher, do you encourage some students to express themselves more often than others? Why or why not? If this is purposeful, why?
- Are there certain students whose interests are focused on more often than others (in terms of activities, movies, media, social media) that are used during discussion or connecting to real world application?

Caring as an Authoritative Act

- Do these interests or activities reflect the identities or lived realities of some students and not others, or some students more than others?

RECONCEPTUALIZING RESPECT

This section explores respect from three perspectives: classroom-conceptions, power-relationships, and an ethic of care framework. First, this section argues that more traditional classroom conceptions of respect reinforce a caring-authority binary, and can necessitate an unrealistic amount of emotional support for both the teacher and the student. Second, this section describes traditional power-based views of respect and highlights how these views are problematic in their focus on White, middle-class culture, which assigns authority to the teacher by default. In addition, this section discusses in more detail the role of authority in student-teacher relationships and offers a form of teacher authority that will help teachers to reconsider caring as an act of authority rather than separate from it. Further, this section argues that re-conceptualizing respect through an ethic of care framework will allow teachers to altogether reimagine respect as 'caring respect.' Finally, the section shows that caring respect is an effective way to promote caring as an act of authority and will help novice teachers integrate their roles as both authoritative and caring figures in school systems where authority is hegemonic and granted by institutions built on racism.

Understanding Respect: Classroom Conceptions

In the classroom, educators often dichotomize respect: identifying respect as either an expression of authority or an expression of caring. Student to teacher respect is often identified through deferential behaviors (authority-based respect) or caring behaviors (mutuality based respect; Goodman, 2009). Authority based respect assumes that teachers should be automatically "listened to" or students should "follow the teacher's rules" simply because they are the authority. In this situation, teachers' authority does not stem from the students' viewing them inherently as authority figures, but the authority is given to them through the institution they serve (Deutsch & Jones, 2008; Goodman, 2009). Yet, the very idea that such institutions as schools can grant authority, and by extension, respect, is controversial, as the very structure of schools reinforces racism (Ladson-Billings & Tate, 1995).

Structural racism, as it is known, adapts to changing sociocultural circumstances (Bonilla-Silva, 1997), and thus such racism is often not explicit. For example, although all teachers are 'granted' legitimate authority by schools, White students regularly challenge the legitimate authority of a teacher of color (Ladson-Billings, 1996; Rodriguez, 2009). This account of legitimate authority suggests a student's (or teacher's) culture and ethnicity influence the perceived relation of authority and respect (Ford & Sassi, 2014; Obidah & Teel, 2001; Pace & Hemmings, 2006; Weinstein, Tomlinson-Clarke, & Curran, 2003). White teachers, with no history of institutional oppression, often conflate their institutional status with authority (Obidah & Teel, 2001). Black students, because of their history of oppression and possible ancestral/generational trauma, believe that authority and respect must be earned rather than automatically granted (Deutsch, 2005; Deutsch & Jones, 2008). Thus, depending on the race and ethnicity of the teacher and students, automatic authority-based respect may not be an appropriate expectation.

In contrast, mutuality-based respect seeks to disassemble all power structures among teachers and students. According to Nelsen, Lott, and Glenn (2000), mutuality-based respect is "a two-way street," that "invites young people to see adults as people who need just as much nurturing and encouragement as they do," (p. 2). That is, students and teachers should respect each other for similar reasons and in similar ways, including equal levels of care and empathy. Although the deconstruction of power boundaries makes mutuality-based respect a more positive alternative than authority-based respect, it is not without limitations. Mutuality-based respect requires a large emotional investment from both teacher and student. As in most teacher-student relationships, the teacher's role is to provide support and care for the students. However, mutuality-based respect expects that students provide care for the teacher as well – both the teacher and the student are simultaneously the ones 'caring' and 'being cared for.' The expectation for students to shoulder the weight of caring for their teachers is not only developmentally inappropriate but puts the teacher at risk for emotional exhaustion (Acker, 1995; Isenbarger & Zembylas, 2006) and burnout (Carson, 2007) as the teacher engages in emotional labor when expectations about caring are not met (Hargreaves, 1998). Novice teachers are particularly at risk for emotional exhaustion and burnout because the first years of teaching invoke the strongest emotions (Intrator, 2006; Liljestrom, Roulston, & deMarrais, 2007) and inexperience in the classroom can lead to teachers' developmentally inappropriate expectations about students' caring behaviors (Chang, 2009; Spilt, Koomen, & Thijs, 2011). Regardless, then, of how students actually behave, if the teacher perceives that caring behaviors are not present or mutual respect is lacking, then the teacher is at risk for burnout. Thus, respect should be examined using a different approach.

Understanding Respect: Power Relationships

Social, interpersonal relationships are traditionally categorized as either vertical (i.e., unequal power relations) or horizontal (i.e., equal power relations; Rubin, Bukowski, & Parker, 2006). As teachers have status as adults, social position within the school, greater knowledge, and the expectation for student obedience (Laupa & Turiel, 1993; Laupa, Turiel, & Cowan, 1995), student-teacher relationships are considered a vertical relationship. Student-teacher relationships are power-imbalanced relationships even though not all teachers may see their role as 'disciplinarians' (Rubinstein, 2010) or agree with the acute power differential. Fostering vertical relationships or establishing authority in the classroom does not preclude caring relationships, or a student-directed environment (Brown, 2004). Yet, many teachers find it difficult to simultaneously navigate caring and authority, even when their students' request it.

In US elementary schools, children often describe respect towards their classmates as "the golden rule," reciprocity ("I'll respect you if you respect me"; Hsueh, Zhou, Cohen, Hundley, & Deptula, 2005), and being "nice" (Shwalb & Shwalb, 2006). However, children at this age do not respect teachers in the same manner; children see their teacher as an authority figure and respect the teacher as such, often through obedience (Hsueh, Zhou, Cohen, Hundley, & Deptula, 2005; Mann, Mitsui, Beswick, & Harmoni, 1994). However, children's understanding of respect towards teachers seems to shift as they become adolescents and enter junior high and high school. This shift occurs, in part, due to the changing perception of the student-teacher power relationship (Eccles, Midgley, Wigfield, Buchanan, Reuman, Flanagan, & Mac Iver, 1993). That is, adolescent students no longer see the teacher as having sole authority; rather, students begin to expect a more personal, horizontal relationship with their teachers (Wentzel, 2010). As presented, respect shifts from concerns of obedience and deference to concerns with reciprocity (Deutsch & Jones, 2008; Jones & Deutsch, 2011), previously highlighted among peers (Hsueh, Zhou, Cohen, Hundley, & Deptula, 2005).

Novice teachers often have a difficult time navigating the power differential of the teacher-student relationship (Aultman, Williams-Johnson, & Schutz, 2009). Instead of coordinating and co-presenting

Caring as an Authoritative Act

stances of authority and caring, novice teachers often vacillate between heavy handed-authority and caring stances in their teacher-student relationships (Shapira-Lishchinsky, 2011; Volkmann & Anderson, 1998). Novice teachers' difficulty in navigating authority and caring is often a reflection of their contradictory beliefs about evaluating students' behavior and creating friendly relationships (Wiggins & Clift, 1995). They believe students can see a teacher as either an authority figure or a caring person, but not both (Smagorinsky, Cook, Moore, Jackson, & Fry, 2004; Veenman, 1984). Pace's (2006) ethnography of a 9th grade English teacher who chose not to get to know her students outside of the academic context because she believed that personally knowing students would undermine her classroom control exemplifies this dichotomous thinking. This typical either/or view of teacher roles and novice teachers' subsequent difficulty in navigating these student-teacher relationships (as they see the need for both vertical and horizontal power relationships) may put teachers entering the field at increased risk for fatigue (Hargreaves, 2000) and burnout (Friedman, 1995, 2000).

Even when novice teachers attempt to balance authority and caring, they may not be successful due to external factors such as race, ethnicity, and culture, as these factors are highly influential in the performance and acceptable boundaries of teacher authority (Ford & Sassi, 2014; Weinstein, Tomlinson-Clarke, & Curran, 2004). In particular, the race/ethnicity of the teacher can influence how students interpret a teacher's behaviors. For example, Ford and Sassi's (2014) case study examining Black and White teachers' authority in an ethnic minority-majority school highlights exactly this point. Although both teachers exhibited a 'warm demander' (high student expectations and not accepting student excuses) teaching persona, the teachers' ethnicity influenced how students responded to each teacher. Students responded positively to the Black teacher's presentation of the 'warm demander persona,' but identified those same behavior traits in the White teacher as 'going hard' on her students. Ford and Sassi (2014) argue that because the Black teacher shared cultural elements with her students, she was able to foster positive teacher-student relationships with the warm demander persona. The White teacher, however, lacked not only cultural similarities with her students but also represented a hegemonic authority that she had not earned. Therefore, for the White teacher to develop a positive student-teacher relationship she had to focus on caring and building trust and approached conflicts 'indirectly.' In sum, issues of race and ethnicity further complicate the relationship between authority and caring in teacher-student relationships. However, if teachers rethink authority in a way that will allow them to integrate, rather than oscillate between, care and authority, then perhaps they can move toward reimagining care in the context of authority as well.

Generally, classroom authority is framed within one of two perspectives: traditional and progressive (see Pace & Hemmings, 2007). The traditional perspective of classroom authority grants that institutions, such as schools, bestow authority on teachers, and teachers use their authority to "cultivate the capacities of those who are themselves not yet authority figures," (Bingham, 2007, p. 455). Education programs often highlight this view of authority and novice teachers embody such a viewpoint without further reflection (McAnuty & Cuenca, 2014). The progressive perspective suggests, contrary to traditional authority that authority should not reside in the teacher, but should instead be given to the students to empower them (Freire, 1970/2005). Both perspectives, however, endorse authority as a finite thing that gives teachers the ability to relinquish it to students over time, if they choose to do so. More so, in both cases, authority can be given or taken away and is independent of the relationship in which it is occurring. Bingham and Sidorkin (2004) offer a third option where authority is not a 'thing' that one person has or does not have; rather, it is a relation dependent upon a dialogic experience. Through their concept of relational authority, Bingham and Sidorkin (Bingham, 2007; Bingham & Sidorkin, 2004) argue that

547

authority cannot be individually held; instead, it only exists within the context of a relationship. This shift in the placement of authority does not necessarily mean that the teacher loses her positional power or that the student-teacher relationship automatically becomes horizontal. Rather, it is the embodiment of the authority that a particular teacher has in a particular relation with her students (Curren, 2005).

Shifting perspectives in authority toward an ethic of care may also help disengage respect from the power relationship. Although the adolescent shift in understanding respect may be associated with shifting student-teacher relationships, not all adolescents view their relationships with teachers as egalitarian, as previously highlighted. Some adolescents see teachers as an unauthorized authority, meaning that they do not accept authority that they have not granted to teachers. This type of demanded authority is especially likely to occur in ethnically diverse schools where White teachers with hegemonic frameworks may show a lack of respect for students of color and their students' cultures and families (Boykin, 1992; Darder, 1991). Indeed, research suggests that adolescents' perception of respect towards teachers varies as a function of gender and ethnicity (Martinez-Egger & Power, 2007). This perception of respect makes it even more important for teachers to identify how students within their schools think about respect in the classroom context, in addition to rethinking authority.

Re-Conceptualizing Respect: Caring Respect

Thus far, this section has considered how respect manifests itself in classrooms and within power relationships but has yet to examine the complex ideology and origins of the word and concept of respect. Respect comes from the Latin root 'respicere,' which means to look back at or to look at again. That is, people respect things that are worth considering, merit attention, or demand to be taken seriously. To differentiate this description from things people also fear and like, respect should also be recognized as object-oriented (Dillon, 1992), meaning that the origin of respect resides within the *person* to be respected, not the giver of respect. That is: "I respect a person because that person is respect-worthy; it has nothing to do with me."

Dillon (1992) and Darwell (1977), both prominent philosophers of respect, suggest that respect comes in two forms: appraisal respect and recognition respect. Appraisal respect is a grading assessment of a person based on a standard of evaluations (known as evaluative respect). Recognition respect suggests that a person should be respected because they have worth. Although there is one type of appraisal respect, which the next section will address, there are four types of recognition respect that need closer examination as well.

Appraisal Respect

The authors suggest that teachers look for respect from students regarding appraisal (evaluative respect), as it involves an evaluation of a person's merit in light of some standard of excellence. Thus, a teacher should receive respect for being an excellent teacher. For students to be able to identify and provide evaluative respect for excellent teaching, teachers will need to help students learn to identify good teaching practices. CRT and cultural competence in teaching suggest that good pedagogy involves transparency (Gay, 2010), meaning teachers should tell students what they are doing and why. For example, let students know that constant quizzing (which may seem like punishment to them) is best practice in cognitive science and helps them in their retrieval of information (Roediger & Butler, 2011). Teachers should explain that what is happening in class is specifically designed to help them learn. This approach

Caring as an Authoritative Act

to teaching allows students to understand why teachers teach the way they do, and also allows students to use their understanding of purposeful pedagogy as a standard of excellence from which to compare.

Although it may seem like a good idea to respect students via evaluative respect (i.e., a teacher respects a student because they are a good student) the authors caution against this approach. Teachers, like all persons who reside in the US, have implicit biases of students. External characteristics such as ethnicity or gender (Riegle-Crumb & Humphries, 2012; Van den Bergh, Denessen, Horntra, Voeten & Holland, 2010) influence whether the implicit bias is positive or negative. For example, teachers identify boys as being better in math and science (Li, 1999) and ethnic majority students are academically better than ethnic minority students (Holder & Kessels, 2017). These implicit beliefs and stereotypes influence teachers' interactions with students (She, 2000). Implicit biases also extend beyond demographics and include cultural models for what good learners (and learning) looks like (Ogbu, 1992). For example, good learners are quiet or follow the rules (Hines-Datiri & Carter Anderws, 2017). The embodiment of the implicit biases for what good learners (and learning) looks like not align with teachers' school demographics or students' cultural behavioral practices (e.g., loud Black girls, Fordham, 1993). This misalignment may mean that the evaluative standard for 'what a good student looks like' may automatically privilege some students over others because of aspects of the self or their communities that they cannot control.

Recognition Respect

Recognition respect, or identifying a person's worth, depends on *why* it is that the person should have worth. Not all recognition respect applies to the classroom. Dillon (1992) identifies four types of recognition respect: institutional respect, directive respect, respect for persons, and caring respect. Institutional and directive respects are not appropriate for an ethic of care-based classroom; respect for persons is necessary, but not sufficient for an ethic of care-based classroom. Instead, teachers should work towards interactions based on caring respect to promote an ethic of care-based classroom.

Institutional respect occurs when a student (or another subordinate) respects a person because of the position they/she/he occupy or their/her/his involvement in an institution. The authors previously discussed this idea as authority-based respect, which often manifests in the classroom as obedience, such as following a teacher's directives or raising a hand before speaking. This type of respect is the most common way that teachers look for respect from students; however, students or subordinates are not directing respect towards the teacher, but towards the position that the teacher holds, or the institution. To reiterate past points, because of institutional racism inherent in the school system and the United States at large, and because of the fraught relation among the privileged having authority over the oppressed, students and parents from oppressed backgrounds may not endorse this type of institutional respect. To reiterate past points, because of institutional racism inherent in the school system and the United States at large, and because of the fraught relation among the privileged having authority over the oppressed, students and parents from oppressed backgrounds may not endorse this type of respect, regardless of who the teacher is as a person or how effectively the teacher teaches.

Directive respect is similar to institutional respect. However, this type of respect is not directed towards people, but towards actions, rules, and procedures. Actions, rules, and procedures outlined by teachers or schools, known as 'directives' are respected through compliance. For example, when a student complies with classroom rules, the student is exhibiting directive respect; that is, the student is respecting the rules, not the person who establishes or enforces the rules. Following established classroom protocols, or maintaining an orderly classroom, then, is not reflective of how the students feel towards the teacher. Instead, it is an expression of how the students feel towards the rules and procedures that the teacher has set in place (and whether or not the students find the directives worthy of their compliance). Thus, respect based on obedience or adherence to rules, procedures, and guidelines, does not represent respect towards a person, but to an institution, position, or procedure.

Respect for persons is the most commonly cited form of respect and is derived from the philosophy of Immanuel Kant (1785), who suggested because of the commonality of humanness that exists within them, all persons should be respected. That is, people should be respected based solely on their personhood. Although the concept of respect for persons is necessary for an ethic of care-based approach, it is not sufficient. Dillon (1992) argues that, at a minimum, respect for persons must be present in the classroom. A teacher needs to respect their/her/his students as people, not as a means to an end, such as a way to increase the school's standing through test scores, or as a way to increase one's salary but respecting them as an end in themselves. This expectation is the minimum standard of care present in an ethic of care.

However, just respecting a student as a person is not enough. Kantian respect for persons respects personhood, not individuality. That is, students should be respected because they have generalized features that encompass what it means to be a person. This conception of respect is problematic for two reasons. First, what it means to be a person is contestable. For example, slaves were not considered people, but property, until 1863; women were limited in their opportunities to be considered individuals (that is, not marriage property) until 1900. Second, respect for persons is respecting an abstract quality that is not limited to an individual. In that way, in respect for persons, individuals are not respected as an end, but as a means to respect what it means to be human.

Care respect (or caring respect), the final type of recognition respect, involves recognizing that each person has a unique and profound value (Dillon, 1992). In a classroom, an example of this is a teacher cherishing their/her/his students. This is not the same as simple caring. Rather, the act of cherishing is in and of itself an act of authority. To cherish, one must recognize that the person's value is fragile and needs special care; thus caring respect requires one to act (or not to act) out of benevolent concern for the person. From the teacher's perspective, there are two points to highlight. First, the teacher as the authority figure should nurture and value what is unique about each student. Second, the teacher should act in a manner that is in the student's best interest (e.g., 'protect' the student), regardless of how the teacher feels about each individual student. Because this is recognition respect and not evaluative respect, there is no emotional (or educative) evaluation at all. At the very least, teachers can recognize that a student is someone's daughter or friend, and use this recognition as a basis for caring respect. The ability to respect anyone, regardless of whether a personal relationship exists, is an aspect of caring respect in which any teacher (or person) can participate.

This classroom use of caring respect, where personal relationships are not necessary, stands in contrast to the ethics of care framework. In Noddings' (2013) ethic of care framework, the teacher and student are in a caring relationship (Noddings, 2013), which implies that they must know each other. However, a strict ethic of care approach would allow a teacher who has trouble sustaining a relationship with a student, or does not have a relationship with the student, to not respect the student, because a relationship is lacking. In caring respect, a teacher does not have to have a relationship with a student at all, as teachers can give caring respect to all persons, not just friends, family, and 'good students.'

In the classroom, caring respect can be embodied by providing attention and taking students' ideas and concerns seriously (even if they seem off-topic). Ignoring or dismissing student ideas or concerns,

Caring as an Authoritative Act

no matter how kindly, is to not respect those students – in many cases it is disrespectful. More importantly, however, caring respect involves recognizing each student in ways that they want to be recognized. Therefore, respecting a student, *because* of who they are, rather than despite who they are, is reflective of how they/she/he want(s) to be perceived. If a student does not do well in class but sees themselves/herself/himself as a star soccer player, or a good friend, then teachers need to recognize and carefully consider that their/her/his interactions with that student cultivate those aspects in that student, rather than lamenting that the student does not do well in class. Caring respect requires people to recognize that humans are not wholly autonomous and that people have the power to make and unmake each other as persons; it asks people to exercise this power wisely and carefully. This notion is important, as teachers often underestimate their influence on peers' perceptions of each other (Audley-Piotrowski, Singer, Patterson, 2015; Farmer, Dawes, Hamm, Lee, Mehtaji, Hoffman, & Brooks, 2017). As the next section suggests, how teachers interact with students regarding social location, authority, and care, influences not just their existence in school, but who they are as individuals.

Re-Conceptualizing Respect: Student Voices

Over the past seven years, the first author has interviewed teachers and students about their experiences of respect and disrespect in classrooms. The authors have noticed a growing gap among how teachers and students conceptualize respect: teachers call for authoritative respect (Audley, 2017) and students call for respect as caring (Singer & Audley, in press). The student insistence of respect as caring is especially true for students of color, who identify teachers' lack of knowledge about social locations as disrespect. This section presents the first author's research on this subject, examining high school students' experiences of respect and disrespect in the classroom.

Methods

For this study, the authors combined two sets of interviews that occurred between 2014 and 2017: adolescents' experiences of disrespect in high school and emerging adults' recollections of disrespectful experiences in high school. The participants came from primarily the Northeast ($n = 17$) and Western ($n = 15$) regions of the United States; 87.1% of participants identified as an ethnic minority, and 59.4% identified as female. Participant ethnic identities included, but are not limited to (in their own words): Jamaican, Indian, Puerto Rican, Mixed, White, Afro-Cuban, Vietnamese, and Chinese-American, among others. Students came from a variety of high schools and colleges (including traditional public high schools, charter high schools, community colleges, public universities, and private universities) and a wide range of socio-economic statuses, representing a diversity of possible social locations. Each student was interviewed for about an hour on topics related to respect and disrespect experiences in high school, using questions such as: "tell me about a time you felt disrespected by a teacher," and, "tell me about a time you felt respected at school." Other specific questions asked depended on the particular study.

To understand how students experienced and reported respect and disrespect with their teachers and in their classrooms, the authors analyzed the interviews using thematic analysis, a common analysis technique that organizes and describes a data set to identify patterns and themes within the data (Braun & Clarke, 2006). First, all interviews were transcribed. Then, initial codes were generated using a theory-driven approach, as the authors were only interested in student-teacher interactions or descriptions and ideas that related to experiences of respect and disrespect. Finally, codes were then organized into themes, which were defined and named.

Results

Four themes were identified: (1) the cycle of disrespect; (2) disrespect as ignorance of social location; (3) disrespect as abuse of authority, and; (4) respect as care. The findings are presented in such a way to highlight often silenced student voices, focusing in particular on the students' words and stories.

The Cycle of Disrespect

Most students acknowledge their active participation in propagating negative classroom interactions in what students refer to as the 'cycle of disrespect.' First, students acknowledge that sometimes students are disrespectful first, and they know it can cause a reaction from the teacher. As a Black high school student stated:

Some kids are real disrespectful, so some kids don't respect teachers as much, like, they just don't want to pay attention, so the teacher will get like frustrated, or start lashing out.

Many students shared that when they felt disrespect from a teacher, even if it were unintentional, the students would disrespect that teacher in return. For some students, experiencing teacher disrespect merited their pushing back or refusing to listen or follow directions in class. For example, when asked about a response to feeling disrespected by a teacher, a (self-identified) multi-ethnic female high-school junior stated:

I come up with an idea just to challenge her on hers. I do that a lot, because when I think my opinion's not being respected or incorporated, not all the time, obviously sometimes students don't get a say, but when it's a good opinion and has a good point and it's just completely shut down because the teacher doesn't want to do it any way but theirs, I definitely will do it again just to play devil's advocate. Even if I agree, I'm like, 'Okay, well how about we do it this way,' and then get the whole class to agree and just repeat the situation.

Other students, however, reported engaging in the cycle of disrespect by not coming to class or not completing assignments. These students reported that when they were academically successful, the teacher was evaluated as successful, and that teacher did not deserve to succeed. In these cases, the students acknowledged that their actions hurt them academically, but that they did not want that teacher to think that they/she/he deserved respect. When asked why they did not want their teacher to think they deserved respect, one student speculated about how students think about respect:

Sometimes, and especially with a lotta, a lotta kids, inner city kids that grew up like in the streets or what not, their biggest thing is respect, and to give it, I mean to get it you have to give it.

Caring as an Authoritative Act

For teachers to receive respect from students then, teachers must first respect students. However, this simple overture can be fraught with difficulties when teachers' social locations differ from their students' social locations.

Disrespect as Ignorance of Social Location

Students highlighted the difficulties of teachers' appropriately respecting them when the teachers' social locations were different from their own. A male (self-identified) Puerto-Rican community college student emphasized this when recalling a story about a time that a teacher wanted to help him with the college process:

She asked me where I want to go to college or what I wanted to do, and then she... went on to tell me I should go to "Local College" because it's close enough to home, that I can have my rice and beans and pork chops three times a week, like I like it, 'cause she knew I was Hispanic. And I was like, you can't say that. You don't know me or my family. I get what she was tryin' to do, but it wasn't right of her to say that, you know?

The key element in this episode of disrespect was not that the teacher was ignorant of the student's culture. The teacher clearly understood fundamentals of this student's background: the importance of family. However, the teacher did not understand her social location, as a White, educated woman. She reduced her student's culture to a food, and because she assumed stereotypical behaviors (most likely because of her assumptions of ethnicity), she overstepped boundaries within the student-teacher relationship. Instead of recognizing the unique individual particularities of this student, and the ways this student was similar to and different from other students with similar social locations, she reduced the student to an ethnic caricature. Besides making assumptions based on students' ethnicity or gender, students also reported teachers' not understanding the "vibe of the class" or the school, and treating them as a whole class, rather than individuals in the class. As one student told of a teacher who entered this class mid-year:

The teacher came in the middle of the year and he didn't know what's going on, but also he never attempted to get the vibe of the class. He came in and was like, 'I'm doing it like this.' He never tried to learn our names in a way. He acted like he never attempted to get to know us. He just came in and was all: 'I'm doing it like this, this and this.'

Disrespect as Abuse of Authority

In addition to ignorance about the students' social locations, students also referred to teachers' lack of awareness about their own social locations, specifically as it related to their use (and often abuse) of teacher authority. When asked about what teachers should know about respect and disrespect in the classroom, a female high school freshman offered sage advice:

Never act like the student is below you, even ... I wouldn't ever say another human being is below someone else, but yes, teachers have more authority over students, but kids will respect you more when you don't exercise that authority, when that authority is just implemented in the classroom, not shown. When authority is shown, students shut down and don't like a teacher.

More importantly, adolescents reported that when teachers established power in the classroom, most students interpreted it as a sign of disrespect. A Latinx high school sophomore reported about an experience of disrespect from teachers:

It was during free work and I made one text to my mom and they belittled me and I think the biggest thing is we're treated like such children and like we are such less than them that they think they want to establish power and I would say that's the biggest form of disrespect I've experienced from teachers.

Teachers' attempting to establish authority through the use of power was a common theme that relates to the literature on how adolescents think about respect (that it is reciprocal; e.g., Hsueh, Zhou, Cohen, Hundley, & Deptula, 2005) and also highlights the changing conception of authority in student-teacher relationships (e.g., Eccles, Midgley, Wigfield, Buchanan, Reuman, Flanagan, & Mac Iver, 1993).

Respect as Care

Other common observations of teacher disrespect were seen through a lack of care – not recognizing the uniqueness of individual students. As one participant noted:

Well... There was a teacher who had heard from one of my middle school teachers on my behavior and since they, they just took what they said and was like, "Oh, that's what this student is," so they would like let's say this half of the classroom is talking, I'm going to be the one to get yelled at in front of the whole class, just because they automatically know that I'm one of the students who would do that and would disrupt and yeah, I've find that disrespectful, because who I was in middle school doesn't mean that's how I am now as a student, and it was your choice not to get to know me or talk to me directly so, I felt it was disrespectful.

Overwhelmingly, students identified teacher respect as caring respect. Over and over again, when the first author asked students to tell about a time a teacher earned their respect, it was because the teacher cared about the student as a unique individual. As a high school junior reported:

Sophomore year all of my teachers were saying my name wrong... I never corrected them... the marking period was over and we're in school and I'm like 'Oh it's too late to correct them on saying my name.'... I would go to first period and she [the teacher] would say my name wrong. Then I'd go to second period and he [the teacher] would say my name wrong. Then third period, ooh she [the teacher] would butcher my name and I was just like 'Aaaahhhhhh." Later [Mr. M] said my name and a friend shouted: 'It's Louwan!' And I was just 'Aaah'... and he was like, 'Wait I've been saying your name wrong this whole time?' And I was like, 'Yeah' and he was: 'No, I'm going to get your name right.' For the rest of the school year he would say my name and he would be: 'Louwan! I'm saying it right!' He would always check in. He was talking to me afterwards and said ... 'Why didn't you ever correct me? Your name is important. You deserve respect. Getting your name right is a sign of respect.' He reinforced [that], it's okay to correct people. You get to choose how to present yourself. And was ... 'Wow, thank you for encouraging' ... he made me realize that it was a bigger thing than I was ... trying to downsize it to. It wasn't like teacher/student relationship but it was: 'I see you as a human being.'

Caring as an Authoritative Act

This story exemplifies caring respect: the notion of having a choice of how one is seen and identified, and seeing the student as a person worthy of respect. Another common refrain, as seen previously in disrespect, surrounds supporting and valuing student ideas. Students equated supporting and valuing their ideas to valuing themselves as people. In response to being asked, "What is one thing you want your teachers to know about earning respect?" one student replied:

I would say that they should just qualify, like make sure kids know that their ideas aren't stupid and that their opinions aren't stupid and that nothing is not valued. I think that the biggest thing is teachers need to just be nice and say like, 'No, I understand. I like that idea,' and even if it's the worst idea ever, just make a white lie and say something good about it. There's got to be something you can say that's nice to the student and then shut it down. Don't just shut it down right away, because the way to maybe not even lost respect, but ruin a student is to just make them feel that they are less and that they are not valued and that they do not have anything to offer.

Taken together, the themes that emerged from these student voices suggest that adolescents are yearning for caring respect from teachers. They want to be recognized as individuals, and they want their ideas to be valued. More importantly, students want teachers to know that pushing authority as power in the classroom undermines the student's ability to respect their teacher, and that youth do not respect in response to authority, but in response to care.

SOLUTIONS AND RECOMMENDATIONS

Talking to Teachers About Caring as an Authoritative Act

The purpose of this chapter was to give novice and pre-service teachers a framework for thinking about respect through caring and recognizing what caring means in light of the power imbalances that characterize student-teacher relationships. There is of course not one solution to such a monumental issue as the way in which the education system operates in the United States. However, the use of an ethic of care in conjunction with an intersectional social justice framework can shift the Euro-centric classroom culture surrounding the way respect is enacted and experienced. Through the use of intersectionality, subjugated knowledge of people of color can be brought forth (Dill & Zambrana, 2009) and discussed in the classroom and among colleagues. Teachers, as leaders, consider others' input, and to a degree, reveal their values, motives, and sentiments concerning a course of action (Atwijuka & Caldwell, 2017). This reframing of respect will allow teachers and other school officials to become accustomed to decoupling respect from authority and power. In addition, identifying social locations will allow teachers to better accept students as unique individuals who have value, and as such, should be heard. By examining schools and classrooms through a CRT framework, schools, administrators, and teachers can establish caring respect as an expected classroom protocol.

The ethic of care – a distinct moral and ethical theory (Atwijuka & Caldwell, 2017) – is a different way of approaching the classroom dynamic. Rather than teaching through classroom management and order, the goal in the ethic of care tradition is to teach through care. This framework of care emphasizes relationships, human needs, and realities in which dilemmas arise (Carmeli, Brammer, Gomes, & Tarba, 2016). Ethical caring, as Noddings (2013) writes, requires effort not present in natural caring – it requires

555

more of a commitment to the cared-for (Noddings, 2013) than traditional caring requires. The authors ask that teachers go beyond this framework of care, and think about the commitment to the cared for differently. Rather than solely focusing on building relationships as classroom practice, teachers should combine the ethic of care with respect for persons, to establish caring respect (Dillon, 1992). It is through caring respect that all students, regardless of background, commitment to the student-teacher relationship, or individual relationships with teachers, can feel valued and empowered. Thinking about respect through the students' perspectives, teachers can simultaneously be figures of both care and authority. Educators must consider a transformation in their teaching so that they are compelled to engage with issues of difference and multiplicity both inside the classroom, and in their daily lives (Hawks & Pillay, 2017).

Educators, especially White educators, must consider their backgrounds and therefore shift their perspective on care in the classroom. Tatum (1997) writes:

Educators all across the country, most of whom are White, are teaching in racially mixed classrooms, daily observing identity development in process, and are without an important interpretive framework to help them understand what is happening in their interactions with students, or even in their cross-racial interactions with colleagues. (p., xv)

This section serves as a guide to help pre-service, and novice teachers embrace caring respect by re-examining their notions of care and authority. Teachers do not have to constantly be rule-enforcing figures with a dominant power relation over their students. Instead, they can co-create an environment in which the students feel individually heard, acknowledged, and respected. Teachers' caring respect for students will be the first step in teachers' earning respect from students as well. The following provides a starting point for teachers to view caring and authority as synonymous, through the enactment of caring respect. Caring respect is accessible to all teachers; it takes a restructuring of how they view respect and their interactions with students.

First, this section will revisit a story that was presented in the previous section and highlight how that conversation could be shifted to reflect caring respect, before providing thought questions for teachers to consider.

Consider the first student story about a misinterpretation of a social location:

She asked me where I want to go to college or what I wanted to do, and then she... went on to tell me I should go to 'Local College' because it's close enough to home, that I can have my rice and beans and pork chops three times a week, like I like it, 'cause she knew I was Hispanic. And I was like, you can't say that. You don't know me or my family. I get what she was tryin' to do, but it wan't right of her to say that, you know?

Revisiting this conversation through the lens of caring respect, the teacher can reconfigure her focus on caring as an act of authority. Instead of making assumptions about what the student wants to do, the teacher should first ask the student about his plans:

Teacher: What are you plans for after high school? Can you tell me more about that and why you are interested in that? How do you want the world to see you?

Caring as an Authoritative Act

After the teacher has an idea of what the student wants, they/she/he can explain to they/she/he how they/she/he sees him, and aspirations that they/she/he has for him. Also, the teacher should acknowledge that the teacher's perceptions of what it means to be a capable student is from their/her/his vantage point as a White, middle-class teacher, and may not be entirely transferrable because of different family situations or cultural expectations:

Teacher: *I see you as a very strong academically oriented student, who has insight and capability. I think if you choose to go to college, you would be successful. What hesitations, if any, or aspirations do you have?*

Finally, regardless of how the student replies, the teacher can let the student know that they/she/he will help him achieve and do what he deems important, even if it is not what they/she/he thinks is best:

Teacher: *What can I do to support you as you think about your life after high school?*

What are other ways in which teachers can respond in a way that highlights caring respect?

Techniques for Discussing Respect in the Classroom

Respect, caring, and authority in the classroom are viewed differently from the students' vantage points than from educators' vantage points. These notions of respect and care extend beyond behavior, and educators must consider their students' (and their own) relative social location. For this approach to be successful, educators must frame respect within a culturally responsive practice. Discussions about respect should happen at both the school and classroom level to affect lasting change. Through the co-creation of enacted respect, teachers can negotiate and define respect with their students. Teachers can, therefore, be a figure of both care and authority. Caregiving requires time and commitment. This caring respect approach may include learning student names, understanding the broader classroom and school community, and not using the power of authority to demand student compliance. One way to begin to cultivate a classroom steeped in caring respect is to have discussions with students about what respect means and to co-create a set of rules based on caring respect.

Questions to ask your class when having a class discussion about respect:

- What makes you unique? How do you want others (teachers and classmates) to see you?
- What are ways in which others students can validate you? How do you want your teacher to validate you?

Questions teachers should ask themselves about how they use power, authority, and respect in the classroom:

- What are ways that you (behaviorally) showed respect to your own teachers, from elementary school, through college?
  - Why did you show respect to said teacher(s)?
  - Why did you show respect in the ways that you did (or did not)?
- Have you experienced an environment steeped in caring respect? If so, what did it look like?

- When authority comes to mind, what do you think of? What does it look like?
- What does caring look like?
- How can you get to know students, even if only a little bit, to be able to recognize their individual characteristics?
- How can educators use their institutional authority to shift notions of respect and care in the classroom on a larger scale?

CONCLUSION

The goal of this chapter has been to demonstrate the notion that effective teachers are, above all else, teachers who care for their students. The authors' aim is to shift commonly accepted notions of respect away from those of authority figures' deserving respect towards respect based on care, relationship, and innate human deservingness. The purpose of this shift in commonly accepted notions of respect is that student success is largely based on whether or not students feel that their teachers care for them. Teaching, by nature, is a caring profession. Novice teachers often misunderstand what it means to be an authority figure in that they believe they must demand respect from their students. Students, however, will likely show teachers respect when teachers create an environment steeped in caring respect in which students can learn. For students to recognize their teacher as caring, the teacher must demonstrate her humanity to her students, and recognize her students for their humanity as well. Students consider a teacher getting to know them as respectful, among other things. Respect is and can be an expression of care by authority.

American culture was founded on inequality, leaving institutional racism embedded throughout Euro-centric society. These institutionalized norms and social mores unintentionally influence educator's views of student respect as obedience and compliance. Considering where the teacher theirself/herself/himself fits into society is imperative in understanding the perspectives, values, and attitudes of their/her/his students. In creating classrooms steeped in culturally cognizant caring respect, teachers must themselves teach culturally sensitive notions of respect. Shifting accepted notions of respect to be based on human deservingness would ideally rid schools of differentials in respect. Taking into consideration the social location of all parties involved in an exchange of respect is imperative in using caring as a pedagogical tool, which includes re-defined notions of authority.

This chapter aimed to re-conceptualize notions of authority so that novice teachers can use this new framework when cultivating a caring environment in their classrooms. Educators need not be the dominant authority figure, but rather a figure of care. In shifting away from traditional expectations of deservingness respect, such as expecting automatic compliance with the teacher's demands, teachers create safe spaces for their students. Through the implementation of caring respect, educators can reconsider the meaning of authority in the classroom setting and society at large. Caring respect can facilitate the prevention of burnout in novice teachers during the turbulent first years of teaching. Caring respect is imperative for the success of the students, teacher, and the classroom as a whole.

ACKNOWLEDGMENT

The authors would like to thank the students and teachers who participated in this research; without their voices and willingness to be vulnerable, this research would not be possible. Also, many thanks should be given to the RCAT (Respecting Children and Teachers) lab group at Smith College for their careful work on this topic, and in particular Kelcie Grenier, Karina Huang and Alexandra Singer for their pilot work on this topic. This research was supported by the Smith College Faculty Compensation and Development Funding.

REFERENCES

Abrams, L. S., & Moio, J. A. (2009). Critical race theory and the cultural competence dilemma in social work education. *Journal of Social Work Education*, *45*(2), 245–261. doi:10.5175/JSWE.2009.200700109

Acker, S. (1995). Carry on caring: The work of women teachers. *British Journal of Sociology of Education*, *16*(1), 21–36. doi:10.1080/0142569950160102

Atwijuka, S., & Caldwell, C. (2017). Authentic leadership and the ethic of care. *Journal of Management Development*, *36*(8), 1040–1051. doi:10.1108/JMD-12-2016-0331

Audley, S. R. (2017). Searching for the golden rule: A case study of two white novice teachers' beliefs and experiences of respect in urban schools. *Manuscript Under Review.*

Audley-Piotrowski, S., Singer, A., & Patterson, M. (2015). The role of the teacher in children's peer relations: Making the invisible hand intentional. *Translational Issues in Psychological Science*, *1*(2), 192–200. doi:10.1037/tps0000038

Aultman, L. P., Williams-Johnson, M. R., & Schutz, P. A. (2009). Boundary dilemmas in teacher–student relationships: Struggling with "the line.". *Teaching and Teacher Education*, *25*(5), 636–646. doi:10.1016/j.tate.2008.10.002

Bingham, C. (2008). *Authority is relational: Rethinking educational empowerment*. Albany, NY: State University of New York Press.

Bingham, C., & Sidorkin, A. M. (Eds.). (2004). *No education without relation*. New York, NY: Peter Lang.

Bonilla-Silva, E. (1997). Rethinking racism: Toward a structural interpretation. *American Sociological Review*, *62*(3), 465–480. doi:10.2307/2657316

Boykin, A. W. (1992). *Reformulating educational reform: Toward the proactive schooling of African American children*. Paper commissioned for "Evaluation and Education Reform: Students At-Risk Study," American Institutes for Research. Available: ERIC Database #ED367725.

Braun, V., & Clarke, V. (2006). Using thematic analysis in psychology. *Qualitative Research in Psychology*, *3*(2), 77–101. doi:10.1191/1478088706qp063oa

Brown, D. F. (2004). Urban teachers' professed classroom management strategies: Reflections of culturally responsive teaching. *Urban Education*, *39*(3), 266–289. doi:10.1177/0042085904263258

Carmeli, A., Brammer, S., Gomes, E., & Tarba, S. Y. (2017). An organizational ethic of care and employee involvement in sustainability-related behaviors: A social identity perspective. *Journal of Organizational Behavior*, *38*(9), 1380–1395. doi:10.1002/job.2185

Carson, R. L. (2007). *Emotional regulation and teacher burnout: Who says that the management of emotional expression doesn't matter?* Paper presented in the annual meeting of American Educational Research Association, Chicago, IL.

Case, K. A. (2013). Developing a transformative and intersectional model of privilege studies pedagogy. In K. A. Case (Ed.), *Deconstructing privilege: teaching and learning as allies in the classroom* (pp. 1–14). New York: Routledge.

Chang, M. L. (2009). An appraisal perspective of teacher burnout: Examining the emotional work of teachers. *Educational Psychology Review*, *21*(3), 193–218. doi:10.100710648-009-9106-y

Collins, P. H. (2004). Learning from the outsider within: The sociological significance of black feminist thought. In S. Harding (Ed.), *The feminist standpoint theory reader* (pp. 103–126). New York: Routledge.

Crenshaw, K. (1991). Mapping the margins: Intersectionality, identity politics, and violence against women of color. *Stanford Law Review*, *43*(6), 1241–1299. doi:10.2307/1229039

Darder, A. (1991). *Culture and power in the classroom: A critical foundation for bicultural education.* New York: Bergin & Garvey.

Darwall, S. L. (1977). Two kinds of respect. *Ethics*, *88*(1), 36–49. doi:10.1086/292054

Delgado, R., & Stefancic, J. (2001). *Critical race theory: An introduction.* New York: NYU Press.

Deutsch, N. L. (2005). "I like to treat others as others would treat me": The development of prosocial selves in an urban youth organization. *New Directions for Youth Development*, *108*(108), 89–105. doi:10.1002/yd.144 PMID:16570880

Deutsch, N. L., & Jones, J. N. (2008). "Show me an ounce of respect": Respect and authority in adult-youth relationships in after-school programs. *Journal of Adolescent Research*, *23*(6), 667–688. doi:10.1177/0743558408322250

Dill, B. T., & Zambrana, R. E. (2009). Critical thinking about inequality: An emerging lens. In D. T. Dill & R. R. Zambrana (Eds.), *Emerging intersections: Race, class, and gender in theory, policy, and practice* (pp. 1–21). Piscataway, NJ: Rutgers University Press.

Dillon, R. S. (1992). Respect and care: Toward moral integration. *Canadian Journal of Philosophy*, *22*(1), 105–131. doi:10.1080/00455091.1992.10717273

Eccles, J. S., Midgley, C., Wigfield, A., Buchanan, C. M., Reuman, D., Flanagan, C., & Mac Iver, D. (1993). Development during adolescence: The impact of stage-environment fit on young adolescents' experiences in schools and in families. *The American Psychologist*, *48*(2), 90–101. doi:10.1037/0003-066X.48.2.90 PMID:8442578

Farmer, T. W., Dawes, M., Hamm, J. V., Lee, D., Mehtaji, M., Hoffman, A. S., & Brooks, D. S. (2017). Classroom social dynamics management: Why the invisible hand of the teacher matters for special education. *Remedial and Special Education*. doi: 0741932517718359

Ford, A. C., & Sassi, K. (2014). Authority in cross-racial teaching and learning (re)considering the transfer-ability of warm demander approaches. *Urban Education*, *49*(1), 39–74. doi:10.1177/0042085912464790

Caring as an Authoritative Act

Fordham, S. (1993). "Those loud Black girls": (Black) women, silence, and gender "passing" in the academy. *Anthropology & Education Quarterly, 24*(1), 3–32. doi:10.1525/aeq.1993.24.1.05x1736t

Frei, J. R., & Shaver, P. R. (2002). Respect in close relationships: Prototype definition, self-report assessment, and initial correlates. *Personal Relationships, 9*(2), 121–139. doi:10.1111/1475-6811.00008

Freire, P. (2005). *Pedagogy of the oppressed* (M. Ramos, Trans.). New York: Continuum. (Original work published 1970)

Friedman, I. A. (1995). Student behavior patterns contributing to teacher burnout. *The Journal of Educational Research, 88*(5), 281–289. doi:10.1080/00220671.1995.9941312

Friedman, I. A. (2000). Burnout in teachers: Shattered dreams of impeccable professional performance. *Journal of Clinical Psychology, 56*(5), 595–606. doi:10.1002/(SICI)1097-4679(200005)56:5<595::AID-JCLP2>3.0.CO;2-Q PMID:10852147

Gay, G. (2010). *Culturally responsive teaching: Theory, research, and practice.* New York: Teachers College Press.

Goodman, J. F. (2009). Respect-due and respect-earned: Negotiating student–teacher relationships. *Ethics and Education, 4*(1), 3–17. doi:10.1080/17449640902781356

Hargreaves, A. (1998). The emotional practice of teaching. *Teaching and Teacher Education, 14*(8), 835–854. doi:10.1016/S0742-051X(98)00025-0

Hargreaves, A. (2000). Mixed emotions: Teachers' perceptions of their interactions with students. *Teaching and Teacher Education, 16*(8), 811–826. doi:10.1016/S0742-051X(00)00028-7

Hartsock, N. C. M. (2004). Comment on Heckman's 'Truth and method: Feminist standpoint theory revisited': Truth or justice? *Signs (Chicago, Ill.), 22*(2), 367–374.

Hastings, R. P., & Bham, M. S. (2003). The relationship between student behaviour patterns and teacher burnout. *School Psychology International, 24*(1), 115–127. doi:10.1177/0143034303024001905

Hawks, M., & Pillay, T. (2017). Institutionalizing an 'Ethic of Care,' into the teaching of ethics for pre-service teachers. *Journal of Critical Thought and Praxis, 6*(2), 66–83.

Hines-Datiri, D., & Carter Andrews, D. J. (2017). The effects of zero tolerance policies on Black girls: Using critical race feminism and figured worlds to examine school discipline. *Urban Education.* doi: 00042085917690204

Holder, K., & Kessels, U. (2017). Gender and ethnic stereotypes in student teachers' judgments: A new look from a shifting standards perspective. *Social Psychology of Education, 20*(3), 471–490. doi:10.100711218-017-9384-z

hooks, b. (2004). Choosing the margin as a space of radical openness. In S. Harding (Ed.), *The Feminist standpoint theory reader* (pp. 153-159). New York: Routledge.

Hsueh, Y., Zhou, Z. K., Cohen, R., Hundley, R. J., & Deptula, D. P. (2005). Knowing and showing respect: Chinese and U.S. children's understanding of respect and its association to their friendships. *Journal of Psychology in Chinese Societies, 6*(2), 89–120.

Intrator, S. (2006). Beginning teachers and emotional drama in the classroom. *Journal of Teacher Education*, *57*(3), 232–239. doi:10.1177/0022487105285890

Isenbarger, L., & Zembylas, M. (2006). The emotional labour of caring in teaching. *Teaching and Teacher Education*, *22*(1), 120–134. doi:10.1016/j.tate.2005.07.002

Johnston, M. (2011). From exclusion to integration: The N.A.A.C.P.'s legal campaign against educational segregation. *Chapman University Historical Review, 3*(1), 23-34.

Jones, J. N., & Deutsch, N. L. (2011). Relational strategies in after-school settings: How staff–youth relationships support positive development. *Youth & Society, 43*(4), 1381–1406. doi:10.1177/0044118X10386077

Kant, I. (2013). Groundwork of the metaphysics of morals. In M. Gregor (Ed.), *Immanuel Kant Practical Philosophy*. New York: Cambridge University Press. (Original work published 1785)

Kolko, V. B. (2003). A history of Jews in higher education. *Journal of the Indiana University Student Personnel Association, 1*(1), 20-33.

Ladson-Billings, G. (1996). Silences as weapons: Challenges of a Black professor teaching White students. *Theory into Practice*, *35*(2), 79–85. doi:10.1080/00405849609543706

Ladson-Billings, G., & Tate, W. F. (1995). Toward a critical race theory of education. *Teachers College Record*, *97*(1), 47–58.

Laletas, S., & Reupert, A. (2016). Exploring pre-service secondary teachers' understanding of care. *Teachers and Teaching*, *22*(4), 485–503. doi:10.1080/13540602.2015.1082730

Laupa, M., & Turiel, E. (1993). Children's concepts of authority and social contexts. *Journal of Educational Psychology*, *85*(1), 191–197. doi:10.1037/0022-0663.85.1.191

Laupa, M., Turiel, E., & Cowan, P. A. (1995). Obedience to authority in children and adults. In M. Killen & D. Hart (Eds.), *Morality in everyday life: Developmental perspectives* (pp. 131–165). New York: Cambridge University Press.

Li, J., & Fischer, K. W. (2007). Respect as a positive self-conscious emotion in European Americans and Chinese. In J. L. Tracy, R. W. Robbing, & J. P. Tangney (Eds.), *The self-conscious emotions: Theory and research* (pp. 224–242). New York: Guilford Press.

Li, Q. (1999). Teachers' beliefs and gender differences in mathematics. *Review of Educational Research*, *41*(1), 63–76.

Liljestrom, A., Roulston, K., & deMarrais, K. (2007). "There is no place for feeling like this in the workplace": Women teachers' anger in school settings. In P. A. Schutz & R. Pekrun (Eds.), *Emotions in education* (pp. 275–292). San Diego, CA: Elsevier. doi:10.1016/B978-012372545-5/50017-4

Mann, L., Mitsui, H., Beswick, G., & Harmoni, R. V. (1994). A study of Japanese and Australian children's respect for others. *Journal of Cross-Cultural Psychology*, *25*(1), 133–145. doi:10.1177/0022022194251008

Martinez-Egger, A., & Powers, W. A. (2007). Student respect for a teacher: Measurement and relationships to teacher credibility and classroom behavior perceptions. *Human Communication*, *10*(2), 145–155.

McAnulty, J., & Cuenca, A. (2014). Embracing institutional authority: The emerging identity of a novice teacher educator. *Studying Teacher Education, 10*(1), 36–52. doi:10.1080/17425964.2013.862493

McLaughlin, H. J. (1991). Reconciling care and control: Authority in classroom relationships. *Journal of Teacher Education, 42*(3), 182–195. doi:10.1177/002248719104200304

Miller, L. (2010). Queer is in the eye of the newcomer: Mapping, performance and place based media. *InTensions Journal, 4*, 1–24.

Nelsen, J., Lott, L., & Glenn, H. S. (2000). *Positive discipline in the classroom: Developing mutual respect, cooperation, and responsibility in your classroom.* New York: Random House, LLC.

Noddings, N. (2013) *Caring: A relational approach to ethics and moral education.* Berkeley, CA: University of California Press.

Obidah, J. E., & Teel, K. M. (2001). *Because of the kids: Facing racial and cultural differences in schools.* New York: Teachers College Press.

Ogbu, J. U. (1992). Understanding cultural diversity and learning. *Educational Researcher, 21*(8), 5–14. doi:10.3102/0013189X021008005

Pace, J. L. (2006). Saving (and losing) face, race, and authority: Strategies of action in a 9th grade English class. In J. L. Pace & A. Hemmings (Eds.), *Classroom authority: Theory, research, and practice* (pp. 87–112). Mahwah, NJ: Lawrence Erlbaum.

Pace, J. L., & Hemmings, A. (2007). Understanding authority in classrooms: A review of theory, ideology, and research. *Review of Educational Research, 77*(1), 4–27. doi:10.3102/003465430298489

Pace, J. L., & Hemmings, A. B. (2006). Understanding classroom authority as a social construction. In J. L. Pace & A. B. Hemmings (Eds.), *Classroom authority: Theory, research, and practice* (pp. 1–32). Mahwah, NJ: Lawrence Erlbaum.

Piaget, J. (1952). *The moral judgment of the child* (M. Gabain, Trans.). New York, NY: Collier Books. (Original work published 1932)

Riegle-Crumb, C., & Humphries, M. (2012). Exploring bias in math teachers' perceptions of students' ability by gender and race/ethnicity. *Gender & Society, 26*(2), 290–322. doi:10.1177/0891243211434614 PMID:24187437

Rodriguez, D. (2009). The usual suspect: Negotiating White student resistance and teacher authority in a predominantly White classroom. *Cultural Studies? Critical Methodologies, 9*(4), 483–508. doi:10.1177/1532708608321504

Roediger, H. L. III, & Butler, A. C. (2011). The critical role of retrieval practice in long-term retention. *Trends in Cognitive Sciences, 15*(1), 20–27. doi:10.1016/j.tics.2010.09.003 PMID:20951630

Roithmayr, D. (1999). Introduction to critical race theory in educational research and praxis. In L. Parker, D. Deyhle, & S. Villenas (Eds.), *Race is. . . race isn't: Critical race theory and qualitative studies in education* (pp. 1–6). Boulder, CO: Westview.

Rubin, K. H., Bukowski, W., & Parker, J. (2006). Peer interactions, relationships, and groups. In N. Eisenberg (Ed.), *Social, emotional, and personality development* (6th ed.; pp. 571–645). New York: Wiley.

Rubinstein, G. (2010). *Reluctant disciplinarian: Advice on classroom management from a softy who became (eventually) a successful teacher.* Waco, TX: Prufrock Press, Inc.

Sadker, M., & Sadker, D. (1994). *Failing at fairness.* New York, NY: Touchstone.

Shapira-Lishchinsky, O. (2011). Teachers' critical incidents: Ethical dilemmas in teaching practice. *Teaching and Teacher Education, 27*(3), 648–656. doi:10.1016/j.tate.2010.11.003

She, H. C. (2000). The interplay of a biology teacher's beliefs, teaching practices and gender-based student-teacher classroom interaction. *Educational Research, 42*(1), 100–111. doi:10.1080/001318800363953

Shwalb, B. J., & Shwalb, D. W. (2006). Concept development of respect and disrespect in American kindergarten and first- and second-grade children. In D. W. Shwalb & B. J. Shwalb (Eds.), *Respect and disrespect: Cultural and developmental origins* (pp. 67–80). San Francisco, CA: Jossey-Bass. doi:10.1002/cd.176

Singer, A., & Audley, S. (in press). Some teachers just simply care:" Respect in urban student-teacher relationships. *CritEdPol: Journal of Critical Educational Policy Studies.*

Smagorinsky, P., Cook, L. S., Moore, C., Jackson, A. Y., & Fry, P. G. (2004). Tensions in learning to teach: Accommodation and the development of a teaching identity. *Journal of Teacher Education, 55*(1), 8–24. doi:10.1177/0022487103260067

Spilt, J. L., Koomen, H. M., & Thijs, J. T. (2011). Teacher wellbeing: The importance of teacher–student relationships. *Educational Psychology Review, 23*(4), 457–477. doi:10.100710648-011-9170-y

Tatum, B. D. (1997). *Why are all the Black kids sitting together in the cafeteria?* New York: Basic Books.

Van den Bergh, L., Denessen, E., Hornstra, L., Voeten, M., & Holland, R. W. (2010). The implicit prejudiced attitudes of teachers: Relations to teacher expectations and the ethnic achievement gap. *American Educational Research Journal, 47*(2), 497–527. doi:10.3102/0002831209353594

Veenman, S. (1984). Perceived problems of beginning teachers. *Review of Educational Research, 54*(2), 143–178. doi:10.3102/00346543054002143

Volkmann, M. J., & Anderson, M. A. (1998). Creating professional identity: Dilemmas and metaphors of a first-year chemistry teacher. *Science Education, 82*(3), 293–310. doi:10.1002/(SICI)1098-237X(199806)82:3<293::AID-SCE1>3.0.CO;2-7

Weinstein, C. S. (1998). "I want to be nice, but I have to be mean": Exploring prospective teachers' conceptions of caring and order. *Teaching and Teacher Education, 14*(2), 153–163. doi:10.1016/S0742-051X(97)00034-6

Weinstein, C. S., Tomlinson-Clarke, S., & Curran, M. (2004). Toward a conception of culturally responsive classroom management. *Journal of Teacher Education, 55*(1), 25–38. doi:10.1177/0022487103259812

Wentzel, K. R. (1997). Student motivation in middle school: The role of perceived pedagogical caring. *Journal of Educational Psychology, 89*(3), 411–419. doi:10.1037/0022-0663.89.3.411

Caring as an Authoritative Act

Wentzel, K. R. (2010). Students' relationships with teachers. In J. L. Meece & J. S. Eccles (Eds.), *Handbook of research on schools, schooling, and human development* (pp. 75–91). London: Routledge.

Wiggins, R. A., & Clift, R. T. (1995). Oppositional pairs: Unresolved conflicts in student teaching. *Action in Teacher Education*, *17*(3), 9–19. doi:10.1080/01626620.1995.10463226

Woolley, M. E., Kol, K. L., & Bowen, G. L. (2009). The social context of school success for Latino middle school students: Direct and indirect influences of teachers, family, and friends. *The Journal of Early Adolescence*, *29*(1), 43–70. doi:10.1177/0272431608324478

ADDITIONAL READING

Case, K. A. (2013). *Deconstructing privilege: teaching and learning as allies in the classroom*. New York: Routledge.

Fasching-Varner, K. J. (2012). *Working through whiteness: Examining white racial identity and profession with pre-service teachers*. Lexington, KY: Lexington Books.

Gay, G. (2010). *Culturally responsive teaching: Theory, research, and practice*. New York: Teachers College Press.

Lawrence-Lightfoot, S. (2000). *Respect*. New York: Basic Books.

Pace, J. L., & Hemmings, A. B. (2006). *Classroom authority: Theory, research, and practice*. Mahwah, NJ: Lawrence Erlbaum.

Parker, L., & Deyhle, D. D., & S. Villenas, S. (1999). Race is. . . race isn't: Critical race theory and qualitative studies in education. Boulder, CO: Westview.

KEY TERMS AND DEFINITIONS

Caring Respect: Valuing, supporting, or not causing harm to a person, in ways that reflect a person's individual characteristics and uniqueness.

Cis-Gender: When the gender that a person was assigned at birth, or that they physically present as agrees with the gender that they identify as.

Critical Race Theory: A framework that recognizes that race has social implications; makes use of the methodologies across the social sciences to come to a deeper understanding of the implications that racial dynamics have on present circumstance.

Intersectionality: The idea that different types of oppression based on categorization exist simultaneously and create more powerful systems of oppression for groups and individuals than if they were to exist separate from one another.

Privilege: Based on certain aspects of personhood, such as race, class, ethnicity, gender, ability, etc., the idea that some people have more or less social power depending on their group identification.

Social Justice: A framework and a political movement with the goal of equity among people in terms of wealth, social class, ability, etc.

Social Location: Refers to an individual's place or location in their society and includes race, class, gender, sexuality, religion, age, education, marital status, and political view.

Structural Inequality: The condition in which certain people are seen as less than in terms of other people and in turn said inequality is perpetuated by commonly accepted notions of inequality inherent in society.

ENDNOTE

[1]   The authors prefer to refer to gender in this chapter in this order so as to situate the genders in an order that reflects intersectionality and the importance of recognizing and lifting marginalized identities.

This research was previously published in Creating Caring and Supportive Educational Environments for Meaningful Learning; pages 154-182, copyright year 2019 by Information Science Reference (an imprint of IGI Global).

Chapter 30
A Decolonial Curriculum Is Everything:
An Afrocentric Approach

Zingisa Nkosinkulu
University of South Africa, South Africa

ABSTRACT

This chapter seeks to map how indigenous people and their indigenous knowledge systems are the most researched and written about in the world, yet they are the least understood. The curriculum of the empire and its scientific explanation justified how indigenous knowledge systems should be approached and viewed as well as who has the authority to justify; hence, indigenous knowledge systems were justified as inferior and not worthy of the standard of European knowledge system. In this chapter, Frantz Fanon's thought will be deployed to illustrate how this division of knowledge justifies the perpetuating dehumanisation of indigenous people under the mask of modernisation and globalisation. By deploying decoloniality, Afrocentricity, and Fanonian thought, this chapter seeks to challenge this curriculum that is based on the history of the conquest of Africa that positioned Africa only as a cradle of slaves and the black bodied as created by God only for the benefit of the Europeans.

INTRODUCTION

Since I was born in the Antilles, my observations and my conclusions are valid only for the Antilles—at least concerning the black man at home. Another book could be dedicated to explaining the differences that separate the Negro of the Antilles from the Negro of Africa. Perhaps one day I shall write it. Perhaps too it will no longer be necessary—a fact for which we could only congratulate ourselves (Fanon [1952] 2008, p.1).

Frantz Fanon's perspective is instrumental to the understanding of the curriculum as a tool that divides the coloniser from the colonised in the colonial/Eurocentric/anti-black world. Fanon's lived experience is testament to this division that influenced his life and thoughts about the existence of the indigenous

DOI: 10.4018/978-1-6684-4507-5.ch030

Copyright © 2022, IGI Global. Copying or distributing in print or electronic forms without written permission of IGI Global is prohibited.

people that he refers to as the colonised or natives in his writings. Indigenous people and their indigenous knowledge systems are the most researched and written about in the world, yet they are still the most misrepresented. This is why Afrocentricity is a suitable paradigm to decolonize the curriculum in relation Fanon's thought. Afrocentricity is a paradigm that positions the Africana subject as the center of hers or his world, it allows the agency and ability to think form an African-centered perspective (Asante 2007; Owusu-Ansah & Mji, 2013). In this regard, Fanon's thought is relevant to the understanding of this epistemic division as something that materialized deliberately for the structure of the "empire" (Hardt & Negri 2000) that was intended to restructure the world to the image of the European logic. The knowledge systems and way of living for colonised people was the fundamental base of creating what transpired to be the curriculum of the empire, with research approaches that are being deployed in academia today. Most research approaches that are being used in the curriculum are based on research and methodologies that were developed and used towards the contribution of positioning black people as objects intended to be owned, used and studied. Under these research approaches, the colonised people's existence and their way of life was studied and used to create disciplines such as anthropology, ethnography, sociology and research methodologies that were used to justify indigenous people as inferior. While other academic disciplines such as science, art and archaeology as well as biology and history were used as a weapon to justify dehumanisation of indigenous people, and the classification of their knowledge systems as primitive and barbaric.

This epistemic division created and justified the existence of what is commonly known as the Global South in which Africa as the victim of colonisation is located under, as the primitive side of knowledge. Fanon understood the language of the centre and periphery that demonstrated these divisions that made the periphery a no man's land, as the "zone of nonbeing" (Fanon [1952] 2008, p.2). The zone of none being is a place without knowledge, a place without history, without spirituality and most importantly a place without humans. As history tells us about what resulted to Africa being named a dark continent, a name that embodies a perception of many fathers of European knowledge such as Hegel. This perception is based on the history of the conquest of Africa that positioned Africa only as a cradle of slaves and black bodies as created by God only for the benefit of European pleasures and development. Narratives of history and of the conquest depicts to us how colonial research and methodologies were supported by the European fathers of knowledge. Fanon takes a different position from the European fathers of knowledge to say that the colonised life is life in the zone of nonbeing, there are beings and there is a different humanity. This chapter takes Fanon's position of thinking beyond the curriculum of the empire by adopting an Afrocentric approach.

LITERATURE REVIEW

Education and its curriculum in most colonised countries is Western, or put differently, after colonisation quality education was only for white people specifically during the apartheid era in South Africa. However, the politics of the apartheid system in South Africa did not exist in a vacuum, their genealogy is connected to all the struggles against colonisation of indigenous societies who were colonised or westernised. Hence, Aimé Césaire posed a very important question that proves to be relevant to the understanding of how the curriculum as the source of knowledge, was appropriated by the colonial master as a tool that builds the empire. However, before this question is posed and answered in this chapter, it will be of great assistance to understand two things, the empire and the curriculum of the empire. As

A Decolonial Curriculum Is Everything

explained by Hardt and Negri (2000, p. vii), "Empire is the political subject that effectively regulates these global exchanges, the sovereign power that governs the world". The empire is the reason why everything is the way it is, it is the reason why the curriculum was and still is appropriated, it is the reason why colonisation, slavery, capitalism, modernisation and globalisation were created as systematic forces that rules the world. "The passage to Empire emerges from the twilight of modern sovereignty" (Hardt & Negri 2000, p. xiii) to position Europe in the centre of the world by reconfiguring ways of building the Eurocentric world, an anti-black world. The hidden thread that is imbedded in this anti-black world highlights that anti-blackness is the fuel that keeps running the machineries that develops what I will term here the curriculum of the empire. The curriculum of the empire is a Eurocentric-asymmetric curriculum that approaches teaching and learning from a westernised perspective. It is a curriculum of lies and distortion, it bounds the Africana subject while it liberates the European subject. It is a curriculum that does not speak to the experience of the Africana subject, it closes indigenous knowledge system outside the curriculum, while it transforms the Africana subject into a black subject as what appears as hyper-slaves. An educated slave of the new system whose skin color precedes being and competence. The curriculum of the empire as one of the vital instruments that is utilized in order to spread and teach the knowledge of the empire is something that most colonised people have in common. It is a curriculum that renders them incompetence.

The curriculum of the empire can be explicated as "Western knowledge has been spread globally and, therefore, it is in all of us who went through at least secondary education" (Mignolo in Gaztambide-Fernández 2014, p.201). However, it has now become an ontological software that is shaping our everyday life because, the "empire is materializing before our very eyes" (Hard and Negri 2000, p. vii). It is in the materialisation of the empire that the world was divided into two oppositional categories namely; world and empire, centre-periphery, master and slave, rich and poor, colonised and coloniser based on black and white as skin color, as well as whiteness and blackness. It is through this Manichean structure of the world that the empire is born as Fanon articulates, "there is a zone of nonbeing, an extraordinarily sterile and arid region, an utterly naked declivity where an authentic upheaval can be born" (Fanon [1952] 2008, p. 2). Following Fanon's remark, it is assumed that there is also a zone of being that Fanon does not mention, it is a space of whiteness, but the empire is born at the cost of the zone of nonbeing, a place of blackness. It is from this place that the colonised people reside, a place where the empire mines knowledge to create its curriculum for the disciplines of knowledge. According to Smith (1999, p. 58-59), p.

Knowledge was also there to be discovered, extracted, appropriated and distributed. Processes for enabling these things to occur became organized and systematic. They not only informed the field of study referred to by Said as 'Orientalism' but other disciplines of knowledge and 'regimes of truth'. It is through these disciplines that the indigenous world has been represented to the West and it is through these disciplines that indigenous peoples often research for the fragments of ourselves which were taken, catalogued, studied and stored.

Judging by Smith's remark, the curriculum of the empire is a curriculum of appropriation, exclusion, single perspective of the world, dehumanisation, epistemic parasite, colonisation and westernisation of the world, it is a curriculum of fragmentation that feeds from what Gordon (2014) calls "disciplinary decadence". The curriculum of the empire was created from traveling experiences, observations, orientation, naming and recording of life, based on dairies and data collection of the colonial master. The creation of the curriculum of the empire in this manner resulted to it being the stone with which the epistemic walls between disciplines were constructed. These epistemic walls produced "an inward path of disciplinary solitude eventually leads to ... disciplinary decadence. This is the phenomenon of turning away from living thought, which engages reality and recognises its own limitations, to a deontologised or absolute conception of disciplinary life" (Gordon 2006, p.86). Disciplinary decadence is based on the "worldview" (Oyewumi 1997) that operates only by the sense of sight, it is a perspective that informs how people view the world based from the Eurocentric logic, it is a view that is grounded on coloniality, it is what I can call coloniality of vision. The concept of coloniality of vision is grounded on the notion of "bad faith (mauvaise foi)" (Sartre [1957] 2003, p. 71, Gordon 1995) and anti-blackness. It does not see the Africana subject as a competent contributor of knowledge and content that can provide the world with a "new humanism" (Fanon 0000). Bad faith means that the European conquer viewed the African and concluded its black, therefore it is inferior, it is black therefore it is animal like, it is lacking a soul, it is not trust worthy, it is their property and most importantly, lets feed of them for our curriculum.

The European presence as the only one prominent in the curriculum of the empire means any other form of knowledge is questioned if whether worthy or not, to be documented as part of the curriculum. This is thinking from the position of the coloniality of vision and the curriculum of the empire that "the discipline becomes, in solipsistic fashion, the world. In that world, the main concern is the proper administering of its rules, regulations, or, as Fanon argued, (self-devouring) methods" (Gordon 2006, p.424). This world that the disciplines projected is a world with multiple faces than what it simply is, it is an anti-black world, a Manichean world, a world that is based on imperialism, it is a world that became an empire. It is an empire of which is created by the creation of colonies. The curriculum of the empire was filtered to the rest of the colonies by missionaries to influence how black people must relate to knowledge, being and power. Through the lens of the Fanonian thought, the curriculum of the empire meant there are "two poles of a world, two poles in perpetual conflict, p. a genuinely Manichean concept of the world" (Fanon [1952] 2008, p.31). This epistemic division was intentionally created to be the operating system of the empire, "a world divided into compartments, a motionless, Manicheistic world, a world of statues, p. the statue of the general who carried out the conquest, the statue of the engineer who built the bridge; a World which is sure of itself, which crushes with its stones the backs flayed by whips, p. this is the colonial world" (Fanon [1952] 2008, p. 50-51). The empire is a colonial world that is divided by colonies where the curriculum of the empire has become an epistemic statue of European presence. The European presence was something that manifested in many different and hidden ways, its footprint was stamped on top of every good discovery in the world. Most importantly, the European presence was imbedded in the mind of the colonised through the curriculum of the empire as the sign of modernity.

The Case of South African Experience

In the case of South Africa as a colony, it is amongst the list of colonial heirs whom the colonial grandfathers left their presence as legacy because it meant that it should exist forever. This settler presence extends as far as the social and political life of the South African people, it can be found on the architecture of buildings, it is on the names of streets and places, it is eaten as food diet and it is seen inside the dreams of the colonised people's mind about their free existence. In this regard Yountae (2017, p.97) indicates that, "the existential impasse of the black person lies, for Fanon, in the fact that his or her existence unfolds in the "zone of nonbeing," a state of perpetual curse". Fanon is a product of the curriculum of the empire who refused to be tamed and rather used its tools to find his way out the colonial subjection. The danger of the curriculum of the empire is that it "brings about essential mutations in the consciousness

A Decolonial Curriculum Is Everything

of the colonized, in the manner in which he perceives the colonizer, in his human status in the world" (Fanon 1965, p. 69). The colonised become hypnotised by the romantic presence of the coloniser in the curriculum who is always depicted as the victor of wars, founder of places and the god of knowledge. The effects of this hypnotism are that it makes the colonised have a different perception of the self and the coloniser. This curriculum hypnotism is similar to the frog that is experiencing paralyses under the snake's watch. In South Africa, the colonised get hypnotised by the presence of the coloniser in the curriculum of the empire and get eaten by modernity by being closed out of the ontological infrastructure that is supposed to grant access to the rights to live.

In the case of South Africa, the issue of the presence of the coloniser in the curriculum of the empire as the victor and the only father of knowledge, is mostly felt by the colonised and its contestation is manifested into resistance movements such as Fees Must Fall, Rhodes Must Fall and Decolonising the Westernised University. South Africa shares a lot in common with many ex-colonised places, as a result, its struggles are linked to similarities of most of the strategies that are taken to combat against imperialism. The movements Fees Must Fall, Rhodes Must Fall and Decolonising the Western University qualify as responding to imperialism, they do present these struggles. However, what these movements have in common is what is fundamentally important, it is what Fanon calls the colonised to do, it is being created by modernity and resisting against modernity. According to Ngugi wa Thiong'o (1993, p.22), "the modern world is a product of both European imperialism and of the resistance waged against it by the African, Asian, and South American peoples". The significance of these movements lies behind embodying the position of the smoke in the English idiom simply paraphrased as "where there is smoke, there is fire". If that's the case, the question that follows is where or what is the fire in the case of these South African student movements of decolonisation? What can be discovered if the fire is explored?

The curriculum of the empire is part of the fire, it is the reason why the aforementioned movements of decolonisation erupted in South Africa. These movements show that there is a problem that needs to be addressed. the building of the empire created these problems as problems that have been long in the making since the collapse of the idea of the world. It can be argued here, the idea of the world "is dead", by world here I don't mean the world in a physical and geographical sense, rather as a conceptual and epistemic place, an open place, a place without borders, where everybody has a place, an open-ended place. When the word "world" is uttered what comes into mind is a globe, it is planet earth, a free and open space, a place for every form of being. The world remained a world until capitalism introduced imperialism to transform it into an empire, during this transformation "the power of the colonialist message, the systems used to impose it and present it as the truth were such that most of the time the colonized had only his own increasingly overshadowed inner conviction to oppose" (Fanon 1965, p.76). The curriculum of the empire has subliminal messages that transforms the colonised subject into a westernised indigenous person. The content that was used to create the curriculum, the objectives of the content and the values of the curriculum are structured in a way that teachers educate from the European point of view. As a result, even indigenous languages are taught in English, from the European perspective. Undergoing for education in a westernised university as a colonised subject could mean a moment of undergoing a metamorphosis. It is a moment of morphing from being an indigenous person, a free human being whose subjectivity is not limited within any form of borders, who is not transformed into a westernised person, from being a person with free subjectivity into an object of European creation.

In history there is always a time for colonised subjects to be doing something for the first time to the point that it becomes their norm and while the historical reasons are normally forgotten or are intentionally omitted. For instance, most cultural elements that most colonised subjects protect as their identity and heritage are elements that resulted as surviving apparatus for slaves or for people in the ghettos and slums. Food, songs, stories, dances, art and language that are still adopted today by colonised subjects as elements of their cultures were created specifically for surviving under a particular kind of oppression or dispossession. In this regard, education and the curriculum are amongst the things that were created during apartheid in the case of South Africa. In this colonial set up, the colonised subject was normally allowed to acquire education that was only technical and only useful for working under the white master until post-1994, colonised people were officially allowed to take education of their choice. An educated black/colonised subject became a dangerous subject under the colonial state because they can obtain their education and use it against the system. In this regard, Fanon highlights how the French were taking over Algeria and brought newspaper for the first time. The government or the comrades against the struggle used these newspapers to communicate or to analyse what the other did or were planning to do. In the case of Algeria, Fanon writes, "the purchase of such a newspaper was thus considered to be a nationalist act. Hence it quickly became a dangerous act. Every time the Algerian asked for one of these newspapers, the kiosk dealer, who represented the occupier, would regard it as an expression of nationalism, equivalent to an act of war" (Fanon 1965, p.81). Asking for a decolonised Afrocentric curriculum in the westernised university can be considered to be an act of war. Every time a black enters at the university he/she is watched with eyes of wonder and resistance, they are accepted under the political sake, till when they leave the university, they wonder and still remain jobless. They remain suspected and unwelcome they "never succeed in gaining recognition as a colleague from the whites" (Fanon [1952] 2008, p.43). Acquiring education for the black people should be equivalent to a political act and a cry for ontological recognition in the eyes of others. However, the curriculum of the empire does not offer any form of epistemological and ontological leap to the colonised figure. Once they become educated under the westernised curriculum they seem to take the position of being a new kind of a sophisticated slave or what Malcom X call a "house Negro".

This does not dispute the important fact that there were some colonised subjects that obtained their education under the curriculum of the empire in a westernised university, whose oeuvre is relevant in today's process of decolonisation and Africanisation as well as in resistance movements. The work they produced after undergoing western training provides intellectual scaffolding and epistemic pillars for the construction of a decolonised and Afrocentric curriculum. Although their western training taught them to train and create others according to the Eurocentric model, they managed to create resistance against the curriculum of the empire, however, their resistance was limited to a certain degree.

LIMITATION OF COMPENSATORY EDUCATION SYSTEM

A response to Africa's need by Africans has resulted to the need to return to the source because, "the call for indigenous approaches to management and leadership falls within the broader cry for an African Renaissance that seeks to reclaim the aesthetics and identity of Africans (Nkomo, 2006; Makgoba, 1999; Mbeki, 1998; Mudimbe, 1988; Nzelibe, 1986)".This was also in line with the theory of Afrocentricity and decoloniality that states that Africa must reclaim itself on its own terms and conduct not according to expertise of the 'Other' (Said 2002, Spivak 1990). To reclaim itself Africa has realised its need to divorce from putting its trust into the curriculum of the empire, by eradicating the act of looking at the Western for solutions. According to Bolden (2005, p.1), "the Inter Action programme seeks to transform Africa through the development of a new generation of leaders who are encouraged not only to take up their

A Decolonial Curriculum Is Everything

own leadership roles but to share their insights and learning to develop and inspire others within their communities". African concepts of community, leadership and family have never promoted individualism and selfishness rather it has promoted Ubuntu. The philosophy of Ubuntu includes the standards of humanism and human solidarity, kindness, and provision to others. The spirit of Ubuntu is central to the way in which the African subject think, speak, act, and interact with other humans. Therefore, Africa with the philosophy of Ubuntu has created interest and contributed to the role of leadership and management in other places across the world.

The impact that the curriculum of the empire had on the African continent has resulted to the slow development of an Afrocentric-Africa that is informed by Ubuntu. The Africa that is present is a Eurocentric-Africa, it is produced and supported by the western logic of modernity and civilisation, it is Africa from the perspective of the West, it is the Africa of the empire. If there is any time to consider the Africa of the empire dysfunctional in its nature of management and leadership that time would be now. Ironically enough, during the time of what is known as time for freedom, democracy and equality in Africa, this dysfunctionality of the African states is not something that begun before the colonial encounter as most wrong European would claim and African's would think, it is something that consequently was derived from the European processes such as colonialism and imperialism. Was Africa dysfunctional and disorganised more after the lines at the Berlin Scramble for Africa conference were drawn to make it what it is today? The African continent is in a situation because of Western interferences. The concepts in the curriculum of the empire even today still divided Africa physically, spiritually, socially, ethnically, economically, culturally and psychologically. The essential task is to explore and discuss what appears to be African dysfunctionality in the attempt to highlight the indigenous approaches which preceded colonialism. The African continent has its own rich history and inheritance way back before the interference of the coloniser. Africa has been led and managed by great men even during the times of wars of resistance against the invasion of the colonisers. Naturally most African cultures require a great level of skill in leadership and management, these ways of living need to function in harmony to keep the indigenous unity together.

According to Nnabugwu and Nwanegbo (2012, p.131), "a major character of the contemporary Africa is the pervasive and overwhelming presence of inorganic and dysfunctional states and structures". Africa's inheritance from the colonisers made it what it is today, it made South Africa and other countries in the continent custodians of the curriculum of the empire, with alien institutions and structures that disorganised it while claiming to organise it. What the curriculum of the empire does not clearly articulate is the fact that the dysfunctional side of African states began during the invasion of the colonisers and it still carries on today. It does not state from the position of the colonised, that different states of Africa have engaged on wars, big projects of large construction and negotiations that displayed a great evidence of skill on African leadership and management even during the resistance against colonial invasion. These big historical events were used to draw solutions from African problems by Africans until the coloniser "emerged without consideration of what the people of Africa wanted or wished" (Nnabugwa & Nwanegbo 2012, p.131). However, before the colonisers came into the picture, the African states were functional in their own way although there is not much written, and research done on African management and leadership in the old days. This is also reflected in the curriculum of the empire by the fact that "within organization studies, theories of leadership and management have generally omitted the voice of the racial 'Other' whether it is Africans or other non-Western perspective" (Nkomo, 2006; Cox & Nkomo, 1990; Nkomo, 1992; Prasal, 2006). Under the curriculum of the empire, there is a great deal of danger posed by what seems to be the fundamental silencing of the non-Western narrative. Literature about approaches to management and leadership might silence the non-Western narrative and provide from anywhere in the world but it does not necessary mean there are no other approaches to management and leadership originating from non-Western concepts.

The hypocritical view that a "98 percent of leadership theory emanates from the United States and has been developed primarily by studying American leaders. Yet, leadership theory is largely represented as universal" (Nkomo, 2006, p. 3) is deceiving and shows the fact that 80% of the curriculum of the empire is Eurocentric. There cannot be a universal leadership rule because situations, places and people are not the same. However, a leader is only great for its time. This idea of taking leadership and management approaches from the West contributes to the concept of Americanising the world. It is the same as taking the curriculum of the empire as the only curriculum in the world. That is America and the rest of the West manipulates Africa to be dislocated from her own roots. The scarcity of literature that reveals management and leadership approaches in African context have been a contributing factor to Africa's delay from her own renaissance. When looking at the curriculum of the empire and its textbooks or in the history of African leadership and knowledge production, only Nelson Mandela and Shaka Zulu are found as leaders (Nkomo 2006, p.4). This is problematic because it can give the impression that these were the only leaders that were considered effective in Africa. In this subject of leadership and management Africa appears in four categories namely; African leadership management, National culture, Africa leadership, African management philosophy (Nkomo 2006). The above summary of African management development reveals that Africa needs to respond to the need of literature that contextualises her development in her own terms. The Africana subject needs to respond to the need to decolonize the curriculum of the empire and change of corrupt leadership and management. In line with this, Alavi (1972, p.61) argues, "it might be said that the 'super-structure' in the colony, is therefore 'overdeveloped' in relation to the structure in the colony, for its basis lies in the metropolitan structure itself, from which it is later separated at the time of independence…The postcolonial state inherits that overdeveloped apparatus of the state and its institutionalized practices through which the operations of the indigenous social classes are regulated and controlled". The African state is in a situation where they appear dysfunctional to the rest of the world because of the foreign leadership and management administrative tools and policies that are taught in the curriculum of the empire.

Institutional and Structural Challenges

Africa is now educating itself to fix the dysfunctional knowledge systems as stated by Thabo Mbeki that "education has an important role to play in the economic, cultural and political renaissance of our continent and in the drive for the development of indigenous knowledge systems. This implies that all education curricula should have Africa as their focus, and as a result be indigenous in its grounding and orientation. To address this state of affairs we need to distinctly Africa knowledge systems" (Mbeki 2005). The development of Africa is hinged on the participation in education of African indigenous knowledge systems and other systems of knowledge. Nkomo (2005, p.19), further argues that "the search for African leadership and management should draw upon the past but must also inevitably be rooted in the present". As much as Africa is seeking ways to develop herself from her indigenous traditions she does not do this in order to stay and remain in the past, but she uses the past in order to understand why things are the way they are in the present. To highlight the point that Africa is not dysfunctional but is organising herself to fix the problems she inherited from the West. Leadership in Africa, p. meaning, impacts and identities argues that "rather that bringing in "expects" from the "developed world" Inter

A Decolonial Curriculum Is Everything

Action embraces Africa wisdom, acknowledging the strength and contributions of all participates and partners, and uses a facilitative, discursive and experiential approach rather thin a more didactic teaching based format (Bolden 2005, p.1). Therefore, Africa's epistemic dislocation has become a call for Africa to find herself through the mist of colonial inheritance. Many attempts are being made by many people who believe that Africa is not where it is supposed to be because it was robbed by other people. This we can say has come to be just one of the general history lessons nothing much but for a new different African scholar like myself, the narrative about Africa is more than just a place for a picnic or something that can simply be buried under the Eurocentric capitalism carpets, it is the heart and mind of the mother earth. African narrative is told by many scholars, researchers, authors, artists and even film makers, but there is still a gap. Instead our historic stories are being told by Western movie producers and actors while our producers and actors starve. For some people the narrative about Africa is a depressing story while to others it's a story of victory, perseverance and optimism.

The depressing side of the story lies on its redundancy and contradiction of the curriculum of the empire. It has also come to be difficult to apply in Africa because government offices that should be improving people with funding and resources to apply their ideas through projects that could facilitate social change and social cohesion are corrupt and irresponsible. Most people in South Africa who are occupying these big government offices took on responsibilities that were new and new to black people. After 1994 new state departments that were not there during the apartheid government were opened and occupied by people with no experience of the job or in that field as a way of prioritising the previously disadvantage. This creates a gap between the offices and those it is supposed to serve, the community of the people. Therefore, this creates a delay in making things happen towards the Africa renaissance.

It is already known why Africa is like this, there are many books explaining this even better than the new scholars and the internet. In South Africa we have museums, statues, artworks, books, poems, tourist attractions and monuments telling the story of the colonisation and apartheid better than some black or white demagogues who are trying to use those stories for political empowerment especially when near to elections. Many people still want to fix Africa into a better Afrocentric-Africa that Africans want, but unfortunately, they still look outside themselves for solutions to their own problems. Some African leaders have lost connection with their ancestors therefore they lose African wisdom. Wisdom is an African element while enlightenment is a European element. The contradiction begins when Africans take the knowledge of the enlightenment as a solution. Current problems in Africa that are the result of resources being looted by the European powers need more than just logical and scholarly debates, but they need wisdom and political will as a radical force that we have inherited through African ancestors. What kept cultures and people united in the old Africa before it was even called Africa was the wisdom that those cultures offered.

African ancestors used African wisdom that can only be found in their different cultures to build strong and united communities until the curriculum of the empire introduced a new vocabulary to the colonised subject. This new vocabulary came with a new reality for most colonised indigenous communities. As stated, the introduction of a new word such as jail, meant that a building structure must be constructed, once its constructed there is a certain set of rules that are set to be followed by citizens in order to avoid the open-trap, jail. It is an open-trap because jails are never full, but they are full of black skin across the world. The set of rules that citizens must follow are called the law and this law is supposed to represent justice. Justice is supposed to be the big brother who is watching everyone to just to others as they would like themselves treated just. In other words, the curriculum of the empire introduced a deviated reality to the colonised subjects, it gave them vocabulary for the colonial reality of torture and lived experience that it is about to experience as the anti-black law of existing. The level of resistance against the European domination that resulted into war in Africa and even in areas like the Eastern Cape in South Africa; the war between Xhosa people, Boers, Khoi khoi, San and British which is not well spoken about or even taught as part of the South African History curriculum, shows a slow level of development. Some of these wars that happened as resistance of colonisation are not well recognised as the beginning of applicable decolonasation, although the first resistance against slave trade, was a decolonial act.

It is scientifically proven that most of our daily life is conducted under the watch of the subconscious mind, the same subconscious mind that dreams and reasons while we are sleeping, which means we do not have full control if we have any control over it. In Xhosa there is a saying that says "*imfuzo iyagqithisa*", which means offspring will live as their fathers lived because naturally there are many things that we unconsciously inherit through our parents who also have inherited them from colonial domination and their parents. These fears, insecurities, psychological dislocation, cultural dislocation and other after effects left by colonial domination are resurfacing through the curriculum of the empire creating a schizophrenic reality effect. This schizophrenic reality is what Dubois ([1903] 2016) calls, "double consciousness" as the result of such mentioned powers. The process of decoloniality is an attempt to escape this schizophrenic-reality which competes with the reality that African people are busy trying to develop for a new Africa. The schizophrenic-reality is a result of psychological and cultural dislocation and European lies that were instilled and are still being instilled in the psyche of the world for domination and capitalism benefits. Thus, Dubois explains well this effect of the curriculum of the empire in the following words:

It is a peculiar sensation, this double-consciousness, this sense of always looking at one's self through the eyes of others, of measuring one's soul by the tape of a world that looks on in amused contempt and pity. One ever feels his two-ness, an American, a Negro; two souls, two thoughts, two unreconciled strivings; two warring ideals in one dark body, whose dogged strength alone keeps it from being torn asunder. The history of the American Negro is the history o9f this strife- this longing to attain self-conscious manhood, to merge his double self into a better and truer self. In this merging he wishes neither of the older selves to be lost. He does not wish to Africanize America, for America has too much to teach the world and Africa. He wouldn't bleach his Negro blood in a flood of white Americanism, for he knows that Negro blood has a message for the world. He simply wishes to make it possible for a man to be both a Negro and an American without being cursed and spit upon by his fellows, without having the doors of opportunity closed roughly in his face ([1903] 201, p. 62-3).

Unfortunately, Africa has been a victim and still is of these colonial forces that are pushed for capitalist benefits of the empire. There is an African proverb that says, "if the is no enemy within the enemy outside can do us no harm". The curriculum of the empire has created black leadership and management in Africa that is redundancy and contradictions in the African narrative or history has created enemies within Africans. It has created divisions in Africa with epistemic borders, geographical borders, global borders, social and political borders and ontological borders.

POSSIBILITIES OF A TRANFORMED CURRICULUM: A DECOLONIAL AFROCENTRIC PERSPECTIVE

Blackness and the curriculum of the empire offers "an existential deviation on the Negro" (Fanon 1952[2008], p. 6), as a position that encourages one to question his or her own existence outside the curriculum. Blackness is the place of the forgotten, a place of the dispossessed and a place of the figure, the one who can be anything, the one with many faces, a place of nonexistence. Blackness and the curriculum of the empire offers two separate realities that are positioned to work together, this combination is a colonial tactic of giving the colonised subjects education that does not speak to their identity, experience and history. It is from the position of the "Afrocentric theory" (Asante 2007, p.10; Bangura 2012, p.110) that the question of the curriculum of the empire reveals that the colonised subjects are not included under the umbrella of nationalism, because as stated by Fanon "history teaches us clearly that the battle against colonialism does not run straight away along the lines of nationalism. For a very long time the native devotes his energies to ending certain definite abuses, p. forced labor, corporal punishment, inequality of salaries, limitation of political rights, etc" (Fanon [1961] 2001, p.119). With Fanon's remark, it is clear some people seem to remain excluded as the idea of the new-nationalism is questionable. This exclusion is manifested in different ways such as being excluded in the curriculum, being excluded in the library archives, being excluded in the art gallery and museums, being excluded from the human register.

The curriculum of the empire is modern thinking because, "modern Western thinking is an abyssal thinking. It consists of a system of visibility and invisibility, the invisible ones being the foundation of the visible ones... The division is such that "the other side of the line" (Santos 2007, p.33) vanishes as reality becomes non-existent, and is indeed produced as nonexistence. Nonexistence means not existing in any relevant or comprehensible way of being", hence the curriculum of the empire as well as modernity are contingent upon the exclusion of the colonised people. Their existence was fueled by nonexistence of the colonised subject because they are both designed and constructed in a way that keeps the colonised subject different and constantly under the state of seeking. Seeking education, seeking a better life, seeking recognition as a human, seeking identity and seeking language to articulate their existence that is always questioned. In this regard Fanon argues ([1961] 2001, p.119), "national consciousness, instead of being the all-embracing crystallization of the innermost hopes of the whole people, instead of being the immediate and most obvious result of the mobilization of the people, will be in any case only an empty shell, a crude and fragile travesty of what it might have been". Meditating deeply on Fanon's remark, it becomes clear in the case of South Africa, that not all South Africans are South Africans, which is to say, not everyone is included under the national identity. This brings under question the notion of a rainbow nation that was coined and introduced by Nelson Mandela as an alternative solution to apartheid's social and political ills. Under the notion of a rainbow nation, what Mandela was stating was that after the fall of the apartheid system African/black people of South Africa must not do what the coloniser did to them, they must consider a more inclusive and assimilative approach.

The rainbow nation as an assimilative approach of being inclusive is a process of becoming, because to assimilate is to become someone or somethings else. In this process, Mandela was arguing that colonised/black people do not have to do what the white people did to them, in other words, in the quest for freedom and justice, the colonised/black figure will not take the position of being the oppressor because the "curriculum was biased toward European knowledge and Western styles of teaching, and that this bias was harmful to the self-esteem and performance" (Binder 2002, p. 1) of the colonised figure. The consciousness of the rainbow nation was limiting as it considers colonised/black people human only to a certain degree, and this degree is the one that is set by the curriculum of the empire. However, the fundamental base of the curriculum of the empire is that it is Eurocentric, and it introduces a version of a Eurocentric-Africa.

Indigenous Knowledge Systems: An Introduction to Afrocentric Perspective

According to Smith (1999, p. 138), "indigenous research approaches problematize the insider model in different ways because there are multiple ways of being either an insider or an outsider in indigenous contexts" (Smith 1999, p. 138). The problem that is faced by the world is the problem of a single side allegory of how Europe is the father of knowledge, being and power amongst everything in the world. When conducting research about the colonised people, it is important to deploy a theoretical framework and methodology that positions colonised/black people as a centre of their own world. Although there are many research tools that can be deployed by colonised/black people to conduct research about their existence, very few or none of them explain the phenomenon from their position as the centre. Afrocentricity as a theoretical and philosophical perspective offers decolonial "actionable perspective" (Asante 2007, p.16). Often the story glorifies the hunter while the hunted is always misrepresented, in this case, Europe is always represented as the centre while other countries are misrepresented as inferior. Therefore, in order to relocate the colonised/black people in general, the African people in particular, it is important to deploy decolonial epistemic perspective as a theoretical framework and Afrocentricity as a methodology. According to Binder (2002, p. 30-31):

The Afrocentric methodology rests on two primary assumptions. The first principle is that analysis of any subject with roots in Africa must begin with "the primacy of the classical African civilizations, namely Kemet (Egypt), Nubia, Axum, and Meroe... Adequate understanding of African phenomena," according to Asante, "cannot occur without a reference point in the classic and most documented African culture... The second major premise upon which Afrocentrism is based is that all people of African descent possess essential cognitive, cultural, and aesthetic characteristics in common. The wife of Molefi Asante, an Afrocentric scholar in her own right, KariamuWelsh-Asante, for example, argues that there is an African Aesthetic, which is "based on seven 'senses' shared by all Africa-descended people around the globe, p. polyrhythm, polycentrism, dimensional, repetition, curvilinear, epic memory, and wholism".

In this regard, Afrocentricity is a suitable methodology because it deals with the colonised/black figure the body and mind level, decoloniality deals with the soul. For most indigenous societies, the soul encompasses essence and essence is being and existence. Therefore, it is important to engage a methodology that poses existential questions as the insider or outsider. The research methodology that is proposed here is still underdevelopment, which is the decolonial Africana existential phenomenology. Phenomenology study is a subjective experienced based research methodology that received a lot of attention in the mid-21st century in the field of qualitative research along with autoethnography because it was regarded as a "process whereby we encounter ambiguity in texts and in all cultural products. We find in the very ambiguity new possibilities for thoughts and actions," (Lundin et al 1985, p. 32). According to Langdridge phenomenology is a study that "aims to focus on people's perceptions of the world in which they live in and what it means to them; a focus on people's lived experience" (Langdridge 2007, p. 4). Phenomenology was popularized in the early 20th century to affirm abstract "realities" (Gable and

A Decolonial Curriculum Is Everything

Handler 2003, p. 376) "lived experience" (Ingold 2000, p. 145) and real life "events" (Zizek 2014, p. 3), as well as the feelings and actions of people. Phenomenology was used by a phenomenologist Maurice Merleau-Ponty's in an essay Cezanne's Doubt, where he "was particularly interested on how Cezanne saw and related to the world and created his paintings the way he did. More especially he was interested to the relationship between the eye and the hand in relation to the creation of the paintings" (Kozel 2013). Phenomenology as a methodology has been applied in various fields of studies including, nursing, biology, psychology, performance arts, therapeutic art and other studies that focus on lived experience. Phenomenology is divided into transcendental, hermeneutic, and existential phenomenology. In most cases existential phenomenology is deployed because it "stresses on the description of everyday experience as it is perceived by the consciousness of the individuals" (Kafle 2011, p.188). In this regard, decolonial Africana existential phenomenological as a methodology draws from existential phenomenology and it is based on the need to the return to lived experience of the colonised people and their consciousness of the world they leave in. Decolonial Africana existential phenomenological is a "research methodology aimed at producing rich textual descriptions of the experiencing of selected phenomena in the life world of individuals that are able to connect with the experience of all of us collectively" (Smith 1997, p.80), specifically black colonised people's phenomenon. Decolonial Africana existential phenomenological study is deployed to affirm theory and practice within the academic research and allows the embodied lived experiences to provide new perspectives. Decolonial Africana existential phenomenology is, "a "gathering" notion under which to situate the articulations (writings, speeches etc.) and traditions of the same, of Africans and peoples of African descendent collectively, as well as sub-discipline—or field-forming, tradition-defining, tradition—organizing reconstructive efforts which are (to be) regarded as philosophy" (Outlaw1997, p.267). Decolonial Africana existential phenomenology as a methodology will be deployed as a method of this study to reflect on "lived experience" (Ingold 2000, p.145) in critical academic setting. Existential phenomenology was deployed by philosophers namely; Edmund Husserl, Martin Heidegger, Maurice Merleau-Ponty, Hans-Georg Gadamer and Paul Ricoeur as a method to reflect on Dasein, which means to 'dwell in the world' or "being-in-the-world" (Heidegger 1962). Decolonial Africana existential phenomenology, in a similar way with African existential phenomenology, according to More is based on "reflections, rooted in black experience, on the boundaries of human existence and the utilization of such reflections to challenges confronting African and African-descended people in Diaspora" (More 2008, p.47). Decolonial Africana existential phenomenological is a critical and creative methodology of no method that resonates well with the intension of this study, which is to diagnose, prescribe and make dead objects come to life and speak or resist. This research is deployed to interpreted black people's lived experience as reflected in their art to understand the culture and being of the black people because "ancient and modern tribal peoples would not distinguish art from artefact or ritual" (Freeland 2013, p. xviii). As it has been proven by various scholars, certain methods prove to carry colonial tools that do not justify the phenomenon of black people. Decolonial Africana existential phenomenological is a research methodology whose intension is to dress and conceal colonised people who have been stripped naked by dirty colonial tricks of research. It is a method to reflect on the notion of being-in-the-anti-black-world.

Decolonial existential phenomenological is a way of turning lived experiences into a critical academic mode and challenge the westernised ways of living, writing, art making and ways of seeing. Decolonial Africana existential phenomenology is a platform to use lived experiences of dehumanised people to formulate counter points of the historic gap created by western domination. However, according to Outlaw, "in the context of such endeavours, persons of the past and present without formal training or degrees in philosophy are being worked into developing canons" (Outlaw 1997, p.266). Decolonial Africana existential phenomenology does not mean the experience of maids, including my experience as a black person; and Fanon's are to be embraced as absolute truth, but it embraces the position that any person's embodied experience when properly contextualised and reflected upon offers perspectives and meaning that speak to other people's realities. Decolonial Africana existential phenomenology seeks to move away from aesthetics to aesthesis (Mignolo and Vazquez 2013). In line with aesthesis, More asserts that "by virtue of the historical fact of racial oppression, colonisation, and ... [bondage], Africana philosophy [and art] raises questions of identity and liberation by focusing on the reality that black ... [figures] are affected by the significance of race and racism" (More 2008, p. 47). The problem with aesthetics according to More's remark on aesthesis, it looks and sees the world through the eyes of race and racism. Meaning through the eyes of race and racism everything else collapses into nonexistence including ontology, law, beauty, reason, history and art when it comes to the black figure. According to Seshadri-Crooks the "scientific basis of race has been thoroughly discredited" and that race is "purely cultural, a construct, and the racialised body would be the imaginary corollary to that construction" (Crooks 2000, p. 12-21). Decolonial Africana existential phenomenology therefore, similar to Africana existential philosophy, as according to More, "consists in reflections, rooted in black experience, on the boundaries of human existence and the utilization of such reflections to challenges confronting African and African- descended people in Diaspora" (More 2008, p.47). One big challenge confronting black colonised people is the challenge of being able to express and articulate the colonial mistreatment in all its subliminal inscription. It is the challenge of lacking tools of excavating coloniality and realise it is not buried underground rather it is surrounding us.

Regardless of what appears as an inability to articulate black people's existence as human beings, Fanonian decolonial phenomenological study "deals with issues of the emergence of the black selfhood, black suffering, embodied agency, freedom, bad faith, racism, and liberation" (More 2008, p.47). By deploying Decolonial Africana existential phenomenology from the positionality of aesthesis in order to make sense and meaning of being-in-the-anti-black-world, Diagne argued that it must deploy what Bergson teaches us on how to make sense about philosopher's thoughts. In regard to making sense with aesthesis, Diagne argues that, "we must begin by taking a step back from ...[its] thought in order to return to its source, weigh the influences that nurtured it. And pinpoint the ideas of which the doctrine is a synthesis" (Diagne 2011, p.00). Diagne's approach to reading philosophers and aesthesis can be linked and viewed in line with decolonial Africana existential phenomenology to read the colonised/black people as a manifestation of a colonial phenomenon from the positionality of returning to its source. From the decolonial Africana existential phenomenology point of view, the difference between a Eurocentric and Afrocentric is how each introduces the world to the viewer by "...looking, seeing and representing visually with the problematic of [racial] difference" (Pollock 1988, p. xvii). This means making sense of the world by deploying all senses of the body to generate knowledge and meaning. It means not only relying only on thinking or seeing as the Western canon has suggested.

Decolonial Africana existential phenomenology makes sense of the world by moving beyond the surface appearance to the deeper essence of the live experience. Hence, "Afrocentrism recognizes no division between the African past and African American history, and regards as ahistorical and mythical any social science that does not trace these continuous African Roots" (Binder 2002, p. 31). In a similar way to the Afrocentrism, decolonial Africana existential phenomenology "...must begin by retrieving the initial attitude, the hermeneutic posture that Senghor adopted from his early writings onwards in order to answer the question (which, as we will see, was also Picasso's), p. What do African mask mean?" (Di-

A Decolonial Curriculum Is Everything

agne 2011, p. 9). Decolonial Africana existential phenomenology comes from a similar position posing a similar question that is connected to the African mask whose meaning is undefined from a colonial gaze, p. what does it mean to exist as a black person in the anti-black world? Decolonial Africana existential phenomenology as a method is a way to move beyond the surface of appearance and get to the essence in attempt to reflect on existential and ontological questions. These questions according to Diagne, can only be answered if, and "when we go back to its source and weigh the influences to pinpoint the ideas of which it is a synthesis…" (Diagne 2011, p.4). Therefore, decolonial Africana existential phenomenology enables objects to think, speak and resist in order to find and embrace the sublime in the grotesque. It "correct[s]… history books for their neglect or oversights of African experience in one of two ways, p. by asserting the preeminence of Africa and its descendants in the course of world historical events, or by underscoring the presence of subjugated African peoples throughout time and the remarkable triumphs of those oppressed over systems of oppression" (Binder 2002, p.31). That is, finding life in being-in-the-anti-black-world and making sense of the lived black experience.

CONCLUSION

In concluding on something that is difficult to conclude about, it is clear that indigenous knowledge systems will continue to suffer as long as the current Eurocentric logic is prevailing, the current anti-black world still stands, and Afrocentricity is absent in the curriculum. This means the is a space open for future research on the topic of decolonising the curriculum by injecting indigenous knowledge systems. The curriculum of the empire is supported by whiteness and white supremacy that positions itself as the defining factor of what is the standard of learning and what is learnt, the standard of knowledge, being, power, beauty and life itself. Decolonisation of the curriculum of the empire means discrediting it from the Afrocentric position by injecting or replacing it with indigenous knowledge systems. It becomes clear that indigenous communities have a serious task at hand, which is to rethink and decolonise their indigenous knowledge systems. Indigenous knowledge systems suffered under western episteme because of its inability to fully articulate the lived indigenous experience, instead of dehumanizing it. This calls for new decolonial existential and phenomenological approaches that are set to recontextualise, reconfigure, rethink and re-membering of the African subject as a human being. In other words, there is a deep need for the decolonisation of the curriculum and repositioning of indigenous knowledge systems as centre knowledge for the indigenous people in the trans-modern world non-Manichean world. This means the remobilisation of African/black/indigenous thinkers and activist who challenged the empire while still located in blackness by deploying indigenous methods and philosophies. Decolonisation/deoloniality is a project that is lead across the world, it is a project for all the colonised subject who are resisting modernity/coloniality under the umbrella of blackness. Therefore, it is important to remember for the colonised subject who engages in the process of decolonisation that, decolonisation/deconiality is only a bridge to help the colonised subject to cross the river of modernity/coloniality and arrive at a particular destination. Hence decolonisation/decoloniality is applied in this article in relation to the Afrocentric perspective, the aim is to epistemologically and ontological arrive to a decolonial Afrocentric curriculum.

REFERENCES

Asante, M. K. (2007). *An Afrocentric Manifesto, p. Toward an African renaissance. Polity.*

Bangura, A. K. (2012). From Diop to Asante, p. Conceptualizing and Contextualizing the Afrocentric Paradigm. *The Journal of Pan African Studies, 5*(1), 103–125.

Binder, A. J. (Ed.). (2002). Contentious curricula. In Afrocentrism and creationism in American public schools. Princeton University Press.

Ce'saire, A. (2000). Discourse on Colonialism (J. Pinkham, Trans.). New York: Monthly Review Press.

Cox, T., & Nkomo, S. M. (1990). Invisible men and women, p. A status report on race as a variable in organisation behaviour research. *Journal of Organizational Behavior, 11*(6), 419–432. doi:10.1002/job.4030110604

Du Bois, W.E.B. (2016). *The Souls of the black folk.* Digireads.com Publishing. (Original publication 1903)

Fanon, F. (1965). A dying colonialism (H. Chevalier, Trans.). New York: Monthly Review Press.

Fanon, F. (2001). The wretched of the earth (C. Farrington, Trans.). London: Penguin. (Original publication 1961)

Fanon, F. (2008). Black skin, white masks (C.L. Markmann, Trans.). London: Pluto. (Original publication 1952)

Ghandi, L. (1998). Postcolonial theory. In A Critical Introduction. Edinburgh University Press.

Gordon, L. R. (1995). *Bad faith and anti-black racism.* Humanities Press.

Gordon, L. R. (2006). *Disciplinary decadence. Living thought in trying times.* Paradigm.

Hardt, M., & Negri, A. (2000). Empire. Harvard University Press.

Lorde, A. (1984). The Master's Tools Will Never Dismantle the Master's House. In Sister Outsider. Crossing Press.

Makgoba, W. (Ed.). (1999). African renaissance. Mafube Publishing.

Mbeki, T. (1998). *Africa: The time has come.* Tafelberg.

Mbeki, T. (2005). *Goals of Higher Education in Africa.* Retrieved from www.utexas.edu/conferences/africa

Mohanty, C. (1984). Under western eyes: Feminist scholarship and colonial discourses. *Boundary, 12*(3).

Mudimbe, V. Y. (1988). *The invention of Africa: Gnosis, Philosophy, and the order of knowledge.* Indiana University Press.

Ndlovu-Gatsheni, S. J. (2013a). Empire, global coloniality, and Arican objection. Berghahn Books.

Nkomo, S. (1992). The emperor has no clothes, p. Rewriting 'race into the study of organizations'. *Academy of Management Review, 17*(3), 487–513.

A Decolonial Curriculum Is Everything

Nkomo, S. M. (2006). *Images of African Leadership and Management in Organisation Studies: Tensions, Contradictions and Re-visions*. University of South Africa.

Nnabugwu, M.B., & Nwanegbo, J. (2012). Dysfunctional state and severance in Africa, p. an analysis in specificities and contradictions. *Ogirisi: A New Journal of African Studies*, *9*, 127-140.

Nzelibe, C. O. (1986). The evolution of African management thought. *International Studies of Management & Organization*, *16*(2), 6–16. doi:10.1080/00208825.1986.11656427

Owusu-Ansah, F. E., & Mji, G. (2013). African indigenous knowledge and research. *African Journal of Disability*, *2*(1), 1–5. doi:10.4102/ajod.v2i1.30 PMID:28729984

Oyewumi, O. (1997). The invention of women, p. making an African sense of Western gender discourse. University of Minnesota Press.

Santos, B. S. (2007). Beyond abyssal thinking from global lines to ecology of knowledges. *RE:view*, *30*(1), 1–33.

Smith, L. T. (1999). Decolonising methodologies: Research and indigenous people. Zed Books.

Spivak, G. C. (1990). The post-colonial critic. Viking.

Thiong'o. (1993). *Moving the centre: The struggle for cultural freedoms*. East African Educational Publishers Ltd.

Yountae, A. (2017). The decolonial abyss: Mysticism and cosmopolitics from the ruins. Fordham University Press.

KEY TERMS AND DEFINITIONS

Africana Existential Phenomenology: It is a kind of phenomenology that allows Africana people to study their subjectivity in relation to the colonial world based on their lived experience. By putting the word decoloniality as a prefix suggest that it is located in the project of decolonisation.

Afrocentricity: An approach that positions African people as the centre of their knowledge production. It allows the African subject to engage the world based on their indigenous knowledge systems.

Blackness: It is a kind of a condition that is created through racism, imperialism and colonisation. It used here from a decolonial epistemic perspective, which believe blackness is a cause and fuel of modernity.

Coloniality of Knowledge: It is a form of colonisation that privileges Eurocentric knowledge over other knowledge systems. It labels indigenous knowledge systems as primitive knowledge that is not at the level of European knowledge.

Decoloniality: It as project of challenging colonisation and racism. Unlike post-coloniality which is located inside modernity, decoloniality comes outside of modernity.

Empire: It is a concept that was invented by Michael Hardt and Antonio Negri (2000) to suggest the global political world that is ruled as one empire, which is controlled by a certain group of people. In the empire, it is only the white subject who is considered a sovereign subject who also qualifies to be the only human.

Frantz Fanon: Is a Black theorist who is known for his work which focuses on the lived experience of the black subject in the colonised world or empire. His work is a critique of colonisation and racism, it allows the black colonised subject to be able to understand their subjectivity in a modern/colonial world.

Indigenous Knowledge Systems: It is a knowledge system that predates colonisation and European modernity. It is an ancient knowledge that is based on the way indigenous people see, think and do in the world based on their culture.

This research was previously published in Ethical Research Approaches to Indigenous Knowledge Education; pages 59-81, copyright year 2021 by Information Science Reference (an imprint of IGI Global).

Chapter 31
Facebook Aesthetics:
White World–Making, Digital Imaginary, and "The War on Terror"

Sadhvi Dar
Queen Mary University of London, UK

ABSTRACT

What is the relationship between digital imaginaries and whiteness? Following recent calls to investigate the juncture between whiteness and the internet, this chapter seeks to provide a critique of imagery posted on Facebook in the aftermath of 'terror attacks' in Paris 2015. The author renders these images as structured by deep forms of white world-making, ways of thinking and feeling that reproduce whiteness as ethically superior, innocent, and in need of preserving at the cost of non-white knowledges and peoples. In this chapter, the author argues that the internet provides yet another site for whiteness to engage in white world-making by extending the white gaze to digital platforms in the service of transforming the violence of Paris into a racialised attack on white innocence. As such, the Paris images are understood as responding to and perpetuating a digital imaginary in which the political capacities of images relate to an ethics of violence to the non-white Muslim body.

INTRODUCTION

The reproduction of whiteness relies on its constitution as an invisible 'raceless' identity, thereby equating white subjects and their specific cultural mores and values with the universality of the human. (Thobani, 2007: 172)

What is the relationship between digital imaginaries and whiteness? Following recent calls to investigate the juncture between whiteness and the internet (Nakayama, 2015), this chapter seeks to provide a critique of imagery posted on Facebook in the aftermath of 'terror attacks' in Paris 2015. Rather than comprehending these posts as a user-reaction to a violent event, I render these images as structured by deep forms of white world-making, ways of thinking and feeling that reproduce whiteness as ethically

DOI: 10.4018/978-1-6684-4507-5.ch031

Copyright © 2022, IGI Global. Copying or distributing in print or electronic forms without written permission of IGI Global is prohibited.

superior, innocent and in need of preserving at the cost of non-white knowledges and peoples. In this chapter, I argue that the internet provides yet another site for whiteness to engage in white world-making by extending the white gaze to digital platforms in the service of transforming the violence of Paris into a racialised attack on white innocence. As such, the Paris images are understood as responding to and perpetuating a digital imaginary in which the political capacities of images relate to an ethics of violence to the non-white Muslim body. The possibility for anti-racist activism on the internet is thus deemed severely mitigated in the context of digital corporations structuring social media platforms - the algorithms that curate online imagery and their viewers' gaze are racist (Noble, 2018).

During/in the aftermath of the Paris shootings (13 November 2015), Facebook became a platform for the production and circulation of photographs, cartoons and filters representing or reacting to the events. These images varied in content and form and a selection became viral. The viral images concentrated attention to the Western European location of the attacks (Paris) and simultaneously challenged notions of nationality and citizenship by their appeal to Facebook-users globally. The viral images varied; some depicted the chaotic aftermath of the shootings (see Image 1), other images portrayed shrines to those who lost their lives in the attacks (see Image 2) and, there were also photos of various international landmark buildings lit up in the colours of the French flag (see Image 3). Other representations included a filter that superimposed the colours of the French flag onto users' profile pictures (see Image 4) and, arguably the most iconic image to emerge on social media newsfeeds was a drawing of a peace sign constructed from the outline of the Eifel Tower (see Image 5).

It is not unusual that Facebook users posted, commented on and shared Paris images after the attacks. Social media has become a platform for sharing affected and affecting imagery immediately after violent events. Indeed, Facebook, alongside other social media platforms (Instagram, Twitter, Flickr, Tumblr), has offered an activist space where users may communicate to build community after experiencing violence (Linder et al., 2016). Others have hailed online community-building as invested with potential policy implications for citizens surviving national trauma (Dufty, 2012). Thus, the spontaneous circulation of Paris 2015 images on Facebook can be rendered a working through of trauma, expressing a need for community-building and as a strategy for recovery. Yet, while these studies have celebrated online community-building as an agentic process that can restore the sanctity and safety of those who have been traumatised, there are other critiques that foreground the political context within which violence is imagined and made sense of.

Thobani (2007: 169) argues that the 'War on Terror' reconfigures "the practices that constitute whiteness through its definition of the West as endangered by the hatred and violence of its Islamist Other". She foregrounds a 'new' imperial imaginary where the deployment of the discourse on 'terror' presents the current 'threat' and 'terrorist' violence as being of global proportions - committed to the destruction of the West at all costs. In this configuration, whiteness is re-centered as innocent of its colonial histories and contemporary complicity in the subjugation of brown and black people. This colonial amnesia is critical to Europe's enduring self-image of a morally virtuous agent that represents a universal humanity invested with the responsibility to restore the rights of, and justice for, oppressed people (Bassel and Emejulu, 2017). In this vein, digital scholars can extend the analysis of explicitly racist posts to those representing European moral goodness where both registers sustain a belief in white innocence and white superiority.

In this chapter, I draw on Fanon's (1961) concept of colonial violence to unpack viral imagery circulated in the aftermath of Paris 2015 and conjoin it to online processes of white world-making. Fanon (1961: 33) articulates how colonial violence targeting black and brown bodies is normalised by a disembodied

Facebook Aesthetics

whiteness that (re)configures itself in the form of universal moralising "values". Connecting these values to digital imaginaries, I employ Ranciere's (2004, 2009) work on the politics of aesthetics to develop a conceptual framework locating Paris 2015 images within a digital communication paradigm that frames colonial violence. Through conducting a semiotic analysis of the Facebook images that draws on an interpretive philosophy, I explore the ways in which social media configures post-traumatic imagery for the purposes of sustaining colonial amnesia.

Whiteness, Colonial Violence and the Internet

Scholars of critical race theory have defined race as a changeable and de-centred configuration comprised of "social meanings constantly being transformed by political struggle" (Omi and Winant, 1994: 55). As such, race is a socially constructed "concept which signifies and symbolizes social conflicts and interests by referring to different types of human bodies", one "constructed and transformed socio-historically through competing political projects" (Omi and Winant 1994: 71). Race is a contested concept because its formation manifests through the political project, a project that is imbricated with forceful dynamics, claims and intersections. Racism is demonstrated in the way formation recreates "structures of domination based on essentialist categories of race" (Omi and Winant, 1994: 71). Extending these debates is scholarship that works with the concept of whiteness. Whiteness is what Ruth Frakenberg (1993) has identified as a structural position of social privilege and power that normalises the benefits racist societies award white groups, as well as normalising white violence (both physical and non-physical) targeting black and brown bodies. The study of whiteness therefore shifts attention away from the scenes of intergroup racial conflict or interracial co-existence to a critique of the "reproduction and maintenance of systems of racial inequality" (Hartigan, 1997: 496).

Culture, including visual culture, in this framework is used in two ways (Hartigan, 1997: 497): "Primarily, it establishes a register apart from individual identity that affects and defines white people collectively while suggesting a broad range of means by which racial matters influence or inform the lives of white people, asserting that they, too, are 'racial'. Secondly, the notion of 'white culture', developed and consistent through the long centuries of white global domination, reifies whiteness as a definable entity." Here, the cultural dimensions of digital life are rendered as central to maintaining the certainty and consistency with which whiteness self-presents itself as innocent. When we employ whiteness as an analytical object to make sense of the seemingly innocuous Paris 2015 imagery, posting such images online can be rendered a racial act of identifying with white innocence in the face of colonial violence.

On social media platforms, communicating one's identity or identification with a community is entangled with multiple acts of showing. These acts are not a one-way process by which opinions or life events are made available and rendered visible to the world, instead they are knotted with Facebook's liberal branding of itself, as a corporation that builds a common world movement[1]. Yet this commonality is framed by a distinctly liberal political economy within which the vocabulary of whiteness becomes the lingua franca for legitimising community-building that restores Europe's innocence. Facebook provides users with the collaborative expertise of bearing witness to global events and traumas, to translate and produce knowledge about events as well as sensing and exposing them. Thus, Facebook has become a space for human sense-making structured by and reproduced through collective forms of visual representation (Matusitz, 2013; Kellner, 2015) that produces value for whiteness. Such forms of visual representation are associated with 9/11 imagery and how the circulation of these images played a central role in shifting the vocabularies of whiteness.

The 'War on Terror' traces its own genesis to the 9/11 attacks. The destruction of New York's iconic twin towers signified that the great Western powers were not infallible, and the transformation of this event into a media spectacle reverberated across the world, repeating the fact of America's vulnerability (Thobani, 2007). The 'War on Terror' was launched by the Bush Administration in close co-ordination with its European and North American allies to reassert its dominance in the world, and as Thobani[2] (2007: 169, my italics) has argued, "the battle to control *the meaning of the attacks* was no less intense than the one waged on the bodies of Muslims named as the enemy". While the Bush Administration sought to enlarge its imperial hold over the oil-producing regions of the Middle East and Central Asia, the twin tower attacks were framed by a discourse of an "epochal assault in the West and its civilizational values" (Thobani, 2007: 169). By arguing Western civilization was under attack for being civilized, whiteness was able to reconfigure itself as innocent, unguarded and exposed while normalising hatred of a fanatic and uncivilised non-Western Other.

While many scholars and activists have sought out Fanon's (1961) thesis on colonial violence to understand decolonial struggles, I adopt a reading of Fanon to account for the coloniser's reproduction of white European culture as innocent and vulnerable. His critique of colonial violence bears a specific significance to the Paris 2015 shootings, since his decolonising politics were borne out of his patent rejection of an expansive and entrenched French colonialism. The writings which I draw on here were formulated during the vicious French-Algerian War (1954-62) when he was writing for the Algerian National Liberation Front in exile from Tunis. These illuminations offer an incisive critique of French colonial society, the struggle against colonialism and the affective registers of colonial relations.

Fanon identifies that the making and re-making of Western culture as civilizing, sensible and innocent is central to coloniser's perpetuating the oppression of global majorities while re-framing decolonial struggles as dangerously unpredictable and therefore a threat to Western civilization. Where the coloniser admits defeat and retreats from colonised land, colonial authority will persist to create a neo-colonial order that privileges white Europeans and Americans. Establishing this neo-colonial order rests on the production and reproduction of Western culture as a universally humanising force that colonised people can relate to rather than resist. This configuring of white European culture enables whiteness to self-present as morally superior to colonised people's as well as leaving open the possibility for the colonised to identify with whiteness – which Fanon argues is an act of colonial de-humanisation.

Bringing Thobani and Fanon's critiques of whiteness together, we can see how notions of witnessing colonial violence and creating community for self-recovery in borderless digital spaces need to become contextualised by the city space of Paris. Paris has long been celebrated by people across the political spectrum as exemplifying a geography of white rebellion. Paris' imaginary evokes the 1789 French Revolution, the student riots of May 1968, and the more recent *gilets jaunes* movement that has sustained a year-long anti-establishment protest. These historical and contemporary events are framed by popular discourses that connect Paris to an ideology of refusal, of dynamic recovery and whitely dissent. By centering these Parisian tropes, France's long history of African - Caribbean colonialism and its continuities with contemporary racial conflicts is made periphery, if not completely denied. For example, France does not record any ethnic data, arguing that it is a colour-blind nation. This position is a historical one and has led to sustained levels of marginalisation and the resulting deprivation of communities of colour (Bassel and Emejulu, 2017). The lack of ethnic data gathering has made anti-racist organizing and advocacy extraordinarily challenging, though communities of colour have built and sustained movements such as *Mwasi Collectif, Indigenes de la Republique* and *gilets noires* to pursue a politics of survival.

Facebook Aesthetics

Further, France's "colonial continuum" has manifested in blatant anti-Muslim legislation, such as the passing of the 2004 law banning religious signs in state schools that effectively outlaws Muslim women from wearing religious clothing (Indigenes de la Republique, 2005). This law was amended in 2010 to ban women from wearing burkas and niqabs in public. France's political racelessness belies its explicit and concerted efforts to suppress Muslim identities and anti-racist activism. The racial morality of France is one that universalises whiteness at the cost of the rights of non-White others. In this political context, witnessing and self-recovery are structured by the whiteness of Paris - a social imaginary that needs to be teased out through an explicit analysis because white innocence has been normalised by the 'War on Terror'. Demarcated from the violence against blackness/brownness, whiteness becomes a moral goodness and the city's survival becomes inscribed through that imaginary. As Facebook users posted images and illustrations depicting their post-traumatic recovery, this act of collective remembering affirmed whiteness's innocence and became redemptive to the black and brown bodies that were framed as causing the violence.

I now turn to the issue of Facebook imagery and its connection to community-building. Drawing on Ranciere's (2004, 2009) critique of aesthetics I build a conceptual framework to make visible the whiteness of the images that structure the users' gaze along essentialist categories of race.

Making Sense of Facebook Aesthetics, Making Sense of Whiteness

(Lest whiteness and blackness become static versions of the marxist superstructure/base paradigm—discrete, separate entities rather than constantly entangled registers—ethnographers must devise means to analyze how whites, as racial subjects, are embroiled in predicaments where the meanings of race are unclear and shifting, subjects of discourses or local idioms that are fashioned in fast-changing sites. (Hartigan, 1997: 502

For Jacques Ranciere, art and community are inseparable because of the singular politics that underscores the very way we imagine these concepts. Ranciere's contribution to art theory is his critique of aesthetics that contradicts the progressive narrative of art moving from 'modern' through to 'postmodern' to 'contemporary' epochs. For what is usually referred to as the 'modern' period, Ranciere comprehends as an 'aesthetic' revolution that continues till today. The emergence of the aesthetic regime came at the end of the eighteenth and beginning of the nineteenth centuries, at the time Enlightenment transformed European politics, philosophy and economies towards operations that were increasingly dependent on slave labour and colonial extraction for wealth creation and industrialisation. Against the heavily regimented structuration of art forms that depicted them as corresponding to 'high' or 'low' art, the aesthetic revolution reframed our experience of it. Most significantly, the aesthetic revolution transformed art into an anti-representational pursuit. As decolonising analyses have shown, this gave rise to the idea that art must play a political role in the mobilisation of imagery to make visible European sensibilities and instil their registers within the viewer's imaginary.

I retain Ranciere's critique of aesthetics, inasmuch I engage with the Paris images as *Facebook aesthetics* – a register of imagery where whiteness assigns roles, practices and capacities to the communities represented (explicitly or implicitly) in the images, while affecting the viewer's sensibilities. I contend that this aesthetic regime transforms the boundaries between art and life because art's function is to produce an affected encounter where viewers are drawn into a relation with Europe as moral superiority. This aesthetic relation is both individual to the viewer who is moved by the image to post, comment and

589

re-post and it is communal because the relation to the image established in this encounter transforms the social boundaries of meaning-making. However, in identifying the online communities that Facebook aesthetics (re)make, we must heed Hartigan's warning to be mindful not to build a structural argument reproducing whiteness as immutable and the idea of European innocence as beyond challenge. Returning to Ranciere's conceptualisation of aesthetic art, the aesthetic regime contravenes the idea that art has an originary interpretation, or a singular meaning. Aesthetic art creates the conditions for dissensus, because it opens up the possibility for the re-ordering of bodies, boundaries and voices that go against traditional patterns. What is supplied to individual senses does not lead to predictable imaginaries. That is precisely why art is at the heart of politics that produce boundaries and communities and why Facebook imagery posted in the aftermath of the Paris 2015 shootings must be understood as a shifting, not cemented, discourse on race.

Whitely Imaginaries / Imageries

The aesthetics of the Paris images are not predicated on their content, the images are aesthetic because they frame post-trauma through an affecting relationship with the image that subjectifies whitely users - turning the white gaze on them and on their sensibilities. We can discern the politics of these images as divisive because community is built by the act of posting or liking the post, so these acts are transformed into an identification with the image. Those whose senses remain undisturbed and untraumatised can be identified within the register of the user who fails to know the trauma of the city's mourning.

Some acts of identification were blatant and obvious. By applying and sharing the profile picture filter that uses the French flag (image 4), the user superimposed two identities: their own and France's. The filter provided the user with a way of engaging in self-recovery by literally becoming the national flag of France. Here, the flag's muted and transparent tones represent the morality of liberalism – of a common humanity that is restrained as well as appropriated. France's humanity can be assimilated into any global user's identity. The proliferation of the flag filter transforms France from the location of a violent event into an imposing and a universally generous force. The profile picture filter is aesthetic because it reconfigures whiteness's reach by producing a post-traumatic community in the service of universalising France's moral superiority and its mourning's global relevance.

An image that was widely circulated on Facebook was a photograph of the damaged glass windows of a restaurant in the Bataclan district, where one of the Paris shootings took place (see Image 2). The restaurant's shattered but exquisitely clean window is punctuated by two sharp bullet holes. Placed delicately within each hole, is a wilting flower: sometimes a rose, sometimes a carnation; but always the flowers placed in the gaping wounds of this once lively café are a shade of love: red, pink or white. This image was circulated and posted on Facebook (alongside other social media and news websites) the day after the Paris attacks. The image performs an economy of attention that reduces the heterogeneity of colonial experience to a single interface between a post-colonial moment and whiteness's innocence. The bullet-holes signify the violation of human life, while the fading roses suggest the benevolent yet assertive democracies of the West. The photograph expresses simultaneous defiance against the terrorists and solidarity with a whitely universal humanity. The image therefore expresses an anti-terror politics and a nostalgic note of collective love, which memorialises a disembodied whiteness while invisiblising the brown body at the centre of the political issue.

The photograph of the bullet-holes and roses draws attention to itself; it defines itself within a particular way of seeing colonial violence. The way the image does this is by functioning as a collage, assimilating

Facebook Aesthetics

at least four disparate, but timely, events: the anti-Vietnam peace rally outside the Pentagon in 1967 (see image 6); the civilized Paris as symbolised by the elegant glass windows; the erratic shooting as signified by the violent glass shatterings, the open, hopeless voids of the bullet holes; and, the post-shooting trauma/nostalgia as connoted by the delicate and velvety red roses that are both deeply romantic and whimsical. The conjoining of disparate, affected histories (whitely peace, colonial violence, romantic mourning) evokes desperate feelings within the viewer. The temporal collage produces a divided community: the non-White-Other-terrorist and the knowing-sensing-White-Parisian.

On Facebook, the consumption and circulation of images produce user newsfeeds of knowable sensibilities that accumulate value when the user identifies with a common recollection of history and a universal reaction to colonial violence. The arranging and re-arranging of Facebook images, through the circulation of them, becomes an "inventory of traces of history" (Ranciere, 2009: 55). Facebook newsfeeds, whether belonging to a single-user or a group, take the listing of images on the webpage as a testimony to a shared experience, a world in common. Facebook enables a collection of images to signify a shared capacity to be affected by white trauma. In this sense, the Facebook user is both the artist and the archivist, being affected and affecting others in their pursuit of promoting Europe's moral reach. This is also how Facebook aesthetics grasp the subjectivity of users in a specific way that is different to an encounter with an art object in an offline space. Facebook aesthetics are operationalised through co-creation that transforms the image into a community-building process. Community-building is accomplished by inviting responses, commentaries and correspondence about the image. Facebook imageries create relations and encounters, as well as an archive of art-objects to be looked at. Value is not only accumulated through the number of likes, but also by how the likes come to signify a community affected by the image. User-initiated commentary of the image provides the semblance of democratic plurality: the liberal tenet of producing community through communicative conflict is evidenced by Facebook making visible and inciting spontaneous vocality.

Social media platforms appear to provide the means to escape structured discourses – to incite a spontaneous break from a visual regime by offering Facebook users the power to select images on their (and others) newsfeeds to like and promote. However, Facebook aesthetics undermine the emancipatory effects of democratic conflict by calibrating newsfeeds to include the most popular or sponsored posts, thus creating racialised archives of meaning that undermines the perceived autonomy of the user. Facebook promotes a visual regime that accumulates value through whitely consensus-building, through users collectively performing an imaginary that colludes with European liberalism.

The White Man's Eifel

In this section, I shift attention from the consumer of Facebook imagery to the producer of it in an attempt to understand firstly, the role of white artists in shaping discourses of colonial violence and secondly, the possibility of Facebook aesthetics for transforming whitely sensibilities. Within liberalism's imaginary, public activity is recognised as a form of civic power that has the potential to disturb political identities, to kilter the structuring forces that divide communities. Thus, management of the visual regime can aid the stratification of liberal subjectivities – between those who have the right to remain civic, sensing beings and those who do not owing to their lack of talent to speak, to listen, to understand. Ranciere (2004: 8) describes the power of aesthetics as invested in those with the "ability to see and who (have) the talent to speak". This position of privilege over the aesthetic regime provides some identities and groups with more reason to speak up and also to be listened to.

In the immediate aftermath of the Paris shootings, allegedly after a minute of learning about the attacks (Wired, 2015), the white French artist Jean Jullien painted an image in his sketchbook of a peace sign using the outline of the Eifel tower (image 5). He spontaneously took a photograph of the image and posted it on his Twitter and Facebook accounts with the caption, "Peace for Paris". Within a matter of hours, the image had gone viral, and by the 17 November 2015, the image had been re-tweeted over 44,000 times, accumulated 163,000 likes on Instagram and had been shared over 22,000 times on Facebook (The Telegraph, 2015). Over the following months, the image was copied and sold on T-shirts, banners, mugs, pens, postcards, and a plethora of purchasable consumables. It was also used as a backdrop for a Coldplay concert, as a logo on the Saint-Etienne football team's kit and was drawn with a plume of white smoke by an anonymous aeroplane pilot over the blue skies of Lyon (Guardian, 2016).

Understanding the aesthetic quality of Jullien's image requires reading the image against the particular discursive configuration of the 'War on Terror' preceding his moment of artistic inspiration. The Paris shootings occurred 11 months after the attacks that took place in the city at the Charlie Hebdo newspaper headquarters. Inspired by Charlie Hebdo's market placement as a satirical and illustrated magazine, artists and illustrators drew cartoons in defiance against the attacks and argued for the protection of art as a mechanism to unlock the public's imagination that can present political arguments beyond the confines of using words or rhetoric. The Charlie Hebdo shootings drew out wide political debates across Europe on the nature of freedom of speech and its enshrinement in democratic states. Central to these debates was the issue of Charlie Hebdo's consistently racist and Islamophobic satire that was defended by French politicians and media personalities as highly evolved but inaccessible and unintelligible to non-French readers. France's great tradition of satire was promoted as innately democratic by Charlie Hebdo's advocates. In these discussions, whiteness's claim over art was reasserted as an integral part of ensuring European democracy and moral values prevail.

In interviews given shortly after the Paris peace sign went viral, Jullien states that the power of images supersedes the written word, that the image is a "universal" language that has a practical role "In selling ideas as much as selling products" (Wired, 2015). As such, Jullien's illustration was a continuation of the Charlie Hebdo defence, but it was also an important departure because it appeared like a corporate logo - a branding of European innocence with the capitalist symbolism of hope and happiness. In stating the equitable relationship between art and branding, Jullien freed himself of his main vocation (to illustrate, to design, to craft) and took on the role of producing great art: he came to occupy "the space of public discussion and take(s) on the identity of a deliberative citizen" (Ranciere, 2004: 40). This position was awarded to a white cis man who had a history of illustrating for corporations to market goods and services.

In one of Julien's interviews, he explains his motivation for painting the image. He states that the image was created, not in his capacity as an artist, but as an expression of a common humanity exerting the need for compassion in the face of terrorism, he states: "It was more an instinctive, human reaction than an illustrator's reaction" (Wired, 2015). Jullien identifies his image as synonymous with living speech; it is a call for dignity in a visual form: a decisive moment of deliberative action represented by a new logo for Paris. Despite, Jullien's insistence that his image is beyond the representational (it is an immediate expression of interiority, not the adaptation of expression to an appropriate form), he relies on the aesthetic regime to brand whiteness's sensibility as consumerist optimism.

Just as the Renaissance movement a few hundred years ago, that sought to distil the complexities of a human story in a single detailed frame, Jullien states his role in society to make his images speak a similarly multifaceted story. However, instead of using the fine layers of oils coloured by colonial commodities (carmine, Indian yellow, ultramarine), built up by the artist and enriched over a period of time,

Facebook Aesthetics

Jullien describes the image as a spontaneous logo created without thought or measurement; without the reasoned sensibility of fine art. Jullien implies in his interviews, traditional forms of European art remove the artist from the realm of spontaneous experience. Jullien's logo addresses, what he believes is, a common need within a community in mourning (peace, hope). To manifest peace, Jullien's logo severs the violence from the event by evoking the happiness and security of a humanity to come. Thus, unlike the democratic leaders, who invoked a 'War on Terror' in the face of American vulnerability, the Paris peace-sign condones a moral gaze that invokes an ethics of violence against the non-White Other without naming it. The humanisation of security has led to liberalism and humanitarianism becoming fused (Duffield, 2007), leading to a re-organisation of life in which an ethics of violence prevails against those non-Whites who do not sense, emote or celebrate Paris's universality. This is a strategy that does not require fixing a location to be destroyed or a mass of people to be murdered, it is part of a political economy that depends on the free circulation of liberal signs; it is creative, imaginative and optimistic.

Jullien's logo operationalised a white gaze that values life on the basis of its potential to be visibly hopeful and vital, here Facebook aesthetics configured whiteness as consumerist and global. Paris was made universally consumable. The movement of Jullien's logo depended on unbridled digital travel, internationalisation and exchange; its virality was also reliant on a distribution of the sensible that drew attention to humanist experiences of hope and happiness. These affects were necessary to purge trauma from whiteness, in order to maintain the fiction of an undifferentiated global community in mourning. The near complete absence of viral Facebook imagery that bears witness to the horrific and ongoing deaths of millions of people in the Arabic-speaking world is no better indicator of the power of online imagery securing political outcomes that benefit whiteness.

Facebook Inc: Curating Whiteness Through an Aesthetics of Paris

The internet has had a profound impact on society and one of its biggest social media platforms, Facebook Inc., is an online network that has accumulated over 1.44 billion monthly active users since its inception in 2005 (Statista.com, 2015). Facebook is a multinational corporation and has online offerings across all countries, except in regions that actively block social media networks[3]. Facebook's impact on society has been analysed by investigating its effect on social relations (Ellison et al, 2011; Ellison et al, 2007), its role in knowledge production (McFadyen et al, 2004) and also its bearing on users' self-esteem levels (Steinfield et al, 2008). These studies have documented the impact of Facebook on how users value each other and experience one another, suggesting that offline social relations are experienced differently, as well as contending online identities are entwined with offline experiences (Hine, 2000).

In this way, Facebook imagery performs a transformation of user experience as it makes a mark on the viewer's subjectivity as well as being marked by it. The image is value-less; it is reproduced efficiently and freely on screens to be viewed and shared infinitely. The image has no monetary value, yet its power is its potential to disaggregate and transform experience. Facebook images of the Paris 2015 shootings engage a white gaze, or a white structure to sense the world. By sharing and posting the image, the user builds a whitely community which responds and transforms whiteness – the images become the focus of political conflict that shape and permeate both user-identities and the institutionalised digital space of Facebook feeds. The diffusion of these images constitutes a universal ethical dimension that is grounded in the liberal politics of bearing witness to a common world: a consensus that may restore meaning and "seal the cracks in the social bonds" (Ranciere, 2009: 122). The power of Facebook aesthetics is its ability to re-configure the boundaries of communities by concentrating the user's gaze toward a particular way of experiencing terrorist events. Facebook art produces an experience of global politics structured through whitely reactions to online images in the form of likes, comments and shares that engage the user's sensibility so that they may experience colonial violence through whiteness's innocence.

Defining art has been a philosophical as well as a political preoccupation for social philosophers, art critics, social activists and artists. Historically, the controversy of defining art has been associated with the need to name it and to thereby distinguish it, in normative terms: to unfold what art should be and what it ought to generate within the senses and souls of its viewers. By introducing the nominal category of 'art', the artistic object is dislocated from the artist who creates it and, instead, is celebrated by way of forming consensus around its disturbing or enlightening qualities as experienced in the artistic encounter. Here, the dislocation is not purely spatial (the art moves from the artist's studio through the walls or archives of a gallery to the online archive of Facebook newsfeeds), but rather it is subjective. When we begin to draw lines between what art is, and what it is not, the viewer is re-drawn as well. For art to be experienced as such, there is a disassembling of the subject: a severing of her cognitive capacities (that attend to the art-object) from her affective experience that structures the encounter. The Facebook user must be able to make sense of the qualities imbued in the pictorial image or sculpture to experience its white power. Thus, defining what art is through the nominal categorising of it is not purely a hermeneutic exercise savoured by the reasoning mind, but also, a political exercise that determines who is recognised as community. I locate the Paris 2015 images within a distribution of the sensible – a distribution that signifies a political economy of bodies, voices and capacities that are reified by imagery and structured by a racialised digital imaginary.

CONCLUDING REMARKS

In this chapter, I have sketched out the relation between the Paris 2015 images (their production and consumption) and the aesthetic regime they (re)produce. Ranciere's (2009) problematisation of the sensible and its relation to art offers a vista to interrogate art that goes viral, allowing a deeper analysis of the subjective dimensions of viral imagery and its relation to the communal politics within which viral art circulates and is consumed. However, Ranciere's thesis is not enough to make sense of the ways Facebook reproduces whiteness as well as how it is reconfigured in the current digital epoch. Fanon's concept of colonial violence provides us with a mandate to go beyond what causes an image to go viral, and to argue for a decolonial analysis of how online aesthetics reconfigure whitely sensibilities that render Europe innocent.

User-activity and the co-created dimension of online art provide the promise of community-building that has the potential to counter hegemonic politics. Indeed, the promise of Facebook is exactly that: to unlock regional boundaries and to affirm anti-racist solidarities. However, political ideas embedded in art can be objectified and extracted to engage a particular gaze for viewing violence and experiencing trauma. When these events happen elsewhere and outside the immediate experience of the individual, the potential for objectification increases dramatically. Immediate experiences or observations can help correct colonial delusions or racial misconceptions, however, the fantasy of a common humanity that a social network recreates instils a belief in whiteness's moral superiority. As such, Facebook imagery signifies a reduction of experience; it's consumption and circulation stand in for an ethical witnessing of Othered bodies who have produced historically rich and alternative definitions of whiteness's sensibility and ethical framing.

Facebook Aesthetics

Facebook aesthetics could acknowledge the impossibility of bearing witness to the non-white Other's trauma, but that would mean embracing trauma as human, rather than something that is to be expunged from cyber-imagination to make room for whitely optimism. This requires the production of content that evolves to manoeuvre outside the white gaze. Five years on from the Paris attacks, we can trace the establishment of counter-hegemonic content that undoes the ethics of violence from the position of the non-White Muslim other. We see the undoing of the white gaze and male tenor in the spoken works of the British poet, Suhaiymah Manzoor-Khan (AKA The Brown Hijabi). She interrupts the whiteness of digital culture, refusing to be categorised by sights of white world-making. She does this by making visual language redundant as she posts performances of her non-page poetry. Her brown orality performs in digital space to undo white gazing. In one of her most viewed posts, she orates a poem called British Values in which she delivers the lines, *"Britain is body-popping outside of the tube, Brick Lane before it was cool, Britain is bilingual, Britain is the burqa, Britain is praying in the changing rooms, Britain has its feet in your sink... Britain is barbaric, Britain has blood on its hands and its back to the wall... Britain is believing in human rights whilst removing them all"*. (Manzoor-Khan, 2019) Here, we witness how colonial trauma is divorced from the belief in white innocence. Colonial violence is sensed outside an ethics of violence, it is reckoned with in a register that is multifaceted, incongruous, visceral. This register for sensing trauma rejects the liberal politics that support Europe's colonial amnesia and cast-off the fantasy of whiteness's purity.

Before aesthetics became the visual regime through which art, the artist and its viewers accrued value, it was the decorative and religious forms of art that were celebrated by social elites. Through the industrialisation of image-making, reproductions of European art became available to those who may not have previously had the means to access an encounter with it. The photographic image appeared alongside the expansion of modern liberalism and the proliferation of the visual regime was cemented in the imagination of a whitely populous. Art became egalitarian in whitely communities while it exercised division and dehumanisation among non-white peoples. Despite the communal sharing of mass-produced art, the pictorial image, in its most classic terms, was and remains an opportunity for calibrated gazing. It's contemporary form potentially undermines the figurative realm of image-making, because its value is accrued by communal acts of knowing, not by the representational qualities of it. The online image builds on this propensity to affect the communal gaze and, simultaneously, the image itself is affected by its viewers who can comment on, photoshop, or edit it. The encounter itself is democratised, freeing the art to speak and be spoken to.

I should make clear here, that I am not aligning the subjective encounter between the viewer and Paris 2015 imagery to what has been described as the concept-less character of the aesthetic experience - or what Benjamin (1936) memorably called 'aura'. For, it is not the subjective pleasure that the image performs within/for the whitely viewer, but the broader structures that reconfigure pleasure sensed by the whitely viewer that are drawn on in the online encounter. Where Benjamin argues that the technical qualities of art pre-form its political and aesthetic qualities, I am proposing that its viewers already recognise the value of whitely imagery because it is consumable and consuming within a liberal political economy. In becoming consumable online, the image does not lose its political power; it constructs new forms of desire within the consumer. The entrance of Paris 2015 imagery online is therefore not a new way of doing politics, but it is part of an emergent political discourse that informs ways of being white.

REFERENCES

Bassel, L., & Emejulu, A. (2018). *Minority Women and Austerity: Survival and resistance in France and Britain*. Policy Press.

Benjamin, W. (1936/1968). The Work of Art in the Age of Mechanical Reproduction. In B. Ardent (Ed.), *Illuminations*. Schocken Books.

Duffield, M. (2007). *Development, Security and Unending War: Governing the World of Peoples*. Polity Press.

Dufty, N. (2012). Using social media to build community disaster resilience. *Australian Journal of Emergency Management*, *27*(1), 40–45.

Ellison, N. B., Steinfield, C., & Lampe, C. (2007). The benefits of Facebook "friends:" Social capital and college students' use of online social network sites. *Journal of Computer-Mediated Communication*, *12*(4), 1143–1168. doi:10.1111/j.1083-6101.2007.00367.x

Ellison, N. B., Steinfield, C., & Lampe, C. (2011). Connection strategies: Social capital implications of Facebook-enabled communication practices. *New Media & Society*, *13*(6), 873–892. doi:10.1177/1461444810385389

Fanon, F. (1961). *The Wretched of the Earth*. Grove Press.

Frankenberg, R. (1993). *The Social Construction of Whiteness: White women, race matters*. Routledge. doi:10.4324/9780203973431

Hartigan, J. Jr. (1997). Establishing the fact of whiteness. *American Anthropologist*, *99*(3), 495–505. doi:10.1525/aa.1997.99.3.495

Hine, C. (2000). *Virtual Ethnography*. Sage. doi:10.4135/9780857020277

Indigenes de la Republic. (2005). *L'Appel des Indigènes*. http://indigenes-republique.fr/le-p-i-r/appel-des-indigenes-de-la-republique/

Kellner, D. (2015). *Media spectacle and the crisis of democracy: Terrorism, war, and election battles*. Routledge. doi:10.4324/9781315633480

Linder, C., Myers, J. S., Riggle, C., & Lacy, M. (2016). From margins to mainstream: Social media as a tool for campus sexual violence activism. *Journal of Diversity in Higher Education*, *9*(3), 231–244. doi:10.1037/dhe0000038

Manzoor-KhanS. (2019). *Facebook*. https://www.facebook.com/watch/?v=396771270918620

Matusitz, J. (2013). *Terrorism and Communication*. Sage.

McFadyen, A. M., & Cannella, A. A. (2004). Social capital and knowledge creation: Diminishing returns of the number and strength of exchange relationships. *Academy of Management Journal*, *47*(5), 735–746.

Nakayama, T. K. (2017). What's next for whiteness and the Internet. *Critical Studies in Media Communication*, *34*(1), 68–72. doi:10.1080/15295036.2016.1266684

Facebook Aesthetics

Noble, S. U. (2018). *Algorithms of oppression: How search engines reinforce racism*. NYU Press. doi:10.2307/j.ctt1pwt9w5

Ranciere, J. (2004). *The Politics of Aesthetics* (G. Rockhill, Trans.). Bloomsbury Publishing.

Ranciere, J. (2009). *Aesthetics and its Discontents* (S. Corcoran, Trans.). Polity Press.

Statistica.com. (2015). Available at: https://www.statista.com/statistics/264810/number-of-monthly-active-facebook-users-worldwide

Steinfield, C., Ellison, N. B., & Lampe, C. (2008). Social capital, self-esteem, and use of online social network sites: A longitudinal analysis. *Journal of Applied Developmental Psychology*, 29(6), 434–445. doi:10.1016/j.appdev.2008.07.002

The Telegraph. (2015). *Jean Jullien: the artist mistaken for Banksy who created the Peace for Paris symbol of solidarity*. Available at: https://www.telegraph.co.uk/art/what-to-see/jean-jullien-peace-for-paris-symbol/

Thobani, S. (2007). White Wars: Western feminisms and the 'war on terror'. *Feminist Theory*, 8(2), 169–185. doi:10.1177/1464700107078140

Wired. (2015). *Meet Jean Jullien, the artist behind the "Peace for Paris" symbol*. Available at: https://www.wired.com/2015/11/jean-jullien-peace-for-paris/

ENDNOTES

[1] Facebook's values include: to "make the world more open and connected" and Mark Zuckerberg, CEO, recently made a statement that Facebook will fund causes that share the corporation's mission of "connecting people and building strong communities" (The Economist, *The New Face of Facebook: How to win friends and influence* people, 9th April 2016)

[2] Thobani's central thesis is that the 'War on Terror' unleashed a cultural war pivoting around gender equality. She argues that gender equality has been Europeanised and that the non-white Other has been identified as inferior owing to the forms of gender inequality prevalent in non-white societies. While her critique of the role of white feminisms in reproducing this racial logic have deeply influenced my thinking on the matter, this chapter does not use a feminist lens to form a critique of whiteness.

[3] These countries include Turkey, Iran, Pakistan, China, Vietnam and North Korea.

This research was previously published in the Handbook of Research on Recent Developments in Internet Activism and Political Participation; pages 139-153, copyright year 2020 by Information Science Reference (an imprint of IGI Global).

Facebook Aesthetics

APPENDIX

Social Media

Figure 1.

Figure 2.

Figure 3.

598

Facebook Aesthetics

Figure 4.

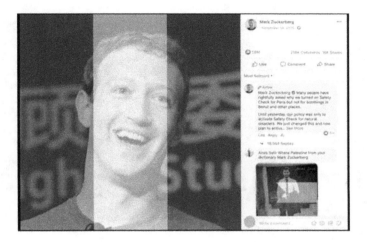

Figure 5.

Figure 6.

Section 4
Utilization and Applications

Chapter 32

Silenced, Shamed, and Scatted:
Black Feminist Perspective on Sexual Trauma and Treatment With African American Female Survivors

V. Nikki Jones
Middle Tennessee State University, USA

Donna M. Dopwell
Middle Tennessee State University, USA

Lauren C. Curry
Black Lesbian Literary Collective, USA

ABSTRACT

The African American experience is grounded in a strong religious tradition that does not adequately address sexual violence against women. This chapter offers perspective on how religiously-motivated heterocentric-patriarchy marginalizes Black female sexual trauma survivors. Recommendations are informed by Black feminisms in order to support culturally congruent practice. These interventions emphasize Black women's lived experience, raise awareness of multilevel oppression, and foster the empowerment of Black women. Basic treatment considerations for African American female trauma survivors and their support systems are provided.

INTRODUCTION

Sexual violence impacts approximately one in three women and one in six men; roughly 1.2 per 1,000 persons are raped or sexually assaulted (Centers for Disease Control and Prevention (CDC), 2016; Morgan & Kena, 2017). Scholarship on sexual violence against African American women remains scarce relative to the considerable research on sexual trauma experienced by European American women. However, there are noteworthy studies that have contributed to understanding Black women's experiences with

DOI: 10.4018/978-1-6684-4507-5.ch032

Copyright © 2022, IGI Global. Copying or distributing in print or electronic forms without written permission of IGI Global is prohibited.

sexual abuse (e.g., Basile, Smith, Fowler, Walters, & Hamburger, 2016; Bryant-Davis et al., 2015; Jones et al., 2015; Kruger, 2013; Perry-Burney, Thomas, & McDonald, 2014; Wadsworth & Records, 2013). According to Bryant-Davis et al. (2015), between 18% and 36% of African American women report sexual assault, but survivors may not disclose the abuse or seek services due to personal, societal, and cultural barriers.

Religion is a cultural factor impacting disclosure of abuse. African Americans traditionally rely on religion for meaning and support in facing trauma, and religious institutions are credited for providing effective coping spaces (Bryant-Davis et al., 2015). However, these institutions can also conceal Black pain and sexual trauma and function as a cultural barrier to reporting sex crimes. Additional religion-related barriers include the power of religion/religious leaders; use of religion to justify abuse; belief that religious leaders will not act in the best interest of participants; fear of harm from abuser, particularly when the perpetrator is a religious leader; and fear of backlash from the religious community following disclosure (Perry-Burney et al., 2014). Patriarchal ideology has significant implications in the suppression or censure of sexual violence because patriarchy is embedded in religious texts that sanction social patterns and subjugate women (Ruether, 1982). Patriarchy is a sociopolitical structure that justifies and promotes male domination of women's bodies. Patriarchy silences women, including those who have survived sexual traumas. Silencing sexual trauma also fuels victim-blaming ideology including myths about harassment and violence that favor the perpetrator and foster poor coping among survivors. Black female trauma survivors, in particular, are routinely shamed and disempowered from sharing their trauma narratives.

While this chapter does not intend to imply that sexual trauma is exclusive to women, African Americans, or religious contexts, this focus is African American female survivors within Abrahamic religions. According to the Pew Research Center (2018b), 79% of African Americans self-identify as Christian thus more attention is shown to this religion. Black women are often simultaneously alienated by religious institutions and erased from mainstream conversations about sexual violence such as #MeToo, which began as the grassroots 'me too.' movement. The 'me too.' movement was initiated by Tarana Burke, an African American woman, and later appropriated into mainstream discussion by American celebrities via social media.

This chapter considers how Black religious institutions minimize sexual violence to preserve Black heterocentric-patriarchy. The chapter also explores how systemic oppression facilitates the need for treatment strategies that support Black women's health and coping processes. In fact, Black feminisms offers a culturally congruent approach to working with Black female sexual trauma survivors. Lastly, this chapter describes how group context, professional cultural awareness, and treatment strategies align with Black feminisms. Note, the terms "African American women" and "Black women" represent women self-identified as Black, of African descent, and of American nationality.

THE HISTORICAL CONTEXT OF HETEROCENTRIC-PATRIARCHY

Patriarchy is a system in which males and masculine persons dominate women and persons perceived as feminine; however, female and feminine allies can also adopt patriarchal values and practices. For example, Townes (2003) argued that 'patriarchy' is a misnomer because White women were so intricately complicit in racial oppression. The intersection of patriarchy and heterosexism exert control over

Silenced, Shamed, and Scatted

labor politics, sex-gender binaries, sex-gender identities, sexual behavior, and relationships (Mies, 2014; Valdes, 1996). Patriarchy is associated with capitalism, colonization, exploitation, and violence against women (Mies, 2014).

White heterocentric-patriarchy is a prevailing system of oppression in the United States. For African Americans, the historical significance of White diasporic heterocentric-patriarchy is evident in institutionalized rape and lynching. When this system predominately lynched Black men and predominately raped Black women, these acts were different expressions of the same racialized social control that centered on labor and profit (Collins, 2004). In order to justify these violent acts, European Americans created and reinforced social constructs of African Americans as aggressive, deficient, lazy, immoral, unhealthy and contagious, sexually promiscuous, and untamed.

Lynching was one of the most brutal ways White heterocentric-patriarchy practiced racialized social control. Most often, the lynching of Black men was a vigilante response to the alleged rape and disrespect of White women. Ida B. Wells-Barnett, an antilynching activist and journalist, hypothesized that a vast majority of sexual relationships between Black men and White women were indeed consensual, if existing at all, and lynching was solely about social control (Giddings, 2008). Lynching served several important tasks such as policing man-woman relationships, controlling economic and political systems during urbanization and industrialization, and intimidating and dissuading Black men from voting (Pfeifer, 1999).

Like lynching, rape was also about labor, profits, and restricting African American self-determination. Research and personal narratives have revealed a high prevalence of rape and sexual violence against African American women by White men (Collins, 2004; King, 2014; Sommerville, 2004). Black women's history is littered with stories of rape, survival, and resilience. For example, in the State of Missouri v. Celia (1855), Celia, an enslaved Black woman, protected and defended herself while being raped by Robert Newsom. After standing her ground, Celia was convicted of first-degree murder by a jury of all White men. Another well-known case involved Recy Taylor, a 24-year-old African American woman. On September 3, 1944 in Abbeville, Alabama, six White men abducted Taylor as she walked home from church and then raped her at gunpoint. None of the men were convicted, and following the trial, Taylor and her family were harassed. The stories of Celia and Recy Taylor are two of many examples of White men's dominance and disregard for Black women's inherent right to protect and control their own bodies. While White men and women primarily lynched Black men for the alleged rapes of White women, White men were free to rape, harass, and exploit Black women with impunity.

Setting the Agenda: African American Women's Overlooked History of Sexual Assault

African Americans have historically placed lynching at the top of the collective social justice agenda. Lynching was prioritized because it garnered public spectacle and resulted in death. Lynchings were graphically violent and cruel events where mobs of predominately White men would hunt, terrorize, torture, and then hang alleged perpetrators. In *Without Sanctuary: Lynching Photography*, James Allen provided photographic records of over 3,000 lynchings of Black men, women, and children from 1882 to 1950. Allen's documentary captures entire White families and communities attending the festive lynching events. There are many lynching narratives; however, the story of Laura Nelson and her teenage son, L. D. Nelson— (sometimes recorded as L. W.)— is especially revealing (Allen, 2000; National Association for the Advancement of Colored People (NAACP), 1911).

Police arrived at the Nelson's cabin in Okemah, Oklahoma to investigate a reported theft of meat. During the visit, L. D. allegedly shot and killed a sheriff. Laura feared for her son's life and disputed that L. D. had murdered the officer. Instead, Laura confessed to the crime. A mob of White men rode into the town and kidnapped Laura and L. D. from their jail cells before they could face a jury. On May 26, 1911, mother and son were hauled approximately six miles outside of town, gagged and hung from a steel bridge across the Canadian River. Laura Nelson's murder was preceded by rape and she became the first woman lynched in Oklahoma (NAACP, 1911). Not one person was ever convicted of Laura's rape or the lynchings. There are postcards and pictures documenting the Nelson lynchings with White adult, child, and infant attendees (Allen, 2000).

Spectators memorialized lynching events with both photographs and collected souvenirs, such as the alleged perpetrator(s) dismembered corpse. Attendees frequently castrated Black men, which was motivated by stereotypes about them as "overly libidinous and aggressive, prone to a racially specific sexual perversion that drove them to rape white women" (Stein, 2015, p. 218). This belief was particularly heinous given that White men raped Black women without such a social construct leveled against them. Because lynching was purportedly about protecting White women, castration symbolized Black male disempowerment and/or White male empowerment. For instance, although L. D. Nelson was not charged with a sex crime, photograph No. 2894 shows that L. D.'s pants had been removed and his genital area was visible (Allen, 2000).

The practice of lynching was social and economic. European Americans conveniently utilized lynching during an opportune historical moment for African Americans. Lynching became more prevalent during Reconstruction and continued beyond the civil rights era when African Americans were seeking upward social and economic mobility (Collins, 2004). The murder of an able-bodied Black male or female laborer could change a family's social, emotional, and financial trajectory. Losing a Black man who could vote, and emotionally and financially support his family was deleterious to his loved ones and community.

While lynching was clearly an issue in need of collective attention and action, a narrow focus on the lynching of Black men overshadowed the sexual violence directed at Black women. Although lynching and rape were equally pervasive, sexual violence— and other forms of gender-specific violence— against Black women rarely received collective examination. Overall, Black women's history with lynching and rape is a nearly invisible and suppressed aspect of African Americans' collective activism. The rationale for suppressing the experiences of Black women must be explored.

Sexual violence has historically received little attention for several reasons. Unlike lynching, rape may be viewed as a gender-specific private shame. Rape could be handled internally by the family or ignored altogether as an individual problem. It is also conceivable that family discord contributed to passive responses to rape. Like lynching, rape could create serious family adjustment issues; however, the rape victim often physically survived the crime and was therefore considered in a better state relative to the lynching victim. While many sexual assault survivors do not experience death, they frequently relive the triggering event. Sexual violence can interfere with mental health and emotional regulation, difficulties with sexual intimacy and pleasure, and self-care (Basile et al., 2016; van Berlo & Ensink, 2000). Such interference can contribute to long-term dysfunction within family life, but also within communities as a whole given the pervasiveness of sexual violence against Black women.

This historical issue of rape also raises the question of whether Black women could be protected. From a heterocentric-patriarchal perspective, men are responsible for protecting women. But, stories about mobs of Black men raiding White towns in pursuit of alleged White male rapists are few and far between, if any exist. As a whole, Black men were systematically disempowered to protect Black women

Silenced, Shamed, and Scatted

from interracial rape. With that said, Black men also raped Black women. Given the historical stigma attached to Black men and rape, many African Americans viewed disclosing rape perpetrated by Black men against Black women as racial disloyalty. This predicament left Black women with little recourse; they could not report rape and receive justice whether a White or Black man committed the crime.

History and African American Studies professor Evelyn Brooks Higginbotham coined the concept *politics of respectability* to denote religious Black women's insistence on cleanliness, politeness, frugality, sexual virtue, and abstention from alcohol (Harris, 2003). In the years following emancipation, politics of respectability were adopted and encouraged to counter stereotypes against African Americans. Wealthy and socially climbing African Americans modeled respectability as a way to emulate European Americans and separate themselves from poor and working-class African Americans. The lack of respectability may also be hypothesized as justification for deemphasizing the rape of Black women. Alternatively, some may have subscribed to the notion that only loose or unrespectable women were raped. The act of rape reflected dirtiness, impropriety, promiscuity, aggression, and many other sexually stereotypical concepts imposed on African Americans. According to Harris (2003), African American women were most likely to utilize and be judged through the respectability lens in both public and private spaces. Therefore, respectability constitutes a significant reason to suppress rape. And while African Americans acknowledged the rape of Black women by White men during slavery and afterword, the rape of Black women by Black men was rarely discussed (Collins, 2000).

On some level, it could also be argued that rape of Black women was normalized among African Americans and Europeans Americans alike. The system was never designed to protect Black women from rape. For one, Black sexuality was viewed as sexually aggressive and promiscuous, which promoted doubts about whether Black women could even be raped. From enslavement through the civil rights era, African American women were largely employed in industries where sexual harassment and aggressive behavior went unrestricted. Black agriculture, domestic, and service workers experienced harassment, molestation, and rape by their employers; and there were generations of Black women—and their fore-mothers— who could recall childhood stories of rape (Collins, 2004). Rape liaisons were responsible for the births of generations of African Americans and deprived Black women from claiming their own sexual identity (Collins, 2000). When considering the children born of such trauma, an ideological stance of 'don't ask, don't tell' also contributed to collective silence surrounding rape.

Intraracial power structure was another reason sexual violence committed against Black women persisted without appropriate social action. One component of African American progress was a consensus view to elevate Black men and masculinity to protect Black women and children. Perhaps, in retrospect, this reasoning may be understandable, but history and existing statistics on rape have revealed that men and masculinity do not create protective factors for Black women. For example, most sex crimes occur in intraracial contexts. Black women are more likely to be raped in their lifetime (21.2%), in comparison to women of other races aged 18 and older (19.3%), by paramours (45.4%) or acquaintances (46.7%) (DuMonthier, Childers, & Milli, 2017). Yet, passionate advocacy against sexual violence remains hardly visible in many Black social justice spaces.

Instead of shifting the Black agenda to collective empowerment, the community approach has expunged issues largely impacted by African American women, girls, and lesbian, gay, bisexual, and transgender (LGBT) individuals. As noted by Collins (2004), some of these groups are deemed to be an embarrassment to the community or flaw upon its progress. From the respectability perspective, rape cannot be spoken of because Black male associates now most often rape Black women. The LGBT experience also cannot be spoken about because gay and transgender people are viewed as unclean and perverted, and most importantly, have the potential to displace heterocentric-patriarchy altogether. This suppression approach is problematic because it does not afford African American women the appropriate concern for their health and wellbeing. Black women aged 18 years and older have reported increased symptoms of depression and stress-related deaths compared to non-Hispanic White women (CDC, 2010; CDC, 2013). Sexual violence can contribute to depression, posttraumatic stress symptoms, and a sequela of maladaptive responses, including increased risky sexual behavior, substance abuse, suicidal ideation, and other self-harming behaviors (Alim et al., 2006; Basile et al., 2016; DuMonthier et al., 2017; Iverson et al., 2013; Jones et al., 2015). Silencing Black survivors can exacerbate the manifestation and severity of these issues.

Intersecting oppression from White men, White women, and to a lesser degree, Black men is complicit in Black women's invisibility (Townes, 2003). Even today in the midst of #MeToo, narratives about and advocacy against rape appear most socially acceptable when received from White women. Tarana Burke, an African American woman activist, originated the 'me too.' movement in 2006 to target Black women sexual assault survivors, as well as other young women of color from lower income communities, through community-led activism (Hill, 2017; Me Too, 2018). Burke explained that the 'me too.' movement was not created for "a viral campaign or hashtag," rather it is a "catchphrase to be used from survivor to survivor to let folks know that they were not alone and that a movement for radical healing was happening and possible" (Hill, 2017, para. 5). Unfortunately, the appropriated #MeToo focuses more on celebrity perpetrators rather than survivors. Black women are largely missing from #MeToo discourse. African American advocacy against sexual violence remains the province of Black women.

Contours of Heterocentric-Patriarchy in Black Religious Institutions

Few studies have explored the impact of Black heterocentric-patriarchy on sexual trauma and harassment within a religious context. If the system of Black heterocentric-patriarchy is the vehicle for which African American sexual survivors are marginalized, then the religious institution is the driver. Abrahamic religion, mainly Christianity, is dominate in African American communities and impacts culture, politics, education, and economics (Weisenfeld, 2015; Pew Research Center, 2018b). Abrahamic religions, such as Christianity, Judaism, and Islam, obtain mobility directly from heterocentric-patriarchy.

The multiform oppression experienced by African Americans makes it difficult, if not impossible, to acknowledge the occurrence of Black heterocentric-patriarchy. Yet, Black feminist discourse has demonstrated that not only does Black heterocentric-patriarchy exist, it is associated with homophobia, sexism, and misogyny (Collins, 2000; Collins, 2004; Neal, 2011). White heterocentric-patriarchy was a harbinger of Black patriarchy and affirms that "Black men [can] be just like White men" within their communities (Collins, 2004, p. 73). Given the omnipresence of White patriarchy, Black male dominance is reasonably difficult to perceive and critique. Black feminist scholarship has shown that Black heterocentric-patriarchy mainly distresses Black women, girls, and the LGBT community (Collins, 2004; Neal, 2011; Smith, 2008; Townes, 2003). Black heterocentric-patriarchy functions similarly to other systems of male domination by denying women equal access to social, political, and economic capital (e.g., religious institutions and organizations); as well as focusing on the ascendancy of males and supporting a worldview that men/masculinity are inherently superior to women/femininity (Jennings, 2017; Jones & Guy-Sheftall, 2015; Neal, 2011; Turner & Maschi, 2015). A key factor of Black heterocentric-patriarchy is prioritizing race over sex and gender. Positioning racial inequality over all other forms of oppression is often favorable to the gender-specific needs of only African American men.

Silenced, Shamed, and Scatted

The women's agenda has focused on White women, like the African American agenda has often equated Black men (Hull, Scott, & Smith, 1982). As opposed to sex-only or race-only considerations, Black feminisms advance intersectionality theory. Intersectionality denotes how race, sex, and other social identities cannot be understood in isolation of one other because oppression is an intersecting system (Essed, 1991; Collins, 2000; Crenshaw, 1989). Intersectionality shifts discourse away from race-invisible or gender-neutral agendas that silence Black women. Much of Black women's experience with rape, sexual violence, and other forms of trauma are informed by race, age, occupation, geographic location, sexual orientation, and gender identity and expression. Black heterocentric-patriarchy has served as a major challenge to organizing collective social action against sexual violence within African American communities. This system, which is advanced by religion-based institutions, controls Black sexual politics, including awareness of and advocacy against sexual violence.

Religion and faith are cornerstones in African American communities. In comparison to the general U.S. population, African Americans are significantly more religious (Pew Research Center, 2018a, Pew Research Center, 2018b). African American women have the highest level of religious commitment and observance (Pew Research Center, 2018a). Although these numbers indicate that African American women are a disproportionate majority of religious participants, with respect to power and control, Black women have historically represented a minority in religion-affiliated leadership roles. African American women often encounter gender discrimination as female clergy; face barriers in assuming leadership roles; and obtain limited preparatory training, mentors in ministry, acceptance, or access to needed resources (Yeary, 2011). The African Methodist Episcopal (AME) Church and Church Of God In Christ, Inc. (COGIC) are two examples of predominately African American denominations that demonstrate gender inequity. It was only after 213 years that the AME church elected Vashti McKenzie as the first female bishop in 2000, followed by the election of Anne E. Henning-Byfield in 2016. Men continue to represent a vast majority of bishops in the AME church. In the COGIC denomination, the presiding bishop, general board, and board of bishops remains male-dominated (Church Of God In Christ, Inc., 2018). While the majority constitutes female congregants, women remain a large minority in the upper echelons of leadership. Efforts to confront Black heterocentric-patriarchy are complicated by a few issues.

The first issue is that Black heterocentric-patriarchy is a typical oppressive system where the majority population lacks awareness. Black heterocentric-patriarchy is minimized within most African American communities. And, to quote Pauline Terrelonge, "many black women [fail] to recognize the patterns of sexism that directly impinge on their everyday lives" (Collins, 2000, p. 86). The lack of consciousness about unequal power distributions creates vulnerability for Black women. In turn, Black female experiences, issues, and trauma become diminished, silenced, and unreal.

A second issue is the need for Black solidarity to counter White supremacy, similar to the need for female solidarity to oppose heterocentric-patriarchy. Black women, men, and children have a shared interest in confronting racial terrorism and White hegemony. America's ubiquitous racial caste system has facilitated collective struggle among Black women and men of all ages. Historically, White feminisms are criticized for misandry and have often not acknowledged the inextricable connection between racism and sexism experienced by Black women (Smith, 2008). However, Black feminisms, including womanism, have addressed this limitation and continues to critique White feminisms for racism and class erasure. Unfortunately, detractors in Black communities have inhibited the adoption of Black feminisms, although Black feminist values are widespread among African Americans (Simien, 2004).

Still, a common value that remains characteristic of African Americans is collective identification. Throughout American history, individuals and systems that have attempted to separate and isolate African Americans have been met with staunch opposition. Unfortunately, advocacy against sexual violence can create division and therefore has not garnered mass support because rape is most common within intraracial contexts. As Charlotte Pierce-Baker (1998) wrote:

I felt responsible for upholding the image of the strong black man for our young son, and for the white world with whom I had contact...I didn't want to confirm the white belief that all Black men rape. Better not to talk about it. And so, I'd kept silent about what had happened to me. (p. 64)

African Americans instinctively protect Black men from racialized stereotypes because acknowledging intraracial sexual violence can sound and feel like abandoning Black men in support of White notions of Black sexual depravity. Additionally, socialization and limited sex education compounds these issues. Similar to other communities, African Americans receive inappropriate sexuality socialization and information on sexual abuse (Tillman, Bryant-Davis, Smith, & Marks, 2010). When content is received, it is often dictated by religious institutions that adhere to patriarchal ideology. Even existing sex education in primary and secondary schools is influenced by religious ideology. All of this contributes to limited awareness and stifled conversations about sexual and domestic violence. The dangers of blind loyalty and poor sex education support maintenance of heterocentric-patriarchy, which very often penalizes African American female survivors. Moreover, women who disclose rape and name their rapists may risk alienation and become shamed into silence by family, friends, and the community— all while the alleged perpetrators receive little, if any, public or community penalties (Collins, 2004). Additional barriers to disclosure include false beliefs about rape; myths justifying male sexual aggression; self-blame; revictimization within legal, medical, and social services; and distrust of legal, medical, and social services (Tillman et al., 2010).

A final issue is power. Power inequity creates major status differences. Within religious institutions, men occupy power to transmit orders downward to women, with little expectation of accountability upward (Perry-Burney et al., 2014). These power inequities offer a bevy of privileges; for example, "Black male ministers whose congregations are usually 70 percent Black female can...enjoy the Sunday dinners, presents, and other benefits that can accrue to men in such situations..." (Collins, 2004, p. 9). Religious institutions legitimize and protect male power structures when rape and sexual violence are silenced.

Because the church plays such a vital role in African American communities, it is often difficult for Black people to address the limitations of the institution. The unequal distribution of leadership and power in African American religious institutions can create several disadvantages for Black women. These women are afforded little control over their personal, familial, and community narrative. For example, rather than seeing rape, sexual violence, and sexual harassment as culprits of male domination, Black heterocentric-patriarchy interprets rape, sexual violence, and sexual harassment as consequences of female temptation (Vaz, 2005). A fundamental role of heterocentric-patriarchy is to control all decisions and narratives. So, it should come as little surprise that religious institutions have largely minimized or ignored rape, abandoned sexual abuse survivors, or refused to participate in the 'me too.' movement (Collins, 2004). With the exception of a few Black female ministers and churches, Black religious communities remain overwhelmingly inactive on sexual violence and harassment.

Silenced, Shamed, and Scatted

BLACK FEMINISMS AND THERAPEUTIC SUPPORT

Black feminisms have provided knowledge, analysis, and critique on patriarchy, misogyny, and homophobia, but have been limited in reshaping sexual and gender relationships among African Americans (Neal, 2011). This chapter aims to show the versatility of Black feminisms for therapeutic treatment, which may begin to address Black women's experience with gender politics, rape, and sexual violence. Black feminisms are strengths-based social, literary, and intellectual thought emergent from and about African American women. According to Collins (2000), Black feminist thought— which is African American women's critical theory— involves bodies of knowledge and sets of institutional practices that actively address the central issues that African American women face. Black feminisms are specific to African American women, thus further enable culturally appropriate evaluation of past, present, and future circumstances that are typically not addressed with traditional approaches.

Using Black feminisms as a guiding treatment framework places focus on African American women's lived experience; fosters Black women's empowerment (the power to think, feel, and do for self); and aims to increase cultural literacy and healthy coping among trauma survivors and their support systems (Jones, 2015). Black feminisms are different from traditional helping approaches because the central task is to address overlapping oppression, understand Black women's history, and emphasize African American women's self-definitions, strengths, and resilience (Collins, 2000; Jones, 2015). Black feminisms are noteworthy for insisting that the changed consciousness of individuals and the social transformation of political and economic institutions constitute the essential ingredients of social change (Collins, 2000). Black feminisms further recognize the sociocultural realities that most Black women encounter, such as interrelated race, gender, and class oppression (Crenshaw, 1989), where race and gender oppression are distinct from the experiences of White women and Black men.

Effective Black feminisms indicate that social change is necessitated by the collective efforts of both women and men. Black feminisms that undermine the contributions of men erroneously advance an agenda of prioritizing gender over race. Instead, Black feminisms' intersectional framework acknowledges that single-issue oppression does not exist; racism and other '-isms' symbiotically produce injustices (Collins, 2000). Black feminisms' principles are applicable to a wide variety of environments and settings, including religious institutions. Since the 1980s, Black female theologists have utilized womanism, which is a feminism, to empower African American Christian women and engage in constructive analysis of White feminisms, racism, Black theology, and patriarchy (Smith, 2008; Townes, 2003). An advantage of Black feminisms within Black religious institutions is that African Americans can find common ground along shared histories and social justice. Black feminisms increase individual and collective consciousness about power and privilege. And when it comes to trauma survivors, Black feminisms can improve receptivity and empathy within religion-based settings.

Group Work

Group work is recommended as an effective method to utilize Black feminisms to treat Black female sexual trauma survivors. bell hooks (1993) described group work as offering a "space where Black women could name their pain and find ways of healing…" (p. 19). Group and collectivist models are significant variables within African American racial identity. African Americans have traditionally shown a strong sense of connection to their racial group and assumed responsibility for the well-being of group members (Carson, 2009). Group work is beneficial to African American women because it offers a safe place to share stories, collectively recover, and create bonds (Jones, 2015). Group context offers spaces that are empowering and less stigmatizing, and foster social support, information gathering, role modeling, and belongingness (Jones & Warner, 2011). Group context is essential to facilitating interventions consistent with Black feminisms. These interventions include professional cultural awareness, psychoeducation, and treatment strategies, such as active listening, externalizing the problem, self-affirmation, deconstruction/co-construction, bibliotherapy, after-session tasks, and social activism.

Professional Cultural Awareness

Working with African American trauma survivors requires professional cultural awareness, critical consciousness, and sociocultural literacy on the part of helping professionals. Professional cultural awareness comprises using a *both/and orientation*, integrating faith, and seeking to racially match helper and client. Helpers who seek to work with this population should fundamentally value Black women, acknowledge intersecting oppression and privilege, and accept a *both/and orientation* when viewing issues (Collins, 2000). This orientation recognizes that Black people are collectively disempowered by White supremacy; appreciates Black women's support of Black male empowerment; promotes Black women's self-empowerment; and advocates against heterocentric-patriarchy. Helpers who employ a *both/and orientation* also do not prioritize gender over race or race over sexual orientation. By using the *both/and orientation*, helpers learn to appreciate the interconnections present in African American women's experience.

Helpers should also integrate faith or meaningful practices in the treatment process because African American experiences are deeply shaped by spirituality, religion, and religious institutions. For example, a helper might explore womanist theology. Womanist theology has both religious and sociopolitical salience to Black women's recovery. Womanist theologists oppose oppressive messages and imagery within religious texts (e.g., Delores Williams' *Womanist Theology: Black Women's Voices*), examine spirituality and activism in relation to Black women's recovery (e.g., Emilie Townes' *Womanist Justice, Womanist Hope*), and offer an ethical model for womanism (e.g., Katie Cannon's *Katie's Canon: Womanism and the Soul of the Black Community*) (Townes, 2003).

Racially/ethnically matching the helper to group participants may further augment professional cultural awareness and client engagement and decrease client dropout (Jones & Warner, 2011). Meyer and Zane (2013) found that clients of color rated race and ethnicity as important culture-specific factors in their mental health care. When culture-specific factors were not included in care, clients of color reported less satisfaction with treatment. Cultural-specific factors included racial match, helpers' knowledge of prejudice and discrimination, and openness to discuss race.

Psychoeducation

Psychoeducation is a common therapeutic model that introduces and educates on social and clinical issues, and supports goal-setting, interpersonal skills, problem solving, and skilled communication (Authier, 1977; Bäuml, Froböse, Kraemer, Rentrop, & Pitschel-Walz, 2006; Brandis, 1998). Lubin, Loris, Burt, and Johnson (1998) found that psychoeducational group therapy positively contributed to treatment effects among a diverse sample of multiply traumatized women. Their psychoeducational model included 15 minutes of helper-directed lecture, one hour of discussion, and 15 minutes of wrap-up (Lubin et al.., 1998). Psychoeducation is a familiar framework for helpers to utilize when working with trauma survivors.

Silenced, Shamed, and Scatted

Psychoeducation is complementary to Black feminisms; for example, conscious-raising activities encourage participants to learn about their own experiences and receive societal and cultural knowledge. Conscious-raising is key to feminist therapies because as Maria Stewart, the first African American woman political writer, declared *for knowledge is power* (Collins, 2000; Richardson, 1987). Although psychoeducation is traditionally didactic and assigns primary authority to the professional helper, this intervention can be modified. When psychoeducation and Black feminisms merge, helpers increase collaboration, recognize patriarchy and racist conceptions of Black women as 'other than the norm,' and avoid suppression of Black women's voice, unlike traditional mental health treatment (Jones, 2016; Jones & Warner, 2011). Modified psychoeducation replaces didactic teaching with experiential learning and encourages active helper-member engagement, independent conscious-raising (Collins, 2000), upward information flow, and reflection.

In Black feminisms, psychoeducation facilitates understanding how historical events shape the current experiences of African American women, analyzes race-gender roles and identity, and discerns healthy and unhealthy coping. For example, a helper and group participants acknowledge and discuss how gendered racism and heterosexism influence oppression. Psychoeducation provides an opportunity for Black women to forge self-definitions and define terms such as trauma, abuse, patriarchy, assimilation, privilege, power, empowerment, resiliency, and gendered racism, which includes intersecting racism, sexism, and other implicit and explicit oppressions (Essed, 1991).

Race-gender role and identity analysis emphasize exploration of Black women's identity development (Jones, 2015; Jones & Warner, 2011). Race-gender role and identity analysis involve race-gender identity and expression; socialization within a patriarchal society; race-gender stereotypes; sex role differences; and misogynoir (Bailey & Trudy, 2018; Brown, 1986; Jones, 2015). For example, participants explore how stereotypical portrayals of African American women undermine support and validation related to sexual violence.

Self-care and coping skills are necessary for all persons, particularly trauma survivors. When psychoeducation focuses on self-care, helpers promote active coping and address unhealthy coping and strain within race and gender-based roles. Recent research on African American women, self-care, and health has demonstrated the adverse impact of the strong Black woman, where Black women are seen as superwomen or Black women adopt the superwoman schema (Jones, 2015; Watson & Hunter, 2016; Woods-Giscombe, 2010). Black women have largely been socialized to stoically self-sacrifice and attend to others before undertaking self-care. Self-sacrifice has become a Black female social norm that benefits heterocentric-patriarchy (Collins, 2000; Lewis, 1989). Therefore, an additional element of psychoeducation explores African American women's self-care tradition, as well as evaluates healthy and unhealthy individual, familial, and collective coping (Jones, 2015; Jones & Warner, 2011).

It is recommended that psychoeducation is recurrent throughout the treatment process. For instance, abuse, patriarchy, and privilege may be revisited during processing of the trauma narrative. Psychoeducation may help reduce stigma about trauma and mental health issues (Pollio, North, & Foster, 1992) and validate Black women's experiences with oppression. Group participants may feel less alone in discussing how their religious setting deals with sexual abuse. Further, psychoeducation has increased client retention rates among adults with mental health disorder and contributed to treatment effectiveness when used as adjunctive treatment (Fristad, Gavazzi, & Mackinaw-Koons, 2003).

Treatment Strategies

Black feminisms do not currently provide a set of treatment strategies (Jones, 2015). However, there are recommended strategies essential to processing trauma or other presenting issues. The following strategies align with Black feminisms.

Active Listening

Active listening, or empathetic listening, is a basic and important communication skill found to increase experiences of feeling understood, satisfaction with conversation, and unconditional acceptance (Weger, Bell, Minei, & Robinson, 2014). Helpers who utilize active listening are attentive, empathetic, and responsive to content (i.e., a participant's message) and process (i.e., non-verbal communication implicit in the message). For African American women who rarely feel heard and understood, active listening accentuates 'I hear you, sis.' As described by Weger et al. (2014), active listening (1) is moderate to high nonverbal attention, (2) reflects the essence of the participant's message using verbal paraphrasing, and (3) poses questions that verify the participant's message was accurately reflected or prompts the participant to elaborate.

Externalizing the Problem

Externalization is a useful narrative therapy strategy that disputes the traditional mental health view of the individual as inherently defective. Because language is suspected of contributing to problem maintenance, externalization detaches the individual from clinical or sociocultural issues (Etchison & Kleist. 2000). This technique is important for trauma survivors because it restrains self-blame. Rather than internalize problems, participants use their personal resources to objectify and personify the oppressive and traumatic experiences. For example, participants are taught to shift perspective from oppressive self-descriptions (I am a sad person) to objective statements (Sadness has told me [fill in the blank] about myself) (Carey & Russell, 2002; Ricks, Kitchens, Goodrich, & Hancock, 2014).

Self-Affirmations

Self-affirmation theory proposes that a primary source of human motivation is attaining and maintaining self-integrity and a sense of worth in situations that threaten integrity (Martens, Johns, Greenberg, & Schimel, 2006). African American women routinely encounter microaggressions, which are everyday interpersonal slights, ranging from insults about their hair and pathologizing commentary on their communication style to assumptions of criminality (Sue et al., 2007; Sue et al, 2008). Self-affirmations offer a constructive way for African American women to counter a daily barrage of microaggressions and negative stereotypes. Self-affirmations such as 'I am beautiful,' "I am worthy," or 'My voice matters' may challenge the internalization of controlling images and messages. Martens et al. (2006) found that self-affirmations can reduce situational threats (e.g., microaggressions) among participants of stigmatized groups. Self-affirmations can also further self-definitions and encourage self-valuation, which are both integral to Black feminisms (Collins, 2000).

Deconstruction/Co-Construction

The multiple interacting systems of oppression faced by African American women warrant participants to question the sociocultural expectations and power dynamics that underlie presenting problems. When helpers use narrative therapy treatment strategies, participants can deconstruct unhelpful stories in order to reconstruct more productive narratives (Nichols, 2009). Deconstruction is breaking down an issue into specific and manageable parts that expose the cultural assumptions or social constructions within the problem. Using externalization, a participant can detach from their problem-saturated story and begin to see life with a new perspective that includes identification of significant events, which were neglected when the participant only focused on problems (Chow, 2015). Reconstruction is generating "new and more optimistic accounts of experience" (Nichols, 2009, p. 290). It is important that past traumas are addressed and validated, but it is equally important that participants are supported in creating life and perspective outside of the trauma. The helper and group participants can engage and collaborate to re-story problem-saturated narratives by analyzing personal beliefs, strengths, events, experiences, and identities connected to a new and helpful alternative story for the future (Chow, 2015; Jones, 2015).

Bibliotherapy

According to Cohen (1993), bibliotherapy is the therapeutic use of literature, with the professional helper as the reader's guide. Black feminist and womanist non-fiction, short stories, poems, and novels are resources that can provide African American women with historical, religious, or literary figures of courage, health, and transcendence (Townes, 2003). A number of Black women writers recount stories and essays about the unique experiences of African American women, including Alice Walker (*The Color Purple*), Zora Neale Hurston (*Their Eyes Were Watching God*), Renita J. Weems (*Just a Sister Away: A Womanist Vision of Women's Relationships in the Bible*), Delores S. Williams (*Sisters in the Wilderness: The Challenge of Womanist God-Talk*), and Maya Angelou (*The Complete Poetry*). Bibliotherapy is an extension of psychoeducation.

After-Session Tasks

Assigning after-session tasks can help participants practice and strengthen skills learned in group sessions. After-session efforts outside of the group and within the natural environment can also reveal each participant's degree of motivation and personal growth. Scheel, Hanson, and Razzhavaikina (2004) have reported that out-of-session actions and compliance are related to positive therapeutic outcomes, and the authors recommend that homework tasks or rituals be developed from participant-helper collaboration. These after-session tasks should offer clear instructions, have cultural relevance, and be queried about at the following session.

Social Activism

African American women are often propelled toward increased self-determination and political activism after recognizing the pervasive impact of heterocentric-patriarchy, resisting the internalization of oppression, and coping with trauma (Collins, 2000). Black feminisms recognize the importance of sociopolitical activism. Collins (2000) conceptualized that Black women's activism has traditionally occurred across two basic levels. The first level involves actions to create Black female influence in existing social systems, or actions to build Black female influence that resists and undermines existing systems. The second level includes individual or collective action to change institutional policies and practices that oppress Black women. Black women's social activism includes participation in social movements, literature, social media and Web 2.0, and creative therapies. The overlapping systems of racism, sexism, heterosexism, and classism provide many opportunities for trauma survivors to engage in advocacy that is meaningful to personal recovery.

SOLUTIONS AND RECOMMENDATIONS

The 'me too.' movement has become large, far-reaching, and positive for many. However, Black women are largely missing in mainstream exchanges. Therefore, a Black feminist critique of the movement engenders the following: first, all women, not just White women, have stories of rape and sexual assault to share. Second, #MeToo has marginalized the voices of Black women by ignoring intersectionality. Third, Black heterocentric-patriarchy, specifically within a religious context, contributes to muting sexual trauma among Black women. All of this results in Black women once again left searching for safe spaces because White women have appropriated the one envisioned by Tarana Burke, and African American communities' have not directly addressed intraracial power structures.

It is necessary for Black feminists to consider the needs of the whole, but this should no longer come at the expense of Black women's needs, welfare, and empowerment. Black feminists must advocate for Black women to have active roles in their neighborhoods and religious communities, and for them to be recognized as equal participants of society. Equality should no longer be considered a matter of allowing women to enter male spaces, rather it should entail the development of new spaces co-created by women. Aside from advocacy for greater equitability with regard to racial leadership roles, progressive religious institutions and organizations must also dispute patriarchal religious ideology regarding women (Yancey & Kim, 2008). In all, Black feminisms must continue to decry heterocentric-patriarchy while concurrently offering solutions that are effective for African American communities.

FUTURE RECOMMENDATION DIRECTIONS

Black feminisms espouse the premise that Black women and men are equal and should be treated as such. Solidarity does not take an *either/or* approach, whereby the needs of African American men are placed above women, children, and others. Black feminisms adhere to a *both/and orientation*, whereby multiform oppression and privilege are examined, and all participants of the community are included in discourse. However, given the solidity of heterocentric-patriarchy, future research should consider whether the *both/and* framework actually protects Black women from systemic sexism. A necessary question is: are African American women being too objective relative to their gender-specific needs?

Black feminisms encompass African American women's theories about empowerment. These social theories were transposed into clinical treatment strategies to support African American female trauma survivors. Black feminisms-informed interventions provide a culturally aware framework for addressing sexual trauma; however, there is limited research on the integration of Black feminisms and sexual trauma within religious contexts. Future research should explore this relationship and consider the ways

Silenced, Shamed, and Scatted

that women are coping with trauma in a heterocentric-patriarchal society. Additionally, studies should examine the religious and spiritual practices that empower Black women and make recommendations to change disempowering practices. Researchers should examine treatment strategies that best address the needs of African American women while avoiding re-traumatization, encouraging empowerment, and strengthening community awareness and engagement.

CONCLUSION

Over 150 ago, Sojourner Truth delivered a powerful speech in which she asked, "And ain't I a woman?" (Collins, 2000, p. 258). Truth's question remains relevant as evidenced by the direction of #MeToo in recent years. Black women have been repeatedly silenced, with their lived experience diminished and healing processes disrupted. African American communities cannot ignore that women and men face oppression in similar and gender-specific ways. But, as crucial as it is for Black women to support Black men, reciprocity is necessary. African Americans must acknowledge and eliminate the practice of Black heterocentric-patriarchy so that Black women may have their voices heard. This chapter has offered a view into the history of heterocentric-patriarchy in the United States. The perpetuation of heterocentric-patriarchy among Black men was reviewed in the context of its effect on Black women. Along with this, the confluence of heterocentric-patriarchy and Black religious institutions was also highlighted. In these institutions, Black women face barriers in attaining leadership positions, endure mistreatment when they enter leadership roles, and are discouraged from participating in activities that would improve their visibility and status.

In this chapter, recommendations were based on Black feminisms as a culturally congruent therapeutic model. The Black feminisms model includes utilizing group work, psychoeducation, and treatment strategies. Professional cultural awareness is further recommended to ensure that treatment meets the unique needs of Black women in a heterocentric-patriarchal society. Overall, Black feminisms can increase empowerment and self-care, while granting Black women safe space to speak their respective truths and access necessary supports.

REFERENCES

Alim, T. N., Graves, E., Mellman, T. A., Aigbogun, N., Gray, E., Lawson, W., & Charney, D. S. (2006). Trauma exposure, posttraumatic stress disorder and depression in an African American primary care population. *Journal of the National Medical Association, 98*(10), 1630–1636. PubMed

Allen, J. (2000). *Without sanctuary: Lynching photography in America*. Santa Fe, NM: Twin Palms Publishers.

Authier, J. (1977). The psychoeducation model: Definition, contemporary roots and content. *Canadian Counsellor, 12*(1), 15–22.

Bailey, M. (2018). On misogynoir: Citation, erasure, and plagiarism. *Feminist Media Studies, 18*(4), 762–768. doi:10.1080/14680777.2018.1447395

Basile, K. C., Smith, S. G., Fowler, D. N., Walters, M. L., & Hamburger, M. E. (2016). Sexual violence victimization and associations with health in a community sample of African American Women. *Journal of Aggression, Maltreatment & Trauma*, *25*(3), 231–253. doi:10.1080/10926771.2015.1079283 PMID:29606850

Bäuml, J., Fröböse, T., Kraemer, S., Rentrop, M., & Pitschel-Walz, G. (2006). Psychoeducation: A basic psychotherapeutic intervention for patients with schizophrenia and their families. *Schizophrenia Bulletin*, *32*(S1), S1–S9. doi:10.1093chbulbl017 PMID:16920788

Brandis, M. (1998). A feminist analysis of the theories of etiology of depression in women. *Nursing Leadership Forum*, *5*(1), 18–23. PMID:10458848

Brown, L. S. (1986). Gender-role analysis: A neglected component of psychological assessment. *Psychotherapy (Chicago, Ill.)*, *23*(2), 243–248. doi:10.1037/h0085604

Bryant-Davis, T., Ullman, S., Tsong, Y., Anderson, G., Counts, P., Tillman, S., ... Gray, A. (2015). Healing pathways: Longitudinal effects of religious coping and social support on PTSD symptoms in African American sexual assault survivors. *Journal of Trauma & Dissociation*, *16*(1), 114–128. doi:10.1080/15299732.2014.969468 PMID:25387044

Carey, M., & Russell, M. (2002). Externalising – commonly-asked-questions. *International Journal of Narrative Therapy and Community Work*, *2*, 76–84.

Carson, L. R. (2009). 'I am because we are:' Collectivism as a foundational characteristic of African American college student identity and academic achievement. *Social Psychology of Education*, *12*(3), 327–344. doi:10.100711218-009-9090-6

Centers for Disease Control and Prevention. (2010). *Summary of health statistics for U. S. adults: National health interview survey, 2010*. Retrieved from http://www.cdc.gov/nchs/data/series/sr_10/sr10_252.pdf

Centers for Disease Control and Prevention. (2013). *Leading causes of death by race/ethnicity, all females- United States, 2013*. Retrieved from http://www.cdc.gov/women/lcod/2013/WomenRace_2013.pdf

Centers for Disease Control and Prevention. (2016). *Facts everyone should know: Intimate partner violence, sexual violence, & stalking*. Retrieved from https://www.cdc.gov/violenceprevention/pdf/NISVS-infographic-2016.pdf

Chow, E. O. (2015). Narrative therapy an evaluated intervention to improve stroke survivors' social and emotional adaptation. *Clinical Rehabilitation*, *29*(4), 315–326. doi:10.1177/0269215514544039 PMID:25142279

Church Of God In Christ, Inc. (2018). *About*. Retrieved from http://www.cogic.org/about-company/

Cohen, L. J. (1993). The therapeutic use of reading: A qualitative study. *Journal of Poetry Therapy*, *7*(2), 73–83.

Collins, P. H. (2000). *Black feminist thought: Knowledge, consciousness, and the politics of empowerment* (2nd ed.). New York, NY: Routledge.

Silenced, Shamed, and Scatted

Collins, P. H. (2004). *Black sexual politics: African Americans, gender, and the new racism*. New York, NY: Routledge. doi:10.4324/9780203309506

Crenshaw, K. (1989). Demarginalizing the intersection of race and sex: A Black feminist critique of antidiscrimination doctrine, feminist theory and antiracist politics. *University of Chicago Legal Forum*, *1*(8), 139–167.

DuMonthier, A., Childers, C., & Milli, J. (2017). *The status of Black women in the United States*. Retrieved from https://iwpr.org/wp-content/uploads/2017/06/The-Status-of-Black-Women-6.26.17.pdf

Essed, P. (1991). *Understanding everyday racism: An interdisciplinary theory*. Thousand Oaks, CA: Sage.

Etchison, M., & Kleist, D. M. (2000). Review of narrative therapy: Research and utility. *The Family Journal (Alexandria, Va.)*, *8*(1), 61–66. doi:10.1177/1066480700081009

Fristad, M. A., Gavazzi, S. M., & Mackinaw-Koons, B. (2003). Family psychoeducation: An adjunctive intervention for children with bipolar disorder. *Biological Psychiatry*, *53*(11), 1000–1008. doi:10.1016/S0006-3223(03)00186-0 PMID:12788245

Giddings, P. J. (2008). *Ida: Sword among lions: Ida B. Wells and the campaign against lynching*. New York, NY: Harper.

Harris, P. (2003). Gatekeeping and remaking: The politics of respectability in African American women's history and Black feminism. *Journal of Women's History*, *15*(1), 212–220. doi:10.1353/jowh.2003.0025

Hill, Z. (2017, October 18). *A Black woman created the "Me Too" campaign against sexual assault 10 years ago*. Retrieved from https://www.ebony.com/news-views/black-woman-me-too-movement-tarana-burke-alyssa-milano

hooks, b. (1993). *Sisters of the yam: Black women and self-recovery*. Cambridge, MA: South End Press.

Hull, G. T., Scott, P. B., & Smith, B. (1982). *But some of us are brave: All the women are White, All the Blacks are men*. New York, NY: The Feminist Press at the City University of New York.

Iverson, K. M., Dick, A., McLaughlin, K. A., Smith, B. N., Bell, M. E., Gerber, M. R., & Mitchell, K. S. (2013). Exposure to interpersonal violence and its associations with psychiatric morbidity in a US national sample: A gender comparison. *Psychology of Violence*, *3*(3), 273–287. doi:10.1037/a0030956 PMID:25232484

Jennings, W. J. (2017). Toward a womanist ethic of incarnation: Black bodies, the Black church and the Council of Chalcedon. *Black Theology: An International Journal*, *15*(1), 79–81. doi:10.1080/1476994 8.2017.1271586

Jones, D., Marks, G., Villar-Loubet, O., Weiss, S. M., O'Daniels, C., Borkowf, C. B., & McLellan-Lemal, E. (2015). Experience of forced sex and subsequent sexual, drug, and mental health outcomes: African American and Hispanic women in the southeastern United States. *International Journal of Sexual Health*, *27*(3), 249–263. doi:10.1080/19317611.2014.959631 PMID:26380592

Jones, L. V. (2015). Black feminisms: Renewing sacred healing spaces. *Affilia, 30*(2), 246–252. doi:10.1177/0886109914551356

Jones, L. V., & Guy-Sheftall, B. (2015). Conquering the Black girl blues. *Social Work, 60*(4), 343–350. doi:10.1093wwv032 PMID:26489355

Jones, L. V., & Warner, L. A. (2011). Evaluating culturally responsive group work with Black women. *Research on Social Work Practice, 21*(6), 737–746. doi:10.1177/1049731511411488

King, W. (2014). "Prematurely knowing of evil things": The sexual abuse of African American girls and young women in slavery and freedom. *Journal of African American History, 99*(3), 173–196. doi:10.5323/jafriamerhist.99.3.0173

Kruger, A., Harper, E., Harris, P., Sanders, D. S., Levin, K., & Meyers, J. (2013). Sexualized and dangerous relationships: Listening to the voices of low- income African American girls placed at risk for sexual exploitation. *The Western Journal of Emergency Medicine, 14*(4), 370–376. doi:10.5811/westjem.2013.2.16195 PMID:23930151

Lewis, E. A. (1989). Role strain in African-American women: The efficacy of support networks. *Journal of Black Studies, 20*(2), 155–169. doi:10.1177/002193478902000203

Lubin, H., Loris, M., Burt, J., & Johnson, D. R. (1998). Efficacy of psychoeducational group therapy in reducing symptoms of posttraumatic stress disorder among multiply traumatized women. *The American Journal of Psychiatry, 155*(9), 1172–1177. doi:10.1176/ajp.155.9.1172 PMID:9734538

Martens, A., Johns, M., Greenberg, J., & Schimel, J. (2006). Combating stereotype threat: The effect of self-affirmation on women's intellectual performance. *Journal of Experimental Social Psychology, 42*(2), 236–243. doi:10.1016/j.jesp.2005.04.010

Me Too. (2018). *About.* Retrieved from https://metoomvmt.org/about/#history

Meyer, O. L., & Zane, N. (2013). The influence of race and ethnicity in clients' experiences of mental health treatment. *Journal of Community Psychology, 41*(7), 884–901. doi:10.1002/jcop.21580 PMID:25400301

Mies, M. (1998). *Patriarchy and accumulation on a world scale: Women in the international division of labour.* New York, NY: Zed Books Ltd.

Morgan, R. E., & Kena, G. (2017). *Criminal victimization, 2016* (NCJ 251150). Report prepared for U. S. Department of Justice, Office of Justice Programs, Bureau of Justice Statistics. Retrieved from https://www.bjs.gov/content/pub/pdf/cv16re.pdf

National Association for the Advancement of Colored People. (1911). Crime. *Crisis, 2*(3), 99–100.

Neal, R. (2011). Engaging Abrahamic masculinity: Race, religion, and the measure of manhood. *Cross Currents, 61*(4), 557–564. doi:10.1111/j.1939-3881.2011.00204.x

Nichols, M. P. (2009). *The essentials of family therapy* (4th ed.). Boston, MA: Pearson.

Perry-Burney, G., Thomas, N. D., & McDonald, T. L. (2014). Rural child sexual abuse in the African American church community: A forbidden topic. *Journal of Human Behavior in the Social Environment, 24*(8), 986–995. doi:10.1080/10911359.2014.953413

Silenced, Shamed, and Scatted

Pew Research Center. (2018a, September 26). *Black men are less religious than Black women, but more religious that White women and men*. Retrieved from http://www.pewresearch.org/fact-tank/2018/09/26/black-men-are-less-religious-than-black-women-but-more-religious-than-white-women-and-men/

Pew Research Center. (2018b, February 7). *5 facts about the religious lives of African Americans*. Retrieved from http://www.pewresearch.org/fact-tank/2018/02/07/5-facts-about-the-religious- lives-of-african-americans/

Pfeifer, M. J. (1999). Lynching and criminal justice in South Louisiana, 1878-1930. *Louisiana History: The Journal of the Louisiana Historical Association, 40*(2), 155-177. Retrieved from https://www.jstor.org/stable/4233571

Pierce-Baker, C. (1998). *Surviving the silence: Black women's stories of rape*. New York, NY: W. W. Norton & Company.

Pollio, D. E., North, C. S., & Foster, D. A. (1998). Content and curriculum in psychoeducation groups for families of persons with severe mental illness. *Psychiatric Services (Washington, D.C.), 49*(6), 816–822. doi:10.1176/ps.49.6.816 PMID:9634164

Richardson, M. (Ed.). (1987). *Maria W. Stewart, America's first Black woman political writer: Essays and speeches*. Bloomington, IN: Indiana University Press.

Ricks, L., Kitchens, S., Goodrich, I., & Hancock, E. (2014). My story: The use of narrative therapy in individual and group counseling. *Journal of Creativity in Mental Health, 9*(1), 99–110. doi:10.1080/15401383.2013.870947

Ruether, R. R. (1982). Feminism and patriarchal religion: Principles of ideological critiques of the Bible. *Journal for the Study of the Old Testament, 22*(22), 54–66. doi:10.1177/030908928200702207

Scheel, M. J., Hanson, W. E., & Razzhavaikina, T. I. (2004). The process of recommending homework in psychotherapy: A review of therapist delivery methods, client acceptability, and factors that affect compliance. *Psychotherapy (Chicago, Ill.), 41*(1), 38–55. doi:10.1037/0033-3204.41.1.38

Simien, E. M. (2004). Gender differences in attitudes toward Black feminism among African Americans. *Political Science Quarterly, 119*(2), 315–338. doi:10.2307/20202348

Smith, Y. Y. (2008). Womanist theology: Empowering Black women through Christian education. *Black Theology: An International Journal, 6*(2), 200–220. doi:10.1558/blth2008v6i2.200

Sommerville, D. M. (2004). *Rape and race in the nineteenth-century South*. Chapel Hill, NC: University of North Carolina Press.

Stein, M. N. (2015). *Measuring manhood: Race and the science of masculinity, 1830-1934*. Minneapolis, MN: University of Minnesota Press. doi:10.5749/minnesota/9780816673025.001.0001

Sue, D. W., Capodilupo, C. M., Torino, G. C., Bucceri, J. M., Holder, A. M. B., Nadal, K. L., & Esquilin, M. (2007). Racial microaggressions in everyday life: Implications for clinical practice. *The American Psychologist, 62*(4), 271–286. doi:10.1037/0003-066X.62.4.271 PMID:17516773

Sue, D. W., Nadal, K., Capodilupo, C. M., Lin, A. I., Torino, G. C., & Rivera, D. P. (2008). Racial microaggressions against Black Americans: Implications for counseling. *Journal of Counseling and Development*, *86*(3), 330–338. doi:10.1002/j.1556-6678.2008.tb00517.x

Tillman, S., Bryant-Davis, T., Smith, K., & Marks, A. (2010). Shattering silence: Exploring barriers to disclosure for African American sexual assault survivors. *Trauma, Violence & Abuse*, *11*(2), 59–70. doi:10.1177/1524838010363717 PMID:20430798

Townes, E. M. (2003). Womanist theology. In R. S. Keller & R. R. Ruether (Eds), Encyclopedia for Women and Religion in America (pp. 1165-1169). Bloomington, IN: Indiana University Press.

Turner, S. G., & Maschi, T. M. (2015). Feminist and empowerment theory and social work practice. *Journal of Social Work Practice*, *29*(2), 151–162. doi:10.1080/02650533.2014.941282

Valdes, F. (1996). Unpacking hetero-patriarchy: Tracing the conflation of sex, gender & sexual orientation to its origins. *Yale Journal of Law & the Humanities*, *8*(1), 161–211.

van Berlo, W., & Ensink, B. (2000). Problems with sexuality after sexual assault. *Annual Review of Sex Research*, *11*(1), 235–257. doi:10.1080/10532528.2000.10559789 PMID:11351833

Vaz, K. M. (2005). Reflecting team group therapy and its congruence with feminist principles. *Women & Therapy*, *28*(2), 65–75. doi:10.1300/J015v28n02_05

Wadsworth, P., & Records, K. (2013). A review of the health effects of sexual assault on African American women and adolescents. *Journal of Obstetric, Gynecologic, and Neonatal Nursing*, *42*(3), 249–273. doi:10.1111/1552-6909.12041 PMID:23682695

Watson, N. N., & Hunter, C. D. (2016). 'I had to be strong': Tensions in the strong Black woman schema. *The Journal of Black Psychology*, *42*(5), 424–452. doi:10.1177/0095798415597093

Weger, H., Bell, G. C., Minei, E. M., & Robinson, M. C. (2014). The relative effectiveness of active listening in initial interactions. *International Journal of Listening*, *28*(1), 13–31. doi:10.1080/1090401 8.2013.813234

Weisenfeld, J. (2015, March). *Religion in African American history*. Retrieved from http://oxfordre. com/americanhistory/view/10.1093/acrefore/9780199329175.001.0001/acrefore-9780199329175-e-24

Woods-Giscombe, C. (2010). Superwoman schema: African American women's views on stress, strength, and health. *Qualitative Health Research*, *20*(5), 668–683. doi:10.1177/1049732310361892 PMID:20154298

Yancey, G., & Kim, Y. J. (2008). Racial diversity, gender equality, and SES diversity in Christian congregations: Exploring the connections of racism, sexism, and classism in multiracial and nonmultiracial churches. *Journal for the Scientific Study of Religion*, *41*(1), 103–111. doi:10.1111/j.1468-5906.2008.00394.x

Yeary, K. H. K. (2011). Religious authority in African American churches: A study of six churches. *Religions*, *2*(4), 628–648. doi:10.3390/rel2040628

Silenced, Shamed, and Scatted

ADDITIONAL READING

Beauboeuf-Lafontant, T. (2009). *Behind the mask of the strong Black woman*. Philadelphia, PA: Temple University Press.

Boyd-Franklin, N. (2010). Incorporating spirituality and religion into the treatment of African American clients. *The Counseling Psychologist, 38*(7), 976–1000. doi:10.1177/0011000010374881

Cannon, K. (1998). *Katie's Canon: Womanism and the soul of the Black community*. New York, NY: Bloomsbury Academic.

Donovan, R. A., Galban, D. J., Grace, R. K., Bennett, J. K., & Felicié, S. Z. (2012). Impact of racial macro- and microaggressions in Black women's lives: A preliminary analysis. *The Journal of Black Psychology, 39*(2), 185–196. doi:10.1177/0095798412443259

Guy-Sheftall, B. (1995). *Words of fire: An anthology of African American feminist thought*. New York, NY: The New Press.

Lorde, A. (1984). *Sister outsider*. Berkeley, CA: Ten Speed Press.

Moraga, C., & Anzaldúa, G. (2015). *The bridge called my back: Writings by radical women of color* (4th ed.). Albany, NY: State University of New York Press.

Semmler, P. L., & Williams, C. B. (2000). Narrative therapy: A storied context for multicultural counseling. *Journal of Multicultural Counseling and Development, 28*(1), 51–62. doi:10.1002/j.2161-1912.2000.tb00227.x

Settles, I. H. (2006). Use of an intersectional framework to understand Black women's racial and gender identities. *Sex Roles, 54*(9-10), 589–601. doi:10.100711199-006-9029-8

Williams, C. B. (2005). Counseling African American women: Multiple identities, multiple constraints. *Journal of Counseling and Development, 83*(3), 278–283. doi:10.1002/j.1556-6678.2005.tb00343.x

KEY TERMS AND DEFINITIONS

African American Woman: A person assigned and/or self-identified as a woman, Black, and of African descent and of American nationality.

Black Feminisms: Black feminisms include perspectives, social movements, and practice theories emergent from and about African American women that emphasize Black women's scholarship and empowerment within social, literary, and intellectual thought.

Heterocentric-Patriarchy: Heterocentric-patriarchy is the systemic domination of social, political, and economic capital by persons assigned and/or self-identified as male and masculine.

Intersectionality: Intersectionality is a framework that acknowledges overlapping oppression across race, gender, sex, class, and other social identities.

Racism: Racism is the ability of one group to use its collective race prejudices to control the livelihood of another group of a different race.

Rape: Rape is the perpetration of unwanted, nonconsensual, or coerced sexual contact against another person.

Religion: Religion is a set of beliefs, values, and practices related to a higher power.

Scatted: To leave or be pushed aside.

This research was previously published in #MeToo Issues in Religious-Based Institutions and Organizations; pages 1-32, copyright year 2020 by Information Science Reference (an imprint of IGI Global).

Chapter 33
Where Our Paths Crossed:
Latina Teachers, Professional Development, and Funds of Identity

Minda Morren López
https://orcid.org/0000-0002-5973-3466
Texas State University, San Marcos, USA

Jane M. Saunders
Texas State University, San Marcos, USA

ABSTRACT

This chapter presents the case of two Latina teachers who worked with Latinx and emerging bilingual students. Their funds of identity are analyzed, and the professional development program is described, including ways it influenced the teachers' ideological clarity and sense of agency. While their experiences were different in many ways, Summer and Ximena's paths crossed through their shared experiences in the professional development program, and they became vocal advocates for language as resource and language as right perspectives in education. This chapter demonstrates the potential in professional development for teachers working with emerging bilinguals and immigrants, how teachers can move towards advocacy work and leadership by examining their own journeys and funds of identity.

INTRODUCTION

That the school has been locked away and walled in as if by a tall fence from life itself has been its greatest failing. Education is just as meaningless outside the real world as is a fire without oxygen, or as is breathing in a vacuum. The teacher's education work, therefore, must be inevitably connected with his (or her) creative, social, and life work (Vygotsky, 1926/1997, p. 345).

DOI: 10.4018/978-1-6684-4507-5.ch033

This chapter has three aims: to explore and explain the burgeoning "funds of identity" (Esteban-Guitart, & Moll, 2014, p.35) of two Latina educators working in a large suburban school district in the southwest United States; to use this as an opportunity for professional development and take down the fence that separates schools from the lived experiences of the larger communities in which they do their work; and to illustrate how pedagogy and language education can be transformed when educators are engaged in this kind of professional development. By understanding ourselves as teachers in relation to the communities in which we teach, we are able to develop ideological clarity (Bartolomé & Balderrama, 2001) in order to better serve our emerging bilingual students.

Specifically, we discuss how two Latina teachers in a literacy graduate program were guided through professional development focused on language and literacy instruction centered in their classrooms and communities utilizing a funds of identity approach. First, we provide an overview of the professional development graduate program, with examples of the curriculum, readings, and assignments. We incorporated team building, scaffolded group interactions, readings, assignments, and teacher reflection that were all designed to uncover funds of identities and to connect teachers to their communities. Then we exemplify the professional development program through two teachers: Ximena and Summer. We make visible their funds of identity and follow their journeys through the two-year program through a case study approach. We provide examples of what they experienced in their respective classrooms and schools and ways they sought to problem-solve or amend their pedagogical practices in order to better serve their multilingual students. We discuss how both teachers engaged in shared leadership and advocacy for their students, emerging bilinguals, and the Latinx community. Finally, we conclude with recommendations for professional development for educators working with multilingual and immigrant communities.

BACKGROUND

"Funds of Identity"

Funds of identity are characterized as a "box of tools people use to define themselves" (Esteban-Guitart, & Moll, 2014, p. 74) that are both internal and external. Moreover, funds of identity are temporal, a process of becoming, created at various times in our lives through a vast range life experiences, including our funds of knowledge, our lived experiences, and other historically created, accumulated, disseminated, and situated resources. Funds of identity can be made visible in artifacts, in chosen activities and academic pursuits, and in a repertoire of behaviors.

"Funds of identity" (Esteban-Guitart & Moll, 2014) was articulated as a means to overcome various limitations in funds of knowledge, including the centrality of families for the individual as well as an overreliance on interviews in students' homes. Funds of identity seek to expand into various social networks and lived experiences of participants. These additional experiences and technologies form relationships and identities in individuals that may differ from that of their family of origin. In other words, participants may embrace, reject or cobble together their own lives and identities with funds of knowledge derived from their families and cultural histories but they also add their own interests, activities, and experiences.

Professional Development

All too often, professional development is disjointed from educators' worlds and local communities. Many professional learning programs do not include teachers' identities and lived experiences and are full of strategies and activities presented as a way to "fix" teachers and hold them accountable for "problems" (Cabson, Shagoury, Smith, & Carpenter, 2005). Effective professional development incorporates teachers' lived experiences and identities, and views these aspects of teaching as integral to success. According to Rogers et. al. (2005), the most effective professional development emerges from classrooms and schools as knowledge generating sites, connected to communities and society. Their research suggests that through community and school based professional learning, transformation can occur and an impact on society can be made. Likewise, renowned educator Michie (2017) urges professional learning that builds relevancy into curricula and works towards justice by centering on teachers' practices around students' lived experiences and communities rather than focusing on outside experts who come in for a one-shot workshop. Similarly, Hurd and Licciardo-Musso (2005) state that teachers must be treated like leaders and given opportunities to practice best teaching practices and reflect on their instruction.

Professional development and learning for educators through university-school or university-district partnerships has been recommended practice for decades. Goodlad (1988) argued that such partnerships provide optimal opportunities for innovation and true reform by combining resources to support mutual goals. Others have found university partnerships as important catalysts for change, especially for teachers of emerging bilinguals, through supportive infrastructure, resources, and individualized learning opportunities (Ek, Machado-Casas, Sánchez, & Alanís, 2010; Flores, Clark, Claeys, & Villarreal, 2007; Slapac, Song, & Chasteen, 2017; Zetlin, MacLeod, & Michner, 1998). In addition, university partnerships have the potential to contribute positively to teachers' identities and agency development (Trent & Lim, 2010).

MAIN FOCUS OF THE CHAPTER

Context and Participants

The South ISD Cohort

The district of South ISD is a district on the outskirts of a large metropolitan area. The district is a mix of suburban and rural communities. At the time of the study, enrollment was just under 14,000 students, 90.5 percent identify as Latinx. Of those, 16% were considered English Learners of various levels of proficiency (at this time, Texas does not disaggregate by levels of proficiency). These demographics show a district that is overwhelmingly Latinx, and below the state average of 19% English Learners.

While the focus of this chapter is on two of the cohort members, the larger group consisted of eight full-time teachers holding a shared interest in literacy. Their teaching experience ranged from 1-22 years, and all but one of the cohorts (who worked as a literacy teacher in a middle school) taught in elementary settings across South ISD. Six members of the group identified as Latina; two as white. Five faculty worked with this cohort. We met with the participants once or twice a week for two years in classrooms, portable buildings, and other school district spaces at night and on weekends and unlike our experiences teaching on a college campus without the cohort model, the group quickly developed a familial dynamic. Students shared stories and food, and helped sustain one another when the work load felt heavy. For faculty, this differed from our experience at the main campus, where students entered the program throughout the school year, registered for courses in different sequences, and only fell into a cohort-like situation near the end of their program when preparing for comprehensive exams. During our two-year collaboration, South ISD began deploying cohort members in a variety of roles in their schools: as literacy interventionists, dyslexia specialists, and master teachers.

After the first year of our cohort, several had taken on leadership roles in schools, serving as literacy specialists or instructional coaches. During class conversations, it was clear they were trying to make sense of what they were reading – about how students develop orthographic understandings that contribute to their later fluency, or the importance of helping immigrant and emerging bilingual students maintain their home languages while developing as readers and writers of English. Unlike teachers we worked with in our program back on the college campus – who represented myriad school districts and priorities – the cohort teachers could draw direct lines between what they were learning, what their experiences were in the district and the local community, and how this could inform their practice. They began to speak in a kind of short-hand as they collectively problem-solved; thus, classroom activities and conversations would often develop into a problem-solving endeavor. The teachers would link back to the readings and test out ideas among the cohort and this led to practical solutions.

Upon completion of the program, students met together the night before graduation to decorate their caps, laugh, and reflect on their experience. We celebrated a second time with family members, kids, and friends the day of graduation. When we followed up with the cohort a few months later to schedule a group conversation, they all rearranged their calendars to ensure they could meet a final time.

Ximena and Summer

The two teachers described here who became the participants in our study, were part of a larger cohort of educators completing a Master of Education/Reading Specialist degree program. The teachers worked in the same school district and reflected similar dispositions toward their students. Upon closer examination, however, we discovered patterns of behavior that we came to see as representative of very different funds of knowledge (Moll, Amanti, Neff, & Gonzalez, 1992) and lived experiences from childhood that seemed to shape their pedagogical orientations. More specifically, we noticed differences of experience related to language, literacy, and culture and funds of identity which, in turn, impacted the capacity of one of the two featured educators initially to enact an agentive identity on behalf of her pedagogical practice *and* her Latinx and emerging bilingual students.

Ximena and Summer (pseudonyms), may appear demographically homogenous – both Latinas of Mexican-American origin born and raised in the same large city in the Southwestern United States, are around the same age, and were Spanish-dominant emerging bilinguals when they began school. Upon closer examination it became evident how their practices and identities differed in significant ways when we met them at the beginning of their graduate program. There are intersections of identities between the two as well as divergent paths. Ximena – whose funds of knowledge included fostering bilingualism and a bicultural identity – started with greater self-assurance about the importance of supporting complex and often competing multilingual and multicultural identities among her students. She had been raised in a bilingual household where her mother interacted with her only in Spanish in an effort to develop Ximena's linguistic and cultural identity as a Mexican-American. Although similarly situated in a Spanish language-dominant home in early childhood, Summer was forced to abandon her home language once she entered school. To support her English-language development, Summer's parents limited her access

Where Our Paths Crossed

to Spanish at home and at school, which had the unintended consequence of constraining her bilingual and bicultural identity. As a result, while Summer's fluency in Spanish is limited today, Ximena's interactions both personally and through her work as a literacy professional allow her to engage in Spanish and English as a part of her daily practice. These differences are representative of differing funds of identity that govern the approaches these two educators employed in enacting their professional identities.

The Professional Development Program

When we began discussions in 2015 to work with South ISD (a pseudonym) to offer our Master of Reading Education program to a cohort of practicing teachers, we seized the opportunity. Instead of meeting at our university an hour away from the district, five faculty taught in schools and professional development spaces within South ISD. In turn, the district gave us permission to research, write, and present with the cohort members studying to become Reading Specialists.

The 36-hour Master of Education (M.Ed.) degree in Reading prepares teachers to serve as literacy leaders within their schools, districts, and local community. Graduates of the program serve as reading specialists, literacy coaches, curriculum developers, consultants, program coordinators, and teacher leaders. Aligned with the program's mission statement, "A community of equity-minded literacy professionals," faculty often conduct research, write, and present with students. We offer courses to strengthen and build on teachers' understanding of theory, research, assessment, and practice within settings that mirror our local school populations. The participants in this research study were part of one cohort where the university partnered with the school district to offer the program onsite over two years. This collaboration arose from discussions between a faculty member and two district leaders who were looking for a way to engage teachers in a rigorous professional development program for emerging bilinguals in literacy. The result was this professional development partnership offered in the district that resulted in a master's degree in reading with a specialization in language and literacy for emerging bilinguals, both recent immigrants and students who had been in the school system for a long time but were still classified as English Learners.

This professional development program began with assignments designed to understand themselves, their students, and their community. This approach is aligned with funds of identity because in each course and throughout the program, teachers are engaged in work that examines their own lived experiences in multiple ways. Funds of identity takes a participants' experience and extracts meaning related to it across their life trajectory in various multimodal ways—drawings, photographs, graphs and symbols, texts, official records such as report cards, etc. (Moll & Esteban-Guitart, 2014). For example, one may depict a time in their lives with a photograph that represents an experience they had or with a symbol. Or draw and write a self-portrait or memoir. Thus, throughout their program, regardless of instructor, teachers engaged in assignments such as: a personal reflective language, literacy, and culture timeline; a literature review related to an area of strong interest within the literacy research; a case study of a student's orthographic development and corresponding intervention, complete with a reflection on their pedagogical decisions in relation to the case study student; and, a multiple case study of emerging bilinguals' language and literacy development over a semester with a plan of instruction. We worked to develop a community of trust and shared goals within the cohort, purposefully incorporating language and literacy research that offered models of additive and culturally affirming pedagogical practices into our coursework along with critical reflection. We developed assignments to help teachers confront their assumptions about their students and local community and reflect on their pedagogical practice through

627

a set of projects designed to leverage growth in the cohort. For example, students were asked to explore their community and unpack its resources for a few different assignments. They interviewed family and community members to better understand the funds of knowledge present within households in their local community; they explored the written language visible within several miles of their schools to gain information about what students saw when going back and forth to school. Cohort members examined the assets of their students and school community, and contemplated ways to incorporate innovations – i.e. drawing on technology, graphic novels or multi-genre pedagogies to enhance their pedagogical practice. Because the cohort was intimately connected with one another, they often leaned in with ideas for solving problems, getting materials for their classrooms, or helping each other prepare for tasks outside of class like interviewing for a literacy position within the school district. These conversations cycled into the class conversation, often in relation to journal articles or texts we were reading.

Throughout the two-year program, teachers collected artifacts that served as part of their comprehensive exam portfolio. Students wrote reflective essays that showed their learning over time, aligned with three areas of emphasis: literacy research; assessment; and literacy for all learners (Texas State University, n.d.). In this manner, students were able to demonstrate their learning both in writing and through an oral presentation.

Methodological Procedures

We study identities by acknowledging micro and macro influences on our participants and by approaching data collection from a multi-method autobiographical approach (Esteban-Guitart, 2012) that includes reflection, visual representations, narratives, and artifacts representing various times in the two participants' lives. This approach is much like a case study (Creswell, 2007) utilized to understand the multiple dimensions of the teachers' experiences. The qualitative data included not only narratives but also drawings, maps, photographs, and writings that were all part of the course assignments and projects. We also analyzed our own field notes and audio transcripts from focus groups. Empirical data presented here capture the teachers' words – written and spoken – as they moved through their two-year professional development in language and literacy. To code the data, we independently read and reread the texts and listened to recorded audio to inductively code units of words that had meaning and we labeled words and phrases for open coding first (e.g., "childhood experiences", "bilingual", "language as resource", "teaching philosophy", "literacy development", etc.) in a technique designed to understand texts after multiple readings (Bogdan & Bilken, 1992). Texts of the participants were compared and codes were defined and categorized into initial themes (Lincoln & Guba, 1985) as each category was reexamined, redefined, and combined with other similar categories. Their words gave rise to several themes (e.g. barriers, agency, shifting identities, background knowledge, teaching others, and advocacy) suggesting the importance of community as a scaffold for the development of agency. In addition, we followed their development of agentive identities. These agentive identities are capable of effecting noticeable change in the multilingual communities in which our teachers worked.

Where Our Paths Crossed

FINDINGS THE TWO CASES: SUMMER AND XIMENA

Summer: Funds of Identity from Lived Experiences

Summer's story as a student is similar to many language learners, and we draw on her experiences to detail a burgeoning identity as a learner and later, a teacher. She moved between Texas and California as a child and characterized herself as an "at-risk" student for a large part of her early grades.

Summer's Background

In a class essay about linguistic and cultural diversity, Summer relays a childhood memory related to a teacher's judgment as she read the word "marijuana" during a round robin reading exercise in her 6th grade class. After using what Summer characterized as her "natural Latina accent" her teacher made a public correction, explaining *"that's not how 'we' say it."* The implication was clear, and in spite of a Mexican classmate assuring the class that his family said the word the same way in his home, Summer was shamed publicly – first by the unpracticed read aloud, and then the mispronunciation.

Before the end of that year, Summer's family moved to Texas and into a school with an almost monolithic Latinx population, a big change from her California school where she was among the minority. In this environment, Summer's memory was of a rash of White teachers who screamed at students they couldn't control and a bifurcated system of floors, with the third floor saved for the "smart" kids and the lower levels for everyone else. Summer endeavored to earn status as a *good* student, eventually working as a volunteer in a summer program during her middle grades years and serving as a tutor to students from her middle school once she moved into high school. She characterizes herself as *"always a teacher"* and says from an early age, *"education as a career chose me."*

In spite of this view, Summer did not initially excel in university studies. Upon graduating from high school, she married, had a daughter, and attempted to take community college classes that would eventually transfer to a four-year university. Lacking support and any kind of a mentor, Summer failed coursework and eventually dropped out, but made her way into the classroom first as a substitute teacher and then as a teacher's aide where she remained for seven years. With the encouragement of her husband, Summer decided to try college work again. She connected with a professor who boosted her confidence and helped her navigate and understand the oft invisible rules of higher education. First in her family to graduate from college, Summer began teaching in 2011. She characterizes this point in her teaching career as in search of a *"bag of tricks"* to help leverage growth in students. Summer relied less on research-based practices than on more experienced teachers to fill this bag, and attempted to control the *"tornado of ideas"* she generated in favor of following district mandates and staying within the lines of the work she saw others doing rather than developing the creative pedagogy she envisioned.

Graduate School

By the time she applied to graduate school in 2016, Summer had taught for four years, first as a 2nd grade teacher and then a 4th grade reading/writing teacher. In spite of her own experience as a language learner, Summer did not always enact a culturally responsive pedagogy. This might reflect the teacher models she had as a EC-12 student, most of whom were White and who did not consider the rich cultural and linguistic backgrounds their students brought to school. For example, throughout her EC-12 experience, the only book she remembered read aloud in class *"with characters like me"* was Gary Soto's *Too Many Tamales*. She didn't think much of this until she began studying culturally rich picture and young adult books that exposed her to a wide range of narrators, cultures, and perspectives. Summer acknowledges she at times carried deficit thinking (Slapac & Kim, 2014; Valenzuela, 1999) about her students and, like her own teachers, did not draw on the resources they brought to school with them. Rather, she focused more on what students could "not do," describing this in a comprehensive exam essay as an example of a "fix the child" mindset.

When we talked in classes about institutional barriers that hamper students' capacity to flourish, particularly those from language-diverse or low-income homes, Summer began to reconsider her practice. Her goal – consistent from her time as a tutor in high school – was "seeing growth" in what students could do, with the teacher as the center of the learning. Graduate coursework helped her recast this as a reciprocal process (Vygotsky, 1986), where students could bring in funds of knowledge (Moll, 2000; Moll, Amanti, Neff, & Gonzalez, 1992) and artifacts of the lived experiences as a resource for learning. Summer began to see herself as a facilitator of activity, rather than the center of it.

Summer: Shifts in Identity and a Change in Practice

Early in the program, Summer exhibited the characteristics of many practicing teachers: she was creative and confident, and sought opportunities to test out what she was learning in our literacy classes with her own students. She was a careful reader of research, and drew on readings to explain and explore her experiences in the classroom. Yet there were tensions between the enthusiasm Summer felt about practices that she was reading about and the reality she experienced working in a school district with a large Latino population – families who struggled economically, who spoke Spanish in the home, and who often did poorly on standardized tests. From the beginning of her time in the program, Summer cautioned that she only had freedom up to a point to teach in the manner she thought might interest and engage her students. And that point was a moving target, drawn by administrators and directly related to test preparation. When one of her professors would push back – and recommend Summer share research with school leaders – she would smile and shrug. *"You just don't know what we're dealing with at my school,"* was her response.

In spite of this, Summer's eyes would light up when we wrote about our identities, cultures, or lived experiences in class assignments. She told stories of fishing with her family, challenges growing up in an impoverished community, her love of travel and pride in her children. When a graduate of our program came into the class to teach the group how to make short movies using AdobeSpark, Summer was the first to test it out and share her work with the class. Having conducted a project in an earlier course that required she experience a home visit to seek out of her student's funds of knowledge (Moll & Gonzalez, 2004), Summer bubbled over with enthusiasm. A rural farming and ranching community (*"the closest grocery story was 15 miles away"*), she learned that her student's family had an encyclopedic understanding of their work. *"Their knowledge was like a Google site,"* she reported, with parents, grandparents, and siblings explaining the role that literacy played in their labor. And, while family members often read and wrote in Spanish, they used this information to keep their farm afloat and pass along information to the younger generation. Summer began to wonder: how can I draw on this in my classroom?

Where Our Paths Crossed

Connecting Research to Practice

The graduate literacy program that Summer was taking part in at our university included several common assignments that students engaged in, regardless of which professor was teaching the course. One of these – the community language and literacy mapping assignment – provided a pivotal shift in Summer's thinking about her students, her practice, and the importance that the Spanish language played in the community where she worked. The community mapping project is modeled after Ordoñez–Jasis and Jasis' (2011) research, which seeks to

chronicle the knowledge produced by teachers about the depth and diversity of language and literacy resources in the neighborhoods surrounding their various urban school sites. Schools are located in dynamic, ever changing communities with both socio-political historical legacies and contemporary resources. As such, community language and literacy mapping is an inquiry-based method that can be utilized by teachers to place literacy learning in context by connecting students' life realities to school instruction. (p. 189)

Summer's exploration of her local community yielded several relevant discoveries. Because of the expanse of land used for farms and ranches, there were few artifacts of literacy to document, other than road signs related to highway exits. There were word-rich texts or literacy resources posted outside of business advertisements like gas stations, tree trimming and removal services, post office placards, and yard signs advertising satellite internet service.

This latter artifact was an important piece of learning for Summer, who later learned through students that they were often forced to drive to a larger town about 20 minutes away to access stable and free Wi-Fi service at a McDonald's restaurant. As part of this assignment, Summer interviewed four different community members, including someone at the post office, two workers at local businesses, and a parent. The local businesses seemed more concerned with stopping shoplifting than in talking with Summer in more detail about the literacy practices of their community. The parent she interviewed explained that while her sons did not read necessarily for pleasure (they were far more interested in entertainment, sports, and playing soccer) they were required to read and "*follow the directions to feed (cattle) and make molasses.*" The parent characterized Summer's principal as "*strict*" and one who "*expects a lot from the students,*" but did not offer specific instances of how literacy was foundational for their learning in school. Summer's takeaway from this project was that the community was filled with Spanish speakers – in fact, she conversed with three of her interviewees in Spanish – and that some of those she interviewed saw her as someone "*who could change things.*" She wrote in her reflection, "*I feel as if I should do something for the community.*"

Challenges to a Culturally Responsive Practice

Yet Summer expressed caution in how to use what she was learning in courses as a basis for her teaching practice. "*I'd love to have students write narratives and explore their lives, but my principal will never allow us to deviate from what our grade level teams decide is best.*" Instead of advocating for practices that captured students' interest, that could sustain them through the writing process, or serve as a scaffold to teach a variety of content, Summer resisted. She blamed the administration, deferring to the collective decision-making of her 4th grade team rather than her creativity or the research she was studying.

Summer was the only teacher among her team studying to become a reading specialist; in spite of this, she still lacked a confident voice and an advocacy stance in her school community.

This was particularly evident as Summer made plans for her action research project required for one of the Capstone courses. Her initial idea was to draw on the background knowledge and lived experiences of her students as a means of developing their writing. Summer's research question was: How can I help my students become better writers by using what they already know? She narrowed this down after watching a video short about a student who completed 365 random acts of kindness in a year's time that she documented through photography and narration. What touched Summer about this video were not just the acts of kindness. Rather, she thought this would be a great way to strengthen students' narrative writing and this could be made public in a lot of different formats: movies, slideshows, info-graphics, or posters. Her goal was to have students write up their impressions of the experience, how it made them feel, and the effects these acts of kindness had on others. Students would then have a tangible artifact of their work after using writer's workshop to strengthen their writing in her classroom.

Summer constructed a literature review in preparation of her action research project, prepared an overview of the project, sent out details about the study to parents that included consent to analyze and write about students' work, and got permission from her school administration to complete this project. At this point, Summer was in her second year of Master's level studies, and her principal readily greenlit the project, confident that Summer would be able to balance preparing students for state-mandated writing tests while completing her research. In spite of this, Summer acknowledged anxiety:

The writing test was around the corner, I felt pressured to drill and kill to get them where they need to be. I know that it probably was not the best practice, but I was afraid to something different at this point. We gave a 20-day countdown to the students, where they reviewed every writing TEKS [the Texas state curricular standards]. It is intense and boy did our students work hard. Since my job is driven by the percent of kids I can get to pass, it's hard not to play along. I save projects like this [the acts of kindness writing project] for before January and after the test. I absolutely hate it. My fear of being considered a horrible teacher because I did not get 80% or better is eye twitching.

Summer had a research-based rationale for pairing writing and photographs – which she was asking students to use to document their acts of kindness – and knew they could contribute to language learning. For example, Cummins and Quiroa (2012) have discovered that photographs used as a scaffold for writing can lessen the cognitive load, freeing up space for students to write more descriptively. Luke, Tracy, and Bricker (2015) also found that the use of multimodal technology and photography "helped motivate and excite the children" (p. 34), and this inspired Summer.

In spite of this enthusiasm, Summer grappled with how to find time for students to work on their acts of kindness project. Testing pushed it aside as the fourth-grade teachers in her school decided to backload the 20 teaching days that preceded the test preparation with targeted test-taking activities. Unfortunately, this three-week period of test review fell directly in the timeframe Summer needed to collect data. She modified her acts of kindness project in two ways: she drew on some of the prewriting strategies other 4th grade teachers were using without changing her students' writing topic. So instead of having students engage in action – completing acts of kindness, documenting these through photography or other means, and then writing up an explanation of what happened, how it made them feel, and what the experience was like for the recipient of the kind act, Summer's students were left with creating bubble maps to develop their writing. Instead of drawing on photographs that demonstrated their action, students ended

Where Our Paths Crossed

up writing more abstractly about the topic, and their writing suffered. Rather than utilizing photographs they took of their own experiences, students looked online for images of kind acts and wrote down notes of what they were seeing in the images.

Summer stuck with her research project. And, after it was interrupted for several days of testing in her school, she came back to her topic. She discovered that while students demonstrated greater capacity in planning their writing, and many included *"better details in their sentences"* Summer also observed that

many were tired of writing... my kids were done. They said, 'Why are we still writing? We already took the STAAR?' [the state mandated test]. My heart broke. The excitement of using pictures was gone. I realized my students were not writing because they enjoyed it; they wrote because they had to at that point. They are not doing their best anymore.

Summer: A More Agentive Identity

One of the benefits of this kind of professional development graduate program is that the teachers from one district took all of their classes together as a cohort over a two year period; this experience engendered frank conversations in classes and a *confianza* (Moll & Gonzalez, 2004) – or mutual trust – that the teachers grew to rely on to help them manage the competing responsibilities of teacher *and* student as they completed our program. Cohort members drew on that common thread when participating in class discussions and advised one another about ways to adapt their practice to meet the needs of students while abiding by the decisions their district and school leadership placed upon them. For example, Summer expressed concern during an in-class discussion about giving students choice when writing instead of staying with a more scripted approach. Class readings suggested that choice could help students find their voice, build writing stamina, and leverage a better performance on standardized tests. But Summer's principal promoted a fairly regimented approach to student writing that limited topics.

Summer felt conflicted. She wanted to test out some of the ideas she was discovering in class readings yet worried she might lose her principal's trust if she went against his lead. Summer asked the group directly, *"Will I get in trouble? And, if it is better for the students to test out a lot of different writing genres, should I risk a reprimand?"* Those with more experience reminded Summer that she was a strong and capable teacher, that she knew her students, and that she should not let the test drive the instruction. Yet Summer's action research project suggested she still had work to do in terms of advocating for what she deemed best for her students.

Teachers studying to become literacy leaders often express tensions that can surface among peers as they transition into positions outside of the classroom, particularly if they are hired into a position of power in the school in which they have an identity as a teacher. We recommend to students they take positions in schools where they have not taught, so they can grow into their new identity as a leader without others seeing them in a former role. Some of our cohort members, however, moved into leadership positions within their schools or worked with educators at new schools whom they knew in earlier jobs. Because of this we require teachers to engage in conversations in our classes where they can practice discussing literacy research and its importance in supporting pedagogical decisions that can leverage growth in student learning. Summer found this to be valuable as she transitioned out of the classroom.

633

Interpersonal Assets

Just a few weeks into the new school year, a teacher expressed concern to Summer about low I-station (a state mandated online literacy assessment) scores among her Spanish-dominant speakers. Seeking advice from Summer, she wondered *"Where do I start? English or Spanish?"* She asked, *"What do you think we should do?"* I-station use was a state mandate, yet Summer reasoned that teachers had to balance what the program data said against effective practices for language learners. She also understood what research suggested regarding the importance of maintaining and developing a student's language or origin while helping them learn English.

It was then that Summer realized she had made the transition from teacher to leader. Drawing on what she had learned in classes, her own understanding of the district, and her lived experience as a language learner Summer responded, *"I think we need to service their Spanish first."* In telling this story Summer expressed pride in herself for *"Standing up for the kids. That's what Dr. López showed us in class, and that is what I learned from the program."* This example is important not only for the likely good it did for the students and the language as right perspective; it is evidence of growth in Summer. While a student in our program, she advocated for students faithfully in class discussions, demonstrated confidence she could help them grow as learners, and sought ways to draw on their experiences to strengthen their connection to work in school. Yet she was grappled with how to realize this kind of practice at times while she was in the classroom, particularly when confronted with decisions made by administrators and district leadership. Her more agentive stance as a reading specialist became an additional set of tools, and this shifted both her funds of identity and potential reach. She now carried expertise that could serve as a resource for other teachers, and in turn the students with whom they work. Summer is now able to see herself as that parent she'd interviewed for the community language and literacy mapping project saw her: as someone *"who could change things."* She wrote in her reflection then, *"I feel as if I should do something for the community."* It seems likely she is.

Ximena: Funds of Identity from Lived Experiences

Ximena's experience may be unique in some ways as a second-generation Latina in the United States. In many of her class papers and projects, Ximena vividly depicted her childhood along the border in Laredo, the city where she was born. She identifies as a simultaneous language learner (Genesee, 2006), growing up on both Sesame Street and Cri-Cri. Raised by a single mother who prioritized bilingualism and recognized the importance of both cultures and with family on both sides of the border, Ximena described these early influences. She recounts a childhood where she *"often traveled 'across' as native Laredoans would call it...my Mexican culture runs deep within my veins, carried through morals, beliefs, and values, and expressed through two languages, Spanish and English."* She depicts her early years as affirming, learning both languages during the early 1970s when bilingual education was proliferating after the Bilingual Education Act of 1968. Her memories are bilingual, bicultural, and she does not recount the early shaming that many other Latinx children have experienced. She describes positive linguistic and cultural experiences in both school and home, despite some of the tensions that arise from living along the border of Texas and Mexico where language is often a marker of status and is full of the complexities of generations of immigrants crossing back and forth.

Where Our Paths Crossed

Ximena's Background

During her childhood, Ximena had the support of a few key family members. Her Spanish-speaking abuelo was an early influence. She describes him as patient and kind, nurturing her inquisitive nature and responding to her constant questions. She recounts stories of him teaching her, especially in the kitchen, as he lovingly showed her how to cook traditional food. Their relationship was reciprocal; he often told her she was his greatest teacher. And what made their time together even more impressionable is that her grandfather was blind. Ximena credits her abuelo with instilling in her the understanding that learning is natural, social, and magical.

After high school, Ximena attended college and became a bilingual teacher; when she entered our graduate program, she had been a highly successful Spanish/English bilingual teacher in the greater metropolitan area for 22 years. She had married a fellow bilingual educator and together they are raising three bilingual children in the same community where they teach. Enrolling in graduate school was a dream she was ready to realize, especially since the program would be held onsite, enabling her to spend less time away from her family.

Graduate School

In her application for the graduate program, Ximena wrote about her philosophy of reading and the skills she has as a reading teacher. She also discussed the textbooks and curricular programs she utilized at her campus to teach reading. Although she discussed the foundations of reading as meaningful and the importance of exposing students to a variety of perspectives, this essay lacked personal details or references to the cultural elements of teaching. Looking back, this was strange because it is not representative of the work she produced in the program; it seems out of character. We believe this may be that prior to enrollment, Ximena imagined graduate school as an academic exercise devoid of identity and culture; as separated from her life and community.

Once enrolled in the program and trust was built with the cohort and her professors, Ximena consistently theorized about community, love, and familia through symbols and references to her bilingual and bicultural Latinidad (Latina Feminist Group, 2001) and in relationship to her teaching and pedagogy. In her first semester, Ximena shared aspects of her identity with the cohort and made connections to the research literature. In an online forum post Ximena wrote:

I was fortunate to have been raised in a bilingual home and education in a bilingual classroom. I now feel grateful that I interacted in such culture and language that I use with my students today. It has made me a stronger teacher in being able to relate and communicate with children and parents, including the undertones that are often lost in translation.

Ximena: Affirming Her Bilingual/Bicultural Identity

While Ximena was consistently confident in her bilingual and bicultural identity, the documented ways in which she evolved as a teacher and literacy leader through this program are related more to affirming her identity through published research. Ximena used research and the literature to confirm her intuitions. Though she had practiced language brokering as a child with her mother, Ximena was not aware of the term for it and the valuable connections to literacy this practice affords children from bilingual and bicultural homes (Orellana, 2001). Reading about language brokers and the various ways teachers can encourage students to bridge home and school with translingual practices (Pacheco, Daniel, Pray & Jimenez, 2019) and translation work (Martinez, Orellana, Pacheco & Carbone, 2008) made sense to her and confirmed her childhood practices as well as her linguistic and literate strengths.

Although the research literature affirmed Ximena's bilingual, bicultural, and biliterate practices, nevertheless it was unexpected that scholars would study families such as hers. She wrote:

I learned that culturally diverse experiences from families and communities such as my own were valued and studied by researchers such as Norma Gonzalez, Luis Moll, and Cathy Amanti (2005). It was quite a surprise to learn about research done on family culture and diversity, a topic that seemed almost inconsequential to me. Family diversity was something I lived, not something I expected others to write about.

And yet reading about it in the research literature helped strengthen her value and belief in connecting language practices between the school, home, and community. For example, reading Ruiz's (1984) work on language orientations resonated with Ximena and she began to use his concept of Language as Resource and Language as Right in her assignments and her discussions to describe her own practices and beliefs.

Ximena: A More Agentive Identity

Reading about her experiences in the research was affirming and another step towards her becoming an advocate for emerging bilinguals and bilingual education as well as a leader in South ISD. In the last two semesters of the program, Ximena began to express more and more how she would advocate for emerging bilinguals in the district through teacher training and community outreach. One of the most salient examples of this is in her community mapping assignment. For this project, Ximena chose to analyze an area around the elementary school where she worked. She walked and documented a two-mile radius around the school on several different occasions, starting from the school and walking outward. She explains her thinking as *"getting a sense of what the children experience…from the inner community of the school to the outer community."* She documented evidence of language and literacy resources in the defined area, such as restaurant marquees, billboards, and also the local flea market. She astutely describes the flea market as a place full of oral and traditional language and literacy practices along with some opportunities for literacy and points out the need for various other skills such as bargaining and knowing prices as you navigate the flea market. She expertly ties these skills to community cultural wealth (Yosso, 2005) and writes, *"we, as teachers, can build upon what Yosso (2005) considers their Linguistic capital by accepting and working with the students' home language and connecting them to the standard school language to help make better connections."* She also advocates for using the community mapping exercise with teachers, and vows to do so once she is in a position to provide leadership and professional development to teachers. She urges:

We need to look deeper into the individual students we are working with. What is their home situation? What seems to be the distractors or inhibitors that are keeping each individual student from academic success? Our campus continuously falls to the bottom of the district list. I am starting to see that some of the missing links are that we lack connection to the students' stories, to their culture, to their community. We lack the attention and "care" that is necessary to focus better on our students. I believe this com-

Where Our Paths Crossed

munity mapping has helped me reflect more carefully on how we can better serve our students and their families... I feel that including the community and family would help nurture our students beyond just the mind. It would help them become part of a larger community, which builds meaning and confidence for who they are and what they are striving to make better. A campus-wide community mapping would help increase conversations about how we can build a better, more inclusive relationship.

The community mapping project helped teachers create connections to the community and to see their school communities through asset-driven eyes. This assignment also connected to their own lives and experiences, opening up conversations about teachers' own neighborhoods, language and literacy practices growing up.

A common practice in Mexican and Mexican-American households is to play the *Loteria* game. As part of their oral presentations at the end of the program, students are urged to use a metaphor or symbolism to represent their journeys. In her presentation, Ximena used the traditional Mexican *Loteria* cards and images to represent her identity along with a picture book about the game called Playing Loteria (Colato-Lainez, 2005). Using la mano (the hand) *Loteria* card, she spoke about her alignment with Vygotsky and social constructivists because she believes students require a supportive and interactive environment in order to learn, much like a family or community structure. She referred to the Mexican proverb, "Dime con quién andas y te digo quién eres" (Tell me who you are with and I will tell you who you are) to illustrate the support she received along her journey as an educator. She wrote:

this dicho is intended to help us be mindful of the company we keep. I can see who I am today because of those who held my hand along my walk through life. As a literacy specialist and leader, I can hold the hands of students and teachers by guiding them through learning about reading.

As a bilingual Latina, Ximena recognizes the importance of affirming students' and teachers' mulitilingual identities and is committed to advocating for her community. Moreover, this shows her evolution as an educator, that she is taking up the call to advocate for students and teachers in her leadership role by guiding them to enact affirming practices with their emerging bilinguals.

While some teachers decide they do not want to become literacy coaches working with adults and instead prefer to continue to work with children as interventionists, Ximena was clear that she felt a duty to share her experiences and knowledge to teach others how to reach students, specifically bilingual and immigrant children. Thus, she created a professional development module for teachers in the district to incorporate interactive strategies for oral language development of young emerging bilinguals, particularly recent arrivals, in bilingual education programs. She described her aims to build capacity with teachers so they can serve emerging bilinguals with this statement. She stated:

I am in a position to coach these teachers with the right tools that include familial capital and culturally sustaining pedagogy, that I envision a more inclusive and diverse learning environment...it's about focusing on what matters to them [students] to build their sense of identity in a diverse world that includes family, friendships, and general interaction with the community that surrounds them. I look forward to guiding teachers through literacy to build on students' strengths, creating strong identities, and eventually helping to build agency to become active participants in their own world.

Ximena uses terms from the research to bolster her ideas and experiences, while maintaining her commitment and advocacy for the community. She maintains her focus on the students and building on their strengths, but also passionately describes advocating for the community by helping teachers see the assets in the Latinx community. While Ximena began the program by writing in her entrance essay about what she could do and her individual philosophy, she exits the program as a leader with agency, a strong advocate for emerging bilinguals; her community.

SOLUTIONS AND RECOMMENDATIONS

In this chapter we provided examples of language learning beliefs and pedagogies these teachers developed as a part of the professional development program aligned with a funds of identity approach. For example, after reading research about the importance of drawing and visualizing to help students craft more vibrant descriptions in their writing, Summer sought ways to incorporate photography and art in her teaching practice. She engaged in an action research project on visual arts and language. Through this work, Summer confirmed that photography and other visual supports were especially valuable for emerging bilinguals. Her experiences and findings align with research that art and photography: provided a scaffold in the writing process; helped students develop their thinking; and facilitated more detailed, impactful language in student writing. Summer, whose funds of identity included a more assimilationist stance of English acquisition reinforced by both her home and school experiences as a child, hesitated when initially adopting culturally and linguistically sustaining pedagogy. Expected to enact a scripted curriculum that valued test preparation over student engagement and creativity, she struggled at first to incorporate the kinds of practices she was studying in courses and hearing about from the other teachers in the cohort. Over time, through personal reflection, readings, and collaboration with the cohort teachers, Summer developed a more critical approach to teaching and a translingual (Canagarajah, 2012), language as right (Ruiz, 1984) approach to teaching the emerging bilinguals in her class.

Summer has moved into a leadership position within the school district since completing this study and she is no longer tied to a monolingual identity. She now enacts a more culturally and linguistically sustaining pedagogy with her students and encourages and teaches other educators to do the same. Ximena's lived experiences and funds of identity were affirmed through the research she studied in the program. While she once relied on her intuition and familiar language practices to serve her pedagogical practice of language as resource and as right (Ruiz, 1984), these were reinforced by a research base – giving her an additional layer of agency. Thus, while it may appear that there was not significant change in both cases, there was a shift for both educators. Equally valuable were the sources of these changes, which we surmise are the direct result of shifting funds of identity that arose through new understandings, tools, artifacts and interactions within this professional development program, engaging with a culturally rich and sustaining research base, reflecting on their own funds of identity, and interacting with each other in a supportive environment. We believe these shifts are instrumental in the development of agentive language and literacy leaders who have the power to positively impact the language and literacy practices of language learners and immigrant students.

Where Our Paths Crossed

FUTURE RESEARCH DIRECTIONS

While the field of education and language education specifically are becoming more diverse and less centered on whiteness (Chávez-Moreno, 2019; Sleeter, 2017), there remain critical areas of study that deserve much more attention. These areas include the study of teachers of color and their identities, of shared leadership where leaders are not only defined as administrators, and of how to prepare teachers to work with language learners and immigrants. There is a continuing need for more research on teachers of color and such research must include the heterogeneity both within and across categories. Moreover, as more research is conducted with and by Latinas, the field of education will benefit from a more robust understanding of the identities of Latinx teachers and how their funds of identity impact their pedagogical decisions. We also must redefine leadership and begin to study the multiple ways educators demonstrate leadership in their communities. Finally, we recognize the need for more studies on preparing educators to work with emerging bilinguals and we plan to extend this research into communities and classrooms to measure the effect of these teachers' practices in this way.

CONCLUSION

One of the implications that surfaced as a result of this study was the necessity of a safe space for teachers to develop their funds of identity where they are not flooded with critique or judgment from others. As part of a larger cohort community, Ximena and Summer engaged in persistent conversations about language diversity, pedagogical efficacy, and how these intersect with the mandates of a classroom's duties and obligations. A contributing factor to Summer's burgeoning agency and ideological clarity is directly related to her interactions and conversations with other teachers in the cohort such as Ximena who had more experience in multilingual contexts and were working in bilingual programs. Thus, the support of the cohort allowed teachers from various program models to imagine the possibilities, exchange ideas, and plan for translingual instruction with each other without judgment.

In addition, Latinas and teachers from any ethnic group will have similarities and differences in their experiences, practices, and identities. This must be acknowledged and taken into consideration when planning professional learning experiences. By including assignments and practices that incorporate funds of identity in our professional development program, teachers were able to develop ideological clarity (Bartolomé & Balderrama, 2001) and became more agentive advocates for their students, in this case Latinx students and emerging bilinguals. Through their own development and leadership, both Summer and Ximena, themselves from historically subjugated positions, and although different, developed awareness and commitment to provide positive educational experiences and to foster and support translingual practices with emerging bilinguals. In this way, their paths crossed. Their early lives and teaching experiences created different funds of identity, and towards the end of the two-year professional development program, they converged as they both expressed ideological clarity on affirming language as a resource and a right for emerging bilinguals.

ACKNOWLEDGMENT

This research was supported by a Texas State University Research Enhancement Grant.

REFERENCES

Bartolomé, L., & Balderrama, M. (2001). The need for educators with political andideological clarity. In R. Maria de la Luz & J. Halcon (Eds.), *The Best for our children: Critical perspectives on literacy for Latino students* (pp. 48–64). New York: Teachers College Press.

Bogdan, R., & Biklen, S. (1992). *Qualitative research for education: An introduction to theory and methods* (2nd ed.). Boston: Allyn and Bacon.

Canagarajah, S. (2012). *Translingual practice: Global Englishes and cosmopolitan relations.* New York, NY: Routledge. doi:10.4324/9780203073889

Chávez-Moreno, L. C. (2019). Researching Latinxs, racism, and white supremacy in bilingual education: A literature review. *Critical Inquiry in Language Studies*, 0–20. doi:10.1080/15427587.2019.1624966

Colato-Lainez, R. (2005). *Playing Loteria.* Lanham, MD: Cooper Square Publishing.

Creswell, J. W. (2007). *Qualitative inquiry and research design choosing among five approaches* (2nd ed.). Thousand Oaks, CA: Sage.

Cummins, S., & Quiroa, R. (2012). Teaching writing for expository responses to narrative texts. *The Reading Teacher*, 65(6), 381–386. doi:10.1002/TRTR.01057

Ek, L., Machado-Casas, M., Sánchez, P., & Alanís, I. (2010). Crossing cultural borders: *La Clase Mágica* as a university-school partnership. *Journal of School Leadership*, 20(6), 820–849. doi:10.1177/105268461002000606

Flores, B. B., Clark, E. R., Claeys, L. C., & Villarreal, A. (2007). Academy for Teacher Excellence: Recruiting, preparing, and retaining Latino teachers though learning communities. *Teacher Education Quarterly*, 34(4), 53–69.

Genesse, F. (2006). *Bilingual first language acquisition in perspective.* Clevedon, UK: Multilingual Matters LTD.

Goodlad, J. I. (1988). School-university partnerships: A social experiment. *Phi Delta Kappan*, 69(3), 77–80. doi:10.1080/00228958.1988.10517847

Latina Feminist Group. (2001). Introduction. Papelitos guardados. Theorizing Latinidades through testimonio. In The Latina Feminist Group (Eds.), Telling to live: Latina feminist testimonios (pp. 1–24). Durham, NC: Duke University Press Books.

Luke, N., Tracy, K., & Bricker, P. (2015). Writing captions as a means of blending text features and digital stories. *California Reader*, 48(2), 29–35.

Martinez, R. A., Orellana, M. F., Pacheco, M., & Carbone, P. (2008). Found in Translation: Connecting Translating experiences to academic writing. *Language Arts, 85*(6), 421–431.

Merriam, S. B. (1998). *Qualitative research and case study applications in education.* San Francisco: Jossey-Bass.

Michie, G. (2017). *Same as it never was: On my (re)turn to teaching.* Keynote at the Conference on English Education (CEE) Summer Conference, Columbus, OH.

Moll, L. (Ed.). (2000). *Vygotskian perspectives on literacy research: constructing meaning through collaborative inquiry.* Cambridge, UK: Cambridge University Press.

Moll, L., Amanti, C., Neff, D., & Gonzalez, N. (1992). Funds of knowledge for teaching: Using a qualitative approach to connect homes and classrooms. *Theory into Practice, 31*(2), 132–141. doi:10.1080/00405849209543534

Moll, L., & Gonzalez, N. (2004). Engaging life: A funds of knowledge approach to multicultural education. In J. Banks & C. Banks (Eds.), *Handbook of Research on Multicultural Education* (pp. 699–715). San Francisco: Jossey-Bass.

Ordoñez–Jasis, R., & Jasis, P. (2011). Mapping literacy, mapping lives: Teachers exploring the sociopolitical context of literacy and learning. *Multicultural Perspectives, 13*(4), 189–196. doi:10.1080/152 10960.2011.616824

Orellana, M. F. (2001). The work kids do: Mexican and Central American immigrant children's contributions to households and schools in California. *Harvard Educational Review, 71*(3), 366–389. doi:10.17763/haer.71.3.52320g7n21922hw4

Pacheco, M. B., Daniel, S. M., Pray, L. C., & Jiménez, R. T. (2019). Translingual practice, strategic participation, and meaning-making. *Journal of Literacy Research, 51*(1), 75–99. doi:10.1177/1086296X18820642

Ruiz, R. (1984). Orientations in language planning. *Journal of the National Association for Bilingual Education, 8*(2), 15–34.

Slapac, A., & Kim, S. (2014). Intercultural conversations. *Kappa Delta Pi Record, 50*(1), 37–41. doi:1 0.1080/00228958.2014.871748

Slapac, A., Song, K. H., & Chasteen, C. C. (2017). Introspections on in-service teachers' intercultural responsiveness skills for English Language Learners. In K. Jones & J. Mixon (Eds.), *Intercultural Responsiveness in the Second Language Learning Classroom* (pp. 181–201). Hershey, PA: IGI Global. doi:10.4018/978-1-5225-2069-6.ch011

Sleeter, C. E. (2017). Critical race theory and the whiteness of teacher education. *Urban Education, 52*(2), 155–169. doi:10.1177/0042085916668957

Texas State University. (n.d.). Retrieved from: https://www.education.txstate.edu/ci/reading-education-masters/aspects/comprehensive-exams.html

Trent, J., & Lim, J. (2010). Teacher identity construction in school-university partnerships: Discourse and practice. *Teaching and Teacher Education, 26*(8), 1609–1618. doi:10.1016/j.tate.2010.06.012

Valenzuela, A. (1999). *Subtractive Schools: U. S.-Mexican Youth and the Politics of Caring*. Albany, NY: SUNY Press.

Vygotsky, L. (1986). *Thought and Language*. Cambridge, MA: MIT Press.

Yosso, T. J. (2005). Whose culture has capital? A critical race theory discussion of community cultural wealth. *Race, Ethnicity and Education*, *8*(1), 69–91. doi:10.1080/1361332052000341006

ADDITIONAL READING

Compton-Lilly, C., Papoi, K., Venegas, P., Hamman, L., & Schwabenbauer, B. (2017). Intersectional identity negotiation: The case of young immigrant children. *Journal of Literacy Research*, *49*(1), 115–140. doi:10.1177/1086296X16683421

Dunsmore, K., Ordoñez-Jasis, R., & Herrera, G. (2013). Welcoming their worlds: Rethinking literacy instruction through community mapping. *Language Arts*, *90*(5), 327–338.

Kohli, R. (2018). Lessons for Teacher Education: The role of critical professional development in teacher of color retention. *Journal of Teacher Education*, *70*(1), 39–50. doi:10.1177/0022487118767645

Lara, G. P., & Fránquiz, M. E. (2014). Latino bilingual teachers: Negotiating the figured world of masculinity. *Bilingual Research Journal*, *2*(38), 207–227.

Lazar, A. M., & Smith, P. R. (2018). *Schools of promise for multilingual students: Transforming literacies, learning, and lives*. Teachers College Press.

Morita-Mullaney, T. (2018). The intersection of language and race among English Learner (EL) leaders in desegregated urban midwest schools: A LangCrit narrative study. *Journal of Language, Identity, and Education*, *17*(6), 371–387. doi:10.1080/15348458.2018.1494598

Paris, D., & Alim, H. S. (2017). *Culturally sustaining pedagogies: Teaching and learning for justice in a changing world*. New York, NY: Teachers College Press.

Saavedra, C. M., & Salazar Perez, M. (2012). Chicana and Black Feminisms: *Testimonios* of theory, identity, and multiculturalism. *Equity & Excellence in Education*, *45*(3), 430–443. doi:10.1080/10665 684.2012.681970

Yosso, T. J. (2005). Whose culture has capital? A critical race theory discussion of community cultural wealth. *Race, Ethnicity and Education*, *8*(1), 69–91. doi:10.1080/1361332052000341006

KEY TERMS AND DEFINITIONS

Community Mapping: Documenting the language and literacy resources in a community.
Confianza: Mutual trust.
Emerging Bilinguals: Students whose dominant language is not English; they are developing bilingualism and may be participating in either a bilingual or ESL program.

Funds of Identity: One's life experiences and histories that form their identity at any given point in time.

Ideological Clarity: Understanding one's beliefs and practices related to education and the educational system.

Language as Resource: The belief that a students' home language is an important resource for learning.

Language as Right: The belief that a student has the right to learn and develop their home language(s).

Latinidad: One's identity and cultural practices around being Latinx.

Loteria: A traditional game played in Mexico and Spanish speaking Latin America that is similar to Bingo. The images represent cultural ideas and lessons.

This research was previously published in Beyond Language Learning Instruction; pages 305-331, copyright year 2020 by Information Science Reference (an imprint of IGI Global).

Chapter 34

Culturally Responsive Teaching and Inclusion for Online Students With Exceptionalities and Other Needs

York Williams
West Chester University, USA

ABSTRACT

Teaching learning-diverse students, English learners (Els), and students with disabilities has become of paramount importance as it relates to each unique student's need, directed by an Individual Education Plan (IEP), 504, English Language Plan, and related services, especially for those students served primarily under the Individual Disabilities Education Act. The students' unique cultural and familial needs also become important used to promote achievement in both the F2F and online educational setting, inclusive of multiple intelligences (MI), learning styles, and appropriate differentiated instruction. As such, the purpose of this chapter is to examine the learners and the diversity that they bring to the online learning community so that instructors may prepare culturally responsive and inclusive pedagogy and online universally designed learner-centered (UDLC) and differentiated practices that include them beyond their disability or exceptionality and to become culturally responsive instructional leaders (CRIL).

INTRODUCTION

As online teaching transforms what higher education looks like for many students, so too are the students transforming how they learn and together practitioners are examining what learning looks like for all students. Especially important are some of the learning diverse students, many who bring with them diverse learning and instructional needs that require accommodations and supports within the online and or distance educational classroom (Hardy & Huang, 2011; Heitner & Jennings, 2016). The literature has rarely engaged what culturally responsive or inclusive teaching and pedagogy looks like for online

DOI: 10.4018/978-1-6684-4507-5.ch034

Copyright © 2022, IGI Global. Copying or distributing in print or electronic forms without written permission of IGI Global is prohibited.

learners who possess special education, linguistically diverse needs and or exceptionalities (Woodley, Hernandez, Parra & Negash, 2017). Additionally, instructional practices must be constructive and co-create a learning environment that entails more than just break out rooms (BORS) and synchronous and asynchronous instruction; but instead must include sacred spaces where learning diverse students from culturally and linguistically diverse (CLD) and exceptional backgrounds can garner the supports that they need in order to be more fully included within all aspects of the online learning classroom (Taliaferro, 2011; Tan et al., 2010; Yi, 2013).

Overall, the during last decade institutions of higher education have seen an increase in online teaching platforms, many that utilize Blackboard, Moodle, D2L and now Canvas (Keengwe & Kidd, 2010). To this end, very little literature has examined the intersections of the learner with this evolving technology including their 'special needs' that are often encapsulated within legal parameters such as the American Disabilities Act (ADA), Section 504 and at the K-12 level, the Individual Disabilities Education Act (IDEA). Students who possess these learning differences are often presented with supports for services and face to face (F2F) assistance across their K-21 experiences that focus on the tools, not the conceptual features of the online classroom space. As such, it is not uncommon for many students with learning disabilities at the higher education or post-secondary education level to avoid online learning altogether for fear of the unknown (Hardin & Huang, 2011). However, given the advent of K-12 online cyber schools and now pop-up online district programs, each has in kind also produced a large number of technologically equipped online learners who also possess learning-diverse needs, in addition to learning disabilities (Chuang, 2016; Hardin & Huang, 2016; Heitner & Jennings, 2016; Sleeter, 2012).

Purpose of the Chapter

Teaching students with disabilities has become of paramount importance as it relates to each unique student's need, directed by an Individual Education Plan (IEP) and related services under the IDEA (2004). The Act also recognizes students' legal right to a Free Appropriate Public Education (FAPE) and their need to demonstrate Adequate Yearly Progress (AYP) consistent with specific and measurable goals as indicated in the IEP. Even within the IEP, the type of instruction and pedagogy used to increase student achievement is of the utmost importance for students with both exceptional and special needs. The effectiveness of the IEP also hinges upon the types of family and community collaboration beyond the students' disability, an area of study that is commonly overlooked (Wang, 2007; Williams, 2013). Hence, on this conceptual schema, the students' unique cultural and familial needs become paramount in promoting achievement in both the F2F and online educational setting, inclusive of multiple intelligences (MI), learning styles and appropriate differentiated instruction. Students with English Learner (El) needs must also be given culturally competent and inclusive consideration within an online learning context. As such, the purpose of this chapter is to examine the CLD learner with exceptional needs and the diversity that they bring to the online learning community so that instructors may prepare culturally responsive and inclusive pedagogy and online Universally Designed Learner-Centered (UDLC) practices that include them, beyond their disability or exceptionality (Rose & Meyer, 2002).

LITERATURE REVIEW

Students who are enrolled in both K-12 and post-secondary educational contexts that include online learning in distance education courses commonly encounter not only transitional obstacles with second language acquisition, but also understanding pragmatic and social internet cues, commonly set up in a typical classroom environment. Whereas the learner may not have traditional experiences with asking questions, cueing, posting, and engaging discussions because of the need for BICS and CALP and more experiences with academic language and in some cases, social language supports (Tan, Nabb, Aagard, and Kioh, 2010; Yi, 2013). The online teaching and learning environment must build supports that are both learning and linguistically inclusively diverse. Lastly, additional considerations of difference must be interrogated that fall across socio-economic status including age, race, level of education, gender, sexual orientation and more (Ke and Kwak, 2013).

Some online learners who have attended high-needs urban schools may not have experienced equitable access to online teaching, instruction and or technology tools commonly associated with the emerging field of distance education (Chaung, 2016). As such, the higher education instructor must assess, ask questions, probe, include beyond observable barriers of difference and engage in more cultural digging in order to unearth the learning curves and differences that these students bring to the online learning environment. Variables that impact the effectiveness of the online learning experience falls across learners at different ages, level of education given how they completed their high school graduation requirements, how long they have attended school prior to matriculating in the online learning environment, resources to software, online learning coaches and the level of motivation and or reluctance with respect to the online learning environment and more (Ke & Kwak, 2013; Sleeter, 2012). Instructors must engage Habits of Mind about the nature of the learners in order to effectively include him or her into the online classroom and or program overall (Sleeter, 2012; Taliaferro, 2011).

According to Tan et al. (2010) while Western and Eastern cultures differ as much between their own subcultures as they do each other, such as when international students begin taking classes in countries different from their home countries, they often face learning challenges. These challenges can become complicated by a lack of knowledge, understanding of the values and language of the teaching culture, and strong values, attitudes and perceptions of their own (2010). Overall, some of these gaps in learning and social-cultural contexts can indeed create wider gaps in online learning and student engagement. On this view, students who are newly immigrated and those who have limited experiences in North America as K-12 students may experience some cultural dissonance as they not only grapple with the commands of the English language, but also how it is utilized within an online learning environment (Tan et al., 2010).

Tapanse, Smith and White (2009) maintain that changes in culture occur faster in the outer layers, labeled practices, than in the core or cultural values, which represent the deepest manifestation of culture. Core cultural values are acquired early in life and are transmitted through generations. Some examples of this difference include cultural values are: good vs. evil, safe vs. dangerous, permitted vs. forbidden, logical vs. paradoxical, rational vs. irrational, among others. Given the diversity of the learner in the online context, instructors will have to interrogate these perceived differences, beyond race, language, disability and sexual orientation, in order to co-create a culturally inclusive online learning environment. Some online activities may include one to one meetings, Mini-Wikis, live sessions, mini-chats and online drop-ins and more that can assist and support the learning diverse and CLD online learner.

According to Heitner and Jennings (2016), cultural differences between faculty and their students can create important challenges that affect the quality and efficacy of online teaching and learning. The authors maintain that faculty who teach online who understand and value culturally responsive pedagogy and have the knowledge and skills to implement best practices in meeting the needs of diverse learners will enhance both teaching. The study used a combined pilot group sample was comprised of 47 completed surveys. The authors reported that the first phase was creating and piloting an assessment instrument for online faculty members designed to measure their knowledge and value of culturally responsive teaching and their use of culturally responsive practices in teaching and advising students of color, military students, LGBTQ students, religious minority students, and international students. The second phase involved administering the instrument via Survey Monkey Pro to a larger sample of online faculty to identify their culturally responsive teaching knowledge and practice and examine differences in knowledge about and value of culturally responsive teaching and use of culturally responsive practices by education sector and degree level taught (p. 59). The instrument the authors created for the study is comprised of statements rated on a 5-point Likert- type scale that focused on awareness of various issues, the extent to which online faculty consider, value, and address culturally responsive teaching in their work.

The authors found no significant between group differences in subscale and overall scores by sector, degree level taught, and gender. The sample was too small to examine differences by other demographic variables. However, the findings are reported as consistent with Culturally Responsive Pedagogy or Culturally Responsive Teaching while creating equal opportunity for academic success for students from diverse cultural backgrounds in the online higher education environment, and acknowledging students' diverse backgrounds, prior knowledge, learning preferences, and experiences to enhance the process of teaching and learning. The authors maintain that partial results have important implications for faculty training, professional development, mentoring, and support. Faculty who teach online who understand and value culturally responsive pedagogy and have the knowledge and skills to implement best practices in meeting the needs of diverse learners will enhance both teaching and learning (p. 68).

Ke and Kwak (2013) suggest that the online learner population in American institutions of higher education is diverse in age and ethnicity. The increased use of web-based education has stretched the scope of the learner population from a homogenous profile of residential students between the ages of 18–24 to one that is intergenerational with a growing number of culturally and linguistically diverse and specifically African American students pursuing college degrees. Ke and Kwak further suggest that there is a concern that minority or older online learners may be disadvantaged online. However, prior research on whether and how culture and age influence online learning and participation is still limited. The authors' mixed-method study examined whether online learning interaction participation, perception, and learning satisfaction would be consistent across varied age and ethnicity groups.

Data were collected via a quantitative content analysis with online interaction transcripts, a comprehensive online learning experience questionnaire, and interviewing. Quantitative data were examined to extract the potential relationships between learners' characteristics and their online interactions and perceptions. Qualitative interviewing gathered learners' experiences and perceptions to consolidate and enrich the interpretation of the quantitative findings. The sample was comprised of 392 students enrolled in 28 online courses at a major university in the United States from across multiple sections of graduate and undergraduate courses in disciplines of nursing, education, business, liberal arts, and sciences. The authors utilized transcript analysis as a dominant data collection method. The survey results indicated that age had a positive and significant relationship with learners' time spent on online learning activities (Pearson r = .21, p < .01). The survey results also indicated that online learners' education levels significantly correlated with the self-reported time commitment toward online learning activities.

The authors report that neither the survey result nor the online discussion transcript analysis indicated a significant correlation between learners' minority/ethnic status and their time-commitment or performance of online discussions and when interviewed most CLD online learners described the intergenerational interactions with their older or younger peers as valuable. The authors also highlighted that quite a few students who spoke English as a second language disclosed high-degree forbearance to cross-cultural situations. However, the finding on the lower degree of satisfaction held by minority students toward the web-based distance education was reported as consistent with related findings that Hispanic students were more disadvantaged online when compared to Caucasian students. The authors maintain that this finding provides empirical evidence to support a critical proposition that the online learning environment should be adaptive or inclusive to support diverse ethnic/cultural group of learners (Ke & Kwak, 2013).

According to Walter (2018), educators must begin the journey of culturally responsive teaching through understanding of who students are and why they operate in the world, and then making decisions about what will be learned based on this information. Across various disciplines and educational settings, this approach is much more student-driven and culturally relevant to students than the more curricular-driven idea of multicultural education, even as this theme relates to music, art and other non-academic subjects. Walter maintains that culturally responsive teaching fundamentally changes what teachers do, because teachers' knowledge of the cultural legacies of themselves and their students can influence the delivery of music content as well as students' ability to gain knowledge, skills, and appropriate dispositions in school environments.

According to Zhang Wu (2017), as the implementer of Culturally and Linguistically Responsive (CLR) pedagogy, the teacher takes the central role in the entire process. Although the curriculum may be dictated by the school system, teachers teach it. To provide quality education that is responsive to students' cultural and linguistic needs, it is important for teachers to adopt a CLR ideology that values diverse cultures and languages as resource. Hollie maintains that educators must strive to become responsive to a variety of students' needs through the use of a creative student-centered pedagogies that transcend race, language, income, gender and nationality (2012). To this end, CLR becomes CRT with the focus on the learner, his needs, strengths and more salient features that encapsulate difference.

Culturally responsive teaching also engages learners in all education contexts even in the flipped classroom. The design practices in flipping the online classroom occurs through creating an environment that acknowledges, celebrates, and builds upon the cultural capital that learners and teachers bring to the online classroom (Woodley, Hernandez, Parra & Negash, 2017). Pedagogy focuses on actively engaging learners in both the construction and teaching of the online classroom, where educators become the active coaches and participants with their students in learning how they learn best. This practice also supports didactic teaching and learning across learners with diverse learning and educational needs.

Learner Diversity and Beyond Difference

Banks et al. (2001) identifies the role that culture plays in education through curriculum and culturally responsive teaching and home school partnerships. Culturally responsive teaching is often understood as a response to traditional curricular and instructional methods that have often been ineffective for students of color, immigrant children, and students from lower socioeconomic families. Culturally responsive family collaboration entails understanding the strengths and needs of students and families and how these needs may be met through dismantling policies and practices that exclude them from fully benefiting from the home school partnership. Culturally responsive teaching in class and online calls attention to schooling norms developed with White middle-class values and expectations that are privileged, while other cultural, racial, and economic histories and community backgrounds are overlooked or degenerated (Varus, 2006).

Rogoff (2003) maintains that culture is complex and dynamic. Culture is much more than holidays, foods, and customs. It reflects our beliefs, how we learn, what we value, and the ways we interact with others. Nor is culture static or unitary. More simply put, students and their families do not just have one culture, but rather multiple cultures. Some views of culture tend to stereotype individuals and box them into categorical identities (e.g., poor black, immigrant, learning-disabled, Latino low-achieving student). A comprehensive definition of culture must include variables across race, ethnicity, language, sexual orientation, age, SES, disability and ability. In order for schools to more competently include and plan for students who may come from non-traditional homes and backgrounds, they must create a safe-space and allies within the school building that confront the "one-size-fits all" paradigmatic view (Williams, 2014).

Culturally responsive family collaboration includes the pedagogy that Gay (2000; 2002) defines within the hallmark of culturally responsive teaching (CRT). Culturally responsive teaching is using the cultural knowledge, prior experiences, and performance styles of diverse students to make learning more appropriate and effective for them. According to Gay, CRT entails meeting the needs of diverse students by relating pedagogy and practice to their strengths and needs. Gay (2000) also describes culturally responsive teaching as having these characteristics:

1. CRT acknowledges the legitimacy of diverse cultures across language, dispositions, habits, attitudes and lifestyles.
2. CRT builds upon collaborative partnerships between the home, school and community of the student.
3. CRT entails learning styles and differences.
4. CRT entails diversities of one's self and others, beyond tolerance.
5. CRT incorporates multicultural literatures, media, artifacts, religions, topics and other values associated with the culture of discussion in order to invoke meaningful dialogue.

For the online classroom to become the primary source of culturally responsive collaboration, it must adopt the aforementioned framework in addition to understanding the unique role that 'learning disability' and ability plays in the lives of students who are eligible for special education, English Learners (Els) services, and/or gifted education (Ford, Grantham & Whiting, 2008; Williams, 2008). All instructors (teachers, counselors, principals, assistants, behavior specialists and more) need to become culturally responsive, through adopting CRT pedagogy and practices, in order to meet the needs of students with special education needs beyond the disability (Banks 2004; Grant, Elsbree & Fondrie, 2004; Gay, 2004; Nieto & Bode, 2008).

According to Bode (2005), Multicultural education encompasses theories and practices that strive to promote equitable access and rigorous academic achievement for students from all diverse groups, so that they can work toward social change. As a process of educational reform in PK-12 schools, higher education, and increasingly in out-of-school contexts, multicultural education challenges oppression and bias of all forms, and acknowledges and affirms the multiple identities that students bring to their learning. A common theme that researchers of multicultural education underscore is that to maintain its critical analysis of power, multicultural education must be constructed within its history and roots in the civil rights movement. Banks has historically advanced a definition of multicultural education as a broad concept and extrapolated on five dimensions (2004). He formulated the five specific dimensions as *content integration, knowledge construction process, prejudice reduction, equity pedagogy, and empowering school culture and social structure* (2004).

Content integration focuses on the infusion of various cultures, ethnicities, and other identities as encapsulated and represented in the k-12 curriculum. The knowledge construction process happens when students engage in critiquing the social positioning of groups through the ways that knowledge is presented, for example in discussing affirmative action policies for historically under-represented minority students in science and medicine. Prejudice reduction entails the praxis of lessons and activities that educators implement to develop inviting and positive images of ethnic minorities so as to improve group relations across various social systems. Equity pedagogy entails modifying instructor's teaching and instructional styles with the focus on promoting academic achievement and excellence for all students. Finally, empowering school culture occurs when the school culture and organization engage in a self-examination of reflective practices with the intent to restructure institutional practices that create barriers for some student groups and particularly CLD students (Banks, 2004). Bode notes that while highlighting the interrelatedness of the five dimensions Banks promotes deliberate attention to each. Additionally, there is a need for the aforementioned theoretical pedagogical approaches to be implemented with fidelity for online learning diverse students who possess special education and ESL learning needs and who come from CLD backgrounds.

LEARNING DIVERSE STUDENTS: SPECIAL EDUCATION AND UNIVERSAL DESIGN AND LEARNING

Instructing learning-diverse students has remained important even under the Every Student Succeeds Act (ESSA) enacted in 2015. Here, students' educational and legal right to the best public school education consistent with their IEP should be driven by High Leverage Practices (HLP) that are used to increase student achievement. The effectiveness of instruction is interwoven with strong student, home and teacher collaboration beyond the students' disability. Overall, students with identified specific learning disabilities benefit not only from rigorous and goal-centered instruction driven by their PLAAFP and learning goals, but also inclusive of CRT and pedagogy beyond the disability, embedded with consistent and culturally responsive family and teacher to teacher collaboration. This involves truly understanding students who have identified learning and other disabilities served under IDEA, along with understanding their various needs and the roles of their classroom teacher.

Teaching students with special needs online and F2F entails teaching to the identified students' needs in order to increase academic achievement, social/life skills, and character. Much of this instruction is driven by specific goals found in the student's IEP. The role of special education became paramount partly as a result of the American Disabilities Education Act's (1990) limited scope to protect the educational rights of students with disabilities within general education settings. Section 504 of The Rehabilitation Act (1973) provides protections for students with Other Health Impairments (OHI) that are not directly covered under IDEA. Students served under Section 504 are eligible for special accommodations to support their learning across educational contexts. One recent example of an implemented special education accommodation is called Response to Intervention. Students at the college level may also carry ADA and Section 504 protections with them to the online learning environment.

Under the Response to Instruction and Intervention (RtII) model, and using a tiered process of intervention in sequential stages, select students' learning needs are targeted intensively in cycles throughout the school year in order to further evaluate how and to what degree they are able to respond and achieve based on this model of instruction (Deno et al., 2009; Fuchs. Mock, Morgan and Young, 2003; Werts, Lambert and Carpenter, 2009). This methodology has decreased the number of students that might have blindly been evaluated and qualified for special education services based on an evaluation without first attempting evidenced based interventions (IDEA, 2004). Special educators must be trained in various teaching areas such as lesson planning design and Universal Design, which will give all students with disabilities equal access to the general curriculum in inclusive classrooms or self-contained settings. But no matter the venue, F2F or online, students with disabilities have a right to a FAPE and to make AYP across all indicators whether these indicators are listed as specific and measurable goals within the IEP or become special considerations of the IEP team. In higher education, under section 504 and ADA, students still have a right to supports necessary to enable them to make progress while accessing the college curriculum and activities. Culturally responsive online teaching entails creating an environment of Universal Design and Learning (UDL) for the student who presents with learning difficulties and includes differentiation.

The concept of UDL has been considered one of the most widely used instructional designs that construct a framework that addresses learner variability by minimizing barriers in the curriculum and CCSS. Through the use of multiple means of representation, engagement and expression, students have multiple tiers of content at their disposal. Lowrey, Hollingshead and Bishop (2017) note that there are however various benefits associated with the use of the UDL framework. Some benefits include teacher-reported increases in teacher efficacy, the efficacy of instruction, and the self-efficacy in reaching diverse learners (Benton-Borghi & Chang, 2012). In this narrative inquiry study, the authors collected stories from general education teachers. Semi -structured interview questions were designed using both UDL and narrative inquiry literature. Four themes emerged across all participants' stories: (a) designing for learner variability, (b) talking about inclusion, (c) teaming fosters success, and (d) differing descriptions of UDL. All of the teachers shared stories about the ways in which the UDL framework allowed them to address various students' needs, provide options, and develop plans to overcome barriers in instruction. Designing for learner variability was a consistent finding across participants and emergent themes which was a primary component of UDL.

Tomlinson (2000) maintains that differentiation consists of the efforts of teachers to respond to variance among learners in the classroom. This pedagogy entails teachers reaching out to students or small groups to vary his or her teaching method in order to create the best learning experience possible (representation, engagement and expression) while differentiating instruction. Accordingly, teachers can differentiate at least four classroom elements based on student readiness, interest, or learning profile: (1) content--what the student needs to learn or how the student will get access to the information; (2) process--activities in which the student engages in order to make sense of or master the content; (3) products--culminating projects that ask the student to rehearse, apply, and extend what he or she has learned in a unit; and (4) learning environment. This may be done with success in an online environment.

Manochehr (2006) suggests that electronic learning (e-learning) is an evolving dynamic and rapidly changing educational opportunity that is the product of advanced information technology environments. E-learning typically refers to using electronic applications and processes to learn which can be done through differentiation in an online teaching and learning environment. These strategies across process, product and readiness can include web-based learning, computer based learning, virtual classrooms and digital collaboration. For example, access to learning via CD-Rom with multimedia capabilities, satellite TV, extranet, internet and intranet can be part of a differentiated lesson. Aspects of online differentiation can be utilized to enhance access to instruction and content for CLD and learning diverse students. As such, differentiating online using various modes of technology integration through e-learning will soon play an essential role at all levels of education from primary school to university.

English Learners and Online Learning

To know language is to know its use in both academic and everyday use. To know language assumes one has the ability to move in and out of contexts where language is used freely and where one also has the ability to be linguistically diverse and ambidextrous. Within the context of online instruction and classroom practice this concept means that instructors must understand that Basic Interpersonal Skills ("BICS") and Cognitive Academic Language Proficiency ("CALP") imply a need for the English Learners ("El") to develop competence and use over a period of time, and not just overnight even considering the convenience of online learning.

For Els BICS entail language skills needed in social situations and includes a day-to-day language needed to interact socially with other people. English learners employ BIC skills when they are on the playground, in the lunch room, on the school bus, at parties, playing sports and talking on the telephone. The CALP entails academic language acquisition which isn't just the understanding of content area vocabulary but CALP includes skills such as comparing, classifying, synthesizing, evaluating, and inferring (Hymes, 1972). Additionally, academic language tasks are context reduced. Information is read from a textbook or presented by the teacher and as a student gets older the context of instruction may become more familiar.

According to Watkins-Goffman and Cummings (1997), the fact that everyday language is different from academic language means that the EL uses a relatively small set of High Frequency and academic words instead of the full range of the English Vocabulary. Additionally, there is a difference in the lexicon and vocabulary Els use vs native English speakers. There are a lot of words in academic language and everyday language and this can present a challenge for Els. Grammatically we use more structured sentence formation and use of active and passive voice in academic language rather than simple everyday language as used in social dialogue. As such, Els will need more time with access to the common core as this relates to not only my own classroom, but also other teachers classrooms in K-12. The authors maintain that we need to make the distinction between everyday use of language and academic language skills since oftentimes teachers may assume that the EL can access the curriculum. They also suggest that most often Els need more time since for academic language they need more time to catch up; possibly up to 5 years, for students to catch up to the academic aspects of language use whereas native speakers of English are usually able to making bigger gains whereas the El student is still playing catch up.

In Dell Hymes' seminal work in ESL "Models of the Interaction of Language and Social Life" he lays out the groundwork for the theories of how language is used in speaking contexts (1975). This adds to this paper around the everyday use of language for Els. Hymes article overall supports his major theoretical concepts focused what he calls a SPEAKING model which includes eight sociolinguistic rules: Situation, Participants, Ends (i.e., goals and outcomes), Acts, Key (i.e., tone), Instrumentalities (e.g., spoken and written), Norms, and Genre (Hymes, 1972). Commonly used as a tool, this hallmark work was used in the academy by researchers to systematically document how people behave in a speech community, which he defines a community as sharing rules for the conduct and interpretation of speech, and rules for the interpretation of at least one linguistic variety. This model has implications for the El as an online learner. The language context should be differentiated and rich so as to support levels of language acquisition. Content should be student-centered and surveys and more activities offered at the beginning of the course to determine if there are Els and learning diverse students within the online learning environment and at what level of comfort is their proficiency level (See Table 1). Such activities noted in Table 1 might become part of a discussion board assignment, a wiki, an online newsletter communication tool or more student-centered and diverse-learning driven pedagogies used to include CLD learners. Finally, multi-modal assessments across second languages can allow learners to develop levels of comfort and familiarity with the content within the online learning environment while also assessing for their knowledge, without fear of failure.

Table 1. Illustrates a 3-point matrix used to explore online student's diversity

Number One	Number Two	Number Three
Internal and External Factors are those variables that impact the diverse students and Els as they engage in online learning. Some of these factors are beyond the students' control.	It is also important to learn about your students' backgrounds including the home, values, culture and language(s).	Understand how Cultural Factors influence how your students learn across contexts.
Some students learn English more quickly than their peers or utilize broken English in spoken and written expression which can be attributed to any number of these factors.	Ask questions about where they come from? • Family • Languages • Cultural Practices and Values	Consider the notion of gender: • Masculinity vs Femininity • Gender roles and stereotypes
Internal Factors • Age • Personality • Motivation	Engage the online student in their first language or try to understand their use of figurative language as much as possible • Take a Spanish or German class; • Learn a few words to share with the class in that student(s) language. • Respect and Value differences in language and customs.	Consider the student's self-concept: • I vs We • Collectivism vs individualism • Extended family vs immediate family • Community vs neighborhood
External Factors • Curriculum • Instruction • Cultural Status • Motivation	Culture is important • Learn your own so that you can appreciate others; • Engage others in online/hybrid classroom cultural exchanges, mini-festivals and activities that include the entire classroom. • Understand the family values and relationships and develop respect about these differences by integrating them into your classroom culture.	Consider diverse cultural traditions: • European values and customs vs non-western • Cooperative learning vs individualistic; orientations to learning; • The value in time: poly vs mono(chronic)

CONSTRUCTING CULTURALLY RESPONSIVE PEDAGOGY AND SKILLS FOR THE 21ST CENTURY ONLINE LEARNER

Taliaferro (2011) maintains that educational leadership interwoven with CRT and 21 Century technologies can enhance online instruction and teaching strategies for CLD learners, non-traditional students and those making progress in the accelerated era of high technology. The rapidly changing demographic landscape of American schools requires that school leadership preparatory programs reconceptualize their role in the preparation of successful school leaders. Accordingly, Taliaferro suggests that given the influx of diverse students attending K-12 and higher education institutions, there is a need to match this subset with twenty-first century leaders that can be culturally responsive in their approach to addressing the language and cultural barrier issues that often exist between teachers and students, including Els.

Villegas (2002) contends that it requires a broader vision, innovative strategies and bold initiatives to prepare students for this conceptual and paradigm shift as they transition from teachers to culturally responsive leaders. Villegas argues that this shift requires educators and diversity stakeholders to develop a broader vision, innovative strategies and bold initiatives to prepare students for this conceptual and paradigm shift as they transition from teachers to culturally responsive leaders. This approach also requires educators to envision their roles as culturally responsive instructional leaders who can lead with pedagogy and practices that close online learning gaps, especially considering historical and localized issues that may confront members of various ethnic and other groups (i.e. finances, geography, Wi-Fi, technology, 21st century skills etc.).

Wilson (1993) discusses the importance of understanding three key themes that underscore the conceptual framework of learning. The first theme is understanding that learning (achievement) and thinking (cognition) are also social activities, especially online, and can be structured by constant interpersonal interaction. Secondly, the resources and online learning tools or those within the particular situation can significantly impact and provide a framework for guided learning and critical thinking. Lastly, in an Erikson conceptual framework, human cognition is somewhat guided by social interaction within the environment. This becomes paramount for instructional leaders to use as a paradigmatic framework wherein differentiation, UDL and CRT are a part of the instruction. To this end, culturally responsive instructional leaders ("CRIL") should create an online learning environment that embodies student-centered teaching and learning strategies (Taliaferro, 2011).

Taliaferro suggests that by providing a contextual learning environment for students that is technological rich will provide them with the opportunity to become familiar with new technologies and be able to incorporate them on a day-to-day basis as school leaders. First, the CRIL can organize the online course around constructivist learning principles and problem based learning (Hung, Jonassen, and Liu, 2008). The Problem Based Learning (PBL) approach enhances learning by providing a highly motivational environment for acquisition of knowledge, which is well received by those who take part in it. Barrows suggest that PBL possess four important objectives: (a) structuring of knowledge for use in a clinical context; (b) development of the student's clinical reasoning processes; (c) development of self- directed learning skills and; (d) increasing the student's motivation for further learning. To this end, the online learning environment can be enhanced to provide learners who present with diverse learning styles and needs opportunities to construct meaning based on their current levels of experience so as to move forward in the learning curve given additional course objectives and learner outcomes.

Taliaferro recommends teachers or CRILs utilize strategies such as having online students work in groups of two or three within a virtual environment which can be used as way to keep students active and focused on their learning. Think-pair share is an active learning technique used in many face-to-face classes but Taliaferro notes that it is rarely used in a virtual environment. The goal is to help students organize prior knowledge, brainstorm questions, or summarize, integrate, and apply new information (p. 18). Taliaferro also suggests Diaries and Journals that can promote continuous reflection throughout the course. For example, journal entries can be self-directed or promoted by an issue, question, or experience posed by the CRIL. Critical Reflective Journals can also be shared amongst the small group who can respond to parts of each other's reflections thereby developing continuous praxis across higher order thinking domains.

Finally, the advent of social media can be a dynamic tool that allows interaction and engagement while also allowing the CLD and non-traditional student to include their unique backgrounds, cultures, heritage, language, religion and beliefs. The use of Twitter has become a popular tool of late, especially since the 2016 Presidential Election, but it may also be utilized as way to include social perspective of difference into the course (Grosseck & Holotescu, 2008). Additional web based tools can be culturally responsive such as web conferencing technologies, Google Hangout to get to know the students face to face, live classroom with Blackboard, D2L, Moodle and more (See Figure 1). Such student centered and learning platform oriented technology can work to enhance the professional and social capital necessary to strengthen diverse learning student's 21st century skills sets.

Figure 1. Illustrates level 1 and 2 activities used to promote CRT in the online classroom

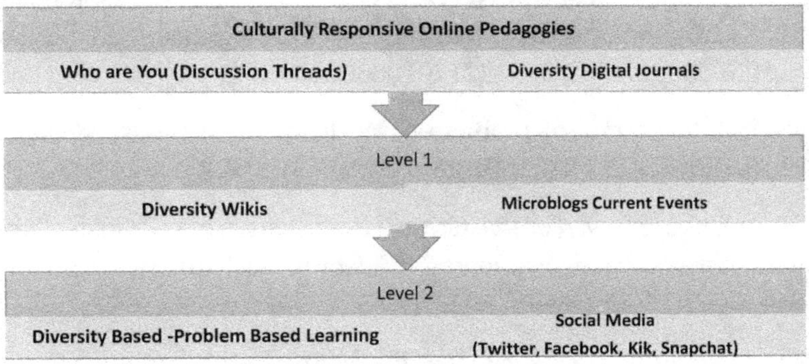

CONCLUSION

In conclusion, it does indeed take more than just access to technology to include students within your culturally inclusive online learning classroom environment. It may require the creation of a cyber community that has at its core culturally responsive and inclusive pedagogical practices that reach and teach beyond the exceptionality so as to include all learners who are in the cyber room. This chapter explored the unique needs of learning diverse students' who come from CLD and other backgrounds with a focus on including them through the process of UDL and culturally responsive pedagogies that reach beyond the disability or exceptionality (Rose & Meyer, 2002; Wang, 2007; Woodly et al., 2017).

Through culturally responsive online teaching from within the CRIL framework, the students will be able to use these technologies to communicate effectively within school community they will one day lead. Moreover, as Taliaferro notes, the infusion of online learning throughout educational training programs also allows for current students who will become CRILs to experience "virtual" learning experiences through varied teaching approaches. Online learning and teaching approaches provides the needed contextual experience for all K-college students that will enrich their course content as well as develop as culturally responsive instructional leadership lens. Part of this lens must be transformative.

Transformative learning must become a part of the CRIL which entails the process of experiential learning, critical self-reflection, and rationale discourse that can be stimulated by people, events, or changes in context which challenge the learner's basic assumptions of the world. Becoming a CRIL who embodies principles of Transformative learning leads to a new way of teaching and instructing within the online learning environment for one's CLD online learners.

REFERENCES

Americans With Disabilities Act of 1990, Pub. L. No. 101-336, 104 Stat. 328 (1990 Act, R. (1973). Section 504. *Public Law*, 93-112.

Banks, J. A. (2004). Multicultural education: Historical development, dimensions, and practices. In J. A. Banks & C. A. McGee Banks (Eds.), *Handbook of research on multicultural education* (2nd ed.; pp. 3–29). San Francisco: Jossey-Bass.

Banks, J. A., Cookson, P., Gay, G., Hawley, W. D., Irvine, J. J., Nieto, S., & Stephan, W. G. (2001). Diversity within unity: Essential principles for teaching and learning in a multicultural society. *Phi Delta Kappan*, *83*(3), 196–203. doi:10.1177/003172170108300309

Barrows, H. S. (1989). A taxonomy of problem-based learning methods. *Medical Education*, *20*(6), 481–486. doi:10.1111/j.1365-2923.1986.tb01386.x PMID:3796328

Benton-Borghi, B. H., & Chang, Y. M. (2012). Critical examination of candidates' diversity competence: Rigorous and systematic assessment of candidates' efficacy to teach diverse student populations. *Teacher Educator*, *47*(1), 2944. doi:10.1080/08878730.2011.632472

Chuang, H. H. (2016). Leveraging CRT awareness in creating web-based projects through use of online collaborative learning for pre-service teachers. *Educational Technology Research and Development*, *64*(4), 857–876. doi:10.100711423-016-9438-5

Deno, S. L., Reschly, A. L., Lembke, E. S., Magnusson, D., Callender, S. A., Windram, H., & Stachel, N. (2009). Developing a school-wide progress-monitoring system. *Psychology in the Schools*, *46*(1), 44–55. doi:10.1002/pits.20353

Ford, D. Y., Grantham, T. C., & Whiting, G. W. (2008). Culturally and linguistically diverse students in gifted education: Recruitment and retention issues. *Exceptional Children*, *74*(3), 289–306. doi:10.1177/001440290807400302

Fuchs, D., Mock, D., Morgan, P. L., & Young, C. L. (2003). Responsiveness-to-intervention: Definitions, evidence, and implications for the learning disabilities construct. *Learning Disabilities Research & Practice*, *18*(3), 157–171. doi:10.1111/1540-5826.00072

Gay, G. (2002). Preparing for culturally responsive teaching. *Journal of Teacher Education*, *53*(2), 106–116. doi:10.1177/0022487102053002003

Gay, G., & Howard, T. C. (2000). Multicultural teacher education for the 21st century. *Teacher Educator*, *36*(1), 1–16. doi:10.1080/08878730009555246

Grant, C. A., Elsbree, A. R., & Fondrie, S. (2004). A decade of research on the changing terrain of multicultural education research. In J. A. Banks & C. A. McGee Banks (Eds.), *Handbook of research on multicultural education* (2nd ed.; pp. 184–207). San Francisco: Jossey-Bass.

Grosseck, G., & Holotescu, C. (2008, April). *Can we use Twitter for educational activities*. In 4th international scientific conference, eLearning and software for education, Bucharest, Romania.

Hardin, B., & Huang, H. F. (2011). A cross-cultural comparison of services for young children with disabilities using the ACEI Global Guidelines Assessment (GGA). *Early Childhood Education Journal*, *39*(2), 103–114. doi:10.100710643-011-0448-y

Heitner, K. L., & Jennings, M. (2016). Culturally responsive teaching knowledge and practices of online faculty. *Online Learning*, *20*(4), 54–78. doi:10.24059/olj.v20i4.1043

Hollie, S. (2012). *Culturally and linguistically responsive teaching and learning: Classroom practices for student success*. Huntington Beach, CA: Shell Education.

Hung, W., Jonassen, D. H., & Liu, R. (2008). Problem-based learning. Handbook of research on educational communications and technology, 3, 485-506.

Hymes, D. (1972). Models of the Interaction of Language and Social Life. In Directions in Sociolinguistics: The Ethnography of Communication. New York: Holt, Rinehart and Winston.

Individuals With Disabilities Education Act Amendments of 2004 (IDEA). U.S.C. §1400 et seq (2004).

Ke, F., & Kwak, D. (2013). Online learning across ethnicity and age: A study on learning interaction participation, perception, and learning satisfaction. *Computers & Education*, *61*, 43–51. doi:10.1016/j.compedu.2012.09.003

Keengwe, J., & Kidd, T. T. (2010). Towards best practices in online learning and teaching in higher education. *Journal of Online Learning and Teaching / MERLOT*, *6*(2), 533.

Lowrey, K. A., Hollingshead, A., Howery, K., & Bishop, J. B. (2017). More than one way: Stories of UDL and inclusive classrooms. *Research and Practice for Persons with Severe Disabilities*, *42*(4), 225–242. doi:10.1177/1540796917711668

Manochehr, N. (2006). The influence of learning styles on learners in E-learning environments: An empirical study. *Computers in Higher Education Economics Review*, *18*(1), 10–14.

Nieto, S., & Bode, P. (2008). *Affirming diversity, The Sociopolitical context of multicultural education* (5th ed.). Boston: Allyn & Bacon.

Qianqian, Z.-W. (2017). Culturally and Linguistically Responsive Teaching in Practice: A Case Study of a Fourth-Grade Mainstream Classroom Teacher. *Journal of Education*, *197*(1), 33–40. doi:10.1177/002205741719700105

Rogoff, B. (2003). *The cultural nature of human development*. New York: Oxford University Press.

Rose, D. H., & Meyer, A. (2002). *Teaching every student in the digital age: Universal design for learning. Association for Supervision and Curriculum Development.*

Sleeter, C. E. (2012). Confronting the marginalization of culturally responsive pedagogy. *Urban Education*, *47*(3), 562–584. doi:10.1177/0042085911431472

Taliaferro, A. (2011). Developing culturally responsive leaders through online learning and teaching approaches. *Journal of Educational Technology*, *8*(3), 15–20.

Tan, F., Nabb, L., Aagard, S., & Kioh, K. (2010). International ESL graduate student perceptions of online learning in the context of second language acquisition and culturally responsive facilitation. *Adult Learning*, *21*(1/2), 9–14. doi:10.1177/104515951002100102

Tapanes, M. A., Smith, G. G., & White, J. A. (2009). Cultural diversity in online learning: A study of the perceived effects of dissonance in levels of individualism/collectivism and tolerance of ambiguity. *The Internet and Higher Education*, *12*(1), 26–34. doi:10.1016/j.iheduc.2008.12.001

Tomlinson, C. A. (2000). *Differentiation of Instruction in the Elementary Grades*. ERIC Digest.

Vavrus, M. (2008). Culturally responsive teaching. *21st century education: A reference handbook*, *2*, 49-57.

Villegas, A. M., & Lucas, T. (2002). *Educating culturally responsive teachers: A coherent approach.* New York: State University of New York Press.

Walter, J. S. (2018). Global Perspectives: Making the Shift from Multiculturalism to Culturally Responsive Teaching. *General Music Today*, *31*(2), 24–28. doi:10.1177/1048371317720262

Wang, M. (2007, March). Designing online courses that effectively engage learners from diverse cultural backgrounds. *British Journal of Educational Technology*, *38*(2), 294–311. doi:10.1111/j.1467-8535.2006.00626.x

Watkins-Goffman, L., & Cummings, V. (1997). Bridging the gap between native language and second language literacy instruction: A naturalistic study. *Bilingual Research Journal*, *21*(4), 380–394. doi:1 0.1080/15235882.1997.10162711

Werts, M. G., Lambert, M., & Carpenter, E. (2009). What special education directors say about RTI. *Learning Disability Quarterly*, *32*(4), 245–254. doi:10.2307/27740376

Williams, Y. (2008). Deconstructing gifted and special education, policy and practice: A paradigm of ethical leadership in residentially segregated schools and communities. In Advances in educational leadership and Policy: K-16 issues impacting student achievement in urban communities. Information Age Publications.

Williams, Y. (2013). *Urban charter schools: African American parents' school choice reform*. Lambert Academic Publishing, Co. KG.

Williams, Y. (2014). Urban charter schools and factors that influence the achievement of students from culturally and linguistically diverse (CLD) backgrounds. *Journal of The Center of Scholastic Inquiry, 3*(1).

Wilson, A. L. (1993). The promise of situated cognition. *New Directions for Adult and Continuing Education, 1993*(57), 71–79. doi:10.1002/ace.36719935709

Woodley, X., Hernandez, C., Parra, P., & Negash, B. (2017). Celebrating difference: Best practices in culturally responsive teaching online. *TechTrends, 61*(4), 470–478. doi:10.100711528-017-0207-z

Yi, Z. (2013). Power distance in online learning: Experience of Chinese learners in U.S. higher education. *International Review of Research in Open and Distance Learning, 14*(4).

This research was previously published in Care and Culturally Responsive Pedagogy in Online Settings; pages 109-124, copyright year 2019 by Information Science Reference (an imprint of IGI Global).

Chapter 35

More Than the Sum of Their Struggles:
Success Factors of First–Generation African American Women With Doctorates

Donna L. Wilson
Equity Options Consulting, LLC, USA

ABSTRACT

Even in 2020, the plight of Black women in higher education saturates the literature. For decades, Black women have been trying to find their place in the academy. This chapter reveals the success factors of five first-generation African American women with Ph.D.s discovered through a narrative inquiry. The theoretical framework used in this study contends that social location and ideas produced by Black women help demystify the orientation of Black women and help illuminate their points of view. This study focused exclusively on capturing the success factors that contributed to the participants successfully navigating their doctoral journey. The findings exposed five success factors and better position the academy to support and replicate mechanisms to foster success and not assumptions of incompetence. This study allowed participants to provide wisdom to future generations and evidence to assist in shaping the trajectory for first-generation African American women doctoral students.

INTRODUCTION

This chapter presents findings from a qualitative research study on the success factors for five first-generation (first in their families to obtain a college degree) African American women who obtained Ph.D.'s in education at predominately white institutions. The sister scholars in this study represented the professoriate in various educational sectors including a military educator, a linguist, a dual language educator, a clinical therapist, and a sex therapist. The contributors to success uncovered through participant interviews include understanding the collective impact of education, being encouraged by an

DOI: 10.4018/978-1-6684-4507-5.ch035

educational figure during their educational journey, having faith in God, demonstrating perseverance, and having solid support systems throughout their doctoral journey.

Historically, Black women have struggled to find their place in society and higher education. Even in 2020, the struggles of Black women in higher education saturate the literature. In history, Black women have been one of the most insulated, underutilized, and subsequently demoralized segments of the scholastic community (Carter, Pearson & Shavlik, 1988). The voices of African American women are often ignored and not reflected positively in the literature. Because academia is historically made up of white, heterosexual, middle-and-upper class, those who do not represent this classification are often "presumed incompetent" by colleagues, students and administrators alike (Muhs, Niemann, Gonzalez, & Harris, 2012).

Using semi-structured interviews, the author, Wilson (2019) captured the success stories of five first-generation African American women with a doctorate, in their own words, through a narrative inquiry—a tool to investigate the ways humans experience the world. This study aimed to change the legacy of invisibility and misperception by breaking the silence and speaking truth to power by intentionally exposing success factors despite the struggles for first-generation African American women who obtained a doctorate degree. hooks (2014) underscored that finding one's voice and using it, especially in acts of critical insurgence and opposition, thrusting past fear, continues to be one of the most authoritative ways feminist philosophy and praxis can change lives. This study gave five women the ability to find and express their voice.

Black women have rich, powerful, transformative, and informative stories to tell. Yet, people have rarely asked to hear those accounts, especially those narratives connected to triumphs, like the ones that were captured in this study. Michelle Obama (2019), former First Lady and a first-generation African American woman with a doctorate stated there is power in authentically sharing your unique story with others to be known and heard. And there's honor in longing to know and understand others. She provided a compelling illustration of the sovereignty of both hearing and providing an avenue for others to share their unique stories with others. Throughout history, storytelling has provided opportunities for enslaved people to preserve memories related to their dialect, reflections, sounds, smells, and textures of their homeland while also staying in touch with friends and family, expanding new kinships, disseminating information across plantations, and obtaining more knowledge about their new environment (Banks-Wallace, 2002).

This chapter does not strive to provide an exhaustive list of success strategies, nor a framework to guarantee success for all Black first-generation graduates who are now Ph.D. students, nor an in-depth description of Black feminist thought, nor a prescribed blueprint for creating success. Instead, it aims to share the counter-stories of five women, sister scholars who refused to allow their past to determine their future and became successful scholars in their own right. Beginning with a brief history of Black women in higher education, this chapter then reviews the significance of the study, highlights the theoretical frameworks anchoring the work, explores the methods, presents the success factors for study participants, offers recommendations on ways to replicate the success in the academy to glean similar results and concludes with reflections on implications for both practice and future research.

Background

Due to the weight of the historical injustices of both Black men and Black women in the quest for knowledge, it will take an intentional effort to undo this unfortunate legacy and to position African American women in a positive, contributory light. Bush, Gafford, Muhammad, and Walpole (2009) indicated that when it comes to underrepresented groups in education at any level, neither women nor men of African American descent have reached their full potential; furthermore, research and scholarship on Black women are usually framed in inferiority, which enables the extended challenges confronting Black women to grow, rather than diminish (Bush et al., 2009).

Literature Review

The history of African American women in higher education is complex and the meaning of higher education has always varied according to the historical time and events (Ihle,1992). In 1833, Oberlin College permitted enrollment of both Blacks and women. However, it was not until 1862 that Mary Jane Peterson became the first Black woman to be awarded a bachelor's degree (Ihle,1992). Fifty-nine years later in 1921, Georgiana Simpson, Sadie Mossell Alexander, and Eva Dykes became the first African American women to receive their PhDs. Research targeted to this population tends to be deficit focused. There appears to be a wealth of information pathologizing the struggles of African American students, particularly highlighting the few who made it to the ivory tower. Bush et atl. (2009) contend that the literature surrounding the professional development of Black female graduate students is practically nonexistent. Even more, there is limited scholarly interest to what contributes to this success. Dowdy (2018) sought to look beyond the negative research reports on Black women and learn from Black scholars who served as role models within their personal and professional spaces. Findings indicated that the role of family, having support beyond the academy, being in service to others and mentoring other young scholars assisted Black women to step into authority and wisdom (Dowdy, 2009).

Although African American women's presence in higher education was not until after the Civil War, there have been significant benchmarks for both Blacks and Black women which are reflected in Table 1 below. The number of African Americans earning doctorate degrees has steadily increased (National Science Foundation, 2018). Conversely, despite this surge in enrollment, there is still limited research on the various success factors that contribute to African American women scholars, especially those who are also first-generation. Researchers studying the impact of race on African American graduate retention found that when students were a part of a support network that affirmed one another and had a space to openly share their experiences, they felt a sense of inclusion and a desire to remain in their program (Gildersleeve, Croon, & Vasquez, 2011).

The purpose of this study was to reveal what the success stories of first-generation African American women who successfully obtained a doctorate degree conveyed. This research gave voice, validation, and credibility to Black women scholars and provided them an avenue to instill guidance and wisdom to future generations and institutions of higher learning. Because the literature is saturated with countless studies on the obstacles and challenges faced by African American women such as isolation, invisibility, intersectionality, and credibility, this study offered a counter-narrative in hopes of shifting the perceptions by highlighting strengths and accomplishments. Marian Wright Edelman (1992) declared that education is for improving the lives of others and for leaving your community and world better than you found it. This study fulfilled the charge and captured the success stories of participants to assist them in inspiring and informing future similarly situated doctoral students, doctoral programs, departments, and researchers on how to promote and replicate mechanisms that foster success.

More Than the Sum of Their Struggles

Table 1. Key events for blacks and black women in higher educaiton

1833	Oberlin College is founded and allows both Blacks and women to enroll.
1844	Oberlin College graduates its first black student, George B. Vashon, who became one of the founding professors at Howard University.
1850	Lucy Ann Stanton is the first African American woman to graduate from college with a certificate in literature from Oberlin College.
1858	Sarah Jane Woodspn Early is the first woman college instructor at Wilberforce University and the only Black woman to teach at a HBCU prior to the Civil War.
1862	Mary Jane Patterson is the first African American woman to be awarded a baccalaureate degree from Oberlin College.
1864	Rebecca Lee, the first Black medical student graduates from the New England Female Medical College. She later worked as a nurse.
1869	Mary Ann Shadd Cary is the first Black woman student enrolled in Howard University's law department, yet, she does not graduate until 1884 at the age of 61.
1881	Spelman College, the first historically Black college for women is founded.
1921	Georgiana Simpson (German philosophy), Sadie Mossell Alexander (economics) and Eva Dykes (English philosophy) became the first African American women to receive their PhDs.
1944	Frederick Douglass Patterson founds the United Negro College Fund.
1961	The term "affirmative action" is coined by Hobart T. Taylor Jr., a black Texas lawyer, who edits President Kennedy's Executive Order 10925, which created the Presidential Committee on Equal Employment Opportunity.
1962	Riots happen at the University of Mississippi due to admittance of the first black student. Federal troops and the U.S. marshals are sent to ensure her entry. Two people are killed.
1969	A suit is filed in Tennessee against the racial segregation in public higher education.
1970	Marian Wright Edelman is the first elected Black woman at Yale University Corporation.
1975	Eileen Jackson Southern is the first Black woman tenured as full professor at Harvard University.
1983	Federal government sues the state of Alabama in an effort to force more desegregation in its system of higher education.
1990	Marguerite Ross Barnett is named president at the University of Houston.
2004	Education Department's Office for Civil Rights publishes report listing race-neutral alternatives to increase racial diversity in higher education. Subsequently, many of the outreach programs highlighted in the report see their funding slashed by the Bush administration.
2008	Michelle Obama is the only First Lady (of any race) to attend an Ivy League for her undergraduate studies.

[1] Key Events in Black Higher Education retrieved from https://www.jbhe.com/chronology/ and https://www.sutori.com/story/timeline-of-the-educated-african-american-woman--WgdjiiwftgJsebDmo8ZMFxpM

Black Feminist Standpoint Theory

Black feminist thought, Black feminist epistemology and Black feminist standpoint theory were the theoretical frameworks supporting this study. These complementary paradigms contend that the world looks different depending on one's social location and the ideas produced by Black women clarify a standpoint of and for Black women (Allen, 2000; Collins,1986).

Among the three complementary frameworks, Black feminist standpoint theory proved to be the most relevant and useful to this study. This theory reflects the accounts of the lived experiences of five first-generation African American women with a doctorate which the author would not have obtained without explicitly discerning their standpoints, seeking their wisdom, and soliciting their recommendations to assist others in being successful.

Black feminist standpoint considers the role and influence of politics and history on shared group experiences. Collins (2000) noted that when the actual language used to illustrate Black feminist thought is criticized, Black women's self- portrayals become harder to attain. This viewpoint focuses less on the individual experience and more on the social conditions that form groups. This standpoint will subsequently influence the recommendations garnered from this study.

History of Black Women in Education

Historically, Black women have fought to have a notable place in society and more specifically, the path of education. The National Science Foundation (2018) highlighted that research related to African American Ph.D. success showed an increase of African Americans earning doctorates. However, despite enrollment increases, there is still limited research on the success factors that contribute to African American women scholars, especially those who are also first-generation. Furthermore, although the enrollment rates for students of color have becomes increasingly more diverse, most of the full-time faculty positions continue to be occupied predominately by white women (Muhs, et al., 2012).

Boukari (2005) indicated that Black American women's scholastic mindfulness arose in the1890s in the South. Their motto, "lifting as we climb", the National Association of Colored Women, established in 1885, symbolized members' commitment to uplift the race by role modeling their resilience and dedication to education (Habiba, 2015). Furthermore, the association was positioned to focus on education, job opportunities, and protection for Black women against sexual assaults from White men in the South (Boukari, 2005). Boukari (2005), further declared that during this period, learning was highly viewed as a means to evade poverty and heighten one's ability to locate a position and impact social inconsistencies and discrimination.

In history, higher education for Black women has been regarded as both a human and civil right (Evans, 2007). An example would be Anna Julia Cooper, born a slave in the mid-1800s who earned her bachelor's degree from Oberlin College, attended graduate school at Columbia, and then in 1925 received her doctorate from Sorbonne University in Paris despite sexism and racism. Instead of basking in her individual scholarly success, Cooper worked to improve higher education by attempting to increase access for African American women because she felt equal access to higher education was an essential part of human growth (Evans, 2007). Mary McLeod Bethune, the founder of Bethune-Cookman College, was an accomplished politician, prominent educator, and prolific author who grew up in the South during the late nineteenth-century, and like Cooper, she comprehended the implications of denied admission to education (Evans, 2007).

Bethune, an advocate for many social issues such as housing, fair labor and citizenship, and peace, dedicated her life to supporting higher education access for all but particularly Black women and insisted that education was a right for all citizens in a democracy (Evans, 2007). Nevertheless, these two views of education created a complementary schema for explaining the academic engagement of previous Black women scholars and these corresponding explanations also provided speculations for increasing educational access in the future (Evans, 2007).

Habiba (2015) noted that Black women in higher education have been instrumental in creating settings for marginalized, underrepresented people of color to tell their stories, and their longing to deal with a variety of socially created systems of oppression is one of the emblems of their Black feminist enterprise. The often-unnoticed contributions made to America by African American women are the primary motivation for why they have taken matters into their own hands (Habiba, 2015). Black women have rallied together and spoken up about social indifferences since the origination of slavery in the United States. They continue to acknowledge injustices related to racism, sexism, classism, and the intersectionality of varied identities. Habiba (2015) pointed out the literature on Black women and their lived experiences are scarce but researchers are finally acknowledging the necessity to record the untold stories of Black women in America. Through life experience, African American women bring significant cultural and social capital they have gained to college campuses (Bush, et al., 2009).

Allen (2002) declared that research should portray Black women in a positive light and free them from preconceived notions. Yet, there is an overwhelming amount of negative research on the status of Black women in academia (Dowdy, 2008). Because Black women have operated as outsiders within the academy (Colins,1986) and are historically portrayed unfavorably within the literature, it was important to examine factors that influenced these women to prevail. Negative perceptions have contributed to disparaging treatment and invisibility for female African American scholars in the academy, yet, they remain victorious.

Overview of the Study

Within academic spaces, women of color, including African American women are often presumed incompetent (Muhs, et al., 2012). Many believe (although few would admit) that the browning of the academy is a result of token hires and the fulfillment of meeting affirmative action quotas. In some situations, an African American woman may be considered as a "twofer"— hired because she could count both as a female and a racial minority and because of this, people with whom she interacts might explicitly or implicitly question her right to be there (Allen, 1995).

While in the academy, Black women often encounter complexities in negotiating their identities as women of color related to being outsiders within the academy and confronting obstacles such as White supremacy, classism, and heteronormativity (Allen, 2012). The identities of Black women are often multidimensional. The concept of intersectionality (examining intersecting forms of discrimination) poses important questions related to the experience of first-generation doctoral students (Holley & Gardner, 2012).

Black doctoral students reported experiencing cultural isolation and tokenism in addition to dealing with institutional and individual racism (Acosta et al., 2015). Additionally, they maintained that faculty and higher education administrators must seek to understand the impacts of programs designed to support Black doctoral students when they face racial domination in higher education (i.e. pervasive ethnocentric curriculum, limited exposed of faculty of color, allocation of funding for research and programs, etc.). Additionally, Acosta et al. (2015) affirmed that work that is targeted toward racial issues must take place within the department and that faculty and administrators in schools and colleges of education must design spaces and opportunities for that to happen. A substantial support tool for Black doctoral students is awareness and acknowledgement of racial issues on the part of institutions (Acosta et al., 2015). Specific to race, some professors and students may adopt a colorblind stance. This colorblind approach, according to Acosta et al. (2015) promotes the idea that race, and racism are not instrumental factors in the experiences of Black doctoral students. Racial and ethnic impartiality in understanding Black doctoral student experiences perpetuates institutional inequity and discounts the genuine needs of Black doctoral students, thus contributing to the limited presence of Blacks in the academy (Acosta et al., 2015).

Method

In the summer of 2019, the researcher spent several months interviewing and collecting the testimonies of five first-generation African American women with a doctorate degree. Their own words revealed experiential truths, the strategies exercised to overcome their obstacles, and what they felt contributed to their ability to successfully complete their Ph.D. programs at a predominately white institution (PWI).

This chapter focuses on the recommendations constructed from the words of wisdom provided by these sister scholars to assist in informing future similarly situated doctoral students, doctoral programs, departments, and researchers on how to promote and replicate mechanisms that foster success for first-generation students in a doctoral program. The author noticed common themes amongst participants, including them being grateful that someone had inquired about their success factors and would capture the how and why they were able to successfully complete a doctorate program when the odds of doing so were stacked against them as first-generation college graduates and Black women.

The Process

Using a random, snowball convenience sample, five first-generation African American women doctoral graduates were selected to participate, based on the prequalification criteria of (a) identifying as a woman; (b) identifying as Black/African American; (c) identifying as a first-generation college graduate; (d) having graduated from a U.S. doctoral program within the last 5-10 years; and (e) obtaining their terminal degree from a predominantly white institution (PWI). The characteristics of these participants are reflected in Table 2 below. Participants who met the above criteria were located throughout the United States.

Table 2. Participant characteristics

Name	Age	Birth Order	Family Composition	Childhood SES/Location	Type of Degree	Age Completed
Lauryn Stedman	53	Oldest	Single mother, two brothers	Poor Segregated Midwest	PhD	52
Pamela Gilmore	59	2nd Oldest	Divorced parents, two brothers, two sisters	Poor, Segregated Midwest	PhD	57
Tamara Givens	40	Oldest	Mother, grandmother, brother	Poor Segregated Midwest	PhD	39
Katrina Benson	42	Oldest	Single mom, sister (teen mom), estranged stepfather	Poor, Rural Southern Coastal Plains, integrated	PhD	36
Marissa Billings	48	Oldest	Married Parents, sister, brother	Middle class South, integrated turned segregated	PhD	46

The Participants

Five African American first-generation female scholars with a Ph.D. participated in this study. All of the women had earned their degrees from education programs at a PWI. One participant did her entire program online and the remaining four at brick and mortar institutions. It took two participants nearly two decades to complete their Ph.D., whereas others were between the 4-6-year range. All of the participants are currently professors and two are also practicing clinical therapists. Participants were given pseudonyms and were invited to review their full narratives. Truncated narratives are with success factors noted are captured below.

Dr. Lauryn Stedman, soldier scholar, and currently a military professor was raised by a single mother in the projects for her first 14 years of life which proved to be challenging at best. The three things that contributed to her success were Christian faith, her drive, her determination, and her belief that she could.

Dr. Pamela Gilmore, a linguistic educator was born into an impoverished family and community but was exposed to educational opportunities early in her formative years. Her success can be attributed to her discipline, determination, commitment to complete her program, and the support of her family.

Dr. Tamara Givens, a triple mastered sexologist who was raised in a poor, segregated, all-Black working-class neighborhood. She attributes the successful completion of her doctoral degree to perseverance; authenticity in owning her Blackness, Black feminism and being unapologetically Black; and having a supportive community.

Dr. Katrina Benson, island girl turned English professor was raised on a poor segregated island in the Southern Coastal Plains region on the United States. Her success factors include her faith in God, her persistence, and having a strong support system.

Dr. Marisa Billings, professor, and clinical therapist grew up in a middle class, dual-parent household. Her success is result of her perseverance, honoring her ancestors, and creating a legacy for her family.

Researcher Background

The characteristics that were most salient for this research were the authors identities as a first-generation African American, Christian, mother-scholar. The author's epistemology stems from the belief that although education is viewed as the "great equalizer," people with similar identities as hers have struggled to access and engage in academic spaces. Viewing education through a historical context, and through the pain of her ancestors, the author often evaluated the cost associated with this quest. Yet, she remains committed to assisting both the academy and individuals to develop strategies to reduce this burden and to shift outcomes to having a higher return on investment. Believing that Black women are more than the sum of their struggles and problems, the counter-story deserved to be told.

As a clinical therapist by trade, the author was acutely aware of the notion of projection and overidentification while conducting this research study. While listening and bearing witness to the very personal stories of the research participants, it was important for the author not to over-identify with them. By understanding and acknowledging her own standpoint and perception, the author was able to prevent presenting results that focused on herself instead of highlighting the stories that arose due to the participants' perspective.

Being four generations removed from slavery, the author understood that the educational trajectory for those who have African ancestry has been turbulent at best. When Black people were held captive and brought to this country against their will, they were not only treated like second class citizens but were prohibited and often punished if they were caught being educated. African descendants suffered so that her yearning for knowledge could someday be fulfilled. The author, an African American, Christian, mother-scholar, dedicated to retelling, preserving, and reshaping the cultural legacy of Black female academics by creating successful educational opportunities for those who share the same lineage as her. Because many people, the author included, rely on books, artifacts, and other tools used in the formal education system to cultivate learning, she was compelled to break down the social and racialized barriers that prevent people like herself from successfully navigating the academy.

As a Black woman scholar who at the time was navigating the academy as a first-generation college graduate and doctoral student, she strongly desired to research a topic that she was passionate about. Often feeling like an outsider within the academy, plagued with the imposter syndrome at times, the author wanted to produce a piece of literature that could serve as both a conduit and a source of encouragement for others.

Data Collection

A narrative inquiry was the chosen methodological approach for this study. Narrative research explores the experiences as expressed in lived and told stories of individuals and provides a rich framework to investigate the way humans experience the world depicted through their stories (Creswell, 2013; Webster & Mertova, 2007). Because narrative inquiry is a context that allows researchers to investigate a person's worldview in their own words, this study involved conducting interviews with African American female first-generation doctoral graduates to explore the factors that contributed to their success. Interviews were the primary source of data collection for this narrative inquiry.

The Interview Protocol

Two semi-structured interviews were conducted via Zoom between 30-90 minutes and allowed participants to provide a chronological account of their educational trajectory, to reflect on the messages they received about education, indicate what inspired them to pursue a doctorate degree, tell when they were inspired to get a doctorate degree, and how being a Black woman helped or hindered their doctoral experience. The second session allowed participants to reflect on a time when they wanted to give up, and what made them keep going, to provide advice to their younger, non-terminal degreed self to ensure success down the road and to share advice to university educators and administrators to ensure the success of future first-generation African American scholars.

To protect confidentiality, each participant was assigned a participant pseudonym. All interviews were recorded. Data collected were analyzed for themes, similarities, and differences across participants and coded to create emergent themes. A participant profile was created, member checked and served as the success narrative of each participant.

Integrity Measures

During the interview process, the author asked participants to expand on significant events and theorize concepts that contributed to their success as a first-generation African American female doctoral graduate. The author followed Lincoln and Cuba's (1985) recommendations for credibility, dependability and confirmability. Credibility was achieved by the collection of the interviews with the five sister scholars, the review of literature and cross referencing the recorded accounts of the success stories of each woman as they navigated through their doctoral programs.

More Than the Sum of Their Struggles

Member checking was performed by the author first checking her transcripts against the audio recordings. The narrative was then sent to each participant. Each sister scholar was asked to not only confirm the receipt of the profile but to also ensure that the information was accurate and if it was not, to make corrections using track changes. This member checking process ensured inter-coder reliability.

The authors advisor also reviewed the success narratives and verified the emergent themes from each participants success narrative.

Data Analysis

During and after each interview, the author scribed field notes to document the interactions. This helped create a bibliographical reconstruction of these events. By writing an analytic abstraction of the interview, the author highlighted: (a) the course of the individual's life; (b) the different assumptions related to those life experiences; and (c) the idiosyncratic and common features of their life (Creswell, 2013). All of the interviews were audio recorded, using two recording devices for backup, and they were transcribed, yielding 160 pages of raw data.

The recordings were then uploaded to Temi.com, a password protected computer-generated system that permitted the audio files to be transcribed. Once the transcriptions were complete, the author read through each page while listening to the recording and made corrections for words or phrases the transcription process had not captured correctly. Without the support of a suitable computer program, it would be unimaginable for a researcher to complete an intensive interpretive analysis and meet the requirements for scientific work (Peters & Webster, 2007). The data collected were analyzed for themes, similarities, and differences across

participants to create an interview transcript, which eventually became a narrative profile. To maintain anonymity, each participant was assigned a participant pseudonym. All interview data was coded to identify themes and/or patterns and recorded accordingly. After the coding was complete, the author constructed a participant profile to retell each participant's success story. The author used the transcript as a guide and each narrative contained an uninterrupted flow of text from the transcripts, with minimal editing. Some text was omitted to protect anonymity and to ensure consistent flow.

Emergent Success Factor Themes

Through this narrative inquiry, the success stories of five African American first-generation doctoral graduates were revealed. Although each of the participants had their own distinctive experiences related to successfully obtaining their Ph.D.'s, through the microanalysis process, five salient themes emerged from interviews with study participants. At the center of this research study were five uniquely different, yet interconnected women who were all first-generation African American Ph.D. recipients.

Although there are limited studies specific to the success factors first-generation African American in Ph.D. programs, findings from this study were consistent with the review of literature, related to first-generation students and they also revealed similar contributors to success which include: (a) collective impact; (b) faith in God; (c) perseverance; and (d) support systems while pursuing a doctorate degree. This study also revealed one new success factor, which was not supported by the literature, (e) exposure to educational gardeners. This section will briefly discuss each of these success factors in Figure 1 below and how they are either supported by or absent from the research.

669

Figure 1.

Collective Impact

Collective impact was a central theme in this study. One example of collective impact for participants meant that they participated in this study as a means of helping the author ascend. This was an opportunity for them to "lift as they climb". Participants such as Pamela and Lauryn, not being too far removed from completing their own doctoral journey, wanted to "pay it forward". Another example was that two participants talked about giving back by teaching at their Alma Mater and feeling obligated to be the "face of diversity" for their students.

McCallum (2017) found that many African American students seek to obtain a degree as a means to "pay it forward" or "give back to the community." For instance, Marissa indicated that she was seeking her degree to impact the legacy of her family. McCallum (2017) also indicated that African American students believed they were empowering future generations of African American scholars by destroying impediments and creating pathways for others to follow. Participants acknowledged that their Ph.D. provided them access to academic tables they were not previously invited to and this would ultimately result in opening more doors for generations to come.

One participant indicated the need to be clear about defining the "why" behind obtaining a Ph.D. was important. Gardner (2013) noted that many first-generation college students were first attracted to pursuing a Ph.D. because of a desire to emulate their mentors, such as an influential professor. Lauryn admitted that "I had never met a sergeant major who was a Ph.D. So, I was immediately impressed by her. I wanted to be like her, and that's when I told myself I would be Dr. Lauryn one day." She is now giving back in her current role and is only positioned to do so because she is a doctoral degree recipient.

Focusing on how one's degree can impact a community or family legacy is significant. The women who participated in this study did so out of obligation to the author although some of them did not know her. The African American community is rooted in a sense of collectivism that steams from slavery. The Black community has a long lineage of women such as Mary McLeod Bethune who dedicated her life to supporting and inspiring other women. Black women's collective cultural capital is enhanced when they work to set one another up for success because they are intrinsically tied to one another by their ancestors.

Exposure to Educational Gardeners

The role of a gardener is to water, feed, fertilize and nurture plants, crops and other vegetation. They also sow seeds when planting new crops. The participants in the study referenced several "educational gardeners" in their lives. The educational gardeners in this study had planted seeds early in the participants' lives and ensured that they had rich educational soil in which to grow and flourish. For Marissa, her early scholastic seeds were planted by her mother, a nun at her school, and one of her aunts. Later in their graduate school journeys, both Marissa and Lauryn had a professor who encouraged them to get a Ph.D. Pamela had a teacher in her formative years that exposed her to opportunities, special events and also encouraged her mother to let her attend a gifted school. Although this theme did not show up in the review of literature, it was revealed to be a significant theme for study participants.

Many of the participants commented that it was these memories that assisted them in having the self-efficacy and drive to excel educationally. The impressions that the early seed planters left on the five participants in this study have had lifelong impacts. Educational gardeners are essential in the lives of students, particularly young, Black female students. Listening to the participants of this study reflect on the level of impact that their early influencers had on their lives, filled the author with both a sense of pride and trepidation. Although delighted to hear that the impacts of seeds being planted could one day flourish into a Ph.D., there was also apprehension knowing that not all kids will have these early seed planters in their life. But they should. Exposing young Black kids, especially girls to programs and people that instill a sense of hopefulness and possibilities is key to inspiring even more first-generation African American college graduate women to become Ph.D. recipients.

Faith in God

McCallum (2017) indicated that when Africans came to America against their will, they remained culturally connected and believed in the interconnectedness of all things, including God. Some African Americans may feel that they were purposefully placed on this path and completing their degree is fulfilling a higher purpose in life. This was true for the participants in the study, especially Tamara and Marissa. Faith in God was a significant finding in this study. For participants, having faith in God meant that they recognized that completing their Ph.D. was by His design, and being obedient to God meant they would fulfill their larger purpose in life.

The concepts of spirituality and faith were also revealed during the literature review process. Study participants mentioned the importance of how faith contributed to the completion of the Ph.D. process. Patton and McClure (2009) examined how spirituality served as the power behind the voices of African American students while attending PWIs.

The author, also a Christian scholar, can attest to the strength one finds when they are navigating spaces through a faith-based perspective. Just like their African ancestors before, many African Americans believe that prayer and seeking direction from God allows one to be fruitful in life. They are rewarded for their faithfulness. Scripture confirms this by stating in Hebrews 10:23 "let us hold unswervingly to the hope we profess, for he who promised is faithful" (New Living Translation).

Perseverance

Perseverance was a central theme in this study. Perseverance for participants meant that they stayed the course, despite the length of time their journeys took, experiencing microaggressions, having a heightened sense of invisibility, and a sense of "otherness" at times while dealing with the intersections of race, gender, and class. In such, Holley and Gardner (2012) highlighted that issues of race and gender often intensified the challenges facing first-generation doctoral students.

However, to counteract these struggles, Tamara created a critical mass with other Black femmes. Tamara indicated that she "gained a good balance on how to absorb microaggressions" by telling herself "if you fight every time somebody calls you a nigga, you are going to fight the rest of your life".

Lauryn stayed the course and indicated that "I purposefully chose a woman for my chair. No one knows our struggles better than we do. Men do not experience the same type of sexism and racism. I wanted women who knew and understood the struggle, and who would be proud of being a part of my success". Lastly, Katrina declared "I knew going in that I had to be successful and I had to achieve no matter what, I could not quit...I knew there would be other women coming after me, I knew that I had to do this, and I didn't mind being first." Findings from this study highlighted that although three of the participants wanted to quit, they endured their struggles and prevailed.

Participants reported having a heightened sense of being visibly invisible within the academy. Due to this, participants found strategies to persevere and make their doctoral journey bearable. For example, Tamara found her voice at the Ph.D. level. She indicated "when I got to my doctoral program, I was like oh y'all can't tell me nothing now because now I understand that it really doesn't matter what I think...I came here to help Black people so that's what I talked about. Take it or leave it. And that process really helped. Seeing the barriers that other people have taken me in has allowed me to free myself to just be who I am." Katrina noted "By you not having any Black professors, it shows me I don't belong here" to circumvent this she stated, " I have to mentally have myself in this place where I say, listen, I'm gonna make a difference, and I have to be here".

Acosta et al. (2015) found that factors such as intrinsic motivation, autonomy, and inner strength impact Black doctoral students' perseverance in their programs. This finding is consistent with the participants in this study. Pamela, for instance, kept going because it was a personal goal. She was motivated to get her degree but not because it was tied to job advancement. Lastly, Acosta et al. (2015) indicated that Black doctoral student persistence at PWIs still occurred despite the lack of cultural diversity and racial aggression in their day-to-day college lives. This was also consistent with the participants in this study.

Although Blacks and Black women, in particular, have endured great struggle while pursuing higher education, they embrace those struggles and persevere. Resiliency is required to endure the extent of isolation, invisibility, microaggressions, and questions of competence that Black women experience in the academy, but the participants in this study demonstrated that it is possible to do.

Support Systems

Having a support system was a contributor to the successful completion of their Ph.D.'s for the participants in the study. For the sister scholars in this study, this meant having spouses, family members, and classmates that could offer support and understanding through their doctoral journey. Pamela received support from her cohort with whom she is still connected with today. Lauryn received support from a mentor and her committee made up of all women with doctorate degrees.

Gildersleeve et al. (2001) studied the impact of race on African American graduate retention and found that when students were members of a support network that acknowledged one another and had a space to openly share their encounters, they felt included and wanted to remain in a program. Furthermore, Gardner (2013) noted that first-generation students should be assisted through a peer mentoring approach. The participants in the study like Katrina sought refuge and support by forging connections with other Black femmes to ensure they would have an impact on the sexology field. Being first-generation established an invisible, often unrecognized external element of a student's life (Holley & Gardner, 2012). Katrina stated that "as a non-traditional student (e.g., living off-campus, having a job and/or family) in my doctoral program, I admit that sometimes I felt like I was less valued. It was apparent that as an African American doc student that me and others who looked like me didn't have the same support systems, especially financial ones as the white students."

Gardner (2013) indicated that adequate federal financial aid is not obtainable to graduate students other than through student loans. This additional debt can be a great stress for many first-generation and African American students, especially women who are also key providers in their families. To ensure that she did not inherit the financial burdens that are often experienced by first-time college students, Lauryn paid for both her undergraduate and graduate education with the GI Bill. She indicated "I decided to go to college, at the military's expense, that was the best expense. That was the best decision ever".

Earning a Ph.D. is traditionally an isolating process. But it doesn't have to be. The sister scholar participants in this study highlighted the importance of creating circles of support and support systems that consist of other Black women scholars, who are similarly situated in doctoral programs who can assist in navigating through the sometimes unfamiliar and tumultuous terrain—the academy.

More than the Sum of their Struggles

From 1976 to 2005, the number of graduate students enrolled in U.S. universities increased from just over 1.3 million to nearly 2.2 million (Bush et al., 2009).

The National Science Foundation (2018) reported that since 2002, women have received slightly more conferred doctorate degrees each year. Similarly, this report noted an increase in underrepresented minorities who are U.S. citizens or permanent residents enrolled in doctoral education. Specifically, the number of doctorates awarded to African Americans increased by 32% from 2006 to 2016 (NSF, 2018).

Furthermore, Okahana and Zhou (2017) noted that the 2015-16 academic year marked the eighth consecutive year in which women earned the majority of awarded doctoral degree level; and 8,807 of those degrees were earned by Black women [A3] (NSF, 2018). Despite the increased degrees, research should produce realistic wisdom that can help liberate African American women in our various community and personal roles within the academy (Carter, Pearson, & Shavlik, 1987).

Black Girl Magic is an expression used to illustrate the universal awesomeness of Black women. Historically, Black women have been told that they are broken, damaged, and everything but magical. Black Girl Magic is a contemporary movement that is embraced by Black girls and women of all ages, socioeconomic classes, and educational backgrounds. Black Girl Magic is an outward expression of the greatness of Black women and their accomplishments, self-acceptance, and self-love. This movement is the current version of the 1960s Black Power moment, except this time, it is exclusively for Black girls and women, a group that has traditionally been silent and almost invisible during the struggle.

In such, this study lifted the veil of silence that has had a crippling effect on how African American women are viewed in the academy, and possibly in the world. As a result of the African American first-generation women with a doctorate participating in this study and telling their success journey, a new perception was hopefully formed for Black women in the academy.

SOLUTIONS AND RECOMMENDATIONS

With insights gained from this narrative inquiry, the following recommendations for practice are provided in hopes to encourage and cultivate new strategies that increase first-generation African American women's ability to successfully complete the doctoral process in a way that promotes agency and resiliency. These recommendations, primarily suited for university administrators, can also be transferred to other institutions fostering academic attainment for first-generation college graduates. These success factors can inspire future scholars and undergraduate programs, college counselors and mentors alike.

Capturing the success stories of first-generation African American women with a doctorate in their own words to assisted participants in inspiring and informing future similarly situated doctoral students, doctoral programs, departments, and researchers on how to promote and replicate mechanisms that foster success.

Intentionally focusing on the success stories of Black female scholars aligned with the aim of Black feminist standpoint theory to engage in acts of resistance in order to shape a new identity for Black first-generation doctoral scholars. By doing so, participants controlled the narrative and drew attention to the positive attributes that Black women contribute to the academy. By keeping the success factors of first-generation African American women as the central focus, the following is recommended through a Black feminist standpoint theory lens: (a) build a more inclusive campus environment that responds to the unique needs of diverse students; (b) offer culturally responsive mentoring; (c) provide information on how to successfully navigate a Ph.D. program; and (d) supervise /advise doctoral students on ways to create their individual network of support.

Implications for Practice

Build a more inclusive campus environment that responds to the unique needs of diverse students. Because the academy is consistently diversifying, it is responsible for ensuring that all members feel welcomed, included, and properly educated. This includes but is not limited to first-generation African American doctoral students. Predominantly white institutions and departments must be cognizant and mindful of the daily microaggressions faced by Black women and other marginalized individuals on their campuses. Microaggressions are unintended and unconscious expressions of racism that still cause harm to the recipient, regardless of the intent. The women in this study had multifaceted identities, including their first-generation status. These intersecting identities often resulted in them feeling like outsiders within the academy. The academy must understand that the United States is not in a post-racial society and that racism, sexism, and tokenism still exists, even on their campuses. The women in this study had multifaceted identities, including their first-generation status. These intersecting identities often resulted in them feeling like outsiders within the academy.

The academy must equip and hold administrators, faculty, and staff accountable for fostering an inclusive and diverse atmosphere by offering ongoing professional development opportunities. Once university staff are properly trained, they must be held responsible to ensure this culture is sustainable.

Having a strong diversity accountability system allows for a greater emphasis to be placed on educational attainment, the benefits the academy achieves through diverse educational exchanges and high-quality research (Williams, 2013). Participants in this study indicated that educational gardeners assisted them in being successful. Once university staff has an integral role in creating a campus of inclusion, they could sow seeds of hope into the lives of first-generation African American women pursuing a doctorate degree.

Offer culturally responsive mentoring. Mentoring is beneficial for both first-generation and African American students to create a sense of belongingness (Allen, 2018; Felder & Baker, 2013; Garner, 2013). Often, faculty of color are assumed to be in the best position to provide this. Black feminist standpoint theory indicates that people in positions of power expect oppressed people to bear the burden of solving all of the diversity woes (Allen, 2000). Inferring that Black people must tread lightly while those in power can ignore what they chose. Because first-generation students have newcomer status in the academy, it may cause them to not ask for help or seek information. The academy needs to ensure that all faculty are suited and positioned to provide mentoring to all students, even those who are from dominant identities.

The sister scholars in this study indicated that having a support system was a key element to the successful completion of their Ph.D. program. Having a culturally responsive mentor to assist with navigating through an unfamiliar process could be tremendously beneficial for future first-generation African American women in Ph.D. programs.

Provide information on how to successfully navigate a Ph.D. program. Similar to the new faculty handbook, students need a roadmap to success. This guide would include issues that are specifically applicable to first-generation doctoral students. All students need to know the rules of the game in order to maximize their cultural capital. Providing this information would allow for sister scholars to "pay it forward" with other future first-generation Black women who are enrolled in a doctoral program. This cultural capital would assist these women in highlighting the collective impact which they were committed to having. Additionally, this information could be greatly beneficial with assisting women in persevering through the program as they might be more determined on completing a process that they are more familiar with.

Supervise /advise doctoral students on ways to create their individual network of support. All doctoral students need support. Consistent with Black feminist theory, participants in this study developed support systems to decrease feelings of isolation and increase a sense of connectivity. Black women may develop social support systems with other Black women to glean the psychological support that White peers cannot offer (Allen, 2000). Universities can serve as resources, connectors, and guides in assisting students in developing a support network.

FUTURE RESEARCH DIRECTIONS

This study about the success factors for first-generation African American women pursuing a doctoral degree, yielded several implications for research and theory, as highlighted below.

Black feminist standpoint theory is committed to using the voices of Black women in their various social positions to identify a standpoint that represents the collective. For this study, participants occupied many roles/identities in addition to their first-generation, Black woman status. For instance, some participants were also mothers, spouses, educators, etc. Black feminist standpoint theory considers the role, the influence of politics and history on shared group experiences, and it would be advantageous for researchers to continue to investigate how these standpoints may be relevant to doctoral success.

This study conducted a narrative inquiry of 5 participants. Although the insights gleaned from this study were informative, the academy may benefit from having a larger pool of respondents. This would be possible if another data collection method was utilized. For instance, by conducting a survey, a researcher would increase the sample size and reach a larger number of first-generation African American doctoral graduates, thereby advancing knowledge, inspiring and informing future similarly situated doctoral students, doctoral programs, departments, and researchers on how to promote and replicate mechanisms that foster success.

This study was designed to capture the success stories of first-generation African American women who had successfully obtained their doctorate from a PWI.

Although participants identified as such, this study neglected to explicitly ask how the participants' first-generation status directly impacted their doctoral process and success. Therefore, a study that explicitly focuses on this aspect of a Black woman's identity, as well as first-generation doctoral students from other minoritized racial identities, could greatly inform the higher education field.

Black feminist standpoint theory invites research to be done to evaluate how Black women engage in acts of resistance to shape a new identity. Participants talked about how they initially needed "to shrink" and be small or to "wear the mask" in order to assimilate into their new academic spaces. However, they actively engaged in resistance and navigated in their new identities. Future research on how first-generation African American doctoral students learn how and when to engage in acts of resistance to shape new identities would be informative.

Many participants noted the isolation they endured at their Predominantly White Institutions (PWIs), especially those who had previously attended Historically Black Colleges and Universities (HBCUs). Future research that examines how a campus with a higher representation of students of color impacts first-generation doctoral completion and feelings of belongingness for African American students as well as for other marginalized populations (for instance, students at Hispanic Serving Institutions) is essential.

The sister scholars in this study indicated that faith in God was a factor that contributed to the successful completion of their doctoral studies. This topic warrants further research as it is an aspect of identity that often matters to Black women and God, spirituality, and/or the Black church as it has played a significant role in the Black community.

CONCLUSION

As a former diversity and inclusion executive administrator, an associate professor, and a first-generation college graduate and Ph.D. student, the author has also witnessed and experienced microaggressions, invisibility, individual and systemic racism like the participants in this study. Through an investigative narrative inquiry, she heard, captured, and retold the stories that shaped the educational trajectories of study participants. Using semi-structured interviews, the testimonies, victories, and triumphs of five first-generation Black women with a doctorate degree, situated throughout the United States were documented.

These stories will help assist the academy in replicating success for future similarly situated first-generation African American Ph.D. students. By focusing on the success factors of first-generation African American women with a doctorate, this study shifted the current perceptions beyond deficit model thinking. This narrative inquiry provided evidence to assist the university in understanding its role in shaping the trajectory and success of first-generation African American women, doctoral students. Storytelling, communication, and language are powerful tools—they can divide people or can unite them. The stories of these five women have provided a voice to the voiceless and displayed power in action for Black sister scholars who are more than the sum of their struggles. The findings from this study will not only shape a new perspective on the capabilities of first-generation African American Ph.D. graduates, but it will also influence and inspire potential doctoral students for generations to come.

REFERENCES

Acosta, M., Duggins, S., Moore, T. E., Adams, T., & Johnson, B. (2015). "from whence cometh my help?" Exploring black doctoral student persistence. *Journal of Critical Scholarship on Higher Education and Student Affairs*, 2(1), 33–48. https://www.researchgate.net/publication/280569810_From_whence_cometh_my_help_Exploring_African

Allen, B. J. (1995). *Twice blessed, doubly oppressed: Women of color in academe*. Paper presented at the Annual Meeting of the Speech Communication Association, San Antonio, TX.

Allen, B. J. (2000). "Learning the ropes": A black feminist standpoint analysis. In Rethinking organizational & managerial communication from feminist perspectives (pp. 177-208). Thousand Oaks, CA: SAGE.

Allen, B. J. (2002). Goals for emancipatory communication research on Black women. In M. Houston & O. I. Davis (Eds.), *Centering ourselves African American feminist womanist studies of discourse* (pp. 21–34). Hampton Press, Inc.

Allen, B. J. (2012). Introduction. In G. Gutiérrez y Muhs (Ed.), *Presumed incompetent: The intersections of race and class for women in academia* (pp. 17–19). University Press of Colorado. doi:10.2307/j.ctt4cgr3k.6

Banks-Wallace, J. (2002). Talk that talk: Storytelling and analysis rooted in African American oral tradition. *Qualitative Health Research*, 12(3), 410–426. doi:10.1177/104973202129119892 PMID:11918105

Boukari, S. (2005). *20th Century Black women's struggle for empowerment in a White supremacist educational system: Tribute to early women educators*. Retrieved from https://digitalcommons.unl.edu/wgsprogram/4/

Bush, V. B., Gafford Muhammad, C., & Walpole, M. (2009). *From diplomas to doctorates: The success of black women in higher education and its implications for equal educational opportunities for all. Sterling*. Stylus Publishing.

Carter, D., Pearson, C., & Shavlik, D. (1987). Double jeopardy: Women of color in higher education. *The Educational Record, 68*(4), 98.

Collins, P. H. (1986). Learning from the outsider within: The sociological significance of Black feminist thought. *Social Problems, 33*(6), S14–S32. doi:10.2307/800672

Collins, P. H. (2000). *Black feminist thought: knowledge, consciousness, and the politics of empowerment*. Routledge.

Creswell, J. W. (2013). *Qualitative inquiry and research design: Choosing among five approaches*. SAGE Publications.

Dowdy, J. K. (2008). Fire and ice: The wisdom of black women in the academy. *New Horizons in Adult Education and Human Resource Development, 22*(1), 24–43. doi:10.1002/nha3.10297

Edelman, M. W. (1992). *The measure of our success: A letter to my children and yours*. Beacon Press.

Evans, S. Y. (2007). *African American women in the ivory tower, 1850-1954: An intellectual history*. University Press of Florida.

Gardner, S. K. (2013). The challenges of first-generation doctoral students. *New Directions for Higher Education, 2013*(163), 43–54. doi:10.1002/he.20064

Gildersleeve, R. E., Croom, N. N., & Vasquez, P. L. (2011). "Am I going crazy?!": A Critical race analysis of doctoral education. *Equity & Excellence in Education, 44*(1), 93–114. doi:10.1080/106656 84.2011.539472

Habiba. (2015). *What does a PhD mean to a African American woman? African American feminism*. Retrieved from https://medium.com/African American-feminism/what-does-a-phd-mean-to-a-African American-woman-7b8b8bb39120

Holley, K. A., & Gardner, S. K. (2012). Navigating the pipeline: How socio-cultural influences impact first-generation doctoral students. *Journal of Diversity in Higher Education, 5*(2), 112–121. doi:10.1037/a0026840

hooks, b. (2014). *Talking back: Thinking feminist, thinking African American*. Routledge, Taylor and Francis Group.

Ihle, E. L. (1992). *African American women in higher education: An anthology of essays, studies, and documents*. Garland.

Lincoln, Y. S., & Cuba, E. G. (1985). *Naturalistic inquiry*. Sage. doi:10.1016/0147-1767(85)90062-8

McCallum, C. (2017). Giving back to the community: How African Americans envision utilizing their PhD. *The Journal of Negro Education, 86*(2), 138–153. doi:10.7709/jnegroeducation.86.2.0138

Merriam, S. B. (2018). *Qualitative Research in Practice: Examples for Discussion and Analysis*. John Wiley & Sons Inc.

Miles, M. B., & Huberman, A. M. (1994). *Qualitative data analysis: An expanded sourcebook*. Sage Publications.

Muhs, G. G., Niemann, Y. F., Gonzalez, C. G., & Harris, A. P. (2012). *Presumed incompetent: The intersections of race and class for women in academia*. University Press of Colorado. doi:10.2307/j.ctt4cgr3k

National Science Foundation - Where Discoveries Begin. (2018). Retrieved from https://www.nsf.gov/statistics/srvydoctorates/

Obama, M. (2019). *Becoming*. Viking.

Okahana, H., & Zhou, E. (2017). *Graduate enrollment and degrees: 2006 to 2016*. Council of Graduate Schools.

Patton, L. D., & McClure, M. L. (2009). Strength in the spirit: A qualitative examination of African American college women and the role of spirituality during college. *The Journal of Negro Education, 78*(1), 42-54. Retrieved from https://www.jstor.org/stable/25608717

Saldaña, J. (2016). *The coding manual for qualitative researchers* (3rd ed.). Sage.

Strauss, A. L., & Corbin, J. M. (1998). *Basics of qualitative research: Techniques and procedures for developing grounded theory*. Sage Publications.

Williams, D. A. (2013). *Strategic diversity leadership: Activating change and transformation in higher education*. Stylus Publishing.

Wilson, D. L. (2019). *Narrative inquiries in doctorate education: Success stories of african american women first-generation graduates*. ProQuest Dissertations Publishing; 2019.

This research was previously published in Challenges to Integrating Diversity, Equity, and Inclusion Programs in Organizations; pages 128-147, copyright year 2021 by Information Science Reference (an imprint of IGI Global).

Chapter 36
Public School Education:
Minority Students at a Disadvantage

Dwayne Small
DePaul University, USA

ABSTRACT

This chapter examines public schools in low income communities in the U.S. by example of two low income high schools in Chicago. It addresses how alliances between U.S. corporations and local government, and public-school officials do not work in the best interest of students of color in low income communities in their pursuit of higher education. The chapter posits that schools for low income communities do not prepare students for white collar corporate positions, putting them at risk of not qualifying for higher education. Considering the claimed school to prison pipeline, the author calls for closing the educational gap between low income and rich public schools in the U.S. by eradicating racism and classism that appears to prevail in U.S. institutions of education.

INTRODUCTION

President Donald Trump, in a meeting with Senators Dick Durbin of Illinois and Lindsey Graham of South Carolina stated: "People coming to the [U.S.] from shithole countries" (Watkins & Phillip, 2018). They were discussing ideas for immigration reform, where emphatically criticized the idea of more Africans and Haitians coming into the U.S., " […]why we want people from Haiti and more Africans in the [U.S.?], the [U.S.] should get more people from countries like Norway" (Watkins & Phillip, 2018). I am not from any African country nor am I from Haiti. I am from Guyana, and my country's GDP is no different from Africa's or Haiti's, so my home country can easily be within the category of shithole countries, too. I came to the U.S. in 1992 and went straight into the Chicago Public School system. What I have learned and continue to learn about public schools, especially in low income communities, is all new to me. While spending four years at Chicago's Morgan Park High School, I never realized that there were various kinds of curriculums: The concomitant, phantom, hidden, tacit, latent, paracurriculum, and the informal (Longstreet & Shane, 1993). I hadn't paid attention to concepts like The goals of public

DOI: 10.4018/978-1-6684-4507-5.ch036

Copyright © 2022, IGI Global. Copying or distributing in print or electronic forms without written permission of IGI Global is prohibited.

Public School Education

education, The restoration of apartheid education across the USA, "The Zero Tolerance Policies and the "School-to-Prison Pipeline" (Smith, 2015, p. 125), which delineate how easily students can go from the classroom and to prison due to the zero tolerance policies, and what schools really teach.

REFLECTIONS OF A U.S. HIGH SCHOOL GRADUATE

My Perspective on Being a Black Youth in a Chicago School

At Morgan Park, I knew I was going on to college. How I was going to get to that point, however, was not clear to me at the time. Looking back at my academic experience, I can strongly conclude that after I had graduated high school, I was not prepared for college academically. I had the experience of not only getting a U.S. public school education; I had also attended high school in Guyana. I will say, from my perspective, the U.S. public schools and the American society in general are divided by race. I find it extremely difficult to understand how a country with two dominant cultures is as different and divided for such a long period of time, with no end in sight for a meaningful reconciliation.

The public schools in Guyana have no such problems with race relations. There are six cultures in Guyana: Indians, Blacks, Amerindians, Portuguese, Chinese, and Mixed. Guyana is divided into ten administrative regions, which, similarly to the U.S, are divided based on culture. However, in spite of the regions being divided based on culture, Guyana's school system and communities are diverse. The majority and minority population across Guyana's communities emerged based on the slave trade followed by the indentured servitude during the 19th century. From 1850–1920, people were brought from India during the indentured servitude to, at the time, British Guyana and the island of Trinidad (Roopnarine, 2011). The present make-up of Guyana's communities is almost the same as when that country was still under British rule. Guyana received its independence in 1966. So, the present make-up of Guyana's schools' population is mixed, but in harmony.

Living in low-income communities across the U.S., however, is considered to be a negative and it comes with quite a few challenges. Many of those communities are blighted. Parents there would prefer to send their children to another location to further their education but too often meet with serious objection by parents in better off urban or suburban communities, who resist increasing a diverse student population. Segregation laws do not exist in the U.S. anymore, but the school system across America is democratically re-segregating. White Americans send their children to majority white schools and Black Americans, in most cases, have no choice but to send their children to majority black schools (Labaree, 2010, p. 180).

I, too, grew up on the south side of Chicago during the 1990s in an area that was considered low income. During my time of residence, this inequity was no different than it is now, the only difference for me was that I did not distinguish between high and low incomes. It was not even on my radar as a recent immigrant in a new and different culture. According to the Illinois report card data for the school year of 2016 – 2017, racial and ethnic diversity for Morgan Park student body stood at white (0.4%), black (97.3%), Hispanic (1.3%), Asian (0.1%), American Indian (0%), two or more races (0.8%), and Pacific Islander (0.1%). Low income students which include the families of students receiving public aid, living assistance, and reduced-price lunches are 87% with a chronically truant statistic of 74.7% (Education, 2017-2018).

Public School Education

I now conclude that I received a full four-year education from Morgan Park, but not enough to develop and sustain me for higher education. However, I took advantage of what I received. I was clueless to paying attention to how deep the corporate world was imbedded into the public schools or if there was a strong divide between Black and White students within Morgan Park. But analyzing this now, in retrospect, Morgan Park was located in a predominately black American community; the majority of my fellow students were black Americans with a few white and Hispanic students.

Inequities in Quality Education

The main purpose for a high school education is for schools to be equitable and offer quality education for all. Labaree (2010) states that, "...democratic equality and social efficiency, its aim is socialization, to provide knowledge that is useful for citizens and workers; from the perspective of social mobility, its aim is selection, to provide credentials that allow access to good jobs, independent of any learning that might have occurred along the way" (Labaree, 2010, p. 17). Studies, however, show that U.S. public schools are the least equal for its students, depending on race and class. Hochschild claims that this is due to "" Nested inequalities" across boundaries of states, school districts, schools within [districts], class within a school, and sometimes separation within a class" (Hochschild, 2003, p. 821). Kozol (2005) said it best when he pointed out the disadvantage of low-income students in public schools receiving an unfair education across the United States. Vaught (2011) described the Martin Luther King, Jr. High School in Jericho, New York as the worst of Jericho public high schools. She stated that this high school was described as "troubled, struggling, chaotic, dangerous, violent, poor, bad, failing, and black" (Vaught, 2011, p.1). When the author took a closer look at this school during an ethnographic study in 2002, it was clear to her that this one school was divided between black and white students, where one culture was excelling academically while the other struggled.

Further examples show an inequitable system experienced by students in Chicago's public schools. One of these students was living in the Ida B. Wells public housing development and recorded life stories. These described what it is like growing up in the ghetto and being a black American. A male student in the housing project spoke of his struggles and fear about the choices he had to make between dropping out or staying in school and going on to college. On a daily these students' stories come from the experiences of being high school students in a racially and ethnically divided American public school. (Hochschild, 2003).

The Colour Divide

Students of colour live in two Americas. "In the ghetto, our laws are totally different, our language is totally different, and our lives are totally different" as one student described it in Chicago (Ayers, Ladson-Billings, Michie, & Noguera, 2008, pp. 8-9). LeAlan never felt American, he felt only what it is like to be a Black American. In his skin, he feels and lives a life of poverty, stress, and expected pain. "As an African American, I have experienced beautiful things, but the majority of the things I've experienced are not beautiful...and I don't even have it as bad as most" (pp. 8-9). Asked why Black Americans are experiencing this dilemma in America in the 21st century and at such an early age, he responded, "why must they look down the road to a future that they might never see? What have my people done to this country to deserve this?" (p. 9). LeAlan continued to argue against the present American system he is taught to love with patriotism, when it is the same system that is detrimental to him and countless

682

Public School Education

Black Americans. This young man lives in the projects not because he chooses to, but because there is no other choice.

A Hispanic student's story is about his passion for filming videos. His primary school teacher taught Juan the craft when he was in seventh and eighth grades. Juan was a natural at handling the movements and creativity of the video camera. When he reached high school, however, he became frustrated with his life. School became boring for him and each semester his academic progress kept declining. His chance of graduating was very slim. He lives on the South Side of Chicago with his family. His father has very little education and his mother is taking classes at one of the city colleges of Chicago. Juan has a part-time job that pays very little, the amount of money he owes to family and friends is much more than he earns. One thing is certain about Juan's father, he is pushing his son to continue his high school education and continue further after graduating. Juan's experience of not being too interested in school happens often to students at his age. Juan, at one time when he was in third grade, wondered who it was "that invented school" (Ayers, Ladson-Billings, Michie, & Noguera, 2008, pp. 12-13). Juan is scared of life. The direction he was going in, what his school was teaching, and why the school system was not paying attention to its students weighed heavy on him and kept him fearful of his future at this crucial age in his development (Ayers, Ladson-Billings, Michie, & Noguera, 2008).

CLASSISM AND RACISM: IT IS A WELL-KNOWN STORY

Scholarly research has been done for over 100 years on race and society (Horton, Martin, & Fasching-Varner, 2017) and there has been almost no change in race unity between black and white Americans within communities and most importantly in public schools throughout the U.S. With the election of 2008 where a black American man, President Obama, was elected to office, one would think that there would be much change within public schools across U.S. cities. The two terms of the former President came to pass with little change to show. As a matter of fact, "the vast majority of children of [colour continue] to live in poverty" (Horton, Martin, & Fasching-Varner, 2017, p. 4) and attend low achieving public schools. It follows that one has to consider the reality that primary and high schools are racist. In order to understand the divide between low-income and rich public schools, "racism is the piece of the puzzle where the power is housed. The concept of race itself is socially constructed, and this construction occurs on the basis of power" (Horton, Martin, & Fasching-Varner, 2017, p. 4). Bridging the divide within the public-school system is an uphill battle. According to Weise, Fine, and Lareau (1993), social class is imbedded in public school children experiences, "but there are also signs that race mediates the impact of class" (Weis, Fine, & Lareau, 1992, p. 5). John Ogbu (1988) pointed out that the "rates of school success are lower for blacks than whites of all social class backgrounds, including privileged black families" (Ogbu, 1988, pp. 163). It is interesting to see that the likelihood of academic success for low-income black and brown students in public schools is not likely. Even for black and brown students whose families are well-off it is more likely than not that their success lacks behind that of white American students.

The divide and inequality in American public schools are steep and come with dear consequences to most black and brown American students. "Social differentiation and power have set the stage in our public schools since the founding of this country," (Horton, Martin, & Fasching-Varner, 2017, p. 12) continues to be a reality. The National Alliance of Black School Educators (NABSE) and the Association of Latino Administrators and Superintendents (ALAS) agree with the American Association of School

Administrators "that poverty and social conditions inhibit the learning of some [black] American children" (Spring, 2011, p. 37) due to the re-segregation. Most white parents take drastic measures to ensure their children attend majority white schools; schools that are racially mixed is also not an often-chosen option selected for white parents. If they live in a mixed upper-class community with a racially mixed public school, they would, but "many have moved or changed schools to avoid it, and white parents consistently choose schools with very few non-Anglo students. Whites who lack other public-school choices are more likely to send their children to private schools" (Hochschild & Scovronick, 2003, p. 45).

The fear among most white Americans as to why they do not want their children in inner city schools relates to their belief that their children would be harmed educationally. One white parent asked, "do you want to lower the quality of my child's education to raise the quality of the inner-city education?" (Caldas & Bankston, 2003, p. 37). Hochschild and Scovronick (2003), state that "some whites fear losing their advantage in the competition for success; as another parent put it in a similar group, when it comes to schooling, changes are all right as long as our kids get to go first'" (Hochschild & Scovronick, 2003, p. 45). This kind of thinking breeds inequalities (p. 45).

There is segregation within the school buildings themselves where students of the same skin colour socialize among their own. These examples of segregation within public schools are no different when most neighborhoods in urban areas remain extremely segregated. "These high levels of racial residential segregation have led to extreme disparities in the quality of public education' (Horton, Martin, & Fasching-Varner, 2017, p. 13). Segregated communities across the U.S. are a major issue and the main cause for poor, undeveloped, and failing public schools because "race plays a major role in communities" (Ostrander & Portney, 2007, p. 173). Most, if not all, public schools receive their funding from the state and federal government, but "most of their major resources are funded through their local property taxes" (Horton, Martin, & Fasching-Varner, 2017, p. 13). So, if the rich communities' constituents are all high earners and the low-income communities are mainly minimum wage earners, property values would greatly differ. According to Horton, Martin, and Fasching-Varner (2017),

Homes located in the suburbs typically occupied by white, wealthier families tend to have higher property values than those located in inner-city neighborhoods, occupied by poorer, minority families. Income and wealth differences in richer suburbs and poorer urban neighborhoods have an astounding effect on the amount of funding local schools receive (p. 13).

Kozol (2005), breaks down the differences in community income. He, states that Edgewood, Texas, a city where 96% of its residents are non-white, can only afford $37 for each student along with funding from the state which creates a combined total of $231 for each child in local low-income public schools. In Alamo Heights, the richest part of the city, spends a total of $543 on each of their students (Kozol, 2005, pp. 241-242). The impact of income disparities is evident.

A major problem in public schools is racism. According to Spring (2011), "since their arrival in this country in 1619, [black] Americans have been subjected to inferior and disproportionate education and other services. First denied and then suffering an inadequate, underfunded, under resourced and separate education" (Spring, 2011, p. 38). Their white counterparts enjoy the hierarchy that has always been in place in the U.S, at the cost of an unequal educational system for black and brown Americans.

It is without argument that the divide within public schools will continue because its black students are not given "the same opportunity to achieve as white students" (Horton, Martin, & Fasching-Varner,

Public School Education

2017, p. 67). The sad reality about these situations in public schools does not end there, they move on to college and university campuses where students in higher education suffer from racial battle fatigue."

COOPERATE BUSINESS AND U.S. PUBLIC SCHOOLS

Since the 1960s, the USA continued an era of desegregation within the public schools in the U.S. The desegregation of U.S. public schools in urban districts shed light to a new problem, 'the line between public schools and private markets [which] turned out to be not so bright, and it gradually became apparent that education is not the primary cause of racial inequality but one of its many interconnected contributors" (Jacob, 1998, p. xii). Scholars have often isolated school desegregation, race, culture, and politics, but not the combined "significant sociopolitical forces as business community influence on education [because...] the flaws of the current literature have come to mirror the failings of Brown itself" (Jacob, 1998, p. xii). In the city of Columbus, Ohio, for example, their "powerful, business-led "growth consensus" that had long shaped [their] political and economic activity in the city [are] provided [with] a development safety valve" (Jacob, 1998, p. xiii). Urban sociologist Harvey Molotoch wrote that "'virtually all U.S. cities," are dominated by a small, parochial elite whose members have business or professional interests that are linked to local development or growth" (Jacob, 1998, p. 77). These corporate elite members use policies, public authority, and private powers to stimulate their economic interest within communities.

The Chicago Public School (CPS) educational system is another example, where business elite and corporate curriculums are alive and well in the classrooms. "CPS policies frame schooling in a language business understands—regulation, accountability, and quality assurance" (Ayers, Ladson-Billings, Michie, & Noguera, 2008, p. 281). Business leaders in corporate companies outline public schools' curricula byway of reforms. Every so often, the idea to reform CPS curricula resurfaces, starting with their educators, policymakers, and onto to students. Some of these reforms are usually in the area of retention, standardized tests, discipline, and literacy curricula and these take place mostly in low-income communities. "This symbolism is highly racialized. In addition to basic mathematical and print literacy, employers are particularly concerned with future workers' attitudes and "work ethic", their reliability, trustworthiness, ability to take directions, and, in the case of in-person service workers, and pleasant manner[s]" (Ayers, Ladson-Billings, Michie, & Noguera, 2008, p. 281). The business communities throughout Chicago wants both public school "students and schools certify for Chicago business that CPS graduates will have the specific literacies and dispositions it demands," (Ayers, Ladson-Billings, Michie, & Noguera, 2008, p. 281) meeting industrial standards.

Besides the corporate business influence in the classrooms, there is the education business. Education companies are the ones that exist on the backs of education. For example, public schools are to reinvest in its institutions and these educational companies would not flourish without funding from departments of education. Education enterprises are the ones who profit from the shortfall of public education. According to Spring (2011), "education business influence school politics in a quest for profit which are in part dependent on government outlays for textbooks, software, equipment, tutoring services, and charter schools" (Spring, 2011, p. 4). The No Child Left Behind (NCLB) act provides "funds to hire for-profit companies to provide supplementary education services to schools, identified as needing improvement, testing, discipline, and restructuring" (Spring, 2011, pp. 4-5). The processes and core curricula that came with the NCLB law only created further inequality in public schools. Out of school suspension for black and Latino students increased 8% and 14 respectively with a 3% drop for white students (Horton, Martin, & Fasching-Varner, 2017, p. 43) in the wake of the NCLB act. These educational for-profit companies also provide tutoring, curriculum restructuring, achievement enhancement, and more, raking in $68.5 billion in 2010 (Spring, 2011, p. 150). They further profit from "high-stakes testing to promote and sort students for careers and higher education and for evaluating teachers and school administrators" (Spring, 2011, p. 5).

The 500 companies and for-profit businesses influence public schools' curriculum because when city public schools fail, vendors like these put receive resources for low-income public schools and add their kind of services. Rothstein (1995) showed that college preparatory programmes are less likely to be found in predominantly minority schools than in majority schools. So, if parents and their children observe their white peers getting the resources, they need that will assist to enter higher education, education companies like charter schools, Kaplan, and Harcourt are low-income parents perceived best options for their child, making these educational institutions profitable organizations. Charter schools, for example, have "4,300 schools in 40 states and the District of Columbia, serving more than 1.2 million students-about 3 percent of all public-school children" (Spring, 2011, p. 167). In some states like Louisiana and D.C., the charter school market shares are 50% and 25% respectively with thousands of families on the waiting list (Spring, 2011). These primary and secondary school organizations can best be described to engage in "extensive range of market-oriented schemes" (Horton, Martin, & Fasching-Varner, 2017, p. 43). The more low-income students fail, the higher the for-profit education corporations' profit (Horton, Martin, & Fasching-Varner, 2017, p. 43).

CONCLUSION

There is no quick fix to the U.S. public schools' divisive system between Black and White students and equality among them. For this system to be fixed by at least beginning a national conversation about race relations, it has to be done from a shared perspective of the value of a quality education for all. Lieberman (1993) said it best, when he mirrored the restructure of the Soviet economy and the upset it caused in the area of the distribution of political power, "the changes required to reform education in the United States, the changes that are needed threaten powerful political and educational interest groups" (Lieberman, 1993, p. 2). The reason why it is difficult for real change in public school education in low-income communities has to do with the interest groups who maintain the status quo for economic benefit. Their show of interest for change will be validated, because the outcome is only cosmetic (Lieberman, 1993).

Donald Trump can speak with distain against minority cultures, exposing that hidden curriculum in the process by favoring white foreign nationals over Black foreigners. As a black immigrant, with two graduate degrees, I see the American society in more bad shape culturally. What has been hidden is now open. Divisive actions by some white Americans in the 21st century is not just now happening, they are based in historical and ideological concepts based on skin colour. But for a while, it was hidden to the larger public. According to Wilson, C, Wilson, M, and Johnson in "…societies such as the USA, race or ethnicity is a maker of significant differences in the distribution of resources and access " (Wilson, Wilson, & Johnson, 2010, pp. 37-58) to a good public education for low-income high school students because race is the dominant and divisive cause of inequality.

Public School Education

Many minority public school students with the support of their parents fight hard to ensure that their children get the best public education being offered within their respective communities. There are more issues to address than lack of corporate social consciousness in the education industry or the prevailing racism and classism that work against people of colour. Issue like the school-to-prison fostered by the hidden curriculum and poor teacher preparations in public schools need to be explored. As one example of a Black man that has overcome the initial struggles created by a poor public-school education, I have dedicated myself to engage in the discourse on education as a means for self and community empowerment. We live in a time when ~isms have moved from behind a veil more so, perhaps than during the Civil Rights era because the USA wanted to believe it had solved its race problem. My experience tells a different story. Educators, administrators, funders, vendors, and elected officials need to join with students and parents to hear stories like mine if we are serious about changing the current state of affair.

REFERENCES

Apple, M. W., & King, N. R. (1977). What Do Schools Teach? *Curriculum Inquiry*, 6(4), 341–358. do i:10.1080/03626784.1977.11075550

Apple, W. M. (2004). *Ideology and Curriculum* (3rd ed.). New York, NY: RoutledgeFalmer. doi:10.4324/9780203487563

Ayers, W., Ladson, B. G., Michie, G., & Noguera, A. P. (2008). *City Kids, City Schools*. New York, NY: W.W. Norton & Company.

Bortis, H., Bardadym, T., & Emmenegger, F. J. (Eds.). (1999). *Social and Political Sciences in the Commonwealth of Independent States*. University Press Fribourg.

Caldas, S. J., & Bankston, C. L. III, (Eds.). (2003). *The End of Desegregation?* New York: Nova Science Publishers, Inc.

Eisner, W. E. (1994). *The Education Imagination: On the Design and evaluation of School Programs* (3rd ed.). Macmillan College Publishing Company.

Giroux, H., & Purpel, D. (Eds.). (1983). *The Hidden Curriculum and Moral Education*. Berkeley, CA: McCutchan Publishing Corporation.

Hochschild, L. J. (2003). Social Class in Public Schools. *The Journal of Social Issues*, 59(4), 821–840. doi:10.1046/j.0022-4537.2003.00092.x

Hochschild, L. J., & Scovronick, N. (2003). *The American Dream and the Public Schools*. New York: Oxford University Press.

Horton, D. H., Martin, L. L., & Fasching-Varner, J. K. (Eds.). (2017). *Race, Population Studies, and America's Public Schools: A Critical Demography Perspective*. New York, NY: Lexington Books.

Jacob, S. G. (1998). *Getting Around Brown: Desegregation, Development, and the Columbus Public Schools*. Columbus, OH: Ohio State University Press.

Kozol, J. (1985). *Illiterate America*. Garden City, NY: Anchor Press.

Kozol, J. (2005). *The Shame of the Nation: The Restoration of Apartheid Schooling in America*. New York, NY: Crown Publishers.

Labaree, D. F. (2010). *Someone has to Fail: The Zero-Sum Game of Public Schooling*. Cambridge, MA: Harvard University Press.

Lieberman, M. (1993). *Public Education: An Autopsy*. Cambridge, MA: Harvard University Press.

Longstreet, S. W., & Shane, G. H. (1993). *Curriculum for a New Millennium*. Needham Heights, MA: Allyn & Bacon.

Ogbu, J. U. (1988). *"Class Stratification, Race Stratification, and Schooling," in Class, Race, and Gender in American Education*. Albany, NY: SUNY Press.

Ostrander, A. S., & Portney, E. K. (Eds.). (2007). *Acting Civically from Urban Neighborhoods to Higher Education*. Medford, MA: Tufts University Press.

Roopnarine, L. (2011). Indian migration during indentured servitude in British Guiana and Trinidad, 1850–1920. *Labor History*, *52*(2), 173–191. doi:10.1080/0023656X.2011.571473

Rothstein, W. S. (Ed.). (1995). *Class, Culture, and Race in American Schools*. Westport, CT: Greenwood Press.

Schubert, H. W. (1986). *Curriculum: Perspective, Paradigm, and Possibility*. New York, NY: Macmillan Publishing Company.

Smith, L. M. (2015). A Generation at Risk: The Ties Between Zero Tolerance Policies and the School-To-Prison Pipeline. *McNair Scholars Research Journal*, *8*(1), 125–141.

Solorzana, D. G. (2004). A Critical Race Analysis of Latina/o and African American Advanced Placement Enrollment in Public High Schools. *High School Journal*, *87*(3), 15–26. doi:10.1353/hsj.2004.0003

Spring, J. (2011). *The Politics of American Education*. New York, NY: Routledge. doi:10.4324/9780203838990

Vaught, S. E. (2011). *Racism, Public Schooling, and the Entrenchment of White Supremacy: A critical Race Ethnography*. New York: State University of New York Press.

Watkins, E., & Phillip, A. (2017). *Trump Decries Immigrants from 'Shithole Countries' Coming to US*. Retrieved from https://www.cnn.com/2018/01/11/politics/immigrants-shithole-countries-trump/index.html

Weis, L., Fine, M., & Lareau, A. (1992). *Schooling and the Silenced "Others"*. New York, NY: GSE Publications.

Wilson, C. L., Wilson, M. C., & Johnson, M. B. (2010). Race and Health in Guyana: An Empirical Assessment from Survey Date. *Caribbean Studies (Rio Piedras, San Juan, P.R.)*, *38*(1). PMID:21553433

This research was previously published in Competency-Based and Social-Situational Approaches for Facilitating Learning in Higher Education; pages 124-135, copyright year 2019 by Information Science Reference (an imprint of IGI Global).

Chapter 37
Race, Class, and Community Cultural Wealth:
Impacts on Parental Involvement Among Black Families in K–12 Public Schools

Evelyn Ezikwelu
University of Utah, USA

ABSTRACT

Culture has been established as an integral part of the successful parental involvement of Black parents in K-12 public schools. This chapter explores the implications of institutional racism and classism against Black parents and how schools as social institutions perpetuate discrimination through the hidden curriculum, which often upholds the dominant culture's values, norms, and beliefs. This chapter also investigates how schools operate within the dominant ideology that upholds the White middle-class form of cultural capital as the standard form of capital, thereby devaluing the cultural skills that Black parents use to help children achieve academic success in school. In addition, the literature demonstrates that the unique forms of cultural capital Black parents draw from to help their children succeed in school challenge the dominant ideology that Black parents lack the required capital for school success and are not interested in their children's education.

INTRODUCTION

Culture is an important factor in successful parental involvement among families of Color in K-12 public schools. Research has established the importance of culture to parental involvement of parents of Color in K-12 public schools (Yosso, 2005). Parental involvement is any form of support from parents toward the success of their children's education (Chapman, 2017) In this regard, parental involvement denotes different forms of learned behaviors that parents use to help their children succeed academically. Yosso (2005) confirms that parents of Color utilize culture-related skills for school involvement. Yosso argues that successful parental involvement of parents of Color in school is derived from their cultural assets

DOI: 10.4018/978-1-6684-4507-5.ch037

Copyright © 2022, IGI Global. Copying or distributing in print or electronic forms without written permission of IGI Global is prohibited.

(2005). Evidence from literature has shown that religion and other forms of community engagement have been cultural sources for Black parents' involvement in schools as ways to help their children achieve academic success (Billingsley & Caldwell, 1991; Lincoln, 1989; Hamilton, 2014). However, the cultures that parents of Color in general bring to schools are often not recognized in K-12 public schools due to the institutional racism and classism that form the foundation of social institutions like U.S. public schools (Yosso, 2005). The discrimination is more evident among the families of Color of low socioeconomic status, who are assumed to lack the necessary skills for successful school involvement, and who are also assumed to not have interest in their children's education (Chapman & Bhopal, 2013; Fernández, 2002; Lareau, 2000; Vaught, 2008). It has been documented that the discrimination affects Black families more in K-12 public schools because of past slavery; hence, there is a historical record of racial discrimination against Black families in the U.S (Bonilla-Silva, 2009; Burton, Bonilla-Silva, Ray; Fultz, 1995; Delgado & Stefanicic 2012). Research has identified the stereotypical assumption that low-income Black parents lack skills for school engagement as a racially driven form of cultural discrimination, which uses cultural capital as a means to divide the low-income Black parents and the White middle-class families in K-12 public schools (Yosso, 2005). To these, I need to emphasize that it is important to critically re-assess the issues surrounding cultural capital in parental involvement between Black and White parents, to ascertain their interconnections with racism and classism, and how they lead to cultural distinctions that devalue Blacks in K-12 public schools. This investigation will help to combat cultural bias against Black parents and promote recognition of those undervalued culture-related skills that Black parents of low-socioeconomic status mostly utilize to effectively support their children's education in K-12 public schools.

Contrary to the hegemonic ideologies that Black parents do not have interest in their children's education, nor possess the required cultural capital to academically support their children, it has been established that schools are highly esteemed institutions for many Black parents, who demonstrate a high parental educational yearning for their children (Anderson, 1988; Willie, Garibaldi & Reed, 1990). Education has been at the center of African Americans' desires since emancipation. Research has confirmed that Black parents and their children have endured serious deprivations to achieve educational equity for the education of Black children (Anderson, 1988; Billingsley & Caldwell, 1991). While Black parents have long been at the forefront of their children's education without much success, Yosso (2005) asserts they are capable and have unique forms of cultural capital such as familial, navigational, resistance, social, and linguistic capital with which to support their children academically.

This chapter will examine culture-related oppressions in K-12 public schools using Critical Race Theory (CRT) and Yosso's (2005) community cultural wealth, to tease out those power dynamics of oppression that recreate and maintain racism and classism. In addition, the Critical Race Theory analytical frame, Yosso's (2005) community cultural wealth, and other literature that demonstrate the positive impact of religion through Black churches in providing alternative sources of cultural strength for Black parents' involvement in schools will be used to answer the following question: Given that Black families of low socioeconomic status are not given equal access for involvement as their White middle-class counterparts, what are the ways through which most Black families navigate and withstand institutional racism and classism and successfully assist in their children's education in K-12 public schools? First, this chapter posits there is a strong connection between parental involvement and culture, and that the connection determines the success of low-income Black parents' involvement in K-12 public schools. Second, this chapter shows Black parents are not given equal involvement access in K-12 public schools due to historical institutional racism and classism that exists in the U.S. Third, this chapter posits that K-12 public

Race, Class, and Community Cultural Wealth

schools as a social institution reproduce and perpetuate systemic racism and classism through the hidden curriculums, which are the forms of values, norms, and beliefs that are detrimental to the success of families of Color because they continuously subject Black families to the hegemonic cultural standard.

Further, through the Critical Race Theory analytical lens and Yosso's (2005) concept of community cultural wealth, this chapter will explore the experiences of some Black parents in K-12 public schools. Particularly, this chapter will contextualize the communal form of community cultural capital to analyze how it is undeviating from cultural values and skills that Black parents acquire from Black churches and social interactions such as community engagement, educational programs, and parent-to-parent forms of social interaction. Although all six forms of community cultural wealth discussed by Yosso (2005) could be applicable when narrating the school involvement experiences of Black parents, this chapter focuses on the communal and social forms of community cultural wealth, to contextualize how they apply to educational programs and social (person-to-person) interactions through which Black parents successfully get involved and help their children succeed in K-12 public schools. For this chapter, the metric for successful school engagement and the success of Black families is school retention. This chapter illustrates some of the knowledge and strengths that most Black families acquire from their church educational programs and friends to help their children succeed in K-12 public schools. In addition, this chapter posits that religion through Black churches shapes Black culture, and as a result, influences the skills Black parents use for school involvement in K-12 public schools. It is important to note that cultural differences exist among Black families in the U.S., as Black families comprise African Americans and African immigrants. Through research evidence, I argue that Black families draw cultural strength from their local churches (Black churches) and through social interactions, for successful school engagements. This is why, for the purpose of this chapter, the author did not consider it significant to differentiate between Black parents' school involvement experiences by immigration status.

These illustrations are used to counter the dominant ideologies that describe Black parents as lacking the kind of cultural capital needed for parental involvement and academic success.

Research has demonstrated that Black parents of low-socioeconomic status are more likely to be ignored in K-12 public schools than White middle-class families due to the ignorance of most White teachers and White school administrators on the unique form of culture they bring with them to public schools (Yosso, 2005). Other scholars have shown that Black parents, particularly those of low socio-economic resources, have cultural skills for effective school involvement with which they assist their children to achieve school success. Therefore, this chapter serves as a theoretical contribution to maintain that Black parents of low-socioeconomic status have cultural skills for successful school involvement. As such, it helps to discover those distinctive forms of cultural capital that are particularly useful for Black parents' support to their children's education, which are often suppressed due to institutional racism and classism that devalue Black cultures. It helps make White teachers and school administrators in K-12 public schools more aware of the need to value the cultures that Black parents bring to schools. In addition, this chapter helps to create cultural awareness and educate White teachers on different forms of cultural skills, such as church community programs and social interactions, as sources of cultural strengths through which poor Black parents help their children achieve school success. Thus, the objective of this chapter is to draw from a variety of literature that challenges the devaluation of cultural skills of Black parents in K-12 public schools. Other literature utilized shows the importance of Black churches' community education programs and other forms of social interaction like friendship among Black parents. These studies are used to demonstrate that their involvement is achieving the objective of school success for their kids despite the institutional racism and classism they face in K-12 public schools.

BACKGROUND

Parental Involvement in Relation to Black Culture

Researchers have broadly defined parental involvement as both home and school activities that parents use to provide educational support to their children. Definitions of parental involvement include different kinds of activities such as involvement at school, homework help, parents' attendance at school events such as parent-teacher conferences, and involving parents in making decisions concerning the education of their children (Alexander & Hernández, 2013; Baquedano-López, 2013; Bowers and Griffin, 2011; Chapman & Bhopal, 2013; Fine, 1993; Ladson-Billings, 1995, 2009; Lareau 2000; Lee & Bowen 2006; Van Galen, 1987; Watson & Bogotch, 2015). These definitions demonstrate that parental involvement entails parents' provision of both home and school academic support to their children for their children's educational success. The definition is expanded by Bowers and Griffin (2011), who include effective communication with teachers as part of the definition of parental involvement. Others have also expanded the conventional definition of parental involvement. Chapman defines parental involvement as

those actions which parents take to provide physical, emotional, psychological, intellectual, and academic support for their child(ren)'s academic success and social well-being. Parental involvement goes beyond actions directly applied to formal education, and extends to the types of activities, systems of support, and areas of wellness that parents access to assist their child(ren)'s engagement with education. (T. Chapman, personal communication, January 4, 2017)

Chapman's recent response on the definition of parental involvement includes all facets of support that parents give to their children to help them succeed in school. By relying on Chapman's definition of parental involvement, this chapter argues that the skills which Black parents bring with them to K-12 public schools are determined by the distinctive cultural skills they have been exposed to over the years.

Parental involvement has been established as an important factor in the educational success of K-12 public school children, particularly students of Color of low socio-economic background, who have substantial drop-out rates (Barnard, 2004; Berger, 1983; Jeynes, 2003; Lee & Bowen, 2006; MacLeod, 1995; Seeley, 1984; Trelease, 1982), and the success of parental involvement among parents of Color has been linked to their culture (Allen & White-Smith, 2018 Usher & Kober, 2012; Yosso, 2005). According to Usher and Kober (2012), families reinforce educational values through their culture, which results in different forms of school engagement by children of different cultural backgrounds. Meanwhile, Usher and Kober (2012) add that students from certain cultures prefer their academic choices be made for them by their significant others such as their parents, unlike the White students who are more likely to be allowed to make school decisions independently. This differentiates the parental involvement between White parents and parents of Color. By making academic decision for their children, parents of Color show dedication to their children's education.

The Roles of Black Churches

To most Black families, the skills for parental involvement could be traced to their relationships and connections to educational programs held at their local churches, widely known as Black churches. It is documented that Black churches bond large groups of African Americans and shape their cultures and

Race, Class, and Community Cultural Wealth

behaviors (Hamilton, 2014). The re-examination of the data on the survey of African Americans by the University of Michigan (Billingsley, in press) demonstrates that almost 70% of African Americans were members at different churches; 77% confirmed that church is very important to them; 80% considered it necessary to send their children to a church at least once every a week, particularly on Sundays; 84% considered themselves religious; 78% said they pray often; and 76% confirmed churches play a key role in their socialization, making Black churches more than just a religious institution for African Americans (Billingsley & Caldwell, 1991). Similarly, Lincoln (1989) expresses that Black churches play major roles, from civilization to freedom, and serve as the mother of African American culture. These roles influence the ways Black churches assist Black families, especially those from low-socioeconomic backgrounds, to create academic success (Hamilton, 2014). In addition, the roles of Black churches support the beliefs of many sociologists, who agree that churches are the most powerful institution of Black people's social lives (Billingsley & Caldwell, 1991). These social lives help African Americans build strong community engagement (Allen & White-Smith, 2018; Blackwell, 1991; Clark, 1990; Drake & Cayton, 1945; Gutman & McLoyd, 2000; Johnson, 1934; Smith, 2014; Williams & Sánchez, 2012). These studies are consistent with Lewis (1957), who argues that Black churches play leading and decisive roles in the lives of most African Americans.

In the same manner, Hill (1971) points out that Black churches play unique roles to instill unique values to most African Americans. The study argues that spirituality plays a key role in African American culture. This is consistent with Smith (2014), who demonstrates that African Americans rely on religious practices as one of their coping mechanisms against racial discrimination in schools. The Merriam-Webster Dictionary defines religion as "a personal set or institutionalized system of religious attitudes, beliefs, and practices" (2002). In addition, the same Merriam-Webster dictionary defines church as "a body or organization of religious believers: Such as a body of Christians." Therefore, this chapter analyzes church as the organization that facilitates religious practices. This chapter recognizes there are different forms of religion with each having its own beliefs and practices. However, for the purpose of this chapter, Christianity as a form of religion is used to demonstrate that Black parents are dedicated to Black churches, with those from low income backgrounds mostly relying on the educational programs that these Black churches establish in their communities to help their children succeed in K-12 public schools.

Additionally, it is important to point that although this chapter is focused on the Black population, which comprises African Americans and African immigrants, in fact, anyone of African descent and a resident in the U.S., it recognizes that African Americans and African immigrants in the U.S. are not the same and do not have the same culture. Nevertheless, evidence from literature has shown that the relationship between African Americans and Black churches are consistent with that of African immigrants residing in the U.S., whose population has increased from 810,000 to over 2.8 million in recent years (Hamilton, 2014; Kent 2007). Twenty percent of yearly immigrants in 1980 were from Africa. Also, between 1990s, and 2005, this number has increased from 36% to 53%. According to an online article, "How Houses of Worship Help Immigrants Adjust to America," by Teresa Matthew (2017), she argues that churches help deliver a course on America 101 to African immigrants to the U.S. She states that the most powerful roles of churches for immigrants are ethnic (cultural), assisting the immigrant families to gain social capital. As an African immigrant residing in the U.S., the author argues that most African immigrants join African American churches (Black churches) and adopt their ways of life So, although a vast majority of these studies on Black churches are mainly on African Americans, is important to note that African immigrant churches also play significant roles in shaping the cultures and skills of Black immigrant parents and assist them in their school involvement and in the educational success of their children in K-12 public schools (Billingsley & Caldwell, 1991). To this effect, Black churches become one of the places for survival for Black people in America.

Roles of Black Churches in the Formation of Black Community Ties

Most often, Black churches are at the center of community activities. Billingsley & aldwell (1991) assert that Black churches are community institutions, due to their involvement in different community engagement services that their congregations benefit from in many ways. Examining how Black communities assist in educational involvement of Black parents and their families, research has shown that Black churches are considered part of African American communities, with almost every Black church holding an educational outreach program that provides educational support for Black congregations (Hamilton, 2014; Lincoln, 1989; Lewis, 1957). This implies that Black churches not only play a significant role in influencing the cultures of Black families, which reflect their beliefs and cultural skills for school involvement, they may offer different forms of academic assistance for Black families' educational success. According to Billingsley and Caldwell (1991), 16% of church programs provide informal educational support to Black children. Also, the study points out that up to 216 Black churches, which are covered in the study, continuously provide 11% of formal educational programs, ranging from head start programs, to elementary and secondary school academic support, to college preparatory and college support programs. Moreover, Billingsley and Caldwell (1991) argue that those Black churches which do not provide formal educational support to their children and youth, directly provide scholarships and mentorship to Black children and Black youth, which operate as an educational program in the community. I argue that both provide significant educational support to Black families and facilitate educational support of Black parents as well as educational success of their children.

Expanding on the significance of educational programs in the community and how Black parents achieve success in their school involvement, a survey conducted by Latunde and Clark-Louque (2016) of 130 Black parents investigating their parental involvement strategies to promote the educational success of their children shows that these parents relied on two major capacities: Some depended on programs and organizations that are especially meant for Black students and their parents, which include educational programs from Black churches. Others depended on other forms of social interaction such as Black social gatherings and socialization through the internet, through friends, and through fellow Black work colleagues. Specifically, Launder and Clark-Louque (2016) point that the African Methodist Church is well known for providing scholarships, mentoring, and tutoring programs for educational progress of their Black congregations. Therefore, the author argues these forms of support promote social interactions among Black parents, as well as the involvement of Black parents from low-socioeconomic backgrounds, who otherwise would not have the financial capability and cultural skills to successfully get involved in their children's education.

Issues of Race, Class, and Hidden Curriculum: Impacts on Black Parents' Involvement

Despite the importance of culture to the successful parental involvement Black parents and the academic success of their children, race and class have been demonstrated as the two major obstacles that create social challenges for families of Color from low socioeconomic status and in K-12 public schools (Bar-

Race, Class, and Community Cultural Wealth

nard, 2004; Berger, 1983; Burton, Bonilla-Silva, Ray, Buckelew & Hordge Freeman, 2010; Jeynes, 2003; Lee & Bowen, 2006; MacLeod, 1995; Seeley, 1984; Trelease, 1982). The author argues that the systemic racism and classism which shape the country's social institutions result in poorer-quality opportunities being extended to families of Color. To that end, there is a need to look at the historical foundations of racism and classism against Black families in the U.S.

Anderson (1988) argues that Black families, since emancipation, have been subjected to other forms of oppression through educational exclusion. Similarly, other scholars have documented that Black students have been legally segregated in the public schools, where they attended inferior public schools that were racially isolated despite the Supreme Court ruling to end educational segregation (Nieto, 2004; Gotanda, Crenshaw, Peller, & Thomas, 1995). Therefore, despite the struggle of Black parents to fully engage in their children's education in the past, they continue to face the problem of exclusion from the best K-12 public schools due to racism (Gotanda, Crenshaw, Peller, & Thomas, 1995, p. 20). Race therefore serves as one of the major reasons that the cultural skills of Black parents are ignored in K-12 public schools.

Black people and their cultures have always been at the forefront of social rejection in the history of the U.S. There is established research that race serves as a societal tool for the distribution of status, power, and prestige (Bonilla-Silva, 2009; Burton, Bonilla-Silva, Ray, Buckelew & Horde Freeman, 2010; Fultz, 1995; Delgado & Stefanicic 2012; McIntosh, 1990; Smith, 1999; Yosso, 2005). Being White alone is a privilege which plays a significant positive role in parental involvement for White parents (Lareau and Horvat, 1999; Delgado & Stefanick, 1997]. As McIntosh (1990) states, "being white is a privilege, norm and invisible" (p.23). Like other social institutions, K-12 public schools promote racial inequality via racial discrimination (Burton, Bonilla-Silva, Ray, Buckelew & Hordge Freeman, 2010).

American society is made up of different ethnicities, cultures, and racial groups, which requires that unfair racial discrimination should be eliminated to achieve social and intellectual development (Bell, Grosholz & Stewart, 2014; Chapman, 2007; DeCuir & Dixson, 2004; King, 1991; Ladson-Billings & Tate, 2006; Lareau & Howat, 1999; Lewis, 2003; Pollock, 2005, 2008; Solórzano & Ornelas, 2002; Woodson, 2006; Bell, Grosholz & Stewart, 2014). The implication is that these forms of racial discrimination apply to people of Color in general, and are not socially recognized. As the argues, these manifestations of racial inequality result in the patterns of operations that socially construct Black parents as unfit for school involvement.

It is not new that Black parents are at the center of discrimination more than other parents of Color. Ladson, Billing and Tate (1995) argue that historically, Black parents from low socioeconomic backgrounds are affected in school by the U.S. policies that reinforce the discrimination against them. To this effect, this chapter demonstrates that the racial and class-related prejudices that Black parents and other parents of Color face in K-12 public schools are systemically embedded schools' hidden curriculum (unseen school practices and policies),. It is important to examine the content of the hidden curriculum to reveal how they reinforce the beliefs and behaviors of school personnel, to understand the foundations of the oppressions that Black parents face in K-12 public schools in the country. Laker (2012) asserts that hidden curriculum is a strong means through which unrevealed norms, values and beliefs are engrained and transmitted to the students through unspoken rules that are used to shape the social relationships in schools.

This is consistent with Bain (1990), who argues that one of the three themes of the hidden curriculum is its effective construction of social interaction. The connection that these authors made between the hidden curriculum and social interactions confirms why Black parents are not socially and culturally accepted in schools. Again, it is connected to systemic racism and classism that have haunted Black families throughout U.S. history. In the same vein, Apple and Apple (2018) contend that schools lean toward ideas that promote economic, political, and cultural tensions in their day-to-day activities with the aim of maintaining an unequal society. These discriminatory activities are kept alive in K-12 public schools through the hidden curriculum. Apple & Apple (2018) argue that the hidden curriculum embodies the dominant forms of social interaction that still exist in schools today. The study contends schools use this means to preserve and circulate the White middle-class form of cultural capital and to recreate forms of consciousness that maintain social control. It is, therefore, a determining systemic principle for those in racial and economic power in social institutions such as K-12 public schools, to relate with Black parents—particularly those from low-socioeconomic backgrounds—in discriminatory ways, to maintain economic and racial domination as well as ownership of cultural capital.

Yosso (2005) states, "cultural capital are those cultural skills, knowledge and abilities that are assumed to be owned by only the effluents in the society" (p. 76). To this, Bourdieu and Passeron as cited in Yosso (2005) argue that some communities are wealthier than others, which is used by the dominant to determine cultural capital availability. According to the study, the wealthy communities reveal White middle-class culture as superior and more in control of social institutions. With this, Bourdieu (1979) maintains that cultural capital is a source of social influence. Further, Bourdieu (1979) claims that White middle-class families face the same lifestyle at school as they live at home; as such, they are familiar with the school environment, and are therefore more likely to succeed than families of Color from low-socioeconomic backgrounds who lack the kind of cultural knowledge needed for school success. To this end, Bourdieu's (1979) narratives of cultural capital seem to be the only determining factor for educational access and success in K-12 public schools. Such a one-sided idea supports the hegemonic ideologies that consider Black families unsuccessful in schools. Therefore, there is a need to explore how systemic racism is constructed against Black parents.

As a theoretical framework that investigates how society uses culture to classify race and power dynamics, Critical Race Theory (CRT) exposes how the racial oppressions of families of Color have become part of the normal operating principles of the dominant group in K-12 public schools. CRT traces these race and cultural oppressions as a means through which the hegemony maintains cultural and power domination. In their analysis, CRT scholars Chapman and Bhopal (2013) state: "Critical Race Theorists recognize that the perspectives of oppressed people have been 'distorted, ignored, silenced, destroyed, appropriated, commodified, and marginalized'" (Bell, 1995, p. 11) as a means to promote White culture and create racial privilege for White families in the U.S. The study further stressed that the oppressions against people of Color are a long-established behavior in both federal and state policies and in school practices. This maintains a one-sided relationship between White educators and those families of Color that are from low-socioeconomic backgrounds, often through cultural devaluation. CRT scholars understand that the blame on parents of Color is used to maintain racial prejudices in public schools (Chapman & Bhopal, 2013), and therefore criticize teachers and school administrators who view people of Color as inferior (Bell 1995; Chang 1993; Chapman, 2007; Delgado 1989; Olivas 1989; Yosso, 2005). With this knowledge, CRT diverts the existing negative research, which label families of Color as culturally deficient, by emphasizing the cultural assets with which families of Color navigate and succeed in K-12 public schools (Solórzano & Solórzano, 1995; Valencia & Solórzano, 1997; Villalpando & Solórzano, 2005; Yosso, 2005).

MAIN FOCUS OF THE CHAPTER

Issues, Controversies, Problems

The sections below provide the overview of the issues and challenges that Black parents face in K-12 public schools.

Issues of Racism and Classism in Schools: Black Parents' Experiences

As discussed earlier, the issues of racism and classism have continued to negatively impact the school involvement of Black parents in K-12 public schools. In a study conducted by Allen and White-Smith (2018) with ten (10) Black parents from a low-socioeconomic status whose children were in K-12 public schools, one of the parents, Ms. Dempsey, narrates the disappointment she experienced due to racial and class-related discrimination. Ms. Dempsey states:

And then I've requested several times, if you have a concern, because his grades are not the greatest right now, if you have a concern or if there's anything going wrong that I should know please communicate with me. This is my name, this is my phone number. I give them everything. First day of the term I send everybody a mass email and let them know who I am. And I won't hear anything until I email them and say okay, I'm looking at [the online grade system] and I see that he has a D and it says he's missing an assignment. Why haven't you contacted me and let me know, you know? I would send emails and I would try to talk to her and she would never return my calls. She failed him last year and he had been saying "I turned in my work, there was no reason for her to fail me." And it was only this year that they sent, like a restructured report card to me that said a mistake was made. And she didn't even apologize to him. There was no apology. It was just like "oops, there was a mistake and now it's fixed." But this was after we browbeat him, punished him for having this bad grade and lying to us and he actually did the work.

Ms. Dempsey's experience of lack of communication with her son's teacher shows that the teacher did not value any contribution that the mother could make to assist her son to succeed in school. Again, Ms. Dempsey's not receiving an apology from the teacher nor the school shows that it is an acceptable behavior to not contact Ms. Dempsey about her child's studies, hence, a systemic form of discrimination. The behavior of excluding Ms. Dempsey is not visibly written as part of the school curriculum.

However, the teacher's and the school's behavior in general show they are acting based on the acceptable belief, norms and values they have that poor Black parents do not have the required skills to positively contribute to their children's school success; hence, their conclusion to exclude Ms. Dempsey from the issues concerning her child's success. Allen and White-Smith (2018) show another Black parent, Ms. Hall, in one of the conversations she had with her son's teacher:

I do remember one teacher telling me, this was at—it probably would have been the ninth grade—that sometimes she has a hard time helping African American students because of the way that they present themselves and so that, you know, I had a problem with that. She was saying that she doesn't take "them" serious because they don't seem like they are serious about school. And she puts her effort towards "those" students and to me "those" students meant the white students and so that kind of bothered me (p. 422).

The White teacher in this conversation draws her belief and conclusion about Black families from the dominant narrative discriminate against Black that Black parents and children from low-income background, and deemed them not interested in school and do not have the kind of cultural capital that is required for school success. As a result, this teacher did not see any reason to try connecting with Ms. Hall to find ways to assist her son to succeed in school. Like Allen and White-Smith (2018), other scholars have recorded the same negative experiences among Black parents in K-12 public schools due to racism and classism. White teachers' negative perception of Black parents and their children is also seen from the way Milner (2006) expresses the experiences of Black parents, as quoted in Howard (2015):

Some parents believed African American children are disproportionately labeled as having attention disorders or other disabilities. They also believed the consequence of labeling, especially around issues of behavior, prevents a child from having a "second chance" in which underlying issues remain unaddressed and low expectations follow a child from grade to grade. This behavior, or way of thinking, has an impact on learning in the classroom (p. 27).

This evidence is in line with other racial and class discriminatory behaviors of most White teachers shown in this chapter on Black families in K-12 public schools, which are rooted in the devaluation of cultures that Black families bring with them to school. This behavior on the part of White teachers impedes the successful parental involvement of Black parents in their children's education.

Discrimination: The Enclosed Cultural Assets of Black Families

As represented in the Figure 1, K-12 public schools are characterized by biased ideas that some parents from minoritized racial groups and class statuses do not have the cultural skills to succeed in schools (Yosso, 2005). It shows that the issues of race, class and cultural validation in K-12 public schools are tied to the biased assumptions of most White teachers' beliefs, values, and norms about who possessed the cultural capital for effective school involvement. Also, the diagram shows that ideas about the cultures and ability of Black parents to be involved in school are drawn from the deficit mindset about the kind of cultural capital these parents bring with them to school, which biases are embedded in the hidden curriculum and are carried out in forms of racism and classism. The diagram shows there is a wide ignorance in K-12 public schools about how community cultural wealth serves as the kind of cultural capital that Black parents utilizes for school involvement. As opposed to White cultural capital norms.

Yosso (2005) challenges the assumption that Black parents lack the kind of cultural capital that is available to the White middle-class families in form of style of speech, knowledge, and dress, which determine school success (Bourdieu, 1979) by introducing the concept of community cultural wealth as the form of cultural capital that families of Color in general draw upon to help their children achieve school success. The first of six forms of community cultural wealth is linguistic capital: Yosso (2005) narrates that this form of cultural capital presents as confidence among students of Color when they appear at K-12 public schools due to their ability to communicate in more than one language such as African-American Vernacular English and African languages. The second is familial capital, which Yosso (2005) argues is the aspect of cultural capital that provides some analytical explanations on some major significant benefits of one's place of cultural origin. To Yosso (2005), familial capital provides the opportunity for a sense of belonging to people of Color, as this cultural origin serves as a place of care. The third is social capital, which she explains as a network of people and community resources

Figure 1. Diagram of the structural representation of biased schooling

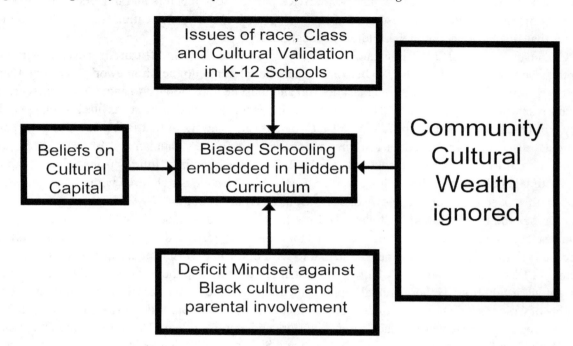

through which families of Color form social relationships with which they succeed in schools. The fourth is navigational capital, which is related to social capital. Yosso (2005) analyzes this as different ways that a network of families of Color form confidence and different ways to solve their related educational needs and problems. These four types of cultural capital are closely related to each other.

The fifth, aspirational capital, according to Yosso (2005), is the type of cultural capital that families of Color utilize to succeed in schools, though they face different barriers and restrictions in U.S public education. Notwithstanding, these parents and their children still maintain strong resilience and perseverance that is embedded in the hope of achieving future educational success. Finally, resistant capital is different forms of resistance that parents of Color teach their children to survive institutional oppressions. She argues that communities of Color use some oral and gestural communications in instilling in their children how to oppose institutional discrimination. Yosso (2005) states, "Parents of Color are consciously instructing their children to engage in behaviors and maintain attitudes that challenge the status quo" (p. 81). Yosso (2005) uses different types of community cultural wealth to explain different avenues through which families of Color withstand racism and classism and succeed in K-12 public schools.

Community Cultural Wealth: Experiences of Black Parents

Chapman and Bhopal (2013) argue that being Black means to succeed at all cost. This provides an insight on the kind of struggles that Black families face in K-12 public schools. Solórzano (1997) argues that racism, whether conscious or unconscious, has a cumulative impact on Black families. Contrary to the hegemonic belief that Black parents lack the cultural capital for school success and do not have an interest in their children's education, Yosso (2005) has shown that the socially marginalized communities of Color are endowed with different cultural skills which they bring to schools to succeed academically.

Chapman and Bhopal (2013) show how some Black parents seek mentors and university resources in their communities as additional resources of survival for their children's education. Taking this initiative shows that Black care about their children's education.

Chapman and Bhopal (2013) illustrate how Julie, a Black woman from an African American background, explains how she made it her duty to help and ensure her children do their homework every night, and do it very well. She says her children must do well and must be in the top list to avoid being categorized as failures because they are Black. "They have to be in the top groups otherwise, as black young people, they will be labeled and fail" (p. 72). As a Black parent, she is aware of that Black families face racial and class discrimination in schools. So, her actions, according the Chapman and Bhopal (2013), will help her child to work harder to succeed in school. As a Black woman, Julie is using familial capital in assisting her children in their school work. She strives to provide her children with all the necessary support they need based on the knowledge she acquired from her culture.

Julie has the understanding that she could not trust her child's academic success to the school as school staff members already have the belief that the child, being Black, does not have as much ability to succeed in school. Black parents understand that K-12 public schools discriminate against their children; therefore, Black parents work very closely with their children to help them succeed. Julie's experience as a parent, in addition to other parental supports mentioned above, challenges the deficit thinking about parents of Color as being nonchalant towards their children's education. Julie's efforts demonstrate that the cultures and experiences of Black parents, nurture and empower them (Delgado-Gaitan, 2001; Delgado Bernal, 2002). This is consistent with Ogbu and Simons (1998), whose study shows how African immigrant parents work extremely hard to assist their children to succeed in school.

Cultural Sources of Strength for Black Parents

In a speech, "The Black Church and the Urban Poor in America," by Dr. Dwight N. Hopkins, the Alexander Campbell Professor of Theology at the University of Chicago Divinity School, on 26 Feb., 2019, Dr. Hopkins stated that educational programs that Black churches establish in Black communities are to change those structures that oppress the racially minoritized and those of low income.

Barrett (2009) uses a representative sample of urban high school seniors to show that religion has a positive relationship with educational outcomes. In an article, "Black Churches Renew a Mission: Education," Susan Chira (1991) demonstrates that most Black churches in Chicago are renewing their long, historic commitment to education by providing after-school programs, summer schools, and family science activities, to assist Black children whose families are living in poverty, and even some children whose families are homeless. The article shows that some of the most ambitious educational programs are from Chicago, where more than 500 churches consistently work to improve science, computer, and math skills of children whose parents attend their churches. Every summer, more than 10 churches offer summer school to approximately 500 children. Church programs also pay for the children's field trips to schools. This assistance serves as a great relief to Black parents' involvement in schools as their children, through these intense programs from Black churches, will develop more confidence to succeed in K-12 public schools. For example, the article shows a 10-year-old student speaking with confidence:

I can't wait to get to school to get A's," said Michael Dameron, 10 years old, his words tumbling out. "Here I got lots of A's, and I like this because it's a church and so if somebody lies here they get struck

Race, Class, and Community Cultural Wealth

down. I like science. We do the solar system, and I found out the Sun is a star. And Mrs. Ervin said Pluto is the smallest planet, but me and him found out Mercury was smaller (Chira, 1991 p. A1).

This kind of opportunity provides the foundations of success for children whose parents are unlikely to have that financial capacity to sponsor their children's educational expenses and to pay for after school programs that will boost academic success of their children in K-12 public schools. This shows a link between Black church educational programs and the involvement of low-income Black parents in K-12 public education.

Another important form of cultural support to Black parents in school involvement is social interaction. This is in of form of friendship among Black parents whose children attend the same school. Research has shown that parent-to-parent interaction among Black parents whose children attend the same school provides a good source of cultural support to the success of Black parents in helping their children succeed in K-12 public schools. Allen and White-Smith (2018) demonstrate how parent-to-parent interaction has been useful in Black parental involvement in K-12 public schools. In the study, one of the Black parents was having some trouble resolving the racially related exclusion she was facing in school. Allen and White-Smith (2018) show that Ms. Powell reversed exclusion of her son from school with the assistance of her friend. Ms. Powell describes her actions:

So what I did was I went with my son, and a really good friend of mine who has known my kids since birth. She's an engineer and so she's got that kind of thinking. That's one and two, I didn't let them rush me. They don't put a time on the hearing. They schedule the hearing for an hour. Who says it's supposed to last an hour? So his hearing was four hours and I sat there and read every exhibit. You know what I'm saying? And then I thought it through, I made my notes, you know and then I consulted with my friend and she had done hers [notes] and I went back and said "You're wrong." And you know what? They could not expel him and not only that, they had to rescind the suspension. They had to reinstate my son in school (p. 425).

Ms. Powell to tapped into community cultural wealth from a place of the strength with her friend to provide her son with the opportunity to continue his studies. Ms. Powell's actions show that she is capable of providing her son with other assistance he needs to succeed and do well in his studies. These communal supports serve as the backbone for Black parents in resisting the institutional oppression of racism and classism they face in school involvement in K-12 public schools.

SOLUTIONS AND RECOMMENDATIONS

When dealing with the challenges of how to improve the educational involvement of Black parents from low socioeconomic backgrounds in K-12 public schools, researchers, White school administrators, Black parents, and Black students could consider the following solutions and recommendations:

To White Teachers in K-12 Public Schools

- **Cultural Awareness:** White teachers should be aware of the importance and the role that culture plays in successful involvement of low-income Black parents in providing academic support to their children.
- **Avoidance of Discriminatory Behaviors**: White teachers should avoid differential behaviors towards to Black parents and White middle-class parents to create equal involvement opportunities for both sets of parents.
- **Critical Consciousness:** White teachers should be aware of both conscious and unconscious behaviors such as beliefs, norms and values that perpetuate the domination of cultures of Black families in schools which often result in negative relationship building between Black parents and White teachers.
- **Cultural Inclusion:** White teachers should be aware of the importance of cultural inclusivity for Black parents' involvement in K-12 public schools. In particular, because White teachers have direct contact with Black parents, they should promote the agenda of their schools' partnership with Black churches, to promote Black parents' involvement and the educational success of Black children.
- **Facilitate Parent-to Parent Social Interaction:** Teachers should initiate ways to bring Black parents together to start social interactions among themselves. This will provide Black parents the opportunities to share their challenges and prospects, which will promote their success of school involvement.

FUTURE RESEARCH DIRECTIONS

The problem analyzed in this chapter has numerous complications. All the information used in this chapter is from secondary data sources, relevant studies already conducted by other researchers. Although most of the low-income Black parents depend largely on the community educational programs established by their local churches and on social interactions such as friendships for their successful school involvement, a lot is still unknown about other forms of strength that will benefit Black parents and other parents of Color, to assist their children achieve educational success in K-12 Public schools. Primary data collection and more study in this area might reveal even more cultural sources and strengths, which will be useful for parental involvement of Black parents, and parents of Color in general.

CONCLUSION

Culture has played a significant role in helping Black parents assist their children's success in school through parental involvement. Despite this active and visible role played by culture to assist Black parents succeed in their effort to provide academic assistance to their children, Black parents' involvement has not been welcomed in K-12 public schools. Instead, most White educators continue to ignore the cultures that Black parents bring with them to schools for school involvement due to institutional racism and classism that have historically worked against Black families in the U.S. These discriminatory behaviors are not seen but are ingrained in the schools' day-to-day activities carried out by most White

Race, Class, and Community Cultural Wealth

teachers, through the hidden curriculum. This is problematic as it continues to support the dominant narrative that Black parents are not interested in their children's educational success and do not have the skills needed to assist their children to succeed in K-12 public school.

The literature carefully reviewed provided an opportunity to examine the interconnection between parental involvement and benefit of Black culture to Blacks parents of low-socioeconomic status, and how institutional racism and classism have historically oppressed and denied Black parents such benefits. Drawing from Yosso's (2005) concept of community cultural wealth and the CRT analytical lens allowed the opportunity to analyze the implications of cultural devaluation of Black parents, and to challenge the discriminatory assumptions that Black parents lack the required cultural capital for successful school involvement. In addition to the contextualization of the six (6) types of community cultural wealth in Yosso (2005), the chapter explored two ways Black parents get involved in their children's education in K-12 public schools. The chapter concludes with a summary of recommendations to White teachers on how to promote culture-inclusivity in parental involvement for Black parents.

It is imperative for schools to ensure that Black parents are provided the opportunity to assist their children by accepting Black culture-related forms of school involvement. Therefore, to support Black parents' school involvement, K-12 public schools should initiate ways to connect with Black churches to understand some of the skills Black parents bring with them to schools for school involvement, as Black parents are dedicated and are influenced by their church community activities. In addition, schools should create ways to build and promote social interactions among Black parents in their schools, as a way to build a forum through which Black parents should share their individual school involvement experiences with one another, for more progress.

REFERENCES

Allen, Q., & White-Smith, K. (2018). "That's why I say stay in school": Black mothers' parental involvement, cultural wealth, and exclusion in their son's schooling. *Urban Education*, *53*(3), 409–435. doi:10.1177/0042085917714516

Anderson, J. D. (1988). *The education of Blacks in the South, 1860-1935*. Univ of North Carolina Press. doi:10.5149/uncp/9780807842218

Apple, M., & Apple, M. W. (2018). *Ideology and curriculum*. Routledge. doi:10.4324/9780429400384

Bain, L. (1990). A critical analysis of the hidden curriculum in physical education. *Physical education, curriculum and culture: Critical issues in the contemporary crisis*, 23-42.

Baquedano-López, P., Alexander, R. A., & Hernández, S. J. (2013). Equity issues in parental and community involvement in schools: What teacher educators need to know. *Review of Research in Education*, *37*(1), 149–182. doi:10.3102/0091732X12459718

Baquedano-López, P., Alexander, R. A., & Hernández, S. J. (2013). Equity issues in parental and community involvement in schools what teacher educators need to know. *Review of Research in Education*, *37*(1), 149–182. doi:10.3102/0091732X12459718

Barnard, W. M. (2004). Parent involvement in elementary school and educational attainment. *Children and Youth Services Review*, *26*(1), 39–62. doi:10.1016/j.childyouth.2003.11.002

Barrett, J. (2009). *Cognitive science, religion, and theology. The believing primate. Scientific, philosophical, and theological reflections on the origin of religion.* Academic Press.

Bell, B. W., Grosholz, E. R., & Stewart, J. B. (2014). *WEB Du Bois on race and culture.* Routledge. doi:10.4324/9780203379509

Bell, D. A. (1995). Who's afraid of critical race theory. *U. Ill. L. Rev.*, 893.

Billingsley, A., & Caldwell, C. H. (1991). The church, the family, and the school in the African American community. *The Journal of Negro Education, 60*(3), 427–440. doi:10.2307/2295494

Bourdieu, P. (1979). Symbolic power. *Critique of Anthropology, 4*(13-14), 77–85. doi:10.1177/0308275X7900401307

Burton, L. M., Bonilla-Silva, E., Ray, V., Buckelew, R., & Hordge Freeman, E. (2010). Critical race theories, colorism, and the decade's research on families of color. *Journal of Marriage and the Family, 72*(3), 440–459. doi:10.1111/j.1741-3737.2010.00712.x

Burton, L. M., Bonilla-Silva, E., Ray, V., Buckelew, R., & Hordge Freeman, E. (2010). Critical race theories, colorism, and the decade's research on families of color. *Journal of Marriage and the Family, 72*(3), 440–459. doi:10.1111/j.1741-3737.2010.00712.x

Chapman, T. K. (2013). You can't erase race! Using CRT to explain the presence of race and racism in majority white suburban schools. *Discourse (Abingdon), 34*(4), 611–627. doi:10.1080/01596306.2013.822619

Chapman, T. K., & Bhopal, K. K. (2013). Countering common-sense understandings of 'good parenting:'women of color advocating for their children. *Race, Ethnicity and Education, 16*(4), 562–586. doi:10.1080/13613324.2013.817773

Chira, S. (1991, September 7). Black churches renew a mission: Education. *New York Times*, p. A1. Retrieved from: https://www.nytimes.com/1991/08/07/education/black-churches-renew-a-mission-education.html

DeCuir, J. T., & Dixson, A. D. (2004). "So when it comes out, they aren't that surprised that it is there": Using Critical Race Theory as a tool of analysis of race and racism in education. *Educational Researcher, 33*(5), 26–31. doi:10.3102/0013189X033005026

Delgado, R., & Stefancic, J. (2012). *Critical race theory: An introduction.* NYU Press.

Dictionary, M. W. (2002). *Merriam-webster.* On-line at http://www. mw. com/home.htm

Drake, S. C., & Cayton, H. (1945). *Black metropolis* (Vols. 1–2). Harper& Row.

Fernández, L. (2002). Telling stories about school: Using critical race and Latino critical theories to document Latina/Latino education and resistance. *Qualitative Inquiry, 8*(1), 45–65. doi:10.1177/107780040200800104

Fine, M. (1993). [Ap] parent involvement: Reflections on parents, power, and urban public schools. *Teachers College Record, 94*(4), 682–710.

Fultz, M. (1995). African American teachers in the south, 1890-1940: Powerlessness and the ironies of expectations and protest. *History of Education Quarterly, 35*(4), 401–422. doi:10.2307/369578

Gotanda, N., Crenshaw, K., Peller, G., & Thomas, K. (1995). *Critical race theory: The key writings that formed the movement.* Academic Press.

Gutman, L. M., & McLoyd, V. C. (2000). Parents' management of their children's education within the home, at school, and in the community: An examination of African-American families living in poverty. *The Urban Review, 32*(1), 1–24. doi:10.1023/A:1005112300726

Hamilton, T. G. (2014). Selection, language heritage, and the earnings trajectories of black immigrants in the United States. *Demography, 51*(3), 975–1002. doi:10.100713524-014-0298-5 PMID:24854004

Hopkins, D. (2019, February 26). *The Black church and the urban poor in America.* YouTube. https://www.youtube.com/watch?v=dypv_9h8slu

Howard, E. D. (2015). *African American Parents' Perceptions of Public School: African American Parents' Involvement in Their Childrens' Education.* East Tennessee State University.

Jeynes, W. H. (2003). A meta-analysis the effects of parental involvement on minority children's academic achievement. *Education and Urban Society, 35*(2), 202–218. doi:10.1177/0013124502239392

Johnson, J. W. (1934). *Negro Americans, what now?* Viking Press.

Kent, M. M. (2007). Immigration and America's Black population: Vol. 62. *No. 4.* Population Reference Bureau.

King, J. E. (2015). Dysconscious racism: Ideology, identity, and the miseducation of teachers. In Dysconscious Racism, Afrocentric Praxis, and Education for Human Freedom: Through the Years I Keep on Toiling (pp. 125-139). Routledge.

Ladson-Billings, G. (1995). But that's just good teaching! The case for culturally relevant pedagogy. *Theory into Practice, 34*(3), 159–165. doi:10.1080/00405849509543675

Ladson-Billings, G. (2009). *The dreamkeepers: Successful teachers of African American children.* John Wiley & Sons.

Ladson-Billings, G. (2009). 'Who you callin'nappy-headed?'A critical race theory look at the construction of Black women. *Race, Ethnicity and Education, 12*(1), 87–99. doi:10.1080/13613320802651012

Ladson-Billings, G., & Tate, W. F. (1995). Toward a critical race theory of education. *Teachers College Record, 97*(1), 47.

Ladson-Billings, G., & Tate, W. F. (1995). Toward a critical race theory of education. *Critical race theory in education: All God's children got a song,* 11-30.

Ladson-Billings, G., & Tate, W. F. (Eds.). (2006). *Education research in the public interest: Social justice, action, and policy.* Teachers College Press.

Laker, A. (2012). *Sociology of sport and physical education: An introduction.* Routledge. doi:10.4324/9780203194119

Lareau, A. (2000). *Home advantage: Social class and parental intervention in elementary education.* Rowman & Littlefield Publishers.

Lareau, A., & Horvat, E. M. (1999). Moments of social inclusion and exclusion race, class, and cultural capital in family-school relationships. *Sociology of Education, 72*(1), 37–53. doi:10.2307/2673185

Latunde, Y., & Clark-Louque, A. (2016). Untapped resources: Black parent engagement that contributes to learning. *The Journal of Negro Education, 85*(1), 72–81. doi:10.7709/jnegroeducation.85.1.0072

Lee, J. S., & Bowen, N. K. (2006). Parent involvement, cultural capital, and the achievement gap among elementary school children. *American Educational Research Journal, 43*(2), 193–218. doi:10.3102/00028312043002193

Lewis, A. E. (2003). *Race in the schoolyard: Negotiating the color line in classrooms and communities.* Rutgers University Press. doi:10.36019/9780813547039

Lincoln, C. E. (1989). *The Black church and Black self-determination.* Association of Black Foundation Executives.

Matthew, T. (2017). *How houses of worship help immigrants adjust to America.* Retrieved from: https://www.citylab.com/ life/2017/08/how-houses-of-worship-are-helping-immigrants-adapt-to-america/535992/

Milner, H. R. IV. (2017). Race, talk, opportunity gaps, and curriculum shifts in (teacher) education. *Literacy Research: Theory, Method, and Practice, 66*(1), 73–94.

Nieto, S.Board of Education for Latinos. (2004). Black, White, and us: The meaning of Brown v. Board of Education for Latinos. *Multicultural Perspectives, 6*(4), 22–25. doi:10.120715327892mcp0604_7

Ogbu, J. U., & Simons, H. D. (1998). Voluntary and involuntary minorities: A cultural-ecological theory of school performance with some implications for education. *Anthropology & Education Quarterly, 29*(2), 155–188. doi:10.1525/aeq.1998.29.2.155

Pollock, M. (2005). Keeping on keeping on: OCR and complaints of racial discrimination 50 years after. *Teachers College Record, 107*(9), 2106–2140. doi:10.1111/j.1467-9620.2005.00586.x

Seeley, D. S. (1993). A new paradigm for parent involvement. *Families and schools in a pluralistic society,* 229-234.

Smith, L. T. (1999). *Decolonizing methodologies: Research and indigenous peoples.* Zed books.

Smith, W. A. (2004). Black faculty coping with racial battle fatigue: The campus racial climate in a post-civil rights era. *A long way to go: Conversations about race by African American faculty and graduate students, 14,* 171-190.

Solórzano, D. G. (1997). Images and words that wound: Critical race theory, racial stereotyping, and teacher education. *Teacher Education Quarterly,* 5–19.

Solorzano, D. G., & Ornelas, A. (2002). A critical race analysis of advanced placement classes: A case of educational inequality. *Journal of Latinos and Education, 1*(4), 215–229. doi:10.1207/S1532771XJLE0104_2

Race, Class, and Community Cultural Wealth

Solórzano, D. G., & Solórzano, R. W. (1995). The Chicano educational experience: A framework for effective schools in Chicano communities. *Educational Policy*, *9*(3), 293–314. doi:10.1177/0895904895009003005

Usher, A., & Kober, N. (2012). *4. What Roles Do Parent Involvement, Family Background, and Culture Play in Student Motivation?* Center on Education Policy.

Valencia, R. R., & Solórzano, D. G. (1997). Contemporary deficit thinking. *The evolution of deficit thinking: Educational thought and practice*, 160-210.

Van Galen, J. A. (1987). Explaining home education: Parents' accounts of their decisions to teach their own children. *The Urban Review*, *19*(3), 161–177. doi:10.1007/BF01111877

Vaught, S. E. (2008). The color of money: School funding and the commodification of black children. *Urban Education*.

Villalpando, O., & Solórzano, D. G. (2005). The role of culture in college preparation programs: A review of the research literature. *Preparing for college: Nine elements of effective outreach*, 13-28.

Watson, T. N., & Bogotch, I. (2015). Reframing Parent Involvement: What Should Urban School Leaders Do Differently? *Leadership and Policy in Schools*, *14*(3), 257–278. doi:10.1080/15700763.2015.1024327

Willie, C. V., Garibaldi, A. M., & Reed, W. L. (1990). *The education of African Americans* (Vol. 3).

Woodson, C. G. (2006). *The mis-education of the Negro*. Book Tree.

Yosso, T. J. (2005). Whose culture has capital? A critical race theory discussion of community cultural wealth. *Race, Ethnicity and Education*, *8*(1), 69–91. doi:10.1080/1361332052000341006

ADDITIONAL READING

Apple, M. W. (2000). The cultural politics of home schooling. *Peabody Journal of Education*, *75*(1-2), 256–271. doi:10.1080/0161956X.2000.9681944

Baquedano-López, P., Alexander, R. A., & Hernández, S. J. (2013). Equity issues in parental and community involvement in schools what teacher educators need to know. *Review of Research in Education*, *37*(1), 149–182. doi:10.3102/0091732X12459718

Bell, D. A., Crenshaw, K., Gotanda, N., Peller, G., & Thomas, K. (1995). Critical race theory: The key writings that formed the movement.

Berlak, H. (2001). Race and the achievement gap. *Rethinking Schools*, *15*(4), 10–11.

Bernal, D. D. (1998). Grassroots leadership reconceptualized: Chicana oral histories and the 1968 East Los Angeles school blowouts. *Frontiers: A Journal of Women Studies*, 113-142.

Bernal, D. D. (2002). Critical race theory, Latino critical theory, and critical raced-gendered epistemologies: Recognizing students of color as holders and creators of knowledge. *Qualitative Inquiry*, *8*(1), 105–126. doi:10.1177/107780040200800107

Bonilla-Silva, E. (2003). 'New racism,' color-blind racism, and the future of whiteness in America. *White out: The continuing significance of racism*, 271-84.

Bonilla-Silva, E., Forman, T. A., Lewis, A. E., & Embrick, D. G. (2003). It wasn't me!: How will race and racism work in 21st century America. *Research in Political Sociology*, *12*(1), 111–134. doi:10.1016/S0895-9935(03)12005-0

Bourdieu, P., & Passeron, J.-C. (1977). *Reproduction in education, society, and culture*. Sage.

Brantlinger, E. A. (2003). *Dividing classes: How the middle class negotiates and rationalizes school advantage*. Psychology Press. doi:10.4324/9780203465479

KEY TERMS AND DEFINITIONS

Black Church: Any religious organization owned and run by Black people of African descent.

Black Families: Those families that are made up of African.

Community Cultural Wealth: This is the unique kind of cultural capital possessed by parents of Color, particularly those of low-socioeconomic status, which they use to achieve school success. This is different from the kind of cultural capital used by middle-class families for school success.

Cultural Capital: Those skills and knowledge acquired through accumulation of wealth, which the hegemony believes to be available to White-middle class families, which to them is the only possibility for school success.

Hegemony: The racial and class domination of one racial group over others.

Hidden Curriculum: Those values, norms, and beliefs that represent the hegemonic ideas, often used for the purpose of domination in the classroom.

Low-Socioeconomic Status: The social categorization of certain individuals to a low socio-class status.

Racial Discrimination: The unfair behavior of treating people differently based on their racial identities.

This research was previously published in Designing Culturally Competent Programming for PK-20 Classrooms; pages 198-217, copyright year 2021 by Information Science Reference (an imprint of IGI Global).

Chapter 38

Building a Racial Identity:
African American Students' Learning Experiences at the Florence County Museum

Eunjung Chang
(iD) https://orcid.org/0000-0001-8148-3873
Francis Marion University, USA

ABSTRACT

This chapter examines African American college students' learning experiences at the Florence County Museum. Looking at several works of art, how do African American students construct their learning experiences in a course-required tour? What personal meanings do they take away from the experience? African American students are voluntarily engaged or only occupied in the works that are related to or connected to their racial roots. They also interpret the works of art from their racial points of view. Therefore, their racial identity as an African American is a key part of understanding their learning experience from the museum. It is important for African Americans not only to see themselves in museum exhibitions but also be able to develop their racial identity and imagine their future through art. It creates equal opportunities for all students from different social, racial, and cultural groups to function effectively in a diverse demographic society.

INTRODUCTION

In public institutions, students' ethnic, cultural, and socio-economic backgrounds are increasingly diverse in the United States. Today students of color account for nearly 45% in elementary and secondary schools (Milner, 2015). Classrooms are consisted of more students of color than ever before. However, the majority of teachers are white, middle class, and female, so students of color are more at higher risk of failing in schools because of bias, ignorance, unfairness, and lack of representation in the classroom (Desai, 2010). Racial disparities present great challenges for students' achievement and success. Black

DOI: 10.4018/978-1-6684-4507-5.ch038

Copyright © 2022, IGI Global. Copying or distributing in print or electronic forms without written permission of IGI Global is prohibited.

students are three times more likely to be referred to law enforcement with levels of racial bias in surrounding communities. They are almost four times as likely to be suspended or expelled from schools than their white peers (Lewin, 2012). Disciplinary actions are also connected to a range of negative life outcomes, including involvements in the criminal justice system (Morrison, 2019). As art educators, we need to pay close attention to this disparity as it addresses to the racial divide that colors the experience of students from public schools to universities.

Recently, the killings of Rayshard Brooks, George Floyd, Breonna Taylor, David McAtee, Tony McDade, and so many others led to national debates over the use of deadly force by law enforcement. These incidents greatly inflamed racism and injustice issues because all of the deaths were African Americans. However, the topic of race is an entirely different story in many schools and classrooms (Desai, 2010). Teachers tend to avoid controversial issues like injustice, discrimination, and racism. When they do take place, classroom conversations on such topics remain simplistic or superficial. There is plenty of research demonstrating that children notice race at a young age and begin to form stereotypes (Dell'Antonia, 2014; Milner, 2015). Therefore, if we do not deal with racial factors in our classrooms, we are telling our students to figure it out themselves. Nadworny (2015) found that students who feel good about their own race do better academically. African American students have suffered from low self-esteem because of society's negative views of African Americans. The development of their self-identification is therefore influenced or limited by their social experiences in conditions of social discrimination, prejudice, injustice, and racism (Young, 2013). The field of art education must re-examine teaching practices to integrate social issues like racism, equity, discrimination, and prejudice into art classrooms. Art educators need to develop appropriate pedagogical methods that bring comprehensive discussions meaningfully and effectively with students and students of color in their classrooms.

In this chapter, I examine African American college students' learning experiences at the Florence County Museum in South Carolina. Looking at several works of art, how do African American students construct their learning experiences in a course-required tour? What do students learn about the works of art? What personal meanings do they take away from the experience? In sum, the objectives of this study are threefold: 1) To examine African American students' learning experiences from the museum; 2) To investigate any learning experience about works of art encountered in the museum; and 3) To evaluate overall students' museum experiences.

BACKGROUND

Historically, museums have been biased toward elite white visitors. The art world has largely ignored or discredited non-European cultures while deifying European-descended artists and culture. According to Crum and Hendrick (2018), a legacy of historic discrimination and cultural exclusion within museum practices has resulted in African Americans attending museums less frequently than white Americans. Researchers found that African Americans visit museums at a rate of 20 to 30% lower than the national norm (Falk & Dierking, 2013). Caucasians, in particular Americans of European backgrounds, were roughly two times more likely to have visited museums than other groups. Several researchers (Acuff, 2020; Crum & Hendrick, 2018; Taylor & Doyle, 2018) demonstrated that museum exhibitions and programs are not culturally relevant for ethnic minority groups. Some possible explanations are lack of relevant objects from their own cultures; negative images of South Asian and African people connected with disasters, poverty, and famine; and a colonial view of history that portrayed African Americans as weak victims and slaves (Hooper-Greenhill, 2001; Khan, 2000). A majority of African Americans see themselves, "not with members of broader society, but with other African Americans" (Rowley, Sellers, Chavous, & Smith 1998, p. 716). African Americans are more likely to attend museum events with a focus on Black culture, specifically designed for a Black audience (Crum & Hendrick, 2018).

In recent years, there has been increased discussion of racial and cultural injustices in art museum education. Over the last twenty years, visitors from museums and galleries have decreased, and the visitors that remain are older and whiter than the overall population (Simon, 2010). There has not been a major increase in museum visit among people of color despite the changing demographics in the United States. Furthermore, neither museum visitors nor museum professionals reflect today's racial diversity of the nation (Crum & Hendrick, 2018). The American Alliance of Museums' (AAM) document *Excellence and Equality* clarified that museums are encouraged to achieve greater inclusiveness in a demographic society and reflect the diversity of the United States (AAM, 1992). Namely, museum professionals are called upon to acknowledge and respect race, ethnic, origin, gender, economic status, and the educational diversity of museum visitors. They are also expected to reflect pluralism in every aspect of their offerings.

Since the early 1990s, the museum field generally has settled firmly into patterns that emphasize successful relationships with visitors, and consequently, the educational role of museums has become significant (Hooper-Greenhill, 1999). AAM suggests that "museum must place education at the center of their public services," and commitment to education must be "clearly expressed in every museum's mission and pivotal to every museum's activities" (AAM, 1992, p. 3). Today most museums are aggressively characterizing themselves as institutions of public learning. They need to demonstrate their educational values to society and justify their very existence. Tom Finkelpearl, New York City's commissioner of cultural affairs, claims that publicly funded institutions have a responsibility and mission to serve a more diverse public (Crum & Hendrick, 2018).

As a result, the heightened interest in education and learning in museums is currently directing educators to investigate educational experiences of museum visitors. A growing body of educators is investigating how an individual makes personal meaning within educational experiences (Adams, Falk, & Dierking, 2003; Black & Hein 2003; Haanstra, 2003; Simon, 2010). They believe that regardless of what the museum staff intends, visitors will continue to make meanings from their own encounters in museums. Personally, different expectations, previous experiences, and levels of perceptual skills mean that a person's museum experiences are personal and individual rather than standard and generic. Museums are expected to respond to the public's needs rather than simply tell the public what curators think they need to know (Falk & Dierking, 2000, 2013; Simon, 2016). As such, understanding the nature of personal meaning making that African American students take away from art museum experiences are significant to art educators for maximizing their learning experiences from a museum visit.

Research Significance, Purpose, and Methods

The challenges of understanding individual learning experiences in museums are raised in the field of museum education. Falk and Dierking (2013) argue that researchers in the field need to make conceptually consistent efforts to answer the following questions: How does learning occur for an individual in museums? What is the process by which learning occurs in a museum? What do people learn and experience in museum exhibit? What do people construct from their museum experiences? What knowledge do they take with them when they leave a museum? These basic questions, which are essential to understanding individual learning experiences in museums, still remain to be answered.

The purpose of this chapter is to investigate African American students' learning experiences from the Florence Country Museum. How did African American students construct their learning experience? In what ways did they create their learning experiences in a required fieldtrip? Students visited a local Florence County Museum, looked at a variety works of art including William H. Johnson, Ethnographic arts, Asian arts, Pueblo pottery, the American Civil War, etc., and described their museum experiences with writing essays. For the study, African American participants were chosen from Introduction to Art, an art appreciation course offered every semester. This is an elective undergraduate course reserved for non-art majors. This study focuses on what students experience during the tour, what they learn about works of art, and what personal meaning they take with them.

Today, almost all museums offer tour programs with various content and themes for different groups of visitors because museum tour provides a basic foundation for museum educational practices. Although a few studies have focused on museum experiences from pre-service and elementary teachers in the field of art education (Black & Hein, 2003; Henry, 2004; Stone, 1995, 1996, 1997, 2001), there are almost no studies about understanding learning experiences of African American college students, especially from non-art majors (Crum & Hendrick, 2018). I hope the findings of this study will be used by museum educators and art teachers in designing meaningful learning experiences for marginalized undergraduate students, particularly African American students.

The Importance of Critical Race and Constructivist Learning Theories

This narrative study is grounded in critical race theory (CRT) and constructivist learning theory (CLT). CRT emerged from primary scholars interested in studying and transforming the relationships between race, racism, and power, especially during the post-Civil Rights period (Desai & Marsh, 2005). It examines critical issues of social justice, economic empowerment, criminal justices, ethnic stereotypes, underserved populations, political power, and cultural racism. CRT is a movement committed to changing and disrupting racism and its associated social, legal, political, and educational consequences as a means for changing dominant systems of racial oppression (McCoy & Rodricks, 2015). Although CRT is fairly new to art education inquiry, it continues to emerge and expand as a theoretical framework and analytical tool for combating racism and other forms of discrimination (Jung, 2015; Kraehe, 2015). It insists that *race* is a key part of understanding today's educational system. Race, the way in which we identify ourselves and are identified by others, affects our lives and opportunities, and defines our feelings, thoughts, and attitudes within society. Race also plays a decisive role in many people being treated differently based on their physical characteristics such as skin color or hair texture.

From a constructivist perspective, learning is seen as a continuous, personal process. Learners begin to experience museums from different cognitive frameworks and create unique individualized experiences. It is also seen as a highly contextual process (Adams, Falk, & Dierking, 2003). In constructivist theory, learning in museums is not just about what the museum intends to teach visitors, but also about what visitors chose to experience from their museum. Learners construct their own meanings and find their own values from the museum experiences. Several empirical studies have demonstrated that museum learning takes place as a result of complicated interactions and interactions of personal (motivations, expectations, interests, concerns, beliefs, & prior knowledge), socio-cultural (social groups or individual), and physical (design, facility, & event) variables (Haanstra, 2003; Falk, & Dierking, 2000). Visitors' learning experiences are built on the interplay of these three contexts because they have varying life

Building a Racial Identity

experiences, different levels of knowledge, and diverse expectations. Black and Hein (2003) studied a guided fieldtrip experiences of college students from different social and ethnic backgrounds and with varying previous art experiences. Findings indicated that some combinations of previous knowledge and degree of experiences, mood, and expectations influenced students' learning experiences. Even in highly structured fieldtrips, students were able to construct personal meaning and gain personal insights into a variety of works of art. In other words, personal meaning-making is an important factor in students' museum fieldtrips.

Museum Education and its Value for African Americans

What is the value of museum learning for African Americans? Research is increasingly demonstrating that "museum education could change people" (Xanthoudai, Tickle, & Sekules, 2003, p.1). Museum learning is "a change in an individual's knowledge, skills, attitudes, beliefs, feelings, and concepts" (Hein & Alexander, 1998, p. 10). Crum and Hendrick (2018) integrated works of art by Kehinde Wiley, an African American male artist, who selects black men in contemporary clothing as the centurial figures in his large-scale portraits. Wiley's signature portraits of everyday black men and woman riff on specific paintings by famous European artists like Titian, van Dyck, and Manet often illustrates his black subjects, who often wear hoodies, sneakers, baseball caps, and gear associated with African Americans. These Wiley's paintings certainly pay attention to the absence of African Americans from cultural and historical narratives (Brooklyn Museum of Art, n.d.). Wiley not only makes the Black male visible in art museums, but also challenges stereotypes of racially marginalized Black men.

Importantly, teachers have to create conscious learning environments by understanding their students as individuals, honoring their different personal experiences and backgrounds, and encouraging self-discovery (Taylor & Doyle, 2018). According to Lee (2012), teachers play a significant role in how students come to understand what it means to respect, understand, and value in society. Lee (2013) signified that teachers' racial attitudes and dispositions towards students of color are "critical components in ensuring equality (equal treatment) and equity (fair and just treatment) in education" (p. 142) and that significantly impacted students' achievement and their understandings toward self and others. Therefore, when all students are able to learn about their own cultural legacies, it creates equal opportunities for all students from different social, racial, ethnic, and cultural groups to function effectively in a diverse democratic society (Young, 2011). One of the most influential art educators Victor Lowenfeld acknowledged the importance of their racial identity by understanding more about their African roots and inheritances (Chang, 2016; Young, 2013). He believed that a person should never deny their backgrounds, but rather address their social, cultural, racial, political, and historical experiences in the arts creatively and sensitively. He used Hampton University's African art collection to emphasize his students' cultural heritage and taught the African American artists who illustrated their struggles with education, culture, economic, and social deprivation in their art (Holt, 2012). African American students had their intrinsic potential to find their own voices in the arts in order to pursue the complexity of their racial identity. Young (2013) said, "as a young man I searched to find meaning in art and the discovery of artists that shared my ethnicity, other commonalities, and interest in art and culture" (p. 52). He believed in the importance of racial identity for African Americans has to be found by learning more about their African roots. He also insisted that all students should know about their own heritages as well as the historical and art historical heritage of others.

How can art educators successfully address issues of race and racism in a college art appreciation course? What is the proper role of art educators in responding to basic social justice issues? When I began my teaching in the American South, I had little idea of where to begin. Since my second year of teaching in 2008, I have assigned my students to take a fieldtrip to a local museum, study a Florence born-African American artist William H. Johnson along with some historical works of art, and write a reflection paper about their learning experiences. I have realized that students deeply engaged with the works of art and came to understand cultural, social, and racial issues of civil rights, social justice, segregation, discrimination, and racism as well as their own heritage and cultural background through the works of art. As a professor at a state university in South Carolina, I regularly have more than 50% African American students from low-income backgrounds. Jung (2015) indicated, "Racism is not just a problem of one university or of the south. Rather, it is a problem that is deeply embedded in the history, culture, and institution of the U.S. society" (p. 216). Therefore, we as educators more broadly need to re-evaluate our goals and contents of teaching in terms of the cultural, ethnic, racial, and social diversity of our students. I think art can be used to elevate and promote awareness of social justice issues; art educators can "facilitate social justice through various media, promote change and clarity, and generate healing, trust, and bridge building" (Gussak, 2010, p. vii). I also agree "if art is not related to their own past experience, to their own goals, the beginning experiences upon which further learning in art can be built will not take place" (McFee, 1998, p. 20). Therefore, it is significant for all students, especially African Americans, not only to see themselves in museum exhibitions but also be able to develop their racial identity and imagine their future through the art.

COLLEGE STUDENTS' LEARNING EXPERIENCES FROM THE MUSEUM

Today Florence Country Museum reflects the region's artistic, cultural, and historical heritage. In particular, it has 20th century African American artist and Florence native, William H. Johnson's paintings, each representing distinct periods of the artist's development. It also has a prestigious collection of Southern Art, including works by Alfred Hutty, Anna Heyward Taylor, Alice Huger Smith, and Elizabeth O'Neil Verner. How did African American students create their learning experiences from the museum? What did they learn from the museum while looking at the works of art? To gain a better understanding of exactly what African American students learned from the museum visit, I analyzed students' unstructured reflection papers that focused on 2-3 favorite works in two pages, format-free submission.[2] Writing activities like reflection papers are useful tool to help the students reflect on their own past, present, and future selves (Taylor & Doyle, 2018).

The work [Evening] just made me think about how life was for me growing up in this county... African American family sat on the bench one evening. It had rakes leaning on a tree. It had a basket of cotton below and a small house. The lady was breastfeeding her baby outside. The first thought that came to my head was life was really hard back then for African Americans... I mean growing up in this county learned that life was not easy. I dealt with a lot of racism from people in my town. I have been called every kind of racist slurs possible. I feel like everyone should be treated equality and given a fair shot at life and being successful. After walking around the museum, I prayed to God and thanked him for making to us, "African Americans." We try so hard to fit in with the others. The others seem to have all the power and life is easier for them. But it has changed things over time so that everyone regardless race, age, gender, sexuality, etc. had a fair shot at life... (Student Trellis, P. – Reflection Paper)

Building a Racial Identity

Figure 1. Evening (1941) by William H. Johnson
Source: "© 2020, Florence County Museum. Used with permission."

William H. Johnson's Evening... just touched my heart so many ways I can actually say I caught myself letting a tear slide down my right cheek. It shows that African Americans had to work hard to get what they wanted, and still to this day we have to work hard in order to get what we want... Gazing at his painting, I could almost envision I am there back during slavery. I could feel the suffering and the sadness coming from the eyes of his work of art... I am an African American, and I know a lot about my background... African Americans who were born into slavery... faced prejudice criticism... everyday life. (Student Mariah, H. – Reflection Paper)

Evening painted with oil on burlap in 1941. Johnson depicted an African American family in South from a personal and historical perspective. It is identified more closely with the rural African American experiences from the 1930s to the late 1940s. Johnson wanted to recapture his experience and used this to express himself through art. Since Johnson himself was born to a poor black family, Evening portrayed well "showing the life of an African American family at that time because most of them were farmers who had nothing else but family or crop." (Student Alexander, M. – Reflection Paper)

Summing up his personal philosophy of art in a Danish interview in 1932, Johnson said, "my aim is to express in a natural way what I feel, what is in me, both rhythmically and spiritually" (Valentine, 2020, para. 17). Using strong colors and silhouettes with simplicity, Johnson illuminated the large hands and spindly limbs of the couple that suggests a life of hard work. Although he left South Carolina home at the age of seventeen, his memories of hard-working black couples were captured in the painting. Born in Florence, South Carolina to a poor African America family, he moved in 1918 to New York where he worked a variety of jobs. While working, he saved money to pay for an art education at the prestigious National Academy of Design. After graduating, he moved to France and absorbed the style of modernism. As a result, his work became more emotional and expressive. During the same period in 1930, he married Danish artist Holcha Krake and spent most of the 30s in Scandinavia. As seen the work *Evening*, Johnson was interested in primitivism and folk art that began to have a noticeable impact on his work (Kantrowitz, 2013).

Looking at the work *Evening*, students expressed their personal experiences, connections, and compassions as African Americans. The work encouraged them to bring critical issues of race and racism, share their individual experiences, understand life of African Americans, and encourage self-discovery. Students Trellis and Mariah reflected their uneasy lives because of racism, inequality, and biases in the United States. Trellis said, "everyone should be treated equality... African Americans... try so hard to fit in with the others. The others [Caucasians] seem to have all the power and life is easier for them." Student Alexander could feel suffering, sadness, poverty, and hardship of an African American family in rural South because they were born into slavery "who had nothing else but family." While walking at the museum, Trellis prayed to God, and Mariah caught a tear down her face.

Opening up the newspapers and websites these days, we find plenty of talk on race issues in mass and social media. Primarily, it is important that teachers understand that racial experiences are real and impact how and why students' social experiences and their worldviews may be different from others. "Awareness is start" (Quinn, 2005, p.189). Lee (2013) regards this realization as a starting point for educators to effectively bridge any racial divide between themselves and their students. Race is a social construct and is enacted in society in different ways (Lee, 2012). Racial silence, therefore, does not transcend racial distinction; rather it continues to disregard and neglect the educational needs of non-Whites (Kraehe, 2015). As Quinn (2005) stated, "What better tools and what better place, than the arts

Building a Racial Identity

and art education?" (p.190). We as educators can create opportunities for our students learn about and address the critical issues of social justice like racism that affect their lives (Dewhurst, 2014; Quinn, Ploof, & Hochtritt, 2012).

Figure 2. Swing Low, Sweet Chariot (1944) by William H. Johnson
Source: "© 2020, Smithsonian American Art Museum. Used with permission."

My favorite painting was titled Swing Low, Sweet Chariot (1944) by William H. Johnson. This work was pleasing to my eye because it was a representation of a Negro spiritual. Shockingly, this song happens to be one of my favorite spirituals. It references back to slavery and the Underground Railroad... (Student Alaria, S. – Reflection Paper).

I really fell in love with the Swing Low, Sweet Chariot... I could actually hear the song through the picture. Swing Low, Sweet Chariot coming forth to carry me HOME"! Johnson had chosen the Negro spiritual because he wanted to define the African American experience in authentic voice (Student Brittany, C. – Reflection Paper)

Swing Low, Sweet Chariot is the song of an African American spiritual of slave origins. "I looked over Jordan, and what did I see/coming for to carry me home/a band of angels coming after me." The song is attributed to Wallace Wills, a slave from Oklahoma. His inspiration was the land beyond the Ohio River in the town of Ripley, Ohio, which was a station on the Underground Railroad. Like other songs of resistance, this song uses encoded language that is familiar to slaves. "Home" could be either heaven or land of freedom. In the Bible, the prophet Elijah was carried to heaven by chariot of fire at the end of his life. A band of angles welcome a man to heaven. Johnson created the painting that is familiar to African Americans, shaping religious figures in Bible (SSAM, n.d). Johnson believed that the power of positive changes in African American life. As Aaron Douglas said, "Let's bare our arms and plunge them deep through laughter, through pain, through sorrow, through hope, through disappointment, into the very depths of the souls of our people... Let's sing it, dance it, write it, paint it. Let's do the impossible" (Urton, 2009, para. 2). This work raised prophetic voices to envision a better future for African Americans.

Students Alaria and Brittany examined a Negro spiritual that imparted Christian values while also describing the hardships of slavery. The discovery of self-identification in the arts was one of the basic factors central for creative expression, and part of this identity for African Americans had to be found by understanding more about their African roots and inheritances. Looking at the painting, students could also share what spiritual songs they would listen, when they feel stress in their lives. Efland (2000) said, "the purpose for teaching the arts is to contribute to the understanding of the social and cultural landscape that each individual inhabits" (p.171). In the search for identity from cultural and social perspectives, he also believed in the significance of art therapy through arts education to develop students' psychological well-being, mental development, and confidence that their own thoughts were valuable, along with their cultural heritage (Lashnoff, 2013).

Moon Over Harlem signified the riot that occurred in New York City in August of 1943. The riot was started due to the killing of Army Private Robert Bandy by a white police officer. This became one of my favorite paintings because it relates to what is happening in America today. With the protest of the grand jury decisions in the police brutality cases happening now, it is just a repeat of history. William H. Johnson captured a moment of history that we are now facing even... (Student Willetta, S. – Reflection Paper)

One that really caught my eye was called Moon Over Harlem... inspired by Johnson's time in New York. Th painting stood out to me because there were black people beaten by white cops at night presumably in Harlem New York. This painting was just so real. I could feel the people hurting... The people that

Building a Racial Identity

were being beaten looked as if they had almost been beaten to death. They were lying on the ground around when appears to be pools of blood beside them... I did not expect for William H. Johnson's work to relate to today's tragedies, with the shootings and innocent lives being taken away by cops who are supposed to protect us... (Student Taylor, S. – Reflection Paper)

Figure 3. Moon Over Harlem (1943) by William H. Johnson
Source: "© 2020, Smithsonian American Art Museum. Used with permission."

Moon Over Harlem commemorated the Harlem riots of 1943. The Harlem race riot began after Robert Bandy, an African American soldier, witnessed an African American woman's arrest for disturbing the peace in the lobby of Braddock Hotel on the southeast corner of 126th Street and Eighth Avenue. A white police office, James Collins, shot and wounded the black soldier Bandy. Rumors were circulated that the soldier has been killed, and the riot was directly occurred against white-owned businesses in Harlem including vandalism, theft, and property destruction. The riot ensued in the community that lasted for two days and resulted six deaths and hundreds injured, with nearly six hundred arrests. Johnson based the figures on photographs of the rioters arrested by white officers, but he ironically painted the police as black men, as if Johnson criticized the people of Harlem who were brutalizing themselves through their own behaviors, manners, and engagements. Students Jessica and Janecia said:

The first thing that popped into my mind was the George Floyd situation. I am not particularly sure why this one popped into my mind so clearly, but it did. I remember seeing people all over the country, painting his face, drawing him and his name on murals and buildings. I remember after his incident people went to the roads and on buildings and sidewalks and wrote "Black Lives Matter." The community created a movement for racial justice. The movements are different now than back then but we as African Americans have to fight for what is right and fight for justice for those who lost their life to police brutality. (Student Jessica, S. – Reflection Paper)

As Black African American kids grow up in the world today, they identify how we are seen and treated as African Americans... Incorporating social justice artworks in a classroom will be a great idea...because you can tell how children are feeling towards the world, physically, mentally, or emotionally, and even how they feel towards innocent people losing their lives. This kind of artwork can work for your community, individually, and even help people come together as one to create something big. Bringing social justice to a community will help a lot...because this is where community comes together as one to create a movement for something that needs to be dealt with in the correct way (Student Janecia, H. – Reflection Paper)

Personally, Johnson faced racism and discriminations living in the United States. Around this time, he created various portrayals of African American life in Harlem and the South – riots, segregation, hard work, freedom, soldiers, important figures, religious themes, etc., and immersed himself in the traditions of the African American culture and heritage. The deaths of African Americans over the use of deadly force by law enforcement are still a big issue in today's society. How has a history of systemic racism in the United States led to what is happening today? How deeply is racism rooted within society? How can we create our country that matters all lives despite their differences of race? What is the purpose of riots or protests within our society? There are many critical questions that we should discuss with students through works of art.

Interpreting Their Experiences and Personal Meaning Making

In this required tour, African American students were eagerly engaged in the works that were related to or associated with their cultural roots among many various works of art from the museum. They interpreted the works of art from their points of view and developed knowledge with the works of art through observation, description, and analysis. They were also challenged to speak up about social, cultural, and racial issues through the works of art in communities. Therefore, their racial identity as African American is a key part of understanding their learning experience from the museum. CRT claims that race is an essential part of understanding educational experiences, especially marginalized African American students. Racism is ordinary and common in everyday experience of most people of color in United States society, because "white Euro American experiences often have been the standard by which all other racial groups' experiences are measured... the experiences and interests of whites are normalized" (Kraehe & Acuff, 2013, p. 297). Races and racisms are social construction in response to shifting a historical and political circumstance by human relationship and thought. In other words, they are not objective, inherent, or fixed (Bryant, Moss, & Boudreau, 2015). Acuff (2020) indicated that "for dark people, the very basic idea of mattering is something hard to conceptualize when your country finds you disposable" (p. 13). Many students are aware of remaining discriminations, negative attitudes, and racial oppression of African Americans. Consequently, it is important for educators that racially responsive teaching plays a critical role how African American students themselves come to understand their ethnic self-esteem, cultural diversity, and social inclusion. It creates equal opportunities for all students from different social, racial, and cultural groups to function effectively in a diverse demographic society.

Moreover, African American students examined the cultural, social, political, and artistic contexts within the works of art from their personal points. As suggested in CLT, this study demonstrated that museum learning experiences were contextual and took place as a result of complicated interactions and interrelations of individual's personal, socio-cultural, and physical contexts. African American students' learning experiences were based on personal contexts because they experienced the museum as a result of their previous knowledge, personal experiences, and particular interests. They also interpreted the works of art in their own ways and personalized them to fit their own understanding and experiences through processes of finding connections and making meaning. As found in previous research from a constructivist perspective, this study demonstrated the importance of personal learning and meaning making as a result of museum visit (Black & Hein, 2003; Haanstra, 2003; Hooper-Greenhill, 1999; Falk & Dierking, 2013). African American students learned in their personal ways, interpreted the information through the lenses of pervious experiences, and personalized it to come to their own understanding. They created unique individualized experiences from their museum visits. Hence, this study emphasized the significance of the personal nature of museum learning experiences that connects to constructivist educators' viewpoint about learning by constructing personal meaning.

DISCUSSIONS AND RECOMMENDATIONS

Art gives people many different understandings of life and the things around them. It brings back old memories and can touch you in many different ways. This will be a memory that I will endure forever. (Student Trellis, P. – Reflection Paper)

We use art to express about social justice in life such as racism, or the unfairness of the color of our skin. That's why we should be fair and listen to other people culture and race stories. When it comes to our identity, we are discovering who we are, not only as individuals but as members of the community defined by our race, gender, and language. (Student Tristian, P. – Reflection Paper)

With increased media attention on police brutality against African Americans, museum educators have questioned the role of museum education in addressing cultural diversity and racial identity (Taylor & Doyle, 2018). Considering present-day social issues, many art educators have written about the needs for all students, especially African Americans, to see themselves in the curriculum; the art curriculum should support black students' basic ability to see their futures not only in the arts but also in the real-world at large. Acuff (2020) shared her experience as a community docent for Mickalene Thomas exhibition, *I Can't See You Without Me*, at the Wexner Center for the Arts as the following:

For an hour, a couple of times a week, I was in the presence of Mickalene's muses, all Black women, different shades of brown, who made me feel strong, visible, relevant, and central to all existence, past, present, and future. Thomas's aesthetic, patterns, and materials felt like home, and she offered a future in which black women could assertively and inconsequently stare back into the eyes of White audience who gazed on them and judged their brown skin. (p. 13)

I include various issues of social justice through different works of art and artists from different racial and cultural backgrounds in my contents of teaching. I believe art education can foster an understanding and serve the purposes of social justice. Therefore, art educators need to develop curriculum in which African American students can find their cultural legacy, recognize their racial identity, and envision their positive future. Racial conversations are one of critical topics for many African American students – how race worked in the past, how race affects their lives, and how it works today (Bolgatz, 2005). I believe such conversations profoundly affect our students' lives and influence to empower to be good citizens in constructing a society where everyone has equal rights. Jacob Lawrence said, "I've always been interested in history, but they never taught Negro history in the public schools… I don't see how a history of the United States can be written honestly without including the Negro" (HumanitiesWeb.org, para. 4). I agree that art can bridge the gap between the African American and white worlds (Kernes, 2007).

FUTURE RESEARCH DIRECTONS

Visiting the Florence Country Museum did change my perceptions on a lot of things about art. It made me realize that art is a way of expressing who we are. It explores where we come from. Art also makes us easier to understand each other. Art can communicate with us. For example, with seeing paintings of wars being fought and slaves it, I gain much sympathy. Art can tell a story that seems real and it can almost be related as a movie that can play over and over just by taking one glance at a piece of works… It was very meaningful experience! (Student Breanna, B. – Reflection Paper)

This visit exposed me to new ideas and important things that I should be familiar with. I learned many ways that artists have expressed their feeling of social justices and I was truly impressed with them all. I think art is an amazing way for people to express their feelings and ideas on social justice issues. Like we have learned earlier in this class, art gives people a voice to express themselves, and people need to express themselves and their feelings on topics like social justices… I always remember to use what I have learned from it in my classroom. (Student Ciera, H. – Reflection Paper)

We as educators broadly need to re-evaluate our content and teaching goals in terms of the cultural and racial diversity of our students. I believe if we are to promote justice, democracy, and academic integrity for students in our schools and to make the quality of life better for them, we need to evaluate our goals of teaching relevant for our students and their needs in our curricula. Many researchers demonstrated that African American students who felt more positive about African Americans and felt more positive being African Americans had higher self-esteem (Marks, Settles, Cooke, Morgan, & Rowley, 2004). As art educators, we need further practical studies about culturally and racially responsive teaching for various students of color. How future teachers define concepts like race, racism, and diversity will ultimately be reflected in their teaching, and their understanding of these concepts' overall impacts in what they choose to include and exclude in their curriculum. I believe we can teach students to understand the challenging issues of race, racism, and social justice in society through a more socially responsive visual art education to connect meaningfully to students' lives and lived experiences. Art educators should be more than teachers to teach 'art subject' in the classrooms.

CONCLUSION

Art education can foster an understanding and serve the purposes of social justice. Today African American artists are energetic participants in a cultural revolution. Driven by needs that are both aesthetic and social, they are in search of cultural identify, self-discovery, and self-esteem (Bowen 2008; Lewis, 2003). Significantly, they are not dominated by the European aesthetic standards, but instead are responding to their own lifestyles by creating art from the depths of their own needs, actions, and reactions (Chang, 2006). They are also unique in their artistic styles and themes depicting personal struggles, political turmoil, cultural conflict, racism, social discrimination, as well as African American music and dance. Young (2013) stated that self-identification of African American artists was often influenced by the history of African Americans in the United States and their struggles against racism, segregation, and injustice.

As seen in this study, in order to create meaningful learning experiences for African American visitors, understanding their racial, cultural, and social contexts are essential because meaningful museum education lies in how museum best can understand them and connect the experiences within the museum into the realms of visitors' real lives. Museums need more inclusive exhibits, education programs, and various staff equipped to discuss art that focuses on the discourses of different culture and race. In the broadest sense, museums perform their educational and public services by supplying learning experiences "by fostering the ability to live productively in a pluralistic society and to contribute to the resolution for the challenges we face as global citizens" (AAM, 1992, p. 6). Today much learning theories acknowledge that according to their previous knowledge, experiences, skills, backgrounds, and expectations, people are active in constructing their own meaning within an education experience. Thus, in museum education today, responsibility for learning often falls more on the learners, but the responsibility of educators is to prepare appropriate learning environments, to act as expert mentors, and to help develop meaningful learning experiences for individuals. Successful museums in the 21st century must communicate effectively with visitors, and inherent in this communication is the museum staffs' ability and willingness to be good listeners and to be willing to make changed based on data that is collected and analyzed.

REFERENCES

Acuff, J. (2020). Afrofuturism: Reimaging art curricula for black existence. *Art Education*, *73*(3), 13–21. doi:10.1080/00043125.2020.1717910

Adam, M., Falk, J., & Dierking, L. (2003). Things changes: Museums, learning, and research. In M. Xanthoudaki, L. Tickle, & V. Sekules (Eds.), *Researching visual arts education in museums and galleries* (pp. 15–32). Kluwer Academic Press.

American Association of Museums. (1992). *Excellence and equality: Education and the public dimension of museums*. American Assoication of Musuems.

Black, M., & Hein, G. (2003). You are taking us where? Reaction and response to a guided art museum fieldtrip. In M. Xanthoudaki, L. Tickle, & V. Sekules (Eds.), *Researching visual arts education in museums and galleries* (pp. 117–133). Kluwer Academic Press. doi:10.1007/978-94-010-0043-7_9

Bolgatz, J. (2005). *Talking race in the classroom.* Teachers College Press.

Bowen, S. (2008). *Recovering and reclaiming the art and visual culture of the Black Arts Movement* (Master's thesis). Available from https://etd.ohiolink.edu/

Brooklyn Museum. (n.d.). *Kehinde Wiley: A New Republic.* Retrieved from brooklynmuseum.org/exhibitions/touring/kehinde_wiley_new_republic

Bryant, L., Moss, G., & Boudreau, A. (2015). Understanding poverty through race dialogues in teacher preparation. *Critical Questions in Education, 6*(1), 1–15.

Chang, E. (2016). Investigating race and racism through African American art and artists. *Journal of Cultural Research in Art Education, 33,* 137–153.

Crum, M., & Hendrick, K. (2018). Black boys and museums: Educators collaborate for cultural awareness through multicultural critical reflection practice. In D. C. Kletchka & S. B. Stephen II, (Eds.), *Professional development in arts museums: Strategies of engagement through contemporary art* (pp. 45–56). National Art Education Association.

Dell's Antonia, K. J. (2014, November 25). Motherlode Blog: Talking about racism with white kids. *The New York Times.* Retrieved from http://parenting.blogs.nytimes. com/2014/11/25/taking-about-racism-with-white-kids/?r=0

Desai, D. (2010). The challenge of new colorblind racism in art education. *Art Education, 63*(5), 22–28. doi:10.1080/00043125.2010.11519084

Desai, S., & Marsh, T. (2005). Weaving multiple dialects in the classroom discourse: Poetry and spoken word as a critical teaching tool. *The Journal of Culture and Education, 9*(2), 71–90.

Dewhurst, M. (2014). *Social justice art: A framework for activist art pedagogy.* Harvard Education Press.

Efland, A. D. (2000). *Art and cognition: Integrating the visual arts in the curriculum.* Teachers College Press.

Falk, J., & Dierking, L. (2000). *Learning from museums: Visitor experiences and the making of learning.* Whalesback Books.

Falk, J., & Dierking, L. (2013). *The museum experience revisited.* Left Coast Press, Inc.

Gussak, D. (2010). Art for life is a way of life, or, personal revelations: Why I needed to work on this book. In T. Anderson, D. Gussak, K. Hallmark, & A. Paul (Eds.), *Art education for social justice* (pp. v–vii). National Art Education Association.

Haanstra, F. (2003). Visitors' learning experiences in Dutch museums. In M. Xanthoudaki, L. Tickle, & V. Sekules (Eds.), *Researching visual arts education in museums and galleries* (pp. 33–48). Kluwer Academic Press. doi:10.1007/978-94-010-0043-7_3

Hein, G., & Alexander, M. (1998). *Museums, places of learning*. American Association of Museums.

Henry, C. (2004). The art museum and the university in preservice education. *Art Education, 57*(1), 35-40.

Holt, A. (2012). Lowenfeld at Hampton (1939-1946): Empowerment, resistance, activism, and pedagogy. *Studies in Art Education, 54*(1), 6–20. doi:10.1080/00393541.2012.11518876

Hopper-Greenhill, E. (1999). *The educational role of the museum*. Routledge.

Hopper-Greenhill, E. (2001). *Cultural diversity: Developing museum audiences in Britain*. Continuum International Publishing Group-Printer.

Jabob Lawrence Quotations. (n.d.). Retrieved from http://www.humanitiesweb.org/ gcq/ID/278

Jung, Y. (2015). Post stereotypes: Deconstructing racial assumptions and biases through visual culture and confrontational pedagogy. *Studies in Art Education, 56*(3), 214–225. doi:10.1080/00393541.2015 .11518964

Kantrowitz, J. (2013). *William H. Johnson's world on paper*. Retrieved from http://arthistorynewsreport. blogspot.com/2013/06/william-h-jobnsons-world on-paper.html

Kernes, L. (2007). *Aaron Douglas: Teacher resources*. Retrieved from http://www.aarondouglas.ku.edu/ resources/teacher_resource.pdf

Khan, N. (2000). *Responding to cultural diversity: Guidance for museums and galleries*. Museums and Galleries Commission.

Kraehe, A. M. (2015). Sounds of silence: Race and emergent counter-narratives of art teacher identity. *Studies in Art Education, 56*(3), 199–213. doi:10.1080/00393541.2015.11518963

Kraehe, A. M., & Acuff, J. B. (2013). Theoretical considerations for art education research with and about "underserved populations.". *Studies in Art Education, 54*(4), 294–309. doi:10.1080/00393541.2 013.11518904

Lee, N. (2012). Culturally responsive teaching for 21st-century art education: Examining race in a studio art experience. *Art Education, 65*(5), 48–53. doi:10.1080/00043125.2012.11519192

Lee, N. (2013). Engaging the pink elephant in the room: Investigating race and racism through art education. *Studies in Art Education, 54*(2), 141–157. doi:10.1080/00393541.2013.11518889

Leshnoff, S. K. (2013). Victor Lowenfeld: Portrait of a young art teacher in Vienna in the 1930s. *Studies in Art Education, 54*(2), 158–170. doi:10.1080/00393541.2013.11518890

Lewin, T. (2012, March 6). Black students face more discipline data suggests. *The New York Times*. Retrieved from http://www.nytimes.com/2012/03/06/education/black- students-face-more-harsh-discipline-data-shows.html

Lewis, S. (2003). *African American art and artists*. University of California Press.

Marks, B., Settles, I., Cooke, D., Morgan, L., & Rowley, S. (2004). African American racial identity: A review of contemporary models and measure. In R. L. Jones (Ed.), *Black Phycology* (4th ed., pp. 338–404). Cobb & Henry.

McCoy, D., & Rodricks, D. (2015). *Critical race theory in higher education: Twenty years of theoretical and research innovations. ASHE Higher Education Report, 41(3)*. Jossey-Bass.

McFee, J. K. (1998). *Cultural diversity and the structure and practice of art education*. National Art Education Association.

Milner, H. R. (2015). *Raci(e)ing to class: Confronting poverty and race in schools and classrooms*. Harvard University Press.

Morrison, N. (2019, April 5). Black students face racial bias in school discipline. *Forbes*. Retrieved from https://www.forbes.com/sites/nickmorrison/2019/04/05/black-students-face-racial-bias-in-school-discipline/#3c2b9e1536d5

Nadworny, E. (2015, April 24). Uncomfortable conversations: Talking about race in the classroom. *NPR Ed*. Retrieved from http://www.npr.org/sections/ed/2015/04/24/401214280/uncomfortable-conversations-talking-about-race-in-the-classroom

Quinn, T.Board of Education. (2005). Biscuits and crumbs: Art education after Brown v. Board of Education. *Studies in Art Education, 46*(2), 186–190. doi:10.1080/00393541.2005.11651789

Quinn, T., Ploof, J., & Hochtritt, L. (2012). *Art and social justice education: Culture as commons*. Routlege. doi:10.4324/9780203852477

Rowley, S., Sellers, R., Chavous, T., & Smith, M. (1998). The relationship between racial identity and self-esteem in African American college and high school students. *Journal of Personality and Social Psychology, 74*(3), 715–724. doi:10.1037/0022-3514.74.3.715 PMID:9523414

SAAM. (n.d.). *Moon over Harlem*. Retrieved from https://americanart.si.edu/artwork/moon

Simon, N. (2010). The participatory museum. Santa Cruz, CA: Museum 2.0.

Simon, N. (2016). The art of relevance. Santa Cruz, CA: Museum 2.0.

Stone, D. (1995). Elementary art specialists' comfort level in teaching in the art museum setting. *Visual Arts Research, 20*(1), 76–81.

Stone, D. (1996). Preservice art education and learning in art museums. *Journal of Aesthetic Education, 30*(3), 83–96. doi:10.2307/3333323

Stone, D. (1997). A comparative study of two art museum tours and their impact on adult learning. *Visual Arts Research, 23*(1), 142–150.

Stone, D. (2001). Using the art museum. Worcester, MA: Davis.

Taylor, J., & Doyle, J. (2018). Constructing identify: A collaborate teacher workshop. In D. C. Kletchka & S. B. Stephen II, (Eds.), *Professional development in arts museums: Strategies of engagement through contemporary art* (pp. 88–97). National Art Education Association.

Urton, R. (2009). *The Harlem Renaissance*. Retrieved from http://robinurton.com/history

Building a Racial Identity

Valentine, V. (2020). *50 years after his death: William H. Johnson's work is showcased in museum exhibitions and rare solo presentation by Michael Rosenfeld Gallery.* Retrieved from https://www.culturetype.com/2020/03/15/50-years-after-his-death- william-h-johnsons-work-is-showcased-in-museum-exhibitions-and-rare-solo- presentation-by-michael-rosenfeld-gallery/

Xanthoudaki, M., Tickle, L., & Sekules, V. (2003). Museum education and research-based practices. In M. Xanthoudaki, L. Tickle, & V. Sekules (Eds.), *Researching visual arts education in museums and galleries* (pp. 15–32). Kluwer Academic Press. doi:10.1007/978-94-010-0043-7

Young, B. (2011). *Art, culture, and ethnicity* (2nd ed.). National Art Education Association.

Young, B. (2013). The importance of self-identification in art, culture, and ethnicity. *Art Education, 66*(4), 51–55. doi:10.1080/00043125.2013.11519232

ADDITIONAL READING

Anderson, T., Gussak, D., Hallmark, K., & Paul, A. (2010). *Art education for social justice.* National Art Education Association.

Buffungton, M. (2019). Changing practice: Culturally sustaining pedagogy in art education. *Art Education, 72*(2), 20–25. doi:10.1080/00043125.2019.1559587

Kletchka, D., & Carpenter, S. (2018). *Professional development in arts museums: Strategies of engagement through contemporary ar.* National Art Education Association.

Kraehe, A., & Herman, D. Jr. (2020). Racial encounters, ruptures, and reckonings: Art curriculum futurity in the wake of Black Lives Matter. *Art Education, 73*(5), 4–9. doi:10.1080/00043125.2020.1789413

Manifold, M., Wills, S., & Zimmerman, E. (2016). *Culturally sensitive art education in a global world.* National Art Education Association.

Tavin, K., & Morris, C. (2013). *Stan(ing) up for a change.* National Art Education Association.

Villeneuve, P., & Love, R. (2017). *Visitor-centered exhibitions and edu-curation in art museums.* Rowman & Littlefield Press.

Young, B. (2011). *Art, culture, & ethnicity.* National Art Education Association.

KEY TERMS AND DEFINITIONS

Constructivism: A theoretical framework that recognizes the learners' understanding and knowledge based on their own experiences.

Critical Race Theory: A theoretical framework that uses critical theory to examine race, racism, and society.

Florence County Museum: Local museum that provides a dynamic exhibition of scientific, historic, and artistic objects are special interest to the people of Florence Country and the Pee Dee region of South Carolina.

Race: A grouping of humans based on physical or social qualities, generally viewed as distinct by society.

Racial Identity: A developmental process in which individuals construct their racial backgrounds from one stage to another as a result of experiences within the mainstream culture.

Racially Responsive Teaching: Teaching of knowledge, beliefs, and values that recognize the importance of racial and cultural diversity of different students in learning.

Social Justice: Justice in terms of the distribution of opportunities and privileges within a society.

ENDNOTES

[1] Information of the works of art and their artists are collected from the museum's exhibitions.

[2] The student comments are exempted from their class assignments. The students' names are pseudonyms.

This research was previously published in Engaging Communities Through Civic Engagement in Art Museum Education; pages 58-77, copyright year 2021 by Information Science Reference (an imprint of IGI Global).

Chapter 39

Mentoring African American Women at Historically Black Colleges/Universities:
Beyond the Misconceptions of Our Identity

Tammara Petrill Thomas
Winston-Salem State University, USA

Michelle Lee Maultsby
South Carolina State University, USA

ABSTRACT

This chapter describes how a considerable milestone for new faculty entering academia has been awarding tenure by the institution of higher education. This is often referred to as the Academy. Tenure-track faculty working towards tenure spend several years honing their craft in the areas of teaching, research, and service. Senior colleagues assume the lead in determining activities, and others who are considered authorities and leaders in the chosen field of scholarship. While HBCUs have provided an enormous source of support for African-American women who are tenure-track faculty, they continue to be underrepresented in the academy and are adversely impacted by the tenure process. Barriers that impede the tenure process of African-American women faculty include societal biases, stereotypes, systemic oppression, and lack of mentorship. This chapter seeks to provide awareness, discuss unique challenges specific to African American women faculty, and existing strategies to negotiating the tenure and promotion processes.

INTRODUCTION

African-American women who serve as faculty within the academy face challenges that are unique to their male counterparts (Herbert, 2012; Lucas & Steinmel, 2009). Contextually, African American women have historically had to bear the weight of stereotypes, and negative perceptions which serve

DOI: 10.4018/978-1-6684-4507-5.ch039

to diminish credibility within professional settings such as predominantly white institutions, colleges, and universities (Grant, 2012; Grant & Ghee, 2015). African-American women continue to focus their efforts to reframe and deconstruct, assumptions, biases, and stereotypes that still exist in today's society (Schwartz, Bower, Rice & Washington, 2003). Moreover, these barriers that African American women contend with in society also tend to find their way in professional settings such as the Academy and serve to impede further her ability to be seen as an equal colleague. Therefore, the African American woman in the academy, who has dedicated her career to thriving in higher learning institutions, finds herself at odds with what society expects her to be, and who she has become through extensive training and development (a professional).

Historically, a majority of tenured black faculty are employed at historically black colleges/universities (HBCUs). Despite the weak attempts of predominantly white institutions (PWI's) to recruit black faculty, there continues to be little change in improving representation. Thus, HBCU's have provided a refuge for black academics to grow professionally, and strive for tenure. However, there are ongoing challenges that are faced by HBCU's. These issues are related to the limited resources, and the difficulty in recruitment of high achieving black students who are enrolling in traditionally white institutions (Mack, 2011; Riley, 2010). Although these challenges persist, a disproportionate representation of black faculty who are women contributes to the pool of role models, which have been found to have a positive influence on student success (Bettinger & Long, 2005; Mack, 2011).

That said, as African-American women in academia make strenuous attempts to negotiate their career, they also have to assert their ability to others in providing premier education with the use of sound pedagogy. To further complicate matters they are also faced with the dilemma of how to convey this message assertively. The aim of this chapter is to address identified disparities, give voice to these phenomena that serve to stagnate the professional growth of African American women in academe and bring awareness to barriers and negative perceptions held. Further, the goal of this chapter is to provide strategies to minimize the impact of these difficulties. Therefore, the objectives of the chapter are as follows:

Objectives of the Book Chapter

1. To increase the awareness of individuals in academia regarding the stereotypes and stigmas placed on African American women.
2. To increase the knowledge and awareness of African American women societal perceptions and negative stereotypes.
3. To raise awareness of African American women of mentoring opportunities, and strategies that will help them navigate through the academic experiences and contribute to their success.

BACKGROUND

It has been a longstanding discussion regarding the importance of diversifying the professoriate on college and university campuses. As recently as 1993, differences in tenure and promotion characterized by gender and race/ethnicity continue to persist, and disparities related to African-American women who are tenured, let alone receive full professoriate ranking, continue to exist within the academy (Oakes, 2008; Perna, 2001). While the magnitude of womens' growth in tenured or tenure-track appointments has grown, African-American women's' growth in tenured or tenure-track appointment is less impres-

Mentoring African American Women at Historically Black Colleges/Universities

sive. According to a study conducted by the Teachers Insurance and Annuity Association of America (TIAA, 2016), which focused on faculty diversity of U.S. colleges and universities found that although there has been an increase in faculty diversity over the last 20 years, most of those increased have not been tenure-track.

According to the "Taking the Measure of Faculty Diversity" report by TIAA Institute provided highlights regarding the proportion of African American women, along with female faculty in other ethnic groups by appointment type. The highlights conducted by TIAAA compared the state of affairs between 1993 and 2013. The report presented findings that suggest in 1993, full-time faculty from underrepresented minority groups working in U.S. colleges and universities made up 8.2%, and of those only 7.1% were tenured, while 10% were on tenure-track.

According to Finkelstein, Conley, Schuster (2016), African-American women tenured full-time faculty has declined from 6.3% to 5.8% between 1993 and 2013. In spite of the benefits that diversity presents, there continues to be underrepresentation of African American faculty, especially those with tenure, within the academy. According to the National Center for Education Statistics (NCES, 2015) in fall 2013, "there were 1.5 million faculties in degree-granting postsecondary institutions. Faculty included in these statistics were assistants, associate, instructors, lecturers, adjunct professors, and interim professors. Of these professors, 79% were Caucasian (43% were male, and 35% were female), while only 6% were African-American. Additionally, among full-time professors, 84% were Caucasian (58% Caucasian males, 26% Caucasian females), and of those only, 4% were African-American" (NCES, 2015).

PROBLEM

Issues that impede efforts of diversification and inclusion of African-American faculty, in general, is complicated, to say the least. African-American women are perpetually underrepresented in the professoriate as compared to White men, and women. However, for African-American women, tenure-track faculty continue to express feelings of alienation from the university, the department, and their colleagues (Henry & Tator, 2012). There are forces within higher education environments that contribute to the dilemma (e.g. financial, governing boards, policies, procedures, staff, societal perception, biases, stereotypes, organizational culture, and so on). There are also individual factors that contribute, which may also provide more context (e.g. issues of commitment, motivation, prioritization, skill, etc.). However, what is clear is that much more work remains to be done. It is without saying, although minimally, there has been a growth in the number of African-American women entering into faculty positions as full-time faculty. To facilitate diversification and integration of African-American women faculty within the field of post-secondary education, and support tenure and promotion efforts, specific strategies, and mentoring activities must consider as a useful, and valuable strategy. The use of well-developed strategies can be utilized to facilitate inclusion of African American women among the ranks of those who have already been awarded tenure, and promotion.

Notwithstanding, being awarded tenure is the paramount goal for many members of the academy, it is important to recognize actions aimed at diversification and inclusion will involve a multi-layered approach. Implementation of a formal review of policy must be implemented, modified, and created on an organizational level to support efforts to increase the number of African-American women who are tenured within academia. Implemented changes at an organizational level will facilitate the process of African-American women, who are newly recruited full-time, tenure-track faculty aimed at equipping them to negotiate the tenure process more efficiently. Further intentional efforts initiated by both the institution's more experienced faculty and new faculty is beneficial in facilitating continued professional development, and eventual appointment of tenure and promotional. Ongoing interactions with individuals who are more experienced in the policies, procedures, culture, and practices of the institution would serve to provide much-needed indoctrination, support, and mentorship.

TENURE AND PROMOTION

Why is tenure so important for African-American women faculty? When a faculty member achieves tenure within an institution of higher learning, it is an indication that the university or college is recognizing an established partnership with the faculty member. Additionally, being appointed tenure acknowledges that the candidate has demonstrated growth, potential, and longstanding commitment to the institution to which they have devoted teaching, research, and service provision efforts. Being awarded tenure and promotion is one of the most noted, and valued accomplishments regarded in American colleges and universities. The process of obtaining tenure is a challenging endeavor that requires, planning, focus, and tenacity. Tenure-track faculty is required in most cases to matriculate through administrative procedures and policies and undergo several levels of review (departmental, college, and administrative). Successful negotiation of these processes more than often requires the support of more experienced colleagues who provide guidance, and mentorship. Research has shown that minorities and women in higher education seem to have positive outcomes when they engage in a collaborative learning experience, which also includes mentors (Kellerher, 2015; Gorman, Durmowicz, Roskes, & Salttery, 2010). Although many institutions attempt to provide objective guidelines to negotiate the process, aspects of the tenure process can be subjective, and open to varied interpretation (Perna, 2001; Persell, 1983; McElrath, 1992). Sue and Sue (2016) has surmised that the oppression and racism in today's society are no longer the overt racism of the past, but it is manifested by an onslaught of offensive slights. Sue and Sue (2016) define microaggressions as those innumerable slights which occur daily and stressors experienced by marginalized groups. Therefore, African-American women who are subject to these assaults may find themselves frustrated and psychologically taxed, which makes the ascension to tenure that much more arduous. It is critical for African-American women faculty to find strategies to negotiate gender microaggressions and hostile environments that are attributed specifically to race and gender. Mentorship can serve to provide support and guidance to African-American women faculty who are new to the academy.

MENTORSHIP

Mentorship has been viewed by many educational researchers as a fundamental component in a variety of professional fields, higher education included (Adedokun, 2014; Kellerher, 2015; Stamm & Buddeberg-Fischer, 2011). Mentorship is also an important part of professional development which is critical for success within academia. Moreover, the engagement in mentoring activities is also built into the institutional culture. There are many definitions of mentorship, and there is no agreed-on definition because the concept and practices vary across disciplines and academic institutions. However, for the purpose of this book chapter, mentorship will be defined according to Blackwell (1989) as:

Mentoring African American Women at Historically Black Colleges/Universities

...a process by which persons of superior rank, extraordinary achievement, and prestige instruct, counsel, guide, and facilitate the intellectual, and career developments of persons identified as protégés... (p. 9).

Mentoring is an activity which denotes a collaborative professional relationship that exists between a less experienced faculty member and a senior faculty member, which aim is an investment in the professional development, and vitality of an early career faculty member. Mentors help early-career faculty (assistant professors) to become indoctrinated into the local campus, and the academic community. Senior faculty assists in various components of acclimation to academia. These contributions may include: clarification of expectations as a newly appointed faculty member; explain relevant institutional, departmental, and program processes (formal and informal); they serve as advisors; provide suggestions for resources for research (e.g. grant writing, writing workshops, proposal review for publication); contribute knowledge that support the areas of teaching, service, research; provide protection from distracting activities and harmful interactions; provide suggestions for strategies to manage time; encourage the development of other mentoring relationships through networking; help assistant professors establish relationships within the academy; and they help to guide assistant professors with the development of a roadmap/blueprint that will guide their progress as they strive for tenure and promotion (e.g. early, 1-2 year, mid, 3-4 years, and late, 5-6 years). This relationship is close, intense, and complex in nature. Also, Mentoring relationships can be either formal or informal (Bussey-Jones, et al.; Ensher & Murphy, 1997). Within these relationships the more experienced professional transfers both social and professional resources that are critical for developing the necessary skills needed to navigate networks that are required for professional success (Kelch-Oliver, Smith, Johnson, Welkom, Gardner, & Collins, 2013). Junior faculty who receive mentoring in academic settings tend to have better research skills, and are more often the recipients of grants, and publications, and also had greater career satisfaction (Kelch-Oliver et al., 2013). Blackwell (1989) asserts that the relationships that exist between a protégé (mentee), and a mentor is similar to that of a parent, in which traits exemplify characteristics such as authority, trust, respect, and intimacy are encapsulated. Although this description insinuates a "child-like" state of new faculty (i.e. junior faculty), the designation affords a form of protected status, reasonable expectations, and provides the much-needed support that a newly hired faculty would require when entering a complex system, which is characteristic of academia. Joining the academy can be a daunting and overwhelming experience. Hill, Castillo, Ngu, and Pepion (1999) discussed the idea of "demystifying the academy," which speaks to learning the nuances of how academia works from one who has the "inside track," so to speak. Therefore, conceptually, outsiders (African-American women), who are aspiring to become tenured faculty will become socialized to the academy's organizational values, rules (formal and informal), and culture.

A better understanding of the expectations is critical to successful immersion into academia, advances the development of a thriving career in academia, as well as provide the foundation for achieving milestones that ultimately lead to appointments that result in higher ranking status such as tenure, promotion, and climatically full professor. However, the concept and practice of mentorship have not been perfected. We understand from the literature that African American women faculty encounter, and experience unique challenges that are related to teaching, research and service. The intersectionality of race, and gender, undergirded by racism and sexism, further complicates the succession of African-American women into higher rankings such as a full professor. Further, these challenges contribute adversely to their ability to access the supports necessary (e.g. mentoring, collegiality) to obtain tenure and promotion. According to Turner & Gonzalez, (2012),

...the intersectionality across gender, race, and ethnicity offers a dynamic and unique window from which to observe the micro and macro processes and nuances that occur within a mentoring relationship (p. [Foreword]).

To fully understand the importance of mentorship, and strive to increase the occurrence of mentorship for African-American women faculty, it is critical that we also discuss the challenges faced in mentorship and issues that result from denied access to a mentoring relationship.

PROBLEMS IN MENTORING

Higher education settings are experiencing an influx of junior faculty comprised of women, minorities, and foreign nationals (Phillips, Dennison, & Cox, 2015; Roberts & Behar-Horenstein, 2012). The diversity of higher education settings is changing, and there is a good reason to alleviate antiquated processes that impede the inclusion of scholars that do not fit the status quo and do not experience the privilege afforded to the White majority. Further, this same group of new minority academics is reporting with more frequency feelings of marginalization, isolation, and exclusion from access to formal mentoring (Darwin & Palmer, 2009; Phillips, Dennison & Cox, 2015; Ragins & Cotton, 1999). Within mentoring relationships the more experienced professional transfers both social and professional resources that are critical when developing the necessary skills needed to navigate networks necessary for professional success (Kelch-Oliver, Smith, Johnson, Welkom, Gardner, & Collins, 2013). Junior faculty who receive mentoring in academic settings tend to have better research skills, and are more often the recipients of grants, and publications, and also had greater career satisfaction (Kelch-Oliver et al., 2013). However, for African American women faculty to take advantage of mentoring networks that exist within the academy, more experienced faculty must demonstrate commitment by granting essential access.

Isolation and Marginalization

In essence, the experience of mentorship acts as a conduit in which senior faculty instills junior faculty with both social and professional skills essential to negotiating academia successfully, while also providing valuable psychosocial benefits (Kay & Wallace, 2009). Limited access to professional interactions with senior colleagues who through more experience possess resources (e.g. networking relationships) poses a barrier. Kay and Wallace (2009), conducted a study which examined gender difference in the mentoring process within the profession of law (also a male dominated profession). Kay et al. research results suggested the following: 1) having multiple mentors, rather than a single mentor, yields career advancement; 2) for intrinsic career rewards psychosocial support is seen as an essential indicator of mentoring quality, which produces a perception of procedural fairness (particularly if the mentor is male); 3) women, as compared to men, gain more through multiple mentors; and 4). Women benefit from close relationships with their mentors, which manifests in higher earnings. The overall conclusion of the study suggests that mentoring relationships that have specific network properties, and provides access to critical resources can yield positive career rewards (Kay et al., 2009). However, a challenge in mentorship relationships relates to the various nuances that may assign unrealistic expectations on the mentor, which impedes their ability to engage in a productive mentorship relationship successfully. According to Kay and Wallace (2009), mentoring has remained mostly focused on this traditional one-to-one model. However, the benefit of a "constellation" (multiple) of developmental relationships, either concurrently, or as a series of "dyadic" relationships may be a better approach to efficaciously capitalizing on the mentorship relationship (i.e. social capital). The benefit of having access to senior faculty is they possess of knowing a larger network of people within the academic environment and can serve as a liaison as it relates to presenting African-American women faculty to other faculty who may at some point in their academic career prove to be a valuable resource. Turner et al. (2014), suggests that it is important for racial/ethnic minority faculty to identify allies within their institutions, which may be done with the assistance of both faculties of color and White faculty and administrators. In other words, establishing larger networks, undergirded with the knowledge that multiple relationships, with more than one primary mentor, will yield more professional benefits. Moreover, the initiative taken by senior faculty and administrators to intentionally facilitate these alliances will further promote inclusion of African-American faculty women faculty into what may be perceived as an impenetrable society. Ultimately, for ethnic/minority women faculty who are faced with the task of integrating into academia, establishing a strong network of fellow academics, and forming a close relationship with multiple mentors, can serve to promote a sense of belonging, and professional satisfaction.

A study conducted by Ensher & Murphy (2010) investigated the role of relational challenged as reported by 309 protégés (mentees) in various stages, and types of mentoring relationships. The Mentoring Relationship Challenges Scale (MRCS) was used to measure three factors of relational challenges which were: "1) Demonstrating Commitment and Resilience, 2) Measuring Up to the Mentors Standards, and 3) Career Goal, and Risk Orientation" (p. 253-266). The study found that the challenges in mentoring relationships can affect the level of satisfaction.

Relational Challenges

Underrepresentation of African-Americans female faculty in higher education continues to contend with interpersonal roadblocks to tenure, unlike their Caucasian counterparts (Chang, Welton, Martinez, Cortez, 2013; Ford, 2011, Hirshfield & Joseph, 2012). Relationship dynamics are bi-products of the mentoring relationship. The mentoring relationship is supported by respect, trust, commitment, honesty, etc. Mentors and mentees work intimately in this collaborative relationship that is reciprocal in nature. Mentees expect to gain the knowledge, support, and guidance, as it relates to acclimation to the academy, and the career trajectory aimed at tenure, promotion, and other professional milestones envisioned by new faculty. Like any partnership similar to that of a mentor and mentee, there can be relational challenges. In light of the unique challenges faced by African-American women in academia, the threat of relational difficulties within the mentoring relationship can be catastrophic for professional development. Relational challenges that are unique to African-American women are the overwhelming majority of White male and female counterparts that hold tenured positions. Therefore, the likelihood of having access to the same gender, let alone same racial background has been extremely hampered. The lack of access to homogenous mentors, and the inability to exercise autonomy in the choice of a mentor can be a barrier for African-American women faculty. A study conducted by Bell and Treleaven (2011) explored the experiences of participants in a mentoring program. The study concluded that it was important for mentees to choose their mentors, and establish their own personal connections, which led to individuals' success in the mentoring program. Mentorship relationship that is "naturally occurring" or informal relationships are considered to yield more positive outcomes, but the downside is the mentorship of senior staff may not be available to all new faculty who are in need of mentorship (Bell, & Treleaven, 2011). Therefore, the approach to establishing a favorable mentoring relationship with mentors who may not be of the same race or gender should be approached with care. Moreover, the perception that on some level a "connection" has been established is critical to the mentor-mentee relationship. A relational challenge is possible due to the presence of distinct cultural differences which can negatively impact the mentoring relationship between a White male senior faculty, and an African-American women junior faculty. Both parties must have mutual respect, admiration, and understanding of the others background, with specific emphasis on the meaning of "White privilege," and the impact it has on the mentees ability to negotiate the world of academia (Turner & Gonzalez, 2014). An awareness of how being a White male in our society affords social privilege and understanding how the advantages that are inherently contingent on this status will embody them with the fortitude needed to be supportive allies and advocates of African-American women faculty. Researchers found that the most common characteristic of an effective mentor is the ability to be altruistic, which speaks to the capacity of the mentor to detach from what they want and focus on considering what is in the best interest of the mentee (Straus, Johnson, Marques, & Feldman, 2014). Additionally, a relational characteristic of an effective mentor indicated by participants was accessibility, and having the ability to identify and support the development of potential strengths in the mentee (Straus, et al., 2014). In keeping with the reciprocal nature of the mentoring process, mentees also have the responsibility of being appreciative, respectful of the mentors, time, deadlines, and other obligations, and also be an active participant in their professional development.

SOCIETAL BIAS

In general, women are expected to endure social norms reinforced by society. These imposed social norms assume that women are to perform as primary caregivers for children (and aging parents), which can serve as a precursor to women's lower likelihood of obtaining tenure and promotion (Perna 2001a; Wolfinger, et al., 2008). For African-American women, society has assigned identities not only based on gender but also race. As a result, societal perceptions of the African-American woman have served to shape expectations, interactions, and the experiences that happen within the institutions of higher learning. Additionally, women and minorities may find post-secondary work environments to be unsupportive and find balancing work and family to be an insurmountable challenge. According to van Anders (2004), in response to perceived barriers, women of ethnic minority backgrounds may self-select away from academia. It would also stand to reason that those same women who may desire upward mobility, as it relates to the pursuit of tenure and promotion, would also find it difficult to negotiate these same unaccommodating environments.

Acknowledgment that social influences contribute to the development of societal biases, which have far-reaching, and adverse consequences for learning environments is critical. Institutions of higher education are microcosms of society, and biases, and prejudices tend to matriculate into organizations like colleges, and universities, thereby creating norms, and organizational culture that promotes and support unfair practices (ASHE Higher Education Report, 2011). Societal perception of who the African-American women are may have provided a negative contribution to how they are seen in higher education settings. These perceptions have served to support long-standing attitudes and beliefs about African-American women. To ensure African American women who are faculty have the best foundation for success in academe it is imperative that inaccurate, biased perceptions and expectations be eliminated within the academy.

PERCEPTIONS AND STEREOTYPES

African-Americans, in general, have found themselves to be the target of stereotypes, and overall negative perceptions, as a group, and separately as men and women. Obviously, there are stereotypes that are negative, as well as those that are viewed as more positive. For example, African-American men are sometimes regarded as aggressive, criminal minded, lazy, unintelligent, while in comparison accomplished athletes, sexually competent, etc. (Czopp & Monteith, 2006; Smith & Hattery, 2006; Steele & Aronson, 1995). African-American women have historically dealt with various stereotypes such as: being non-sexual; nurturing; family-oriented Mammies; hostile; angry; antagonistic Sapphires; overly sexual, the Superwoman or the "Strong Black Women" who is an extreme multi-tasker; possessing an unwillingness to ask for help; and a promiscuous Jezebel (Moore, 2012; West, 1995). Unfortunately, these stereotypes continue to be reinforced through media (e.g. television, news, music), which has only contributed to the perpetuation of these stereotypes. According to Amodio & Devine, (2006), individuals can make associations quickly by the ongoing continuation of constant exposure material that reinforces ideas. As a result, individuals can form biased perceptions, and begin to see these perceptions as global agreed upon "truths." These flawed perceptions and stereotypes impact not only the groups that are the target of these negative beliefs, but they can also affect people on an individual level. In other words, individuals within the group can experience anxiety that in some way their behaviors will confirm the negative stereotype, also known as stereotype threat (Moore, 2012; Steel & Aronson, 1995). The perpetuation of biased stereotypes towards African-American women can be substantially damaging to their professional careers because it can influence how their colleagues and students engage with them. Research conducted by Weitz and Gordon (1993) indicated that Caucasian college students characterized African-American women as boisterous, aggressive, forthright, argumentative, intelligent and aggressive. For some these characteristics may be seen as positive attributes, but in most cases, these descriptors associated with African-American women are not seen as strengths. Thus, taking prior research into account, it would appear that perceptions of African-American women, as it relates to race, would have an adverse impact on how colleagues within the academy view her, while also causing an adverse impact on the development of mentoring relationships.

Gender Stereotypes

Negative stereotypes and perceptions serve to stigmatize African-American women and contribute to others forming biases as relates to the what is believed to encapsulate the identity of African American women. Unfortunately, unfounded perceptions transcend into the workplace settings like institutions of higher learning, and these negative perceptions can impact how African American women faculty are perceived.

African-American women faculty are often scrutinized on appearance, such as hairstyles, attire, body language, and behavior (Ford, 2011). These inequalities and criticisms are couched and justified by what is seen as institutional/departmental, and societal expectations for professionalism, hence "normal". The idea of what is regarded, or believed to be normal within the Academy presents an overwhelming obstacle for African American women faculty because they can be singled out as an outsider, a deviant, or illegitimate. Moreover, these inequalities serve as barriers that question the intellectual abilities, competence, and overall credibility of underrepresented female faculty (Delgado-Bernal & Villalpando, 2010; Ford, 2011). Unfavorable viewpoints and subjective assessment can color tenure review, and tenure and promotion. Moreover, an idiosyncratic assessment not in keeping with transparent and objective standards can also be professionally catastrophic (Agathangelou & Ling, 2002; Baez, 2000; Lising, 2002). Lastly, if African-American women faculty are perceived by their colleagues as defective, intellectually inadequate, and ideally not a good fit for academe, the likelihood of being actively adopted and invited to engage in a mentoring relationship by "seasoned" academics is highly unlikely.

Intersectionality

Crenshaw, (1991), discussed intersectionality as the connection that exists between the social constructs of race, class, and gender. Often averages of the faculty are reported quantitatively, which make the information being presented appear to be significant. For example, research studies are presented on the number of African-American women faculty, in comparison to the number of White women faculty. In these cases, the analysis of the data is not additive when considering the outcomes of White women faculty in higher learning settings, as compared to the outcomes of African-American women faculty. Crenshaw's (1991) research discussed how the intersection of social identity and systems of oppression, domination, and discrimination could lead to the development of multiple identities. Further, characteristics such as gender, race, ethnicity, disability, etc. can also intersect. African-American women are vulnerable to the maladies that are imposed by the intersection of two prejudices: sex, and race. The concept of intersectionality proposes that to understand an individuals' privilege and societal perception all aspects of simultaneously interacting identities must be considered. Conceptually, understanding the contribution of intersectionality is important. Recognizing the impact of intersectionality, as it relates to the experience of African-American woman faculty acknowledges that certain characteristics that are possessed are not isolated, cannot be considered independently, but each overlaps in concert and provide meaning. As a result of societal characterization of the identity of African-American women, the existence of slights, discrimination, and biases are perpetuated. The term *identity politics* (Heyes, 2016), denotes that simply being a member of a particular oppressed group (i.e., woman, African-American, etc.), can place the group member at risk for cultural domination which is manifested by incidence of stereotyping, experienced invisibility, or being assigned one's group identity. These adverse occurrences take place without considering the individualized differences of each person within the group. The premise of political identity is centered on leveraging these assumptions, by creating new and affirming group and self-concepts, while also standing in solidarity, which in turn provides a place of "safety". An illustration of this solidarity is supported by the collective agreement among African-American women faculty that there are disparities in their experiences as they work towards achievement of professional goals. Moreover, illumination of these injustices provides compelling rationale for in-depth analysis, as well as demand for change, and action.

Systemic Barriers

According to Hughes and Howard-Hamilton (2003), systemic racism is perhaps the greatest obstacle faced by African-American women in higher education (p. 98). Institutional forms of racism can manifest in both overt and covert ways. They may also appear in the form of microaggressions (Sue & Sue, 2016). Sue and Sue (2016) explain microaggressions as casual degradation of any marginalized groups which take place in the daily life of people who belong to the group. An example of a microaggression is when a Black man enters a high-end department store, and notices overly attentive salespersons shadowing

Mentoring African American Women at Historically Black Colleges/Universities

him around the store. These types of assaults are pervasive within the culture of the work environment. It is the plight of African American women faculty who work in institutions of higher education where these assaults are so common place that a state of apathy has developed and the violence is maintained. Factors that work against the promotion of African American women faculty in institutions of higher learning has been forthcoming (Evans, 2007; Few, Piercy, & Stremmel, 2007; Harley, 2008). However, more research is warranted. Several factors have been identified as barriers to tenure for African American women. It is apparent that organizational culture is a major contributor to the cultivation and maintenance of roadblocks which continue to act as formidable barriers for African American women faculty who desire tenure within the academy. Lack of visible role models, stereotype threat, tokenism, racism, inequities in pay, and alienation (to name a few), have all been identified as barriers. However, perceptions, stereotypes, and organizational culture will be discussed as contributing factors.

STRATEGIES FOR IMPROVING MENTORING RELATIONSHIPS FOR WOMEN AT HISTORICALLY BLACK COLLEGES AND UNIVERSITIES (HBCU)

Okawa (2002) indicated that individuals tend to work better together when they have similar cultural experiences. Although there continues to be limited availability of colleagues that share the same race and gender, there are opportunities for African American women to develop variations of mentoring experiences with the resources that are available. Moreover, tenured faculty should maintain an ongoing posture of support that makes it evident that they are receptive to investing in the growth and development of African American women faculty regardless of gender and race.

As indicated earlier in the chapter, mentoring relationships can have a very positive effect on the advancement of careers for African American women in academia. Therefore, it is imperative that Historically Black Colleges and Universities (HBCU) help provide an environment that supports the development of African American women so that they may flourish in this setting. To assist in creating such an environment that is supportive, three strategies have been identified. The strategies consist of the following: 1) creating an organizational culture that is conducive for mentoring 2) management of competencies and 3) developing effective communication techniques.

CREATING AN ORGANIZATIONAL CULTURE CONDUCIVE FOR MENTORING

An important aspect of faculty development is understanding of the organization in which they teach and its culture. This culture, commonly known as organizational culture, is often deemed as the social environment that exists within the university and can affect the productivity of faculty. It is defined as, "shared values and beliefs that give members of an organization meaning and provide them with a structured set of rules for behavior" (Mathis, Jackson, Valentine and Meglich, 2015, p. 13). These core concepts are entrenched in the organization and affect the employee's self-concept, expressed opportunities and methods for developing strategies for future endeavors. Cultures specific to institutions of higher education include collegial, managerial, developmental and negotiating. Collegial culture is formed from "faculty disciplines and consists of scholarly engagement, shared governance, decision-making, and rationality. Managerial culture is developed based on the mission and vision of the university and focuses on goals and purposes, effective supervisory skills, and fiscal responsibility. Developmental culture concentrates

739

on personal and professional development and negotiating culture emphasizes the establishment of policies and procedures that are equitable and egalitarian. It also focuses on interest groups, mediation, and power" (Kezar & Eckel, 2002, p. 439). Organizational culture ultimately informs faculty of how they should interact with other faculty members. If developed in a positive, beneficial manner, organizational culture can foster effective working affiliations and enhance mentoring relationships.

HBCUs are recognized as having a culture that promotes the development of minorities, including African American women. Noteworthy to mention, they were among some of the "first institutions to allow women access to college" (Allen, Jewell, Griffin, & Wolf, 2007, p. 268). The established culture also parallels that of a community where all those involved are charged with the responsibility of empowering students to change their lives and the society in which they live. However, when addressing faculty mentoring relationships at HBCUs, the culture has been identified vastly different. Wilson (2011) contends that the administrative culture continues to be a growing concern for faculty, alumni, and stakeholders. It is noted that there is a "detectable disenchantment with some organizational deficiencies, ranging from inefficient business practices to a failure to maintain quality control and high standards of customer service in frontline offices such as admissions, financial aid, and public relations" (Wilson, 2011, p. 2). Shared governance among faculty has also decreased, thereby affecting decision making on critical issues within the institutions (Lewis, 2011). The research also purports that inadequate resources have been documented as an area of concern for faculty professional development (Allen, Jewell, Griffin, & Wolf, 2007; Lewis, 2011; Wilson, 2011). All the conditions as mentioned above can play a vital role in the ability and willingness of senior faculty to mentor junior faculty. Given this, it is imperative that HBCUs continue to foster a culture of community and learning by providing intellectually challenging and stimulating environments and strong institutional leadership. Environments that support mentoring can be accomplished by intentionally developing, and incorporating a culture that encourages and welcomes the change.

Kezar and Eckel (2002) conducted a study on six institutions analyzing the effect of the universities culture on strategies that were implemented for change. The following strategies were implemented to enact the cultural shift: senior administrative support, collaborative leadership, robust design, staff development, and visible actions. Senior administrative support consists of the academic leadership team that can provide support regarding fulfilling major institutional obligations. Their involvement ensures the provision of resources needed by faculty and also develops mechanisms for accountability. Effective leadership by this team can help facilitate a conversion of cultural change where needed. Collaborative leadership involves incorporating both senior administrators and faculty and developing a joint effort throughout campus from beginning to end in the change process. Robust design constitutes developing a plan for change incorporating goals and objectives, which are constantly evolving based on the need of the institution. It allows for new innovative ideas from various individuals that will provide opportunities for change and advancement. Staff development consists of providing faculty with opportunities to obtain more knowledge and awareness directly related to the desired change. Staff development can include training specific to the individual need as well as departmental. The use of peer training or mentoring is also very vital to this process. Visible actions involve allowing faculty to see how the changes in processes have affected the culture. When visible change begins to take place, it can alter the attitudes of others as well as motivate them to become more proactive and involved in the process. Incorporating activities that faculty can be a part of also gives a sense of involvement and builds trust. The themes of the Kezar and Eckel article appear to be consistent with other viewpoints of organizational culture at universities including those of HBCUs. Although the above study was not conducted at an HBCU, incorporating

Mentoring African American Women at Historically Black Colleges/Universities

these strategies into the existing HBCU culture can help facilitate a more conducive culture that promotes well-developed faculty and the ability to have effective mentoring relationships.

PERSONAL AND PROFESSIONAL MANAGEMENT OF COMPETENCIES

To maintain an effective mentoring relationship, there are responsibilities that the mentor and mentee must be able to perform. One of those major responsibilities for the mentee is to have the ability to apply acquired skills and knowledge to job tasks and successfully carry out those functions. This is commonly known as managing competencies. Given the mentoring relationship, the mentor will guide the mentee in several critical steps to help build this function. These steps include:

1. Develop a clear goal for your academic career.
2. Develop specific objectives, activities, and set reasonable timelines.
3. Develop a support system.
4. Be aware of your strengths and weaknesses.
5. Identify resources that are readily available.
6. Effectively manage interpersonal relationships. Be approachable.
7. Identify barriers that may affect the outcome of your goal and methods for overcoming them.
8. Identify how to change the barrier into an opportunity to achieve the goal.

Develop a Clear Goal for Your Academic Career

Successful mentoring will require that the mentee is aware of what their actual goal is for their academic career. Once identified, the process of setting goals will help the individual to be proactive in their career and to assess their productivity and whether they will be successful (Trees, 2016).

Develop Specific Objectives, Activities, and Set Reasonable Timelines

Once the overarching goal has been identified then steps must be created to develop specific objectives and activities to reach those goals. For example, if the junior faculty's goal is to obtain tenure, then they must identify the criteria for promotion and ascertain how they will achieve it. Within this description should be a method of excelling in the four major areas for promotion include teaching, research, service and professional development. A detailed, realistic timeline for accomplishing these four tasks should also be outlined. The university faculty handbook can also be a guideline for specific timelines and may include specific criteria for promotion, (i.e., three research articles per year) (Mylona, Brubaker, Williams, Novielle, Lyness, Pollart, Dandar & Bunton, 2016).

Develop a Support Team

There are many pragmatic benefits to developing a support system and having supportive relationships. These benefits including having access to people who are knowledgeable, who can provide guidance and a sense of comfort when needed and who can make the mentee more buoyant in times of stress. Research has also shown that there are other benefits in having a "linkage of supportive relationships: indicating those with robust social support networks have better health, live longer lives and report higher well-being" (School of Social Work, 2017). The support team should also be inclusive of a cohesive team that can help the mentee reach their goals such as other faculty and administrative support.

Be Aware of Strengths and Weaknesses

An important aspect of self-awareness is the ability to recognize personal strengths and weaknesses. Identifying and using our strengths helps maximize our potential and increases self-esteem. Consequently, identifying weaknesses can be more difficult than identifying strengths. Pointing out the things you are good at is easier than pinpointing the deficient areas and things you are not naturally as proficient. However, it is essential to recognize these weaknesses to ensure the proper skills are in place to be successful. Take weaknesses into account when making career decisions. If a particular job function is in areas that you are not as skillful, and perhaps deficient, then reconsider pursuing this task if it is an unrealistic one. If there is uncertainty about a particular area of weakness, put a plan in place for assessment. For example, after completing a project, ask what went well and what could have done better.

Identify Resources That Are Readily Available

In order for the faculty member to be successful, they must identify resources that are available to them. This can be accomplished by creating a professional development plan that outlines the faculty member's needs that are consistent with job-related functions. Items identified in the plan can range from supplies, equipment, workshops, training, and technology. Once identified, the plan should be cross checked with the administration to ensure that these resources will be readily available.

Effectively Manage Interpersonal Relationships: Be Approachable

A strong interpersonal relationship will require reciprocity by both the mentor and mentee. Rules of thumb for cultivating an interpersonal relationship will entail: showing appreciation for the relationship; continuous contact via different methods of communication such as text, phone calls or emails; being dependable and available; respect boundaries; and having a willingness to accept constructive criticism.

Identify Barriers That May Affect the Outcome of Your Goal and Methods for Overcoming Them

Identifying barriers early on in the process of setting goals will help the faculty member to conquer them. Recognize that often they are stemmed from internal fears and discomfort when taking risk. These barriers consist of things such as comparing oneself to others, striving for perfectionism, having an unhealthy need for approval, impatience, and simply having a fear of failure. Rieger (2011) contends that barriers stem from five major causes: fear, information flow, short-term thinking, misalignment, and resources. An individual can start eliminating their impediments and improving their performance by "assessing the root cause, manifestation, and impact of them, then prioritizing them based on their influence and how difficult they will be to remove. Though barriers can seem insurmountable, it's important to remember that because they were created internally, they can be knocked down internally" (Rieger, 2011, p.3).

Identify How to Change the Barrier Into an Opportunity to Achieve the Goal

Once the individual has identified the barriers and how to overcome them, they can easily transition into changing this obstacle into new found opportunities. For example, as opposed to comparing oneself to others, focus on areas of strength and highlight distinct talents and attributes that are sought after by organizations. Instead of concentrating on the things that promote fear, understand that it is a defense mechanism that sets in to address failure. Embrace failures as lessons that were necessary to learn to improve performance.

EFFECTIVE INTERPERSONAL COMMUNICATION

As indicated earlier in the chapter, various viewpoints and stereotypes have characterized African-American women as, aggressive, forthright, argumentative, and aggressive. Although these characteristics may be viewed as positive attributes (intelligent), in some cases, these descriptors associated with African-American women are often viewed in a negative connotation and may affect the interactions among African American women faculty and their mentors. Given this perception, it is imperative to establish effective communication as early on as possible in the mentoring relationship.

An advantageous method for examining interpersonal communication among African American women is the social exchange theory. The social exchange theory is "based on the premise that individuals weigh the costs and rewards associated with a particular relationship to determine whether the relationship should be maintained or terminated" (Myers, Know, Pawlowski, & Ropog, 1999, p. 71). This communication process allows for the transfer of resources and rewards, which can be advantageous for both the mentee and mentor. It's particularly important given the culture of the HBCU that African American women feel the benefits of this relationship.

African American women have also often been misunderstood when communicating. Due to the expressive nature of their nonverbal cues, they have been deemed as being loud, boisterous and angry. In actuality, most times they are responding out of distress. Strumska-Cylwik (2013) describes a clear distinction between stress in communication and communication under stress. Stress in communication refers "directly to mutual communication which mainly turns out to be governed by the level of stress that accompanies it. Communication under stress focuses on people communicating with each other who are under stress affecting their general well-being, physical sensations and behavior" (p. 420). It is further purported that when individuals are experiencing distress, it is more difficult for them to effectively communicate. Given the demanding nature of academia and the rigorous criteria for promotion, African American women often find themselves in very stressful situation and responding accordingly. However, these responses can be misinterpreted and negatively affect interpersonal relationships. In an attempt to effectively convey communications, the use of comprehensive methods of responding when discussing difficult topics will be beneficial for African American women. These methods include probing for clarity, being direct, reflecting on thoughts and feelings, and interpreting in an effort to obtain the most optimal information (Rajmohan, 2015). The use of these methods can help to alleviate misinterpretations of emotions and communication.

CONCLUSION

African-American women continue to focus their efforts to reframe and deconstruct long-standing assumptions, biases, and stereotypes that still exist in today's society (Schwartz, Bower, Rice & Washington, 2003). Moreover, these barriers that African American women contend with in society also tend to find their way into professional settings such as the Academy, and serve to impede further her ability to be seen as an equal colleague. Furthermore, mentoring relationships may be difficult to cultivate because of these associated stereotypes. As a result, strategies for improving interpersonal relationships are identified as crucial component for these relationships to be successful.

FUTURE RESEARCH

Future research is warranted regarding the organizational culture and change of historically black colleges and universities. There is also need to continue to assess the misconceptions of mentoring African American women and methods for delineating those ideas. More rigorous study of existing mentoring programs, communication styles and their effect on African American women. Additionally, assessing the differences between mentoring programs of African American women at Historically Black Colleges and Universities versus that of predominantly white institutions is another area to address.

REFERENCES

Adedeokun, A. D. (2014). *Mentoring, leadership behaviors, and career success, of African American female faculty and administrators in higher education.* Retrieved April 29, 2017, from http://search.proquest.com/docview/1504639769/

Agathangelou, A. M., & Ling, L. H. M. (2002). An unten(ur)able position. The politics of teaching for women of color in the U.S. Retrieved May 19, 2017, from http://www-tandfonlincom.proxy.lib.uiowa.edu/doi/abs/10.1080/14616740022000031562

Allen, W., Jewell, J., Griffin, K., & Wolf, D. (2007). Historically black colleges and universities: Honoring the past, engaging the present, touching the future. *The Journal of Negro Education, 76*(3), 263–280.

Amodio, D. M., & Devine, P. G. (2006). *Stereotyping and evaluation in implicit race bias: Evidence for independent constructs and unique effects on behavior.* Retrieved May 3, 2017, from http://psycnet.apa.org.proxy.lib.uiowa.edu/journals/psp/91/4/652

ASHE Higher Education Report. (2011). *Women's status in higher education: Background and significance.* Retrieved April 1, 2017 from http://eds.a.ebscohost.com.proxy.lib.uiowa.edu/ehost/pdfviewer/pdfviewer?sid=1b32238b-193c-4404-b4b7-8bca93a93f3b%40sessionmgr4009&vid=1&hid=4202

Baez, B. (2000). Race-related services and faculty of color: Conceptualizing critical agency in academe. Retrieved May 10, 2017 from http://eds.a.ebscohost.com.proxy.lib.uiowa.edu/ehost/pdfviewer/pdfviewer?sid=4876bd75-dbbb-4956-b1eb-b577afae1d79%40sessionmgr4007&vid=1&hid=4205.

Bell, A., & Treleaven, L. (2011). *Looking for professor right: Mentee selection of mentors in a formal mentoring program.* Retrieved April 12, 2017, from https://linkspringer-com.proxy.lib.uiowa.edu/article/10.1007/s10734-010-9348-0

Bettinger, E., & Long, B. (2005). *Do faculty serve as role models? The impact of instructor gender on female students.* Retrieved June 5, 2017 from https://www.aeaweb.org/articles?id=10.1257/0002828057746670149

Blackwell, J. E. (1989). *Mentoring: An action strategy for increasing minority faculty.* Retrieved April 28, 2017, from http://www.jstor.org.proxy.lib.uiowa.edu/stable/pdf/40249734.pdf

Bussey-Jones, J., Bernstein, L., Higgins, S., Malebranche, D., Paranjape, A., Genao, I., ... Branch, W. (2006). Repaving the road to academic success: The IMeRGE approach to peer mentoring. *Academic Medicine, 81*(7), 674–679. doi:10.1097/01.ACM.0000232425.27041.88 PMID:16799297

Chang, A., Welton, A. D., Martinez, M. A., & Cortez, L. (2013). Becoming academicians: An ethnographic analysis of the figured worlds of racially underrepresented female faculty. *Negro Educational Review, 64*(1-4), 97–118.

Crenshaw, K.W. (1991). *Mapping the margins: Intersectionality, identity politics, and violence again women of color.* Retrieved June 2, 2017 from http://socialdifference.columbia.edu/files/socialdiff/projects/ArticleMapping_the Margins_by_Kimblere_Crenshaw.pdf

Czopp, A. M., & Monteith, M. J. (2006). Thinking well of African Americans: Measuring complimentary stereotypes and negative prejudice. *Basic and Applied Social Psychology, 28*(3), 233–250. doi:10.120715324834basp2803_3

Darwin, A., & Palmer, E. (2009). *Mentoring circles in higher education.* Retrieved April 20, 2017, from http://www.tandfonlinecom.proxy.lib.uiowa.edu/doi/abs/10.1080/07294360902725017

Delgado Bernal, D., & Villalpando, O. (2002). An apartheid of knowledge in academia: The struggle over the "legitimate" knowledge of faculty of color. Retrieved May 10, 2017 from http://www.tandfonline.com.proxy.lib.uiowa.edu/doi/pdf/10.1080/713845282?needAccess=true

Ensher, E. A., & Murphy, S. E. (2010). The mentoring relationship challenge scale: The impact of mentoring state, type, and gender. *Journal of Vocational Behavior, 79*(1), 253–266. doi:10.1016/j.jvb.2010.11.008

Evans, S. Y. (2007). *Women of color in American higher education.* Retrieved May 6, 2017 from http://www.nea.org/assets/docs/TAA_07_13.pdf

Few, A. L., Piercy, F. P., & Stremmel, A. J. (2007). Balancing the passion for activism with the demands of tenure: One professional's story from three perspectives. *NWSA Journal, 19*(3), 47–66.

Finkelstein, M.J., Conley, V.M., & Schuster, J.H. (2016). Taking the measure of faculty diversity. *Advancing Higher Education,* 1-18.

Ford, K. A. (2011). Race, gender, and bodily (mis)recognitions: Women of color faculty experiences with White students in the college classroom.

Gorman, S. T., Durmowicz, M. C., Roskes, E. M., & Slattery, S. P. (2010). Women in the academy: Female leadership in STEM education and the evolution of a mentoring web. *Forum on Public Policy Online, 2*, 1–2.

Grant, C. (2012). *Advancing our legacy: A Black feminist perspective on the significance of mentoring for African American women in educational leadership.* Retrieved May 3, 2017, from http://www.tandfonline.com.proxy.lib.uiowa.edu/doi/abs/10.1080/09518398.2011.647719

Grant, C. M., & Ghee, S. (2015). Mentoring 101: Advancing African-American women faculty and doctoral student success in predominantly white institutions. *International Journal of Qualitative Studies in Education, 28*(7), 759–785. doi:10.1080/09518398.2015.1036951

Harley, D. (2008). Maids of academe: African American women faculty at predominately white institutions. *Journal of African American Studies, 12*(1), 19–36. doi:10.100712111-007-9030-5

Harley, D. A. (2008). Maids of academe: African American women faculty at predominantly white institutions. *Journal of African American Studies, 12*(1), 19–36. doi:10.100712111-007-9030-5

Henry, F., & Tator, C. (2012). Interviews with racialized faculty member in Canadian universities. *Canadian Ethnic Studies, 44*(1), 75–99. doi:10.1353/ces.2012.0003

Herbert, S. S. (2012). *What have you done for me lately?: Black female faculty and "Talking Back" to the tenure process at PWIs.* Retrieved April 3, 2017 from http://eds.b.ebscohost.com.proxy.lib.uiowa.edu/ehost/pdfviewer/pdfviewer?sid=c2093e56-554c-446c-b55f-657c6a959cbc%40sessionmgr107&vid=1&hid=121

Heyes, C. (2016). *Identify Politics.* Retrieve June 2, 2017, from https://plato.stanford.edu/archives/sum2016/entries/identity-politics/

Hill, R. D., Castillo, L. G., Ngu, L. Q., & Pepion, K. (1999). *Mentoring ethnic minority students for careers in academia: The WICHE doctoral scholars program.* Retrieved May 3, 2017, from http://journals.sagepub.com.proxy.lib.uiowa.edu/doi/abs/10.1177/0011000099276007

Hirshfield, L. E., & Joseph, T. D. (2012). *We need a woman, we need a Black woman: Gender, race and identity taxation in the academy.* Retrieved April 17, 2017 from http://eds.b.ebscohost.com.proxy.lib.uiowa.edu/ehost/pdfviewer/pdfviewer?sid=2b127026-6b4b-4a0d-8221-464600d31d0a%40sessionmgr104&vid=1&hid=121

Hughes, R. L., & Howard-Hamilton, M. F. (2003). Insights: Emphasizing issues that affect African American women. *New Directions for Student Services, 2003*(104), 95–104. doi:10.1002s.110

Jean-Marie, G., & Brooks, J. S. (2011). Mentoring and supportive networks for women of color in academe. *Women of Color in Higher Education: Contemporary Perspectives and New Directions, 9*, 91–108.

Kay, F. M., & Wallace, J. E. (2009). *Mentors as social capital: Gender, mentors, and career rewards in law practice.* Retrieved April 17, 2017 from http://onlinelibrary.wiley.com.proxy.lib.uiowa.edu/doi/10.1111/j.1475- 682X.2009.00301.x/full

Kelch-Oliver, S., & Johnson, W. Gardner, & Collins, (2013). Exploring the mentoring relationship among African American Women in Psychology. Retrieved May 3, 2017 from http://eds.b.ebscohost.com.proxy.lib.uiowa.edu/ehost/pdfviewer/pdfviewer?sid=53ca064c-737b-41af-a20b-bcd4fa14793%40sessionmgr103&vid=1&hid=121

Kelleher, S. E. (2015). *A case study of the perceptions of faculty in a formalized mentoring program.* Retrieved May 2, 2017 http://media.proquest.com/media/pq/classic/doc/3970178731/fmt/ai/rep/NPDF?_s=wb3juJutmgdTG53vNEF6a9gfROM%3D.

Kezar, A., & Eckel, P. D. (2002). The effect of institutional culture on change strategies in higher education. *The Journal of Higher Education, 73*(4), 435–460.

Lewis, V. (2001). Faculty participation in institutional decision making at two historically black institutions. *The ABNF Journal,* 33–40. PMID:21675667

Lising Antonio, L. (2002). Faculty of color reconsidered: Reassessing contributions to scholarship. Retrieved May 3, 2017 from http://muse.jhu.edu.proxy.lib.uiowa.edu/article/14873/pdf

Lucas, K., & Steimel, S. J. (2009). Creating and responding to the generalized other: Women miners' community-constructed identities. *Women's Studies in Communication, 32*(3), 320–347. doi:10.1080/07491409.2009.10162393

Mack, K. M., Rankins, C. M., & Winston, C. E. (2011). *Black women faculty at historically black colleges and universities: Perspectives for a national imperative.* Retrieved June 5, 2017 from http://www.sswoc.net/wp-content/uploads/2012/03/Black_Women_at_HBCUs- Perspectives.pdf

Mathis, J., Jackson, J., Valentine, S., & Meglich, P. (2015). *Human Resource Management* (15th ed.). Boston, MA: Cengage Learning.

McElrath, K. (1992). *Gender, career disruption, and academic rewards.* Retrieved from http://www.jstor.org.proxy.lib.uiowa.edu/stable/pdf/1982015.pdf?refreqid=excelsior:44083ecf8acec4dfc3248008f92360cc

Moore, J. A. (2012). Love styles utilized by African-American men as predicted by stages of racial identity and perceptions of African-American women [Doctoral dissertation].

Myers, S., Knox, R., Pawlowski, D., & Ropog, B. (1999). Perceived communication openness and functional communication skills among organizational peers. *Communication Reports, 12*(2), 71–83. doi:10.1080/08934219909367712

Mylona, E., Brubaker, L., Williams, V., Novielli, K. D., Lyness, J. M., Pollart, S. M., ... Bunton, S. A. (2016). Does formal mentoring for faculty members matter? A survey of clinical faculty member. *Medical Education, 50*(6), 670–681. doi:10.1111/medu.12972 PMID:27170085

Oakes, J. L. (2008). *Tenure and promotion differentials for women faculty and faculty of color at public two-year colleges in the United States.* Retrieved April 12, 2017 from http://journals.sagepub.com.proxy.lib.uiowa.edu/doi/pdf/10.1111/j.1471-6402.1983.tb00615x

Okawa, G. Y. (2002). Diving for pearls: Mentoring as cultural and activist practice among academics of color. *College Composition and Communication, 53*(3), 507–532. doi:10.2307/1512136

Perna, L. (2001a). The relationship between family responsibilities and employment status among college and university faculty. *The Journal of Higher Education*, 72(5), 584–611. doi:10.1080/00221546.2001.11777115

Perna, L. W. (2001). *Sex and race differences in faculty tenure and promotion.* Research in Higher Education, 42(5). Retrieved May 3, 2017 https://link.springer.com.proxy.lib.uiowa.edu/article/10.1023/A%3A1011050226672

Persell, C. H. (1983). *Gender, rewards, and research in education.* Retrieved May 2, 2017 from http://journals.sagepub.com.proxy.lib.uiowa.edu/doi/pdf/10.1111/j.1471-6402.1983.tb00615.x

Phillips, S. L., Dennison, S. T., & Cox, M. D. (2015). *Faculty mentoring: A practical manual for mentors, mentees, administrators, and faculty developers.* Retrieved April 12, 2017 from http://site.ebrary.com/lib/uiowa/reader.action?docID=11170677

Ragins, B., & Cotton, J. (1999). Mentor functions and outcomes: A comparison of men and women in formal and informal mentoring relationships. Retrieved from http://psycnet.apa.org.proxy.lib.uiowa.edu/journals/apl/84/4/529

Rajmohan, T. Interpersonal competencies of executives in service organizations. *KIIT Journal of Management*, 11(11), 75-94.

Rieger, T. (2011). Overcoming barriers to success. *Business Journal, 3*, 1–3.

Riley, J. (2010). *Black colleges need a new mission.* Retrieved June 7, 2017 from https://www.wsj.com/articles/SB10001424052748704654004575517822124077834

School of Social Work. (2017). Developing your support system. Retrieved May 17, 2017 from https://socialwork.buffalo.edu/resources/self-care-starter-kit/additional-self-care-resources/developing-your-support-system.html

Smith, E., & Hattery, A. J. (2006). *Hey stud: Race, sex, and sports.* Retrieved April 14, 2017 from http://link.springer.com.proxy.lib.uiowa.edu/article/10.1007/s12119-006-1013-5

Steele, C. M., & Aronson, J. (1995). Stereotype threat and the intellectual test performance of African-Americans. *Journal of Personality and Social Psychology*, 69(5), 797–811. doi:10.1037/0022-3514.69.5.797 PMID:7473032

Straus, S. E., Johnson, M. O., Marquez, C., & Feldman, M. D. (2013). *Characteristics of successful and failed mentoring relationships: A qualitative study across two academic health centers.* Retrieved June 1, 2017 from https://www.ncbi.nlm.nih.gov/pmc/articles/PMC3665769/

Strumska-Cylwik, L. (2013). Stress and communication (i.e. on stress in communication and communication under stress). *The International Journal of the Arts in Society*, 6(3), 419–441.

Sue, D. W., & Sue, D. (2016). *Counseling the culturally diverse: Theory and practice* (7th ed.). Hoboken, New Jersey: John Wiley & Sons, Inc.

TIAA Institute. (2016). Research overview. Taking the measure of faculty diversity. Retrieved June 30, 2017, from https://www.tiaainstitute.org/sites/default/files/presentations/2017- 02/faculty_diversity_overview_0.pdf

Toutkoushian, R. K. (1999). *The status of academic women in the 1990s: no longer outsiders, but not yet equals.* Retrieved June 2, 2017 from http://eds.a.ebscohost.com.proxy.lib.uiowa.edu/ehost/pdfviewer/pdfviewer?sid=9d4fad8a-b742-4f9c-82ee-f6645b892b6c%40sessionmgr4009&vid=2&hid=4202

Trees, L. (2016). Designing and implementing a mentoring program focused on knowledge transfer. *KMWorld*, 11-13.

Turner, C. S. V., & Gonzalez, J. C. (2012). *Foreword. Modeling mentoring across race/ethnicity and gender: Practices to cultivate the next generation of diverse faculty.* Retrieved April 2, 2017, from http://site.ebrary.com/lib/uiowa/reader.action?docID=11035814

Turner, C. S. V., & Gonzalez, J. C. (2012). *Modeling mentoring across race/ethnicity and gender: Practices to cultivate the next generation of diverse faculty.* Retrieved April 3, 2017, from http://site.ebrary.com/lib/uiowa/reader.action?docID=11035814

U.S. Department of Education, National Center for Education Statistics. (2015). *The Condition of Education 2016* (NCES 2016-144), Retrieved May 15, 2017 from https://nces.ed.gov/programs/coe/indicator_csc.asp

U.S. Department of Education, National Center for Education Statistics. (2016). *The condition of education 2016: Characteristics of postsecondary faculty.* Retrieved April 3, 2017 from https://nces.ed.gov/fastfacts/display.asp?id=61

van Anders, S. M. (2004). Why the academic pipeline leaks: Fewer men than women perceive barriers to becoming professors. *Sex Roles*, *51*(9/10), 511–521. doi:10.100711199-004-5461-9

Walker, N. (2016). Missing leadership: Mentoring African American women in higher education [Doctoral dissertation].

Weitz, R., & Gordon, L. (1993). Images of Black women among Anglo college students. Retrieved from http://link.springer.com.proxy.lib.uiowa.edu/article/10.1007/BF00289745

West, C. M. (1995). Mammy, Sapphire, and Jezebel: Historical images of Black women and their implications for psychotherapy. Retrieved from http://psycnet.apa.org.proxy.lib.uiowa.edu/journals/pst/32/3/458

Wilson, J. (2011). A multidimensional challenge for black colleges. *The Chronicle of Higher Education*, *9*, 1–3.

Wolfinger, N. H., Mason, M. A., & Goulden, M. (2008). Problems in the pipeline: Gender, marriage, and fertility in the ivory tower. *The Journal of Higher Education*, *79*(4), 388–405. doi:10.1080/00221546.2008.11772108

KEY TERMS AND DEFINITIONS

Awareness: Being conscious of your own and societies worldviews, and the disparities that exist as it relates to women, faculty, and mentorship.

Bias: A prejudice in favor of or against a person, or group as compared to another group, which is typically unfair and slanted.

Gender Microaggressions: Everyday slight, put downs, invalidations, and insults that are directed specifically toward women.

Intersectionality: Describes the overlapping or intersecting social identities and related systems of oppression, domination, or discrimination.

Marginalized Groups: Groups that are excluded from the dominant culture, and denial of access due to race, gender, etc.

Mentee: Faculty who are trained, advised or counseled by a senior person with credibility within their profession.

Mentor: Experienced or senior faculty who serve as a guide in academia in the areas of research, teaching, advisor, resource, organizational culture, and role model.

Microaggression: Everyday slights, insults, slurs, invalidations that occur.

Organizational Culture: Taken for granted values, assumptions, expectations that characterize the organization and its members.

Relational: Concerning the connection or interactions that impact the way in which two or more people understand each other and engage.

Stereotypes: A preconceived notion about a specific group of people.

Stereotype Threat: When individuals of marginalized group fear that they may inadvertently confirm a bias, or stereotype assigned to their group.

Tenure: An indefinite appointment that can be terminated only for cause or extraordinary circumstances.

Underrepresentation: Despite the importance of diversity, the number of minority faculty is lacking.

White Privilege: The unearned advantages, and privileges that are afforded people of White European descent.

This research was previously published in Faculty Mentorship at Historically Black Colleges and Universities; pages 97-125, copyright year 2018 by Information Science Reference (an imprint of IGI Global).

Chapter 40
Minority Students in Computer Science:
Barriers to Access and Strategies to Promote Participation

Jung Won Hur
Auburn University, USA

ABSTRACT

Over the past decade, a number of collaborative efforts to expand computer science (CS) education in U.S. K-12 schools have been made (e.g., CS 10K and CSforAll). Despite various efforts, minority students, such as African Americans and Hispanics, still face unique barriers to accessing CS courses, resulting in the underrepresentation of minorities in the field of CS. This chapter reviews factors affecting minority students' interest in and access to CS learning and identified barriers, such as a lack of CS courses offered in schools, students' lack of self-efficacy in CS, and a lack of role model who can encourage minority students to study CS in college. The chapter also introduces the culturally responsive teaching (CRT) framework, followed by a discussion on how teachers can incorporate CRT strategies to create culturally responsive computing learning environments where minority students' engagement and success in CS are promoted.

INTRODUCTION

The increasing demand for computer science (CS) related jobs has allowed K-12 schools, universities, government, tech industry, and nonprofit organizations to work together to broaden participation in CS in the United States (Brown & Briggs, 2015). According to the U.S. Bureau of Labor Statistics (2020), employment of computer and information technology jobs is projected to grow about 12 percent from 2018 to 2028, which is much higher than the average growth for all occupations. Expanding CS learning opportunities is more than meeting the employment demand. Margolis and Goode (2016) claim, "Knowledge of computing is important across all types of fields and jobs, but knowledge about computer

DOI: 10.4018/978-1-6684-4507-5.ch040

Copyright © 2022, IGI Global. Copying or distributing in print or electronic forms without written permission of IGI Global is prohibited.

science is also a critical component of civic life and democratic participation.... [Computer science] allows one to intervene and innovate in today's world" (p. 52). Similarly, Webb et al. (2017) state that the emphasis on CS is essential to educate active creators and producers who can lead cultural change as opposed to generate passive consumers of technology. In order for a nation to continue to innovate and progress, providing K-12 students with the opportunity to learn CS is important (Google & Gallup, 2016; Yadav, Gretter, Hambrusch, & Sands, 2016).

Over the past decade, a number of collaborative efforts to expand CS learning opportunities have been made, reporting positive results. For instance, *CS 10K* and *CSforAll* initiatives, funded by the National Science Foundation, have allowed new curriculums to be developed. These initiatives have also provided teachers with more professional learning opportunities to learn how to teach CS (Brown & Briggs, 2015; Margolis & Goode, 2016). The New York City (NYC) Department of Education launched the *CS4All* initiative in 2015, and the evaluation survey reported that approximately 55% of NYC schools provided students with some kind of specific CS instruction during the 2016-2017 academic school year (Villavicencio, Fancsali, Martin, Mark & Cole, 2018). According to the College Board (2018), almost 136,000 students took at least one AP CS exam in 2018, a 31% increase from 2017. The number of Black students who took one of AP CS exams increased about 44% from 2017, and the number of Hispanic students increased 41%.

Despite various efforts to provide CS learning opportunities to all K-12 students, minority students, such as African Americans (Black is also used interchangeably in this chapter), Hispanics (Latino is used interchangeably), and American Indians, still face unique barriers to accessing CS courses, resulting in the underrepresentation of minorities in the field of CS in the U.S. (Sax et al., 2018). According to the report by Google and Gallup (2016), Black students (47%) are less likely than their White counterparts (58%) to have CS classes at their schools, and Black (58%) and Hispanic (50%) students are less likely than White peers (68%) to use a computer at home. Despite NYC's effort to diversify students in CS education, more wealthy schools that include fewer minority students reported that they have offered CS instruction, indicating a lack of minority students' opportunities to learn CS (Villavicencio, Fancsali, Martin, Mark & Cole, 2018).

In order to broaden participation and to diversify the future CS field, understanding barriers that minority students face to gain access and ways to promote minority students' interest and participation in CS is critical (Goode, 2007; Wang, Hong, Ravitz, & Moghadam, 2016). Consequently, this chapter reviews factors affecting minority students' interest in and access to CS followed by synthesizing various studies and projects promoting minority students' learning of CS. The chapter also introduces culturally responsive teaching and discuss how teachers can incorporate this teaching method to promote minority students' participation and success in CS classes.

UNDERREPRESENTATION OF MINORITY STUDENTS

Barriers to Having Computer Science Learning Experiences

Although African Americans and Hispanics represent 27% of the U.S. population, they only make up 16% of the science, technology, engineering and math (STEM) workforce. In terms of college or advanced degree, just 7% of African Americans and 6% of Hispanics hold a bachelor's degree or higher in a STEM field (Funk & Parker, 2018). This indicates a potential lack of minority role model who can

Minority Students in Computer Science

encourage minority students to pursue a degree in CS. Google and Gallup (2016) report that while Hispanic students are more interested in CS than their White peers, they are less likely to have access to an adult who works in a STEM field, potentially less likely to have a direct role model who can encourage them to study CS.

A number of scholars have examined barriers of minority students to accessing CS learning to tackle the lack of diversity issue. For instance, Wang, Hong, Ravitz, and Moghadam (2016) analyzed a survey examining experiences and perceptions of 1,673 students, 1,685 parents, 1,013 teachers, 9,693 principals, and 1,865 superintendents in the United States. The researchers found that most participants do not have a clear understanding of what CS is (e.g., thinking that CS is about creating a document or a presentation). Black and Hispanic students and parents are less likely to understand CS than their White peers, potentially contributing to the underrepresentation of these groups in the CS field. Similarly, Buzzetto-More and Ukoha (2010) surveyed students enrolled in computer applications courses at two Historically Black Colleges and Universities (HBCU) and reported that minority students lack appropriate knowledge necessary to select a CS related major. These findings indicate that minority students and parents do not clearly understand what CS is, and the lack of CS knowledge possibly affects minority students' decision to major in CS. Goode (2007) argues, "Without understanding of computer science, its interdisciplinary connections, and an explicit bearing to youth interests, few students not already enamored with computing end up pursuing these courses" (p. 69).

Students' self-efficacy has been identified as an important factor contributing to students' interest, choice, and persistence in CS. Bandura (1997) defines self-efficacy as "beliefs in one's capabilities to organize and execute the courses of action required to produce given attainments" (p. 3). Self-efficacy does not refer to one's actual skills or abilities; it is one's judgment that he or she can achieve a specific task in a given condition (Lin, 2016). According to Bandura (1977), self-efficacy affects human behaviors such as choice of activities, persistence, effort, and achievement. Students with high self-efficacy are more likely to enthusiastically participate in and complete a task as compared to those students with low self-efficacy (Lin, 2016).

Students' self-efficacy is related to their CS career choice as those students who believe they would be successful in studying CS are likely to select CS as their major (MacPhee, Farro, & Canetto, 2013). Lent, Lopez, Sheu, and Lopez (2011) examined the relationship among self-efficacy, interest, and intention to persist in CS and reported that "interests were well predicted by self-efficacy, and intentions to persist in computing were directly linked to self-efficacy, interests, and supports and barriers" (p. 189). The survey study by Wang, Hong, Ravitz, and Moghadam (2016) reported that more than half of principals and teachers agreed that students who are good at math and science would be more successful in CS. Hispanic students (28%), however, are less likely than White (40%) or African American (50%) counterparts to rate themselves as confident in science. The researchers claimed, "With students' low ratings of their own skills in math and science, teachers and principals may be less likely to encourage these students to pursue CS" (p. 648).

Studies have also identified a lack of CS courses as a critical barrier (Google & Gallup, 2016; Wang & Moghadam, 2017). Martin and Scott (2013) present that schools serving large numbers of minority students are less likely to offer rigorous CS courses than more affluent school systems. Even though CS courses are offered, these minority-serving schools tend to focus on basic computer applications or developing typing skills (Goode, 2007). Scott and White (2013) explain that compared to white students, African American and Latino students are three times more likely to attend schools that lack resources, technology access and advanced CS courses. In addition, the study by Wang, Hong, Ravitz, and Moghadam (2016) reported that Black students are less likely than White or Hispanic peers to have a CS learning opportunity at school.

Minority students' lack of technology access at home is a concern. According to Perrin and Turner (2019), Black and Hispanic adults remain less likely than White adults to own a traditional computer or have a high speed internet connection at home. Schaffhauser (2020) summarized a study from Carnegie Mellon University and the Massachusetts Institute of Technology and reported that African American students are eight percent less likely to have access to a high-speed internet connection at home. They are four percent more likely to have no internet access. Without internet access, students are less likely to be exposed to various possibilities that technology can provide (e.g., accessing to free coding sites https://code.org/; https://scratch.mit.edu/), which might lead to the lack of interest in CS.

The negative perception about CS is another barrier. The field of CS is often stereotyped as a career that is technologically oriented and antisocial, not involving communal goals such as helping community members or working with others (Master, Cheryan, & Meltzoff, 2016). Charleston, Charleston, and Jackson (2014) contend, "The culture of computer sciences is strikingly individualistic. Such a culture is often alienating to African Americans, who are likely to cite social support as a major influencer in their decision to pursue careers in computer sciences" (p. 402-403). Wong (2016) also presents that young students, including those who are digitally skilled, consider CS as an area that is not for "someone like me" or an "out of reach" field due to their perception that CS is for those who are extremely intelligent or have a lot of resources.

Researchers have claimed that in order to attract more underrepresented minority students to the CS field, providing them with mentors and helping them feel a sense of belonging is critical (Charleston, Charleston, & Jackson, 2014; Strayhorn, 2012). Having a role from the same ethnic group not only help minority students imagine themselves in that professional role, but it also helps them dismiss stereotypes about CS (Goode, 2008). Sense of belonging involves a person's belief that she/he is a valued member of an academic community whose presence and contribution are important (Rattan, Good, & Dweck, 2012). Positive racial climates and peer and faculty interactions are related to a high level of sense of belonging in a school environment (Johnson, et al., 2007). Meeuwisse, Severiens and Born (2010) reviewed previous studies related to minority students' sense of belonging and concluded, "ethnic minority students appear to feel less at home in their educational programs compared to majority students, and that this feeling may result in negative student outcomes, such as poor study progress and early withdrawal" (p. 532).

Broadening Participation in Computer Science

In order to provide minority students with opportunities to be exposed to the concepts and practices of CS and to promote interest in pursuing a CS degree, scholars have developed CS projects and new CS curriculums for K-12 students. For instance, Ericson, Engelman, McKlin and Taylor (2014) developed a project called Rise Up 4 CS, designed to help African American students in Georgia pass the Advanced Placement (AP) Computer Science (CS) A exam. The project included several strategies to attract African American students' interest in CS, including giving students a chance to visit a college campus, having undergraduate student role models, engaging in a competition, and providing financial incentives. The researchers reported that almost 70% of students who took the AP CS A exam passed, and students who met all the completion requirements for the project showed statistically significant changes in attitudes toward CS.

Minority Students in Computer Science

Magerko et al. (2016) promoted students' interest in CS by implementing a program called EarSketch (http://earsketch.gatech.edu). This program allowed students to compose music through computational music remixing while learning computing concepts. The researchers reported the evaluation study with approximately100 high school students who were engaged in a 10-week module with EarSketch. The results showed that both minority students and majority students demonstrated statistically significant growth in various constructs, including attitude towards success in CS, motivation to complete a task, and intention to persist in computing.

Dettori, Greenberg, McGee, and Reed (2016) reported the impact of Exploring Computer Science (ECS) curriculum implementation in Chicago schools. ECS is a high school introductory CS curriculum and professional development program developed by researchers at the University of California, Los Angeles. The program focuses on assisting students in developing problem-solving skills, critical thinking skills, and creativity. The researchers reported the impact of ECS implementation, highlighting the large number of underrepresented group enrollment: almost half of the students in the ECS course were girls (48%), and more than half of the participants were Hispanic (36%) or African American (19%). They also reported the results of a survey of 349 students: about 74% of participants indicated that ECS increased their interest in taking another CS course or majoring in CS in college. The researchers also conducted a survey of 61 teachers and reported, "the percentage of teachers feeling fairly to very well prepared to teach females, racial and ethnic minorities, and students from low socioeconomic backgrounds increased from 61 to 69 percent, from 50 to 64 percent, and from 55 to 73 percent, respectively" (p. 13).

Price, Albert, Catete, and Barnes (2015) presented the results of post-course survey of 399 students who participated in the Beauty and Joy of Computing (BJC) course. BJC is an introductory CS curriculum developed at the University of California, Berkeley. BJC combines pair-programming labs with various lectures and readings, and it also includes optional technology modules such as GameMaker and AppInventor activities. The survey findings indicated that over 80% of underrepresented minority students reported that they would recommend the course to a friend. However, significantly fewer minority students reported an interest in taking more CS courses as compared to White and Asian students.

Qazi, Gray, Russell, and Shannon (2019) created a project called ECSAlabama to provide rural high-minority high schools in Alabama with an opportunity to learn CS. A total 52 in-service teachers received training on ECS, and these teachers offered a CS course to almost 1,500 students, approximately 80% of them were minority students. The researchers conducted an evaluation study and reported that the ECS professional development increased teachers' self-efficacy in teaching CS, and students' interest in CS also improved after participating in the ECS curriculum.

Universities have also created new projects to attract underrepresented groups (e.g., female and ethnic minority) to CS and STEM fields. For example, Burg, Pauca, Turkett, and Santago (2016) introduced the STEM Incubator Program, designed to attract and retain non-traditional students in the CS field. The program included four components: (a) one-hour course including a variety of topics such as mobile apps for campus life and wearable sensors development for health application, (b) hands-on activities in a collaborative work environment, (c) faculty and peer mentoring, and (d) lending experimental equipment at no cost. The enrollment data showed positive female students' enrollment although the number of African-American and Hispanic students was not high due to the low number of race diversity in the school campus. The findings also demonstrated that program participants continued to partake in research and experimental projects with faculty beyond the initial STEM Incubator course.

Washington, Burge, Mejias, Jean-Pierre, and Knox (2015) discussed a university and industry partnership program, Google-in-Residence (GIR). It was designed to provide students in a HBCU with an opportunity to engage in Google's Computer Science Summer Institute (CSSI) curriculum with an aim to increase the number of students who apply for Google Summer internship and full-time positions. Through the partnership, an introductory CS course was taught by a Google software developer. Additionally, students in the researchers' department were encouraged to participate in CS Bootcamp, a peer tutoring program conducted by CS undergraduates. Students could attend CS Bootcamp four days per week to receive assistance to review CS concepts that they were learning in CS classes. The researchers concluded that both GIR and CS Bootcamp not only improved students' performance in CS courses but also increased interest in CS among students both within and outside of the CS department.

Goode (2008) shares strategies that have been useful for her project team to attract more minority and female students to CS. She emphasizes the purposeful recruitment of underrepresented populations. Due to the lack of CS knowledge among teachers, administrators, and school counselors, minority students are less likely to be encouraged to participate in a CS class. A CS teacher needs to meet with students who might enjoy CS activities individually or as a group and to explain how CS can be fun and useful. Goode (2008) explains the power of social group recruitment strategy, where one or two people from a small group can attract their friends to a CS class. Showing a clear pathway in CS is important in facilitating student interest, such as explaining courses that students need to take, providing internship opportunities, and sharing salary information of people in the CS field.

Without effective teachers, students are less likely to be engaged in a CS class. Providing teachers with continuous professional development on CS is thus very critical (Goode, 2008). CS teachers feel isolated because they are often only one CS teacher in a school. To tackle this teacher isolation issue, Yadav, Gretter, Hambrusch and Sands (2016) highlight the importance of creating a virtual community of teachers, a place where teachers not only share classroom practices and teaching resources, but also engage in a rich discussion and reflection on teaching CS.

Most K-12 CS teachers did not have a formal CS learning experience and self-taught CS content, making them feel less confident in their content knowledge and pedagogical skills (Goode, 2008; Yadav, Gretter, Hambrusch & Sands, 2016). It is critical to provide them with many CS professional development opportunities that focus on both content learning as well as engaging CS teaching methods. For instance, the Computing at School (CAS) Hub in the United Kingdom provides CS teachers with a chance to learn practical ideas of teaching CS from experienced teachers and to engage in learning CS pedagogical tools and assessment strategies with other teachers and researchers (CAS, 2013). Providing more programs like this is important to support CS teachers' professional development (Yadav, Gretter, Hambrusch & Sands, 2016).

CULTURALLY RESPONSIVE TEACHING IN COMPUTER SCIENCE

Culturally Responsive Teaching (CRT)

Creating innovative CS programs for minority students is important to boosting their interest in CS. However, if CS lessons provided are not culturally responsive, minority students will be less likely to enjoy CS learning, negatively affecting their decision to study CS in college. Scholars have argued that providing culturally responsive teaching is one of the most effective ways to meet the needs of diverse

Minority Students in Computer Science

learners (Harmon, 2012). African American students often learn best in a learning environment where the atmosphere is personal, relational, and encouraging (Ladson-Billings, 1994). Kuo, Belland, and Kuo (2017) report, "African American students are considered as high context learners who have a preference to work in groups rather than work independently or individually. Participating in a learning community appears to increase the chance of academic success among African-American students" (p. 37).

Garcia and Chun (2016) explain that Latino students demonstrate better academic performance in a culturally responsive learning environment. They tend to work well in small groups as opposed to individual learning, and social interaction is important to support Latino students' learning. Teachers' attitudes toward minority students also affect students' academic performances. Students perform better when teachers share high expectations and positive perceptions on their ability (Ware, 2006). These findings indicate that educators' understanding of culturally responsive teaching (CRT) is important to promote minority students' learning of CS.

CRT is a pedagogical framework that recognizes and infuses the culture of students who have been historically marginalized and socially alienated from their public education (Milner, 2007; Vavrus, 2008). It is an equal educational opportunity initiative that acknowledges differences among diverse ethnic groups and promotes academic success of students of color (Gay, 2013). Due to the lack of minority students' voices in dominant narratives about education, CRT emphasizes that "knowledge can and should be generated through the narratives and counter-narratives that emerge from and with people of color" (Milner, 2007, p. 391). Thus, CRT is designed to make learning more culturally relevant and effective by integrating teachers' active use of cultural knowledge and experiences of students from diverse cultural groups (Jackson, 2015).

Gay (2010) defines CRT as "using the cultural knowledge, prior experiences, frames of reference, and performance styles of ethnically diverse students to make learning encounters more relevant to and effective for them" (p. 31). It starts with acknowledging positive contributions that culturally diverse students are making in classroom learning, such as their unique experiences, insights, and perspectives (Warren, 2013). Ladson-Billings (1995) introduces a similar framework, culturally relevant pedagogy (CRP). CRP is a model that not only emphasizes student achievement but also helps students accept and affirm their cultural identity. Ladson-Billings (1995) explains, CRP "provide(s) a way for students to maintain their cultural integrity while succeeding academically" (p. 476). In education, both terms (CRT and CRP) are often used interchangeably (Morales-Chicas, Castillo, Bernal, Ramos & Guzman, 2019).

To provide CRT, teachers must learn accurate content about the lives, cultures, experiences, and challenges of ethnically and racially diverse groups in the U.S. society (Gay, 2013). A lot of information about ethnic groups available via textbook and media is not up-to-date, so teachers need to make an effort to learn accurate information about the culture of diverse students whom they are serving. They also need to understand ethnic groups' cultural values, communication styles, and social structures, and how they affect their learning in classrooms. For instance, teachers need to understand a particular group's communication styles between adults and students, and how it could influence the interaction between students and a teacher (Gay, 2010). The miscommunication or a lack of cultural understanding increase the possibility of students' academic failure (Ware, 2006).

Gay (2013) explains that restructuring beliefs in the ability of minority students is essential to providing culturally responsive teaching. She claims, "CRT requires replacing pathological and deficient perceptions of students and communities of color with more positive ones" (Gay, 2013, p.54). Griner and Stewart (2012) discuss that minority students such as African American children are significantly overrepresented in special education programs, specifically in the areas of mild intellectual disability, learning

Minority Students in Computer Science

disability, and emotional/behavioral disorder, while they are underrepresented in gifted programs. A study by Reeves (2006) reported that studies examining teachers' attitudes toward English language learners (ELLs) showed their unwelcoming, negative, or ambivalent attitudes due to their concerns about the lack of time to address unique needs of ELLs and perceived intensification of teacher workload. Culturally responsive teachers do not consider differences as either good or bad. They instead focus on promises and potentials of culturally diverse students and encourage them to accomplish complicated tasks by sharing high expectations for these students (Boykin, Lilja, & Tylerm, 2004; Ladson-Billings, 2014).

Students' perceptions of their cultural values greatly influence how much they care about their academic and nonacademic activities (Scott & White, 2013). When teachers share a high level of interest and respect for students' cultures, students are more likely to be engaged in schooling. When teachers share high expectations toward minority students and share diverse teaching strategies, scholars have found positive effects on students' self-efficacy and academic performance (Garcia & Chun, 2016) as well as psychological wellbeing (Cholewa, Goodman, West-Olatunji, & Amatea, 2014). In a CRT environment, culturally diverse students demonstrate academic growth as an outcome of classroom instruction and learning experience. These students can further develop cultural competence, an ability to appreciate and celebrate their cultural origin. A CRT learning environment is also beneficial to majority students as it allows them to learn some facts about another's culture (Ladson-Billings, 2014).

Culturally Responsive Teachers

Culturally responsive teachers connect class lessons to students' cultures and create a learning environment that is encouraging and caring (Vavrus, 2008). These teachers tend to believe that students from a nondominant cultural group are capable learners even though the way they think, act, and interact are different from the dominant cultural group (Villegas & Lucas, 2002). Culturally responsive teachers consider their work to be deeply connected with the communities where they teach, and they agree that knowledge is co-constructed between students and teachers (Ladson-Billings, 1995; Thomas & Warren, 2015). They make a considerable effort to develop personal relationships with their students and families (Harmon, 2012). Miller and Mikulec (2014) claim, "When teachers commit to culturally responsive teaching, not only do they become effective content teachers, but they also take on the responsibility of developing the learners' happiness and well-being" (p. 18).

Villegas and Lucas (2002) share six characteristics of culturally responsive teachers. First, they are socioculturally conscious, meaning that they recognize multiple ways of perceiving reality. They also acknowledge that the ways students think are influenced by their location in the social order. Second, they share affirming views of students from diverse cultures. These teachers "acknowledge the existence and validity of a plurality of ways of thinking, talking, behaving, and learning" (Villegas & Lucas, 2002, p. 23). Third, they demonstrate their commitment and skills to act as change agents. They have a clear vision of their own roles as teachers and share a moral obligation to help all students succeed, not just some. They actively work for greater equity in education and increase access to learning for all.

Fourth, they share constructivist views of learning. They understand that students generate meaning based on their prior knowledge, beliefs, and experiences. Villegas and Lucas (2002) argue, "The knowledge children bring to school, derived from personal and cultural experiences, is central to their learning" (p. 25). Fifth, teachers try to know about students' experiences both inside and outside school to engage them in a knowledge construction process. They try to learn students' past schooling experiences and family backgrounds and include students' experiences in learning activities. Finally, they design learning environments in which CRT is practiced. Some CRT examples include "building on students' personal and cultural strengths, helping students examine the curriculum from multiple perspectives, using varied assessment practices that promote learning, and making the culture of the classroom inclusive of all students" (Villegas & Lucas, 2002, p. 27).

Ladson-Billings (1995) observed culturally responsive teachers and reported similar characteristics. These teachers (b) believe all students are capable of academic success, (b) think that pedagogy is an art, which is unpredictable, changing, and always in the process of becoming, (c) consider them as members of the community, (d) define teaching as a way to give back to the community, and (e) believe that teachers' primary responsibility is to pull knowledge out.

Culturally responsive teachers are aware that their students are already experts on their prior experiences and life worlds, and they use students' previous knowledge as a scaffold to support students' academic achievement (Gay, 2013; Thomas & Warren, 2015). They also demonstrate caring and empathy. Caring teachers do not necessarily mean nice or kind teachers. They are "teachers who are unwilling to tolerate underachievement (Rychly & Graves, 2012, p. 45). These teachers care so much about students' growth, and they hold all students to the same rigorous standards. Empathetic teachers show an ability to understand the learning environment from their students' perspectives (Rychly & Graves, 2012). They share genuine concerns about students' emotional and cognitive learning and utilize various strategies to raise quality student-teacher interactions (Warren, 2018).

Gay (2013) explains that teachers have anxiety about applying CRT due to the lack of confidence in providing appropriate support to culturally diverse groups. She argues that becoming a culturally responsive teacher is a personal and professional endeavor that involves continuous learning. The learning process starts with a continuous reflection on teachers' own biases and privileges, and how these affect their interactions with students (Scott, Sheridan & Clark, 2015). Pre-service teachers often lack "conception of, interest in, and concern about cultural and racial diversity" (Milner, 2006, p. 352). Some do not know about their own cultures and are not aware of the prejudices they hold toward other cultures (Kidd, Sanchez, & Thorp, 2005). To help pre-service teachers develop CRT skills, Kidd, Sanchez, and Thorp (2008) suggest integrating various pedagogical activities in teacher education. These include "(a) readings focused on issues of race, culture, poverty, and social justice; (b) internships in diverse communities; (c) interactions with diverse families; (d) critical reflection; and (e) dialogue and discussion" (p. 326).

Gay (2013) encourages teachers to accept the redistribution of knowledge and power. This means that teachers do not need to aim to be an ideal, all-knowing, teacher. Their role is to support students' construction of knowledge by creating a learning environment that engages students in questioning, interpreting, and analyzing problems that are meaningful to students (Villegas & Lucas, 2002). While teaching, teachers need to not only teach accurate information about students' cultures but also invite students to share their own cultural stories. Teachers should not only learn about culturally diverse students but learn from them (Ladson-Billings, 2014). Harmon (2012) argues, "Teaching is believing in one's own teaching and ability to influence the achievement of students" (p. 13). Instead of avoiding or worrying about teaching culturally diverse students, teachers need to be flexible, open minded, and make a continuous effort to build a connection with culturally diverse students. Teachers also need to gain a better understanding of their own culture as well as their own students' cultures. Irizarry (2007) argues, "Culturally responsive pedagogy is about more than what teachers need to know about a specific group of students; it also involves who they need to be and who they need to continuously become" (p. 27).

Applying CRT to Computer Science

To help minority students become engaged in CS, scholars have emphasized providing culturally responsive computing lessons. Based on their experiences working with minority students and the CRT framework, Scott, Sheridan and Clark (2015) introduce a revised framework called, Culturally Responsive Computing (CRC). CRC is based on five tenets. First, all students are capable of digital innovation. Some teachers believe that minority students are less likely to be successful in CS, offering only low-level tasks. CRC requires challenging this deficit thought process and encourages teachers to set high expectations for minority students and to regularly communicate with students that they can and will achieve a high-level standard. Second, CRC learning environments should support the transformational use of technologies. Students are expected to go beyond simply using a tool. They are encouraged to analyze design issues of the tool, envision their own design, create their own tool, and critique classmates' designs to provide constructive feedback. Many existing tools are designed without input from users who have diverse needs and backgrounds. Providing minorities with the opportunity to design their own tool can not only help minority students be interested in the design aspect of CS but also make new technology tools be useful for a wide range of consumers (Hur, Andrzejewski, & Marghitu, 2017; Kafai, Searle, Martinez, & Brayboy, 2014).

Third, CRC learning environments encourage students to reflect on self along with various intersecting sociocultural lines with the aim of technical innovation. In this environment, students are encouraged to critique many social issues such as what they know about equity, equality, race, and resource distribution. Through discussion with peers and mentors, students are encouraged to identify their multiple selves, being motivated to develop digital products that "actively challenge essentialist notions of their self and their communities" (Scott, Sheridan & Clark, 2015, p. 426). Scott and White (2013) created a program called COMPUGIRLS based on CRC. Students were engaged in a student-centered, social justice related, and real-world activity in COMPUGIRLS (e.g., using geographic information systems (GIS) to identify neighborhood food availability). A few studies have examined the impact of COMPUGIRLS, reporting students' increased critical awareness in terms of how technology platforms perpetuate privilege and inequality and heightened interest in becoming a technology innovator (Ashcraft, Eger, & Scott, 2017; Scott, & White, 2013).

Fourth, CRC encourages students to create counternormative images of themselves using various digital tools. Students are initially expected to study how others and the media perceive them, and then create a product that challenges the negative perceptions toward minorities or women. While promoting consciousness about social or political issues in computing can be beneficial, Morales-Chicas, Castillo, Bernal, Ramos and Guzman (2019) explain that it can also provoke controversy. They claim, "With this in mind, educators are encouraged to take into account their own positions of power and biases when raising sociopolitical consciousness in computing" (p. 133). Finally, CRC promotes community involvement. The success of CRC is not evaluated based on the number of minority students who major in CS, but how they can develop a digital tool that ultimately advances their communities. Scott, Sheridan and Clark (2015) claim, "the CRC context guides students in recognizing their communities as valuable foundations that must be included in the success formula" (p. 427).

Another approach that incorporates CRT into CS is called ethnocomputing (Tedre, Sutinen, Kähkönen, & Kommers, 2006). The concept is proposed based on the study of ethnomathmatics by D'Ambrosio (1985). Similar to math, computing is not culturally neural, and computing principles are shaped from culturally informed logic. For instance, an email or folder icon used in many computer programs are

Minority Students in Computer Science

symbolic expressions of items used in the western world, and these items are not universal symbols being used across the cultures. Tedre, Sutinen, Kähkönen, and Kommers (2006) contend:

We computer scientists need to trace the historical and societal constructions of the computational practices of different cultural groups.... We must examine the relationships between language, society, arts, tools, artifacts, and computing technology. We must rethink how to teach the use and development of technological tools in culturally relevant ways. (p. 129)

Kafai, Searle, Martinez, and Brayboy (2014) proposes an approach to ethnocomputing that incorporates electronic textiles (e-textiles). The incorporation of e-textiles is designed to help students learn about engineering and computing by connecting the concepts of engineering and computing with Native arts and craft. E-textiles connect "crafting practices such as sewing and decorative beading that have a long history in many indigenous communities to computing and engineering practices" (p. 241). The authors integrated e-textiles into a 10-week unit in a Native arts class and a 2-week intensive summer camp. After studying the experiences of students in these classes, the authors concluded, "providing all students with design agency to imagine forms of computation responsive to their interests and identities has the potential to provide embodied learning experiences that allow students to see themselves as successful stakeholders of the digital age" (p. 245). Morales-Chicas, Castillo, Bernal, Ramos and Guzman (2019) also highlight that computing should be taught considering cultural contexts, and the artifact design process should be made considering the needs of the local community.

Eglash, Bennett, O'donnell, Jennings, and Cintorino (2006) introduce a culturally relevant design tool called Culturally Situated Designed Tools (CSDTs). They are web-based software applications that allow students to create simulations of cultural arts (e.g., Native American beadwork, African American cornrow hairstyles) by applying mathematical principles. CSDTs aim to help students utilize a synthesis of math, computing, and culture in a creative way by providing them with an environment where they can take advantage of their cultural identity development in ways that can promote academic performance. The researchers used CSDTs with 8-12 grade minority students (mostly African American and Latino students) from low-income families and reported that the use of CSDTs positively affected students' attitudes toward information technology careers.

CONCLUSION

"Diversifying computer science is a critical and important task. It is not just an issue of equity for underrepresented groups, but increased representation is vital for the continued growth and development of our economy" (Goode, 2007, p. 85). In order to explore ways to promote CS learning of minority students, this chapter reviews barriers to accessing CS education and explores various projects that promote minority students' interest in CS. The reviews of previous studies suggest that providing minority students with an engaging and rigorous CS learning experience is critical. Unless students understand what CS is, it would be very hard for them to be interested in studying CS. Consequently, policy makers, teachers, and administrators should make a great effort to provide all students with an engaging and rigorous CS learning opportunity in K-12 schools to help students learn what CS is, ultimately promoting their interest in studying CS.

Providing effective CS lessons can be possible only when teachers are confident in teaching CS. To help teachers develop CS knowledge and pedagogical skills, continuous teacher professional development should be provided. In order to help CS teachers share experiences and resources with other CS teachers, creating an online professional teacher community is recommended (Yadav, Gretter, Hambrusch & Sands, 2016). Additionally, educational researchers should continue to work with practicing teachers and conduct classroom level research, identifying the needs of students and teachers and suggesting effective CS teaching strategies. Most school administrators and school counselors lack knowledge of CS; helping them learn what CS is important to assist them in guiding minority student' decision to study CS in college (Goode, 2008).

To help minority students be successful in CS classes, incorporating CRT strategies is recommended. The key idea of CRT is to facilitate academic success of culturally diverse students without compromising their cultural identity (Gay, 2013; Ladson-Billings, 1995). Teachers should demonstrate culturally sensitive caring and empathy and share their high expectations toward culturally diverse students in order to help them demonstrate a high level of academic performance. Scott and White (2013) argue that by helping teachers integrate CRT strategies in CS classes, we may be able to attract more diverse students in the field of CS.

REFERENCES

Ashcraft, C., Eger, E. K., & Scott, K. A. (2017). Becoming technosocial change agents: Intersectionality and culturally responsive pedagogies as vital resources for increasing girls' participation in computing. *Anthropology & Education Quarterly*, *48*(3), 233–251. doi:10.1111/aeq.12197

Bandura, A. (1977). Self-efficacy: Toward a unifying theory of behavioral change. *Psychological Review*, *84*(2), 191–215. doi:10.1037/0033-295X.84.2.191 PMID:847061

Bandura, A. (1997). *Self-efficacy: The exercise of control*. Freeman.

Boykin, A. W., Lilja, A. J., & Tyler, K. M. (2004). The influence of communal versus individual learning context on the academic performance of African-American elementary school students. *Learning Environments Journal*, *7*, 227–244. doi:10.100710984-004-3294-7

Brown, Q., & Briggs, A. (2015). The CS10K initiative: Progress in K-12 through "exploring computer science" part1. *ACM Inroads*, *6*(3), 52–53. doi:10.1145/2803178

Burg, J., Pauca, V. P., Turkett, W., & Santago, P. (2016). A STEM incubator to engage students in hands-on, relevant learning: A report from the field. *Proceedings of the ACM Conference on Innovation and Technology in Computer Science Education*, 142–147, 10.1145/2899415.2899461

Buzzetto-More, N., Ukoha, O., & Rustagi, N. (2010). Unlocking the barriers to women and minorities in computer science and information systems studies: Results from a multi-methodological study conducted at two minority-serving institutions. *Journal of Information Technology Education*, *9*(1), 115–131. doi:10.28945/1167

CAS. (2013). *Running a computing at school hub*. Retrieved from https://www.computingatschool.org.uk/data/uploads/Hub_OperationsManual.pdf

Charleston, L. J., Charleston, S. A., & Jackson, J. F. L. (2014). Using culturally responsive practices to broaden participation in the educational pipeline: Addressing the unfinished business of Brown in the field of computing sciences. *The Journal of Negro Education*, *83*(3), 400–419. doi:10.7709/jnegroeducation.83.3.0400

Cholewa, B., Goodman, R. D., West-Olatunji, C., & Amatea, E. (2014). A qualitative examination of the impact of culturally responsive educational practices on the psychological well-being of students of color. *The Urban Review*, *46*(4), 574–596. doi:10.100711256-014-0272-y

College Board. (2018, August 27). *Number of females and underrepresented students taking AP computer science courses spikes again*. Retrieved from https://www.collegeboard.org/releases/2018/number-of-females-and-underrepresented-students-taking-ap-computer-science-courses-spikes-again

D'Ambrosio, U. (1985). Ethnomathematics and its place in the history and pedagogy of mathematics. *For the Learning of Mathematics*, *5*, 44–48.

Dettori, L., Greenberg, R. I., McGee, S., & Reed, D. (2016). The impact of the exploring computer science instructional model in Chicago Public Schools. *Computing in Science & Engineering*, *18*(2), 10–17. doi:10.1109/MCSE.2016.39

Eglash, R., Bennett, A., O'donnell, C., Jennings, S., & Cintorino, M. (2006). Culturally situated designed tools: Ethnocomputing from field site to classroom. *American Anthropologist*, *108*(2), 347–362. doi:10.1525/aa.2006.108.2.347

Ericson, B., Engelman, S., Mcklin, T., & Taylor, J. Q. (2014). Project rise up 4 CS: Increasing the number of black students who pass advanced placement CS A. *Proceedings of the 45th ACM technical symposium on Computer science education*, 439-444. 10.1145/2538862.2538937

Funk, C., & Parker, K. (2018). *Diversity in the STEM workforce varies widely across jobs*. Retrieved from https://www.pewsocialtrends.org/2018/01/09/diversity-in-the-stem-workforce-varies-widely-across-jobs/

Garcia, C., & Chun, H. (2016). Culturally responsive teaching and teacher expectations for Latino middle school students. *Journal of Latina/o Psychology*, *4*(3), 173–187. doi:10.1037/lat0000061

Gay, G. (2010). *Culturally responsive teaching: Theory, research, and practice* (2nd ed.). Teachers College Press.

Gay, G. (2013). Teaching to and through cultural diversity. *Curriculum Inquiry*, *43*(1), 48–70. doi:10.1111/curi.12002

Goode, J. (2007). If you build teachers, will students come?: Professional development for broadening computer science learning for urban youth. *Journal of Educational Computing Research*, *36*(1), 65–88. doi:10.2190/2102-5G77-QL77-5506

Goode, J. (2008). Increasing diversity in K-12 computer science: Strategies from the field, ACM. *SIGCSE Bulletin*, *40*(1), 362–366. doi:10.1145/1352322.1352259

Google Inc. & Gallup Inc. (2016). *Diversity gaps in computer science: Exploring the underrepresentation of girls, Blacks and Hispanics*. Retrieved from https://goo.gl/PG34aH

Griner, A. C., & Stewart, M. L. (2013). Addressing the achievement gap and disproportionality through the use of culturally responsive teaching practices. *Urban Education, 48*(4), 585–621. doi:10.1177/0042085912456847

Harmon, D. A. (2012). Culturally responsive teaching though a historical lens: Will history repeat itself? *Interdisciplinary Journal of Teaching and Learning, 2*(1), 12–22.

Hur, J., Andrzejewski, C. E., & Marghitu, D. (2017). Girls and computer science: Experiences, perceptions, and career aspirations. *Computer Science Education, 27*(2), 1–21. doi:10.1080/08993408.2017.1376385

Irizarry, J. (2007). Ethnic and urban intersections in the classroom: Latino students, hybrid identities, and culturally responsive pedagogy. *Multicultural Perspectives, 9*(3), 21–28. doi:10.1080/15210960701443599

Kafai, Y., Searle, K., Martinez, C., & Brayboy, B. (2014). Ethnocomputing with electronic textiles: Culturally responsive open design to broaden participation in computing in American Indian youth and communities. *Proceedings of the 45th ACM technical symposium on computer science education,* 241–246. 10.1145/2538862.2538903

Kidd, J. K., Sanchez, S. Y., & Thorp, E. K. (2005). Cracking the challenge of changing dispositions: Changing hearts and minds through stories, narratives, and direct cultural interactions. *Journal of Early Childhood Teacher Education, 26*(4), 347–359. doi:10.1080/10901020500413304

Kidd, J. K., Sanchez, S. Y., & Thorp, E. K. (2008). Defining moments: Developing culturally responsive dispositions and teaching practices in early childhood preservice teachers. *Teaching and Teacher Education, 24*(2), 316–329. doi:10.1016/j.tate.2007.06.003

Kuo, Y. C., Belland, B. R., & Kuo, Y. T. (2017). Learning through blogging: Students' perspectives in collaborative blog-enhanced learning communities. *Journal of Educational Technology & Society, 20*(2), 37–50.

Ladson-Billings, G. (1994). *The Dreamkeepers: Successful teachers of African American children.* JosseyBass.

Ladson-Billings, G. J. (1995). Toward a theory of culturally relevant pedagogy. *American Educational Research Journal, 32*(3), 465–491. doi:10.3102/00028312032003465

Lent, R. W., Lopez, F. G., Sheu, H. B., & Lopez, A. M. Jr. (2011). Social cognitive predictors of the interests and choices of computing majors: Applicability to underrepresented students. *Journal of Vocational Behavior, 78*(2), 184–192. doi:10.1016/j.jvb.2010.10.006

Lin, G. Y. (2016). Self-efficacy beliefs and their sources in undergraduate computing disciplines: An examination of gender and persistence. *Journal of Educational Computing Research, 53*(4), 540–561. doi:10.1177/0735633115608440

MacPhee, D., Farro, S., & Canetto, S. S. (2013). Academic self-efficacy and performance of underrepresented STEM majors: Gender, ethnic, and social class patterns. *Analyses of Social Issues and Public Policy (ASAP), 13*(1), 347–369. doi:10.1111/asap.12033

Magerko, B., Freeman, J., Mcklin, T., Reilly, M., Livingston, E., Mccoid, S., & Crews-Brown, A. (2016). Earsketch: A steam-based approach for underrepresented populations in high school computer science education. ACM Transactions on Computing Education, 16(4), 14:1-25. doi:10.1145/2886418

Margolis, J., & Goode, J. (2016). Ten lessons for computer science for all. *ACM Inroads*, 7(4), 52–56. doi:10.1145/2988236

Martin, A., & Scott, A. (2013). Engaging underrepresented students in computer science: Examining the effectiveness of a 5-week computer science course in the SMASH academy. *Proceedings of the International Conference Frontiers in Education: Computer Science and Computer Engineering*, 362-366.

Master, A., Cheryan, S., & Meltzoff, A. N. (2016). Computing whether she belongs: Stereotypes undermine girls' interest and sense of belonging in computer science. *Journal of Educational Psychology*, 108(3), 424–437. doi:10.1037/edu0000061

Meeuwisse, M., Severiens, S. E., & Born, M. P. (2010). Learning environment, interaction, sense of belonging and study success in ethnically diverse student groups. *Research in Higher Education*, 51(6), 528–545. doi:10.100711162-010-9168-1

Miller, P. C., & Mikulec, E. A. (2014). Pre-service teachers confronting issues of diversity through a radical field experience. *Multicultural Education*, 21(2), 18–24.

Milner, H. R. (2006). Preservice teachers' learning about cultural and racial diversity: Implications for urban education. *Urban Education*, 41(4), 343–374. doi:10.1177/0042085906289709

Milner, H. R. IV. (2007). Race, culture, and researcher positionality: Working through dangers seen, unseen, and unforeseen. *Educational Researcher*, 36(7), 388–400. doi:10.3102/0013189X07309471

Morales-Chicas, J., Castillo, M., Bernal, I., Ramos, P., & Guzman, B. L. (2019). Computing with relevance and purpose: A review of culturally relevant education in computing. *International Journal of Multicultural Education*, 21(1), 125–154. doi:10.18251/ijme.v21i1.1745

Perrin, A., & Turner, E. (2019, August). Smartphones help black, Hispanics bridge some-but not all-digital gaps with whites. *Pew Research Center*. Retrieved from https://www.pewresearch.org/fact-tank/2019/08/20/smartphones-help-blacks-hispanics-bridge-some-but-not-all-digital-gaps-with-whites/

Price, T. W., Albert, J., Catete, V., & Barnes, T. (2015). BJC in action: Comparison of student perceptions of a computer science principles course. *Research in Equity and Sustained Participation in Engineering, Computing, and Technology, 1-4*, 1–4. Advance online publication. doi:10.1109/RESPECT.2015.7296506

Qazi, M., Gray, J., Russell, M., & Shannon, D. (2019). ECS4Alabama: A state-wide effort to provide access to authentic computer science education in predominantly rural and high minority schools. *Proceedings of the 50th ACM Technical Symposium on Computer Science Education, 1279.* 10.1145/3287324.3293866

Rattan, A., Good, C., & Dweck, C. S. (2012). "It's ok — Not everyone can be good at math": Instructors with an entity theory comfort (and demotivate) students. *Journal of Experimental Social Psychology*, 48(3), 731–737. doi:10.1016/j.jesp.2011.12.012

Reeves, J. (2006). Secondary teacher attitudes toward including English-language learners in mainstream classrooms. *The Journal of Educational Research*, 99(3), 131–142. doi:10.3200/JOER.99.3.131-143

Rychly, L., & Graves, E. (2012). Teacher characteristics for culturally responsive pedagogy. *Multicultural Perspectives, 14*(1), 44–49. doi:10.1080/15210960.2012.646853

Sax, L., Blaney, J. M., Lehman, K. J., Rodriguez, S. L., George, K. L., & Zavala, C. (2018). Sense of belonging in computing: The role of introductory courses for women and underrepresented minority students. *Social Science, 7*(8), 122. doi:10.3390ocsci7080122

Schaffhauser, D. (2020, May). Poverty, race linked to lack of internet for students. *The Journal.* Retrieved from https://thejournal.com/articles/2020/05/14/poverty-race-linked-to-lack-of-internet-for-students.aspx

Scott, K. A., Sheridan, K. M., & Clark, K. (2015). Culturally responsive computing: A theory revisited. *Learning, Media and Technology, 40*(4), 412–436. doi:10.1080/17439884.2014.924966

Scott, K. A., & White, M. A. (2013). COMPUGIRLS' standpoint: Culturally responsive computing and its effect on girls of color. *Urban Education, 48*(5), 657–681. doi:10.1177/0042085913491219

Strayhorn, T. L. (2012). *College students' sense of belonging: A key to educational success.* Routledge. doi:10.4324/9780203118924

Tedre, M., Sutinen, E., Kähkönen, E., & Kommers, P. (2006). Ethnocomputing: ICT in cultural and social context. *Communications of the ACM, 49*(1), 126–130. doi:10.1145/1107458.1107466

Thomas, E. E., & Warren, C. A. (2015). Making it relevant: How a Black male teacher sustained professional relationships through culturally responsive discourse. *Race, Ethnicity and Education, 20*(1), 87–100. doi:10.1080/13613324.2015.1121217

U.S. Bureau of Labor Statistics. (2020). *Computer and information technology occupations.* Retrieved from https://www.bls.gov/ooh/computer-and-information-technology/home.htm?view_full

Vavrus, M. (2008). Culturally responsive teaching. In T. L. Good (Ed.), 21st century education: A reference handbook (Vol. 2, pp. 49-57). Los Angeles: Sage. doi:10.4135/9781412964012.n56

Villavicencio, A., Fancsali, C., Martin, W., Mark, J., & Cole, R. (2018). Computer science in New York City: An early look at teacher training opportunities and the landscape of CS implementation in schools, *Research alliance for New York City Schools.* Retrieved from https://research.steinhardt.nyu.edu/scmsAdmin/media/users/ks191/CS4All/CS4All_Report.pdf

Villegas, A. M., & Lucas, T. (2002). Preparing culturally responsive teachers: Rethinking the curriculum. *Journal of Teacher Education, 53*(1), 20–32. doi:10.1177/0022487102053001003

Wang, J., Hong, H., Ravitz, J., & Moghadam, S. H. (2016). Landscape of K-12 computer science education in the U.S.: Perceptions, access, and barriers. *Proceedings of the 47th ACM Technical Symposium on Computing Science,* 645-650. 10.1145/2839509.2844628

Wang, J., & Moghadam, S. (2017). Diversity barriers in K-12 computer science education: Structural and social. *Proceedings of the ACM Technical Symposium on Computer Science Education.* 615–620. 10.1145/3017680.3017734

Ware, F. (2006). Warm demander pedagogy: Culturally responsive teaching that supports a culture of achievement for African American students. *Urban Education, 41*(4), 427–456. doi:10.1177/0042085906289710

Warren, C. A. (2013). The utility of empathy for White female teachers' culturally responsive interactions with Black male students. *Interdisciplinary Journal of Teaching and Learning*, 3(3), 175–200.

Washington, A. N., Burge, L., Mejias, M., Jean-Pierre, K., & Knox, Q. (2015). Improving undergraduate student performance in computer science at Historically Black Colleges and Universities (HBCUs) through industry partnerships. *Proceedings of the ACM Special Interest Group on Computer Science Education (SIGSCE)*. 10.1145/2676723.2677277

Webb, M., Davis, N., Bell, T., Katz, Y., Reynolds, N., Chambers, D. P., & Sysło, M. M. (2017). Computer science in K-12 school curricula of the 21st century: Why, what and when? *Education and Information Technologies*, 22(2), 445–468. doi:10.100710639-016-9493-x

Wong, B. (2016). 'I'm good, but not that good': Digitally-skilled youth's identity in computing. *Computer Science Education*, 26(4), 299–317. doi:10.1080/08993408.2017.1292604

Yadav, A., Gretter, S., Hambrusch, S., & Sands, P. (2016). Expanding computer science education in schools: Understanding teacher experiences and challenges. *Computer Science Education*, 26(4), 235–254. doi:10.1080/08993408.2016.1257418

This research was previously published in the Handbook of Research on Equity in Computer Science in P-16 Education; pages 88-104, copyright year 2021 by Information Science Reference (an imprint of IGI Global).

Chapter 41

"Just Listen to What the Panthers Are Saying":
A History of the Black Panther Party From Its Vision and Perspective

Valeria Carbone
University of Buenos Aires, Argentina

ABSTRACT

Within the American Black Movement, the Black Panther Party (BPP) became the most prominent and influential organization of the 1960s and 1970s. The movement initiated in Oakland (California) and captured the attention of politicians, journalists, intellectuals, and scholars. From a documentary corpus that shows its protagonists' perspective, this chapter aims to focus on the actions, goals, and development of the Black Panthers: what they did, how and why they did it, and what they represented to the Black freedom struggle. It offers an analysis of their tactics and strategies of struggle against police brutality, poor housing and living conditions, unemployment, poverty, and structural racism. The authors aim to show how the BPP went from being a local grassroots organization to a national and highly popular political party for collective action, much more complex and influential than what the collective memory and the dominant historiography have shown.

INTRODUCTION

The Black Panther Party (BPP) and the movement it initiated in the mid-1960s captured the attention of politicians, journalists, intellectuals and scholars. Many authors from the right and from the left, tried to analyze the history and legacy of a group that conquered the popular imagination and the country's attention for two decades.

The most extended historiographical trend characterized the Black Panthers as the most violent version of the Black Power movement, heading the "radical" (and erroneous) turn that the Civil Rights Movement took after 1965, an analytical paradigm that has prevailed until today. In this historiographi-

DOI: 10.4018/978-1-6684-4507-5.ch041

Copyright © 2022, IGI Global. Copying or distributing in print or electronic forms without written permission of IGI Global is prohibited.

cal interpretation, however, the history of the BPP plays a very small role. Jama Lazerow and Yohuru Williams stated that "much of what we now call 'histories' of the Party are crafted by activist-scholars – former leaders, high profile members, or supporters – in which recollection collapses into data collection, scholarship into subjective analysis, history into memory" (Lazerow & Williams, 2006, p. 4).

Most historical works have focused on what was characterized as the "apogee" period of the BPP (1966-1972), with limited references to the subsequent "decline" years. Considering the premise that although the organization lingered on until 1982 the government's repressive tactics had weakened the Panthers considerably by 1972 (Wendt, 2006, p. 162), research has mostly focused on topics such as:

- The BPP as the embodiment of black radicalism and its role in the end of non-violence and civil disobedience, main characteristics of the Civil Rights Movement of the 1950s and 1960s.
- The role played by the notions of "violence" and "armed self-defense" both in the rhetoric, activism and organization of the Party, as in its rise and fall.
- The centrality of "machismo", gender relations, and the role of women within the Party.
- The role of systemic institutional repression in the advent and disappearance of the BPP.

These lines of research emerged from what historian Joe Street has identified as three periods in the historiography of the BPP (Street, 2010). The first period (from the end of the 1970s through the 1980s) was dominated by (auto)biographic accounts written by participants and observers of the BPP in action. These productions offered insight into the BPP leadership but included relatively little on the Party's rank and file. The nineties brought works that focused on local BPP chapters, its community work and the experiences of BPP's rank and file. A third period emerged in the early 2000s with publications that focused on the Party's legacy and contribution to African American and American culture beyond its political program and violent image.

These works fell mostly short at offering a comprehensive view of the Black Panther Party as a national phenomenon. Likewise, they largely leave aside the analysis of tactics and strategies of struggle and resistance, and forms of community organization in the 1970s and early 1980s, years in which the Panthers had to fight against a fierce repression and persecution, sabotages and infiltrations by the FBI, and the relentless murder and imprisonment of leaders and activists.

OAKLAND IN THE 1960'S AND THE EMERGENCE OF THE PARTY

The BPP was the product of the activism and mobilization of the black community throughout the 1950's and 1960's, as well as of the impact of the socio-economic situation on African Americans. It was Huey P. Newton who contextualized the emergence of the organization in the political and socio-economic reality of Oakland in the aftermath of World War II:

The great exodus of poor people out of the South during World War II sprang from the hope for a better life in the big cities of the North and West. In search for freedom, they left behind centuries of southern cruelty and repression. The futility of that search is now history. The Black communities of Bedford-Stuyvesant, Newark, Brownsville, Watts, Detroit, and many others stand as testament that racism is as oppressive in the North as in the South. (Newton, 1973, p. 14)

In the mid-1960s, Oakland and other urban-industrial centers in the North and West part of the country were going through a deep economic crisis. High unemployment rates particularly affected an increasing black community. The population index grew considerably during and after the war, due to mass migration in search of job opportunities and better living conditions. In those years, families like Newton's migrated from southern states like Louisiana, Texas, Oklahoma and Arkansas to Oakland, home of shipyards, war industries, transportation and manufacturing, making the black population soared from 8,462 to over 20,000 (Spencer, 2005, p. 302). But when employment opportunities started to decrease, it seemed that black people "were no longer wanted" (Newton, 1973, p. 14).

Due to residential racial segregation practices of real estate and white property owners, and as the white middle class flew to the suburbs, West Oakland became home to 84 percent of Oakland's African American population. Other factors that contributed to this were racial discrimination in the private market, the banking industry's discriminatory policies in allocating real estate loans, and restrictive covenants barring black people from model suburbs created by federally sponsored wartime construction programs. By 1959, almost half of Oakland's families lived below the poverty line, in depravation or worst. By 1966, unemployment was more than twice the national average and almost half the entire work-eligible flatland population was unemployed or sub-employed (Spencer, 2005, pp. 302-303).

THE *BLACK PANTHER PARTY (FOR SELF-DEFENSE)*: FROM AN EMBLEMATIC LOCAL COMMUNITY ORGANIZATION TO A NATIONAL MOVEMENT (1966-1974)

The *Black Panther Party for Self-Defense* was founded in 1966 in Oakland (California) by Huey P. Newton and Bobby Seale. They were classmates at Merrit College, a black university, and were partners in activism: they actively got involved in the Civil Rights Movement during the early sixties, were members of the Soul Students Advisory Council (a group formed by the Revolutionary Action Movement, the paramilitary arm of Malcolm X's Organization of Afro-American Unity) and participated in the North Oakland Service Center, a unit of federal anti-poverty programs (Newton, 1973, pp. 110-115). According to Franz Schurmann, Newton and Seale formed an organization that became:

A revolutionary vehicle made up of three elements: a small but dedicated cadre of workers who are willing to devote their life full time to the goals of the organization; an organized structure through which the cadre can function; and revolutionary concepts which define and interpret phenomena, and establish the goals towards which the political vehicle will work. This is one side of the practice. Its other indispensable side is "the building of a community structure", the development of basic survival programs for the people amongst whom the Party lives and serves and derives nourishment. [...] As Newton says, "they have to see first some basic accomplishments in order to realize that major success are possible." (Schurman, 2009, pp. xxxii-xxxiii)

The BPP considered black population the moving force of a grassroots movement centered on black urban ghettos throughout the country (Hilliard & Cole, 1993, p. 118). Many of its most active members were young, some taking their first steps in political activism, others with a vast track-record in Black nationalists' organizations and civil rights groups. Highlighting that the BPP became a powerful grassroots organization is important because it is what allowed the Party to survive until the 1980s. Its leaders were subjected to police, judicial and governmental persecution, were imprisoned and killed, or

"Just Listen to What the Panthers Are Saying"

were forced to choose the exile. Without the active involvement of the rank and file, the systematic state repression they were subjected to would have inevitably doomed the party's fate from the beginning. Added to these was the internal fracture towards 1971 because of divergences on tactics and strategies. Despite all of this, to a greater or lesser extent, the Party continued its activities until 1982.

BLACK PANTHER PARTY'S PLATFORM AND PROGRAM

Newton and Seale wrote the *Ten Point Program* (*What we Want, what we believe*) to set the Party's goals and what was needed to achieve them. Considered as a "survival program" - not revolutionary nor reformist (Newton, 2009, p. 20) -, the ten point platform summoned those groups to which the BPP spoke to (that is, the poor blacks of the urban ghettos), and showcased their most pressing socio-economic needs. Listing long-standing demands, the program was designed of a Party to serve as a basis for a "structured political vehicle of transformation" that would implement strategic actions for political purposes (Newton, [1971] 2009, p. 451). According to Newton, reaching the ultimate Party goal ("revolution") was a process and black people had to survive until they could achieve that total transformation. "Therefore, we need a survival kit: The ten-point program" (Newton, 2009, p. 21), which would allow them to "exist" and get to the end of the revolutionary process.

The ten points established the goals and ideological principles that would frame the struggle. From a class perspective, they demanded

1. "Freedom", as in political power and autonomy.
2. Full employment. If the Federal Government or American businessmen could not comply with that task, "the means of production should be taken from (them) and placed in the community".
3. Reparations: compensatory payment to the descendants of African slaves.
4. Decent housing, or the possibility to form housing / land cooperatives with government aid, to make housing accessible.
5. Education and vindication of the role of Black people in American history.
6. Exception from military service for Blacks, so they would not be forced to defend "the white racist government of America". This directly referred to the escalation of the war in Vietnam, and the high levels of recruitment among African Americans who, in the mid-1960s were 20% of the war's casualties (Appy, 2013).
7. End to police brutality and repression in the black community, and recognition of black's constitutional right to bear arms in order to organize for self-defense.
8. Freedom for all black men held in federal, state, county and city jails, who had not received a fair trial.
9. Fair trials by juries of peer group, in other words, by people "from a similar economic, social, religious, geographical, environmental, historical and racial background (...) a jury from the black community from which the black defendant came."
10. "Land, bread, housing, education, clothing, justice and peace."

The Ten Point Program finished up referring to the right to rebellion and the revolutionary overthrow of the government, legitimized by the Founding Fathers in the Declaration of Independence of 1776:

We hold these truths to be self-evident, that all men are created equal; that they are endowed by their Creator with certain unalienable rights; that among these are life, liberty, and the pursuit of happiness. [...] But, when a long train of abuses and usurpations, pursuing invariably the same object, evinces a design to reduce them under absolute despotism, it is their right, it is their duty, to throw off such government, and to provide new guards for their future security. (The Black Panther, 1969, p. 16)

Many of the declamations in the Ten Point Program were shared by other black organizations at the time. What distinguished the BPP in the very beginning was their emphasis on point seven of the program: armed self-defense against violence and police brutality. The BPP's emphasis on this issue deeply resonated within the black community, despite class differences. Point 7 was promptly reinforced by the "Executive Mandate No. 1" (1967, May 2), in which the Party stated that, given that "the racist power structure of America has but one policy: repression, genocide, terror and the big stick", black people, as an oppressed community "determined to gain their freedom by any means necessary", had the constitutional right to bear arms for defensive purposes (Newton, 2009, pp. 7-8). This led to the formation of "police patrols" to monitor police actions in black neighborhoods. They carried weapons, tape recorders, video cameras, the Constitution and law books and dedicated themselves to roaming ghetto streets to observe and control police actions. Being one of the first, most popular and publicized actions of the BPP, they sought to legitimize the idea of black self-defense to gain popular support.

The theatricality of the patrols wandering the streets and their verbal confrontations with the police, added to a famous episode in Sacramento, made the interest and support for the Party increase rapidly and considerably. In 1967, a delegation of Panthers openly carrying guns made statements to reporters covering Republican Governor Ronald Reagan's visit to the Sacramento Legislature. After thirty Panthers enter the Legislature building to protest the sanction of a bill (later signed into law) that would ban public carrying of loaded firearms in urban areas (the Mulford Act), the group read Executive Mandate n° 1 in front of the cameras (Lee, 1996). According to Newton, after Sacramento "from all across the country calls came to us about establishing (BPP) chapters and branches... in a matter of months we went from a small Bay Area group to a national organization..." (Newton, 1973, pp. 150-151).

FROM RESISTANCE TO REVOLUTION: RACISM, RACE AND CLASS IN THE IDEOLOGY OF THE BPP

"You can't have capitalism without racism". These words by Malcolm X (1964) were one of the basic premises of the ideology of the Black Panther Party: institutional racism and the racial oppression that it entailed, represented the fundamental basis of the inequality and economic oppression to which black people were subjected to. In *On the Ideology of the Black Panther Party* (1969), Eldridge Cleaver, Minister of Information and ideological referent of the organization between 1967 and 1971, stated that the ideology of the Party was the product of the "historical experience of Black people and the wisdom gained by Black people in their 400-year long struggle against the system of racist oppression and economic exploitation, interpreted through the prism of the Marxist-Leninist analysis by our Minister of Defense, Huey P. Newton" (Cleaver, 1969, p. 1). Newton was who determined the ideological and methodological parameters of the BPP. His interpretation, which sought to adapt the principles of scientific socialism "by and for black people", combined elements of Marxism-Leninism and black nationalism, which he initially characterized as "revolutionary black nationalism".

"Just Listen to What the Panthers Are Saying"

This ideology was articulated based on the dynamics of the interrelation of racism, race and class struggle. Newton considered that, when it came to the problem of racism, Marxism-Leninism offered little help, since it mistakenly assumed the homogeneity of the proletariat, the working class and the lumpen proletariat, when in reality capitalism appealed to the differences created by racism "to make money by keeping black and white people divided. Then they can pay black workers less and keep White workers fighting the blacks rather than uniting to fight the bosses" (Why Pigs Perpetuate Racism, 1969, p. 5). Therefore, it was necessary to have an ideology that considered the reality of racism and race in the Marxist analysis.

The ideology of the BPP evolved to fit the ever-changing situation of the black community in the United States of America (Cleaver, 1969, p. 2). Following the teachings of Kim Il Sung and Mao Tse-tung, both of whom "applied the classical principles of Marxism-Leninism to the conditions in their own countries and thereby made the ideology into something useful for their people" (Cleaver, 1969, p. 5), the BPP rejected the ideas that were not relevant to the realities of Black Americans, and assumed others to put theory into action. The Party's ideology also reflected the teachings of Malcolm X and – showing the impact of Maoism and the global influence of the Chinese cultural revolution – of Mao Tse-tung, Ho Chi Minh y Kim Il Sung. Newton also took on the ideas of Franz Fanon and on "Guerrilla Warfare" by Ernesto "Che" Guevara, in order to develop his own vision with which to address and transform the reality of black people in the United States.

Below we analyze some of the main premises of the Panther's ideology, and the notions that determined their tactics and strategies of struggle and resistance.

Revolutionary Intercommunalism

By 1970, Newton had abandoned the "black revolutionary nationalism" (nationalism plus socialism) idea to embrace "Revolutionary Intercommunalism". Historian Nikhil Pal Singh has characterized Intercommunalism as a concept that Newton developed to refer to a "deterritotialized conception of liberation", in which small groups like the Panthers could participate with other oppressed "communities", like the Cubans and the Vietnamese, in the struggle for freedom and liberation (Singh, 2004, p. 198).

Newton considered that, as a consequence of the transformations produced by capitalism globally, nations - as territorial and political units - had been deeply affected in terms of their internal organization and borders. Intercommunalism saw the world as a body of communities dominated directly or indirectly by the Imperial Power (the United States of America) and its ruling class. The transnationalization of capital had turned nation-states into organizations that were obsolete to fight the Imperial Power, and it was no longer possible to talk about struggles for national liberation. Thus, every liberation movement worldwide would serve the ulterior goal: liberation from imperialist oppression. In this context, Black Americans were the ones at the vanguard, not only for being in the heart of the Empire but for its more than 400 years of struggle and resistance (Hilliard & Weise, 2001, pp. 234-240). In this conceptualization, "the vanguard of the vanguard group" was the BPP, who would teach the correct approach to struggle to carry out the revolution (Newton, 2009, pp. 15-16), and would lead the poor and oppressed to the era of "Revolutionary Intercommunalism". This era, the prior stage to communism, would be the phase in which a "higher level of consciousness" would be experienced in which the people of the world would "seize the means of production and distribute the wealth and the technology in an egalitarian way to the many communities of the world" (Newton, 2009, pp. 31-32).

In this classist and anti-capitalist analysis, the notions of race and racism played a central role. In "To the Black Movement" (1968, May 15), Newton refers to the United States of America as a classist society, organized by a system of racial hierarchy in which Black people had historically been relegated to the lowest echelon, had no social mobility and lacked opportunities to move into the higher classes. Blacks were an oppressed community because of their blackness, and the exploitation that automatically came with it (Newton, 2009, pp. 90-93). The capitalists used the philosophy of racism "to support their wicked oppression" and to disseminate the national ideology that "some citizens are better than others because of differences in physical and social characteristics, and therefore have a right to exploit the others" (Newton, 2009, p. 91). This philosophy of racism had pervaded the poorest white people, often the most racist, because they were afraid "that (they) might lose something or discover something that (they) does not have". So, blacks were non other that a threat to them (Newton, 2009, p. 153).

A Nation Within a Nation: The Black Community as a Colony

The situation of black people in the United States was of a colonized subject. And the ghetto was the colonial territory inside North America. African Americans constituted a colony within the territory that was to be liberated, as liberation movements in the Third World were leading their struggle for de-colonization and independence. Therefore, and privileging the inherent right to self-determination, the black struggle was part of the global national-liberation movement against colonialism and imperialism. In this context, the police were a "force of occupation" (Newton, 1967, p. 4), the armed wing of a racist system that would use every tool at its disposal to keep besieging, oppressing and exploiting the black community.

Despite this line of argument, and unlike many other black nationalist groups, the Black Panther Party never advocated secession or separatism. Historian Robin D.G. Kelley has observed that describing black people as colonial subjects was a way of characterizing the materialist nature of racism. More a metaphor than an analytical concept, self-determination was understood to mean community control within the urban environment, and not necessarily the establishment of a black independent nation (Kelley, 2002, p. 95). As Huey P. Newton would put it, the call for self-determination or self-rule did not mean "independent rule, independent of others, located geographically together, but self-rule" (Foner, 2002, p. 250).

The Party's Class Composition

It is from the internal colony (the ghetto) from where freedom fighters would come to fight the final battle for liberation. The ghetto - a racial space of poverty, underdevelopment and violence - was mainly inhabited by blacks who were "on the margins of society". Thereby, and even though historiography has been inclined to assess that the BPP was composed of and appealed to the "black lumpen proletariat", the truth is that the rank and file of the Party was the black working class. For Cleaver, the "lumpen" category was very broad and considered the employed and unemployed workers, the millions who had no political representation, the ones that lacked an organization or were unorganized, and those who did not own or control any capital or means of production, those whose "daily life is a hustle to make it by any means necessary in the struggle to survive" (Cleaver, 1969, p. 4). The "lumpen" were:

"Just Listen to What the Panthers Are Saying"

That part of the "Industrial Reserve Army" held perpetually in reserve; who have never worked and never will; who can't find a job; who are unskilled and unfit; who have been displaced by machines, automation, and cybernation, and were never "retained or invested with new skills"; all those on Welfare or receiving State Aid. Also the so-called "Criminal Element", those who live by their wits, existing off that which they rip off. (...) In short, all those who simply have been locked out of the economy and robbed of their rightful social heritage. But even though we are Lumpen, we are still members of the Proletariat. (Cleaver, 1969, p. 7)

The lumpen proletarians were the "left wing of the proletarians" (Newton, 2009, p. 26) and, therefore, their vanguard. The right wing of the proletarians was the organized labor movement, and the factory where their struggle took place. But for the 'lumpen', the struggle was in the streets, where they would carry out the revolution through guerrilla warfare tactics, even at the behest of the right wing of the proletariat (Cleaver, 1969, p. 4).

In his interpretation, the majority of the black population fit into the "lumpen" category: they were a growing set of cheap, unskilled labor, with little influence or collective political power. Technological development, the need it created for skilled labor, the lack of qualification of black workers, and the rising unemployment of unskilled labor would make blacks chronically unemployed, and they would inevitably increase the ranks of the lumpen proletariat. Ergo, all black workers were potentially "lumpen" (Newton, 2009, p. 28)[1]. So, it was about promoting the interests and organizing the "Black have-nots, who represent about 98 percent of Blacks in America" (Foner, 2002, p. 52). This included both the lumpen and the proletariat. This racial and class rhetoric was appealing not only to the most dispossessed members of society, but to workers, students, middle-class professionals, war veterans and intellectuals.

Interracial Alliances and Coalitions

According to Bobby Seale, the BPP invoked for alliances and coalitions with all the people and organizations who wanted to move against the power structure. He stressed that it was not a race struggle, but a class struggle between the massive proletarian working class and the small, minority ruling class. "Working-class people of all colors must unite against the exploitative, oppressive ruling class. So let me emphasize again - we believe our fight is a class struggle and not a race struggle" (Seale, 1970, pp. 42-43). Similarly, Newton considered what he called "strategic coalitions" as an essential part of the revolutionary process:

The only way that we're going to be free is to wipe out once and for all the oppressive structure of America. We realize we can't do this without a popular struggle, without many alliances and coalitions, and this is the reason that we're moving in the direction that we are to get as many alliances as possible of people that are equally dissatisfied with the system. (Foner, 2002, p. 72)

The formation of class, interracial, alliances and coalitions were a necessary strategy (Foner, 2002, p. 250)[2] in which African Americans – under the BPP's leadership – were to be "the vanguard". And the role of other parties and organizations, particularly predominantly White groups, was to support and aid the black movement (Foner, 2002, pp. 55-56). While this banishes the myth of the BPP as an "anti-white" organization of black supremacists, and even taking into consideration their belief in the convenience of interracial alliances, the Party could not overcome its identification as a Black organization. The Panthers not only recognized themselves as an *All-Black Party* (Foner, 2002, p. 55)[3] but also considered that the "double black problem" (being black and being poor) could only be overcome through racial solidarity:

The BPP is a Black organization because we feel that we have a Black problem. Our problem is unity at this point. We have to unite among ourselves (...) The White revolutionists realize that they're exploited politically and economically, more politically than anything else, but we (Black people) suffer from racism also. We have to man our own group to straighten out our own problems of Black people and Black colonies, and we welcome support. (The Black Panther, 1969; Hilliard, 2007, p. 13)

As an All-Black organization, the BPP could make alliances with radical groups, poor whites and other ethnic groups under class terms, but could not be an "organization of organizations". Creating a single organization in which class solidarity prevailed over racial solidarity did not seem feasible, giving true meaning to one of its popular slogans: Black Power to Black people, Brown Power to Brown people, Red power to Red People, Yellow power to yellow people... white power to white people (Sonnie & Tracy, 2011, p. 74).

TACTICS AND STRATEGIES OF STRUGGLE

With the Ten Point Program as a guide, the BPP developed a diverse set of tactics and strategies in order to "stop the White racist power structure from grinding the life out of the Black Race through the daily operation of this system which is design to exploit and oppress Black people" (The Black Panther, 1967, p.4; Hilliard, 2007, p. 4).

The first one was perhaps the most theatrical and impactful: patrolling the police force of Oakland. Police patrols constituted community self-defense groups that roamed the ghettos to control the police and keep them "from misusing their tremendous power over the neighborhood" (OUI Magazine, reprinted by The Black Panther, 1978; Hilliard, 2007, p. 136). Not only it was an organizational tactic in terms of recruitment but addressed the need for self-defense tactics to stop police abuse and repression.

In the Party's ideology, the notion of self-defense was not an end in itself, but a tool - among others - to be used to get to the final stage of the revolution. Newton wanted blacks to see the virtues of disciplined and (opt for) organized self-defense, rather than the "spontaneous and disorganized outbreaks and riots" (Newton, [1971] 2009, p. 452), so common since the summer of 1964.

Since the BPP always kept the use of guns within legal limits, when the Mulford Act (1967) repealed a law allowing public carrying of loaded firearms, the Party put an end to the armed patrols (Newton, 1973, pp. 146-152). With the sanction of the law, the notions of self-defense, guerrilla warfare and armed struggle ceased to constitute the backbone around which the BPP organized their activities. With the symbolic elimination of "for Self Defense" from its party denomination (Hampton & Fayer, 1990, p. 453), the main strategy became the survival programs.

Before focusing on the survival programs, we should take a moment to discuss The Black Panther Intercommunal News Service, the news organ that published *The Black Panther,* the Party's newspaper. Becoming the "official voice" of the BPP, it was an important tool to raise political consciousness and articulate the struggle. Its weekly publication gave coherence and cohesion, linking the different and distant chapters and branches of the Party. It was the primary source of information about the organization, indoctrination, communication and consistent revenue stream. One of the basic requirements of

"Just Listen to What the Panthers Are Saying"

the BPP membership was selling the newspaper, as well as the participation in newspaper reading and discussion workshops (Hilliard, 2007, p. vii). Acts to sabotage the newspaper's production, selling and distribution were very common, and the its selling was among the main reasons of Panthers arrests. Being the media that provided reliable information on the work, community programs, demonstrations, and other activities of the Party, at one point the *Black Panther* became the third-largest Black circulating newspaper in the United States, behind the *Amsterdam News* and *Muhammad Speaks* (Jeffries, 2006, p. 195), and had subscriptions and sales in China, Cuba, Scandinavia, Western Europe, Africa, South America, the Middle East and Vietnam (Hilliard, 2007, p. vii).

Besides the important work of political education and information *The Black Panther* allowed, the BPP certainly pursued two other types of strategies: one we could consider (a) "revolutionary" and the other one (b) "reformist".

The Survival Programs

During 1967 and 1968, the Party started to focus on the implementation of social community programs. Known as *survival (pending revolution) programs* or *Serve the People programs*, they sought to educate and organize the struggle of the black community, face the absence of the state and the lack of social programs in the ghetto, and help meet the most pressing and daily needs of the community. Understanding politics as "the desire of individuals and groups to satisfy their basic needs first: food, shelter and clothing and security for themselves and their loved ones" (Newton, 2009, p. 87), these programs had a pressing political purpose: they were the organizational tool that would serve to bring people to the level of class consciousness required to establish a socialist society (Newton, 1974, p. 11). These programs combined essential social services, cadre training and grassroots organizing. They required the involvement of hundreds of volunteers and were the way of accessing an organization strongly discredited, attacked and vilified by the government and the media. Some inside the BPP believed that the Survival Programs diverted the Party from their main goal: carrying out armed revolution against the government. But for some others, the programs accurately reflected "the original true vision of the BPP".

Despite this internal discrepancy, the popularity of the BPP evidenced the failure of government social programs and the shortcomings of the laws approved in the context of the Civil Rights Movement. By 1973, the BPP had more than 60 model programs that provided social services, food and clothing, healthcare, assistance to children and the elderly, legal and labor counseling, community workshops and kindergarten, primary and secondary level education. The Panthers even founded their own school. In January 1971 the Intercommunal Youth Institute was established to educate children and to provide them with "quality and meaningful" education. In 1974 the institute's name was changed to Oakland Community School (OCS). The OCS was approved by the Board of Education of the State of California and instructed children from ages 2 to 11. In September 1977, California Governor Edmund "Jerry" Brown Jr. and the California Legislature gave OCS a special award for "having set the standard for the highest level of elementary education in the state" (Abron, 1998, p. 185).

But all of this depended on fundraising. One source of income was the sale of *The Black Panther* and other products such as posters, reading materials and books produced by the Party. Since no advertising was sold, newspaper sales and subscriptions were vitally important. They collected money and products from merchants and businessmen, urged to collaborate with the Party and their survival programs. They also received donations from "wealthy White philanthropist, humanitarians, and heirs to the corporate monopolies" (Newton, 1974, p. 11), and even from important Hollywood stars and celebrities (Shames,

2006, p. 13). Other revenue came from fundraising rallies, talks and conferences, and from White leftists' organizations in the West Coast, such as the Communist Party and the Socialist Worker's Party (Wilson, 2006, p. 193).

Some of the money went to the financing of the many community programs, but mainly was used for legal expenses and bail bonds of incarcerated Party members. As Newton acknowledged in an interview with OUI Magazine in 1978, bails and legal expenses ended up being "a real financial drain on the Party" (Hilliard, 2007, p. 135). BPP's local chapters were not likely to get the kind of money the Oakland headquarters did. Judson Jeffries highlights that fundraising was often a challenge for most of these local chapters. Relying on the sale of newspapers, Panther literature and merchandising - a constant, albeit minimal, source of income -, they operated on a very limited budget. So, given the lack of revenue, the fact that they were able to provide the volume of services and programs they did is a very impressive achievement (Jeffries, 2006, p. 199).

Electoral and Political-Institutional Strategies

To mobilize and organize the black community politically and electorally was about filling a void at the national level: the lack of representation in the power structure. The strategy of working within the limits of the political system and through institutional channels was about achieving power that could be transform into actions whose effects were economic: the redistribution of resources and wealth. Thus, the BPP ended up accepting elections as a legitimate strategy of struggle. The first step in this direction was organizing registration rallies. This was not just to increase the political power of the organization. Registering is essential to be selected as a jury in judicial proceedings. So, this was the only way to guarantee black people the possibility of being judged by their peers.

When it came to alliances, the BPP attempted a (failed) merger with the Student Nonviolent Coordinating Committee (SNCC), a popular group of young black nationalist, with the goal to form a powerful organization with strong bases in the North, the West and the South (Newton, 1973, pp. 154-155). That combined with the Party's rapprochement to "moderate" groups and personalities like Martin Luther King, Jr. Simultaneously, under the leadership of the charismatic Fred Hampton - Deputy chairman of the Illinois Black Panther Party - the Chicago chapter of the BPP built an important coalition with "street gangs" such as the Puerto Rican Young Lords and the Latin Kings that put the political establishment and the FBI on high alert (Ogbar, 2006, p. 216). By 1969, the Chicago BPP, the Young Lords and the Young Patriots – a gang of poor white Appalachian youths from the city's Uptown section that adopted the ideology and praxis of the BPP (Foner, 2002, pp. 239-243)[4] - formed the *Rainbow Coalition*. For Bob Lee, co-founder of the original Rainbow Coalition, the latter soon became "just a code word for class struggle" (Sonnie & Tracy, 2011, p. 80). This might have been the reason why this major coalition effort had a short life. After the brutal assassination of Hampton in 1969, the Young Lords fragmented into two different organizations, and the Young Patriots disbanded after the mass arrest of their leaders. These, added to the onslaught of state repression, made the Rainbow Coalition disappeared by 1970.

The BPP also had an interesting but brief alliance with (the predominantly White) *Peace and Freedom Party* (PFP), an anti-war and pro-civil rights organization. Despite the fact that in 1971 Newton had established the Party line that BPP members would never run for political office, but would endorse and support candidates that could prove were acting "in the true interest of the people" (Newton, 2009, p. 50), the alliance with the PFP was seen as a "tactical move". The decision allowed Newton, Seale and Kathleen Cleaver to run for public office at the local level and even for the presidency of the United States

"Just Listen to What the Panthers Are Saying"

(Sonnie & Tracy, 2011, p. 63).[5] In order to legitimize the new strategy, in 1972 the Party recognized that even though getting involved in electoral politics would not eradicate "the many ills which afflict Black and poor people in this country... we realized that, still, many positive gains could be achieved by Black and poor people utilizing our collective vote for those political candidates who truly represent our interests" (Panthers sweep Berkeley elections, 1972, p. 2).

Despite the agreement and subsequent dissolution of these and other alliances and coalitions with political organizations and worker's unions, the BPP continued to invoke the electoral strategy. In 1972 they won four out of nine seats in the elections for the Berkeley Community Development Council Board of Directors, an agency with a billionaire budget to re-distribute in social programs. This victory was especially significant as the BPP announced Party members' candidacy one day before the scheduled elections (Panthers sweep Berkeley elections, 1972, p. 2). After this victory, and now following the premise that voting showed "the power of the people", a mean to exercise the control of the community, they won six out of eighteen appointments in the elections for the West Oakland Planning Committee, which was responsible for providing citizen's input on how the $ 4.9 million budget was to be used in providing social services and urban renewal financing in West Oakland (Burke & Jeffries, 2016, p. 182).

That same year, the BPP made a controversial decision that meant a breaking point for the Party. Seale announced his candidacy for Mayor of Oakland and Brown for a City Council seat, both running as Democratic Party candidates. Per Newton's request, the Party decided to close all its chapters and branches and ordered its members to relocate to Oakland and fully devote themselves to Seale and Brown's campaigns. Even though a few chapters did persist, for most practical purposes the BPP was once again a local community organization based in Oakland.

Even though both candidates lost their political bids (Seale forced a runoff election and Brown came in close second for City Council), the BPP continued given prominence to the electoral strategy by supporting the candidacy of the democrat Ron Dellums for U.S. Congress and of Shirley Chisholm for President of the United States in the California Democratic primary election of 1972 (Hilliard, 2007, pp. 70-75).

THE NATIONAL AND TRANSNATIONAL IMPACT OF THE BPP

Even though it is hard to determine the BPP's membership throughout the years, it is believed that by 1970 the Party had as many as 5,000 active members. With at least 40 offices and more than 100 chapters throughout the country (United States Congress, 1971)[6], the Panthers outside of Oakland followed the line set by the national headquarters and immersed themselves in community service projects (Jeffries, 2006, p. 196). It is to note that this alleged membership seems to underestimate the larger influence and grassroots support of the Party. Some BPP rallies drew up to 10,000 people and, according to a Wall Street Journal poll, by 1970 at least 60% of the black population felt the Panthers represented their interests (Panther Supporters, 1970, p. 1).

On the international front, chapters of the BPP were established in Algeria, Israel and New Zealand. Affiliated groups were organized among black soldiers in Vietnam. The Party also had the public support of the governments of North Vietnam, Cuba, Algeria, Korea and China, and of international organizations and political groups from Great Britain, Ireland, Germany, Switzerland, Netherlands, Africa and Latin America. Panther "solidarity committees" were formed in countries like England, France, Denmark, Norway, Finland and Sweden. And, last but not least, the BPP inspired the emergence of insurgent indigenous organizations in England, Bermuda, Israel, Australia and India, and it fostered close relations with liberation movements in Africa (Zimbabwe, Mozambique, South Africa) and Asia (Vietnam, Palestine) (The Black Panther, 1974, p. 8; Terry, 1970; Free Huey Demonstrations in Scandinavia, 1969, p. 12).

In Latin America, the BPP had closed ties and political relations with Cuba (where in addition to ideological inspiration, several Panthers found refuge over the years (Bloom & Martin, 2013, p. 351)[7], and connections to Brazil and Uruguay. In a 1970 interview with *Sechaba*, the official organ of the African National Congress of South Africa, Newton said that they were particularly interested "in the strategy being used in Brazil, which is an urban area" and that they were planning to draw on that (Newton, 2009, p. 205). The Minister of Defense was referring to the actions of a few underground guerrilla organizations that were acting since mid-1960s in big cities like Rio de Janeiro, São Paulo and Belo Horizonte. These groups found inspiration in the "Mini Manual of the Urban Guerrilla", originally written in 1969 by Carlos Marighella, one of the leaders and founder of the Ação Libertadora Nacional (National Liberation Action, ALN), a Brazilian guerrilla movement formed in 1968 to stand against the military government of 1964–1985. Marighella's theories on urban guerrilla warfare contemplated large cities as a key point of support for the armed revolt against "the government, the big businesses and the foreign imperialists, particularly North Americans" (Marighella, 2002, p. 4). In January 1971, right before the ideological split within the Party, Field Marshal Donald Cox quoted Marighella in order to promote violence and immediate guerrilla warfare against the US government:

Today, to be an assailant or terrorist is a quality than ennobles any honorable man because it is an act worthy of a revolutionary engaged in armed struggle against the shameful military dictatorship and its monstrosities… Guerrilla Units (self-defense groups) must be formed and blows must be struck against the slave master until we have secured our survival as a people. (Bloom & Martin, 2013, p. 358)

For its part, the Black Liberation Army, the armed wing of the BPP, adopted some of its urban guerrilla tactics and strategies from the Tupamaros National Liberation Movement, a urban guerrilla organization founded in 1963 in Uruguay (FBI, 1974, p. 21). In "Break the Chains", a 1973 pamphlet from the National Committee for the Defense of Joanne Chesimard and Clark Squire (also known as Sundiata Acoli and Assata Shakur, two well-known BLA members), this organ stated that they were "a people's army", the equivalent "to the Tupamaros of Uruguay, Frelimo of Mozambique, or the NLF of Vietnam" (National Committee for the Defense of Joanne Chesimard & Clark Squire, 1973, p. 14).

GOVERNMENT REPRESSION

According to Michael McCarthy, an active member of the Party in 1969-1971, when the survival programs started to show that they were popular and successful, "that's when the government moved in" (Lee, 1996, 51:54 min). As happened to many other "radical" organizations of these years, the BPP was subjected to police surveillance, infiltrations, sabotage, and the most brutal repression. From a survey of *The Black Panther* and other local newspapers, Panthers and even people related to the Party were constantly detained and imprisoned under a multitude of criminal charges ranging from assault, robbery, public disorder, resisting a police officer, carrying weapons, (attempt to) homicide, traffic violations, illegal sale of the newspaper, reading material and other Party paraphernalia and even under "criminal anarchy" charges (Jeffries, 2006, p. 203)[8].

"Just Listen to What the Panthers Are Saying"

Inevitably, this affected the dynamics and development of Party activities, its growth and institutional strengthening, the use of financial resources and its public image. Not only did they suffer confiscations in numerous police raids, but their leaders were imprisoned for long periods of time, had to be exiled or were killed in confrontations with the police or in police custody. In a 1976 interview with Louis Tackwood, a black Los Angeles Police Department informant that infiltrated the BPP back in the 1970s, stated that "during this period, the police were shooting Panthers left and right [...] They were shooting them down as fast as they could find them, and the verdict would always be 'justifiable homicide' [...] there were so many Panthers getting shoot and killed that there was no way of keeping up who was getting killed when" (Hilliard, 2007, p. 144).

The year that the BPP experienced its greatest popularity and growth was also the year that the Party suffered the strongest repressive surge against it. In 1969, 233 out of 295 FBI counterintelligence operations were levied against the Panthers (Shames, 2006, p. 141). The 1976 Senate Select Committee on Government Intelligence found that in 1969 alone, 27 Panthers were killed by police and that 749 were arrested or jailed (Marable, 1991, p. 112). Thus, the BPP had to resort to the constant recruitment of new members, which made infiltration quite frequent, difficult to control and even estimate. This was the reason why in 1969, the Party's Central Committee decided to carry out an internal purge to expose and expel those to be believed snitches and confidential informants of the government.

Espionage and infiltration were valuable tools to generate a climate of mistrust and paranoia, that triggered serious problems and dissent within the organization (Jeffries, 2006, pp. 206-207). This was possible partly because of the split between Newton and Cleaver, related to tactics and strategies of struggle, that created two irreconcilable factions among Party members. How each of them came to their position and how it led to the Party's split is a long and complicated story that we cannot address here. For our purposes, we will summarize it in that Cleaver (exiled in Algeria since 1968) believed that the right strategies were armed struggle and guerrilla warfare, while Newton considered it was time to focus on strengthening the survival programs in order to build a strong and enduring political organization.

On his corner, J. Edgar Hoover deemed that any act – even those illegal and unconstitutional –was justified to eliminate the organization that "without question, represents the greatest threat to the internal security of the country" (Black Panther greatest threat to US security, 1969). In order to provoke dissent, discord, and decimate the Party, the FBI and police departments nationwide appealed to all kinds of tactics – including political assassinations, shootings, bombings and any other gross violation of civil liberties and human rights – to "prevent a coalition of militant black nationalists groups and to prevent the rise of a Messiah who could lead the black masses" (Marable, 1991, pp. 111-112).

These FBI operations occurred in a context in which the BPP, being only 4 years old, was emerging as that Messiah. In 1970, a Time Magazine survey revealed that 63% of Blacks believed that the American political system was "rotten" and had to change completely "for blacks to be free" (63% of Negroes Despair of Being Free, Poll Says, 1970, A4). The same source revealed that 31% (40% among youth) considered that only the retort to violence would bring them equality, and 9% (about 2 million) identified themselves as "revolutionaries". At the same time, the New York Times recognized Bobby Seale as one of the top three African-American leaders of the time (Blacks Found to Favor Working through System, 1970, p. 86), and the Wall Street Journal revealed that 60% of the black population supported the goals and strategies of the BPP, especially its survival programs (Panther Supporters, 1970, p. 1). This would explain the numerous FBI memos, which - once declassified - revealed how infiltrated agents were responsible for promoting discord, dissent, fostering violence, discrediting, damaging and disrupting party activities.

By 1970, with Cleaver in Algeria, Newton took full control of the Party, and ordered the withdrawal of militancy to Oakland, not without numerous objections This led to defections of members who, unhappy with Newton's leadership and decision, and feeling closer to Cleaver's position, left the party and joined other black organizations, or continued their struggle from the underground.

BLACK LIBERATION ARMY

The sixth rule of the Black Panther Party stated that "no party member can join any other army or force other than the Black Liberation Army (BLA)" (Rules of the Black Panther Party, 1968, p. 7), acknowledging the latter as the Party's armed wing. The emergence of the BLA coincided with the preeminence of the political-electoral strategy and the moderation of the Party's position regarding armed self-defense and the retort to violence.

Newton considered that, although the appeal to guns had served its purpose as a catalyst for popular support, many had converted them in the axis of the struggle (Hampton & Fayer, 1990, p. 518). The reevaluation of arm struggle and its relegation as merely a defensive tactic reinforced the idea that the BPP did not want to be acknowledge or characterized as a paramilitary force. That was actually reserved for the BLA.

The BLA indeed consider armed struggle as an end in itself. Self-defined as a political-military front, it was a clandestine paramilitary force whose main strategy was urban guerrilla warfare. Assata Shakur, a member of the BLA who in 1972 would be convicted of the killing of a police officer and ended up escaping to Cuba, gave this definition of the BLA:

The BLA is not an organization: it goes beyond that. It is a concept, a people's movement, an idea. Many different people have said and done many different things in the name of the BLA. The idea of a Black Liberation Army emerged from conditions in Black communities: conditions of poverty, indecent housing, massive unemployment, poor medical care, and inferior education. The idea came about because Black people are not free or equal in this country. Because 90% of the men and women in this country's prisons are Black and Third World. Because 10 year-old children are shoot down in our streets. Because dope has saturated our communities, preying on the disillusionment and frustration of our children. The concept of the BLA arose because of the political, social and economic oppression of Black people in this country. And where there is oppression, there will be resistance. (Shakur, 1987, p. 169)

This underground apparatus was decentralized, with autonomous cells in different cities (even operating from prisons around the country) that were referred to by different names at different times (Umoja, 2006, p. 227). In a way, the BLA was broader than the BPP. They were the vanguard of the Black Liberation struggle in America. Their goal was to militarize Black people in order to create a popular army that would work for the "physical elimination of oppression" (National Committee for the Defense of Jo Anne Chesimard & Clark Squire, 1973). To achieve this goal, they carried out operations against the "internal enemies of the black community": traffickers, criminals and the police.

The fate of the BPP and the BLA was linked to the disagreement and latter split between Newton and Cleaver. Many Panthers from different chapters supported Cleaver's view, and after Newton's purge of the Party, the BLA went underground. While they shared many of the BPP's ideological and politi-

"Just Listen to What the Panthers Are Saying"

cal positions, the BLA considered that the correct strategy was "revolutionary violence" and "armed struggle", and not the institutional path through electoral policy (Black Liberation Army, 1976, pp. i-ii).

Under the leadership of Geronimo 'Ji Jaga' Pratt (former Panther of the Southern California chapter), the BLA set up an underground railroad to help comrades being sought by local and federal police forces and focused on establishing guerrilla units all over the country (Umoja, 2006, p. 228). Between 1970 and 1984, the BLA staged at least 36 incidents: attempted plane's hijackings, armed robbery to banks and businesses (called "expropriation acts"), hostage-taking, bomb attacks, and confrontations with the police that ended up in officers and Panthers' killings in cities like New York, New Jersey, Los Angeles, San Francisco, New Orleans, Atlanta and Detroit (Muntaqim, 1979). One of their boldest operations took place in April 1974, when they attempted the assault of Tombs City Jail (New York), to free a group of comrades serving a life sentence (BLA Communique No. 14, 1974). In the early 1980s, countless BLA members were in jail on charges of conspiracy (Black Liberation Army Communique, 1983, July 16), and others were still wanted by the police under various criminal charges (NY police hunt members of the Black Liberation Army, 1981, p. 3). One of the last BLA actions we were able to register took place in 1983, when a BLA unit bombed South African Airways headquarters in Long Island and the IBM building in New York, in the context of the Anti-Apartheid movement (United Freedom Front, 1984, pp. 1-2).

THE BROWN YEARS (1974-1977)

Newton's persona was too important to be easily dismissed. Between 1972 and 1974, he led the BPP in a very controversial and dictatorial way. The bibliography states, almost unanimously, that Newton used the Party's resources and revenue to carry out criminal activities and finance his addictions. This led to Seale's departure from the Party in 1974, an attitude imitated by many high-ranked members of the BPP.

In 1974 Newton decided to flee to Cuba after being indicted one more time for the killing of 17-year old Kathleen Smith. And it was Elaine Brown who took charge and rose to national leadership. The new BPP's chairperson initiated a period (from August 1974 through June 1977) in which the BPP showed impressive stability and strength.

With the exception of Brown's autobiography, only a few works have focused on these years. And the main premise seems to be that under Brown's leadership the Party enter its decline period. Historiography mostly ignores them, and they refer to the 1974-1977 years as a transitional period until Newton's return. However, primary sources analysis evidences that these was a period of stability, preeminence of the electoral and institutional strategy and of the consolidation of the BPP at the grassroots and local level. Taking on a moderate and "politically correct" rhetoric, the BPP prioritize the survival programs, electoral politics, and the formation of alliances with political organizations and unions, making the Party a leading political force. This was accompanied by the rise of many women to prominent hierarchical roles (Ortiz, 1993, p. 178). All of these lead to Brown being elected in 1976 as an official delegate to the New York Democratic National Convention from California, where she openly and harshly criticized some democrats (like Andrew Young and Jesse Jackson) and their collaborationist politics. She stated that they misled people into believing that the Democratic Party represented the interest of poor and oppress people and she called on those "still in the Democratic Party to leave and begin to work with all the poor and working people of this country to build our own political party" (The Democratic Party has abandoned Black People, 1976, pp. 1, 8). Fully oriented now towards a reformist approach to politics, the BPP became the Party of reference to which many candidates turned to for political support for local and national elections.

In three years, Brown became one of the most prominent political figures in the West Coast. Installed in the ranks of the San Francisco Democratic Party, Brown was appointed as an advisor to the cabinet of Lionel Wilson, the first African-American Mayor, and as a member of the Executive Committee of the newly formed Oakland Council for Economic Development (OCED) (Elaine Brown warns businessmen: jobs, housing or no city center, 1976, p. 1). But what enshrined the absolute "transition from revolution to politics" during the Brown era was the lawsuit filed by the Party and the "Committee for Justice for Huey P. Newton" for US$ 100 million against the FBI, the CIA, the police force and other federal agencies such as the Internal Revenue Service (IRS) (Nationwide support urged for BPP suit against FBI, 1976, p. 1), in the belief that "the system" would compensate the Panthers for the fierce violence and repression conducted by the same system that now welcomed a reformed BPP.

THE OUTCOME (1977-1982)

In July 1977, Newton returned to the United States to regain control of the Party. As a result, and after working to dismiss all charges against him, Brown resigned from the organization. With her departure, the 1977-1982 years became "Newton-centric". *The Black Panther* exponentially increased the "cult of personality" of its leader. The centrality of Newton, his judicial situation, his past, present and future, the lawsuit against the repressive state and federal agencies and the fundraisings needed to sustain the judicial processes seized the reality of the Party, even over the survival programs. This led to a massive estrangement of members and supporters. On his part, Newton focused on his legal problems and on promoting what would become his doctoral dissertation, elaborated in those years. In 1980, he received his PhD from the University of California (Santa Cruz) for *War against the Panthers. A Study of repression in America* on the persecution and political repression of the BPP (Newton, 1980).

Even though many survival programs continued providing services thanks to the work and contributions of Party members and volunteers, the political and electoral preeminence of the BPP quickly dissipated. On September 9, 1980, the Intercommunal News Service published the last issue of *The Black Panther*. Ironically, its main headline was "Black Community organizes against Police Brutality": black protest was happening nationwide against cover-up of police murders, triggered by the assassination of a 17-year-old black youth by a White Philadelphia policeman (Black community organizes against police brutality, 1980, pp. 1-4). Two years later, one of the most important and longest standing Black Panthers initiative found its sad ending. The *Ockland Community School* (OCS) closed amid allegations that US$285,000 in federal and state grants had been misused (Barclay, 1983, p. 40) (The Black Panther, 1980; Hilliard, 2007, p. 147)[9]. The closing of the OCS put an end to an intense period of struggle initiated fifteen years earlier, in which the Black Panthers became the symbol and paradigm of Black resistance in the United States.

"Just Listen to What the Panthers Are Saying"

CONCLUSION

In 1990, the United Coalition against Racism, a student anti-apartheid organization at the University of Michigan, published an opinion piece in the *Michigan Daily* publicizing the screening of *The Murder of Fred Hampton*, a 1971 documentary film about the life and brutal death of Fred Hampton in Chicago. During the original film's production, the young leader of the Illinois BPP was fatally shot on December 4, 1969, in an illegal pre-dawn raid at his apartment by the Chicago Police and the FBI. The article asserted that:

Myths continue to pervade our understanding of the Panthers. The images in the history books depict the Panthers as armed and dangerous, empty of any explanations of the tactical necessity of armed struggle. Nor do we learn of their work in the community: breakfast programs, cop watches, assisting the elderly, and Black Youth Education Programs. The Panthers were a threat because through their work they exposed the racist infrastructure of this entire society. […] Our knowledge of historic struggles will enable us to continue those struggles and be better prepare for those we must wage today. ("United Coalition against Racism," 1990, p. 4)

The BPP becoming reveals a lot about the experience of struggle of the black community throughout the 1970s. The fact that the Party was primarily a grassroots organization oriented to mass mobilization whose goal was to satisfy Black population's most pressing (class) needs was what allowed it to survive the time it did. Despite the adversities and violent repression that the Panthers suffered, the Party was the vehicle through which the black population, in different parts of the country, took action, organized collectively and resisted through political activity and community programs.

The BPP has probably been the best organized local (African American) political party in the United States and embodied a true movement with peculiar and diverse local expressions. While remembered for its radical position and revolutionary ideology, the BPP proved to be a political force that appealed to a multiplicity of strategies and tactics of struggle in search of social change, whose key was the satisfaction of class demands of the black population. At the same time, they sought to show the racism of a system that provided unequal services for the rich and the poor – mostly blacks and other ethnic minority groups - and to fight against the inherent racism of American political and economic power structure.

In a plethora of tactics, the construction of coalitions and interracial alliances was considered not only possible but desirable. However, the centrality of race in the organization of the resistance attempted against the conformation of these alliances. Considering its ideological position, and even though the Party did not discriminate when it came to offer their services, "they did encourage individuals to organize around problems in their own particular community. Black people must organize black people, white people must organize White people, brown people must organize Brown people on the road to a 'Rainbow Coalition' that could represent the disparate need of all those so allied" (Williams, 2006, pp. 186-187).

Even though race did not seem to prevent per se the possibility of forming interracial organizations, it did exist the possibility of interracial alliances subordinated to racial identity. This required the BPP to affirm itself as the vanguard. Party leaders believed that the gap between races would force African Americans to assume a leadership role in any coalition. The differences in living conditions of black communities and other ethnic groups required separate but still connected movements, in which whites constituted the "secondary partner". Thus, in a way, the BPP tried to transcend the idea of race and, by invoking some fundamental principles of Marxism-Leninism, elaborate a class ideology that incorporated the peculiar problem of race and racism in the United States.

Judson Jeffries affirmed that state repression and law enforcement's abuse of authority prevented the BPP from devoting the time, resources and manpower needed to build a long-lasting mass political organization. "Between 1968 and 1971, numerous Panthers were killed by local police. Today, there are more Black Panthers in prison than from any other left-wing group" (Jeffries, 2006, p. 218). While we agree on the devastating effects of the state and federal repression against the BPP, we believe that the Party still managed to build a lasting grassroots movement, that reinvented itself by implementing a myriad of tactics and strategies that were based on that brutal repression and that adapted to the local needs of the city in which the Panthers developed their activities. It is likely that their legacy is more related to their rhetoric and methods of struggle than to their political action program and the development of a complex ideology that placed them at the forefront of the fight against capitalism, imperialism and colonialism.

Without hesitation, the most important and lasting strategy that the BPP implemented were the survival programs. These initiatives showed the true class side of the organization's struggle, the pivotal role of the rank and file for the success of the movement, the complex organization of the Party, and reinforced the notion that these were programs for the community that worked thanks to the actions of the community. Last but not least, the legacy of the Black Panther Party must also be estimated in the influence it had in other heterogeneous organizations that identified with their spirit, ideology and / or their methods of organization and resistance: The Republic of New Africa, the Dodge Revolutionary Union Movement (DRUM) and the League of Revolutionary Black Workers (from the Detroit auto industry and other industrial sectors), the Young Patriots, the Young Lords, the Brown Berets, the American Indian Movement (AIM), the Congress of African People (CAA), the Black Liberators, the Black Students Alliance (BSA), and even in the movement of black rural workers from southern states like Alabama and Mississippi.

REFERENCES

Abron, J. N. (1988). Serving the People: the Survival Programs of the Black Parther Party. In C. E. Jones (Ed.), *The Black Panther Party (Reconsidered)*. Baltimore, MD: Black Classic Press.

Appy, C. G. (2013). Vietnam: una guerra de clase [Vietnam: a war class]. In P. Pozzi & F. Nigra (Eds.), *Huellas Imperiales: De la Crisis de 1929 al Presidente Negro* [Imperial Footprints: From the 1929 Crisis to the Black President]. Buenos Aires: Imago Mundi.

Barclay, D. (1983, October 12). Black Panthers. *The Day*.

Black community organizes against police brutality. (1980, September 9). *The Black Panther, 20*(9).

Black Liberation Army. (1976). *Message to the Black Movement: A political statement from the Black underground*. Author.

Black Liberation Army Communique. (1983, July 16). *Freedom Archives*.

Black Panther greatest threat to US security. (1969, July 16). *Desert Sun, 42*(296).

"Just Listen to What the Panthers Are Saying"

Blacks Found to Favor Working through System. (1970, March 30). *The New York Times.*

Bloom, J., & Martin, W. (2013). *Black Against Empire: The history and politics of the Black Panther Party.* University of California Press.

Brown, E. (1993). *A Taste of Power: A Black Woman's Story.* Anchor.

Burke, L. N., & Jeffries, J. L. (2016). *The Portland Black Panthers: empowering Albina and remaking a city.* University of Washington Press.

Cleaver, E. (1969). *On the ideology of the Black Panther Party.* The Freedom Archives.

BLA Communique No. 14. (1974). *The Freedom Archives.*

Elaine Brown warns businessmen: jobs, housing or no city center. (1976, December 11). *The Black Panther, 16*(6).

FBI. (1974, October). The Legacy of Carlos Marighella. *Law Enforcement Bulletin.*

Foner, P. (2002). *The Black Panthers speak.* New York: Da Capo Press.

Free Huey Demonstrations in Scandinavia. (1969, September 4). *The Black Panther.*

Hampton, H., & Fayer, S. (1990). *Voices of Freedom: An oral history of the civil rights movement from 1950s through the 1980s.* New York: Bantam Books.

Hilliard, D. (2007). *The Black Panther Intercommunal News Service (1967-1980).* New York: Atria Books.

Hilliard, D., & Cole, L. (1993). *This side of Glory.* Little, Brown and Company.

Hilliard, D., & Weise, D. (2001). *The Huey P. Newton Reader.* New York: Seven Stories Press.

Jeffries, J. L. (2006). *An unexamined chapter of the Black Panther History.* Urbana: University of Illinois Press.

Kelley, R. D. (2002). *Freedom Dreams: The Black Radical Imagination.* Boston: Beacon Press.

Lazerow, J., & Williams, Y. (2006). *Search of the Black Panther Party: New perspectives on a Revolutionary Movement.* Duke University Press. doi:10.1215/9780822388326

Lee, L. L. (1996). *All Power To The People - The Black Panther Party & Beyond.* Academic Press.

Marable, M. (1991). *Race, Reform and Rebellion: The Second Reconstruction in Black America, 1945-1990.* Jackson, MS: University Press of Mississippi.

Marighella, C. (2002). *Mini-Manual of the Urban Guerrilla Warfare.* Montreal: Abraham Guillen Press & Arm The Spirit.

Muntaqim, J. (1979). *On the Black Liberation Army.* Montreal: Abraham Guillen Press & Arm The Spirit.

National Committee for the Defense of Joanne Chesimard and Clark Squire. (1973, September). *The Freedom Archives.* Retrieved from http://freedomarchives.org/Documents/Finder/DOC513_scans/BLA/513.BLA.Break.De.Chains.pdf

Nationwide support urged for BPP suit against FBI. (1976, July 31). *The Black Panther, 15*(16), 1.

Newton, H. (1967, May 15). The Functional definition of politics. *The Black Panther.*

Newton, H. (1973). *Revolutionary Suicide.* New York: Writers and Readers.

Newton, H. (1974, September 9). Black Capitalism re-analyzed. *The Black Panther.*

Newton, H. (1980). *War against the Panthers: A Study of Repression in America.* University of California Santa Cruz Press.

Newton, H. (2009). On the Defection of Eldridge Cleaver from the BPP and the Defection of the BPP from the black communit. In L. M. M. Marable (Ed.), *Let Nobody Turn Us Around: An African American Anthology* (pp. 449–451). USA: Littlefield Publishers. (Original work published 1971)

Newton, H. (2009). *To die for the people: the Writings of Huey P. Newton.* San Francisco: City Lights Books.

NY police hunt members of the Black Liberation Army. (1981, May 2). *The Afro American.*

of Negroes Despair of Being Free, Poll Says. (1970, March 30). *The Washington Post.*

Ogbar, J. O. G. (2006). Rainbow Radicalism: The rise of the radical ethnic nationalism. In P. R. Joseph (Ed.), *The Black Power Movement: Rethinking the Civil Rights-Black Power Era.* New York: Routledge.

Ortiz, R. D. (1993). New Memoirs on the Black Panther Party (Book reviews). *Social Justice (San Francisco, Calif.), 20*(1/2).

Panther Supporters. (1970, January 13). *Wall Street Journal.*

Panthers sweep Berkeley elections. (1972, June 10). *The Black Panther, 8*(12), 2.

Rules of the Black Panther Party. (1968, September 7). *The Black Panther, 2*(5).

Schurman, F. (2009). Foreword. In H. Newton (Ed.), *To die for the people: the writings of Huey P. Newton.* San Francisco: City Lights Books. doi:10.1016/B978-1-84334-473-5.50011-2

Seale, B. (1970). *Seize the time: the story of the Black Panther Party and Huey P. Newton.* Penguin Random House Grupo Editorial.

Shakur, A. (1987). *Assata: an autobiography.* Chicago: Lawrence Hill Books.

Shames, S. (2006). *The Black Panthers.* New York: Aperture Foundation.

Singh, N. P. (2004). *Black is a country: Race and the unfinished struggle for Democracy.* Cambridge: Harvard University Press.

Sonnie, A., & Tracy, J. (2011). *Hillbilly Nationalists, Urban Race Rebels, and Black Power.* Brooklyn: MelvilleHouse.

Spencer, R. C. (2005). Inside the Panther Revolution. In K. Woodard & J. Theoharis (Eds.), *Groundwork: Local Black Freedom Movements in America.* New York: New York University Press.

"Just Listen to What the Panthers Are Saying"

Street, J. (2010). The Historiography of the Black Panther Party. *Journal of American Studies, 44*(2), 351–375. doi:10.1017/S0021875809991320

Terry, W. (1970, October 8). Bringing the War Home. *The Harvard Crimson.*

The Black Panther Party Research Project. (n.d.). Retrieved from http://web.stanford.edu/group/black-panthers/programs.shtml

The Democratic Party has abandoned Black People. (1976, July 24). *The Black Panther, 15*(15).

Umoja, A. O. (2006). The Black Liberation Army and the radical legacy of the Black Panther Party. In J. Jeffries (Ed.), *Black Power in the Belly of the Beast.* Urbana, IL: University of Illinois.

United Coalition against Racism. Fred Hampton's Murder. (1990, January 15). *The Michigan Daily.*

United Freedom Front. Communique No. 8: Bombing of IBM Offices, N.Y. (1984, March 19). *Freedom Archives.*

United States Congress. (1971, 92nd Congress, 1st Session). *House Committee on Internal Security, Hearings on the Black Panther Party, Gun-Barrel Politics: The Black Panther Party, 1966-1971.* Washington, DC: United States Government Printing office.

Wendt, S. (2006). The roots of Black Power? In P. Joshep (Ed.), *The Black Power Movement: Rethinking the Civil Rights-Black Power Era.* New York: Routledge.

Why Pigs Perpetuate Racism. (1969, April 27). *The Black Panther, 3*(1).

Williams, Y. (2006). White Tigers, Brown Berets, Black Panthers, Oh My! In J. Lazewor & Y. Williams (Eds.), *In Search of the Black Panther Party: New perspectives on a Revolutionary Movement.* London: Duke University Press.

Wilson, J. (2006). Invisible Cages: Racialized Politics and the Alliance between the Panthers and the Peace and Freedom Party. In *In Search of the Black Panther Party: New perspectives on a Revolutionary Movement.* London: Duke University Press.

ENDNOTES

[1]   "If the ruling class remains in power the proletarian working class will definitely be on the decline because they will be unemployables and therefore swell the ranks of the lumpen, who are the present unemployables. Every worker is in jeopardy. . . ."

[2]   "There's also an equal need for these Blacks to work in very close working coalition and close communication with their class brothers, regardless of color, regardless of whether you're for or against intermarriage, whether you want to live in Beverly Hills or Watts or Oakland or Washington, D.C., it doesn't make any difference. The need is for a constant maintenance of a correct class line" – Huey P. Newton.

3 "As far as our party is concerned, the Black Panther Party is an all-black party, because we feel as Malcolm X felt that there can be no black-white unity until there first is black unity" – Huey P. Newton.

4 The BPP also formed coalitions with dozens of other white organizations that had adopted an ideology, rhetoric and organizational structure that reflected Panther influence, such as the White Panther Party (Michigan), the John Brown Party (California), and Rising Up Angry (Chicago).

5 In 1968, and in a very controversial decision, the PFP nominated Eldridge Cleaver for president of the United States and PFP's Peggy Terry as his running mate. Newton, incarcerated at the time, run for a seat in Congress for California's 7th District; and Seale and Kathleen Cleaver run for Oakland 17th Assembly District and San Francisco 18th Assembly District respectively. The Cleaver-Terry ticket won just 0.4% (28,000) of the votes in the election that Richard Nixon won with 43% of the vote.

6 Number of BPP chapters in each state: California (15), Colorado (1), Connecticut (3), Delaware (1), Distrito de Columbia, Illinois (3), Indiana (1), Iowa (1), Louisiana (1), Maryland (1), Massachusetts (3), Michigan (2), Minnesota (1), Mississippi (1), Missouri (1), Nebraska (1), New Jersey (4), New York (3), New York City (7), North Carolina (1), Ohio (5), Oklahoma (1), Oregon (1), Pennsylvania (3), Tennessee (1), Texas (2), Washington (1) and Wisconsin (1).

7 Cuban support for the BPP was strong during the late 1960s. When Cleaver fled to Cuba as a political exile in late 1968, Cuba not only provided safe passage and security but promise to create a military training facility for the Party outside Havana. This was consistent with the active role Cuba had played supporting African American leaders throughout the sixties, when it sponsored the broadcast of Robert Williams radio program "Radio Free Dixie" and his newspaper, the Crusader, when it welcome Stokely Carmichael in 1967 for the Organization for Latin American Solidarity, as well as many other black intellectuals, and even Newton and Gwen Fontaine, who lived in Cuba until 1977.

8 "Criminal Anarchy" was describe as "the advocating or teaching, in any manner, in public or private, of the subversion, opposition or destruction of the government of the United States... by violence or other unlawful means".

9 In 1980, Ericka Huggins, Director of the OCS, started denouncing a number of attacks, and break-ins at the OCS and the Oakland Community Learning Center, another BPP program, stating that there was a conspiracy to destroy both Party educational programs. According to Huggins, there were forces "who oppose our school and our community services" and were using the Party's period of financial crisis "to increase their efforts against us".

This research was previously published in Historical and Future Global Impacts of Armed Groups and Social Movements; pages 98-127, copyright year 2020 by Information Science Reference (an imprint of IGI Global).

Chapter 42
Teaching Safety, Compliance, and Critical Thinking in Special Education Classrooms

Lilly B. Padía
https://orcid.org/0000-0001-6135-074X
New York University, USA

ABSTRACT

Special educators are tasked with teaching students with disabilities to understand and adhere to social norms for their own safety and acceptance in society. This chapter explores ways special educators can teach critical thinking alongside these social and cultural norms in order to support student agency. One special educator shares her experiences working with students with disabilities in urban public schools as she grapples with teaching her students what they need to know to be safe, while also teaching to challenge oppressive social and behavioral expectations.

INTRODUCTION

In my first year of teaching, a four-year-old student looked up at me in confusion and pointed to the sign on the bathroom door that had a picture of a person with two legs and the word "BOYS" written beneath it. "This is the boys' bathroom?" he asked me. "Yes," I replied. "I have to use this one?" "Yes," I replied. "Why?" he asked. I had an internal meltdown. I was fresh out of a program at New York University where I studied Social & Cultural Analysis. I spent three years running a women's empowerment group in a New York City high school. I facilitated workshops designed to understand gender as a spectrum and challenge the gender binary. I read David Valentine's Imagining Transgender (2007) in my coursework and grappled my way through a course on Disability and Sexuality in American Culture. Everything I stood for and believed said that this beautiful little boy should not have to confine himself to the box of boyhood to gain bathroom entry. And yet, as I stood there, it took all of three seconds to re-compose myself. As a first-year teacher responsible for the cultural understanding and societal movements of six kindergarten students diagnosed with Autism, I knew my response and my teachings would socialize

DOI: 10.4018/978-1-6684-4507-5.ch042

Copyright © 2022, IGI Global. Copying or distributing in print or electronic forms without written permission of IGI Global is prohibited.

this black-skinned Dominican boy who would grow up to be a black-skinned Dominican man who would not be safe walking into a bathroom labeled "WOMEN" or "GIRLS." Visions of police arresting him, tackling him, or worse flashed through my mind. When I opened my mouth to respond, it was to say, "Because that is what the sign says."

The purpose of this chapter is to examine how disability is constructed and understood as something negative in schools and to explore the possibilities for transforming this narrative of disability as a deficit. I offer vignettes of students and teachers grappling with what disability means that highlight the tensions that arise when teachers find themselves torn between feeling the need to teach strict adherence to rules in order to keep kids safe and teaching critical thinking to challenge these rules and norms. This chapter offers personal narratives from experiences teaching students diagnosed with Autism Spectrum Disorder, Intellectual Disabilities, and Emotional Behavioral Disorders in a public elementary school in an urban Northeast city. I offer insight rooted in classroom and school-wide practices and an analysis of how institutional special education policies and practices manifest in interpersonal interactions in the school system.

A twelve-year-old Black student on the Autism Spectrum entered my office last year. Tears were streaming down his face. He said, "I'm scared the police will hurt me." Another teacher, a White woman, responded in the moment by saying, "If you listen to the police and do what they tell you, they won't hurt you."

My experiences in the public schools in the Bronx have constantly affirmed the need to prepare educators to support students' development of critical consciousness and realization of agency. This teacher's response, while well-intentioned, missed the mark; it reinforced a narrative that every young person of color who is harmed by the police is harmed because they failed to comply with directions. It lacked a nuanced understanding that sometimes it is the color of a person's skin that makes them unsafe, and their actions cannot ensure their safety. This is a difficult and frightening conversation to have for many adults, let alone with children, but acknowledging these realities is an important component of preparing our students to be critically conscious, engaged, aware citizens. It is essential that educators understand how power dynamics operate. They must be trained in identifying the ways their own relationship to power may blind them from comprehending the realities students experience. If educators do not understand the way that power operates on ideological, institutional, interpersonal, and internalized levels, they cannot empower young people to understand and realize their own relationships to power—and how to simultaneously be critical consumers of societal norms and remain physically safe in a society that often renders their bodies dangerous. This is particularly pertinent for teachers in the field of special education; we must teach our students how to be safe and successful in the current culture of power (Delpit, 1995) while simultaneously challenging and reimagining said culture of power.

Rethinking disability calls into question everything we know about special education. As the disability rights movement and disability studies scholarship have flourished, the field of Disability studies in education, commonly referred to as DSE, has emerged (Ware, 2001). Disability Studies in Education offers new paradigms for understanding disability, which pose questions that challenge the very foundation of the field of special education. A growing body of literature is emerging to address this exciting new discourse, including how educators can attend to the intersections of Critical Race Theory and Disability Studies in special education (Connor, Ferri, & Subini, 2016). This chapter connects to the larger theme of the book as it explores the intersections of ability, race, class, gender, and sexuality in special education. My call for a paradigm shift that reimagines special education stems from my time spent working within the public special education system, both as a teacher and as a teacher development coach, my

Teaching Safety, Compliance, and Critical Thinking in Special Education Classrooms

experiences working with quick-start Teacher Preparation programs, like the NYC Teaching Fellows, my experiences teaching graduate students, and my background in social justice education.

The next time a first-year teacher is asked by her student with Autism why he can't use the girls' bathroom, I want her to have a community of educators, a canon of theories, and a plethora of tangible lesson and unit plans to draw on to guide her response. Special Education is in itself a project of justice, and not a separate entity to be infused with elements of equity and justice. Our project must create a sphere in special education that renders, "because that's what the sign says" an obsolete response.

POWER AND DISABILITY IN SCHOOLS

To understand special education, we must first understand how disability is defined within society and within the institution of schooling. Two models are useful in helping us understand disability: the medical model of disability and the social model of disability. The medical model of disability involves diagnosis and treatment or intervention. It understands disability as something within an individual that can be identified, diagnosed, treated, cured, and/or mediated through medications, therapies, surgeries, and other medical and psychological interventions. This model addresses disability as a deficit or deviance from a norm, and the interventions and treatments prescribed are intended to help restore or create an approximation of "normalcy" in the person with a disability. The social model of disability posits that individuals have impairments, but only become disabled once the environment is not set up to accommodate or include them (Shakespeare, 2006). The hallmark example is that a person with a physical impairment who requires a wheelchair only becomes disabled upon encountering a building she needs to enter that has stairs but no ramp or elevator; she is disabled by the environment, not by her impairment. Since Shakespeare's publication of the social model of disability, there have been several critiques, including those that claim there are natural barriers in the world that have nothing to do with a human-created environment, such as mountain ranges or oceans. While the social model has typically been applied to physical disability, examining how the school environment disables students can help shift the narrative in special education away from "fixing" students with disabilities towards revamping the school system to be more inclusive and responsive to all students.

Disability in schools, particularly in terms of special education, is by and large read through a medical model of disability. Students access disability-related services when they are diagnosed by a psychologist according to criteria set forth by the Diagnostic Statistical Manual (DSM). Reimagining special education from a social model of disability would depathologize individual students and generate collective responsibility for ensuring that the classroom is an inclusive, affirming place for students with all different physical, cognitive, and social/emotional developmental trajectories. Disability studies in education, critical special education, and DisCrit (disability studies and critical race theory in education) all offer transformative paradigm shifts for the field of special education. It is important to note that the school system is not solely responsible for this deficit model of thinking about disability. This chapter will explore how the notion of disability as inferior is maintained from multiple directions, from the institution of school itself to peer interactions to family beliefs.

"You didn't know that? It's 'cause you're 'Ed'."

"Ed" is an abbreviation my students in the South Bronx use to indicate Special Education status. This comment is reflective of the ways disability and special education have become coded as dirty, undesirable, inferior subclasses within the educational system. Special education functions like a dirty word in many schools today. In the same vein that the word "retarded" has been utilized in popular, casual discourse to indicate inferior mental status or capacity, "ed" has become a colloquialism employed by students to reify a hierarchy of cognitive superiority. This chapter will explore how special education and disability are defined, constructed, and maintained through the school system as negative deficits in need of institutional cure, intervention, and/or treatment. Special education constructs and reifies disability as a deficit through discourses and policies of "least restrictive environments/least intensive services." These policies position the ultimate goal for students with disabilities as conforming to and/or "attaining" academic and social skills and ways of being that mirror those of their nondisabled peers—at least in perception, if not in actuality.

Disability studies in education has expounded on these models to examine the ways in which sociocultural contexts shape the experience of disability (Baglieri, Valle, Connor, & Gallagher, 2011). The distinguishing feature between disability studies and DSE is an attention to the practical application and demands of schooling (Taylor, 2007). While disability studies traditionally centers around physical differences, disability studies in education moves us into the realm of cognitive and social-emotional ability and difference. It requires that we move away from thinking about deficits in our students and instead examine how our teaching practices can cultivate more inclusive, supportive spaces for all students (Naraian & Schlessinger, 2017). DSE does not place the onus of improving educational spaces solely on individual educators. It highlights the need to include disability as a category of diversity in culturally relevant curricula—which often address identities of race, class, gender, and language, but has yet to fully include disability identities—and holds that disability is to be studied as part of the civil rights movement and is a civil rights category (Connor, Gabel, Gallagher, & Morton, 2008).

Special education covers a wide range of disabilities and learning needs. Some students qualify for special education services through cognitive diagnoses that align with psychological disorders in the Diagnostic Statistical Manual (DSM). Other students are labeled with emotional behavioral disorders (EBD), some of which align to psychological disorders in the DSM and some of which are purely educational classifications that hold no merit outside of the school system. Because there is such a wide range of justification for and definition of disability in schools, there are also distinct narratives surrounding disability that emerge. For students diagnosed with emotional behavioral disorders, there is a pervasive narrative of "returning" to or "relearning" "normalcy," because emotional behavioral disorders are often associated with traumatic life experiences that produce what are read as maladaptive behaviors and unreasonable or irrational responses to experiences, situations, and interactions.

Juxtaposed with the narrative of "returning" to normalcy is the narrative of "becoming" or "developing" normalcy. For students determined to be born with cognitive differences, this is the standard narrative, which is predicated on the belief that an individual with a cognitive disability is born with an inherent deficit, and it is the school's responsibility to help the student "overcome" that deficit in order to become more "normal" and function in a way that mirrors neurotypical functioning (Silberman, 2015)—in school and society. Interventions like those in special education seek to transform a person into a new and different standard of being and behaving that is considered "normal." Clare (2017) complicates the notions of becoming normal and returning to normalcy by highlighting that, for many people who were born with disabilities, the proposed desired state of normalcy never existed. Instead, what happens is an imagined, hegemonic state of normalcy. He says,

Teaching Safety, Compliance, and Critical Thinking in Special Education Classrooms

But for some of us, even if we accept disability as damage to individual body-minds, these tenets quickly become tangled, because an original nondisabled state of being doesn't exist. How would I, or the medical-industrial complex, go about restoring my body-mind? ...it arises from an imagination of what I should be like, from some definition of normal and natural (p. 15).

A hierarchy of disability is created, wherein students with emotional disorders are read as more cognitively capable than students with cognitive disorders—both by the school system and amongst themselves. In the school I worked at in the Bronx, students with emotional behavioral disorders would typically either assume responsibility for students with cognitive disabilities, performing tasks like holding their hands to help them onto the bus, or would attempt to distance themselves from those with cognitive disabilities, going so far as to refuse to participate in a yearbook project because they "don't want to be in a yearbook with THOSE kids." This scenario demonstrates the complexities of conflating all disabilities, as well as the ways hierarchy of ability become reified as students and their families attempt to balk the negative perceptions associated with disability. Even within disability pride and disability rights activism groups there is discord; some people with physical disabilities prefer to distinguish themselves from people with intellectual and cognitive disabilities because they do not want their physical impairments to be associated with mental inferiority.

We can see how a web of power operates through interpersonal interactions that occur between parents and students, parents and the school system, amongst students, and between educators and students. When parents who do not want their students to be marked as "different" refuse to consent to psychological evaluation—which cannot legally occur in schools without parental consent—disability is upheld as something undesirable and inferior. Parents may not trust the school system due to perceptions of the school as racist, classist, and discriminating based on language; their own cultural factors may impact their suspicions of a school system that suggests that their child has a disability. The message is encoded thus: a suggestion of disability is a suggestion of defect. We cannot read disability as detached from other marginalized identities; particularly in the school system, the intersection of race, gender, sexuality, class, and ability manifest in differential teacher expectations, student tracking, and segregated public schools, to name a few. Power traverses through student comments about special education (use of the word "retarded") to belittle, shame, or dismiss the "other" and serves to reinforce the notion of disability as deficit and defect.

One of the key components of DisCrit and critical special education is an attention to intersectionality (Crenshaw, 1991). Ability cannot be separated from race, class, sexuality, gender, language, and other elements of identity—particularly in the school system. The anecdotes in this chapter are born from a place of grappling with intersectionality in a system that likes to compartmentalize identity and "issues" in order to address them (read: fix them and/or render them more "normal").

A framework that I find particularly helpful to understanding all forms of oppression, but particularly disability, is the "Four I's of Oppression" (Grassroots Institute for Fundraising Training, 2012). The Four I's of Oppression are: Ideological, Institutional, Interpersonal, and Internalized. Ideological oppression involves widespread thoughts, ideas, and beliefs that justify and uphold the oppression in question. Institutional oppression involves the policies, practices, and structures that legally prescribe and maintain the oppression in question. Interpersonal oppression is typically the easiest to identify, because it involves person-to-person interactions of discrimination that demonstrate the oppression in question. Internalized oppression defines the way that oppressed people come to believe oppressive ideological ideas about themselves. Table 1 and Table 2, offer examples that I created of how the Four

I's of Oppression (Grassroots Institute for Fundraising Training, 2012) function in the school system to help demonstrate its utility as a framework.

Using the Four I's of Oppression to understand special education is useful; power functions through special education on each of the four levels and identifying the different levels can help us determine where and how to intervene to transform education to make it liberatory and affirming for all students.

Table 1. The 4 I's of English-only education in the United States

Issue	English-only education in the United States
Ideological	The ideologically oppressive element of English-only education is the notion that English is superior to all other languages. The belief that English is the best and only language that should be used in the United States, and that if you want to be American you need to learn English, underpins the concept of English-only education.
Institutional	Policies, practices, and laws that reify the supremacy of English, such as state exams that are only offered in English, college applications only being accepted in English, schools that teach limited content to English as a New Language students because of the belief that until they learn English, they are neither ready nor deserving of rigorous academic content, are all institutionally oppressive aspects of English-only education.
Interpersonal	When monolingual English-speaking students tell other students to "go back to [insert home country here]. This is America, we speak English here," they are demonstrating an interpersonally oppressive element of the notion of English-only [education].
Internalized	When an English learner student believes that they are less intelligent than their monolingual English-speaking peers because they do not have a full grasp on the English language, they have internalized the belief that English is the superior language and their worth is dependent on their relationship to English.

Table 2. The 4 I's of disability as inferior in education

Issue	Disability as inferior in education
Ideological	The belief that disability is undesirable and inferior is the foundation of this form of oppression. Students are considered successful when they either "pass" as "normal"/nondisabled or "overcome" their disability to function just like their nondisabled peers within the school system. This belief adheres to a medical model of disability that positions the individual student as deficient and needing to be fixed, rather than focusing on how to change the school environment to be more inclusive and supportive of all students.
Institutional	Policies, practices, and laws that reify the supremacy of nondisabled students and reinforce the ideologically oppressive notion that there is something wrong with disability make up this category. The policy of moving students towards "less restrictive environments" and "less intensive services" and the mainstreaming of students who demonstrate behaviors and academic markers understood as developmentally "normal," as measured against their nondisabled peers are one example. The segregation of students with disabilities into self-contained classes that focus solely on vocational training as a post-school option, rather than providing information about college as well as vocational jobs, is a practice that reinforces the notion that students with disabilities are only capable of certain things. (The push for college as the ultimate goal for students in general education and the suggested lower value of vocational jobs is a connected problem.)
Interpersonal	When students mock other students by calling them "ed" or "special ed," this is an example of peers reinforcing the inferiority of disability. When parents or guardians refuse psychological evaluation for their child who might need services because "there's nothing wrong with my kid," this upholds the ideologically oppressive message that there is something wrong with having a disability diagnosis.
Internalized	When a student with a disability believes that they are less intelligent, less cool, and less capable than their nondisabled peers, they have internalized the ideologically oppressive belief that having a disability makes you inferior to nondisabled people.

Teaching Safety, Compliance, and Critical Thinking in Special Education Classrooms

MAIN FOCUS OF THE CHAPTER

Teaching for Safety and Liberation: Compliance vs. Critical Thinking in Special Education Pedagogy

The opening example of my student Eduardo, a four-year-old dark-skinned boy with Autism who wanted to know why he couldn't use the girls' bathroom, began me on my journey of thinking critically about special education. My quest as a teacher became centered around honing my skills to answer the following question: How do I teach my students the skills they need to be physically safe in a world that believes they are dangerous, while simultaneously teaching them those beliefs are wrong? I came into teaching with grand thoughts of teaching histories of people that don't show up in textbooks, of discussing how power operates and how we can disrupt it. What I found was beautiful, curious, energetic, engaged young people who had difficulty with the concept of "you" and "me," who did not sit in their seats for more than two minutes at a time, who could only sometimes follow single-step directions, and even then it was with the use of picture symbols of photographs for support. I had to rewire my understanding of teaching—and of social justice.

During my first two years of teaching, I threw myself into honing my pedagogy. The learning curve was steep. I had a background in social justice education, housing rights organizing, youth empowerment work, and racial justice education, but special education was foreign to me. I committed myself to learning different communication systems, from PECS (Picture Exchange Communication Systems) to Augmentative & Assistive Communication Devices (AAC devices), basic sign language, how to make my classroom responsive to different sensory needs, how to differentiate my classroom materials, and how to tap into students' motivations. Velcro and laminating paper became my new best friends; I laminated and velcroed words and images to all my books to make them interactive and give students opportunities to respond. I worked with the speech teachers and school counselors to make communication systems with students' parents and families who were also struggling with behaviors at home.

One student, Mateo, would cry until he had difficulty breathing. He spoke fewer than 20 words when he began with us in September. The first time we sat down with his mom, she broke down crying, explaining that she felt it must have been something that she did to cause his autism (he had a twin brother in general education). He would hit his siblings and get easily agitated. She was beside herself. We made a communication log that showed his behavior at school and added a column for home; if he did well at home, he would get five minutes of choice time during breakfast at school. If he did well at school, Mom would give five minutes of play time as soon as he got home from school.

My notions of creating a social justice curriculum highlighting multiple histories and structures of power classroom quickly melted away. I spent those first couple of years dedicating myself to learning how to communicate with and nurture the learning of my young students on the Autism spectrum. But something did not sit right with me. My coworkers were some of the biggest-hearted, most compassionate people I had ever met. So why did I feel like our work was so limited? I felt like we were teaching students to prescribe to behaviors understood as "normal," and while that was important for their safety, it felt paternalistic. In teaching students that there was a correct way to behave in society, we were removing their agency. Students are often told not to flap their hands or make certain noises because it is not seen as "normal." Heilker and Yergeau describe "autism as a rhetoric" that complicates and challenges our notions of socially accepted communication (2011). I began to realize that simply teaching prescription to socially acceptable norms, while it helped keep students safe to a certain degree, was not socially just.

I decided to find social justice education spaces to help me pick up where I had left off. I attended events run by a collective of self-proclaimed radical educators. But try as I may, I could not seem to find spaces that attended to my students. The extent of the overlapping conversation on social justice pedagogy and special education seemed to be the overdiagnosis and overpathologization of Black and/ or Latinx students into special education. The conversation was about special education's role in the school-to-prison pipeline for students of color. And while this is a pressing issue, this dialogue served to do two things: 1) marginalize Black and/or Latinx students with real and significant cognitive and psychological disabilities, and 2) reaffirm disability as something negative, lesser, and undesirable. This chapter looks at my personal experiences teaching and learning from students with disabilities in order to reimagine special education as a program that could be more socially just and culturally responsive.

When Teaching Compliance Is Not Enough

Our students do not operate in a silo just because they have a disability. They watch the news, they hear and comprehend conversations being had around them, and they have questions.

As mentioned in the opening of this chapter, last year a distraught teacher brought one of her students, a twelve-year-old black boy diagnosed with Autism Spectrum Disorder, into my office. He had tears pouring down his cheeks.

"Tell Ms. Padía why you're scared, Christopher," she said. He looked up at me with tears still in his eyes. "I'm afraid the police will shoot me."

His teacher told me that another teacher had been in the room when he first made the statement and had immediately told him not to be afraid—that if he followed the directions the police gave him, he would be safe.

I can understand the urge to quell a student's fears, but I am concerned that the educator in question either did not believe the student could comprehend the complexities of reality, or that she herself genuinely believed what she told him to be true. When we sugarcoat reality for our students with disabilities, we are actually making life less safe for them. Particularly for our Black and/or Latinx students with disabilities, their bodies will be read as dangerous in a society that has a deep fear of black and brown bodies.

I was teaching fifth grade when Tamir Rice, an eleven-year-old Black boy, was shot and killed by a white police officer in Cleveland, Ohio, for playing in a park with a toy gun that was mistaken by the officer for a real weapon. During Morning Meeting one day in November of 2014, a student shared that he felt scared because he saw on television that a boy had been killed in a park. I had not been prepared during my teacher training to talk about how to navigate racism, ableism, physical danger, and interactions with law enforcement, yet here I was, the teacher of a class of eight fifth graders with Autism, all of whom were Black and/or Latinx, six of whom were boys, about things they could do to be safer in the world—and situations that could be dangerous for them, despite any and every action they could take to try to be safe. A student wrote on his Do Now that morning, "We get love. No guns. We are happy. A good day." My students were clearly aware of the dangers facing them in the world.

Teaching Safety, Compliance, and Critical Thinking in Special Education Classrooms

Because of my background in social justice education, I was able to facilitate these conversations, though I am certain I fumbled my way through at times, Through my community organizing and youth empowerment work, I had received training to unpack and examine my own relationship to power, privilege, and oppression, as well as how to facilitate that process for others. Had I not experienced this training, I would have been completely lost when these topics came up with my students. I became deeply concerned with the lack of attention to systems of power and oppression in special education discourse. From special education teacher training to professional development to curricular choices, these conversations are crucial. While the perspective often seems to be that students with developmental disabilities or delays are not ready for or able to handle such complex, intense conversations, it is precisely because of their cognitive and/or psychological disabilities that these conversations must take place; it is literally a matter of life and death.

Special education, particularly for students with significant disabilities, must address the implications of the material and information that is being taught on the physical safety of the students. While teaching students of color with disabilities that they should not play with toy guns in public does nothing to transform or liberate society from oppressive, racist notions, it does the work of addressing the urgency and immediacy of their physical wellbeing. The larger projects of dismantling white supremacy, unlearning racial bias, developing and/or increasing awareness around manifestations of and responses to different disabilities, must occur. In the meantime, we have a responsibility to our students to teach them about the harsher realities of the world in order to help them be as safe as possible. Survival is not the end goal and is certainly not conflatable with liberation, but in the immediate, existence is resistance.

Teaching Politeness for Safety: How Polite Qualifiers Support Student Voice in an Adultist, Ableist World

Helping my students navigate the world in the safest way possible means walking a line between prescribing to norms of power and subverting them. One strategy for students to get their needs heard and met by adults is to use what I call "polite qualifier" words when communicating their needs. Brown and Levinson's Theory of Politeness highlights strategies that employ politeness to acquire desired results (1987). Polite words are used to help secure one's wants or needs. Saying, "No, thank you," tends to be heard much more calmly and positively than a straight "No." "May I use the bathroom, please?" is more likely to elicit the desired affirmative response than, "I need to use the bathroom." This is not to say that it is correct that students must ask for permission or use these polite qualifiers, but teaching them to traffic in what is read as respectful discourse can help them obtain what they need from adults and gate-keepers of power.

I had a kindergarten student in one of my classes whom all the adults in the building seemed to want to hug. They would always ask him for a hug or open their arms when they saw him in the hallway. Whether because of his Autism or because he simply did not want to hug them, he got extremely agitated whenever anyone would try to hug him. He would scream, "No!! Don't touch me! Get away!" whenever anyone would try to embrace him. The adults would get offended, tell him to calm down, to lower his voice, to not use such a tone with grown-ups. He was well within his rights; no one should be touched if they do not consent. There is a larger conversation that must occur around teaching affirmative consent to both students and teachers. In the immediate moment, though, I recognized that teaching him the polite qualifier of "Thank you," to turn his screaming into a "No, thank you," would help him communicate and receive the results he desired from the communication. And it worked. We practiced saying, "No,

799

thank you. I don't like hugs," when people asked him for a hug. The responses were overwhelmingly positive. "Ay, bendito," "You're so precious," and other exclamations of adoration followed his polite communication. The polite qualifier of "thank you" transformed a situation that had been hostile for my student into one in which he was physically safe and his needs and wants were heard and honored.

Toya would get extremely agitated and throw the nearest item in reach at someone anytime they said, "shh." Something about that sound really set her off and upset her. The first couple of weeks that she was in my class, I dodged several pencils that came flying at my head. The class teaching assistant, who was fortunate enough to have quick reflexes, found himself barely making it out of the path of a stapler that she sent hurling his way. We worked together to develop a response to someone who said "shh" that did not entail flinging an object at their head. She began to respond with, "Excuse me? I don't like the sound "shh." It makes me upset. Could you please not say it?" The first few times this occurred, she had tears pouring down her face as she struggled to get the sentences out. Eventually, she became accustomed to using her words instead of becoming physically agitated when she heard the sound. While some of my colleagues disagreed with my approach and argued that she needed to get used to the sound, because "shh" is something she may encounter in the world outside the school building, using qualifiers to explain her aversion to the sound helped her get her needs met and kept everyone physically safe. If she heard the sound, "shh" in the outside world, hopefully she would be able to verbally explain her discomfort instead of throwing an item at the person making the sound. This was not just for the other person's safety; a stranger might not be aware that she has Autism and might respond to her physical response with more physical aggression. This reaction could be extremely dangerous for her. Using polite qualifiers helped her communicate herself in terms that people understood, respected, and honored.

This is not the ultimate goal. Teaching our students to use polite qualifiers to keep them safe in a system of power that dehumanizes and devalues them is certainly not teaching towards a liberatory society. It is a project in social justice, though, because it balances the tensions of helping our students with significant disabilities employ their agency as much as possible in an oppressive culture of power while we work to transform said culture.

Disrupting "Normalcy": Fixing the System vs. Fixing Individual Students

Louis Althusser's assertion that the School is an Ideological State Apparatus (1977) positions the education system as a dominant, top-down force that reinforces set social hierarchies. Special education is designed to help students emulate the actions, behaviors, and thought patterns of neurotypical students. This archetypal student is an ideal that the school system trains young people to adhere to, internalizing and reproducing messages that are beneficial to the maintenance of capitalism and a given system of dominance that benefits the State.

Students with disabilities graduate from high school and complete undergraduate college degrees at lower rates than their nondisabled peers (Bureau of Labor Statistics, 2015). These discrepancies in typical markers of achievement between special education students and general education students, such as high-school graduation and completion of a college degree, point to the strength of School as an Ideological State Apparatus. In a medical model of disability, which is most commonly found in schools, lower performance and achievement levels of students with disabilities might be attributed to deficits within the individual students with disabilities. This medical model that faults and blames students with disabilities for this difference in performance is an element that perpetuates the status quo. A social model of disability would challenge these dynamics by shining a light on the institution of school, on its

Teaching Safety, Compliance, and Critical Thinking in Special Education Classrooms

structures and pedagogical approaches for special education, in order to examine how the school system and teaching practices can be adapted to support success of all students. Special education programs provide students with work training, rather than college preparation (Trainor, 2017). Students with significant disabilities were often denied access to schooling prior to the first iteration of IDEA in 1975, and while IDEA mandates that schools allocate resources for educating all students with disabilities, significant improvement in achievement for students with disabilities has not been demonstrated to scale (Council for Exceptional Children, 2015). While it is important to acknowledge that a restrictive definition of "success" that devalues certain labor in favor of higher education is highly problematic, it is also important to acknowledge that we live in a society that places hierarchical value on higher education. When certain students—in this case students in special education—are presumed unqualified and unfit for continued education, the school system reinforces a system of dominance that elevates some students by providing them with options and limits others by offering them minimal options.

As students become aware of their disability diagnosis, they become part of and become active agents in a new identity of "students with disabilities." Whether they are internalizing and absorbing messages of shame about disability from their peers and an institutional structure informed by a deficit framework or are developing agency, self-advocacy skills, and a sense of pride in their full identity, many young people undergo a process of discovering and realizing a new sense of self once they are aware of their disability diagnosis.

Placing disability status in school in conversation with student self-concept might help us understand how special education status and disability classification currently function as oppressed identities within the education system. Can we read disability status through a lens of self-concept, wherein students are aware of their marked difference, whether due to explicit information about their diagnostic label or derogatory comments from peers, and oftentimes, particularly in inclusive settings, spend their time "passing" as neurotypical? If we understand special education status as a contributing factor to a new sense of self, the question of a student's relationship to disability comes into play. The way that language is used to discuss disability is a point of contention in many spaces. Some advocate for "person-first language," calling for speaking about a person with a disability, to highlight that the person is a whole person and the disability is one facet of their personhood. Others, particularly in the disability pride movement, argue that their disability is a central part of their identity and cannot be extracted, and that there is pride in their disabled identity. Therefore, they prefer to be referred to as disabled people, claiming the term and identity of disability may be one way that individuals attempt to assert their agency in a system that repeatedly denies their personhood and agency. The way young people are treated and assigned meaning within the school system may be dependent on the degree to which their disability is perceived and/or obvious to others (Clare, 2017). Conceptualizing identity and agency for students in special education begs the following question: How does a perceived, visible disability, as opposed to an invisible one, impact a student's consciousness and sense of self?

I was teaching a class of fourth graders diagnosed with Autism Spectrum Disorder several years ago. I was in the middle of a lesson on division. We watched a Brainpop video (Brainpop is an educational website that houses cartoon videos explaining different academic concepts in simple terms through the characters of a robot and a boy). One student, Vincent, began laughing very loudly at the video in what sounded like a forced laugh and slapping his knee in a seemingly exaggerated way. When I asked him to please laugh a little more quietly, he responded "I can't help it. I have Autism." He had learned that people would have different—and oftentimes "lower"—expectations of him because of his diagnosis and was able to speak to those expectations. In a way, he was advocating for himself, challenging the notion

801

that he needed to prescribe to normative standards of behavior and comportment. He likely could have controlled his volume, especially given his metacognitive awareness, but he chose to communicate in a way that felt most comfortable for him and used his disability to push back against the expectations of conformity to "normalcy" that the school system imposed on him.

The hierarchy that emerges within the category of "students with disabilities" between emotional and cognitive disorders is complicated by this notion of perceived dis/ability. Extending the notion beyond the walls of the school building brings a host of new—and often opposing—realities; students with emotional behavioral disorders are often read as cognitively capable, and therefore individually responsible and culpable for all actions, regardless of struggles they may have due to their emotional disability, such as with impulse control or emotional regulation. This factors into what is commonly referred to as the "school-to-prison pipeline," wherein students are enabled by the school system to engage in behaviors, such as physical outbursts or refusal to follow directions, that are accepted within the school environment as manifestations of disorder or disability, but are criminalized in public spaces. The discord between the school system's allowance for behaviors deemed permissible in school and the criminal justice system's punishment for the same behaviors can be read as a manifestation of School as an Ideological State Apparatus (Althusser, 1977). The school system, in this instance, is essentially setting young people up for a relationship with law enforcement and the carceral system that is precarious at best and doomed at worst. While special education typically serves as a project to attempt to help students return to normalcy or become more normal, in this case, rather than attempting to teach students "normal" and expected codes of conduct, students with emotional behavioral disorders are read as inherently deficient and therefore incapable of "normal" behavior. In this example, the school system's deficit orientation towards disability leads to differential expectations for students labeled with disabilities, which creates a literal physical threat to and danger for students.

The summer after my first year of teaching, I was assigned to teach a class of fourth and fifth graders diagnosed with Emotional Behavioral Disorders (EBD). My class during the school year had been kindergarten students with Autism, so this was a completely new and different educational environment for me. One of the difficulties of being a special education teacher is the wide array of diagnoses and learning differences that students have. My degree in teaching with a focus on students with disabilities officially made me qualified to teach students diagnosed with Autism, Intellectual Disabilities, Multiple Disabilities, Emotional Behavioral Disorders, Other Health Impairments, and other disabilities. In practice, I was completely unprepared to teach most (if not all) of these students. Still, I was excited about the opportunity to teach a different group of students and develop my pedagogy. I walked into a classroom of students who were extremely bright, engaged, thoughtful, excited and eager learners, and who also became agitated and expressed their frustration in physical ways. Furniture and fists got thrown in the classroom almost daily. On one particularly intense day, an eleven-year-old boy picked up a table and hurled it across the room, slamming it into the wall. I snapped.

"These rules are not in place just to control you. These rules are here because there are similar rules outside of these walls. If you throw something when you get angry outside of school, you can get shot or arrested or both. It is okay to be upset. It is okay to express your frustration. But doing that with physical aggression is only going to get you hurt in the long run. If you continue to react like this when you get frustrated, you could end up in prison or dead."

Everyone froze. They stared at me. The student who had thrown the table was breathing heavily. Finally, he spoke.

Teaching Safety, Compliance, and Critical Thinking in Special Education Classrooms

"Okay, miss. I'm sorry."

He sat down in his seat and two other students jumped up to return the table to its proper place. My one-minute speech did not alleviate the cycles of trauma and systemic oppression in their lives. It did, however, seem to offer a candor they had not received from teachers before. For a couple of hours, our classroom operated with the quiet hum of calm engagement and joy. The next day, two sets of students had to talk to the counselor because they got into physical altercations. My diatribe was a start, but needed to be accompanied with a curriculum about systems of power and how to disrupt them, social-emotional curriculum that affirmed students' emotions and experiences while teaching socially accepted forms of expression, and an ongoing dialogue that provided students with the space to explore their frustrations and learn different coping strategies.

Resistance is a critical component of the way in which power functions (Foucault, 1990). Disability studies in education presents the possibility of special education as a liberatory tool to transform the system of schooling. Currently, it seems that special education serves to reify the inequities that already exist and to reproduce them in a way that is cloaked in access and equality (Trainor, 2017). Althusser discusses individual teachers who are committed to liberation and try to challenge the oppressive nature of schooling, but for him this struggle is futile, as the Ideological State Apparatus is so powerful (1977). Foucault's assertion that people can resist power to redefine and redistribute its parameters and forces presents a more hopeful framework for reimagining what special education could look like. For example, disproportionality and the overdiagnosis and overpathologization of black and brown students into special education is a real issue that many researchers and scholars have highlighted in recent years (Harry & Klinger, 2014). The disproportionality argument is at odds with a disability studies framework because it positions special education and the need for it as something inferior and negative, implying that being in special education is something undesirable. A paradigm shift that utilizes both a Foucaultian notion of resistance and a disability studies framework would suggest that there is nothing value-negative about disability (Barnes, 2016).

SOLUTIONS AND RECOMMENDATIONS

Developing Critical Consumers: Nurturing Both Understanding and Critique of Societally Accepted Concepts

The year I taught a comprehensive Christopher Columbus unit to my fifth graders was a turning point I will never forget. I taught my students that Christopher Columbus did not discover the Americas because people were already living there, that Leif Erikson and the Vikings were actually the first people of European descent to land in the Americas, and that the arrival of Columbus and his men to this land led to destruction, death, and colonization. We read accounts from different sources and students were introduced to the creation of Columbus Day as a national holiday. We explored the rationale that Columbus was a hero and that he was a villain and then students decided on and constructed their own stance. All my students arrived at the conclusion that Columbus was more a villain than a hero (except for one student, whose name also happened to be Christopher. The rationale he gave for Columbus being a hero was "He is amazing; his name is Christopher").

803

I developed my pedagogical stance as I taught:

1. Students must be exposed to, be able to identify, and be able to explain the societally accepted notion (i.e. Christopher Columbus discovered America, thus we celebrate him on Columbus Day).
2. Students must be presented with multiple sources and varying perspectives on the notion (i.e. accounts presenting Columbus as a great explorer, accounts presenting Columbus as a facilitator of genocide, accounts celebrating his contribution to the world's interconnectedness, accounts explaining his contribution to European colonization of indigenous peoples).
3. Students must be provided the opportunity to explore and construct their own opinions and thoughts using the sources they have read.
4. What I failed to teach my students was what might happen to them if they disagreed with the societally accepted norm. My class aide, who stayed with the students during my prep periods when other teachers taught the class, pulled me to the side one day after the students had been in Social Studies class with another teacher.

"I feel bad for the kids," he said. "Ms. Rodriguez was so frustrated with them today."

"Why? What happened?" I asked.

"Well, she taught them that Christopher Columbus discovered America. And she kept asking them, 'Who discovered America?' and getting upset when they didn't respond 'Christopher Columbus.' But you've been teaching them that he did not discover America. So they were confused."

I felt awful. Here I was, thinking I was doing this radical thing, teaching my students with significant disabilities to think critically about Christopher Columbus. What I had neglected to do was prepare them for the backlash if and when their critical thinking clashed with the hegemonic way of viewing the world. I realized that my pedagogical approach needed a final step:

5. Students must be able to put their own opinion(s) in conversation with the societally accepted notion(s).

Teaching students to critique a social norm has to follow the same sort of backwards design that we as educators are taught to use for lesson plans or unit plans, a philosophy that you plan a unit or lesson by beginning with the end goal and planning backwards from that point. If we are to lead students to a desired outcome of thinking critically, we must ensure that they have all the skills, tools, and background information necessary to complete the task. Teaching critical thinking, particularly for students with significant disabilities, entails first teaching an understanding of exactly what the social norm is. It is tempting, particularly for someone who is social justice minded, to teach students what we believe to be the true history and viewpoint—which oftentimes is different from the widely understood history and viewpoint. While this may feel like the just thing to do, for our students with significant disabilities, neglecting to also teach them the socially accepted norm(s) is actually an act of injustice. As I experienced in my Christopher Columbus example, I needed to teach my students an understanding of the social norms of Columbus in order for them to be active participants in a critical discourse.

FUTURE DIRECTIONS

Educational researchers need to center on how the school system sets expectations for students (whether the expectations be due to race, socioeconomic status, ability, the intersections of multiple identities, etc.). Studies show that teachers hold lower expectations regarding academic success and performance for students with disabilities (Cook, 2001), so the overdiagnosis of black and brown students into special education indicates yet another excuse for lowering expectations for students of color—and lowering accountability for teachers to educate students of color—and students with disabilities—with a rigorous, high quality education. A reimagining of special education and disability is interwoven with a transformation of expectations for all students. An intersectional understanding of deficit theory in education (Connor, Ferri, Annamama, 2016) will acknowledge the ways students of color, students who speak languages other than English, students with disabilities, queer students, and poor students get conflated and assigned similar and interlocking positions of inferiority. Under a medical model of disability and diagnosis, students who are positioned as non-normative are constantly required to adhere to the norms set forth by the school system in order to be acknowledged as fully human. Any deviance from the "norm" is read as defiance, incompetence, or inability, and blame is assigned to individual students. While existing research highlights the implications of criminalizing these deviations, we need to continue to build alternatives that affirm, sustain, and develop students' strengths and differences.

While students are being punished and blamed for deviance from a "norm," the school system actively marks students with disabilities as different through a process of infantilization. This can be seen in the example of sex education; students in special education typically do not receive the same (often times state-mandated) sexual education curriculum as their general education peers. Students are stripped of their agency and neither recognized nor treated according to their age. Because students may have cognitive disabilities that impact their cognitive development, meaning they sometimes do not follow what is understood to be a "normal" development trajectory, they are read as younger than their age and thus incapable of accessing and/or handling the same content and responsibilities as their peers in their same age group. This phenomenon is particularly salient when it comes to educational content that is deemed both necessary and highly sensitive as students age, such as sex education. Special education students in self-contained classes often do not receive sexual education, even when it is mandated for general education students in the same age group/grade (McDaniels & Fleming, 2016). Future research and curriculum development should address this dynamic of infantilization and exclusion from curricula that provide vital information for developing independence and agency.

Special education currently serves to reify and reproduce an understanding of disability as a deficit. It is intended to be an equalizing tool contributing to equity and justice, certainly in terms of the laws by which it is driven (Council for Exceptional Children, 2015). As Althusser asserts, there are certainly teachers engaged in the project of challenging the status quo (1977), particularly special education teachers who are committed to equity for all students. As educational research and pedagogical knowledge continue to grow, an integration of disability studies and special education will be instrumental in transforming the schooling system into one that truly honors, affirms, and values all expressions and abilities. Development of curriculum that explores how to convey age-appropriate topics and content to students, rather than assuming the content is too advanced or too mature for students with disabilities, is a crucial element of this future research.

CONCLUSION

"We have so much work to do." This is a phrase that I hear repeatedly with regard to special education, from the mouths of school staff to parents of students to community activists. There is so much work to do. From shifting the narrative away from disability as deficit and towards difference as asset to including students and families in the dialogue to centering social justice pedagogy conversations around dis/ability, we have so much work to do. We are in a moment where culturally responsive teaching (Ladson-Billings, 1995) is recognized as essential for effective pedagogy. Ability is currently a missing piece of the puzzle. Bringing conversations about dis/ability into curricular discourse on equity will ensure that all educators, students, and families are working together towards empowerment, agency, and growth for all our young people.

This chapter has highlighted my experiences as a special educator in the Bronx working with students with a range of disability diagnoses. The emerging narrative speaks to the inextricable links between dis/ability and other identities. Special education does not and cannot operate in a silo; issues of race, class, language, gender, and others interact with disability to produce unique and important realities for our students. It is our job as educators to teach students skills that function on multiple levels: to keep them safe in a society that neither understands nor accommodates disability, and to teach them to be critical consumers of the norms, ideals, and messages put forth by society. Positioning disability as difference, and not as deficit, is crucial in ensuring pedagogical practices that serve to affirm, support, develop, and liberate all students. It's time to get to work.

REFERENCES

Althusser, L. (1977). Ideology and Ideological State Apparatuses (Notes towards an Investigation). In *Lenin and Philosophy and Other Essays* (2nd ed.; pp. 123–173). London: New Left Review Editions.

Baglieri, S., Valle, J. W., Connor, D. J., & Gallagher, D. J. (2011). Disability Studies in Education. *Remedial and Special Education*, *32*(4), 267–278. doi:10.1177/0741932510362200

Barnes, E. (2016). *The Minority Body: A theory of disability*. Oxford Univ Press. doi:10.1093/acprof:oso/9780198732587.001.0001

Bourdieu, P. (1977). Structures and the Habitus. In *Outline of a Theory of Practice* (pp. 72–87). Cambridge, UK: Cambridge University Press. doi:10.1017/CBO9780511812507.004

Bureau of Labor Statistics. (2015). *People with a disability less likely to have completed a bachelor's degree*. United States Department of Labor.

Clare, E. (2017). *Brilliant imperfection: Grappling with cure*. Durham, NC: Duke University Press. doi:10.1215/9780822373520

Connor, D. (2013). Who "Owns" Dis/ability? The Cultural Work of Critical Special Educators as Insider–Outsiders. *Theory and Research in Social Education*, *41*(4), 494–513. doi:10.1080/00933104.2013.838741

Connor, D. J., Ferri, B. A., & Annamma, S. A. (2016). *DisCrit: Disability studies and critical race theory in education*. New York: Teachers College Press, Teachers College, Columbia University.

Connor, G., Gabel, S. L., Gallagher, D. J., & Morton, M. (2008, September-November). Disability studies and inclusive education: Implications for theory, research, and practice. *International Journal of Inclusive Education*, *12*(5-6), 441–457. doi:10.1080/13603110802377482

Cook, B. G. (2001). A Comparison of Teachers Attitudes Toward Their Included Students with Mild and Severe Disabilities. *The Journal of Special Education*, *34*(4), 203–213. doi:10.1177/002246690103400403

Council for Exceptional Children. (2015). *Federal outlook for exceptional children: Fiscal year 2015*. Washington, DC: Council for Exceptional Children.

Crenshaw, K. (1991). Mapping the Margins: Intersectionality, Identity Politics, and Violence against Women of Color. *Stanford Law Review*, *43*(6), 1241. doi:10.2307/1229039

Ferri, B., & Connor, D. (2005). *Tools of exclusion: Race, disability, and (re)segregated education*. New York: Teachers College Record.

Foucault, M. (1990). The history of sexuality: Vol. 1. *An introduction*. New York: Random House.

Grassroots Institute for Fundraising Training. (2012). *Four I's of Oppression*. Retrieved from http://www.grassrootsfundraising.org/wp-content/uploads/2012/10/THE-FOUR-IS-OF-OPPRESSION-1.pdf

Harry, B., & Klingner, J. K. (2014). *Why are so many minority students in special education?: Understanding race & disability in schools*. New York: Teachers College Press.

Heilker, P., & Yergeau, M. (2011). Autism and Rhetoric. *College English*, *73*(5), 485–497. Retrieved from http://www.jstor.org.proxy.library.nyu.edu/stable/23052337

Ladson-Billings, G. (1995). Toward a Theory of Culturally Relevant Pedagogy. *American Educational Research Journal*, *32*(3), 465–491. doi:10.3102/00028312032003465

McDaniels, B., & Fleming, A. (2016). Sexuality Education and Intellectual Disability: Time to Address the Challenge. *Sexuality and Disability*, *34*(2), 1–11. doi:10.100711195-016-9427-y

Shakespeare, T., & Davis, L. J. (2017). The social model of disability. In The disability studies reader. New York, NY: Routledge.

Silberman, S. (2015). *NeuroTribes*. New York: Avery.

Swain, J., & French, S. (2000). Towards an Affirmation Model of Disability. *Disability & Society*, *15*(4), 569–582. doi:10.1080/09687590050058189

Taylor, S. (n.d.). Introduction: Before It Had a Name. *Disability Services and Disability Studies in Higher Education*. doi:10.1057/9781137502445.0002

Trainor, A. (2017). *Transition by Design*. New York: Teachers College Press.

Valentine, D. (2007). *Imagining transgender: An ethnography of a category*. Durham, NC: Duke University Press. doi:10.1215/9780822390213

Ware, L. (2001). Writing, Identity, and the Other. *Journal of Teacher Education*, *52*(2), 107–123. doi:10.1177/0022487101052002003

This research was previously published in Social Justice and Putting Theory Into Practice in Schools and Communities; pages 227-244, copyright year 2020 by Information Science Reference (an imprint of IGI Global).

Teaching Safety, Compliance, and Critical Thinking in Special Education Classrooms

APPENDIX

Chapter Questions

1. When do you first remember becoming aware of disability? How has that impacted your perspective on disability?
2. What social codes of conduct and rules of appropriateness do you see in society?
   a. Which, if any, of those do you think students should be taught to follow?
   b. Which, if any, of those do you think students should be taught to challenge?
   c. Why?
3. Which of the author's vignettes did you most appreciate? Why?
4. How will you apply specific new understandings from this chapter to your work in school settings with all students, including those with disabilities?

Chapter 43

Overcoming the Layers of Obstacles:
The Journey of a Female African American Physicist to Achieve Equity, Diversity, and Inclusiveness

Helen C. Jackson

https://orcid.org/0000-0003-4958-197X

African Scientific Institute, USA

ABSTRACT

This chapter documents the experiences in the journey of an African American female physicist. They correspond to those in documented studies of other African Americans and females in both the specific field of physics as well as the broader area of all STEM. When scaled with the norm of these groups, there is a thread of consistencies in the obstructions and difficulties that seem to be common to the underrepresented. This writing, which is adopted from the author's previous contribution to a similar topic, seeks to continue to reinforce the challenges women of color have experienced in pushing for advances obtained thus far. The scientific Ph.D. community is an area that many have felt was immune to the difficulties faced by African Americans on the lower end of society. It is evident that our society is neither "post-racial" nor "post-sexist," even on the higher intellectual turf. With a level playing field that is established by removing the obstacles that systemic racism creates—obstacles like unfair roadblocks—accomplishing one's dreams is attainable.

INTRODUCTION

After climbing a great hill, one only finds that there are many more hills to climb. I have taken a moment here to rest, to steal a view of the glorious vista that surrounds me, to look back on the distance I have come. But I can rest only for a moment, for with freedom comes responsibilities, and I dare not linger, for my long walk is not yet ended. (Mandela, 1975)

DOI: 10.4018/978-1-6684-4507-5.ch043

Overcoming the Layers of Obstacles

Addressing sexism, women have had to wait on society to evolve in order to experience equity and inclusion, particularly in STEM fields. The recognition of scientific brilliance and high technical competence are characteristics African American women are gaining but are still fighting to have recognized as attributes. The book and movie *Hidden Figures* exposed to the world their brilliance, pinpointing the fact that Space Race successes were due to the computational genius of African American women like Katherine Johnson back in the 1960's—who, by accurately calculating the correct flight trajectories, bears responsibility for the first American astronaut's orbiting of the moon (Hidden Figures, 2016).

In the author's field of physics, there have been only 3 female Nobel laureates in 117 years—none of which were African American—as opposed to 206 men. The most recent female is Donna Strickland (Nobel Media, 2018). Yet the author personally knows of Nobel-worthy African American females who have changed the course of science their fields—women like ophthalmologist and inventor Patricia Bath (A&E Television Networks, 2018).

Addressing racism: History is adorned with African American inventors and scientists who have made world-changing contributions despite the obstacles that surrounded them (McFadden, 2018). For women of African descent, the fight is against a double-edged sword. The anti-discrimination laws— laws which resulted from the civil rights movement of the 1970s through the 1980s, and which opened some doors—assisted in bulldozing down the locked doors of STEM. Now, there is still a big question mark as to whether there is equity once inclusion has been achieved. Despite a rich history of having been contributors in all arenas, African Americans—though many decades after Jim Crow formally ended—are poorer and have harder lives than do their counterparts in White society.

African Americans still face racism at every turn. They are not necessarily viewed with admiration, but rather as if under a magnifying glass that is expected to reveal some fault. There is no guarantee that they can count on the support of White females; as it is, often the contrary is the case. As former President Barack Obama recently stated in his speech on the 50th memorial of Bloody Sunday (as echoed in Mandela's quote above), the Civil Rights movement did not end decades ago but is an ongoing movement—a work still in progress (Obama, 2015).

Discriminatory practices thrive in climates that insist that a lack of advancement is due to a lack of adequate intelligence, skills, or motivation. Nonetheless, for the underrepresented, while moving forward with all the faculties—such as brain power, ambition, and diligence—required to accomplish and succeed in their goals, their crossing the bridge to success is still not a given. Too often, those in the higher-level technical arena, if of African descent, must double or triple prove themselves over and above what is required of Whites. This is a systemic problem for Blacks and women and is discussed at length in a report entitled "Double Jeopardy" (Williams, Phillips, & Hall, 2014). Additionally, amongst a significant segment of the scientific community, African American females are still stereotyped and perceived as being outside of the realm of "the best and brightest," which the technical field pursues. The same words can come out of the mouth of a White male and an African American female; however, the former statement is accepted as credible and brilliant and the latter is subject to many levels of what is sometimes never-ending scrutiny. In the discussion of the term which the above-mentioned report coined as "Prove it Again" (Williams, Phillips, & Hall, 2014), the authors discuss how the resulting unfair requirement stems from the perception of what is and is not credible and scientifically brilliant by the scientific community in their maintenance of the status quo. Others' perception of scientific/technical worth has been documented in studies such as one entitled "Merit alone is not enough" (Eichler, 2012), and is further discussed throughout this chapter as well. So, for the underrepresented in these situations, acceptance of credibility is not based on merit but rather on personal preference and bias, which is highly unscientific and illogical. Unfortunately, discriminatory thinking is hardwired into the minds of too large a segment of society. Though often vehemently denied by culprits, their bias is explicitly racist and sexist—period.

If success were based on merit alone, the status of STEM opportunities for African Americans and women would be very different. In the same article by the previously-referenced Eichler (2012), it was acknowledged that merit alone will not put one ahead of their professional peers. Not everyone can get through or around "the good old boys'" system. In some of these environments, power is in numbers, and the underrepresented are just out-numbered. As for government-instituted remedies, affirmative action efforts are—all too often (though not always)—staging shows set up to appease. They do a poor job of resolving the issues of fairness for all the underrepresented within a STEM group. In fact, due to sometimes insincere implementation, too often these programs birth another set of problems.

Since the election of our first Black president, it has come to light that racial tension and injustices against African Americans have both escalated and exposed hidden animus in some arenas—triggering an outcry for social justice. This is in conjunction with the arrival of on-the-spot cameras built into cell phones; and instant exposure on social media platforms. What may not be known is how those in STEM fields have been affected in parallel but on a different plane. In particular, those seeking Ph.D.'s in the hard/physical sciences (which have always been White-male dominated) are suffering—despite their intellect and the quality of the metrics they possess for success.

At the time of this writing, the previous US president—Barack Obama—put forth more STEM-related initiatives than any US president known to date. Despite this, there has been and still is a huge disparity in these fields—such that African Americans are still disproportionately underrepresented.

The reasons for this disparity are complex, but it is not because there is somehow any less capability or brain power in African Americans. After making it through the many levels of difficulties that African Americans face—difficulties such as inequality in K-12 education; and a greater percentage of poverty and of single-parent families—there is still a tremendous racial and, if female, gender firewall to surmount. All of this is encountered once one has been proven just as technically competent as one's White counterparts.

All the outside world sees are the small numbers of African Americans advancing in STEM while living in a time in which so many are saying that society has become "post-racial." Certainly, certain women have forged throughout STEM to the highest levels; but somehow, the rule of sexism in our society has not been abdicated. And, though it is certainly assumed that certain supposedly intelligent scientists would not be bigots in their interactions with African American females, history begs to differ. Most of Academia cooperated with Jim Crow in enforcing its discriminatory practices. Many African Americans still today come from a blood line that was not allowed to attend public education until the Brown vs. Board of Education ruling was fully enacted. Many Americans still have parents and grandparents that had considered women as being second class, especially in the STEM arena. For African Americans, just a few generations ago, the available schools were whatever the southern descendants of slaves could build, or whatever Catholic charities provided.

Overcoming the Layers of Obstacles

BACKGROUND

How Culture (Gender Roles and Stereotypes) Can Affect Black Female Professionals

One's journeys and pathways are strongly affected by the cultural norms in which individuals find themselves embedded. The same cultural/religious aspects of African American female life which make her as strong as steel—and often, even stronger than necessary—can be roadblocks to success. In the lower echelons, even when the benefits of the structure of a marriage existed, it was often founded in a subculture where a woman's career aspirations were—by requirement—sanctioned and permitted only at the whim of the husband. Too often, abuse was so normal it was accepted. These cultural mutations did and do exist as unwritten norms. For so many, left with children to rear alone, being a single-parent mother in the African American subculture had come to be another norm (Ursula & Drake, 2016).

The Disproportionately Heavy Yoke

All too often, with the now-older generations, when culture converged with science, the traditional roles a woman held trumped her career aspirations.

While it has been proven that women with children can do so successfully, the needed support system for the author in the early years of her career was lacking.

The traditional role that many women play can be a challenging juggle with a demanding STEM career. To add insult to injury some women, in particular African American women, have been culturally cast into the role of care giver. They care for the generation before, below and every stray family member who has minimally achieved in life. Aspects of this are detailed in the book *Too Heavy a Yoke* (Barnes, 2014). Generationally, many still have family rooted from a time when success and opportunity for African Americans existed only to a minimal extent. Because of this, there is a "savior-like" profile attached to an even barely successful STEM family member. Certainly, not all African American female professionals are tied to this "yoke." Seemingly, though, the pressure to cope with this set of demands—compounded with the extra burden of proving oneself both as a female and as an African American in a technically challenging field—can be a deal-breaker in terms of success. Just as support is needed in the career arena, so also is it needed in her role in the family structure—however broad this family structure may be.

THE MYRIAD OF OBSTACLES

Both sexism and racism discriminate and are among a collage of areas of discrimination. Sexism is broad, and spans races. It is international. Yet for us, it is racism (as has been concluded by the author and by her African American female contemporaries) that is the most dominant factor of the two. It stands out in bright flashing neon lights over sexism in our domains. Racist behavior that damages us is not always done by individuals who purposely or consciously hate. So, it should be useful to analyze racism—as the academic superiors and employers have a smorgasbord of discriminatory behaviors from which to choose. An African American female can suffer from a multiplicity of these harmful biases, which have been described as being intersectional. In a study done on the science of racism (Gelman, 2012), it was shown

813

that the way people categorize individuals is hardwired in their brains. Race is the trait that leaves the most dominant impression on the brain (according to this and other scientific studies). Gelman's research points out that race, above all other areas which can trigger discriminatory responses, is most strongly and incorrectly "essentialized." This essentialized type of categorization induces an automatic rapid-fire association in the brain that often leads to very derogatory assumptions about an individual of a given race. The result can be that the victim can be value-judged based on pre-wired groupings, because of their race. If an individual—such as an African American female—is intersectionally underrepresented, this bias is compounded. If s/he wants to be in a field that African Americans are stereotyped as being good at, that may be good. However, if they want to forge forward to become a respectable scientist, s/he will have to overcome the effects from stereotypes that degrade his/her intellectual capability.

So, in the generations that have evolved since "quality" education (or, at least marginally similar education) became available, it should be known (as reports in this area are made) that the fact that only small numbers of certain minorities earn STEM degrees is a statistic not due to laziness, insufficient motivation, or lower intellect. Figure 1 plots the percentages of underrepresented minorities (African American, Hispanic, and Native American males and females) in STEM fields by degree level (American Physical Society, 2015).

Figure 1. Percentage of degrees in STEM fields earned by underrepresented minorities (American Physical Society, 2015)

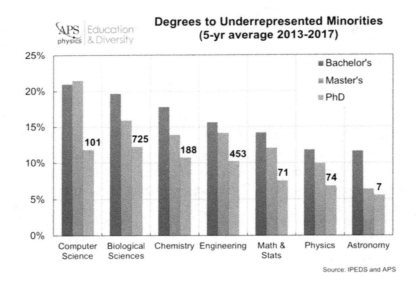

The causes of the low numbers presented above are recorded in two reports: Jackson, APS (2015) and the Journal of Blacks in Higher Education (2006). In the latter report, it was said that an all-time high had been reached as compared to previous decades—and that it is not obvious that the increasing numbers are countered by obstructionism. However, as documented in many other reports to date, discriminatory practices are keeping the numbers lower.

Overcoming the Layers of Obstacles

Ironically, in contrast to the 2006 report, a later report by Associated Press writer Jesse Washington indicates that the number of Blacks going into math and science careers was shown to be decreasing relative to previous years (Washington, 2011). African Americans—though comprising a full 12% of the population—comprise only ~2% of all STEM Ph.D.'s (National Center for Education Statistics, 2015). For instance, less than 1.9% of doctoral degrees in physics were awarded to African Americans (ibid.).

To further subtract from the numbers, once a STEM career has been achieved by an African American, there is no guarantee of remaining in that career. Regarding retention, in another article published in 2014 by the American Institutes for Research and as shown in Figure 2, those most likely to leave STEM fields are women and Blacks (Turk-Bicakci, 2014).

Figure 2. Retention and departure in STEM based on gender and race (American Institutes for Research, 2014)

The findings were as follows:

Women are more likely than men to leave STEM (19% versus 16%). Blacks are more likely than other races and ethnic groups to leave (21% compared with 17% of whites, 14% of Asians and 14% of Hispanics). (ibid.)

This is supported by a 2018 report done by PEW Research (Funk & Parker, 2018), which found affirmative action for African Americans—while being reluctantly implemented upstream—is up against the countercurrent of workplace racism downstream.

Stereotypes and Roadblocks

In retrospect, before learning much of anything else, and upon re-entering the academic and workplace environment, the first certainty discovered by the author was that amongst the indefinites was a definite. This definite was that of being heavily stereotyped and being presumed incompetent.

Incidentally, *Presumed Incompetent* is the title and subject of a recent book edited by Gabriella Gutierrez y Muhs et al. (Gutierrez y Muhs, Flores Neiman, Gonzales, & Harris 2012) that speaks to this topic and documents the experiences of women (particularly women of color) in the academic world. Years before this came to be documented and affirmed as an issue, this issue was the elephant in the room upon walking through the doors (doors which had technically been opened). It seemed the only way to overcome this obstacle was to work twice as hard—even thrice as hard—and overly prove that for which White males were given the benefit of the doubt. The experience of "prove it again" requirements is a common thread experienced in particular by African American female scientists, because prewired perception betrays the mind of their scientific peers as to whether their research is legitimate. So be it—for now it had to be this way. It was then determined by these scientists to do what was needed to achieve their sought-after goals.

Once the author was back on the path—following a postponement (which lasted over a decade) due to "traditional" maternal responsibilities—to completing the graduate physics education program and working as a research physicist, the feeling was that of being a data point in the database of stereotyping statistics. With regard to the interpretation of social statistical data and statistical correlation, the current era is plagued by stereotyping; despite the fact that as a nation there have been some efforts to exit from this. One side of a given argument grabs data and uses it to justify one's own biases or preferences. Some major fallacies of these statistical analyses of social data need to be examined.

Statistics and Discrimination

All statistical models can be understood to be averaged simplifications. Proceeding from this concept, correlation does not equal causation (Beebee, 2009). The presence of a correlation between African Americans and their minimal presence in STEM fields does not implicate an organic causal connection based on their aptitude.

There are many hidden and complex variables not involved in the characterization of social data. Characterizing individuals based on group-level data can lead to ecological fallacies, which in turn can lead to stereotyping that is damaging and sometimes dangerous. The rapid-fire association mentioned above, which categorizes people, can be very demeaning. Each individual should be subject to distinct individual analysis as opposed to being clumped into an aggregate group that is often labeled with negative stereotypes. This hurts those scientists aspiring to enter STEM fields because such behavior can lead to unfair elimination—if not initially, later down the road or whenever harmful assumptions are made based on such modus operandi.

Related to this is the characterization of statistical outliers. As a scientist, the author has found valid outlier data; and often, discovery lies in outliers; so whether or not to dismiss or include them needs evaluation. To say that an intellectually outstanding African American female is a statistical outlier ought to be interpreted as grossly offensive—regardless of the available data.

Overcoming the Layers of Obstacles

An example of incorrectly analyzing social data would be to say that significantly more people are killed by auto accidents than in plane crashes or among troops in combat. If plane crash deaths are considered as being outliers with respect to the total number of deaths, incorrect analysis of this could lead to fallacious conclusions. One airplane crash is profoundly serious and needs much attention. One loss of life within a troop is serious and warrants much evaluation and attention as to why, even though such death could be said to be outliers in the total number of non-disease-induced deaths of the nation's total population.

This current time period is supposedly an enlightened high-tech era. One-size-fits-all oversimplifications are unacceptable. More accurate modelling in the realm of social behavior is needed to avoid stereotyping. Often with certain news channels, statistics appear to be used and evaluated based on pre-existing nonscientific biases and to subsequently legitimize a perhaps false or weak concept.

And to those who don't hold themselves accountable to scientific thought—for example in some political or religious realms—the generalizations and subsequent damage are still unacceptable. History has proven how tragic this can be.

Racial Slurs and the Misuse of Statistics Involved in Stereotyping

To further establish these claims, the issues faced by some women and many African Americans are neither irrelevant outliers nor statistical oversimplifications. Stories have been told by far too many who have had to endure the racially derogatory name-calling by those in university and laboratory environments. It is not anomalous. After having to double-prove or even triple-prove oneself above and beyond one's White counterparts, African American females are still further ostracized. It was said to a female African American Ph.D. physics student, for example, "You better not mess up like Obama." The statement was loaded with unhealthy stereotypes that she reminded them of Obama (whom they considered a mess-up), and additionally that they did not like President Obama. The author was told that people like "her kind" had a poor work ethic. This was even though there were many years of documented success, which resulted from consistently putting in 16-hour days. These are cruel examples of stereotyping based on the misuse of statistical data coming from biased individuals. A more disrespectful example was the author being compared to a cockroach, which is more beneficial being smashed, since it is generally an unwelcomed pest.

Consequences: Long Delays

For the author in this same setting, upon finally defending and passing the Ph.D. defense (after years of "prove-it-again" delays), there was an awe as to how someone "in this (undervalued) category" could assemble and analyze all that technical information. The dissertation research was extraordinarily long, being one of the longest in the school's history. However, the "prove it again" requirement (Williams, Phillips, & Hall, 2014) for which African American females must go through was a main reason for the extra lengthiness that resulted in the amassing of significantly larger-than-normal data sets. Out of caution, the invitation to attend the Ph.D. defense in virtual mode was extended to credible scientists from around the country and the globe. This was done in spite of the vow by a key Ph.D. committee member that the author would never be passed, even if the outside scientific community was so impressed and awarded her the Nobel Prize for this research. With the more objective assessment from the rest of the international scientific community, the hope was that the aggregate bias would be less intense. Such assumptions were correct.

Stereotyping Can Lead to a Lack of Support

After all, why should someone who is innately not up to par be supported? Stereotyping can be exhibited both openly and passive-aggressively and can translate into "you don't belong here" or "you will never make it." It can be discouraging enough for some in the underrepresented category to walk away from STEM before they get started—in order to migrate to a more welcoming environment, where such an individual is not just minimally tolerated (Campos 2010). Having people who support you—and who themselves have experienced at least some sort of gender, ethnic or racial bias—presupposes a better guarantee for the needed support.

Some Roadblocks Are Career Deal-Breakers

Scientists need to "publish or perish" their research findings and get their name out in the open. In most environments, for the typical researcher, there is minimal obstruction to this. However, with a combined atypically-high-security academic and workplace environment, darts from both environments had to be dodged. The chain of approval was outrageously lengthy to get a paper approved and out to a journal. Some of the technical approval staff of that chain did not have a clue about the technical depth of what was written for submission. Novel material is something that one wants to publish, and this was an even bigger problem. Even without the extra barrier created by stereotyping, some supposedly seasoned authorities are reluctant to approve material that does not align with the current norm or with what they are capable of understanding. With the stereotyping that can occur especially with an African American female, novel and significant findings can be marginalized, trashed, or called erroneous, simply because of from whom it is coming. In the previously-mentioned report (Williams, Phillips, & Hall, 2014) as well as from personal observation, it has been documented that accepting exceptional findings from a minority female is downplayed or dismissed.

The Road to a Roadblock

Reflecting on one incident where the author was very excited about the long-toiled-for research findings and wanted to publish the results, the "powers that be" of the research group said that in no way would they approve publishing this material, because it would be an embarrassment to the organization. A few years later, a distinguished researcher from a prestigious institution in Boston came and presented his findings, which concurred exactly with the author's previously-rejected results. This researcher from Boston got to be credited as being the first to come out with this. There is no doubt that had it been originally handed to them by a White male, the author's group would not have quickly rejected the research findings. In turn, this organization would have had this "first-to-discover" credit and would have benefited by utilizing the results to enhance the technologies being developed.

Overcoming the Layers of Obstacles

General Consequences of Stereotyping

Because of stereotyping, for women and underrepresented minorities, merit alone will not enable one's advancement and success. As a disclaimer, there are women who stereotype and buy into the marginalization of other women, over 50% of them, due to deeply ingrained cultural and/or political views. This compounds the problems faced, in particular, by African American females. In the previously mentioned report by Eichler (2012), which addressed meritocracy, the presumption that the underrepresented would be further ahead if they tried harder was debunked. Likewise, the notion that "such individuals" are not further ahead because of lesser qualifications, which overlooks the discriminatory stereotyping roadblock, was also dismantled.

Multiplicity of Effects

As a corollary to the first section above (where the science of racism was introduced), researchers such as Leonard Mlodinow have identified the power that subconscious prejudices are at play that marginalize in gender stereotyping (Mlodinow, 2014). This study showed that for a man and woman delivering the same scientific script, it was determined by the student audience that the man was of superior qualifications. How much more of a diminution would an African American woman suffer, as she is cast down intersectionally! In the recently heated maze of 2016 through 2018 political discourses, it has been shown on the world stage that men are believed over women—period. Moreover, African Americans are not given the benefit of the doubt, which—in life-or-death situations—has led to their death.

Lack of Support

Regarding the author's personal story, in the world of someone growing up in housing projects or other domains in the range of poverty, compounded with a dismantled family, structures were not in place to support the goal of being a physicist. Some with this background, even in STEM, were looked at as oddities who slipped through the cracks. There were no parents cheering them on, because the family of origin was in shambles and no one understood what a physicist was. For the author, with a main guardian being the classic "ghetto grandmother" figure who was first a cotton picker and then a maid, the ability to understand what the nerdy grand-daughter was aspiring to be was out of reach.

Support for the STEM Novice

For many of the underrepresented, once navigating through an intense battlefield of obstacles to make it into the STEM environment, the next level of difficulties must be tackled. Today's science is highly collaborative. It is complex and intertwined. Initial guidance and support is a critical necessity. It was also found that, for African American females (as opposed to those of other categories), support is something that was most lacking. Some initial reactions to walking into a graduate quantum mechanics class or a high-energy radiation test lab were: "You're in the wrong place. Can I direct you to where you are trying to go?" In this situation, the assigned support staff was just as traumatized over the "intrusion" into 'their' elite club. The relayed feelings were that it would just be a matter of time before this unfit intruder would be eliminated—so why waste valuable time in offering support efforts?

Overcoming the Layers of Obstacles

Lack of Support Can Be a Byproduct of Stereotyping

Lack of support is a major roadblock to overcome, which was addressed in a previous section. Academia is the first landing ground for those aspiring to a STEM career. When transferring from a Ph.D. graduate institution in 2008, one of the items that pierced the heart was the very frustrating pockets of negative racial bias. Upon eventually transferring to two other schools, it was concluded that this was not an isolated southern university problem but a nationwide problem of institutional racism by members of society that are not expected to have this bias. As will subsequently be emphasized, an important clarification needs to be made: Some of the biggest and most important advocates for the underrepresented have been White males. Ironically, discriminatory behavior is often enacted by other minorities and females. In STEM fields, discriminatory behavior is still disproportionately troubling because it only takes one or two people situated in strategic decision-making positions in the path of a prospective STEM worker to ruin one's efforts or career. There is still enough of a remnant of such individuals who feel it is their obligation to preserve the exclusive and elite nature of, for example, Ph.D. physicists, to present an obstacle. So many are still unnecessarily and unfairly thrown into battle for what could otherwise be a smoother ride.

The Men's Club

First, the "hard" physical sciences at the Ph.D. level have traditionally been a men's club. So, the Tier One hurdle for acceptance into that is getting past the gender barrier, if one is female. Secondly and most strongly, the racial barrier requires some special rites of initiation for Blacks. The mandate is to be razor sharp and leave no stone unturned—because even if one is currently tolerated by one's present contemporaries, on the other side of the next door the situation could be worse. One thing that many African American parents nail into their children is "you cannot be wrong—you must be perfect." It turns out that "perfect" is relative and often is still not enough.

From Murky Waters for the Ultra-Filtrates to Tokenism

Upon making it through the initial filters of the elimination process, it is time to go to work. Once situated in the workplace, life and work can range from near perfect to a nightmare. In some of these environments, many of the diversity initiatives hurt and victimize people rather than provide a pathway to their success. This is because they are implemented not by the creators of the diversity initiatives but rather by random middle management—who are often hostile to diversity and inclusiveness. They can be a conglomerated mess of just putting up a poster child. In the era of the 1980's to 2000, in the recent aftermath of the Civil Rights laws, diversity and Affirmative Action was better celebrated instead of being greeted with drudgery. The enthusiasm for it has fizzled. Its efforts now are minimally quantitative and not qualitative, so "the box can be checked" to please higher ups in human resources who always seem more enthused about diversifying their workplace than are the middle management with whom the individual must interact. Once the "box is checked," other underrepresented individuals (African Americans in particular) enter these domains at their own risk, since they are no longer needed. A term "tokenism" has been coined and is demonstrated by the arbitrary "checking of the box" routine. If one is not the "selected" one chosen for display, one's future could be grim. A talented and diverse workforce that produces excellence is far from the goal in the implementation of "forced diversity," which hinges on tokenism. Tokenism is bad because it pits minority against minority. On the flip side, it in fact ap-

Overcoming the Layers of Obstacles

pears to be a threatening situation if the middle management for the underrepresented STEM individual, because they often lack the level of education of those they manage, are prone to suffer intimidation. Female management and professional colleagues have been shown to discriminate just as must as their male counterpoints do. So therefore, the solution is not in arbitrarily hiring more female management—it is in hiring fair, honest, and intelligent staff members who see the value of a diverse workforce.

The Quota Game

Once the minimal "quota" is met, the possibility of a strategic elimination process is initiated by those who feel threatened. This is more of a racism issue than an issue of sexism, as White females and other minorities—instead of African Americans—are sought out to fill quotas. Because of the privileges and the associated level of comfort that are traditionally given to the dominant groups—which, in some organizations, include White females—a technically well-groomed minority poses a threat. In such situations, there is no exploration of how to better utilize the talent available. Rather, it is just a "dog and pony show" based on token diversity—put on to showcase to upper management. There is also vicious turf-protecting tactics, as often the level of seniority enjoyed by the intimidated manager cannot be matched outside of the organization, should they have to leave or be reassigned.

Basic Facts

For a worker who is undervalued, finding support may be difficult. In comparing women with African Americans, statistical data findings are similar but are more exaggerated regarding the lack of support African American women have in the STEM workplace. As for careers, among the findings in the report by the American Institute for Research (AIR), researchers Tanenbaum and Upton (cited in American Institutes for Research, 2014) found that

1. Men were more likely than women to secure a position upon earning their STEM Ph.D.'s—but among those with secured positions, women were more likely than men to begin their careers in academia;
2. At the same time, males were significantly more likely than females to secure the more prestigious or difficult-to-obtain academic position: faculty at a research university; and
3. Being married and having children suggests a disadvantage in securing a position at a research institution—for both men and women.

In fact, having children is a strike against women in STEM (Tanenbaum, 2014)—but so is being childless.

The Consistent Lack of Support

Lack of support has been a consistent marker once past the master's degree. Relating back to the author's often difficult personal journey, Fisk University and NASA were positive experiences in terms of support. The first was a Historically Black College and/or University (HBCU) and the second was one of NASA's east coast centers with a very rich history of diversity.

The author has observed those who have started from some bottom entry-level position and have risen to the top in their STEM profession. This is mostly observed for men—and for a much smaller subset of women. Often, women are picked for a display of token gestures; and when this is the case, their rise is problematic. African American women, in general, upon reaching a certain level, are held under a microscope—and there seems to be an anticipated wait for failure or stumbling.

I have observed the support given to White males throughout my career, wishing I could garner the same level of support from my contemporaries. For me, it's been a "sink or swim" and "you are on your own" environment through which to navigate.

Black females are the least supported of any group in my field. Very importantly, and as previously emphasized, when there was enough support for a successful outcome, this was often due to assistance from a White male, as that was virtually all that existed for nuclear physics in my environments. There is a need for more such individuals. Since the process leading to success can often be described as a political jungle with untreaded territory for the underrepresented STEM student or worker, support is not optional. It can be a task identifying and maintaining such support when it is not built into a program. It is a test above and beyond one's technical ability. It is an endurance test of constantly reprocessing the rejection and marginalization, while maintaining belief in one's abilities and seeking one's goals.

The Issue of Geography

For the author, one leg of the journey involved changing Ph.D. institutions and relocating to a Midwest military research lab, so that both employment and completion of her studies would be allowed. This ushered in two wars to fight; the issues already in Academia and now a rigid military STEM workplace. In the physical sciences in this Midwest military laboratory, it was a very White male dominated environment. This move marked the crossover from shallow to deep waters.

Geography Is Critical But Not Constrained

Racism is nationally systemic, but it is easier to make it across shallow waters than through deep waters. This is the case now, as it was in the earlier days of the Civil Rights movement. More of the east coast institutions appear to be comparatively better at both retaining and graduating African Americans in STEM. While such success occurs in institutions nationwide, there seems to be a strong link to how progressive an area is in terms of civil rights and how many African American high-level-STEM professionals are produced.

For the author, it was previously erroneously thought that discriminatory problems existed because of living in the south. Many are not schooled about the Midwest, the "new" South; it is dotted with former "Sundown town" strongholds (Loewen, 2006). Upon arriving in the area, it was observed that, apart from a handpicked few, Affirmative Action seemed to be something for White females and immigrants. In at least two institutions, it was observed that the democratic process did not exist if you were African American. The climate was one of fear and intimidation. The democratic process is one for which traditional academia is touted. For those from more progressive settings, perhaps these experiences may be categorized as being far outside the norm. Because the setting was a military academic institution, this was compounded by the initially surreal entrance into a mangled world of drill-sergeant types waiting to rip the unsuspecting victim down to their inner core—while at the same time maintaining 'face,' functioning in a well-outfitted (funded) scientific environment. Negative categorization was multi-faceted.

Overcoming the Layers of Obstacles

Once again considered double jeopardy from another angle, as a financially strapped graduate student and the single (widowed) mother of a seriously ill daughter, the immediate label was "dead upon arrival." It took innocence and audacity to enter into this guarded, rigid world.

Survey of the Land

Taking an excerpt from a blog post contribution of mine at the time (Jackson, 2014):

After 6 years in the Midwest, moving from Nashville, I feel so emotionally and spiritually drained. I feel as though I have landed in alien hostile territory. In the South the lines were clearly drawn, but up here there is a big theatre where the lines between reality and falsity were blurred; you can be subtly destroyed, and no one notices. One can be left beaten and bleeding on the side of the road and it is not noticed. A big portion of African Americans seem to be joyfully content despite the lack of achievement, socially lobotomized, functionally rendered ineffective and in a state of domicile contentedness, as beneficial educational programs are gutted, districts gerrymandered (79% of them) (Cooper, 2015), and the unarmed gunned down. When poked, both sides like to roll over and play dead rather than invoke a response.

Additionally, there is a trend to bring on board non-native born individuals of color in lieu of native-born African Americans. While the acceptance of the intellectual capability of any person and any people of color and of African descent is to be applauded, it is suspected that the "powers to be" in many institutions are more comfortable in choosing someone not rooted in Jim Crow and American slavery. Such individuals also appear to be less damaged, as many of us who are deeply rooted here are still in recovery mode. Also, this does not correct the disparity that African Americans face.

Nationally Systemic

In all fairness, geography is not necessarily a pre-test because some experiences are ubiquitous geographically, even if they are less tolerated in some areas. While there is a forward movement in parts of this overall mechanism of change, the operation of the vehicle of change seems to be currently subject to the forces of a "magnetic" reversal. That is, in some places, the race relations, progress and the associated civil rights seem to have reverted back 40 years. Whether or not this is a temporary transient will have to be seen.

Specific Experiences

The author gives some specific experiences that line up with those of other aspiring or established African American STEM individuals, which pinpoints that in environments functioning under systemic racism, that the difficulties aren't linked to the technical capabilities of the individual.

In progressing into both the workplace and the Ph.D. completion path, the most unexpected things continues to happen as guidance and support is sought. Perhaps it was unusual to have a drill-sergeant-type advisor, since at the Ph.D. level one is dealing with a professional adult student. Lines can be crossed in interactions that diminish the individual's dignity with derogatory racial or gender insinuations.

Marginalization 101

One such example involves a conversation with the Ph.D. advisor about more good data results being now available. The response, in front of other people, was: "Your data is crap, and it's about time you started doing some good work." This data, incidentally, had already been sanctioned by the organization's chief scientist as a novel discovery.

Disregard and Disrespect

Another example of a typical recurring playout of the micro-aggressive and demeaning treatment was the impromptu cancelling of scheduled appointments. These appointments were the only way advising and counseling meetings could occur. The scheduled arrangement would be trumped by any student or person deemed more important than the author, which was effectively anyone. At that time, as the only African American Ph.D. student in the department for most of the time there, this behavior looked suspect. This appointment cancelling occurred far too regularly. It often occurred after waiting by the advisor's office for a lengthy amount of time for a scheduled appointment—only to be bumped by another student (who would, of course, be a White male) randomly showing up. With the requirement to give regular updates to sponsors, the delays this caused always cast a negative shadow upon the author. As opposed to almost 95% of the Engineering Physics department's student body who was not employed, scheduling appointments meant the author taking time off from work.

Delays and Setbacks

The heart and soul of an experimental physicist is doing experiments. The wait in line to use the equipment (in this case, an accelerator owned jointly by the research lab and the Ph.D. student's institution) was critical to performing and completing one's research. Being bumped out of line was another delay that often would lead to 6 months or more each year, due to being given last priority over the other students and researchers. These delays added up to years. It is not usual for researchers to have to wait in line to do experiments on equipment that does not have duplicates. But usually, when the one who is scheduled gets to the front of the line, going forward is allowed. It became obvious that this line was "status" coded. Perhaps it was mingled with some other "coding" that resulted in disregard based on certain other categories. Excuses for constantly being thrown back to the end of the line were given without apology. Excuses included this one: The students that bumped the author were working within a time frame for completion. This is mentioned because this process (being bumped to the end of the line, to have to start over on the wait list)went on for five years. The author was thrown back down into the bottom of the queue each quarter—four times a year. Explanations given to supporting sponsors were not acceptable to them and were written off as foot dragging. Since apparently the only scenarios the sponsoring management had ever experienced had involved only White students and employees, the notion that discriminatory behavior was being engaged in by these residing smart engineers and scientists was ruled out.

Overcoming the Layers of Obstacles

Other Infractions

There was a laundry list of negative experiences. Most of them, upon talking with fellow African American physics students in hostile institutions, were similar. One simple thing that most other graduate students can take for granted is having a desk at which to sit. Things like tuition assistance (a given for most graduate physics students because of their being in high demand) and the use of laboratories owned by the school for the express purpose of research were rights that were also denied.

Personal Cost and Resolve

While able to work around most of these situations, at a cost of personal time and money, the most damning and hurtful experiences was the verbal abuse. Getting into the specific episodes of marginalization, an example of the verbal abuse from an advisor is given. Words hurt, and "the power of life and death is in the tongue." The greatest damage done during slavery and Jim Crow was not was done to the body, but to the mind. It took very strong mental acts of reconstruction to reject what was regularly being delivered—and reverse into the brain a different message of capability and self-worth. This loud verbal downplaying was projected outward in the presence of those in authority, who naturally believe the more established individual. There is then the task of further proving oneself against the word of the respected person. The author came into this graduate and research environment with a very good professional and technical resume—but this fact had no redemptive power to rescue her from these onslaughts.

Orchestrating Change That Leads to Broadening Participation

The author, to change policy in the PhD institution on behalf of both the author and those in similar paths, was assured that negotiations to change institutional problems had occurred. Official investigations were mandated, which resulted in uncovering subtle systemic racism. Lack of inclusion and equity was found to be a big problem. This a powerful barrier to African Americans seeking their PhDs. New policies were adapted that monitored and protected the vulnerable from sequestration in a hostile environment. However, the personal cost, the delays and setbacks, and the fighting for equity and change, lead to a very long process for obtaining a PhD. This delay was a red flag to prospective future employers, who were always White male and who generally had no experience in such levels of obstructionism.

Marginalization in the Workplace

The author's post-PhD workplace experiences reinforced the fact that systemic racism is a national problem. While the title "PhD" earned a higher level of respect than previously, those on the sidelines—who resented giving this level of respect to a woman who was a member of a supposedly "inferior" intellectual race—explored a path to vengeance, being unable to come to grips that this African American could be legitimately capable and skilled. The author observed strategically placed stumbling blocks. The same pattern of marginalization experienced while in graduate school was observed. Much-needed support systems were nonexistent. The conclusion was that this situation was not necessarily representative of the whole of corporate America. However, despite all the wonderful-sounding lip service, America is in transition—sometimes moving forward; sometime spiraling downward.

Total positive change is still a work in progress.

Overcoming the Layers of Obstacles

SOLUTIONS AND RECOMMENDATIONS

The Need for Role Models

Role models can guide, inspire, and mentor. It is somewhat natural to want a role model that looks like oneself, but that does not have to be the case. Decades ago one, had to be flexible with that requirement if one was minority and/or female. As a young girl, Physicist Marie Curie was the only choice the author was aware of. Curie had an inspiring story, being a nuclear physicist, wife and mother. The author's decision had been made by the age of twelve to become a nuclear physicist. Early in the author's career, at the bachelor's degree level, level there was a mentor relationship while at NASA with the mathematician Dr. Valerie L. Thomas. Dr. Shirley Jackson, who is a renowned particle physicist, was later revealed as being someone to emulate.

When studying role models, young girls can look at their lives of role models and see what was overcome and what was achieved. Like many recent and somewhat crippled descendants of Jim Crow, there was a frustration. Most African Americans of the author's generation were born into, and were surrounded by, much more hostile territory to traverse—and huge walls to tear down—before making it to first base. More than being dealt a bad hand, it can be viewed as being just a different hand. There are multiple pathways to success. The author hopes that sharing the challenges and the bumpy road will particularly encourage those from nontraditional backgrounds. With a level playing field that is established by removing the obstacles that systemic racism creates—obstacles like unfair roadblocks—accomplishing one's dreams is attainable.

As a resident of the inner-city slums, without either parent by junior high school, the author was speaking French, Italian, Portuguese, Russian, and Swahili. IQ tests a few years later were found to be 143. While a junior in high school, the SAT was taken—and the author earned a perfect score.

The problem was that, as a young girl, nobody cared about all of that. Caught in a vicious fight for survival, choices were made to work maid jobs, five-and-dime-store jobs, or whatever was available to maintain minimal subsistence. Fighting off thugs on the way home was not by choice. So, in this world, nobody cared about being a high achiever. However, there were the author's dreams that were never going to be satisfied until the halls of academia could be graced by her efforts in quantum mechanics, electrodynamics, and nuclear interactions.

Today, there are, in fact, many African Americans in STEM who can be displayed and emulated as role models. Their names need to be as popular as Black entertainers and athletes. Popular culture, while improving in this area, is—at present—doing a poor job of promoting them. There are many females in STEM to serve as role models for females as opposed to decades ago. The author was fortunate at the very end of the Ph.D. process, after two changes, to get a brilliant female physicist as the lead advisor. This professor was, in fact, the only female professor in a very long graduate school experience—one spanning three schools.

Remedies

Since this chapter is mainly addressing the issues of professional and Ph.D. levels in STEM, solutions applicable to those in that phase of their career will be suggested.

Overcoming the Layers of Obstacles

Broaden Participation in STEM for the Underrepresented

I have given data on the percentage of degrees as well as the retention rates for African Americans, keeping in mind that African American females are double minorities. In recent years, there has been a call to "broaden participation." Programs have sprung up across most universities, government agencies (such as The National Science Foundation), and research institutions to address this, at least at some level. These efforts should be continued and be held accountable by stakeholders to ensure that African American women are included.

Create a Database of Supporters From Which to Choose

As part of a remedy for the intermediate tier, which is finishing graduate school, institutions favorable to (having strong support and mentoring systems for) African Americans are being identified and are key in increasing the numbers of master's and Ph.D. graduates, particularly for areas like physics. This database can be generated from STEM networking mechanisms.

Creation of Bridge Programs

As a case in point for the correction of a disparity and its remedy, in 2007, Vanderbilt University had not graduated an African American Ph.D. physicist in roughly 35 years. Nearby, an HBCU Fisk University partnered with Vanderbilt University and decided to form a "Bridge" Masters-to-Ph.D. program to rectify this (Fisk, 2015). The program identified Vanderbilt programs and professors willing to offer support and additional mentoring if needed. Regardless of race, gender, or ethnicity, a percentage of the students still do not make it, for several reasons. However, given a support system and a non-hostile climate, students from underrepresented groups do very well.

Due to the trigger of stereotyping, to the then-associated lack of support, and to hostile environments—especially encountered by African Americans—it has been observed that it is not unusual for African Americans to have enrolled in 3 or more graduate schools to complete their Ph.D. In contrast, Whites who generally find welcome arms and support are enrolled in one institution until the completion of their degree. This unstable-looking school hopping is an effort to find a supportive environment, not an easier pass. Those who lack technical confidence or enough motivation usually abandon the pursuit of an advanced degree early on. Some African American physicists (after taking as long as 12 years to complete their degrees-as opposed to Whites taking 3–6 years), have completed their degrees and gone to work in research laboratories in Europe, where they appear to be more welcome.

As a Nation, We Must Study and Understand Implicit Bias

Perhaps as a nation we should pause and do as Starbucks did, and mandate implicit bias training (Nordell, 2018). Academic institutions and STEM departments should also engage in anti-bias training. This training should expose the dangerous sexist mindset that begs the question: Why is a man's testimony more credible than a woman's? (Branigin, 2018).

Work on Retention

Figure 2 is a representation of the retention in STEM based on gender and race (American Institutes for Research, 2014). The discussion in this chapter can give a credible illustration of why the numbers for workplace retention are lower for both females and African Americans. Workplace retention can be aided by programs in HR that address disparities and specific needs for women and minorities. This may vary from institution to institution.

Strong Self-Esteem Is a Must

Despite the harshness of the environment one may find him/herself in, grit iron determination and self-confidence is a must. According to Gandhi:

Man often becomes what he believes himself to be. If I keep on saying to myself that I cannot do a certain thing, it is possible that I may really end by really becoming incapable of doing it. On the contrary, if I have the belief that I can do it, I shall surely acquire the capacity to do it even if I may not have it at the beginning. -Mahatma Gandhi (Easwaran, 1997)

FUTURE RESEARCH DIRECTIONS

An excellent report referenced throughout this chapter (Williams, Phillips, & Hall, 2014) has some guidelines for moving forward. Underrepresented STEM individuals and their management and environments need to be honestly monitored. The data from such monitoring should guide future corrective efforts. General solutions have been presented; but awareness of the totality of particular, unique problems of intersectional groups should be addressed. Scenarios which are camouflaged in supposedly "progressive" environments, along with a set of metrics for progress, need to be honestly analyzed. As evidenced by data, many areas of STEM still suffer from a lack of diversity, equity and inclusion. This can occur unknowingly under the watch of very caring upper management. A one-size-fits-all path is not suggested. However, based on the information presented in this book, mandates for change should be researched and implemented.

CONCLUSION: STEM RACISM IS SYSTEMIC

Nonetheless, the continued fight can forge us—and is forging us—into a new, more inclusive, and more equitable era. Perhaps unsurprisingly, many of the author's STEM acquaintances who came through the doors in the 1980's—right after the doors were opened—find some of these experiences foreign. And yet, by contrast, the civil rights movement of the 1960's and 1970's did not penetrate every crack and crevice. For that matter, entire geographic areas of the country seemed to have been bypassed. The strongholds of progressive thinking on the East and West coasts, as well as in some of the largest cities, picked up the mantle. However, systemic racism is in America's DNA—as is the unconscious bias that accompanies it.

Overcoming the Layers of Obstacles

Despite sincere efforts to "broaden participation" on behalf of the underrepresented, the remedies for overcoming the disparities are layers deep. According to a Pew Research study (Funk & Parker, 2018), African Americans are plagued with issues that keep them from advancing to their full potential in the workplace—due to, among many things,

1. **Insufficient attention** given to workplace diversity;
2. **Discrimination** in recruiting, hiring, and promotions;
3. **Workplace discrimination** based on race; and
4. **Treatment from coworkers** that has hampered success.

As long as the power brokers of the country—who are still mostly White—set, as their own agenda, the keeping of power in the hands of the Whites (whether due to fear or to whatever host of self-justifying reasons), we will just continue to keep on discussing these problems and never deliver on solutions.

So, we still exist in an era where systemic racism is still running rampart. The use of appropriate role models can lead to solutions, as such role models demonstrate how to break through barriers and achieve the desired diversity, equity, and inclusiveness. An immediate solution for bypassing much grief would be for a graduate school candidate or job applicant to thoroughly research a prospective institution for its track record on inclusiveness and diversity. If one is already situated in a less-than-ideal environment, even more immediate solutions include bringing visibility regarding a hostile situation to those who can change it, as well as joining in the chorus of those seeking to rectify troubling discriminatory practices.

REFERENCES

A&E Television Networks. (2018, February 9). *Patricia Bath—inventor, doctor, educator*. Retrieved from https://www.biography.com/people/patricia-bath-21038525

American Institutes for Research. (2014, March 6). *Among new STEM Ph.D.'s, women likelier to join academia, but men get more faculty jobs*. Retrieved from http://www.air.org/news/press-release/among-new-stem-ph-d-s-women-likelier-join-academia-men-get-more-faculty-jobs

American Physical Society. (2015). *Underrepresented minorities in physics*. Retrieved from http://www.aps.org/programs/education/statistics/urm.cfm

Barnes, C. W. (2014). *Too heavy a yoke*. Eugene, OR: Oregon Cascade Books.

Beebee, H., Hitchcock, C., & Menzies, P. (2009). *The Oxford handbook of causation*. New York, NY: Oxford University Press.

Branigin, A. (2018, September 28). *Brett Kavanaugh and America's insistence on white male virtue*. Retrieved from https://www.theroot.com/brett-kavanaugh-and-americas-insistence-on-white-male-v-1829387000

Campos. (2010, March). *Bayer Facts on Science and Education XIV: Female and minority chemists and chemical engineers speak about diversity and underrepresentation in STEM*. Retrieved from http://www.igert.org/system/content_item_assets/files/579/Bayer_Facts_of_Science_Education_Executive_Summary.pdf?1269877505

Cooper, J. (2015). *Civil rights and equality*. Retrieved from https://cooper.house.gov/issues/civil-rights-and-equality

Cuddy, A. J., Fisk, S. T., & Glick, P. (2004). When professionals become mothers, warmth doesn't cut the ice. *The Journal of Social Issues, 60*(4), 701–718. doi:. 00381.x doi:10.1111/j.0022-4537.2004

Easwaran, E. (1997). *Gandhi the man: The story of his transformation* (3rd ed.). Tomales, CA: Nilgiri Press.

Eichler, L. (2012). *You can't get ahead on merit alone*. Retrieved from http://www.theglobeandmail.com/report-on-business/careers/career-advice/you-cant-get-ahead-on-merit-alone/article4226012/

Fisk Vanderbilt Bridge Program. (2010). *Get the preparation you need to earn a Ph.D.* Retrieved from http://www.vanderbilt.edu/gradschool/bridge/descript.htm

Funk, C., & Parker, K. (2018, January 9). *Women and men in STEM often at odds over workplace equity*. Retrieved from http://www.pewsocialtrends.org/2018/01/09/women-and-men-in-stem-often-at-odds-over-workplace-equity/

Gutierrez y Muhs, G., Neiman, Y. F., Gonzales, C. G., & Harris, A. P. (2012). *Presumed incompetent: The intersections of race and class in academia*. Boulder, CO: Utah State University Press.

Jackson, K. (2006). *The status of the African-American physicist in the Department of Energy National Laboratories*. Retrieved from http://www.aps.org/publications/apsnews/200205/backpage.cfm

JacksonZ. (2014, September 3). *Journey on*. Retrieved from https://www.collectedyoungminds.org/single-post/2014/09/03/Journey-On

Loewen, J. W. (2006). *Sundown towns: A hidden dimension of American racism*. New York: Touchstone Publishers.

McFadden, C. (2018). *31 Highly Influential African American Scientists*. Retrieved from https://interestingengineering.com/31-highly-influential-african-american-scientists

Mlodinow, L. (2014). *Overcoming unconscious bias*. Available from http://www.thebigidea.co.uk/overcoming-unconscious_bias

National Center for Education in Statistics. (2015). *Fast facts—Degrees conferred by sex and race*. Retrieved from https://nces.ed.gov/fastfacts/display.asp?id=72

Nobel Media. (2018). *Donna Strickland—facts*. Retrieved from https://www.nobelprize.org/prizes/physics/2018/strickland/facts/

Nordell, J. (2018, May 2) Does Starbucks understand the science of racial bias? *The Atlantic*. Retrieved from https://www.theatlantic.com/science/archive/2018/05/starbucks-unconscious-bias-training/559415/

Obama, B. (2015). *Selma: Remarks by the president at the 50th anniversary of the Selma to Montgomery marches*. Retrieved from https://www.whitehouse.gov/the-press-office/2015/03/07/remarks-president-50th-anniversary-selma-montgomery-marches

Overcoming the Layers of Obstacles

Shetterly, M. L. (2016). *Hidden figures: The American Dream and the untold story of the black women mathematicians who helped win the Space Race.* New York, NY: William Morrow. Retrieved from https://www.harpercollins.com/9780062363596/hidden-figures/

Tanenbaum, C. (2014). *Early academic career pathways in STEM: Do gender and family status matter?* Retrieved from http://www.air.org/resource/early-academic-career-pathways-stem-do-gender-and-family-status-matter

The Journal of Blacks in Higher Education. (2006). *Doctoral degree awards to African Americans reach another all-time high.* Retrieved from http://www.jbhe.com/news_views/50_black_doctoraldegrees.html

Thomas, U., & Drake, J. (2016). *Critical research on sexism and racism in STEM fields.* IGI Global. doi:10.4018/978-1-5225-0174-9

Turk-Bicakci, L. (2014, July 9). *Women, blacks most likely to leave STEM careers, new research by AIR finds.* Retrieved from http://www.air.org/news/press-release/women-blacks-most-likely-leave-stem-careers-new-research-air-finds

Washington, J. (2011). STEM education and jobs: Declining numbers of blacks seen in math, science. *Associated Press.* Retrieved from http://archive.boston.com/news/education/higher/articles/2011/10/23/declining_numbers_of_blacks_seen_in_math_science/

Williams, J. C., Phillips, K. W., & Hall, E. W. (2014). *Double jeopardy? Gender bias against women of color in science.* Retrieved from www.lifeworkflow.org

This research was previously published in Women's Influence on Inclusion, Equity, and Diversity in STEM Fields; pages 76-107, copyright year 2019 by Information Science Reference (an imprint of IGI Global).

Section 5

Organizational and Social Implications

Chapter 44
Men and Women Against the Other

Kalina G. Spencer
John Carroll University, USA

ABSTRACT

The purpose of this chapter is to discern the oppressive and prejudicial treatment inflicted on Black students at John Carroll University, a private white institution. This chapter will outline instances of oppression, culturally and racially insensitive behavior, and lack of solidarity that one student of color in particular experienced throughout her four years of attendance. The goal of this chapter is not only to inform others of the treatment of this student, but to encourage students of color to advocate for themselves and pursue their education regardless of the obstacles they may encounter.

INTRODUCTION

As stated by human rights activist Malcolm X, "The most disrespected woman in America, is the Black Woman. The most un-protected person in America is the Black Woman. The most neglected person in America, is the Black Woman" (X, 1962). This was a distinguished quote from a speech given by Malcolm X. It is a statement with which I agree and have lived experiences. Through many aspects of everyday life, such as career, education, and social life, black women are constantly reminded that they are "third class citizens" and that even though they do everything right, it is still not enough (Cooper, 2018). As a woman of color, I did not realize how little my existence meant to others until I attended college. My college years should have been a pleasant and exciting time in my life, however it only proved to be discouraging and negatively revealing. Throughout this chapter, I want to describe how as a woman of color I persevered through my struggles, tribulations and anguish at a private religious white institution.

I was primarily raised by my mother, and my grandparents in Cleveland, Ohio. I have always been very grateful that I have a family who continuously stressed the importance of school and having an education. Growing up, I was always told that an education is something that cannot be taken away from you. It is something that you have earned and it will always carry merit. With that in mind, I strove to

DOI: 10.4018/978-1-6684-4507-5.ch044

Copyright © 2022, IGI Global. Copying or distributing in print or electronic forms without written permission of IGI Global is prohibited.

Men and Women Against the Other

excel in academics. I have always found academics and the idea of learning riveting as I read endlessly in hopes of learning something new each day. When it was time for me to apply for college, I began choosing between my r*each* schools, schools that were highly likely of getting into, and schools that I knew for sure I would be accepted into. The *reach* schools were schools that I did not feel were likely to accept me due to admissions expectations. John Carroll University in University Heights, Ohio fell into my "likely" category. Although John Carroll was not a "goal" school, it was still on my radar and I would have been happy to be accepted. Prior to being accepted to John Carroll, I had very little knowledge of the campus culture. I prioritized time to research the majors and programs that the university offered, yet I knew nothing about the culture of the school itself. I did not know much about Catholicism to begin with and I did not know anything at all about the Jesuits.

John Carroll is a Catholic university centered on the principles of Jesuit education. One of the primary principles of a Jesuit education is the frequently stated motto of being, *men and women in solidarity with others*. That principle grew in part from the 29th Superior General of the Society of Jesus, Fr. Hans Kolvenbach's assertion:

When the heart is touched by direct experience, the mind may be challenged to change. Personal involvement with innocent suffering, with the injustice others suffer, is the catalyst for solidarity which then gives rise to intellectual inquiry and moral reflection. (Inspiring Quotes, n.d.)

The experience of personally being involved with others, who have suffered and continue to suffer injustices, can bring about solidarity with the other—*creating men and women for others*. Throughout my undergraduate experience at John Carroll University, I did not experience solidarity from my white peers, but more so faculty and staff. I was fortunate to have professors who were understanding of injustices I face as a black woman.

During my college search process, my mom and I scheduled a tour of John Carroll University (JCU). I was asked to fill out a form prior to coming to campus which asked me a series of questions such as my current school, major of interest and where I was from. When I arrived on campus, I was introduced to my tour guide who was currently a senior at JCU. This young lady was also a woman of color. She seemed very happy to be a student there and had nothing but great things to say about the institution. I was also very intrigued when she told me all of the clubs and activities that she was involved in such as Greek Life, for example. She gave my mom and me a tour around campus for about twenty minutes and when it was time for lunch, she guided us to the cafeteria where she said I would meet a few other students who could tell me more about the school. The student I spoke with in the cafeteria was also another young woman of color. She was at the time a sophomore and delighted in giving me pointers for my freshman year. As she was talking, I caught my eyes wandering around the cafeteria looking at the other college students.

I remember seeing many students with tall plates of food and that definitely grabbed my attention, but I did not see many black people in the cafeteria. It was not until I got in the car with my mom that I realized I did not see anyone in that cafeteria, other than my tour guide, who looked like me. At eighteen years old I did not find that problematic, but more so strange because I had always attended school with black students. I convinced myself that there must be black people at the school and that modern-day segregation could not possibly exist. In a sense I was right. Obviously, there were not any Jim Crow laws or blatant segregation laws in effect at JCU What I did not know is there is a thriving racist culture at the institution and how much of a plague it actually is to the institution and its students.

Men and Women Against the Other

I grew up going to schools that were predominately black and although I had many great teachers who were white, I have always had peers who looked like me. Although I was used to having peers who were also black, we certainly did not always share the same interests or values. For example, my peers and I did not like the same things such as entertainment and I rarely met anyone who shared my passion for playing string instruments and reading for leisure. In fact, I was bullied for years as a child because of how "different" I appeared to be. I remember being in middle school and asking my mother to look into high schools with a reputation for having high academic standard, such as Hathaway Brown or Hawken.

I had conjured up the idea that I needed to go to school with students who had equivalent goals and dreams as I had, students who thought things such as orchestra and environmental science were interesting. The alarming part is that I evoked this kind of thinking all on my own because at such a young age I had not been exposed to anything divergent. With that being said, I did not know that as a woman of color, I would have difficulty finding my niche regardless. I would have never thought that simply being a woman of color would allow others to constantly question my intelligence, worth and significance. I also did not discern that escaping one environment, in hopes that the other environment would accept me, would be unrealistic.

It was not until the second semester of my freshman year that I began to fully discern the environment to be terribly toxic. Perhaps my judgment prior to this realization was clouded with my long list of expectations for college and I did not yet see or even understand how I was viewed by others on campus. That summer prior to enrolling at JCU I resolved to make a lot of friends. A resolution made to ensure that I would leave behind the quiet person I had been in high school. I had expectations to meet boys, go to parties, and have my first drink. Soon, however, I discovered the campus culture, and I pushed those things to the very bottom of my list of expectations and priorities. I found myself confronting microaggressions from my peers. The feeling of being in a classroom and realizing that there was always an *empty* seat next to me in all my classes. Only when the instructor intervened with his or her special seating arrangements would I find myself seated next to a peer.

Group work was always sure to find me not selected to be in a group or with a partner. I was grateful to those few professors who somehow knew and understood cultural issues and therefore assign groups or partners. That helped to reduce being marginalized within my classes and reduced the instances of being blatantly avoided or ignored. Unfortunately, most of the professors at JCU are themselves culturally quite similar to the white students they are entrusted to enlighten. Microaggressions emanated from both students and professors.

One professor in particularly seemed to take to heart Fr. Kolvenbach pronouncement. I took the freshman seminar course taught by a most caring and dedicated professor. Many of my peers perceived her instructional methods as "forced" participation. In reality it was precisely what Fr. Kolvenbach suggested—enabling people to step outside their comfort zone in order to have personal interactions with the other. The course dealt with many topics of urban life and how as a Jesuit school, we are called be influential in creating a better community. Given the course focus, it was not surprising that some students chose to remain silent, until forced to participate. Conversely, other students were extremely verbal, often speaking from a data free environment that resulted in ignorant comments and questions related to the black community. My peers' pronouncement about the black community informed me that they were crudely prejudice. That realization created a level of discomfort suggesting that I did *not belong*. I began to reevaluate my college career at JCU and I wondered if I should stay or if I should transfer to a school where there are more students like me, and where diversity is actually implemented into the school culture.

Studying While Black

An analysis of my situation as an intelligent, high achieving student who graduated from a predominately white high school, and now enrolled in a university that lacked an appreciation of cultural diversity concluded with my decision to tough it out. There was the realization that I should not try to run away from JCU, prejudice people are everywhere. It was too apparent that my peers at JCU viewed me as "different." My difference seemed to give some peers permission to engage in blatantly racist behavior towards me and other students of color. For example, on a November night during my freshman year, a white male decided to run into my neighbor's dorm room and shout "nigger" in her face multiple times. We were two women of color who had met early on in our enrollment at JCU and the incident left us fearful, angry, and violated.

The verbal assault by a white male was an invasion and violation of space occupied by a black female. Given there were only four black females living in a dorm with four floors for males and one floor for females our apprehension was real and warranted. The incident was clearly a racist attack targeting a student because she was black. The young woman who had been verbally violated and her roommate contacted the police and made a report of the incident. Perfunctorily, the police went around to rooms nearby to ask if anyone had seen or heard anything. Thereafter, there was no update as to whether the perpetrator was identified, or if there were any consequences. I felt certain that if a black male or female were accused of such an abusive offense, there would have been more effort to find the culprit and expel the abuser.

This incident was similar to the Charleston church shooting in which a young white male unleashed gun fire on black church members simply because of their race. Their space, privacy and lives were invaded and attacked because of their race and unfortunately, that is what happen to this student in her dorm room. That same lack of concern manifested by the police was shared by some of the white students on the floor. Some JCU white students did not seem to be able to develop empathy for the black female students who were affected by the verbal assault. That lack of empathy clearly indicated these people were not in solidarity with the other. Moreover, this showed me that students of color, especially women, are not valued at JCU. I wondered what would be next and feared it would be worse. I feared that I might be targeted for a physical rather than a verbal attack. Given our small number, four black women, none of us felt safe. After the incident, I walked from class to my dorms in fear that I could be harassed, beaten, mugged, raped, or even killed, simply because of the color of my skin. While having these traumatizing thoughts, I discerned I could not depend on campus police or even my black male peers to protect me. Unfortunately, the black woman is not protected—it is her duty to protect herself.

Living on that floor made clear what it must be like to work in a hostile environment. There were not many people who could or would empathize with my lack of comfort. On multiple occasions, I would hear loud bangs on my dorm room door and being too afraid to get up to check it out, I would lie in bed hoping whoever it was would go away. I began going home every weekend because of how frightened I had become at school. This experience silenced me. I regret not using my voice to express to the institution how fearful I was to be in my own dorm room and how I did not even feel protected by the people who were hired to protect me and every other JCU student. At that point it became very difficult to accept that after the entire college application process and the joyous feeling when I received my acceptance letter to JCU, that I was now feeling as though I was in danger and that I should leave in order to protect myself.

A Compromise and a Challenge

I decided to commute my sophomore year because I felt as though I needed a break from the campus culture and I also did not want to merely walk away from the situation. I thought it would be best for me to be with my family and in an environment where I felt welcomed and loved. Commuting was very different and at times difficult because I did not yet have a car to drive myself to class. I would spend the entire day on campus if my classes were spread out and would usually spend the majority of my time in the library in a secluded study space. I started to feel very disconnected from the school because I did not live on campus. I would think to myself that this is just one more thing my peers can add to their list of things that make me different as JCU is predominately a residential campus. I already felt different and mistreated because I am a woman of color, but not having the resident connection to the campus added to my perception that my peers were viewing me even more as an outsider.

Sophomore year quickly became one of the most challenging years of my brief life. I continued to focus on my perceived differences between my peers and myself to the point of becoming overly anxious. That situation began to erode my mental health and I found I was increasingly anxious and angry with my peers. In retrospect, I must concede at that point my own mental state rather than any specific behaviors on the part of my peers, was the primary cause of my disquiet in the situation. Any perceived slight, real or imagined became amplified.

Early on in the school year, I realized I was on the verge of a mental health melt down.

My anxiety and anger continued as the school year wore on. Attempts were to analyze my situation of being a commuter and the ongoing disconnect I felt with my peers. I began to develop this relationship between not living on campus and the disconnect with my peers and proceeded to the conclusion that my choice to commute is what resulted in me feeling isolated. However, I observed my peers very closely and I would notice that there were many other students who also commuted, but were not excluded as I was. I began to ponder over whether it had anything to do with me as a person, such as my personality, my level of intellect or my appearance. I felt the exclusion specifically from my white female peers in the Education program.

The Teacher Education Cohort

The major of Early Childhood Education at JCU, like most universities was a white-female dominated major. Many of my peers in that program had already made their decision as to who they would interact socially and academically. It was not uncommon for some students to have gone to the same high school or to be roommates at JCU. Their closeness and closed spaces damaged my self-esteem because I felt as though whenever there was an opportunity to collaborate that I would always be marginalized.

One spring semester, we all took a course focused on specific early childhood concepts we were learning. We were to identify concepts during our time in our field placements. Our final project was a group assignment and I was matched with three other girls. Two of the girls were generally very friendly, but the other one clearly preferred not to have me in the group. My perception ensured that my contribution to the project would surpass the requirements. I was charged with observing the students in my field placement in order to determine how the students employed various math strategies the teacher had taught. I had taken massive quantities of notes on the topic and carefully crafted a Power Point presentation that incorporated the most relevant information. When I was certain the presentation fulfilled the assigned task, I sent it to the other group members. During the presentation however, I did not feel that my peer or the other class members valued my contributions. All of my care to ensure a quality presentation was actually minimized.

Rising From the Ashes

It was exhausting trying to initiate conversation with my peers or even working with them. I could not successfully collaborate with my peers as they continued to devalue and marginalize me and eventually, the situation began to negatively affect my academic achievement. Notably, during most group projects I was not included in the decision-making process. That relegated me to the position of complying with decisions or directives of my peers. It is a frustrating situation working in a culture that creates an illusion of inclusion while consistently marginalizing the other. The realization that these same groups of girls, most of whom I had shared courses with since sophomore year, had continuously excluded me, created a deep sense of anger, frustration and sadness. Feeling hopeless and alone, I unfortunately had a mental breakdown and attempted suicide in April 2016.

Memories of the JCU campus are still vivid. Walking across the campus and smiling at other students and remembering how most did not smile back. Most never acknowledged my existence, as they never made eye contact. I was invisible. During my weeklong confinement to a mental ward in hospital I had time to reflect on my college experiences. There came a realization that the isolation of the mental ward, the loneliness and seclusion, was more endurable than the conditions I suffered at JCU. After a week of hospitalization, I returned to school to finish the semester. As I reflect on this time in my life, I wonder if my peers realized how their behavior affected me as not only a person, but as a student, a daughter, a friend and an employee. After months of intense talk therapy, I came to the conclusion that much of my depression came from the rejection and exclusion I faced in my life. I did not know prior to seeking help that I have been dealing with this kind of conflict my entire life and I did not have the skills to confront the issues. The way I was treated by peers at JCU affected me greatly and caused me to question not only my place at JCU, but my existence.

It quickly became apparent that nothing changed. Despite having been in hospital for a week, I still made my contribution to the group project that was due the first week of my return. Though I should not have been, I was surprised that my peers chose not to give me credit for the work I contributed. I was finally beginning to realize what I could expect from this group of future educators and with that realization I somehow managed to only be annoyed rather than being truly upset. With that situation behind me, I made the decision to return to JCU for my junior year. I decided I would graduate from John Carroll University no matter what the race relations might be.

A Path to Actualization

At this point in my life I was learning how to manage my depression more efficiently so, by the fall the beginning of my junior year, I was ready to return to campus. Life however, had more obstacles. During much of October, I had to witness my mother's health decline. My grandmother and I spent a good part of each day traveling to and from the hospital in order to be with my mother. Those conditions began to heavily weigh on me. Going to hospital before my classes in the morning and then again in the evenings after work was a non-stop carnival ride.

Men and Women Against the Other

I was beginning to have trouble focusing on my studies. Increasingly, I found myself trying to complete assignments early in the morning before I left home or late in the evenings when I returned home. Unfortunately, there were also times when I did not complete assignments on time and this caused me to have uncomfortable conversations with my professors. I had convinced myself that my professors would treat me similarly to how my peers treated me and would simply not care that I was going through a difficult time.

To my great surprise I was wrong and my professors with the exception of one, were all very understanding. In an attempt to advocate for myself, I decided to speak privately with the one professor who seemed quite unsympathetic to my plight. I met with her after class and my explanation elicited a statement from her that I should not expect *special treatment*. The irony of her statement was not lost on me. I had endured special treatment at JCU since I first ventured on the campus. Being marginalized, made to seem invisible, having my academic contributions minimalized, were all examples of special treatment. That type of special treatment from peers and some JCU faculty created a feeling of powerlessness and rage. That conversation with the professor and her lack of empathy and support was a strong catalyst that spurred me on and made me even more determined to graduate. Additionally, I began to contemplate how to be more proactive in advocating for myself against the injustices.

Throughout my time at John Carroll, I recall that many of my peers in this group/cohort had Italian heritage. It was not until my junior year when I noticed that Italian heritage and Catholic religion were very prevalent among John Carroll students. These two identifying factors contributed to much of the culture at John Carroll. There were many of times that these same peers emphasized and glorified their Italian heritage and at the same token disregarded the heritage of people of color. It was almost as if I could not be proud of my African heritage because it was not seen as significant by my peers. An example of this is during a literacy course taught by a JCU graduate when I finally saw the perception my peers had for black literature. The assignment required each student to present a Newberry Prize winning book and summarize the book and explain why they picked it. Many of my peers chose books written by Italian authors (many of which were Italian folk tales). I was very interested in the books my peers chose and I even contributed to discussion to show my interest. The book I chose was written by a black author, Julius Lester called *To Be a Slave*. I had a feeling that my choice would make my peers uncomfortable, but this book was significant to me because it tells multiple stories and accounts about something my own ancestors endured. Although I supported my peers during their presentations, I did not receive the same support from them or my professor. Instead, I did not receive any contributions or participation during my discussion and my professor did not encourage my peers to do so. Before presenting for this assignment, I emailed my professor about this specifically. In the email I told my professor that I was nervous about the book I chose and that I was nervous about how my peers would react to my presentation in hopes that my professor would encourage my peers to be supportive. This was a significant example of the microaggression and exclusion I faced as a student of color. My peers displayed microaggressions in their behaviors by the subtle action of not participating or supporting a peer. Their behaviors also showed exclusion because their actions made me feel as though I was not a peer of theirs.

Spring semester of my junior year proved to be a significant turning point. That semester I took a required course for all education majors. The course titled, Multicultural Education in Pluralistic Society was not only interesting, but more importantly for me, powerful because of the significant content taught. The professor who taught the course would become and remain a key person in my life. She *saw* me, my potential and re-awakened in me the knowledge of my worth as an intelligent black woman. In that course I grew as a student and person. The course focused primarily on white privilege in American society and its correlation to education. I enjoyed this course because not only did it discuss the past and current issues in society in regard to marginalization of people of color, but it embraced many of the achievements and advancements that people of color have made in society. In this course we discussed topics such as the modern effects of the Civil Rights Movements. We also discussed people who have made great contributions to the black community which included black authors such as Toni Morrison, Alice Walker, James Baldwin, Maya Angelou, etc. I was elated to teach my peers about these important figures as many of them have never read any of their works. I personally felt that authors such as the ones listed are important in the field of education regardless of age group.

The professor emphasized that participation was a key course requirement—meaning failure to participate would negatively impact the course grade. For the first time my white female peers seemed to have difficulty participating in the open class discussions. In every, other course in which I had been their classmate they spoke frequently with great self-assurance, from a position of power. I am sure the content of the multicultural course made many of my peers very uncomfortable. Normally, open, eager, confident young women were now quiet and guarded. They seemed very unsure of themselves. Observing their transformation made me realize how important it is to talk about these kinds of topics. Further, I realized how comfortable the content made me as it afforded me the opportunity to speak in the first person of the mistreatment of people of color in our society. I also realized that when my peers chose to remain silent, it highlighted the reality of them having white privilege. They could choose not to discuss issues of racial discrimination, oppression and not acknowledge how education is impacted. Moreover, their silence, like the silence of many white Americans, contributes to the continued racial oppression of people of color.

One of the most memorable days in the multicultural course occurred when the professor began the class discussion by asking, "Can people of color be racist?" Silence consumed the room. After some few minutes, the professor persisted and repeated the question. Finally, a peer raised her hand. She stated in the affirmative, that people of color could be racist just like white people and proceeded to "justify" her response. I felt empowered to provide a rebuttal informed by the course text, my own intuition, and an informal discussion I had previously had with the instructor. My response noted that people of color and black people in particular, could not be racist in a society that is built on white supremacy. In a white supremacy society, all of the resources--political, financial, educational, and legal, are controlled by white people who ensure the ongoing oppression of people of color. Lacking the tools to enact racist behavior on white people, people of color can never be racist in a society that adheres to white supremacy. My peers' thoughts on this topic showed the privilege she assumes as a white female. It showed privilege because regardless of how ignorant she thought her comment was, she still felt entitled to state it, not recognizing that she may offend someone in the room. In this instance, I felt offended because of her lack of consideration toward me being one of the only two black people in the room.

As I was explaining my point, my peer attempted to interrupt me, but I refused to let her to silence me. For the first time in my career as a college student, I did not feel embarrassed or awkward after speaking in front of my peers. I believe I delivered my argument in an articulate and respectful manner and that my peers, willingly or not, were able to comprehend my explanation. That day I walked away from class realizing that my voice is very powerful and that I do have the ability to speak up for myself and other students of color. By speaking up and challenging the false assertion of a peer, I was able to show that I had a powerful, informed voice that is just as valid as anyone's in the class. It became clear that many of my white peers were not willing to have discussions about racism. My thoughts are that my

Men and Women Against the Other

peers realize that racism is wrong and should not be tolerated, but because it is not a trend to discuss and combat it, they would rather sit in silence. I am not certain if they realize their silence is only exercising their white privilege and making racism stronger. When this kind of behavior is displayed in classrooms, professors should be adamant that each student contributes to the conversation in some kind of way so everyone can hear everyone's thoughts and opinions and there can be an open discussion.

Unfortunately, events of that day were not the beginning of a new era in my relationship with my peers. Sadly, there were still more challenges ahead for me. Those ongoing challenges crystalized for me that I would never find acceptance among my white female peers. Being a female and black put me squarely in double jeopardy socially. It reminded me of the feminist movement that some white women embraced as they fought for women's rights. In the process of fighting for their rights, they rarely felt solidarity with women of color who fared far worse than white females socially. Indeed, white women have historically and currently shown that they are just as likely as white males to oppress black women.

Dating back to slavery, there were white feminists who had no interest in abolishing slavery, but simply wanted to gain their own rights. In *Relating to Privilege: Seduction and Rejection in the Subordination of White Women and Women of Color*, the author states that white women did not want to eliminate the racial hierarchy, but rather sustain it and the factors that helped it thrive such as segregation and white privilege (Hurtado, 1989). According to a New York Times article, *How the Suffrage Movement Betrayed Black Women*,"… suffragists outside the South used the racism in the Jim Crow states as an excuse for their discriminatory treatment of their black suffragist sisters" (Staples, 2018). This quote resonates with me as a woman of color, because similar to the women's suffrage movement, education majors were predominately white women. As such we were all just women trying to reach the same goal of one day becoming educators. However, the prejudical behavior of my peers made it clear that I was not perceived as an equal.

I was already involved in the program as a mentor to freshman students at John Carroll, so the director of the program was very familiar with me as a student there. When I spoke with the director about the situation, he expressed his concerns and apologies of the overall issue of not being given adequate feedback, but rather being disparaged. His advice to me was to write a letter to the School Psychology program director and to also schedule a meeting and he assured me he would be able to attend as my advocate. He was not just an advocate because he knew me, but because I had been a part of CSDI since my freshman year and he has followed my academic achievements and progress because of that. When I finally received a reply from the director, we scheduled a time to meet. While in the meeting I informed him about the comments made by the faculty member and why I took offense to them. The director was very understanding and shocked that a staff personnel would say such things to a candidate. He offered his apologies on the behalf of the faculty member and the program and assured me he would have a discussion with this individual. He proceeded to express his regret of my rejection and I was also told by the director to send a copy of the letter I wrote for the meeting so he could have it on file and that he would follow up with me on the issue.

Unfortunately, I never received a follow up email from the director. I am hopeful that my suggestions were taken into consideration and I was very proud of myself for having the confidence to share with them about my experience as a student at John Carroll University. During my four years at John Carroll, I noticed the lack of students and staff of color and the overall lack of appreciation for diversity. It would cause one to wonder if this school even values people of color and if so, how do they make them feel a part of the institution? These are valid questions considering there were very few faculty members of color at John Carroll. There was minimal representation of students of color and it seemed as though John Carroll did not see the importance of changing the matter in question.

Repeatedly during my time at JCU, I felt as if no one saw me. My feelings of invisibility coincide with an article written in Psychology Today titled, *Are Black Women Invisible* by Dr. Melissa Burkely. In the article, the author explores why black women feel invisible in social settings and she came to the conclusion that it is because "black women do not fit prototypical image of the stereotype target" (Burkely, 2010). The author points out that because black women are not typically used as participant groups or samples in research, it has caused them to become invisible in most settings. Black women despite the physical and economical oppression have endured in this nation, somehow are not seen as the typical target of oppression. Black women are the most oppressed group in the United States and the abuse and marginalization faced by black women dates back to slavery.

CONCLUSION AND RECOMMENDATIONS

My final days at JCU found me empowered to advocate for myself and other students of color. Self-advocacy empowered me to meet with the Dean of Students Affairs. During the meeting I shared with her the history of my experiences, with students and professors, and how those experiences had negatively affected me. The realization that my negative interactions no doubt stemmed primarily from my racial identity should be a concern for the institution. I explained to her my sorrows of not feeling accepted or valued by so many others at John Carroll. My experience highlighted to her that JCU does not do a good job of promoting diversity. The university fails utterly to promote inclusion whether in hiring of faculty of color or showing representation of students of color on the campus. Further, I advised her to attend to the specifics I shared with her in order to begin to create an environment that would be more inclusive to *students who look like me*. Students of color will always attend JCU and they should feel protected and welcomed rather than ostracized because of the color of their skin. In closing I shared with the dean my future aspirations to attend graduate school. Our meeting ended with her committing to investigate my concerns and she expressed her appreciation for my suggestions. Lastly, the dean directed me to the Center for Student Diversity and Inclusion (CSDI) for assistance regarding applying to graduate school at JCU.

My concerns, experiences and suggestions to create a climate at JUC that truly exemplifies men and women for others, were obviously shared by many other students of color, the sprinkling of faculty of color and the white allies. The amplification of all those voices resulted in a working-group comprised of administrators, faculty, staff and students that was empowered to create a sweeping blue print for the creation of a more diverse campus dedicated to inclusive excellence. Once completed, the document was approved by the new university president, and then passed on to the board members for their approval and enactment. If the proposed academic changes, mandatory procedures, new documentation processes and professional development training are followed, JCU many one day properly claim it embodies its motto of *men and women for others*.

My suggestion to my white peers is to utilize their white privilege to benefit others who do not have the same resources and opportunities. People of color have very little resources and ability to make substantial changes without white people, therefore when a white person sees that a person of color is experiencing injustice then they should help them voice their opinions. It is important for John Carroll to commend and eulogize inclusion and to assure students of color that they are valued and protected

Men and Women Against the Other

by the school. Many of the students of color I knew at John Carroll had similar feelings as I did, that we were alone and unvalued. I believe faculty and staff also have a huge responsibility of helping students feel that they are a part of the institution. Professors can do this by encouraging inclusive groups and assigning students to work with peers whom they typically do not work with. This strategy in itself will help promote diversity within the classroom and modify some of the social norms many students are used to. Ultimately, it is important to have substantive conversations about not only racism, but also topics such as homophobia, xenophobia, sexism, etc. When topics such as these are not discussed they become much bigger issues because people, with privilege, in particular are not willing to address them. When people with privilege are willing to discuss problematic topics and situations then change becomes easier to achieve.

As I reflect on my time at John Carroll, I realize that if I may have advocated for myself sooner, then my college experience would have been different. It may have been a more positive and fulfilling experience, however, at the time I did not have the skills or confidence to advocate for myself. As a college freshman, I was unsure of who to present my concerns to and how to present them effectively. Also, one of my main concerns was to be accepted socially and I did not want to do anything that may jeopardize making friends and getting to know people. I now realize that in order to learn from that mistake, I must support and advocate for others who are having the same or similar difficulties. It was a very lonely journey which has made me dedicated to making sure other students of color do not have to feel that way. Actions that I can personally take to be in solidarity with others is to be as empathetic and understanding as possible. Regardless of race, class, or achievements, each and every person is or has gone through something in their lives and we all deserve to have an empathetic person in our lives. It is important that I am in solidarity with others because it was something, I wish I had throughout my undergraduate career.

It is my hope that by sharing my experiences as a woman of color who attended and graduated from a religious, predominately white university, other students may read this and find inspiration. They should know that though they may have similar struggles, they should not despair, but continue to fight for what they so richly deserve. Each of us must have the same level playing field. Being that my ancestors endured so much for me to be in the place that I am in, I have found it my duty to be an advocate for every and any student of color who have experienced similar situations. Lastly and most importantly, what matters is not so much that we as black females are *liked,* rather we must be acknowledged as the diverse, capable deserving humans that we are. We can accept nothing less.

ACKNOWLEDGMENT

It is not easy to raise children to become decent, independent, enlightened adults. The cost of raising a child is in the hundreds of thousands of dollars. That is just the beginning. The most difficult part is the time, energy, love, fear and dedication that is vital to shaping a young person. When I reflect on how I came to be the accomplished, educated, caring black adult female I am, I realize there were many hands that shaped me. Those persons deserve my recognition and thanks for all they have done. There are several people I wish to publicly acknowledge for their ongoing love and support through the years. Without them, I would have given up completely. Their deep, unshakable belief in me has brought me to where I now stand on solid ground. My mother, Lisa, and grandparents Geneva and Emanuel, who are huge inspirations in my life. Their love and encouragement is one of the main reasons I have achieved academic success. I watched each member of my family work extremely hard to provide me with the opportunities that many little black girls did not get to have. With that said, they are pivotal in my success and I will never to be able to thank them enough for all they have done for me. I would also like to acknowledge my former professor Dr. Theron Ford, who was a force in making sure I was a successful student in the Education program and that I developed into a well-rounded professional. Lastly, I would like to acknowledge the black staff on campus (groundkeepers, Einstein bagels and Starbucks employees). Without their daily encouraging words and smiles, I am not certain how I would have made it through each day.

REFERENCES

Burkley, M. (2010, December 8). *Are Black Women Invisible?* Retrieved from https://www.nytimes.com/2018/07/28/opinion/sunday/suffrage-movement-racism-black-women.html

Cooper, B. (2018, May 15). *What Happens When Making All the Right Choices Just Isn't Enough?* Retrieved from https://www.nbcnews.com/think/opinion/being-blackwoman-america-means-realizing-doing-everything-right-may-ncna874171

Hurtado, A. (1989). Relating to Privilege: Seduction and Rejection in the Subordination of White Women and Women of Color. *Chicago Journals, 14*(4), 833-855. Retrieved from http://www.jstor.org/stable/3174686

Inspiring Quotes. (n.d.). *Peter Hans Kolvenbach Quotes and Sayings.* Retrieved from https://www.inspiringquotes.us/author/5468-peter-hans-kolvenbach

Staples, B. (2018, July 28). How the Suffrage Movement Betrayed Black Women. *The New York Times.* Retrieved from https://www.nytimes.com/2018/07/28/opinion/sunday/suffrage-movement-racism-black-women.html

X, M. (1962). *Who Taught You to Hate Yourself?* Speech presented at Funeral Service of Ronald Stokes, Los Angeles, CA. Retrieved from https://www.youtube.com/watch?v=z_q_Z9A0RuQ

KEY TERMS AND DEFINITIONS

Diversity: The state of being diverse; variety.
Exclusion: The process or state of excluding or being excluded.
Inclusion: The action or state of including or of being included within a group or structure.
Marginalization: Treatment of a person, group or concept as insignificant or peripheral.

Microaggression: A statement, action or incident regarded as an instance of indirect, subtle, or unintentional discrimination against members of a marginalized group such as a racial or ethnic minority.

Oppression: Prolonged cruel or unjust treatment or control.

Privilege: A special right, advantage, or immunity granted or available only to a particular person or group.

Representation: The action of speaking or acting on behalf of someone or the state of being so represented.

This research was previously published in #MeToo Issues in Religious-Based Institutions and Organizations; pages 56-75, copyright year 2020 by Information Science Reference (an imprint of IGI Global).

APPENDIX: QUESTIONS FOR DISCUSSION AND REFLECTION

Review the chapter and identify specific incidences of the key terminology.

1. Please share if you have ever experienced instances of any of the key terminology. How did that experience make you feel and how did you handle the situation?
2. Reflect on the incident in the dormitory and posit the intent of that behavior. Identify and discuss recent incidents reported in the news that are similar to the dormitory event.
3. What does Fr. Kovelbach mean by saying we should be men and women in solidarity with others? Give specific instances when you have seen that actualized.
4. Are there currently situations nationally or internationally where the need for solidarity with the other is most urgent? Brainstorm actions you could take to be in solidarity with those who most need support and voices to address their plight.
5. Why is it imperative to have ongoing substantive discussion about racism and sexism? Why do we not have such discussions? Identify ways that some people interrupt or end such discussions?
6. Provide specific actions professors or teachers must take to ensure that every student in the class is made to fill that he or she belongs.
7. The author finally found her voice in a course specifically focused on issues of race, class and culture. Review the chapter and identify specific incidents during which the author might have been more pro-active in advocating for herself.

Chapter 45

Sustaining Our Diminishing Teachers of Color in Urban and Suburban Schools:
A Crisis of an Othered Identity

Karen D. Griffen
Creighton University, USA

Aaron J. Griffen
https://orcid.org/0000-0003-0459-6182
DSST Public Schools, USA

ABSTRACT

This chapter emphasizes the importance of implementing culturally competent recruitment and retention practices, which suburban schools and systems can use to ensure that all students have a well-trained and high-quality teacher of color. Changes in teachers' expectations for student success and strategies in managing administrative and behavioral tasks are all required of all novice teachers. Methods of recruitment, strategies of organization management, and student demographics should be factors in supporting the approaches to implement culturally competent policy change, impacting the outcomes for teachers of color and the student's they serve. A positive organizational culture to include culturally responsive instructional leadership, adequate teacher salary, and critical professional development are determinants for sustaining high-quality teachers of color not only for students of color but for all learners. An emphasis on valuing the cultural identity of teachers of color in suburban schools will be emphasized as a preventative measure for the othering of teachers of color.

DOI: 10.4018/978-1-6684-4507-5.ch045

Copyright © 2022, IGI Global. Copying or distributing in print or electronic forms without written permission of IGI Global is prohibited.

INTRODUCTION

Principals are accountable for rigorous learning for all students. Excuses are not acceptable, particularly in turnaround schools, despite research that indicates that it takes a long term commitment for consistent school leadership and staff retention to fully turnaround a school in the long term (Hoxworth, 2017). School leaders guide their staff through the challenges posed by an increasingly complex environment. Teachers of color are experiencing burnout due to conflict, high job demands, high-stake accountability of assessments, boredom, negative student behavior, student trauma, and management's style of leadership.

This, however, is not simply an Urban-defined issue, but a Suburban concern as well. Every year, the recruitment of teachers steadily increases. School principals of Urban-defined public schools are accountable for improving student academics and the school's culture while addressing social and emotional issues of students and staff. Annually, schools receive a federal evaluation which rates the school on assessment results, student attendance, teacher turnover rate, student discipline, and student mobility. When schools receive negative evaluations, schools receive negative publicity which then makes it more difficult to gain and maintain sustainability.

Once sustainability is lost, student academics decline and the school's culture digresses. Therefore, this chapter emphasizes the importance of implementing culturally competent recruitment and retention practices, which Suburban schools and systems can use to ensure that all students have a well-trained and high-quality teacher of color. An emphasis on valuing the cultural identity of teachers of color in Suburban schools will be emphasized as a preventative measure for the othering of teachers of color.

BACKGROUND

It is common for Urban-defined schools to have negative reputations. When a school building is aesthetically unattractive, needing renovations and repairs, and the residing neighborhood of the school is believed to be dangerous and unsafe, employing high-quality educators is almost impossible. "The persistence of multigenerational poverty is the most villainous explanation for these continuing disparities, with structural racism as its regular sidekick". (Edly & Darling-Hammon, 2018). The school building should be functional with adequate resources. With the exodus of people of color from Urban to Suburban areas, definitions of Urban are now becoming blurred. Urban-defined schools are described as having a majority minority population demographic above 65% with a Free and Reduced Lunch population about 50%. Moving to the Suburbs, many have found, does not necessarily remove one from a Low SES status and a question of identity and belonging becomes glaring.

While an Urban-defined school can substantially improve with a supportive public policy, the actuality of Suburbanization is necessary to help mandate the needed changes. School policy should be written to design a school as a "safe haven" for students, teachers, and administrators where the cultural identity of all stakeholders are intact and valued. Teachers of color often bring alternative pedagogies to the school environment that counter traditional thoughts of schooling and learning as they introduce children of color to "culturally relevant" instructional practices (Ladson-Billings, 1994). Teachers should have a sense of satisfaction; students should be healthy and learning as the whole child; and administrators should have a sense of security in remaining in their roles. This is the ongoing description of Suburban schools in affluent areas. However, teachers of color in these Suburban settings often experience feelings of isolation, marginalization and frustration through a lack of being valued as professionals (Lee, 2013).

Suburbanization of Children and Teachers of Color: Gaslighting and Othering

The *Suburbanization* of children of color is having a profound impact on how we view their education. Long has been the notion and ideal that predominantly White schools – "Affluent Defined" were the pillars of public education. Yet, Black and Brown children who are moving into these schools from Urban-defined schools suffer similar academic inequities. In Black Suburbanization: American Dream or New Banlieu, Johnson (2014) shares several studies indicating that this sudden Suburbanization of traditionally Urban defined students are having a profound impact on Suburban schools, communities and school systems. "For minority groups, there are potentially troublesome implications of moving to the suburban context in terms of political fragmentations" (p. 3).

Johnson is referring to how the migration to Suburban areas work against people of colors' ability to mobilize their interests, politically. By moving to areas with minimal representative of their interests, they are essentially politically invisible. For teachers of color, the impact to moving to a Suburban school mean that they will have less people with whom they can connect both professionally and personally due to a difference in cultural identity and cultural values. "Teachers of color do not feel adequately supported professionally in their schools which intensifies their sense of invisibility" (Leary, 2015). This results not only in the feeling of invisibility but also being *othered* because their values do not match those of the working environment.

According to Jensen (2011), "Othering occurs when ethnic minority identities are always situated within specific social contexts and conditioned by them." (p. 65) The social contexts that situate those identities are systems, policies, actions and beliefs that work to define the identity of ethnic minorities as anything other than normal. Most recently, Serena Williams, considered quite possibly the greatest Tennis player of all time, argued with the referee, called him a thief, and smashed her racket. She received three violations and was fined $17,000. Several male and female analysts and tennis players argued that a male player would not and has not ever received the violations she received. To add insult, the referees are now threatening to boycott Serena's matches because they felt the referee was not supported.

Serena Williams is an example of *othering* because African-American female students are receiving harsher punishment for behaviors their White female and male peers also portray. According to Blake, Butler, Lewis & Darensbourg (2011), "Disproportionate discipline appears to be a pervasive problem for Black girls that begins in elementary and extends through high school" In comparison to Hispanic and White girls, Black girls are more likely to be suspended from school (as cited in Blake et al, 2011, p. 92). Furthermore women teachers of color suffer from implicit and explicit strategies grounded in *Whiteness* (Rademacher, 2018) called *Gaslighting* (Roberts & Andrews, 2013), where women of color, particularly African American women, are labelled as aggressive, angry, pushy and rude for behaviors their White female peers display. Examples are raising their voice to make a point, disagreeing in a meeting, expressing frustration, and providing a counter argument. "By repeatedly and convincingly offering explanations that depict the victim as unstable, the abuser can control the victim's perception of reality while maintaining a position of truth-holder and authority". (Roberts and Andrews, 2013).

Teachers of color and children of color ultimately have to navigate these socially constructed spaces by developing Consciously Constructed Identities (Lee, 2013). These identities are designed to protect their personal life from professional life by creating a work place identity, a professional identity that they were comfortable with revealing with colleagues (p. 7). Griffen and Carrier (2017) promoted a concept called *Compliant Ambiguity*, which they argue African American male students and adults must enact so that they will not receive negative work place and school consequences:

Compliant ambiguity results when communities and schools fight to dismantle the pipeline through policy modifications and grassroots protests of school reform. I become compliant in order to fit into the mainstream and not be a part of the pipeline. My compliance then eradicates my uniqueness, so that I am part of the whole and no longer exceptional. I become ambiguous. (p. 6)

These "survival" strategies actually work against the students of color and teachers of color, for they further diminish their ability to operate confidently in work or school environment.

Gaslighting (Roberts and Andrews, 2013) and *Othering* (Jensen, 2011) in a Suburban learning environment are only two of many efforts that result in low teacher of color efficacy, high teacher of color turnover, and ultimately burnout. To combat these feelings and efforts that diminish teacher of color ability to be successful, Suburban school leaders and system leaders must utilize culturally responsive leadership practices to build trust among all teachers (to include teachers of color); emphasize critical professional development to build teacher efficacy and prevent teacher burnout; and implement policies and practices that value the cultural identity of teachers of color and the students of color they will serve.

SUSTAINING TEACHERS OF COLOR IN SUBURBAN SCHOOLS

Educational trends are shaping and stretching the decisions that must be made in our schools today, and educational leaders should be prepared to manage and approach issues that are occurring today. More students arrive in Suburban schools from dysfunctional families, foster homes, and homeless shelters. Suburban educational leaders are not equipped with the necessary skills to run day to day operations and other issues as they deal with diverse child protective service issues, discipline issues, and diversity issues. These issues were once only defined in Urban schools. Kozol (1992) revealed that "almost three fourths of Black and Latino students attend schools that are predominantly minority", and more than two million, including more than a quarter of Black students in the Northeast and Midwest, "attend schools which we call apartheid school" in which 99 to 100 percent of students are non-white (p. 19).

Suburban School Practice and the Relationship of Trust Among the Teachers

According to the National Center for Educational Statistics (2018), 82 percent of teachers are white, 8 percent Hispanic, 7 percent are Black, and 2 percent are Asian. As the historically White Suburban schools are becoming more diverse, efforts are being made to hire a more diverse teaching pool. However, diversifying the pool is not sufficient so long as teachers of color do not feel supported in their schools professionally (Lee, 2013). When any teacher does not feel supported professionally, they develop distrust. Trust is essential in any workplace, but particularly for teachers of color who are already recognized as the *token representative* of their cultural group. (p. 2) Supports are necessary in aiding the management of any school, regardless of economic status. Hypothetically, supports and funds are provided, but Suburban principals like their Urban-defined peers are now in need of strategic management education and guidance to ensure that resources are dispersed appropriately and equitably.

- **Strategic planning for onboarding.** Principals should use strategic planning as a process for managing change in student achievement and school culture. Strategic planning provides leaders a systemic, structured, and collaborative approach to identify and examine current issues and

Sustaining Our Diminishing Teachers of Color in Urban and Suburban Schools

trends (Guerra, Zamora, Hernandez, & Menchaca 2017.) Using strategic planning as a part of the onboarding process allows teachers and members of the learning community opportunities to participate, collaborate, and engage in meaningful conversations and meaningful activities. Active participants of onboarding are impacted with hope, optimism, and resilience. Hope provides the determination to achieve goals, optimism recognizes the positive performance impact in work settings, and resilience has the capacity to rebound or bounce back from adversity, conflict, and failure (Yousseff & Luthans, 2007).

Strategic planning is the framework for setting expectations, understanding standards, creating a mission, setting goals and preventing conflict. In addition, strategic planning, which shares the vision of an organizations bureaucratic structure to organize the complex tasks of educating diverse groups of students, is usually centralized using a hierarchy or authority, identified division of labor among personnel, policies, rules and regulations. Incorporating cultural competence as a part of strategic planning for the onboarding process allows for cultural identity to be considered. This is not a simple as having a leader of color onboard a teacher of color or a teacher of color onboard a teacher of color. This means the entire process is culturally competent, removing barriers and obstacles to a sense of belonging and acceptance as a part of the organization. Regulations such as dress code, particularly, hairstyle, clothing attire, and facial hair are potential barriers. Maintaining such a bureaucratic system that recognizes and celebrates one primary culture over all others could be at the expense of professionalism, trust, and teacher efficacy.

Griffen (2018) calls for principals to be culturally responsive instructional leaders, where they empower and allow teachers to take part in the building and investment of their own self-discovery. This means, that teachers of color have a voice and are active participants in the design of their instructional practices and curriculum scope and sequence. Teachers of color recognize their unique ability to communicate differently with culturally different learners. It is imperative for Suburban school leaders to recognize this. Excessive administrative authority, status quo approaches, and one size fits all practices will prevent teachers from conducting their work and establishing trust in the school community (Moran, 2016).

- **Trust is the mediating factor.** Teachers expect to have leaders who are competent and well-trained. At the same time, when teachers feel supported, typically they will support the principal's vision. When teacher's support the principal's vision, there is a relationship of trust between the teacher and the principal.

Educating large and diverse groups of students takes more than the role of the principal. It is necessary to cultivate a trusting orientation from the principal, teachers, students, and parents. Lee (2013) recommends that "Before bringing in teachers of color, a school needs to honestly examine its culture to identify its strengths and weaknesses as they think about their level of commitment to school diversity" (p. 3). Tschannen-Moran (2016) states,

Schools would be better served by exercising their administrative authority with a professional orientation, extending adaptive discretion to teachers in the conduct of their work, and adopting practices that lead to strong trust among school leaders, teacher, students, and parents. (p. 218)

Goddard, Salloum, & Berebitsky (2009), view trust as a mediator of multiple factors including race, economics, gender, biases, and misinterpretations. Each of these factors are barriers teachers of colors have historically had to navigate daily, in U.S. Society. As Tschannen-Moran refer to schools, trust must be authentic as schools today face pressure from external environments, internal issues, and bureaucracies of change. Therefore, it is essential that Suburban schools are truly invested in building the trust of all teachers, including teachers of color. This means being self-aware of their own biases they may have and how they relate to others. Maxwell (2013) shares, "When people feel liked, cared for, included, valued, and trusted, they begin to work together with their leader and each other" (p. 47). To avoid feelings of *othering*, trust has to be established among all teachers. Therefore, in order for trust to mediate these constructs and barriers to the vision of the school such as race, economics, gender, biases, and misinterpretations, principals must not only consider but celebrate the impact teachers of color will have on the entire learning and professional environment. This means acknowledging that the cultural differences of all teachers and ensuring a working environment where teachers of color are free to be their authentic selves in all spaces. Discomfort of the majority population should not be considered when creating these spaces. The space is already safe and prepared for their success. Considering their discomfort will only maintain the status quo and the *othered* identity of the teachers of color. Trust will be lost and never gained.

- **Teachers of color feelings of distrust**. There are detriments in Suburban schools that can create distrust. As previously noted, teachers like to be a part of the decision-making process of the school. Teachers of color want to be included, especially in regards to decisions about their growth and future on the campus. Teachers in general feel as though they are capable of doing their jobs without being micromanaged. According to Goddard, Salloum, & Berebitsky (2009).

social systems characterized by low trust suffer from inefficiencies associated with the creation and enforcement of formal contracts; in contrast, groups characterized by comparatively higher levels of trust tend to achieve goals more efficiently because fewer scarce resources are devoted to the creation and maintenance of formalized agreements (p. 295).

A culture of compliance interferes with teachers' development needs for learning and growth. When bureaucratic practices such as common lesson plans, common instructional strategies, and common ways for disagreement are strictly enforced, teachers lose their flexibility, innovation, and adaptability. Furthermore, anxiety increases, communication alleviates, conflict occurs, teachers become withdrawn and trust is lost or never developed. Next, the teacher of color becomes dissatisfied with their role because of the addition of high demands as she or he suffers from burnout.

Teacher Efficacy and Burnout

Today's society is forever changing, and there is a perceived social pressure to every profession, occupation, or job. In the teacher's life, there are personal challenges, social challenges, and professional challenges. Various challenges create emotional stress, loss of enthusiasm, depression, and physical illness. Colomeischi (2014) research study states, "It is important to identify the psychological resources and their relation with burnout syndrome to overcome all challenges and to develop a fulfilling teaching career." (p. 1068). There are many school districts which college graduates can choose to apply to become a teacher. It is important for the candidate to know what kind of school and what kind of children

Sustaining Our Diminishing Teachers of Color in Urban and Suburban Schools

which he or she would like to teach. A teacher's efficacy belief impacts his or her capabilities to bring about the desired outcome of student engagement, learning, and influence of students. When teachers are given autonomy, trust, and innovation, teachers tend not to say they are burned out.

- **Teacher of color burnout.** "Teacher burnout is recognized as a prolonged exposure to emotional and interpersonal stressors on the job, often accompanied by insufficient recovery, resulting in previously committed teachers disengaging from their work". (Steinhardt, Jaggars, Faulk, & Gloria, p. 420, 2011) Within Urban-defined schools, teachers are often found to pursue a specific program for reading and math curriculum, and there is a limited autonomy for innovation and creativity within the specific program. Suburban teachers are now faced with a similar categorization due to the *Suburbanization* of Urban-defined students. These teachers are now facing the same few opportunities to make choices and decisions in the reality of their job as their Urban-defined peers. For teachers of color, the *token representatives* on the campus, this exasperates their working life.

Teachers of color tend to bear an extra emotional and cognitive burden due to their token status. They suffer from *stereotype threat,* the self-fulfilling prophecy where people of color suffer from the constant fear of failure that perpetuates a negative stereotype about their groups (Steele, 1997). Examples of stereotype threat are African Americans "not being good at math", thusly, they fail math. They all bear the burden of participating in a cultural stereotype. *Gaslighting* examples of anger, aggression, and loudness result in teachers of color, especially African American women having to navigate their *othered* identity.

Teachers of Color experience a multitude of the following factors according to Milner and Hoy (2003):

(a) the teachers' experience of social and collegial isolation, (b) the burden of invalidating stereotypes among colleagues and students, (c) the importance of students' and parents' perceptions and response, and (d) the role of successful self-reflective experiences. (p. 267)

In addition, after school activities such as teacher meetings, parent meetings, supervising extra-curricular activities, lesson planning, and professional developments or trainings make the day long for all teachers.

For teachers of color, these additional activities only add to their traditional role as the disciplinarians on their schools teams. According to Shafer (2018),

Black teachers often had a distinct ability to manage "difficult" students, and colleagues often asked them to supervise and help these students during planning periods or after school. But because of this work, black teachers felt they were often seen as enforcers rather than educators — that they were overlooked in opportunities to advance professionally. (p. 5)

This multidimensional work is becoming less rewarding and compensations are becoming minimized if at all earned in addition to feelings of being devalued when they do not receive financial or social recognition.

- **Teacher of color efficacy.** In Urban-defined schools, there has been noted a lack of community and teachers becoming isolated, who try to thrive by themselves. There is a non-willingness to share, give praise to others, or give respect to their colleagues and subordinates. Over time, Suburban teachers have now begun to feel unaccomplished, depersonalized, and exhausted which becomes burnout. For teachers of color, this becomes exemplified as they must also navigate an unfamiliar cultural plain which was established prior to their arrival. Griffen & Carrier (2017) laments,

As a Black professional, I remain a part of the pipeline since Black professionals cause anguish; this, in turn, drives the oppressor to create situations and conditions to conceal my presence. I am forced to choose between being an American who is defined by upward mobility or being defined as an African whose existence is divisive (p. 21).

This is felt by both the teachers of color and the students of color as their cultural identity is not considered as a determiner of success. They are thus being forced to assimilate to communication and movement styles that are unfamiliar. As a result, teachers of color, who are often tokenized to check a box in recruitment and, for the skills and values they bring, are being forced out of Suburban schools either by burnout or "run out".

When teachers are engaged and valued, and they feel supported by administration, they are somewhat satisfied with their job. Supporting teachers' belief on self-efficacy motivates the teacher. Perera, Granziera, & McIlveen (2017) explains, "For teachers high on openness, inclinations towards intellectually curiosity and preference for variety may trigger exploration of diverse teaching engaging students and using effective instructional strategies" (p. 172) Innovative teachers of color want to take risks with their students and use approaches that are not assigned of specific math programs and reading programs. Suburban leaders need to ensure safe spaces for teachers of color to share what they do not know through dialogue, discussion and inclusive planning practices (Griffen, 2018). Inclusive planning means that every voice matters and is included in the work and reflection on the work. Prior knowledge and personal experiences are tools teachers of color develop to engage and stimulate thinking of students of color. Teachers' of color efficacy builds a connecting relationship among themselves and the student which builds the students confidence, and the teacher feels accomplished.

Status Quo Bureaucracy and Teachers of Color

Results from annual evaluation reports shapes the perception of the Urban-defined school. Low test results, high teacher turnover, and high student mobility are detriments that are placed on principals for poor management of academics and culture. As the proverbial carrot is placed in front of the principal's face, and the stick is on the back-side of the principal's body, students become the audience. Young African American and Latino/a/x children in Urban-defined schools, perceive their schools "good" when their teacher and leaders treat them fairly and show them that they care about them. Teachers of color are committed to their teaching role because they care about the lives of poor children and want to make a difference in their lives. Teachers of color tend to teach with a social justice lens and approach. At the same time, poor test results and bureaucratic policies can remove teachers and administrators from high-poverty Urban-defined schools. Black principals leave for Suburban schools because of better pay and less stress from having to constantly address struggling Urban-defined learners (Johnson, Lewis, & Griffen, 2013).

- **Training for teachers of color.** The United National Educational Scientific Cultural Organization require that an effective school system include healthy and motivated students, well-trained teachers, adequate resources, relevant curriculum, and a safe learning environment. To be well-trained, teachers of color must receive culturally responsive professional development which allows them to thrive as they are versus being molded into a Suburban replica. Critical professional development practices allow for differentiation to occur and promotes empowerment of participants to take part in their learning. The governance and management of schools must be participatory, and there must be respect and engagement with local communities and cultures (Kraft & Furlong, 2015). For example, training staff on culturally responsive pedagogy in response to an increase in diversity among students and asking teachers of color for strategies they employ and/or resources they implement will add value to them as professionals.

Ideally, schools are reviewed annually using measuring devices such as a unified improvement plan and a performance framework. Theses measurement tools are developed by school officials, school officers and administrators, and school community members. Teachers of color should be asked to take part in these plans as experts to address achievement gaps that exist in Suburban schools between children of color and their White peers. Chernoski (2015) recommends that teachers from Suburban schools shadow teachers at Urban-defined schools to support in their ability to teach the increasing diverse population. Teachers of color in the Suburban school could serve as exemplars for White teacher.

- **Teachers of color and school climate.** A study of third-graders perception of school climate was conducted by two researchers. This study was completed before the "No Child Left Behind Act of 2001". The results of the survey concluded that both African American and Latino students saw their primary teachers as nurturing, and their teachers' classroom as fun. Defoe and Carlson (1997) stated, "African American children viewed teacher-child relations as the most important dimension of school climate." Besides acknowledging best efforts, caring teachers listened to children and were available to comfort and help with school and personal problems.

Latino children stressed teacher fairness, caring, and praise for effort as well as the importance of moral order, Defoe and Carlson (1997). When teachers of color must follow rigid routines and explicit instructions in how to care for children and how to instruct students, this causes low teacher and student of color moral. Failure of Suburban school leaders' willingness to recognize the differential ability of teachers of color as an asset will affect the relationship among teachers of color, non-teachers of color and students in Suburban schools.

IMPLICATIONS FOR SUSTAINING TEACHERS OF COLOR IN SUBURBAN SCHOOLS

Principals, teachers, and other educational leaders are realizing that poverty and language barriers in urban schools are unacceptable excuses for low student performance. Like their Urban-defined peers, Suburban districts are having difficulty hiring the needed personnel to assist students with language barriers. The students are not taught in their native language, and their native language is the only language spoken at home. Therefore, the students are limited in English and test results show they are more than one grade level behind their peers.

Dropout Prevention and Graduation

When these students reach 4th grade, they are unable to read a simple children's book, and many children of poverty of limited English are unable to solve a practical math problem due to language barriers. By the time they reach high school, they are frustrated and drop out of school and not graduate. According to the National Center for Educational Statistics (2018), in 2016, the African American student dropout rate was 6.2% and the Hispanic student dropout rate was 8.7%. In contrast, the White student dropout rate was 5.2%. These are all significant declines from 2000 when the African American dropout rate was 13.1% and the Hispanic dropout rate was 27.8%. The decline in dropout rates and the increase in graduation rates to 84%, the highest it has been since 2011 (NCES, 2018) can be attributed to the focus in the recruitment and hiring of teachers of color.

Now, before anyone argues that the recruitment, hiring and retention of teachers of color have no bearing on the graduation rate increase because the White graduation rate improved as well to 88%, there are several studies that indicate having at least one teacher of color during their educational career increases all students change to graduate and reduces their likelihood to drop out. According to a Johns Hopkins Study, Rosen (2017), "Having at least one black teacher in third through fifth grades reduced a black student's probability of dropping out of school by 29 percent, the study found. For very low-income black boys, the results are even greater – their chance of dropping out fell 39 percent." (p. 1). Furthermore, there is evidence that White students having at least one teacher of color disrupts one sided portrayals of people of color as incompetent (Anderson, 2015).

Academic Achievement and Incentives

Kraft and Furlong (2015) suggests, "To provide the means for elementary and secondary schools to do the best they can for each student, policy analyst and policy makers need to address a number of problems and issues". (p. 345) When the root causes are addressed and resolved, school communities can possibly benefit from high quality teaching. High quality teachers of color in Suburban schools can ensure that all students succeed in reading, writing, and mathematics. High quality teachers of color in Suburban school settings should empowered to provide equitable and inclusive environments that are healthy, supported, engaged, challenged, and safe. All students are supported cognitively, socially, mentally, and emotionally. As the educational system progresses, evidential procedures such as testing must continue to undergo and measure student achievement or student growth. However, what evidential procedures can measure the outcome of the whole child? In other words, there should be more than assessment results that determine if a teacher is "well-trained" or "highly-qualified".

Students' data and test results are reported for every school in the state. Therefore, a student cannot escape remediation. For example, in Texas, students who failed state assessment in the 3rd grade, 5th grade, and 8th grade were retained. Students cannot graduate without passing the state assessment. Some school districts end up retaining students several times. Most of the students who were retained were African American students, Hispanic students, and students of poverty (Heilig & Darling-Hammond, 2008). High poverty Urban-defined schools with high populations of student failures result to loss of employment for administration and teachers. Loss of employment then attribute to high teacher turnover and high administration turnover.

There are other correlations of poverty such as poor health, inadequate housings, high crime rates, single-parent families, and drug abuse. Some families are unemployed, homeless, and labeled as dysfunc-

Sustaining Our Diminishing Teachers of Color in Urban and Suburban Schools

tional. These factors contribute to African American and Hispanic children having difficulties focusing on learning. Teachers of color tend to have a keener eye on the academic abilities of children of color than their White peers (Ladson-Billings, 2004). This may hold true for teachers of color having a keener sense of academic abilities of low social economic status White children who tend to suffer from similar or same system marginalization practices that negatively impact their schooling.

Having teachers of color will have further long term benefits for the recruitment of students of color to educational programs. One must see themselves in order to formulate a vision that they too can achieve that outcome. Having White male teachers in STEM subjects has produced a cadre of White male applicants to STEM majors in college. By not having teachers of color as an active participant and designer of schooling experiences for students of color, we will continue to have difficulties diversifying the teaching force. For Suburban schools, this may prove even more costly. Although there is a number of low-Social Economic Status (SES) students and students of color entering Suburban schools that are historically White, those middle class students of color are suffering as well.

In her study on middle class African American students in gifted and talented course, Williams (2009) pointed out that they suffered from the same discriminatory and low expectation practices that their Urban defined peers of color experienced. In fact, Toldson (2019) shares how White teachers who teach in majority Black schools have low expectations placed on them and suffer from the same *stereotype threat* as their students. Therefore, the notion that White schools are superior for education promotes the notion that students of color not being successful is due to their own fault and bad White teachers, not that of the White environment that *others* those students and the one or two teachers of color they may have.

Implications for Future Study

Urban-defined students benefit from teachers who are the same nationally or the same culture as they are because the teacher of color becomes their role model. Suburbanized students of color would benefit from teachers of color as well due to the possibility of *stereotype threat* (Steele, 1997) and being *othered* (Jensen, 2011). The Department of Education has reported that only 18% percent of our teachers are teachers of color. Also, the Department of Education (2016) expresses, "We have an urgent need to act. We've got to understand that all students benefit from teacher diversity. We have strong evidence that students of color benefit from having teachers and leaders who look like them as role models and benefit from the classroom dynamics that diversity creates. But it is also important for our White students to see teachers of color in leadership roles in their classrooms and communities." (p. 1)

Racial Diversity in the Suburban School and Teacher Preparation Programs

As simple as this sounds, this is a complex issue to address as a nation. As a nation, our diversity and inclusion create innovation. Varied backgrounds, experiences, and perspectives work and learn together. The reason that NASA has been so successful is because they employ people from every race, ethnicity, culture and background to achieve their breakthroughs (Carson, 1990). The more diverse the environment, we can be competent problem solvers. The Department of Education (2016) shared a variety of information regarding the state of racial diversity in the workforce: (p. 3-4)

- The workforce is 82% white in public schools.

- Education leaders are also predominantly white. In 2011-2012 school year, only 20% of public school principals were individuals of color.
- There are less graduates with bachelor's degrees. In 2011-2012, 43% of public high school graduates were students of color, whereas 38% of bachelor's degree students of color.
- A large majority of education majors enrolled in college institution programs are white. Most teachers of color enroll in alternative teaching programs.
- Seventy-three percent of bachelor's degree students majoring in education completed a bachelor's degree six years after beginning postsecondary education.
- Teacher retention rates are higher among white teachers than for African American and Hispanic teachers.
- Two percent of individuals who are preparing to be teachers are enrolled at Historical Black Colleges or Universities (HBCUs), but 16% percent of all black teacher candidates attend HBCUs.
- Alternative routes to teacher certification tend to enroll more racially diverse populations of candidates than traditional teacher preparation programs. Forty-two percent of teacher candidates enrolled in an alternative teacher preparation program were individuals of, color.

The majority of public school teachers are White and female. The gender gap in education is a whole other area for which we would recommend further studies. In particular, the impacts of male teachers of color on students of color and their White peers should be considered. Though the United States is largely a patriarchal society, and the majority of school leaders are White male, the classroom settings and curriculum implementers are female. Griffen and Carrier (2017) have argued that *Compliant Ambiguity* is a growing phenomenon among African American males in school settings and in in everyday work life, where they are not allowed to be their authentic selves, forced to adhere to policies that devalue their cultural identity and masculinity in order to survive the prison pipeline.

There are more African American students graduating from college with a Bachelor's degree; however, African American college students who earn Bachelor's degrees are not majoring in education. At the same time, typically African American and Hispanic college students are earning their Bachelor's degree in six years instead of four years. Once their six-year Bachelor's degree is earned, African American and Hispanic college graduates may not enter into an alternative teacher certification program (They may work in another field besides education). As the college graduate participates in the alternative teacher certification program outside the school day, he or she has the same accountability as the certified teacher. Generally, the alternative certified teachers earn at least seven-thousand dollars less that the starting certified novice teacher, and student loans must be repaid. Further studies could include the impacts of economic and workplace stress as correlates of teacher of color burnout and fatigue.

Teacher preparation programs must report to the Higher Education Act (HEA) Title II reporting system student demographic information. The Department of Education (2016) reported, "Black enrollees were concentrated in programs located in the Southeast, mid-Atlantic, and Arizona, while Hispanic enrollee were concentrated in the Southwest, Florida, and New York area. Candidates who end up teaching in elementary and secondary school do not necessarily teach in the region the program is located." (p. 13) Teacher candidates are often unable to obtain a teaching position in their region and are recruited by teaching agents such as Teach for America. The teaching agent contracts with Urban-defined school districts to employ candidates of alternative teaching programs. A study on displacement and homesickness on novice teacher of color success outcomes in Suburban schools is recommended.

SOLUTIONS AND RECOMMENDATIONS

Education reforms, which policymakers and others have proposed, debated, and originated over the quality of education, are still left on the table for implementation for policy change. Whether it is merit pay, teacher certifications, salaries, school choice or testing, status quo will remain or no action alternative will be made (Kraft & Scott, 2015). The goal is to propose a viable solution to ensure all children receive a quality education and school systems sustain quality and well-trained teachers.

Teacher and Administrative Stipends to Maintain Sustainability in Suburban Schools

Finding and sustaining qualified and well-trained teachers of color should be the goal when identifying determents of a Suburban school, serving a diverse population of learners. Not all Suburban schools will meet the described characteristics of an Urban-defined school due to the fact each school is unique and poses different demographics and geographical locations. For instance, two schools may have 44% poverty, including free and reduce lunch rates. However, one school may have more than 10% limited English proficient speaking students while the other has 10% students of color and 5% limited English proficient speaking students. On the surface, one may say that because they are 44% poverty, they must be Urban. Yet, they are 91% White. Urban is a moniker used to define schools with high poverty and a high student of color population. This disparity in understanding warrants that Suburban school leaders need training in educating diverse populations even if the population is majority White. The school with only 10% limited English proficiency is in an Urban area compared to a Suburban or Rural area. The school also has a relatively high proportion of students of color, and the school has a relatively high proportion of students who are identified as having special needs. Depending on the location of a Suburban school relative to an Urban-defined school, close by, the demographic may be drastically different.

For example, gentrification in historically Black and Brown areas in major metropolitan cities like Denver, Houston and New York are now forcing a diverse groups of residents into the Suburban areas. This growing Surbanization is one of many reasons why Suburban schools are having to address diversity issues. Along with children of color, there is an increase in Limited English Speaking students, Refugee students and historically impoverished families who are no longer able to afford the increasing rent prices in the inner city. Along with these traits, a [Suburban] school can been designated as "High Need" by their residing state (Russo, 2004).

Culturally Responsive Policy Alternatives

Three policy alternatives that should be considered to solve the issue of recruiting and sustaining teachers of color for high impoverished low social economic schools need to be considered for Suburban schools as well. Such culturally responsive alternatives are student loan forgiveness, high demand educational role stipends or high demand content assignment stipends, and social economic and status rate pay. These alternatives can be analyzed for strategy, equity, and technical impacts. Relevant criteria for evaluating the teacher of color's proficiency may vary based on experience, the pathway of certification, interior factors, and exterior factors that result from a baseline analysis. Supporting the given background information, it is highly recommended to implement a suitable alternative that can sustain and recruit teachers for high-impoverish schools.

Alternative 1: Student loan forgiveness. Due to systemic racism that have negatively impacted people of color and other marginalized groups historically, the student loan debt among these groups has created a national debt concern. The total student loan debt in the United States is $1.48 Trillion (Student Loan Hero, 2018). According to Berman (2018), "Wiping away $1.4 Trillion in outstanding student loan debt for the 44 million Americans who carry it could boost GDP by between $86 billion and $108 billion per year on average for the 10 years following the debt cancellation (p. 1). Therefore, a student loan forgiveness program would allow teachers of color opportunities to live a comfortable lifestyle and provide opportunities to further their education by earning graduate degrees.

Simultaneously, the forgiveness program also lessens their stress with struggling to repay an unwanted debt. Clearing unwanted debt provides a financial opportunity to purchase a home or extend their learning through graduate studies. However, the teacher of color must meet a set of rigid requirements to secure a student loan repayment such as remaining in the same school for a minimum of 5 years in an elementary, 3 years in a middle school and 4 years in a high school. The reason for the different years is for the number of years students attend those particular levels. The reason for the number of years is for sustainability and consistency. This will support with retaining teachers of color and allow students to see the same teachers for a number of years.

Alternative 2: High demand educational role or high demand content assignment. A baseline analysis will identify trade-offs of teachers who work in high poverty schools. Considerations should be granted for potential problems likely to emerge in Suburban schools that were once thought to be seen only in low-income schools: high trauma, toxic stress, and systemic racism. Social, economic, and political stances should be imbedded into a differential criterion. We know that Urban-defined schools lack the recruitment of attaining highly skilled teachers in specific needed areas. This is now the case in Suburban schools. (Department of Education, 2016). Thinking ahead, it is imperative to become innovative in designing approaches that will benefit children of color ensuring there will be quality schools available for their well-being and the contribution of their future. Approaches will include not only recruiting and hiring teachers of color, but making them an intricate part of the school environment, beyond the token representative. Teachers of color should have a standing voice in curriculum and programing decisions (Griffen, 2018) and be called upon as content experts within and outside of their cultural identity. Failure to do so will ensure that teachers of color will continue their othered status.

Alternative 3: Social economic status rate. This approach serves the purpose of providing financial equity for teachers of color as they are encouraged to be role models, leaders, and quality teachers for students of color in Suburban schools. Educational leaders must undergo cultural competency training and critical professional development (Ford, 2010; Griffen, 2018) to build their skills and expertise with understanding culture, diversity, and challenges of impoverish children and their families. Usually teachers and administrators work extended hours and additional work days to meet the obligations for student achievement. Teacher leaders and teachers with tenure usually share the rewards and benefits in teaching students in low social economic schools. However, pay equity would do well for sustaining teachers of color who have the extra stress and burden of being the cultural representative on the campus.

Recommendations for Alternative Teaching Programs, Colleges, and Universities

Alternative teaching programs may last from six-weeks to two years. It is suggested that teaching programs provide seminars and request recommendations upon accepting teacher applicants. Ideally, applicants of color need to be made aware of expectations of today's modern school system and how they fit and do not fit in the system as it has historically been developed. This includes sharing that the profession in which they are going has a historically damaging Eurocentric view of education and it is not currently designed for students of color to be successful. Furthermore, teaching programs should ensure that applicants of color are able to access alternative views to educational success, to include culturally responsive pedagogy, multi-cultural instructional strategies, and ways to develop self-efficacy.

At the same time, colleges and universities should restrict the amount of student loan imbursements. Schools should only distribute the needed amount for housing and food, courses, and books and supplies. Additional amounts which consume automobiles and vacations are catalyst of students graduating in debt. In the long-run, there will be less money for the federal government to consider as "forgiveness".

FUTURE RESEARCH RECOMMENDATIONS

There remains an emerging trend where not only are there less teachers of color entering education as field, but more teachers of color are leaving the profession in general as shown in this chapter. This trend is not relegated only to Urban schools, however. Future research should be conducted on the exodus of suburban teachers of color due to changes in licensure and downsizing as a result of educational funding gaps between majority minority suburban schools and majority white suburban schools. Alternative teaching programs in addition to (not in comparison to) teacher preparation programs at colleges and universities should be topics of study when researching the exodus of suburban teachers of color from both majority minority and majority white suburban schools.

CONCLUSION

Urban-defined schools have a shortage of high quality teachers to teach low-income students of color. With the growing Suburbanization of students of color, Suburban schools are now competing from the same limited pool of diverse candidates. The majority of teachers in the United States are White due to less African American and Hispanic graduates majoring in education. There are less college graduates of color compared to high school graduates of color. Currently, the college graduate of color is graduating with a Bachelor's degree in six years compared to White college students graduating in four years (The Department of Education, 2016).

Most Urban-defined teachers of high poverty schools participate in alternative teaching programs. Some programs induct teacher candidates during a rapid summer program, or some alternative teaching programs mandate additional studies of post-bachelorette course of content. Either way, the teacher candidate decides to obtain a teacher's certification, neither program prepares the teacher candidate for low-poverty students' learning and classroom behavior. These now becoming Suburban issues. At the same time, low-poverty administrators are not prepared to strategically manage a chaotic system while leading the novice alternative certified staff of teachers. Again, Suburban administrators are now faced with the same concerns. The excited novice teacher of color is frustrated, exhausted, and unmotivated. A lack of training and experience leads poor organizational behavior which then student achievement and organizational culture never stand a chance to improve (Schaufeli &Bakker, 2004).

While the hungry struggling novice teacher of color gives an effort to teach poor Urban-defined students, accountability of high-stake assessments test still exists. Teachers of color, who choose to teach in Suburban schools, are now faced with the same high-stake assessments where there is an increasing achievement gap between students of color and their White peers at high performing affluent schools. The frustrated teacher of color either walks out and quits, or the resigns and leaves the profession all together. As the turnover rate increases, and student mobility increases, the principal's job may be threatened. The central office bureaucrats develop more initiates which are mandated for the principal and the school community. Distrust, burnout, ineffectiveness, inexperience, lack of support, high job demands, and conflict are all left in the inside the cold and dark broken-down schoolhouse with crying children everywhere needing a supportive school policy to make effective changes.

Culturally competent alternatives and culturally responsive approaches are needed by policymakers to attract and sustain high-quality teachers of color in Suburban schools. Influences using high equity consciousness and values may be a challenge as high-power internal educational stakeholder share alternatives to less-interested stakeholder. A reminder of the purpose of the public-school systems could bring awareness to less-interested stakeholders that our school system is troubled with ineffective and outdated policies and procedures. Without the intervening of community stakeholders, particularly those of color, it could cost our nation of taxpayers more than money in the end. The cost will be the loss of teachers in general, but more specifically our teachers of color not only for students of color but for all learners.

REFERENCES

Anderson, M. D. (2015). Why schools need more teachers of color – for white children. *The Atlantic*. Retrieved from: https://www.theatlantic.com/education/archive/2015/08/teachers-of-color-white-students/400553/

Berman, J. (2018). Canceling $1.4 trillion in student debt could have major benefits for the economy. *MarketWatch*. Retrieved from: https://www.marketwatch.com/story/canceling-14-trillion-in-student-debt-could-have-major-benefits-for-the-economy-2018-02-07

Blake, J. J., Butler, B. R., Lewis, C. W., & Darensbourg, A. (2011). Unmasking the inequitable discipline experiences of Urban Black girls: Implications for Urban educational stakeholders. *The Urban Review*, *43*(1), 90–106. doi:10.100711256-009-0148-8

Chernoski, S. (2015). The importance of black teachers in mainly white schools. *Medium*. Retrieved from: https://medium.com/@nsjersey/the-importance-of-black-teachers-in-mainly-white-schools-fa212919a703

Colomeischi, A. A. (2014). Teachers' burnout in relation with their emotional intelligence and personality traits. *Procedia: Social and Behavioral Sciences*, *180*, 1067–1073. doi:10.1016/j.sbspro.2015.02.207

Darling-Hammond, L., Berry, B., & Thoreson, A. (2001). Does teacher certification matter? Evaluating the evidence. *American Educational Research Association*, *23*(1), 57–77.

Sustaining Our Diminishing Teachers of Color in Urban and Suburban Schools

Department of Education, United States of American. (2016). *The state of racial diversity in the educator workforce*. Retrieved from: https://www2.ed.gov/rschstat/eval/highered/racial-diversity/state-racial-diversity-workforce.pdfLinks to an external site

Diamond, J. B., & Spillane, J. P. (2002). *High stakes accountability in urban elementary schools: Challenging or reproducing inequality*. Evanston, IL: Institute for Policy Research, Northwestern University.

Ford, D. Y. (2010). Culturally responsive classrooms: Affirming culturally different gifted students. *Gifted Child Today, 33*(1), 50–53. doi:10.1177/107621751003300112

Griffen, A. J. (2018). Enacting African American Legislative Voice: A program design toward the development and recruitment of African American educational lobbyists. *American Journal of Qualitative Research, 2*(2), 74–102.

Griffen, A. J. (2018). A call for principals as culturally responsive instructional leaders (CRILs). *Forest of the Rain Living Education eMagazine*. Retrieved from: https://www.forestoftherain. net/2018- summer- edition- living-education-emagazine-vol-xx.html

Griffen, A. J., & Carrier, I. C. (2017). The disestablishment of African American male compliant ambiguity: A pipeline essay. *Intersections: Critical Issues in Education, 1*(1), 17–30.

Guerra, F. R., Zamora, R., Hernandez, R., & Menchaca, V. (2017). University strategic planning: A process for change in a principal preparation program. *NCPEA International Journal of Educational Leadership Preparation, 12*, 83–97.

Helilig, J. V., & Darling-Hammond, L. (2008). Accountability Texas-style: The progress and learning of urban minority students in a high-stake testing context. *American Educational Research Association, 30*(2), 75–110.

Hoxworth, L. (2017). 5 myths that inhibit school turnaround. *UVA Today*. Retrieved from: https://news.virginia.edu/content/5-myths-inhibit-school-turnaround

Jensen, S. Q. (2011). Othering, identity formation and agency. *Qualitative Studies, 2*(2), 63–78. doi:10.7146/qs.v2i2.5510

Johnson, K. S. (2014). 'Black' suburbanization: American dream or the new banlieue? *The Cities Papers*. Retrieved from: http://citiespapers.ssrc.org/black-suburbanization-american-dream-or-the-new-banlieue

Kozol, J. (1992). *Savage inequalities*. New York: Harper Perennial.

Kraft, M. E., & Furlong, S. R. (2015). *Public policy: Politics, analysis, and alternatives*. Thousand Oaks, CA: Sage.

Ladson-Billings, G. (1994). *The dream keepers*. San Francisco, CA: Jossey-Bass.

Leary, D. (2017). Teachers of color in Suburban schools. *Partners in Learning*. Retrieved from: http://performancepyramid.miamioh.edu/node/1365

Lee, V. J. (2013). Teachers of color creating and recreating identities in suburban schools. *Qualitative Report, 18*(8), 1–16.

Lewis, C. W. (2017). *Black lives matter: Promising teaching practices*. Retrieved from: https://youtu.be/xxnzrubm3E0

Milner, H. R., & Hoy, A. W. (2003). A case study of an African American teacher's self-efficacy, stereotype threat, and persistence. *Teaching and Teacher Education, 19*(2), 263–276. doi:10.1016/S0742-051X(02)00099-9

National Center of Educational Statistics. (2018). *Preprimary, Elementary and Secondary Education*. Retrieved from: https://nces.ed.gov/programs/coe/pdf/coe_coi.pdf

Perera, H.N., Granziera, H., & McIlveen, P. (2018). Profiles of teacher personality and relations with teacher self-efficacy, work engagement, and job satisfaction. *Personality and Individual Differences, 120*(1), 171-178.

Rademacher, T. (2018). To future white teachers, here's a resource guide so you don't have to ask your co-workers to explain racism. *Education Post*. Retrieved from: http://educationpost.org/t o- future-white-teachers-heres-a-resource-guide-so-you-dont-have- to-ask-your-co-workers-to-explain-racism/

Roberts, T., & Andrews, D. C. (2013). A critical race analysis of the gaslighting against African American teachers considerations for recruitment and retention. In D. J. Carter-Andrews & F. Tuitt (Eds.), *Contesting the Myth of a Post Racial Era: The Continued Significance of Race in U.S. Education*. New York: Peter Lang.

Rosen, J. (2017). With just one Black teacher, Black students more likely to graduate. *Johns Hopkins University*. Retrieved from: http://releases.jhu.edu/2017/04/05/with-just-one-black-teacher-black-students-more-likely-to-graduate/

Russo, P. (2004). *What makes any school an urban school?* New York: Center for Urban Schools.

Schaufeli, W. B., & Bakker, A. B. (2004). Job demands, job resources, and their relationship with burnout and engagement: A multi-sample study. *Journal of Organizational Behavior, 25*(3), 293–315. doi:10.1002/job.248

Shafer, L. (2018). The experiences of teachers of color. *Usable Knowledge: Harvard Graduate School of Education*. Retrieved from: https://www.gse.harvard.edu/news/uk/18/06/experiences-teachers-color

Slaughter-Defoe, D., & Glinert-Carson, K. (1996). Young African American and Latino children in high-poverty urban schools: How they perceive school climate. *The Journal of Negro Education, 6*, 59–66.

Steele, C. (1997). A threat in the air: How stereotypes, shape intellectual identity and performance. *The American Psychologist, 52*(6), 613–629. doi:10.1037/0003-066X.52.6.613 PMID:9174398

Steinhardt, M. A., Jaggars, S. A., Faulk, K. E., & Gloria, C. T. (2011). Chronic work stress and depressive symptoms: Accessing the mediating role of teacher burnout. *Stress and Health, 27*(5), 420–429. doi:10.1002mi.1394

Student Loan Hero. (2018). *A look at the shocking student loan debt statistics for 2018*. Retrieved from: https://studentloanhero.com/student-loan-debt-statistics/

Toldson, I. A. (2019). *No bs (bad stats): Black people need people who believe in black people enough not to believe every bad thing they hear about black people.* Boston, MA: Brill/Sense.

Tschannen-Moran, M. (2009). Fostering teacher professionalism in schools: The role of leadership orientation and trust. *Educational Administration Quarterly, 45*(2), 217–247. doi:10.1177/0013161X08330501

Watkins-Johnson, J., Lewis, C., & Griffen, A. J. (2013). The exodus of Black principals from urban to suburban schools. *The International Journal of Diversity in Education, 13*(2), 63–75. doi:10.18848/2327-0020/CGP/v13i02/58054

Williams, T. (2009). *Save our children: The struggle between Black parents and schools.* African American Images.

Youssef, C. M., & Luthans, F. (2007). Positive organizational behavior in the workplace: The impact of hope, optimism, and resilience. *Journal of Management, 33*(5), 774–800. doi:10.1177/0149206307305562

Ziezulewicz, G., Freishtat, S., & Baker, S. (2016). Suburban school districts face challenges diversifying teacher ranks. *The Courier News.* Retrieved from: http://www.chicagotribune. com/ suburbs/elgin-courier- news/ct-ecn-teacher-diversity-classroom-st-0228-20160226- story.html

ADDITIONAL READING

Gay, G. (2018). *Culturally responsive teaching: Theory research and practice.* New York, NY: Teachers College.

Griffen, A. J. (in press). *The power of a praying principal: An attitude of faith, hope, meaning, purpose, and spirituality in schools.* Ontario, Canada. *Word and Deed.*

Kafele, B. K. (2018). *Is my school better because I lead it?* Alexandria, VA: ASCD.

Toldson, I. A. (2019). *No bs (bad stats): Black people need people who believe in black people enough not to believe every bad thing they hear about black people.* Boston, MA: Brill/Sense.

KEY TERMS AND DEFINITIONS

Burnout: The emotional and mental exhaustion, weariness, and fatigue that results bouts of depression, anxiety, and overwhelming feelings of hopelessness.

Cultural Competence: The intentional and specific acknowledgment and implementation of culturally responsive and culturally relevant practices in all planning, evaluation, assessment and decision making.

Cultural Identity: How an individual personally identifies, which may be counter to the defined categorization or label provided by U. S. and/or Western Civilization social constructs.

Cultural Responsiveness: Ensuring and promoting culturally safe environments through the enactment of policies which support and promote individuals to be fully themselves by recognizing and acknowledging their unique and individual cultural identity.

Efficacy: One's innate belief in their ability and skill to accomplish tasks, goals, and assignments.

Gaslighting: Manipulation tactics performed by individuals in order to create a psychological and emotional advantage through lies and fear over a perceived yet unrealized threat to their position, power, or privilege.

Othering: The intentional and unintentional exclusion of an individual or group based on differences in culture, gender, race, ethnicity, non-binary, class, and ability.

Stereotype Threat: The perceived self-fulling prophecy of imminent failure that people of color, particularly African American men and women, endure as a result of a history of systemic oppression and discriminatory practices that have successfully excluded them and impeded upward mobility and career advancement.

Strategic Planning: A decision making process that includes conducting needs assessments, collecting data, soliciting input from impacted stakeholders, and aligning goals of implementation with timely and measurable outcomes.

Trust: Acceptance of one's given word and promises as infallible and believable.

This research was previously published in African American Suburbanization and the Consequential Loss of Identity; pages 86-115, copyright year 2019 by Information Science Reference (an imprint of IGI Global).

Chapter 46
What Is It Like to Be a Minority Student at a Predominantly White Institution?

Lucila T. Rudge
University of Montana, USA

ABSTRACT

This study examines the differences in experiences and perceptions of campus climate of 38 minority students enrolled in a predominantly white institution (PWI). African American students, Native American students, gender and sexually diverse students, students with disabilities, Latinx students, and international students participated in the study. About half of the participants reported negative experiences with racism and discrimination on campus whereas the other half reported the opposite. Attribution to discrimination theory informed the theoretical framework of this study and the data analysis. Policy recommendations to improve the climate of diversity on university campus are provided.

INTRODUCTION

This study examines the experiences and perceptions of campus climate of 38 minority[1] students enrolled in a predominantly white institution (PWI) of higher education in the U.S. Research indicates that minority students' experience can be distinctively different from that of the dominant groups at PWIs (Bennett, Cole, & Thompson, 2000; Griffith, Hurd, & Hussain, 2019). Having a minority status can add additional pressure to minority students that goes beyond the regular stresses usually expected in an academic institution of higher education (Smidt et al., 2019). At a PWI, minority students can feel isolated, underrepresented, stereotyped, misunderstood, and discriminated. They can feel like "guests in someone else's house" (Turner, 1994, p. 356). The absence of diversity views in the curriculum, minimal ethnic faculty representation, and misunderstanding of diversity enhance the stresses faced by minority students at a PWI (Mills, 2020; Sue et al., 2007; Smedley et al., 1993). According to Gusa (2011), "PWIs do not have to be explicitly racist to create a hostile environment…unexamined historically situated White

DOI: 10.4018/978-1-6684-4507-5.ch046

Copyright © 2022, IGI Global. Copying or distributing in print or electronic forms without written permission of IGI Global is prohibited.

cultural ideology embedded in the language, cultural practices, traditions, and perceptions of knowledge allow these institutions to remain racialized" (p. 465). Furthermore, PWIs tend to privilege the voices and perspectives of Western scholars and marginalize the voices and perspectives of non-dominant groups (Dhillon et al., 2015; Patton et al., 2007; Sue et al., 2007). When these normative "messages and practices remain subtle, nebulous, and unnamed, they potentially harm the well-being, self-esteem, and academic success of those who do not share the norms of White culture" (Gusa, 2011, p. 471).

Despite significant evidence concerning the hardship of minority students' experiences at PWIs, not all minority students perceive PWIs as hostile and "racialized." Some students may not even notice the White cultural ideology in the practices and norms of the university. Others might purposely deny or ignore acts of discrimination and instead focus on pleasant experiences. In this study, we found such variability in the experiences and perceptions of campus climate among participants. While many minority students did report an array of challenges and discriminatory acts on the university campus, several others reported exactly the opposite. To examine the differences in participants' experiences and their perceptions of campus climate,[2] I draw on the work of social psychologists on attributions to discrimination (Crocker & Major, 1989; Major & Dover, 2016; Major & Sawyer, 2009). Below I discuss the theory and research of this field of study.

THEORETICAL FRAMEWORK

Attribution theory is concerned with the ways in which individuals explain events and people's behavior. Research on attributions to discrimination examines how people respond to social disadvantage and negative treatment and how specific examples are explained (Crocker & Major, 1989; Major & Dover, 2016; Major & Sawyer, 2009; Schmitt et al., 2014). Major, Quinton, and McCoy (2002) define attribution to discrimination as having two primary elements: a) a judgment that treatment was based on social identity or group membership; and b) a judgment that treatment was unjust or undeserved. Events are prone to be attributed to discrimination when both elements are present. In other words, "people are most likely to say that they were discriminated against when they feel they were treated *unfairly* because of their social identity" (Major & Dover, 2016, p. 215). According to social psychologists, perceptions and attributions to discrimination are often subjective, disputable, and dependent on a number of psychological factors. Research in this area reveals that

...two people can often see or experience the same event and explain it quite differently, depending on their cultural beliefs, expectations, location in the status-hierarchy, and personality characteristics. This is particularly true when discrimination is ambiguous. Thus, people who are chronically high in stigma consciousness or race-rejection sensitivity are more vigilant for prejudice cues and likely to interpret ambiguous events as discrimination (Major & Dover, 2016, p. 224).

The characteristics of the event as well as the characteristics of the people involved in the event play an important role in the attribution to discrimination. For example, people tend to have prototypes or expectations for the types of events that constitute discrimination, such as being treated unfairly by an out-group member (Baron, Burgess & Kao, 1991; Branscombe & Baron, 2016). The more an event resembles the prototype, the more likely it will be labeled as discriminatory. Status-asymmetry between the people involved in the event also plays a role in the attribution to discrimination (Simon et al., 2013).

What Is It Like to Be a Minority Student at a Predominantly White Institution?

When the perpetrator is of a higher status than the victim, events are more likely to be attributed to discrimination. Members of chronically oppressed groups tend to regard negative actions from high-status perpetrator as discriminatory practices and interpret ambiguous events as discrimination (Major & Dover, 2016; Major & Sawyer, 2009).

Individual beliefs, experiences, knowledge, expectations, and group identification are also significant factors in the attributions to discrimination. Individuals' beliefs about why differences in status exist in society, such as the belief that social hierarchy is legitimate or that success is based on hard work (meritocracy), will most likely influence individuals' perception of an outcome as being deserved or discriminatory (Major & Dover, 2016; Major & Sawyer, 2009). Research shows that the more a person believes in individual mobility (Major et al., 2002) or individual preferences/choices (Stephens & Levine, 2011), the less likely they are to attribute negative experiences to discrimination. Group identification can also strongly impact how people perceive an event. Individuals "differ in the extent to which they are chronically aware of or sensitive to the possibility of being a target of negative stereotypes and discrimination because of their group membership" (Major & Dover, 2016, p. 222). Individuals who chronically identify with their in-group often perceive the event through a group lens and are likely to interpret ambiguous events as discriminatory (Major & Dover, 2016). More over, individuals who are high in stigma consciousness and sensitive to race-based rejection expect that their behavior will be judged according to their group membership, and most likely will feel discriminated in face of a negative situation. Experience and knowledge of discrimination also play a role in how individuals interpret negative events. Individuals who have had many experiences with discrimination linked to their group membership tend to be more sensitive to acts of discrimination directed to their group, and consequently be more prone to attribute negative actions to discrimination (Medoza-Denton et al., 2002). Finally, research shows that when individuals are more knowledgeable and aware of pervasive discrimination against a particular group, they are more likely to recognize and report actions of discrimination (Hirsh & Lyons, 2010).

The need for belonging and social inclusion can have an opposite effect on how individuals interpret events. People may minimize, underestimate, or even deny acts of prejudice or discrimination in order to bond and feel connected with others. Carvallo and Pelham (2006) argue that the social costs and risks of rejection involved with acknowledging discrimination are too high and threaten the need for social inclusion. Thus members of disadvantaged groups may find a range of excuses or explanations to ignore or minimize discriminatory acts in order to feel valued and accepted by a group. Finally, the fear of discrimination and uncontrollable negative treatment and the need for self-protection may lead members of stigmatized groups to engage in a number of strategies to avoid encounters with prejudicial treatment (Schmitt & Branscombe, 2002). Groups with invisible stigma, for example (e.g. white homosexuals, individuals with invisible disabilities), may attempt to pass as members of the privileged group to avoid encounters with prejudicial treatment.

METHOD

Design and Data

This study used a focus group research design. Focus group research draws on respondents' attitudes, feelings, beliefs, and experiences of a topic (Morgan, 1996). It is particularly suited for obtaining several perspectives about the same topic and gaining insight into people's shared understanding of everyday life. The purpose of this study was to qualitatively assess the climate of diversity on campus and learn from participants how the university could improve the experiences of minority students on campus. 38 students voluntarily participated in the study. It included African American students, Native American students, gender and sexually diverse students, students with disabilities, Latinx students, and International students. We conducted six 60-minute focus group sessions. Each student participated in at least one focus group; one student participated in two sessions. All focus groups were recorded and transcribed and are the sole data for this study.

The study was conducted in a mid-size research university in the West of the United States, with 75% of its student population identified as White. Native Americans represent the largest ethnic minority on campus (5%), followed by international students (4%) and Latino-Hispanic students (3%). African American/Black students represent the smallest ethnic minority on campus (1%). The university campus is located in a small town, known for its friendly, progressive and liberal community.

Analysis

Discourse analysis was used as a method for analyzing students' responses. Discourse analysis is the analysis of language in use (Van Dijk, 2014). It considers the relationship between language and the contexts in which it is used. More specifically,

Discourse analysis examines patterns of language across texts and considers the relationship between language and the social and cultural contexts in which it is used. Discourse analysis also considers the ways that the use of language presents different views of the world and different understandings. (Paltridge, 2012, p. 2).

Discourse analysis is by nature interpretative and explanatory. In the analysis presented in this study, I describe student's experiences and perceptions of campus climate, interpret their discourse in the focus group sessions, and explain their responses according to research on attributions to discrimination.

FINDINGS/DISCUSSION

Overall, international students, Latinx students, and gender and sexually diverse students described their experiences on the university campus as very positive. They perceived the campus climate as friendly, welcoming, and accepting of diversity. Native American and African American students, and students with disabilities, on the other hand, reported very negative experiences on campus. They mentioned numerous encounters of prejudicial treatment, endemic discrimination on campus, and lack of representation of minority perspectives in the curriculum. In the following sections, I describe into more detail partici-pants' perspectives and analyze their experiences and perceptions of campus climate into more depth.

Native American Students

Five Native American students participated in the focus group. Four of them were tribal members raised in the reservation. One of them was a non-tribal member raised in a white Irish Catholic community. The

What Is It Like to Be a Minority Student at a Predominantly White Institution?

four tribal member students reported strong dissatisfaction with the programs and the support provided for Native Americans by the university, whereas the non-tribal member student, although aware of the problems raised by his colleagues, did not demonstrate much concern about these issues. Furthermore, similar to other empirical studies, the tribal member students reported experiences of racism on the university campus and difficulties in navigating cultural and institutional differences (Chee, Shorty, & Kurpius, 2019; Dell, 2000). Their attributions to racism came in "the form of feelings of isolation from being singled out based on race, being stereotyped by faculty, staff, and students on campus, and inaccurate information regarding American Indians in textbooks" (Makomenaw, 2012, p. 857). Finally, the four tribal member students reported preference in having relationships with Native American faculty, staff, and students as it gave them a sense of belonging and comfort (Ibe, 2020; Tierney, 1995). The non-tribal member student did not express any preference about relationships. Instead, he commented that his experiences on the university campus were positive, with no instances of racism. He loved his classes and had never had any issues with professors.

Multiple factors could have determined the differences in perceptions of campus climate between the non-tribal and tribal member students. When examining their responses through the lens of attributions to discrimination, the tribal member students displayed very strong group identification, high stigma consciousness, and sensitivity to race-based rejection, whereas the non-tribal members presented very low group identification and no signs of stigma consciousness. The two excerpts below illustrate the contrasting differences between students with regards to in-group identification.

...from what I know from my own tribe, we were integral in many, many, many things that have happened in this United States. And the country that it was previous, and the people who had it previous to that. So when I don't even hear a holistic viewpoint, or it's brushed over as the Columbian Exchange, or any number of things to make what happened sound really good on paper, it becomes academic. For everybody else around when you say 18 million people died, that's an academic number. Not for me. For me that's family members. For everybody in this room that's Native, that's a family member that died. That's somebody that had to go on a long walk that they didn't deserve to go on.

My experience has been completely different from yours. They talk about the cultural shock, I'm from [.....], man. I come from a white, Irish Catholic community altogether. So coming over here was like 90% of the people I meet and talk to, or even sit next to in class are Native Americans. I don't really... I hear other people talk about they see racism and stuff like that, I just... a lot of times I'm not seeing it myself. It's what you make of it. I don't know, I've just had a completely different experience I imagine, from anybody, because I was already acclimated to being a total minority.

According to research on attributions to discrimination, individuals who chronically identify with their ingroup often perceive the event through a group lens and are likely to interpret events as discriminatory (Major & Dover, 2016). It is evident in the first excerpt that the tribal member student perceives the lack of American Indian representation in the history class through his group lens; he identifies deeply with his American Indian heritage and history for him is much more than historical facts, it is a personal matter. On the other hand, it is very likely that the non-tribal member has experienced similar incident in a class but in the conversation, he made no comments about the lack of representation of American Indians in the curriculum. Additionally, as portrayed in the second excerpt, he claims to have not seen any racism on campus, which shows that he does not attribute inaccurate information about American

871

Indians in the curriculum as a form of racism, as the others do. It is also interesting to note the differences in perception regarding representation of Native Americans on campus. The non-tribal member student commented that 90% of the people he meets on the university campus are Native Americans, whereas the tribal member students expressed strong dissatisfaction with the low representation of American Indians on campus. This is another example of how the level of identification with the ingroup can influence one's perception of the situation.

High stigma consciousness, sensitivity to race-based rejection, and experience with discrimination were also determinant factors in how the tribal member students perceived the campus climate. According to theorists of attributions to discrimination, individuals who are high in stigma consciousness, who are sensitive to race-based rejection expect that their behavior will be judged according to their group membership, and most likely feel discriminated in face of a negative situation (Major & Dover, 2016). Additionally, individuals who have had many experiences with discrimination linked to their group membership tend to be more sensitive to acts of discrimination directed to their group, and consequently be more prone to attribute negative actions to discrimination (Medoza-Denton et al., 2002). The excerpt below illustrates the profound experience of discrimination of one of the tribal member students, and how this experience has shaped his perception of all university professors. It also illustrates the negative effects of high stigma consciousness and sensitivity to race-based rejection to one's life. The passage begins after I had asked him to clarify if he had experienced discrimination with one or various professors.

With one professor, but it boiled down to other professors, because I found that's how every professor perceived me as. So that's why I get upset with every professor whether they're like that or not, I get really pissed off at them. Because I think that that's what they're thinking. Just because of that one professor who told me not to even come here.... Then it would make you, with that mentality, think you're getting put down by one professor then you're going to go around and think that this other professor is going to end up putting me down, so I'm not going to try hard in here. So you classify professors based off that one professor that will put you down, and he'll spoil it for everybody else.

The negative experience of this student with one professor was so overpowering that he now perceives all interactions with professors as negative, prejudicial, and harmful. This experience has most likely increased his stigma consciousness, making him even more sensitive to race-based rejection to the point that he does not seem able to interact with a non-Native American professor without feeling judged and discriminated.

African American Students

Three African American students participated in the focus group. All of them reported having had negative experiences on campus, including various instances of racism and discrimination, stereotyping, racial discrimination in curriculum content, and strong discomfort with the low number of students of color on campus. Similar to other empirical studies, the African American students felt marginalized, devalued, and deterred to fully participate in academic activities (James, 2017; Kuykendall, 2020; Levister, 2001; Rankin & Reason, 2005; Suarez-Balcazar et al., 2003; Whitmire, 2004). They expressed pervasive experiences with racial discrimination that extended beyond campus life, and commented that they "get marginalized everyday." The three students appeared to be very high in stigma consciousness and race-rejection sensitivity. They seemed very knowledgeable about issues of prejudice, racism, and

What Is It Like to Be a Minority Student at a Predominantly White Institution?

discrimination (Major & Dover, 2016). Finally, the students displayed strong identification with the African American community, despite one of them been adopted by white parents and another one been raised by a white mother. The excerpts below illustrate the struggle of these two students raised by white parents and how difficult it can be for black individuals to ignore racism in society.

And there would be times where I knew that something wrong was happening. I didn't know it was racism, but I knew something wrong was happening. I didn't want to tell my mom. Because she was white, and all the rest of my family was white that I knew. And then even contextualizing that. I didn't really start to understand what racism looked like until I started looking at feminism and queer studies and stuff, and developed a way to discuss it. Because it was happening all around me, but I didn't know what it was... I think if you don't have the vocabulary for it... if this is the norm, the expectation, then it's really hard to see what's happening.

It's just interesting where people who adopt people, and I can attest to that for my younger years, that I kind of ignored being African-American, but now it's just you can't ignore who you are. And anthropologically I've studied more about where I come from, instead of just going out there and going, "I'm Polish and I don't know my dad, but I'm black!" That's how I used to be. But now I get a lot more insulted when people come up to me and say things wrong about me.

Both students experienced racism growing up but had no knowledge or "vocabulary" for it as they were surrounded by white families. Despite the lack of knowledge and identity with the Black community in the early years, they sensed something was happening but could not name it or visibly identify it. As they grew older they sought to educate themselves to try to understand what was happening around them. The more knowledge they acquired, the more aware and sensitive they became to insults of discrimination and racism. Their experiences validate Major & Dover's (2016) argument that as "minorities become more educated about and aware of the potential for discrimination, they maybe more likely to recognize and report discriminatory treatment" (p. 223). In the passage below, we see another example of the effects of being knowledgeable about discrimination, and how such knowledge can lead to higher stigma consciousness and greater sensitivity to these issues to the point of hindering a student to fully participate in class.

But the thing that really bothers me, is this is a barrier. An actual barrier to our access to this work. There was a lab that we were doing in anthropology, and I almost didn't go. Now, not going would have meant that I would have lowered my letter grade. But I almost didn't go, because based on my previous two or three months of experience with this particular professor, I knew how it was going to go before I got in the room. And so my access to that particular piece of information that was absolutely valuable and I needed to learn, was barred by my feeling threatened and having anxiety about what was going to happen when I got in the room. And it was validated. I got in the room and it happened exactly like I thought it was. It was...the onus was on me to sift through the racism and sexism and homophobia, and get to the one little grain of natural scientific information that I needed from that particular course. And the same thing happens anywhere else. And you know the natural response is to shut your brain down and just be like, I'm not hearing this, this isn't happening.

This student was very knowledgeable about issues of discrimination and could easily identify acts of racism, sexism, and homophobia, since he also identified as a homosexual. His knowledge of the dominant cultural ideology embedded in the anthropology class led him to expect and anxiously dread the forthcoming experience of "racism, sexism, and homophobia."* As Gusa (2011) argued, an environment does not have to be explicitly racist to create a hostile environment. Unexamined historically situated White cultural ideology, embedded in the language and perceptions of knowledge, is a form of discrimination that may cause as much distress as explicit and direct racists acts. In fact, all African American and Native American students, with the exception of the non-tribal member student, were outraged with the pervasiveness of Eurocentric White views in the anthropology curriculum.

Students with Disabilities

Ten students with visible and invisible disabilities (e.g. cognitive disabilities) and the mother of a student with disability participated in the focus group. All of them, with a few exceptions, were very dissatisfied with the lack of handicapped accessible buildings on the university campus and the lack of knowledge from professors to accommodate students with disabilities. Similar to Marshak and his colleagues' (2010) findings, participants in this study described numerous difficulties and barriers to seeking and utilizing disability support services on campus. Many of them avoided disclosing their disabilities to professors fearing discrimination (Momboleo et al., 2015). Overall, most participants in this focus group seemed high in stigma consciousness, very sensitive to prejudice-based rejection, and fearful of prejudicial treatment. Stigma for people with disabilities is more complex than the other minority groups, as it involves "individual bodily differences, negative evaluation of and adverse reactions to those differences by others, and negative socio-emotional outcomes for individuals with disabilities" (Green, 2007, p. 330). Hence, the emotional well being of individuals with disabilities is affected not only by the existence of the impairment itself but also by the public attitude towards disability. Several students in this group mentioned how hurtful and damaging it can be to disclose their disabilities to "uneducated" professors and how it can affect their self-esteem.

I would say discrimination is a very big aspect of our lives. Discrimination by other students and faculty, and professors...And I find that discrimination is very deteriorating. And it's very alive and well on the campuses of [...], and it very much upsets me. Every semester I have to burn it all off, the negativity, and go back in and push that smile out. And it's exhausting. I should be concentrating on studying and growing. But I have to concentrate on interactions with professors. How are they going to do this, how are they going to do that?

It is evident in this passage, the emotional stress this student faces every semester as she enters a new class. She dreads the professor's response to her disability needs and feels distressed and exhausted to deal with these issues every new course. Many others have echoed similar experience. The fear of discrimination and prejudicial treatment led several students to delay or avoid disclosing their disability in class. This kind of behavior is not uncommon among students with disabilities. According to Hartman-Hall & Haaga's (2002), students with disabilities who are high in stigma consciousness may reduce their willingness to seek help in fear of more negative treatment from members of privileged groups. Such reluctance in disclosing the disability is illustrated below, in the voice of two students, who would rather

What Is It Like to Be a Minority Student at a Predominantly White Institution?

pass as members of the privileged group and face some disadvantage in their learning, than disclose their disabilities and confront prejudicial treatment.

My teacher did not know for two years that I'm a TBI. When he found out I'm a traumatic brain injured with PTSD, he looked at me like, wow, I've got to help her. And he did. But I didn't want to come out with it, because of some other past experiences with my professors that have really just...

... most of the time I don't even show my professor unless I see that I am really struggling. I always wait until the first exam. And then if I see it's going to... because I'm allowed time and a half. And if I really need it, then I'll go to them. They'll say, "You should have come at the beginning." I don't want to, because then you get this interaction going on that I don't want to deal with. But if I absolutely need it...

Although most students with disabilities who participated in this focus group had negative experiences to share, there was one particular student who only had positive experiences to report:

I've been so fortunate. I'm so fortunate I haven't had some of the experiences some of these people have had, and I'm sorry about that. The only person I've had an unfortunate experience with is my disabilities coordinator. That's another deal. But when you're disabled and you have to have help going in and out of doors when you're in a scooter or wheelchair, you always have to depend on other people to help you. And all of us with disabilities understand that we have to depend on other people. And I always feel like I wish I could give something back to this nice person that always gets the door for me at this thing.... So something to say I appreciate you. I'm disabled and I hate to ask for help, but you did it anyway. You're an angel, thank you. I'm just trying to figure out ways to bring us together and smooth out that hostility kind of, that sometimes brews between able-bodied and disabled. I just thought that would be kind of fun.

This particular student had no complains about the buildings, no problems with professors, and was very grateful to everyone who assisted her. She even proposed a "light and fun" awareness training. The student has muscular dystrophy and her symptoms did not appear until later in life. She mentioned that she was very active prior to this illness and that she sympathizes with people that don't understand her disability, as she said, "they could never understand because they've never been in the situation." Her comments indicate that she is very low in stigma consciousness and has low identification with the disability group. Furthermore, because her disability appeared late in life, she may have limited knowledge and experience of the discrimination usually associated to the disability group. These factors, in addition to her disability being very apparent, to the point of eliciting pity from passerby, may explain why her response was so positive and different from her colleagues.

Gender and Sexually Diverse (GSD) Students

Four gender and sexually diverse students participated in the focus group—a White male who self-identified as homosexual, a White female who self-identified as asexual, a White female who self-identified as lesbian, and an African American who self-identied as pansexual. Unlike the three groups discussed above, the GSD group reported very positive experiences on campus. The only exception was the African American student whose experience seemed very different from their[3] peers. Nonetheless, they did not speak much in this focus group (they participated in another focus group) and their subtle complains were often overshadowed by their colleagues' optimistic view of the campus climate. The three GSD students reported that most experiences on the university campus with professors and students had been very positive. They comented that people in the university are usually very open-minded, liberal and accepting. While the African American and Native American groups complained about the endemic discrimination on the university campus in comparison to other universities, the GSD group raved about the openness and acceptance they encountered on campus. Although there were some slight acknowledgements of homophobia on the university campus, those were usually justified as "single acts" or just "misunderstanding."

From what I've heard there are often simply misconceptions and stereotypes that come into play. However I haven't heard of a whole lot of open animosity, simply misunderstanding.

So I definitely agree with […] in that it's misunderstanding, it's a lack of knowledge when it comes to any kind of disagreement.

The perception of the three White students was quite different from the African American student, who later commented that these students were "making it sound like flowers and daisies." These students' perception also differed from a student in another focus group who complained about the "pervasive hetero normative" on the university campus. The positive response of the three White students is contrary to other research findings that claim that sexual minority college students is still highly stigmatized and discriminated on university campuses (Rankin, S. R., Weber, G., Blumenfeld, W., & Frazer, S., 2010) and the target of sexual harassment (The Association of American Universities, 2015). A number of factors might have influenced these students' perceptions of campus climate. Maybe for them, the university campus is more open to GSD students in comparison to their past experiences in high school. Most gender and sexually diverse high school students have devastating experiences in schools during their adolescence, with little alternative to scape discrimination (Sadowski, 2003), whereas in college, "you have a lot more power in deciding who is around you and who knows about you," one of them commented. Nonethelsess, when examining their responses through the lenses of attributions to discrimination (Major & Dover, 2016; Major & Sawyer, 2009), three factors emerge as possible explanations for their positive perceptions of campus climate: the need for belonging, low group identification, and having an invisible stigma. The three GSD students are white with access to most White privileges (McIntosh, 1989), as opposed to the African American student. In addition, they had the option to hide their sexual preference (invisible stigma), which would allow them to pass as members of the privileged groups.

I don't think that I have a whole lot to add to any feelings about on-campus discrimination or being afraid for my own well being, or anything like that. Because people just perceive me as another straight white male, I blend in really well.

I feel like mine is pretty similar, although I do identify as asexual and there's nothing about that that's an obvious giveaway so no one bugs me about it.

Schmitt & Branscombe (2002) argue that groups with invisible stigmas may often pass as members of the privileged group to avoid encounters with prejudicial treatment. Thus, by having the option of not disclosing their sexual preference, these students most likely had avoided many instances of direct

What Is It Like to Be a Minority Student at a Predominantly White Institution?

discrimination. Low identification with the GSD group may also have played a role in their perception of discrimination. The two female students who identified as lesbian and asexual had no strong connections with the GSD group and did not regard their sexuality as their main identity. In fact, of the few negative responses reported by this group, most of them were related to the GSD community.

I never wanted to make, and I continue not to make my sexuality part of my main identity. I don't want to be like that gay person that is super gay....Yeah, because I've had really negative experiences with people who promote themselves on that platform and that platform only, and it's really annoying. And it gives people who are part of the community a bad name... what I strive for, just being a person within a community of accepting people, and not basing it on sexual identity has really helped me...And it's also made me realize that there are people, many more than probably any of us realize, that are curious. And that are just looking for somebody to ask questions with and to answer questions, and to explore with...

The low identification of this student with the gay community is evident in her statement. Besides not positioning her sexual orientation as her social identity, she despises the behavior of some members of the gay community who overemphasizes their sexuality. Moreover, by not ascribing to her sexual identity, she feels warmer and more accepting to the "curiosity" of the hetero community and is able to justify "disagreements" as "misunderstandings." Finally, the need for belonging and social inclusion (Carvallo and Pelham, 2006) might have also influenced their perceptions and experiences on campus, particularly for the male homosexual student. This student was born and raised in the university town. He is very involved with the university campus gay community and proud of the openness and liberalism of both his town and university. If he made any negative comments during the discussion, they were directed at the GSD community instead of the university.

In terms of the community, I would say that [refers to the town] is of course a liberal bastion in [refers to the state], and on top of that we're very, very community-oriented. And so I think that with that comes more of an acceptance and a willingness to accept everyone, and involvement. I don't care who you are as long as you are willing to put in work for your community and make it a better place. Growing up here, that's what I always experienced.

And I think that sometimes a lot of the prejudice that people associate with the GSD community is propagated by the GSD community itself. Because it is a large community, but it is an uncertain and not incredibly stable community.

The deep connection of this student with his town and university surfaced several times during the discussion. He seemed very proud of the liberalism of the university and the openness of his town to accept everyone who wants to make the community a better place. If there were any problems related to the GSD community, they were the ones causing the problems and the ones to blame for the prejudice and discrimination associated with the community. His deep connection to his town and university and his need for social inclusion might explain why he minimizes and underestimates acts of prejudice and discrimination toward the GSD group and instead, blames the community for it.

Latinx Students

Four Latinx students participated in the focus group: a couple from South America, who came to the U.S. to do their graduate studies; a male student from Mexico, who moved to the country in 2007, and a female student from Central America, who immigrated to the U.S. when she was seven years old. Similar to the GSD group, these four students were also very pleased with the university campus and with their interactions with professors and students. They commented that people on campus were very friendly and welcoming. If they experienced or noticed any negative interactions, they attributed them as isolated acts of prejudiced individuals— "there's always going to be bad people, not just here, anywhere. So I just think a few bad apples cannot ruin my overall view." On the whole, the Latinx group appeared determined to minimize or brush off any form of discrimination they encountered either on campus or off campus.

Based on the theory of attributions to discrimination, a number of factors could have influenced these students' experiences and perception of campus climate. First, the South American couple and the Mexican student had very low identification with the Latinx minority group. They did not even consider themselves as part of a minority group:

"I grew up in a different country where I wasn't a minority. So being here and being a minority, I guess I just don't have that in my head. I just have my identity."

Second, the South American couple had been in the U.S. for just two years, which one could argue is a short time for developing stigma consciousness and sensitivity to race-based rejection, especially if they have been in a privileged position in their home country. Finally, the Mexican student spoke fluent English, which seem to have afforded him acceptance and inclusion into the dominant group, a privilege that many immigrant students may not share. Moreover, his proficiency in English allowed him a status above his international peers to the point of even sympathizing with the perpetrators.

I heard a couple of odd experiences from a couple of people I know. But it's mostly regarding people making fun of them or criticizing they have an accent. Truth be told, yes, they do have a very thick accent. So I don't know, I mean, I don't know how to put that. No one should be made fun of, but I think it helps a lot if you speak the language fluently and correctly.

Although this student feels uncomfortable to criticize the lack of fluency of his international peers, he agrees that having a thick accent can be a problem, and by agreeing with his American friends, he assures his membership in the privileged group. This same student disagreed with a comment I made about some Latinx students feeling isolated on campus. He thought that people just needed to know where to look to find the right relationships. In his view, it was up to the individual to look for these opportunities. His view was echoed by the other Latinx student who argued that most of her relationships on campus emerged because of her own effort and desire to make new friends.

For me, I'm a social butterfly. So if I see somebody who is maybe interacting in the class more, and I want to learn more, I'll maybe go talk to that person say hey. Just try to talk and get to class early so that if anybody else comes to class early I can at least try to talk with them before class. That's how a lot of my strong relationships formed.

What Is It Like to Be a Minority Student at a Predominantly White Institution?

This student, unlike the others in this group, mentioned several instances of prejudice and discrimination she had experienced in the U.S., including the university. She described having been kicked out of a program by a professor for no sound reason, shouted out several times to "go back to her own country," and yelled at a bar with statements such as "Get that black out of the bar!" Despite clear evidence of acts of discrimination, she insisted in justifying these events as isolated actions of individuals who do not accept other cultures.

Anyway, other than that, seeing a couple people here and there who just don't really accept other people of different cultures, I've never had a problem. I love it here, I've always gotten along with all my teachers and received the same amount of help, I feel, as everyone else. So I truly feel safe. It's a great learning experience here.

Her determination to focus on the positives despite many encounters of racism and discrimination in her life is apparent. Her need for social inclusion (Carvallo and Pelham, 2006) appeared to be a key factor in her wiliness to dismiss these events as isolated incidents. As quoted above, she regards herself as "a social butterfly." She loves the campus, "feels as everyone else," and "feels safe" in the community. Why would she risk her membership in this White community complaining about racism? As Carvallo and Pelham (2006) argue, the social costs and risks of rejection involved with acknowledging discrimination are too high and threaten the need for social inclusion. Members of disadvantaged groups may engage in various strategies to ignore or brush off discriminatory acts in order to feel valued and accepted by a group. In her situation, being accepted in the White community appears to be far more important than dwelling on acts of discrimination. Hence, her insistence in minimizing these negative incidents or dismissing them all together. Finally, a belief in social mobility might also have influenced her disposition to ignore instances of discrimination. Research shows that the more a person believes in individual mobility, the less likely they are to attribute negative experiences to discrimination (Major et al., 2002). This student is an offspring of immigrant parents, who most likely endured great discrimination as they settled in the country with very limited English. Her mother "tells [her] stories but [she doesn't] like to hear them." She is now fluent in English and a college student. She has succeeded despite encountering racism and discrimination throughout her life. Why would she criticize a social system in which she has thrived and prospered?

International Students

Twelve international students participated in the focus group: seven students from East Asian, three from Africa, one from the Middle East, and one from South America. Similar to the last two groups, these students were also very happy with the university campus environment and the support from the International Office. They mentioned that people were very friendly and welcoming and professors were very supportive to accommodate their needs. The only negative comments made by this group were related to the university Residence Halls. Several students encountered problems in their dorms and felt that they had to do all the "accommodation" to adapt to the lifestyle of their American roommates. As Lee and Rice (2007) argue, "international students confront an array of cultural adjustments but the responsibility is often left to the student to 'adjust' or 'adapt' to the host culture" (p. 386). Nonetheless, overall, these students seemed quite pleased with their experiences on campus and determined to overcome any discomfort to make the most of their educational experience abroad. All of them stated very clearly that they came to the U.S. with the specific purpose to study and then return to their home country. If they encountered difficulties or lack of accommodation from a professor, they felt it was upon them to adapt. If they heard comments embedded in stereotypes or wrong information about their culture, they justified as ignorance and an opportunity for educating others. None of the factors concerning attributions to discrimination discussed earlier was apparent in this group, not even between the two Black students from Africa. The purpose and determination to accomplish their goal, the temporary nature of their experience, and the assumption that they were responsible for adapting to the host culture were the most evident explanations for their positive perception of campus climate. There was however, a noticeable difference in English language proficiency among these students, which appeared to have impacted some of their experiences on campus. Those who were very proficient in English looked very self-confident, showed no reluctance to speak, and described no problems in participating in class discussions. The students with very limited English, however, were very quiet, only spoke when a question was directed at them, and participated very little in class. Lack of English proficiency is one of the greatest barriers for international students, as it affects both their ability to succeed academically and their ability to engage socially with others (Andrade, 2006; Andrade & Hartshorn, 2019). Nonetheless, despite the language barriers, none of them reported dissatisfaction with the campus life.

CONCLUSION

This study examined the differences in experiences and perceptions of campus climate of minority students enrolled in a predominantly white institution of higher education through the lens of discrimination attributions (Crocker & Major, 1989; Major & Dover, 2016; Major et al., 2002; Major & Sawyer, 2009; Schmitt et al., 2014). Nearly half of the students reported strong dissatisfaction with their experience on campus while the other half reported the opposite. The variability in students' experiences and perceptions of campus climate was present within and across all minority groups. Students who demonstrated great dissatisfaction with their experiences on campus and a negative perception of campus climate (tribal member students, African American students, and students with disabilities) appeared to be high in stigma consciousness, sensitive to race-based rejection, and fearful of prejudicial treatment. They all have experienced pervasive discrimination in life and demonstrated strong identification with their in-group. Knowledge and awareness of theory and research related to prejudice, racism, and discrimination also appeared to have played a role in the students' negative perceptions of campus climate (African American students). Conversely, students who reported positive experiences on the university campus and optimistic views of campus climate, showed no signs of stigma consciousness, no apparent sensitivity to prejudice-based rejection (3 GSD students, Latinx students, non-tribal member student), and low identification with their in-group (2 GSD students, non-tribal member student, Latinx students). The need for social inclusion and the privilege of an invisible stigma also appeared to have contributed to the positive experiences and perceptions of campus climate of some students (1 GSD student, 2 Latinx students). Finally, the international students' perspective was very distinct from the other five focus groups. None of the factors concerning attributions to discrimination was apparent in this group. Instead, a clear focus and purpose of study, the temporary nature of their experience, and the responsibility for adapting to the host culture seemed to have played a more significant role in their perceptions of campus climate.

LIMITATIONS

Limited contact with the students (60-minute focus group session) is the main limitation of this study. Although the discussions provided strong clues to draw an analysis of students' responses based on theories of attributions to discrimination, a more in-depth interview would allow for a richer and more in-depth investigation of the history behind their experiences and perceptions of campus climate.

RECOMMENDATIONS FOR UNIVERSITY POLICY

This study was sponsored by the university's Diversity Advisory Council to examine the experiences and perceptions of campus climate of students from minoritized groups, assess the climate of diversity at the university, and learn how the university could improve the experiences of diverse groups of students on campus. Despite the limitations of the study, findings were robust enough to provide recommendations for improving the experience of minoritized groups on campus. The following recommendations were provided.

Strengthen and expand the support centers for each minoritized group. Students reported that these centers have been instrumental in helping them navigate the challenges they faced at the university.

Students felt protected, supported, and understood. They appreciated having a space to meet students of similar racial background and having adults to guide them through difficult moments.

Make greater effort to recruit and retain students, faculty and staff from diverse backgrounds. Students of color, similar to other studies conducted at PWIs, felt isolated, underrepresented, and stereotyped on campus. The sense of social alienation and "ethnic isolation" that students of color experience at PWIs can lead to a dramatic drop in academic performance and many may eventually leave the university. Increasing the number of people of color on campus can help ameliorate the feeling of isolation and alienation that students experience at PWIs.

Provide greater academic and personal support for Native Americans. For many Native Americans enrolled in the university, this was their first educational experience outside the Indian reservation. The tribal member students felt unprepared to navigate the university system and overwhelmed with the challenges to adapt to the campus culture. Although these students appreciated the support provided by Native American mentors, they expressed the need for more mentors with experience working with tribal communities at nontribal universities to help them navigate the academic system.

Provide educational programs for students, faculty and staff about diversity, equity and inclusion. Incidents of bias, stereotypes and discriminatory acts were felt by students across peers, faculty, and staff. Providing a broad range of educational programs about diversity, equity and inclusion is key to reducing discrimination and fostering a more inclusive community. The university should consider making diversity training programs a requirement for students, faculty, and staff.

Provide specific workshops for faculty to advance awareness of diversity. Students reported numerous complains about faculty and urged that we recommend specific diversity training for professors on campus. Complains included: biased curriculum with lack of representation of diverse cultural groups and social identities, inability to properly accommodate students with disabilities, singling out minority students during class discussions, inability to handle students' oppressive behavior in class, gender bias, and inability to use appropriate language when referring to people from minoritized groups. Having experiences such as these in a course can greatly affect the academic performance and emotional wellbeing of minority student. The university should consider requiring colleges to provide specific workshops for faculty to make their curriculum and classroom practices more inclusive.

Many of the recommendations cited above are now common practices in various universities across the United States. Diversity and antiharassment training for students, faculty and staff is now mandatory at many universities. However, the way it is implemented, particularly when conducted online, is often ineffective leading to no significant change. To make diversity trainings more effective, universities would need to create more long-term trainings where participants are invited to reflect on their own bias, privilege, and behaviors.

ACKNOWLEDGMENT

I would like to thank Heather Smith for her work and support in this study.

REFERENCES

Andrade, M. S. (2006). International students in English-speaking universities adjustment factors. *Journal of Research in International Education*, *5*(2), 131–154. doi:10.1177/1475240906065589

Andrade, M. S., & Hartshorn, K. J. (2019). *International student transition: A framework for success.* Cambridge Scholars Publishing.

Baron, R. S., Burgess, M. L., & Kao, C. F. (1991). Detecting and labeling prejudice: Do female perpetrators go undetected? *Personality and Social Psychology Bulletin*, *17*(2), 115–123. doi:10.1177/0146167291017000201

Bennett, C., Cole, D., & Thompson, J.-N. (2000). Preparing teachers of color at a predominantly white university: A case study of project TEAM. *Teaching and Teacher Education*, *16*(4), 445–464. doi:10.1016/S0742-051X(00)00005-6

Branscombe, N. R., & Baron, R. A. (2016). *Social Psychology: Understanding human interaction United Kingdom*. Pearson.

Carvallo, M., & Pelham, B. W. (2006). When friends become friends: The need to belong and perceptions of personal and group discrimination. *Journal of Personality and Social Psychology*, *90*(1), 94–108. doi:10.1037/0022-3514.90.1.94 PMID:16448312

Chee, C. L., Shorty, G., & Robinson Kurpius, S. E. (2019). Academic stress of Native American undergraduates: The role of ethnic identity, cultural congruity, and self-beliefs. *Journal of Diversity in Higher Education*, *12*(1), 65–73. doi:10.1037/dhe0000094

Crocker, J., & Major, B. (1989). Social stigma and self-esteem: The self-protective properties of stigma. *Psychological Review*, *96*(4), 608–630. doi:10.1037/0033-295X.96.4.608

Dell, C. A. (2000). *The first semester experience of first semester of American Indian transfer students* (Unpublished doctoral dissertation). Montana State University.

Dhillon, M., Rabow, J., Han, V., Maltz, S., & Moore, J. (2015). Achieving consciousness and transformation in the classroom: Race, gender, sexual orientations and social justice. *Sociology Mind, 5*(2), 74–83.

Green, S. E. (2007). Components of perceived stigma and perceptions of well-being among university students with and without disability experience. *Health Sociology Review, 16*(3-4), 328–340.

Griffith, A. N., Hurd, N. M., & Hussain, S. B. (2019). "I didn't come to school for this": A qualitative examination of experiences with race-related stressors and coping responses among black students attending a predominantly white institution. *Journal of Adolescent Research, 34*(2), 115–139. doi:10.1177/0743558417742983

Gusa, D. L. (2011). White institutional presence: The impact of whiteness on campus climate. *Harvard Educational Review, 80*(4), 464–490.

Hartman-Hall, H. M., & Haaga, D. A. (2002). College students' willingness to seek help for their learning disabilities. *Learning Disability Quarterly, 25*(4), 263–274.

Hirsh, E., & Lyons, C. J. (2010). Perceiving discrimination on the job: Legal consciousness, workplace context, and the construction of race discrimination. *Law & Society Review, 44*(2), 269–298.

Ibe, L. (2020). *The languages of belonging: Heritage language and sense of belonging in clubs and organizations*. https://digitalcommons.calpoly.edu/mllsp/51

James, D. (2017). Internalized racism and past-year major depressive disorder among African Americans: The role of ethnic identity and self-esteem. *Journal of Racial and Ethnic Health Disparities, 4*, 659–670.

Kuykendall, T. (2020). *All eyez on me: the socialization experiences of African Americans at predominately white institutions* (Undergraduate Honor Thesis). University of Arkansas.

Lee, J. J., & Rice, C. (2007). Welcome to America? International student perceptions of discrimination. *Higher Education, 53*(3), 381–409.

Levister, R. L. (2001). *Blacks in gowns: A qualitative study of African American students' persistence at predominantly white college and universities* (Unpublished doctoral dissertation). University of Utah.

Major, B., & Dover, T. (2016). Attributions to discrimination: Antecedents and consequences. In T. D. Nelson (Ed.), Handbook of prejudice and discrimination: 2nd edition (pp. 213-239). Psychology Press.

Major, B., Gramzow, R. H., McCoy, S. K., Levin, S., Schmader, T., & Sidanius, J. (2002). Perceiving personal discrimination: The role of group status and legitimizing ideology. *Journal of Personality and Social Psychology, 82*(3), 269–282.

Major, B., Quinton, W. J., & McCoy, S. K. (2002). Antecedents and consequences of attributions to discrimination: Theoretical and empirical advances. *Advances in Experimental Social Psychology, 34*, 251–330.

Major, B., & Sawyer, P. (2009). Attributions to discrimination: Antecedents and consequences. In T. D. Nelson (Ed.), *Handbook of prejudice and discrimination* (pp. 89–110). Psychology Press.

Makomenaw, M. V. A. (2012). Welcome to a new world: Experiences of American Indian tribal college and university transfer students at predominantly white institutions. *International Journal of Qualitative Studies in Education: QSE, 25*(7), 855–866.

Mamboleo, G., Meyer, L., Georgieva, Z., Curtis, R., Dong, S., & Stender, L. M. (2015). Students with disabilities' self-report on perceptions toward disclosing disability and faculty's willingness to provide accommodations. *Rehabilitation Counselors & Educators Journal, 8*(2), 8–19. PMID:31008459

Marshak, L., Van Wieren, T., Ferrell, D. R., Swiss, L., & Dugan, C. (2010). Eploring barriers to college student use of disability services and accommodations. *Journal of Postsecondary Education and Disability, 22*(3), 151–165.

Mendoza-Denton, R., Downey, G., Purdie, V. J., Davis, A., & Pietrzak, J. (2002). Sensitivity to status-based rejection: Implications for African American students' college experience. *Journal of Personality and Social Psychology, 83*(4), 896–918.

Mills, K. J. (2020). "It's systemic": Environmental racial microaggressions experienced by Black undergraduates at a predominantly White institution. *Journal of Diversity in Higher Education, 13*(1), 44–55.

Morgan, D. L. (1996). *Focus groups as qualitative research* (Vol. 16). Sage publications.

Paltridge, B. (2012). *Discourse analysis: An introduction.* Bloomsbury Publishing.

Patton, L. D., McEwen, M., Rendón, L., & Howard-Hamilton, M. F. (2007). Critical race perspectives on theory in student affairs. *New Directions for Student Services, 120*, 39–53.

Rankin, S. R., & Reason, R. D. (2005). Differing perceptions: How students of color and white students perceive campus climate for underrepresented groups. *Journal of College Student Development, 46*(1), 43–61.

Rankin, S. R., Weber, G., Blumenfeld, W., & Frazer, S. (2010). *2010 state of greater education for lesbian, gay, bisexual and transgender people.* Campus Pride.

Sadowski, M. (2003). Still in the shadows? Lesbian, gay, bisexual, and transgender students in U.S. Schools. In M. Sadowski (Ed.), *Adolescents at school: Perspectives on youth, identity, and education* (pp. 117–135). Harvard Education Press.

Schmitt, M. T., & Branscombe, N. R. (2002). The meaning and consequences of perceived discrimination in disadvantaged and privileged social groups. *European Review of Social Psychology, 12*(1), 167–199.

Schmitt, M. T., Branscombe, N. R., Postmes, T., & Garcia, A. (2014). The consequences of perceived discrimination for psychological well-being: A meta-analytic review. *Psychological Bulletin, 140*(4), 921–948.

Simon, S., Kinias, Z., O'Brien, L. T., Major, B., & Bivolaru, E. (2013). Prototypes of discrimination: How status asymmetry and stereotype asymmetry affect judgments of racial discrimination. *Basic and Applied Social Psychology, 35*, 525–533.

Smedley, B. D., Myers, H. F., & Harrell, S. P. (1993). Minority-status stresses and the college adjustment of ethnic minority freshmen. *The Journal of Higher Education, 64*(4), 434–452.

Smidt, A. M., Rosenthal, M. N., Smith, C. P., & Freyd, J. J. (2019). Out and in harm's way: Sexual minority students' psychological and physical health after institutional betrayal and sexual assault. *Journal of Child Sexual Abuse*, 1–15.

Stephens, N. M., & Levine, C. S. (2011). Opting out or denying discrimination? How the framework of free choice in American society influences perceptions of gender inequality. *Psychological Science*, *22*(10), 1231–1236.

Suarez-Balcazar, Y., Orellana-Damacela, L., Portillo, N., Rowan, J. M., & Andrews-Guillen, C. (2003). Experiences of differential treatment among college students of color. *The Journal of Higher Education*, *74*(4), 428–444.

Sue, D. W., Capodilupo, C. M., Torino, G. C., Bucceri, J. M., Holder, A. M. B., Nadal, K. L., & Esquilin, M. (2007). Racial microaggressions in everyday life: Implications for clinical practice. *The American Psychologist, 62*(4), 271.

The Association of American Universities. (2015). *Report on the AAU campus climate survey on sexual assault and sexual misconduct*. Westat.

Tierney, W. G. (1995). Addressing failure: Factors affecting native american college student retention. *Journal of Navajo Education*, *13*(1), 3–7.

Turner, C. (1994). Guests in someone else's house: Students of color. *Review of Higher Education*, *17*(4), 355–370.

Van Dijk, T. A. (2014). *Discourse and knowledge: A sociocognitive approach*. Cambridge University Press.

Whitmire, E. (2004). The campus racial climate and undergraduates' perceptions of the academic library. *portal. Portal (Baltimore, Md.)*, *4*(3), 363–378.

ENDNOTES

[*]   It is important to note that this student is also homosexual, which adds greater weight to his experiences of discrimination.

[1]   The term minority refers to those individuals who are underrepresented or historically marginalized in society.

[2]   Campus climate is defined in this study as the attitudes, behaviors, and practices of faculty, staff, administrators, and students concerning respect for diversity and students' needs.

[3]   The pronouns they/them/there are being used as a singular pronoun for the student who self-identified as pansexual.

This research was previously published in Behavioral-Based Interventions for Improving Public Policies; pages 191-209, copyright year 2021 by Information Science Reference (an imprint of IGI Global).

Chapter 47
Agnotology and Ideology:
The Threat of Ignorance and Whiteness Ideology to Transformative Change

Victorene L. King
Divergent Consulting, USA

ABSTRACT

During periods of local and national unrest, leaders engage in discussions surrounding the reexamination of old policies and the consideration of new policies. Their changes to policies and procedures may be symbolic to silence objections or performative to feign new awareness, but symbolic and performative changes will not lead to transformative change. So how does a nation fix a problem of which many of its citizens are mostly ignorant? How do organizations redress inequitable hiring practices when they believe America is a meritocracy where everyone has the same chance of succeeding? How do educational institutions restructure teaching practices when the predominately White teacher workforce continues to resist talking about race? Transformative change will require the unexamined power of Eurocentric culture and thought that normalizes the marginalization, oppression, and subordination of Communities of Color and other groups of people based on gender, class, and citizenship to be completely exposed and then abolished.

INTRODUCTION

In banking, there has long been the practice that bank tellers study multiple examples of genuine currency in order to accurately identify counterfeits. The ability to recognize counterfeit money is one of the minimum requirements bank agents are required to learn to reduce overall risk to the institution (Lauer, Dias, & Tarazi, 2011). Imagine what would happen to the stability, infrastructure, and foundation of one bank agency if all its agents were incorrectly trained to identify counterfeit money as genuine currency. All incoming and outgoing financial transactions would be measured against the fake money and tenders would no longer be worth their actual value.

DOI: 10.4018/978-1-6684-4507-5.ch047

Copyright © 2022, IGI Global. Copying or distributing in print or electronic forms without written permission of IGI Global is prohibited.

Agnotology and Ideology

Now imagine an entire nation intentionally working to legitimize the enslavement of millions of Black bodies and the continual oppression and marginalization of People of Color by creating virtually the same dilemma: the inability to identify truth from deception. What would happen if an entire nation was deliberately and strategically kept ignorant of its history through the suppression of particular events and narratives or through the careful preservation of distorted perceptions to maintain systems that benefit only a few (Logue, 2013)? What if some forms of information were maintained by those with power to "keep people of African descent in undesirable places" (Ruffin, 2010, p. 12)? The suppression of information, or the distortion of the truth, or the manipulation of facts to serve a purpose that befits a particular belief over another is precisely what some scholars aim to understand when they study the production of ignorance; a study referred to as agnotology.

This chapter will analyze the intersection of agnotology and Whiteness Ideology, and their combined threat to an organization's ability to effectively implement diversity, equity, and inclusion efforts.

This chapter is broken into five distinct sections:

1. Brief summation of Critical Race Theory (CRT)
2. Agnotology Defined
   a. Examples from the past and present
3. Ideologies Defined
   a. Whiteness Ideology
   b. Ideologies of Poverty (Individual and Structural)
4. A Study of Ideologies within a School District
5. Rethinking the Design of Diversity, Equity, & Inclusion Trainings in Organizations & Schools
   a. Critical Thinking Framework

The juxtaposition of agnotology to Whiteness Ideology provides leaders committed to racial and social justice an alarming point of interest because Whiteness Ideology can go undetected by most white Americans as it serves as the very infrastructure of society while agnotology will intentionally misguide and thwart any efforts to unveil and dismantle the existence of Whiteness Ideology. Whiteness Ideology is analogous to the bank teller's training described earlier. Whiteness Ideology has been the exemplar by which many white Americans base their assumptions and decisions, and grounds their beliefs on. Because the production of Whiteness Ideology has been reproduced for hundreds of years, as we will see throughout the chapter, it is often the case that when white Americans are confronted with an alternate narrative, one that is supported by historical events and validated by true accounts from participants challenging the exemplar, the new accounts are rejected.

As seen in the figure below, agnotology and Whiteness Ideology will be the two overarching concepts that will be deeply examined using critical theory as the framework to ground the work throughout this chapter. Thus, the basic tenets of critical theory warrant a brief review.

Critical Race Theory

Critical theory builds on the classical writings of Karl Marx who argued society is built on relationships of power and should be examined critically. "The goal of conflict/critical theory is to reduce inequalities such as gender stratification, ethnicity/ "race" stratification, sexual identity discrimination, age discrimination, and international inequalities" (Tashakkori & Teddlie, 2010, p. 84). In 2001, Solórzano and Delgado Bernal described five themes that would be used to heighten awareness around racism within critical theory. These themes have been used and referenced by scholars as Critical Race Theory (CRT). Critical race theorist, Bell (1995) stated that he and other proponents of CRT "seek to empower and include traditionally excluded views and see all-inclusiveness as the ideal because of our belief in collective wisdom" and went on to express that "we emphasize our marginality and try to turn in toward advantageous perspective building and concrete advocacy on behalf of those oppressed by race and other interlocking factors of gender, economic class, and sexual orientation" (pp. 901-902).

Figure 1. Concept Organization
Source: Adapted from Kohli, R. & Solórzano, D. G. (2012). Teachers, please learn our names!: Racial microaggressions and the K-12 classroom. Race Ethnicity and Education, 15(4), 441-462.

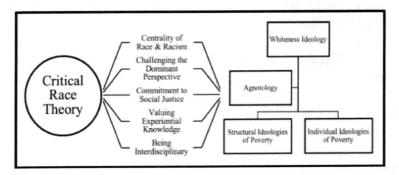

Similarly aligned with this thinking, Kohli and Solórzano (2012) summarized those five tenets in this way:

1. *Centrality of Race and Racism.* All CRT research within education must centralize race and racism, including intersections with other forms of subordination such as gender, class, and citizenship.
2. *Challenging the Dominant Perspective.* CRT research works to challenge dominant narratives and re-center marginalized perspectives.
3. *Commitment to Social Justice.* CRT research must always be motivated by a social justice agenda.
4. *Valuing Experiential Knowledge.* CRT builds on the oral traditions of many indigenous Communities of Color around the world. CRT research centers the narratives of People of Color when attempting to understand social inequality.
5. *Being Interdisciplinary.* CRT scholars believe that the world is multi-dimensional, and similarly research about the world should reflect multiple perspectives. (p. 445)

Applying those five tenets, the objective of this chapter is to create a tension within the White community between the need to slow down and critically interrogate knowledge and the urgency to reevaluate the narratives, experiences, and traditions of indigenous Communities of Color and other communities who have been marginalized, in order to realize transformative change.

Specifically, the chapter will outline several instances of agnotology taken throughout history that exemplify the outcomes from the creation of disinformation and misinformation. The chapter will also provide an overview of Whiteness Ideology to establish a general understanding of its influence over other

Agnotology and Ideology

ideologies. Findings from a recent study by the author, examining a Midwest school staff's ideological perspectives about the causes of poverty, will then be examined to illustrate agnotology and ideological beliefs in an educational setting. While several examples, including the research findings, draw from educational settings and perspectives to illustrate agnotology and ideologies throughout the chapter, the principles can be applied to various organizations. Furthermore, "how society responds to poverty and its related issues is conditioned by its public attitude toward the poor and the people's perceptions of the root cause of the problem," thus many scenarios and the forthcoming recommendations can also be applied to other organizations and leadership settings (Adeola, 2005, p.4).

BACKGROUND

Agnotology

In his 2008 book, *Agnotology: The Making and Unmaking of Ignorance*, Robert Proctor coined the term *agnotology* to describe the study of ignorance, its production, and its reproduction. Within the last decade there has been a growing interest from epistemologists to examine and understand "how and why various forms of knowing have "not come to be," or disappeared, or have been delayed or long neglected, for better or worse, at various points in history" (Proctor & Schiebinger, 2008, p, 3). One characteristic of agnotology is the intentional creation of misinformation and disinformation or the deliberate omission of information for the purpose of maintaining power, which is often referred to as structural ignorance. "Ignorance, allied with power, is the most ferocious enemy justice can have;" and while the term agnotology only emerged in the 21st century, various forms of structural ignorance have been used as weapons to oppress and marginalized communities for hundreds of years (Baldwin, 1998, p. 445).

Agnotology: Examples from the Past

During Ida B. Wells' lifetime in the late 19th into the early 20th centuries as an African American journalist, newspaper editor, and abolitionist, she daily bore witness to the dehumanization of Black people through the mass production of false reporting from the White press. Given the importance of an accurate recounting of history and the implications resulting from the persistence of structural ignorance, an extended citation from Wells' biography is vital:

We have Frederick Douglass's history of slavery as he knew and experienced it. But of the time of storm and stress immediately after the Civil War, of the Ku Klux Klan, of ballot-box stuffing, wholesale murders of Negroes who tried to exercise their new-found rights as free men and citizens, the carpetbag invasion about which the White South has published so much that is false, and the Negroes' political life of that era–our race has little of its own that is definite or authentic. (Wells, 2020, p. 4)

Like many abolitionists' writings of historical events, Wells provided numerous references to the press publishing fictional accounts of events. Some of the writings published were in an effort to stop the westward movement of Blacks so they would stay in Memphis and contribute to its economy, some were attempts to justify crimes against Blacks, but in every case, they were attempts to fan the flames of racial prejudice.

Wells' life's purpose and work was to provide investigatory reporting on events that were either incorrectly covered in the White press or not covered at all. In fact, Ida B. Wells explained in her autobiography that she began documenting her life's experiences specifically for future generations of Black people because she was all too aware of the "lack of authentic race history of Reconstruction" (p.3). It is this same history that many White Americans cannot accurately recall today, because beyond a cursory nod to Wells and other People of Color during Black History month, redressing the narrative in educational settings requires a degree of effort not currently exerted systemically, which will be discussed more fully later in this chapter.

Agnotology: Examples from the Present

Structural ignorance oppresses more than just marginalized *racial* groups. In 2009, the "Don't Say Gay" bill required school personnel to notify families if a student disclosed information about their sexuality that could be deemed as a safety concern. In fact, the Senator of Missouri argued that the "... act of homosexuality is very dangerous to someone's health and safety" (Barbeauld, 2014). This form of misinformation is an example of agnotology that was purported by someone with legal authority and power to marginalize and villainize those who identify as LGBTQ+.

In the same way, policies–and ultimately educational curricular decisions–that forbid discussions of sexuality-related topics in schools are influenced by resistance to LGBTQ+ inclusiveness and repress and oppress LGBTQ+ students in educational settings. These attempts to create school policies requiring educators to avoid or silence conversations about sexuality is a direct effort to keep people ignorant. Such policies overtly "eliminate crucial discussion of the historical and contemporary realities, struggles and contributions of gay, lesbian, bisexual, transgender, curious, and questioning communities in schools and fosters the formation of ignorant, closed communities" (Logue, 2013, p. 48).

Often referred to as misinformation or fake news by the media, the intentional production of inacurate and false claims have damaging outcomes. During the 2016 Presidential election, the now current President of the United States often misrepresented the immigrants crossing the Mexican border as criminals, drug dealers, and rapists. While these statements were fact-checked and clarified by many new agencies and reporters, there are reports suggesting their impact has been alarming. In a report titled, Mexican Immigrants Face Threats to Civil Rights and Increased Social Hostility, the authors expressed "The extreme degree of hostile rhetoric and the mounting evidence of its pernicious effects, however, are particular to the Trump administration and may be responsible for an increase in hate crimes against Latinos in 2017" (2019, p.7).

Four years later, that same administration would not only reject evidence and reports from experts in the Center for Disease Control about the threat a novel coronavirus would have on national health and safety but would downplay the virus by comparing it to the common flu. The administration's outright disavowal of the facts regarding the virus' threat and mortality rate resembled the tobacco industry's effort years ago to exploit public uncertainty over the causal links between tobacco and cancer- an issue that is no longer debated as fact or fiction. Nevertheless, the end-result was over 180,000 American lives lost to a virus, which some in power continue to spread false information about.

Educational and political systems and the press are not the only institutions culpable in agnotology's vitality. The next section will explore how one's ideological preferences will influence their willingness to reject or cling to misinformation.

Agnotology and Ideology

Ideologies

Oftentimes, people are unaware of their own ideologies as they are unconsciously held, shaped, and instilled. McClosky (1964) defined ideology as a "system of beliefs that are elaborate, integrated, and coherent, that justify the exercise of power, explain and judge historical events, identify political right and wrong, set forth the interconnections (causal and moral) between politics and other spheres of activity" (p. 362).

Ideologies are reinforced from birth through media and news, in schools through curricula choices, and through traditions connected to celebrations and lamentations. Therefore, when information is presented that does not align with one's ideological perspective, oftentimes an individual will experience mental resistance to the information. "One of the crucial elements of ideology is that it compensates in the mind for a deficient reality" (Barlow & Barlow, 1995, p. 107). Logue's (2013) position that "whites are able to think of themselves as good while in fact acting in racist ways" is an example of how the mind will work to compensate for false realities (p. 47) Logue goes on by stating that one's, "misrecognition of themselves as morally innocent when it comes to matters of race is supported by structuralized ignorance's whites fail to recognize," (p. 47).

There are as many ideologies as there are religions, political stances, countries, and cultures within those countries. "Periods of change and upheaval have brought about the birth of new ideologies and the reorienting of old ideologies" (Sakensa, 2009, p. 68). The next section will examine Whiteness Ideology and its dangerous and insidious influence on the consciousness of people in the United States.

Whiteness Ideology

Whiteness is constructed through social understandings about how people are supposed to look and behave, conduct themselves sexually, gender identify, and so on (Flores, 2016; Theoharis & Haddix 2011). Whiteness Ideology has existed for centuries and is so deeply woven into the fabric of American society it is undetectable: "even thinking about Whiteness takes a deliberate conscious effort that most White Americans simply never attempt" (DeCuir-Gunby, 2006). In DiAngelo's book, *White Fragility*, she posited Whiteness Ideology is intentionally masked because it is more powerful and useful when it goes unrecognized and unchecked.

Historically, schools across the western United States in the 18th centuries for Native Americans and Mexicans provide an example of overt Whiteness Ideology. The American schools' purpose was intended to strip "indigenous people of their language and culture, and replace it with English, European clothing and Eurocentric cultural values" (Kohli, R. & Solorzano, D., 2012, p. 443). Presently, examples of Whiteness Ideology may be more subtle:

Many Students of Color have encountered cultural disrespect within their K-12 education in regards to their names. While the racial undertones to the mispronunciation of names in schools are often understated, when analyzed within a context of historical and current day racism, the daily insults that, as a form of racism, support a racial and cultural hierarchy of minority inferiority. (p. 441)

White people may argue their racist responses are unconscious or that their intention is not to oppress People of Color through their words or actions; nevertheless, Whiteness, "elevates Whites and Whiteness Ideology to the racial apex" (Matias, 2020, p. 134). Consequently, its toxicity cascades down across all areas of society. The pervasive nature of Whiteness Ideology in education exists in the way of tracking, honors and gifted programs, punitive disciplinary protocols, and at every level beginning with whom is accepted into teacher preparatory programs.

Whiteness Ideology in Teacher Preparatory Programs

Often, in discussions about school desegregation, white people fail to recognize how they managed to benefit from the displacement of Black teachers and Black administrators. Instead, "white teacher candidates become the heroic liberal warriors who will save students of Color from failing" (Matias, 2013, p. 54). Unsurprisingly, the educational system effectively reinforces Whiteness Ideology in both overt and covert ways that deserve greater examination because the populations of students of Color is increasing even as the number of ethnically and linguistically diverse teachers is decreasing (Marx, 2004, p. 31).

In 2012, upward of 74% of the enrolled teacher candidates in traditional programs were White (U.S. Department of Education, 2016). In the teacher preparation stage, future teachers are taught by predominantly White professors. While many education preparatory programs include courses related to cultural competency or diversity, those courses are taken as separate programs and are rarely considered core to the curriculum (Sleeter, 2017). This separation of coursework reifies how race, ethnicity, and culture are set apart from the sum of learning and simultaneously altogether not part of the dominant White narrative.

Furthermore, many teacher certification requirements are based on a Eurocentric curriculum. This may not only dissuade candidates of Color from applying but may also eliminate them altogether, as uncovered in Kohli's research. Kohli (2013) observed that candidates who held a degree in ethnic studies were unable to pass the social studies content exam in the California Subject Examination for Teachers (CSET). CSET assessed content knowledge of a curriculum that only minimally acknowledged People of Color in general, and was *completely* absent of content related to U.S. Latinos when, at the time, the state comprised of approximately 40% of people who identified as Hispanic or Latinx (U.S. Census Bureau, 2010).

Some educators are presenting non hegemonic content to their students, but they are often met with resistance and pushback in the form of poor course evaluations, White emotionality, or disengagement from White students. These responses reflect a standard or expected response that researchers have observed when Whiteness Ideology is brought up in discourse (Matias, 2020; Sleeter, 2017; Barlow & Barlow, 1995; DiAngelo, 2018). Moreover, multiple studies have found a predominantly white teacher workforce leads to increased learning, achievement, and opportunity gaps (Sleeter, 2017; Matias, 2020; Ingersoll & May, 2011). White educators cannot deny their culpability.

An examination of prevailing ideologies about the causes of poverty illustrates this ugly truth in both people's deficit beliefs about people experiencing poverty and how widespread Whiteness Ideology is in the American subconscious.

The next section of this chapter will explore the grievous way Whiteness Ideology influences reality and harms all its citizens. By critically examining an ideology that is situated within a cornerstone of the American Dream, overwhelming evidence supports the notion that White people revere the ideal of their hard work earning them their personal prosperity and at the same time refuse to "acknowledge that they did so off the backs of People of Color" (Matias, 2020, p. 68).

Agnotology and Ideology

Individual and Structural Ideologies Surrounding Poverty

There are multiple views of poverty's origination, ranging between *individualistic* and *structural* causes. These two ideologies present a natural dichotomy, and they encompass strategies and pedagogical methodologies many educators rely on when they interact with students experiencing poverty. Social scientists have traced American ideologies related to poverty to several sources, including protestant ethics and the core American values stressing activity and work, independence, individualism, achievement and success, free enterprise, and the lingering conservative ideology rooted in social Darwinism. There is a preponderance of evidence that American attitudes toward the poor are negative, which partly explains the government's reluctance to address poverty more aggressively (Adeola, 2005; Bullock, 1999; Feagin, 1975; Gans, 1995).

Two prevailing poverty ideologies–Individual and Structural–were explored in a recent research study examining one Midwest school district's staff's perceptions. The two ideologies do not establish a binary; however, they do portray a pattern in behaviors, attitudes, and even political positions (Gorski, 2016; Nilson, 1981). "Ideologies, belief systems, value systems, and their policy outcomes generally come in opposing pairs . . . individualistic vs. structural . . . all reflecting the same basic cognitive conflict" (Nilson, 1981, p. 532). As such, both ideologies can be linked to policy choices. An example of an individualistic view is the 1996 "Welfare to Work" law, which requires people receiving benefits to obtain employment or attend job training. Whereas, strategies such as increasing wages and the enforcement of equal opportunities emanate from the structural explanation, though people holding structural views are seldom in a position of power to bring about change (Bremeyer, 2008, p. 235).

Individual Ideology

By the early to mid-19th century, the prominent ideology of American Individualism and Whiteness Ideology was firmly ingrained in the United States. It was commonly believed that "poverty was an undesirable character flaw that could be remedied with concerted action" (Orser, 2011, p. 535). Intensifying this stance was the belief that people fought hard to earn their superior status. Their efforts included an "emotional investment" (Nilson, 1981, p. 353). American Individualism "extoll[ed] the virtues of the oppressed to adapt and survive" (Orser, 2011, p. 539). Thus, traditional values and beliefs about an individual's opportunity for achievement have historically influenced American perceptions about the poor (Nilson, 1981; Orser, 2011; Wilson, 1996).

Religiously-inspired reform efforts have also set out to "cure the social ill" of poverty (Nilson, 1981, p. 535). Some studies have found that religious conservatives are more likely than others to hold individualistic views of poverty (Bremeyer, 2008; Nilson, 1981). Religion's influence on the individual ideology is the belief that one's freewill influences God's favor or wrath. Therefore, a person can control her or his perilous or prosperous outcomes (Bremeyer, 2008, p. 229). A person's fortune or misfortune is a result of faithful adherence to scripture, personal effort and discipline, or a willingness to confess sins.

Predictably, many who uphold these beliefs also tend to discount structural explanations of poverty as irrelevant and "shifting the blame" (p. 229).

The core of this ideology as it relates to the causes of poverty is the assumption that the individual is distinctively the problem or the solution; the individual has the capacity to change her/his situation if s/he exerts enough effort. This meritocratic ideal is manifest in individualism: the belief that in America, intelligence, effort, and grit would be celebrated and rewarded, and one's effort alone would be enough.

Those who live up to this ideal would be rewarded with privilege equal to their effort and inherent status over others.

Structural Ideology

In contrast to individual ideologies, a structural view of the causes of poverty is the belief that the poor suffer from circumstances largely beyond their control, such as a shortage of jobs, inadequate schools, or discrimination (Wilson, 1996). This ideology has an awareness that the existing structural conditions keeping certain people in a cycle of poverty cannot be resolved as easily and quickly as suggested by those who prescribe to an individualistic belief system (Gorski, 2016, p. 383). Structural views acknowledge the existence and persistence of inequitable distribution of resources both implicitly and explicitly in many systems to keep the current structure as the status quo. They also believe that "poverty is a way of positioning some at a disadvantage that simultaneously enriches a few, impoverishes others, and marks the poor with symbols of marginality, failure, and otherness" (Spencer-Wood & Matthews, 2011, p. 1).

One of the hallmark identifiers of those with a structural view is the acknowledgment of the fallacy that education is the great equalizer, as the fallacy often falls into a meritocracy paradigm that hard work and effort is rewarded (Blankstein, Noguera, & Kelly 2016; Marsh, 2011). Marsh (2011) argued:

Many have fallen prey to a pervasive, favorite myth in the United States today, one that holds that problems of social justice, including and especially poverty, can be solved through education. They cannot. And believing that they can does considerably more harm than good. (p. 605)

Blankstein, Noguera, and Kelly (2016) did not argue against rewarding hard work and talent. Rather, they point out that often the same groups of people are being recognized and rewarded while others who have put in the hard work are overlooked due to circumstances outside of their control. They wrote: "in most schools throughout the United States, a child's race, socioeconomic status, and zip code continues to predict not only how well he or she will do in school but also the quality of school he or she will attend" (p. 13).

Finally, in the literature related to structural views of the causes of poverty is the acknowledgment of historical prejudice and pervasive biases against marginalized groups. In fact, it is exceedingly difficult to find discussions on structural perspectives on poverty that do not include issues related to groups marginalized by dominant White culture. Spencer-Wood and Matthews (2011) argued this is because "impoverishment is a complex process involving the interaction of capitalism, patriarchy, and racism to produce structurally a set of economic, social, and political positions" (p. 1). If we look back further, Nilson (1981) similarly noted the policies that emerged from the War on Poverty in 1965 were focused "on disadvantaged minority groups, especially Blacks," not just class (p. 532). In summary, those who maintain a structural view believe society cannot ignore the potential threat of holding to a deficit and individualistic view of poverty.

The next section will examine a recent research study conducted by the author examining the ideological perspectives held by school staff about the causes of poverty. Heightening the collective awareness and creating a dialogue about educator views on the causes of poverty may lead to improvements in the educational practices and ultimately better support students experiencing poverty.

Ideological beliefs about the causes of poverty held by current and future educators should present a level of urgency that educational leaders must attend to. An educator's ideological position, whether it is

Agnotology and Ideology

within her/his conscious awareness or not, determines the extent to which her/his instructional practices further exacerbate the impact poverty has on the academic, social, emotional, and physical development of school-aged students. In fact, Gorski (2016) suggested that "no set of curricular or pedagogical strategies can turn a classroom led by a teacher with a deficit view of families experiencing poverty into an equitable learning space for those families" (p. 381). Thus, the need to better understand how an educator's beliefs about the causes of poverty impact their decisions, both consciously and unconsciously, is important to this body of work and across educational settings.

A STUDY OF A DISTRICT'S IDEOLOGIES ABOUT THE CAUSES OF POVERTY

A recent study was conducted to measure school staff's perceptions about the causes of poverty in order to gain a deeper understanding about ideologies in a diverse, midsize school district in the Midwest. Over 44% of the educators within the research site took an anonymous survey which included a selection of modified questions from the National Public Radio and Kaiser Kennedy School Poll: Poverty in America. The modifications drew upon the Feagin Poverty Scale, which measures perceptions of the causes of poverty (Feagin, 1975). Feagin developed an 11-item survey using a Likert-type scale that included three ideological dimensions: individualistic, structural, and fatalistic explanations. Yung and Weaver (2010) stated, "the three constructs identified by Feagin have been widely used and modified in several studies which measure people's attitudes toward poverty and/or poor persons" (p. 175). Adapted to fit the researcher's needs, 18 Likert-type survey items aligned to a specific ideology related to the perceived causes of poverty: structural or individual.

While analyzing the data, the author identified an area needing further study for two reasons. First, this area was identified because of the responses' impact on the overall outcome data; participants who selected "I don't know" on 10 or more items made up one-third of the overall survey responses. Second, the researcher wanted to understand the types of items to which the respondents indicated they did not know how to respond. Table 1 provides the frequency with which participants responded to survey questions with "I don't know" equal to or more than 10 times in the online survey, and those who responded in the same way less than 10 times. As an important point of reference, respondents were asked to answer 30 total of Likert-type items within the 18 questions.

Because of the number of respondents selecting they did not know how to respond to several survey items, the researcher needed to determine if all the questions and prompts in the online survey were written in a way that could produce valid results. Through this process, there were three questions the researcher decided to eliminate from the data, because it seemed clear the questions were either poorly written and confusing to participants, or the participants did not have enough background knowledge to answer the questions. Ultimately, only three questions and their corresponding data were eliminated, and 30 items were kept and used for analysis.

Table 1. Respondents selecting "I don't know"

	# of Respondents	Percent
"I Don't Know" responses greater than or equal to 10	82	47.1
"I Don't Know" responses less than 9	92	52.9

The researcher divided the data into two tables to demonstrate the variables, with a mean (average) above or below 2.5 because they had a data range from one to five based on the Likert-type scale. By separating the data, it became clear which items the participants more strongly *disagreed* with, indicated by a score of one or two (as seen in Table 2), and which items the participants more strongly *agreed* with, indicated by a score of four or five (seen in Table 3). For instance, from Table 2, the data suggested staff did not perceive that circumstances and/or the distribution of wealth as a cause of poverty; nor did they believe that people experiencing poverty work. They also believed there were opportunities available for the poor to work. Thus, the responses implied participants believed there was a lack of effort and motivation from people experiencing poverty. These beliefs align within individualistic ideologies as described earlier, which reverse hard work and, by proxy, Whiteness Ideology because it is the framework how white America has operated for centuries.

Table 3 echoes the data in Table 2, but in a more nuanced way. For example, there was strong disagreement about whether there was a lack of opportunities for the poor presented in Table 2, but when participants were asked if they believed the poor actively sought to improve their lives (M = 3.11), had a desire for achievement (M = 3.2), or were motivated (M = 3.33), the mean was closer to the middle with a low standard deviation. Furthermore, the response "I Don't Know" corresponded to the value three. Generally speaking, on one hand, the district believed that jobs and opportunities are available for the poor, and on the other hand, they did not know if the poor were motivated.

These data reflect the preference toward the option to claim ignorance versus making sense of incongruent information by claiming ignorance. Matias (2013) wrote about this cognitive dissonance in her discussions about White emotionality. She posited it is actually the White person's shame at witnessing the false claim of equality in the U.S., regardless of skin color, that causes a person to respond with such open hostility and animus. These data may represent the effort several participants made to acquit themselves of the ignominy of knowing *there were not actually* the opportunities available for the poor to work as their responses indicated, thus they selected they *did not know* if poor people sought to improve their lives or desired better for themselves.

Table 2. Strongly disagreed with variable (sorted by the mean less than 2.50)

Variable	n	M	SE	SD
Circumstances	171	1.67	.04	.64
Drug Abuse	173	2.43	.08	1.13
Medical Bills	173	2.02	.06	.89
Too many jobs being part-time or low-wage	172	1.98	.07	.93
Distribution of wealth in society is uneven	169	1.76	.05	.78
The society lacks social justice	167	2.19	.06	.73
The poor are exploited by the rich	167	2.38	.05	.80
The poor lack opportunities due to the fact that they live in poor families	169	2.06	.04	.74
The government's difficulty to provide infrastructure	168	2.48	.04	.69
The government's corruption	169	2.42	.04	.72
The lack of adequate health services	170	2.11	.06	.79
Most poor people in the US work	173	2.06	.05	.75

Agnotology and Ideology

Table 3. Strongly agreed with variable (sorted by the mean greater than 2.51)

Variable	N	M	SE	SD
People not doing enough	172	3.24	.08	1.14
A shortage of jobs	172	2.81	.08	1.16
The welfare system	170	2.98	.08	1.07
Too many immigrants	173	4.03	.07	1.01
Poor people lacking motivation	173	3.63	.08	1.14
Decline in moral values	173	3.32	.09	1.26
The poor are born inferior	168	3.61	.04	.57
The poor are not motivated	168	3.33	.05	.69
The poor waste their money on inappropriate items	167	2.91	.05	.64
The poor lack the ability to manage money	168	2.79	.05	.69
The poor do not actively seek to improve their lives	167	3.11	.05	.59
Loose moral values among the poor	167	3.10	.04	.61
The poor lack the need for achievement	168	3.20	.06	.64
Most poor people in the US don't work	165	3.82	.06	.79
Hard to get work	170	2.57	.08	1.10
Job are available if you are willing to work	167	2.59	.07	1.02
Poor people have it easy because they can get government benefits without doing anything in return	170	3.71	.08	1.06
Poor people have hard lives because the government benefits don't go far enough to help them live decently	171	2.56	.07	1.04

While the overall data did not yield statistically significant findings which would have suggested the staff leaned toward one ideology over the other, the author believed the data may present a hidden threat that should not be ignored or overlooked. The frequency participants chose to indicate they did not know what they believed about people experiencing poverty and what those uncertainties suggested about their views is both troubling and alarming.

Taking a deeper look into the data, the researcher noted that each question (30 items) on the online survey had a minimum of eight and maximum of 111 of the 173 participants who selected Don't Know. As reflected in Table 4, there is a notable break between the frequency Don't Know was selected for *individual* ideologies compared to *structural* ideologies. Six of the 11 statements presented in the table, with at least 99 participants submitting Don't Know responses, are aligned with an individual ideological position, and over half of the top Don't Know responses are aligned with the individual ideology. The researcher used the frequency of at least 50 participants selecting Don't Know as the cut-off because it was close to the average number (M = 49.5) of times participants selected Don't Know.

Similarly, five of the 11 statements with over 50 participants selecting the Don't Know option on the Likert-scale were structural. However, it was unclear to participants whether the government's ability to provide support and infrastructure impacted a person's socio-economic status. One statement that was very close to meeting the criteria to be included in these data, with a frequency of 48 participants selecting they Don't Know, was: **The poor are born genetically inferior** (the next highest frequency was a 36). The researcher strongly believed this datum, even though it did not meet the mean (*M*) cut-off, needed to be highlighted in the body of research as the statement reveals a surreptitious characterization many White Americans place on marginalized communities and groups (Adeola, 2005).

Table 4. Frequency don't know responses were selected by 50 or more participants

Statement Item	Number of Respondents	Ideology Alignment
The poor are not motivated	76	Individual
The society lacks social justice	55	Structural
The poor are exploited by the rich	84	Structural
The poor waste their money on inappropriate items	109	Individual
The poor lack the ability to manage their money	99	Individual
The government's difficulty to provide infrastructure	76	Structural
The poor do not actively seek to improve their lives	111	Individual
The government's corruption	89	Structural
Loose moral values among the poor	108	Individual
The poor lack the need for achievement	94	Individual
The lack of health care services	82	Structural

Agnotology and Ideology

Based on the data analysis, the author created a working hypothesis: "There Is a Connection Between Individual Ideology Items Related to Poverty and the Frequency with Which the Response, 'I Don't Know' Was Selected." The purpose of describing the conclusion as a working hypothesis is grounded in post-positivist theories of research. Whereas positivist research posits a certain degree of confidence in an outcome leading to the formulation of conclusions, post-positivist research accepts "that theories, background, knowledge and values of the researcher can influence what is observed" (Smeyers & Smith, 2014, p. 208). This framing is especially important because post-positivist research also allows for counter-storytelling methodologies. Storytelling and counter-storytelling are often seen as "Other"-centered research, which is grounded in values that are not acceptable in positivist research, but central to the tenets of Critical Race Theory (Delgado, 1995). Stemming from the working hypothesis, the author submits that in order to engender more equitable classrooms, school leaders and teachers should consider the following question: *Why are so many people unclear about individualistically-positioned statements compared to structurally-positioned statements?*

Based on the number of participants in the study selecting Don't Know responses (as seen in Table 4), the author speculates that they were selected deliberately, but there is no method for making any definitive claims. However, Larrian's definition of ideology is useful here: "a particular form of consciousness which gives an inadequate and distorted picture of contradictions, either by ignoring them, or by misrepresenting them" (1983, p. 12). Perhaps the participants did not like acknowledging their beliefs that people experiencing poverty were not motivated, lacked a desire to improve their situation, or were genetically inferior, so they chose to hide behind the Don't Know option.

Agnotology and Ideology

Whether participants selected Don't Know so they might remain neutral or it was their honest admission of ignorance, at the heart of this body of research is the ethical obligation to understand, acknowledge, and address what educators may not know related to the causes of poverty because what they *Don't Know* has serious implications for students experiencing poverty. The author believes it is incumbent on people in positions of authority and leadership, alongside the community they lead in, to understand the possible implications of findings such as those observed in this district so that next steps can be developed and monitored. Other recommendations and suggestions are discussed next.

What Comes First When Solving Problems: Addressing Agnotology or Ideology

As mentioned earlier in the chapter, there is a complexity within this entire conversation. At a macro-level, which is driven by personal and communal, political and religious ideologies, exists the implications of agnotology. At the same time, Whiteness Ideology is invisible to the majority of people in the U.S. but deeply influences society. Does a school committed to effectively implementing diversity, equity, and inclusion focus first on redressing the disinformation that is reinforcing ideological strongholds or try to unpack the impact of Whiteness Ideology? Put another way and more specific to the previously described study: Should a district first focus on training and professional development for staff intended to train them to meet the diverse social, emotional, physical, and academic needs of students or implicit and unconscious bias? The author posits that while the work should be done deliberately and simultaneously, which will take time, there is an urgency that leaders must engage in now. Educational theorists provide some helpful observations into this discussion that are worth examining and relevant for all organizations committed to equity, diversity, and inclusion.

In response to challenges Professors Barlow and Barlow experienced with their mostly White students breaking through barriers during course discussion about ideologies of race and crime, they began to examine Perry's stages of critical-thinking. Perry (1970) outlined stages of critical thinking that have been widely applied and shared to develop similar progressions of critical thinking within various fields to help people move into conversations they otherwise would not have been able to cognitively and emotionally handle. These stages are 1) Dualistic View, 2) Multiplicity, 3) Contextual Relativism, and 4) Commitment (p. 106). Each will be discussed in turn.

Dualistic. In this stage, people see theories, ideas, or events as good or bad and right versus wrong. They build their trust in advisors and seek out mentors or relationships with those who have similar beliefs. In this stage of critical thinking, White people in America are not able to recognize Whiteness Ideology nor, therefore, the systemic nature of racism, deficit ideologies about people experiencing poverty, and the Dominant narrative is used as a filter through which all other information is received. Thus, people experience cognitive dissonance when counter-stories are shared and move into various forms of White fragility or Whiteness emotionality (DiAngelo, 2018; Matias, 2020). For this very reason, educational researchers suggest that most college undergraduates only move into the next phase by the end of their senior year or remain in this phase (Barlow and Barlow, 1995; Belenky et al., 1986).

Multiplicity. In the second phase, people build a tolerance for those they would consider as Other and those who do not hold the same viewpoints and develop a willingness to listen and consider alternative perspectives. In many organizations, people in the multiplicity stage are content with just getting here, so they invest in microaggression and implicit bias training and book studies that teach tolerance. However, this level of critical thinking alone will not be enough to threaten inequity and systemic injustice because these activities may not directly challenge the behaviors, beliefs, and actions of liberalists. Another defining aspect of Critical Race Theory is the critique of liberalism because in order to "counter racism and White supremacist ideologies, liberalism is not a mechanism for substantive, real change" (Theoharis & Haddis, 2001, p. 1335). Whites need to understand the origin of their Whiteness in order to recognize when, where, and how it shows up to protect its power.

Contextual Relativism. Gallagher (1998), drawing on Perry's framework, described people at this level of critical thinking as "disillusioned with didactic instruction" (p. 15). They appreciated accessing information that was supported by other academic theories and, " . . . disciplined argumentation, and the standards of excellence in different fields of study" (p. 15). During this phase, White people would be more cognitively and emotionally available to thoughtfully engage in discussions that challenge their privilege and their power. Here, they would seek out counter-stories from communities of Color. They would want to examine and challenge the reasons behind a society that would strategically silence, distort, and manipulate the narratives of so many communities of Color, including other intentionally and historically marginalized groups such as gender, class, and citizenship. It is in this level of critical thinking that people could begin to identify the absence of Other narratives as an intentional exertion of Whiteness Ideology and White supremacy's power and influence to keep people ignorant.

Commitment. Perry's (1970) final stage of critical development reflects the recognition that problems, ideas, phenomena, theories, and differences can be approached within a variety of frameworks. They can also identify the differences in frameworks, and when information is presented, they can see which framework it is most closely aligned to and how it connects. Thoma (1993), who further modified Perry's critical thinking developmental stages, posited that when people move beyond the *contextual relativism* stage, they are able to "independently make and commit to choices of ideas and actions" and that " . . . knowledge is not absolute and that even the methodologies of specific disciplines are imperfect" (p. 133). Either version of this stage of development functions in the Critical Race Theory grounding this chapter because what many White people presently know about the world is *only* known and experienced through the lens of Whiteness Ideology. Deconstructing this ideology will lay bare the gross misrepresentation of the heroes and villains in American history and who benefits from the American Dream. As Frederrick Douglass (1852) stated in an oration:

"I am not included within the pale of this glorious anniversary! Your high independence only reveals the immeasurable distance between us. The blessings in which you this day, rejoice, are not enjoyed in common. The rich inheritance of justice, liberty, prosperity and independence bequeathed by your fathers, not by me.

If organizations are to become spaces where more critical thinking and justice-based discourses happen, individuals must first see the social contradictions that Whiteness Ideologies have tried to erase or hide through the acknowledgment of agnotology. The presentation of counter-stories becomes evermore paramount because the current monocultural history is unable to address the contradictory experiences of People of Color. It is arguably set up to support ideological interpretations that protect Whiteness Ideology. Leaders must then be aware that when these contradictions are revealed and presented openly, White fragility and Whiteness emotionality responses will be activated. White people afraid of losing the power and privilege that was stolen from communities of Color will make claims that these counter-stories are attempts to erase history instead of recounting the true story. Thoma (1993) summarizes Perry's warning that at any point on the stages of critical thinking people:

Agnotology and Ideology

. . . may suspend, nullify or even reverse the process of growth . . . may pause for a year or more, often quite aware of the step that lies ahead . . . as if waiting or gathering his forces. . . . He may entrench himself, in anger and hatred of "otherness," in the me-they or we-other dualism of the early Positions. . . . He may settle for exploiting the detachment offered by some middle Position on the scale, in the deeper avoidance of personal responsibility known as alienation. (p. 135)

The desire to revert back to dualistic behaviors is natural for those raised in Whiteness Ideology. One's internal dissonance may likely be amplified externally by the cruel expressions of those experiencing resistance to the same change.

FUTURE RESEARCH DIRECTIONS

Rethinking the Design of Diversity, Equity, and Inclusion Trainings in Organizations & Schools

Central to CRT is the action of pressing forward and against these White emotional responses. Efforts to threaten injustice and inequity are not without challenge, but there are examples that can be used as models and guide future research (Theoharis & Haddis, 2011; Barlow & Barlow, 1995). Barlow and Barlow's research applying critical-thinking frameworks while teaching undergraduate students in criminal justice or criminology courses, we can see the intentional organization of their course materials. Their work offers leaders an exemplar and model that can be replicated.

They organized content to best prepare students to contextualize issues of freedom, social justice, race, and crime. Grounding the issues that were sensationalized in the media or distorted by inaccurate news reports in historical contexts allowed the students to identify contradictions and then begin to challenge their own assumptions informed by agnotology and ideologies. For example, students learned about the 1914 Harrison Act and the 1937 Marijuana Taxes Act. They learn that the former targeted Chinese immigrants who were competing for the same jobs as White people during an economic decline and that the latter act targeted Mexican immigrants and was passed during a labor war between fruit growers in California and Mexican migrant workers. Students were able to see this and many other historical examples demonstrating suppression of communities of Color developed by racist policies and legislation. They examined these events as they also studied the War on Drugs. Thus, moving students out of dualistic and multiplicity stages of critical-thinking into constructive relativism and commitment.

Similarly, when we examine the findings from Theoharis and Haddis' (2011) study of six White urban principals committed to creating more equitable places for students of Color, we see a similar strategy used with staff members. Each of the six principals spent years examining their own power and privilege, and engaged in intellectual work around race. Though without naming it as such, they worked their way through a critical-thinking framework before they began talking about it with their staff. What is notable about these school principals is they did not allow staff to opt out of the discussions about race and privilege–demonstrating their full *commitment* to CRT. They brought race into every aspect of the conversation–discipline data, hiring and promotion practices, and tracking. They unpacked areas where, as a district, they had individually and collectively tried to distort the truth about each of those practices. The principals recentered every conversation so it could no longer be a separate discussion. Though unmandated in school policy, the leaders expected her/his staff to confront issues of race.

These examples suggest areas of improvement for leaders and researchers. One area worth immediately researching is higher education. Examining how to apply both CRT and critical-thinking frameworks into courses is an area educational theorists and researchers committed to diversity, equity, and inclusion ought to invest time. For example, when we train students in business programs, are those students also taught to examine how corporations in the U.S. have benefited from prisons full of Black and Brown bodies to manufacture its merchandise? Are they taught to compare this current practice with the historic practice of Black workers being forced to work off their debts to White people after slavery ended? This process would require educational institutions to research and reevaluate their diversity and ethics courses.

These types of learning experiences can only happen as leaders in all sectors come to the realization that structured ignorance, created in part by Whiteness Ideology, is working against, not with, their diversity, equity, and inclusion efforts. Organizations ought to evaluate the frequency and types of experiences that move people into spaces that challenge their thinking while equipping them with the skills to endure and manage the discomfort long enough for growth to occur.

Additional research into the compounding effect Whiteness Ideology has on agnotology or vice versa warrants exploration. Developing tools or inventories to assess the degree to which people are influenced by Whiteness Ideologies may also be worth further exploration. This may help organizations better identify those they want in positions leading their Diversity, Equity, and Inclusion (DEI) efforts, leading their school districts, or creating policies and procedures.

Finally, this chapter only breached the surface in examining structural ignorance in education, politics, and the press. But they are not the only institutions culpable of spreading misinformation and disinformation. Religion and science are also fields warranting further exploration, as they have also played a devastating and lasting role on Communities of Color. Likewise, there are many ideologies, and this chapter only *briefly* examined Whiteness Ideology, related to poverty. These, and particularly race and criminology ideologies as well as genetic and other forms of deficit ideologies, warrant further research and discussion.

CONCLUSION

Having a better working understanding of agnotology and Whiteness Ideology, organizations may be more equipped to develop a stronger more effective framework for addressing their DEI efforts. Organizations may then also begin to identify that some of their policies and procedures were based on erroneous information and assumptions. Unless leaders have these understanding, they become like the bank agent who was supposed to be trained to identify counterfeits by repeatedly studying and examining authentic currency, but instead was trained using a counterfeit from the beginning. Thus, like the bank agent who is moving through her entire career measuring all currency against the counterfeit, leaders who never examine agnotology's efforts to distort truth and deception, or even their own ideologies, are simply misleading their organization.

As evidenced by findings from the study on ideologies surrounding the causes of poverty held by school staff, there is a need for leaders to better understand how the ideologies held by their employees impact their organization's diversity, equity, and inclusion efforts. Whiteness Ideology has most certainly influenced those ideologies; Critical Race Theory requires leaders to lead their organizations into the work of abolishing it. Perry's Critical-Thinking Framework offers a model that allows leaders to me-

Agnotology and Ideology

thodically and strategically acknowledge agnotology through historic counter-stories and narratives by Communities of Color, while simultaneously and deliberately addressing Whiteness Ideologies.

REFERENCES

Adeola, F. (2005). Race and class divergence in public attitudes and perceptions about poverty in USA: An empirical study. Jean Ait Belkhir, Race. *Gender and Class Journal, 12*(2), 53–80.

Baldwin, J. (1998). *No name in the street. Collected essays*. Library of America.

Barbeauld, P. H. (2014). Don't Say Gay Bills and the Movement to Keep Discussion of LGBT Issues out of Schools. *JL & Educ., 43*, 137–146.

Barlow, M., & Barlow, D. (1995). Confronting ideologies of race and crime in the classroom: The power of history. *Journal of Criminal Justice Education, 6*(1), 105–122. doi:10.1080/10511259500083351

Belenky, M. F., Clinchy, B. M., Goldberger, N. R., & Tarule, J. M. (1986). *Women's ways of knowing* (Vol. 986). Basic Books.

Bell, D. (1995). *Who's afraid of critical race theory. U.* L. Rev.

Blankstein, A. M., Noguera, P., & Kelly, L. (2016). Excellence through equity: Five principles of courageous leadership to guide achievement for every student. Alexandria, VA: ASCD.Bremeyer, T. (2008). Religious affiliation and poverty explanations: Individual, structural, and divine causes. *Sociological Focus, 41*(3), 226–237.

Brimeyer, T. M. (2008). Research note: Religious affiliation and poverty explanations: Individual, structural, and divine causes. *Sociological Focus, 41*(3), 226–237. doi:10.1080/00380237.2008.10571332

Bullock, H. E. (1999). Attribution for poverty: A comparison of middle class and welfare recipient attitudes. *Journal of Applied Social Psychology, 29*(10), 2059–2082. doi:10.1111/j.1559-1816.1999.tb02295.x

DeCuir-Gunby, J. T. (2006). Proving your skin is white, you can have anything: Race, racial identity and property rights in Whiteness in the Supreme Court Case of Josephine DeCuir. In C. Rousseau & A. Dixon (Eds.), *Critical Race Theory in Education: All God's children got a song* (pp. 89–111). Routledge.

Delgado, R. (Ed.). (1995). *Critical Race Theory: the cutting edge*. Temple University Press.

DiAngelo, R. (2018). *White fragility: Why it's so hard for White people to talk about racism*. Beacon Press.

Douglass, F. (1852). *The Meaning of July Fourth for the Negro* [Oration]. Retrieved from: https://www.ushistory.org/declaration/more/douglass.html

Feagin, J. R. (1975). *Subordinating the poor: Welfare and American beliefs*. Prentice-Hall.

FitzGerald, D., Lopez, G., & McClean, A. (2019). *Mexican Immigrants Face Threats to Civil Rights and Increased Social Hostility* [Scholarly project]. Center for Comparative Immigration Studies. Retrieved August 31, 2020, from https://ccis.ucsd.edu/_files/conference_papers_present/CNDH-final-3.4.19.pdf

Flores, N. (2016). A tale of two visions: Hegemonic Whiteness and bilingual education. *Educational Policy, 30*(1), 13–38. doi:10.1177/0895904815616482

Gallagher, S. A. (1998). The road to critical thinking: The Perry scheme and meaningful differentiation. *NASSP Bulletin, 82*(595), 12–20. doi:10.1177/019263659808259504

Gans, H. J. (1995). *The War Against the Poor. The Underclass and Antipoverty Policy.* Basic Books.

Gorski, P. (2016). Poverty and the ideological imperative: A call to unhook from deficit and grit ideology and to strive for structural ideology in teacher education. *Journal of Education for Teaching, 42*(4), 378–386. doi:10.1080/02607476.2016.1215546

Henderson, K. (1998). Researching Diverse Populations. *Journal of Leisure Research, 30*(1), 157–174. doi:10.1080/00222216.1998.11949823

Ingersoll, R., & May, H. (2011). *Recruitment, retention and the minority teacher shortage.* Academic Press.

Kohli, R., & Solórzano, D. G. (2012). Teachers, please learn our names!: Racial microaggressions and the K-12 classroom. *Race, Ethnicity and Education, 15*(4), 441–462. doi:10.1080/13613324.2012.674026

Larrian, J. (1983). *Marxism and Ideology.* Macmillan. doi:10.1007/978-1-349-16999-3

Lauer, K., Dias, D., & Tarazi, M. (2011). Bank agents: risk management, mitigation, and supervision. *Focus Note, 75.*

Logue, J. (2013). Sanctioned curricular ignorance as a challenge to critical educational communities. *Philosophical Studies in Education, 44*, 44-49.

Marsh, J. (2011). The literature of poverty, the poverty of literature class. *College English, 73*(6), 604–627.

Marx, S. (2004). Regarding Whiteness: Exploring and Intervening in the Effects of White Racism in Teacher Education. *Equity & Excellence in Education, 37*(1), 31–43. doi:10.1080/10665680490422089

Matias, C. E. (2013). On the" flip" side: A teacher educator of color unveiling the dangerous minds of White teacher candidates. *Teacher Education Quarterly, 40*(2), 53–73.

Matias, C. E. (2020). Surviving Becky(s): Pedagogies for deconstructing Whiteness and gender. Lanham, MD: Lexington.

McClosky, H. (1964). Consensus and ideology in american politics. *The American Political Science Review, 52*(58), 361–382. doi:10.2307/1952868

Nilson, L. (1981). Reconsidering ideological lines: Beliefs about poverty in America. *The Sociological Quarterly, 22*(4), 531–548. doi:10.1111/j.1533-8525.1981.tb00679.x

Orser, C. Jr. (2011). The archeology of poverty and the poverty of archeology. *International Journal of Historical Archaeology, 15*(4), 533–543. doi:10.100710761-011-0153-y

Perry, W. G. (1970). *Forms of intellectual and ethical growth in the college years: A scheme.* Academic Press.

Agnotology and Ideology

Proctor, R. N., & Schiebinger, L. (2008). *Agnotology: The making and unmaking of ignorance*. Academic Press.

Ruffin, K. (2010). *Black on Earth: African American Ecoliteracy Traditions*. The University of Georgia Press.

Sleeter, C. (2017). Critical race theory and the Whiteness of teacher education. *Urban Education*, *52*(2), 155–169. doi:10.1177/0042085916668957

Smeyers, P., & Smith, R. (2014). *Understanding education and educational research*. Cambridge University Press. doi:10.1017/CBO9780511920714

Spencer-Wood, S., & Mattews, C. (2011). Impoverishment, criminalization, and the culture of poverty. *Historical Archaeology*, *45*(3), 1–10. doi:10.1007/BF03376843

Tashakkori, A., & Teddlie, C. (Eds.). (2010). *Sage handbook of mixed methods in social & behavioral research*. Sage. doi:10.4135/9781506335193

Theoharis, G., & Haddix, M. (2011). Undermining racism and a Whiteness ideology: White principals living a commitment to equitable and excellent schools. *Urban Education*, *46*(6), 1332–1351. doi:10.1177/0042085911416012

Thoma, G. A. (1993). The Perry framework and tactics for teaching critical thinking in economics. *The Journal of Economic Education*, *24*(2), 128–136. doi:10.1080/00220485.1993.10844786

U.S. Census Bureau. (2010). Retrieved from https://www.census.gov/quickfacts/fact/table/CA,US/RHI225219

Wells, I. B. (2020). *Crusade for justice: The autobiography of Ida B. Wells*. University of Chicago Press.

Wilson, G. (1996). Toward a revised framework for examining beliefs about causes of poverty. *The Sociological Quarterly*, *37*(3), 413–428. doi:10.1111/j.1533-8525.1996.tb00746.x

Yun, S. H., & Weaver, R. D. (2010). Development and validation of a short form of the attitude toward poverty scale. *Advances in Social Work*, *11*(2), 174–187. doi:10.18060/437

ADDITIONAL READING

Barlow, M., & Barlow, D. (1995). Confronting ideologies of race and crime in the classroom: The power of history. *Journal of Criminal Justice Education*, *6*(1), 105–122. doi:10.1080/10511259500083351

Delgado, R. (Ed.). (1995). *Critical Race Theory: the cutting edge*. Temple University Press.

Gorski, P. (2016). Poverty and the ideological imperative: A call to unhook from deficit and grit ideology and to strive for structural ideology in teacher education. *Journal of Education for Teaching*, *42*(4), 378–386. doi:10.1080/02607476.2016.1215546

Kohli, R., & Solórzano, D. G. (2012). Teachers, please learn our names!: Racial microaggressions and the K-12 classroom. *Race, Ethnicity and Education*, *15*(4), 441–462. doi:10.1080/13613324.2012.674026

Matias, C. E. (2020). Surviving Becky(s): Pedagogies for deconstructing Whiteness and gender. Lanham, MD: Lexington.

Sleeter, C. (2017). Critical race theory and the Whiteness of teacher education. *Urban Education, 52*(2), 155–169. doi:10.1177/0042085916668957

KEY TERMS AND DEFINITIONS

Agnotology: The study of ignorance, its production, and its reproduction.

Critical Race Theory: A framework for examining society and culture as they relate to race, law, and power.

Ideology: A system of beliefs and ideals. They are instilled at an early stage in life and reinforced throughout a person's life through media, religion, politics, education, and social interactions. A person's ideological beliefs and positions may change.

Individual Ideology: The belief that a person can experience the American Dream of prosperity and success if s/he works hard enough and exerts enough effort.

Perry's Critical-Thinking Framework: A framework for cognitive development for higher order thinking.

Structural Ideology: The belief that the system is set up in a way that only some groups of people will experience success and prosperity, and that regardless of the amount of effort someone exerts, s/he may continue to experience poverty.

Whiteness Ideology: The unexamined power of Eurocentric culture and thought that normalizes the marginalization, oppression, and subordination of Communities of Color and other groups of people based on gender, class, and citizenship.

This research was previously published in Challenges to Integrating Diversity, Equity, and Inclusion Programs in Organizations; pages 165-185, copyright year 2021 by Information Science Reference (an imprint of IGI Global).

Chapter 48

I Can't Breathe:
The African American Male With Emotional Disabilities in Education

Richard D. Williams
https://orcid.org/0000-0002-7966-6854
American University, USA

April J. Lisbon
Spotsylvania County Public Schools, USA

ABSTRACT

This chapter is a critical analysis using African American Male Theory (AAMT) to examine and critique the status of the African American male with an emotional disturbance in the American education complex. This chapter expands upon AAMT by applying a critical lens to various AAMT tenants. A vignette of Ahmad, a young African American male, shows the injustice endured by many African American male students. A review of literature on the mental health of African American students and equity in education provides for a rich discourse. This chapter also provides implications for further discussion and recommendations for practitioners.

INTRODUCTION

The plight of the African American student has been one of oppression since the inception of the United States, and the transatlantic slave trade stole millions of Africans from their homes and forced them into centuries of bondage. That bondage has transcended society through oppressive policies, beliefs, and pedagogies. In a time when African American male student's mere existence is criminalized, fetishized, and their culture paradoxically exploited and hated, this paper aims to address the plight of the African American male with an emotional disturbance in the American education complex. Utilizing African American Male Theory (Bush & Bush, 2013), this chapter explores the juxtaposition of being Black with a mental illness in the American educational complex and its impact on the identification, supports, and outcomes of African American males with an Emotional disturbance.

DOI: 10.4018/978-1-6684-4507-5.ch048

Copyright © 2022, IGI Global. Copying or distributing in print or electronic forms without written permission of IGI Global is prohibited.

African American males have a uniqueness that is inherent in their African heritage, and the intergenerational transmission of trauma endured over hundreds of years of oppression within the American context (Bush & Bush, 2013). African American males often navigate social norms within the African American community that are resistant to mental health concepts (Miller & Bennett, 2011). Mental health in the African American community has a complicated history that straddles the absolute need for care, religious traditions, an oppressive and culturally ill-equipped mental health system (Miller & Bennett, 2011).

Within the American educational complex, African American children face disproportionate suspension rates, deficit model policies, oppressive pedagogies, both a bastardization and resistance of their culture and culturally misaligned educational supports (Ford & Russo, 2016; Artiles, 2011). Even with the introduction of Positive Behavior Intervention and Supports (PBIS), African American male students with emotional disabilities face unparalleled challenges in accessing those positive supports, cultivating positive relationships with their white peers and teachers, and avoiding the school-to-prison pipeline that entraps millions of students (Artiles, 2011).

A thorough discussion, with an exemplar, identification of root causes for these challenges within the context of the conceptual framework within the African American community and the American educational complex will anchor a discussion of diversity in education, specifically African American male students with an emotional disturbance. In the discussion of educational diversity, systemic oppression, cultural misalignment and other challenges to the individualized success of African American male students with an emotional disturbance will illuminate possibilities for the improvement of the American educational complex towards embracing and honoring the African American male student with ED and promote success within school and community.

CONCEPTUAL FRAMEWORK

AAMT was established by Bush and Bush in 2013, "Introducing African American Male Theory (AAMT)" in the Journal of African American Males in Education. The theory advances of six tenets summarized as (a) using an ecological approach to understanding the individual and collective experiences, behaviors, outcomes, events, phenomena, and trajectory of African American males; (b) there is a uniqueness of being male and of African descent; (c) African culture, consciousness, and biology continues to influence African American males; (d) African American males are resilient and resistant; (e) Race, racism, classism, and sexism have a profound impact on African American males; and (d) AAMT should be used in the pursuit of social justice (Bush V. & Bush, 2013).

To further implement AAMT in the literature, Bush and Bush (2013) noted that the AMMT model is founded in Bronfenbrenner's interconnected environmental systems theory. With this foundation, AAMT developed a 6-level ecological system. In the heart of the systems lies the microsystem, divided into an inner which represents personality, sexual orientation, beliefs, etc., and the outer which includes family, community, school, etc. Separating the micro from the mesosystem is the first instance of a subsystem. This subsystem includes supernatural and spirit, and unconscious archetypes. The mesosystem includes the interactions between the inner and outer microsystem and the first subsystem. The exosystem holds concepts such as unemployment and access to health care, leading to the macrosystem of cultural hegemony, Black nationalism, laws and policies. The fifth system is the chronosystem, which encompasses

I Can't Breathe

(de)segregation, and change in family structure. The sixth and final system is a second instance of the subsystem in which Bush and Bush (2013) allow for 'unknown non-matter.'

While AAMT is a relatively new theory, the tenets promoted within it directly combat the pervasive and debilitating deficit approach the educational complex takes when viewing African American male students. This chapter highlights the resiliency of African American males. Zimmerman et al. (1999) advanced a new approach to viewing resilience in urban African American male adolescents. Zimmerman et al. (1999) argued that research on the mental health of African American male adolescents has focused on risk factors, problem behaviors, and related consequences and contrasts that path of research with a focus on circumventing negative outcomes. Resilience is defined as factors and processes that disrupt the trajectory from risk factors to negative outcomes including psychopathology (Zimmerman et al., 1999; Zimmerman & Arunkumar, 1994). Resilience is referred to as both maintaining a healthy development and recovery from trauma. African American male students with emotional disabilities and those who have challenging behaviors learn in a traumatic educational environment, traumatic society, and many continue to achieve individual success. The resilience of the African American male with emotional disabilities is examined further in this chapter through a case study and review of barriers for success.

Ahmad: Trauma or Just Bad?

Ahmad is an African-American male middle schooler whose educational career began at age five. He attends a school that is ethnically diverse within a middle-class neighborhood. In his school district, parents have a solid educational stake in identifying school climate, norms, and the overall culture.

Ahmad comes from a single parent family where his mother works 40 hours per week. He infrequently sees his father on the weekends as he lives in another city. Ahmad comes from a supportive family and resides with his grandmother and two siblings. He is actively engaged in team sports and has won several awards for his athleticism and leadership skills. Ahmad takes pride in his work and has a strong desire to please adults whom he feels respect him.

Ahmad's first two years of school were no different than his peers. He was respectful of teachers, respectful of peers, and enjoyed being in school. Ahmad was doing grade level work without any difficulties, and he presented as being a model student. However, Ahmad's behaviors began to shift towards the end of his second-grade year when his teacher went out on leave unexpectedly. Ahmad liked his second-grade teacher as she would often call on him to be her helper to assist with passing out papers or taking things to the office. When his teacher left that year, Ahmad became defiant towards the long-term substitute teacher and administrators. He was sent to the office three times that year in order to help him process his actions and 'see' how his actions impacted his classmates and staff. Ahmad enjoyed the one to one attention provided to him, and after the third incident, the behaviors stopped, and he ended his second-grade year without any additional incidents.

Over the years, his teachers felt like he was capable of doing grade level work, but his inability to handle conflict often caused him to be suspended. By the end of Ahmad's third grade year, he had been suspended ten times for infractions related to (1) insubordination; (2) fighting with and without injury; (3) destruction of school property; and (4) inappropriate language towards staff. Ahmad's parents determined that he needed to spend more time with him, and both parents agreed that Ahmad should move to another school system with his father to see if this would help improve his behaviors. Ahmad initially responded well to the change in his fourth-grade year; however, after the Christmas break, his behaviors

909

were no different than his third-grade year. At the end of his fourth-grade year, Ahmad moved back with his mother, grandmother, and two siblings to a new home and a new school district.

Ahmad's behaviors during his fifth-grade year decreased tremendously. He attended a school where he responded well to his teachers and his peers. Ahmad's family felt like the new home and school were the fresh start Ahmad needed to be back to 'normal.' Ahmad is now in sixth grade, and his behaviors have re-emerged. His behaviors escalate each nine-week period. Ahmad's discipline folder is large, and many of the behaviors seen in middle school are reminiscent of behavioral patterns that were evident during his third-grade year.

Ahmad's teachers indicate that they have provided many interventions to support his educational needs with limited responses. Most of the interventions implemented are scripted based on district approved tools. Ahmad also works with his school counselor this year, in fourth grade, and he responds well in the one to one setting. He is articulate and is able to provide the school counselor with strategies to assist him in the classroom setting. However, when someone accidently gets into his personal space or his classroom teacher says something that comes off as 'disrespecting' him, Ahmad is easily angered and begins lashing out.

The school is unsure whether or not Ahmad has an outside mental health diagnosis as his mother infrequently attends school conferences or responds to school phone calls. Ahmad's mother feels like the school is not academically challenging her son enough as at home, he does not exhibit these behaviors. Ahmad's mother believes her son is no different than any other ten-year-old boy who is active and likes to 'rough house' around. She has a job that will not allow her to take the excessive calls from the school.

The school's position is that with Ahmad's ongoing behaviors over the years he should be referred for special education services as he may need a 'little help' to manage his emotional and behavioral difficulties. His mother does not support the need of special education services as her own brother received special education services to help him with his 'behaviors' and he is currently incarcerated. Ahmad's mother chooses not to disclose if Ahmad or anyone in his family has a mental health diagnosis as (1) it is family business and (2) she does not want the school to use it as a reason to put him in special education.

Generational Trauma in African-American Communities

The narrative surrounding African American families often focuses on poverty, incarcerated fathers, single mothers raising their babies, and trauma related to community violence. This narrative perpetuates a stereotype that African American families are the byproducts of a broken family system (Assari, 2018; Griffin, Botvin, Scheier, Diaz, & Miller, 2000). Yet, the underlying question or concern is when did this trauma start and how did we, as a community get here.

According to Hill (2001), most African American families tend to raise their children with American values so that their children are socialized within the dominant White culture while preserving what is left of their African history. Hill expressed:

Black parents value honesty, academic success, and family responsibility and teach these values to their children. In addition, they are likely to embrace culturally distinct values, which include extended kin networks, respect for the elderly, and mutual cooperation and sharing. These Afrocentric values are rarely included in studies of child socialization or deemed important by the dominant society (p. 504).

I Can't Breathe

By denying what African American families value most for their children by the dominant White culture is to deny the very existence of the African American culture. This in turn may create a space where African American children devalue their identities and their African ancestry in an effort to fit in with the dominant White culture, a phenomenon often described as *acting White*. (Durkee & Williams, 2015).

In thinking about Ahmad and his story, Ahmad grew up in a very close-knit family. Most African Americans live with extended family or have close family ties (Hill, 2001). Although his parents were not together, they ensured that both parents were visible in his life. Ahmad's family unit consists of his maternal and paternal grandparents, aunts, uncles, and a host of cousins. Ahmad grew up in a neighborhood that was rough and where trusting the police was a challenge due to the hostility scene within the community. Ahmad knew that he should respect his elders as this is what his parents and grandparents taught him.

When entering school as an early learner, Ahmad obeyed his teachers. He followed the rules to the best of his abilities as a preschooler. Yet his high level of engagement and rambunctious behaviors were deemed to be disruptive to the learning environment. According to Wright and Ford (2016), "African American children represent 18% of preschool enrollment, but 42% of the preschool children suspended once, and 48% of the preschool children suspended more than once" (p. 7). The pre-criminalization of African American males is rooted in a space that when compared to other ethnicity groups, African American males are at a higher rate of being accused of wrongdoings by their European American teachers and other adults in position of authority (Bentley-Edwards, Thomas, & Stevenson, 2013).

Ahmad's story is no different than some African Americans who have experienced inherent racism in schools. According to Williams and Williams-Morris (2000), racism significantly impacts the mental health of African Americans in three keyways. First, it impedes the overall social economic status of individuals contributing to less resources within predominantly Black communities. Second, discrimination within ones environment may elicit psychological and physiological responses that impact the overall psyche. Third, being seen in a negative light because of one's culture might create a space where African Americans create unfavorable self-evaluations of who they are as individuals. Compounded with the explicit bias of systemic institutional racism, trusting a system that is *supposed* to protect you, yet often neglects you, makes it more challenging for African Americans to seek out community resources for mental health related issues. Hankerson, Suite, and Bailey (2015) stated that the "Medical experimentation on African Americans during slavery laid a foundation of mistrust towards health care providers" (p. 23). The concerns of African Americans are rooted in generational trauma, which in turn may influence their perceptions of healthcare providers of any kind.

Therefore, most African American families chose not to discuss mental health issues outside of the home environment for fear that it may be used against them in a negative light. This perpetual fear is rooted in the very fabric of American history creating a space where differentiating between generational trauma and situational trauma is a very thin line. This line then flows into the academic setting where parents and teachers have to determine if the behaviors seen within a child is due to an emotional disability, choice based, or systemic racism within education. For many African American males who may exhibit difficulties with emotionally regulating their behaviors, more times than not, it is assumed that such behaviors are related to an emotional disturbance compared to another classification like gifted identification (Owens, Ford, Lisbon, Jones, & Owens, 2016). Yet for some students, their behaviors may be in response to being under stimulated academically and not because they are just bad (Wright, Ford, & Young, 2017).

Characteristics of ED

Historically, special education services have been under scrutiny due to the overrepresentation of African American students, specifically males, identified as being disabled. Out of these students identified with educational disabilities, African American males are disproportionately identified with an emotional disability or ED (Owens et. al, 2016). Unfortunately, when schools fail to consider the impact of trauma and mental health concerns associated with behavioral outbursts, some students are assumed to be emotionally disturbed when this may not be the most appropriate classification to meet the needs of the student. It is one reason why it is important that a clearer understanding of the definition of an emotional disability is outlined in order to provide better support and services to meet these students' unique needs.

According to the Section 300.8 (c) (4) of the Individuals with Disabilities Education Act (2004), an emotional disturbance is characterized by one or more of the following for an extended period of time that adversely impacts the education of a student:

1. An inability to learn that cannot be explained by intellectual, sensory, or health
2. factors.
3. An inability to build or maintain satisfactory interpersonal relationships with peers
4. and teachers.
5. Inappropriate types of behavior or feelings under normal circumstances.
6. A general pervasive mood of unhappiness or depression.
7. A tendency to develop physical symptoms or fears associated with personal or school
8. problems.

There are some mental health conditions such as schizophrenia that can fall under the classification of an emotional disability. However, those whose behaviors are more socially maladjusted would not meet this classification.

Although the current language in the definition of emotional disturbance is flawed, it still fails to take into account how debilitating social and emotional problems really are. For example, some individuals may not be unwilling to learn. Instead a student may not be emotionally available to learn because of issues associated with childhood trauma, which is different from an 'inability' to learn (Oelrich, 2012). Not all trauma is visible to the eyes. The manifestation of what we see in the classroom settings may be hereditary and/or environmental. Labeling a child for something that is outside of their control and/or *criminalizing* their behaviors with harsh disciplinary actions can lead to detrimental results (i.e. higher risk of suspensions or dropping out of school) if the correct treatments are not available to remediate their emotional and mental health needs.

Criminalization of African American Males in K-12 Education

There is insurmountable research that addresses the disproportionality rate of African American males either identified in special education and/or suspended from school compared to the dominant White culture. This research has been addressed by both Black, White, and Brown scholars. Yet with all of the research in tow, African American males like Ahmad, continue to be profiled in the classroom. Such discourse not only leads to questions regarding one's academic abilities but also leads to a narrative that some African American males are too bad to be academic scholars (Owen et al., 2016).This body of

I Can't Breathe

research also leaves the question-- are the incongruent treatments of African American males and the dominant White culture in K-12 education still leading our African American males through the school to prison pipeline?

According to Mallet (2017), "The impact of the school-to-prison pipeline is substantial, involving millions of young people. Of the 49 million U.S. students enrolled in the 2011-2012 academic year, 3.5 million students experienced in-school detention, 1.9 million students were suspended for at least one day, 1.6 million students were suspended more than one time, and 130,000 students were expelled" (p.564). Unfortunately, African American males are more than 3.3 times as likely to be suspended or expelled from school compared to their White peers (Lewis, Butler, Bonner III, & Joubert, 2010). This is highly alarming as African American males receive more office referrals than their White peers, yet making up less than their overall school populations (2010).

Yet our current educational system is not fully equipped to handle the overwhelming demands of students especially those with trauma and/or mental health needs (O'Reilly, Svirydzenka, Adams, & Dogra, 2018). Many of these students do not have access to outside community resources to address mental health needs. Furthermore, although schools may have mental health teams in place, more times than not these individuals are doing other duties that would preclude them from offering counseling-based services to those in need. For example, school psychologists are trained to provide both individual and group counseling services. However, their schedules do not afford them the flexibility to serve in this role as they are either participating in meetings, testing students for suspected disabilities, or doing significant paperwork in order to be in compliance with district and state guidelines (Lisbon-Peoples, 2014).

Without the necessary resources in place, more students will not receive the support and services they need to address their underlying trauma. The longer the underlying trauma remains, the more some students will physically lash out in anger in an attempt to feel heard and acknowledged (Gibbons et al., 2012). Additionally, Jacobsen, Pace, and Ramirez (2016) suggested that school discipline does not reduce the level of physical aggression in children.

Therefore, in order to combat racial profiling within our K-12 educational system, we must re-evaluate our current educational practices to ensure equitable treatment of all students based on their needs and not their identified race. A deeper dive into cultural responsiveness and educational stakeholders' personal assessment on race and racial identity will be one of many keys to stabilizing the mental and emotional well-being of African-American male students as well as ensuring that the school to prison pipeline is no longer a part of our educational discussions. Until we as a society state that we want more for all of our students, not only in words but actions, we as a society will continue to perpetuate the stereotype that African Americans, especially males, are a *threat* to the dominant White culture (Simson, 2013).

Treatment of African-American Males in K-12 Education

Sitting around the table as staff members discuss Ahmaud's needs, rather than discussing his strengths academically and/or behaviorally, his teacher leads with the ongoing behaviors he exhibits. She discusses the number of times she has remediated his behaviors, provides an exhaustive list of the interventions she has tried within a two or three week period, and explains that Ahmaud's behaviors are a disruption to his learning, her instruction, and the learning of the other students in the classroom setting. As Ahmaud's mother listens to everything that is *wrong* with her child, she internally questions if there is anything that is *right* about her child.

The team considers Ahmaud's thick disciplinary file and immediately asks the question, is it time to assess this child for special education services. Why? The team feels that he simply needs a *little help* to get his behaviors under control not realizing that special education services will change the narrative of this young man's educational life for the rest of his life.

This narrative is not related to Ahmaud alone and is often seen in K-12 education on a regular basis. Bal, Betters-Bubon, and Fish (2019) stated that African American males are referred for special education services for emotional difficulties two to three times more likely than their White classmates. This level of disparity within referrals for special education and/or discipline expresses the underlying fact of White fear (Irby, 2014). According to Irby, "Black boys are a problem from the moment they enter the school door because of the threat their presence in the student body poses to the natural basis of Whiteness" (p. 790). By viewing African American males through a deficit lens, being less childlike and even animalistic compared to their White peers, special education services may be used as a vehicle to separate or segregate these youth from the general education population (Goff, Jackson, Di Leone, Culotta, & DiTomasso, 2014).

Rather than looking at Ahmaud's behaviors and that of other African American males as a threat, we as educators must shift our focus on considering (1) the cultural upbringing of the child; (2) how our own implicit bias may shape how our students perceive our intentions; and (3) how our lack of cultural sensitivity may reflect on our delivery of instruction and overall engagement with our African American students. By reflecting on our own biases and what we are willing to do to create change within ourselves, we then open up the door to clearly listen to the needs of our students while creating a safe learning environment where our African American males are thriving and not just surviving. If we do not, we will continue to hear the cries of our African American males with emotional disabilities-- 'I can't breathe'.

EDUCATIONAL EQUITY

Equity in education for African Americans has been a continual struggle in this country from inception. African Americans have just recently escaped legal Jim Crow and bondage, and currently endure social and systemic racism in an ever-intensifying manner. With the landmark Supreme Court decision in *Brown v. Board of Education*. The tides were thought to be changing, however, schools across the nation are still segregated, and there is a dire need for equity in all aspects of education. Momentum has been gained for students with disabilities, with the passage of PL 94-142, which is now the Individuals with Disabilities Education Act (IDEA) that guaranteed a free and appropriate education for all students, regardless of ability. This victory could have been the knight in shining armor for African American students with disabilities, but in reality, things have at minimum maintained or at worst, degenerated into further inequity (Ford & Russo, 2016). Ford and Russo (2016) also noted that disproportionality has remained stable for some 40 years, since the U.S. Department of Education's Office of Civil Rights began tracking placement in special education data.

African American males are still the most over referred, identified, and represented population in special education, especially those identified as Emotionally Disturbed (ED) (Ford & Russo, 2016). In 2013, The U.S. Department of Education released its 37th Annual Report to Congress, in which it stated African American students are twice as likely to be identified as ED as compared to others. In 2011, Artiles noted that boys represented about 80% of the ED population. African American students

I Can't Breathe

are more likely to be placed in segregated settings, attend lower funded schools, and live in poverty (Artiles, 2011; Ford & Russo, 2016).

The impact of special education, especially for African Americans is tremendous. Students placed in special education typically experience low academic performance, high dropout rates, high levels of contact with the juvenile justice systems, and limited access to college as compared to their nondisabled peers (Artiles, 2011). With a subpar education with these disappointing outcomes, African American males students with ED, enter a society that already criminalizes and oppresses them, without a proper and supportive education.

When examining factors that lead to racial inequity, Sciuchetti (2017) identified numerous school and teacher-based factors. These factors include school climate and culture, referral and assessment practices, the discrepancy model versus the response to intervention model, lack of a diverse teaching force, and deficit thinking of teachers. When looking more broadly, Artiles (2011) noted how the classic distributive model of justice in education has remained color blind, marred with maldistribution and misrecognition. These color blind and marrings are a direct result of what Ross (1990) identified as *White innocence* and *Black abstraction*. White innocence is described as the perpetual argument of contemporary white innocence, or that contemporary white culture is not to blame and is therefore excused of obligations to address the over 400 years of oppression committed by the dominant culture against African Americans. Black abstraction can be conceptualized as the absolute refusal to view Blacks as real and dynamic in a social context (Ross, 1990).

Artilies (2011) furthers his critique of inequity in education with an examination of disability policy. Historically, disability policy and programming has been conceptualized in the medical lens which attempts to cure and trace disability to individual traits (Aritiles, 2011). This reliance on the medical lens perpetuates the deficit and individual ownership theory of disability. The medical model also fails to recognize, through white innocence and black abstraction, the heterogeneous nature of students with disabilities, to include race, gender and socioeconomic status.

Coupled with the epidemic of institutional racism and perpetual racism, African American Males with an ED are unjustly and immorally subjected to a subpar education. African American male students suffer through an education with an ill-equipped, culturally inept, and severely inadequate diversity of educators. To combat this grave injustice, we must adopt culturally responsive and affirming practices, diversify the teaching force, diversify the body of policy makers and advocate for the appropriate education for African American males with an ED.

IMPLICATIONS

This chapter has provided a deep conceptualization of African American males with an ED in education. With the use of AAMT, the authors have provided a body of contextual theory to affirm the precarious state that African American males with an ED currently learn. This chapter has opened the proverbial door open for a critical analysis of the state of African American males with ED in the American educational complex. Implications of the need to further explore both culturally responsive and affirming policies of practice are inherent. The tenants of AAMT should be thoroughly evaluated and applied within future educational research on African American male students. This chapter's limitation is the focus on resiliency of African American male students with emotional disabilities despite the various institutional, social, and other barriers that have created an unhealthy, oppressive, and generally challenging learning environment. The resiliency of African American male students with emotional disabilities should be applauded and used to uplift these students. The use of AAMT and related theories must increase to combat and eradicate the prevailing deficit lens these students are forced to matriculate through. The uniqueness that of African American males- their history of struggle from the inception of the United States and before, the strong family, community, and spiritual bonds that the African American community has created to withstand hundreds of years of oppression, violence, and death, and the ability for African American males to hold this weight yet still reach the highest elected office or support their family must be celebrated and used to uplift. Further discussion on the use of culturally sensitive testing, standardized by norms that truly reflect the sociocultural needs of African American students. More implications lie in the need for improvements in teacher preparation and ongoing training. Uncomfortable and unsettling discourse on the history, impact, and contemporary effects of this nation's use of systemic racism and oppressive tactics to subjugate African American males must commence immediately.

Aside from racial implications, the implications of a broken special education system must also be taken into account. Culturally incongruent assessments and systems are leading to the overidentification of African American males as ED. The response to intervention process many schools and systems have adopted has been implemented without fidelity and without the appreciation of the nuance of behaviors. Response to intervention is more widely used for academics, however it is increasingly being used to identify ED (Artiles, 2011). This practice is irresponsible, as response to intervention protocols were not designed for the behaviors and social/emotional development. Positive behavior intervention and support (PBIS) programs have been hijacked by the dominant White culture and have been misused through the implementation of culturally isolating and insensitive policies (Williams, Giffen, & Williams, In press). Williams, Griffen, and Williams (In Press) evaluate a culturally responsive model for PBIS. Culturally responsive PBIS (CRPBIS) is slowly beginning to gain traction in practice and research. CRPBIS and other culturally responsive practices force the dominant White culture and general education complex to recognize, affirm, and promote the culturally based behaviors of all culturally diverse learners. By engaging in culturally responsive practices, the education complex can begin to reverse its oppressive and degrading practices against African American males and other diverse student populations.

RECOMMENDATIONS FOR PRACTITIONERS

In order to begin the discussion of supporting the mental health needs of African American males in a culture that often polices their moves out of prescribed generational irrational fears, the following recommendations are suggested. First, is to move away from the mentality that some African American males are damaged, aggressive, and should be restrained because of one's own fears or misconceptions of Black masculinity (Bryan, 2018; Basile, 2020). Instead, as educational stakeholders and those who support the needs of African American males should reframe the conversation and determine how underlying trauma, institutional racism, and/or genetics influences the lens in which these young males see and view themselves and the world around them. By looking at African American males through a holistic eye and not a part of their 'story', we are then better able to create support and services that meet their overall needs.

I Can't Breathe

Secondly, some African American males are less responsive, for example, when 'talked at' instead of being 'talked to'. Those who are talked at often find themselves in a position where they must defend or resist the discourse experienced within their educational environment in an effort to maintain their sense of self-identity (Allen 2017). This may be cumbersome for those with emotional disabilities as they rely heavily on the outcomes of their environment to determine how they may intrinsically respond to a situation. Engaging in a respectful dialogue where the child feels heard and respected not only alleviates the pressure within the external environment but how the child views his ability to handle future incidents.

Third, ensure that the supports and services offered are culturally responsive. For example, the art of music and dance is a strong part of the African culture. Therefore, activities that are hands-on in conjunction with 'talk therapy' may be appropriate in order to gear the effectiveness of the work you as the educator is providing to the student. A one size model does not fit each child so understanding your own knowledge base on culturally responsive practices as well as personal biases towards working with African American males, including those with emotional difficulties, will influence your application of these practices (Peters, Margolin, Fragnoli, & Bloom, 2016; Bryan 2017).

Finally, more mental health services are required to assist African American males to ensure their emotional stability. Behavioral interventions and/or medical interventions may be appropriate in helping to create balance. Without balance there is no peace of mind and vice versa. With the level of trauma African Americans, especially males, have historically experienced, it is important that balance is restored so that these young men are able to effectively live and lead a healthy life both in and outside of the classroom.

CONCLUSION

The current status of African American males with an ED is a state of emergency. These bright and capable young men are criminalized at an early age, in a setting that is a safe haven for the dominant White culture, which should be a safe haven for all. Through the affirmation and inclusion of African American males, in their totality as described in AAMT, and their disabilities, the education complex will take one small step towards equity. The American education complex must purge itself of White innocence by critically evaluating and eradicating systemic and individual racism. The American education complex must end the practice of Black abstraction and move towards understanding, affirming, and including African American culture into schools. Education policy makers must review the current definition of emotional disturbance and the evaluation process. Assessments must be normed by the cultures and communities in which a student belongs, not the dominant White culture. The criminalization of African American males in education must end immediately. The response to intervention model must be re-evaluated for ED and systemic shifts made to accommodate culturally responsive practices. African American males are the embodiment of a rich heritage and culture. African American males must be treasured and not criminalized and overidentified. African American males bring such joy and richness to education, it is up to the dominant White majority to shed oppressive tactics and biased views and embrace these beloved children.

REFERENCES

Allen, Q. (2017). "They Write Me Off and Don't Give Me a Chance to Learn Anything": Positioning, Discipline, and Black Masculinities in School. *Anthropology & Education Quarterly*, *48*(3), 269–283. doi:10.1111/aeq.12199

Assari, S. (2018). Diminished economic return of socioeconomic status for black families. *Social Sciences*, *7*(5), 74–84. doi:10.3390ocsci7050074 PMID:32832108

Bal, A., Betters-Bubon, J., & Fish, R. E. (2019). A multilevel analysis of statewide disproportionality in exclusionary discipline and the identification of emotional disturbance. *Education and Urban Society*, *51*(2), 247–268. doi:10.1177/0013124517716260

Basile, V. (2020). Standin'tall: Criminalization and acts of resistance among elementary school boys of color. *Race, Ethnicity and Education*, *23*(1), 94–112. doi:10.1080/13613324.2018.1497964

Bentley-Edwards, K. L., Thomas, D. E., & Stevenson, H. C. (2013). Raising consciousness: Promoting healthy coping among African American boys at school. In *Handbook of Culturally Responsive School Mental Health* (pp. 121–133). Springer. doi:10.1007/978-1-4614-4948-5_9

Bryan, N. (2017). White teachers' role in sustaining the school-to-prison pipeline: Recommendations for teacher education. *The Urban Review*, *49*(2), 326–345. doi:10.100711256-017-0403-3

Bryan, N. (2018). Shaking the bad boys: Troubling the criminalization of black boys' childhood play, hegemonic white masculinity and femininity, and the school playground-to-prison pipeline. *Race, Ethnicity and Education*, 1–20. doi:10.1080/13613324.2018.1512483

Durkee, M. I., & Williams, J. L. (2015). Accusations of acting White: Links to Black students' racial identity and mental health. *The Journal of Black Psychology*, *41*(1), 26–48. doi:10.1177/0095798413505323

Gibbons, F. X., O'Hara, R. E., Stock, M. L., Gerrard, M., Weng, C. Y., & Wills, T. A. (2012). The erosive effects of racism: Reduced self-control mediates the relation between perceived racial discrimination and substance use in African American adolescents. *Journal of Personality and Social Psychology*, *102*(5), 1089–1104. doi:10.1037/a0027404 PMID:22390225

Goff, P. A., Jackson, M. C., Di Leone, B. A. L., Culotta, C. M., & DiTomasso, N. A. (2014). The essence of innocence: Consequences of dehumanizing Black children. *Journal of Personality and Social Psychology*, *106*(4), 526–545. doi:10.1037/a0035663 PMID:24564373

Griffin, K. W., Botvin, G. J., Scheier, L. M., Diaz, T., & Miller, N. L. (2000). Parenting practices as predictors of substance use, delinquency, and aggression among urban minority youth: Moderating effects of family structure and gender. *Psychology of Addictive Behaviors*, *14*(2), 174–184. doi:10.1037/0893-164X.14.2.174 PMID:10860116

Hankerson, S. H., Suite, D., & Bailey, R. K. (2015). Treatment disparities among African American men with depression: Implications for clinical practice. *Journal of Health Care for the Poor and Underserved*, *26*(1), 21–34. doi:10.1353/hpu.2015.0012 PMID:25702724

Hill, S. A. (2001). Class, race, and gender dimensions of child rearing in African American families. *Journal of Black Studies, 31*(4), 494–508. doi:10.1177/002193470103100407

Individuals with Disabilities Education Improvement Act of 2004, Pub. L. No. 108-446, Stat. 118 (2004). Retrieved from http://idea.ed.gov

Irby, D. J. (2014). Revealing racial purity ideology: Fear of Black–White intimacy as a framework for understanding school discipline in post-Brown schools. *Educational Administration Quarterly, 50*(5), 783–795. doi:10.1177/0013161X14549958

Jacobsen, W. C., Pace, G. T., & Ramirez, N. G. (2016). *Even at a young age: Exclusionary school discipline and children's physically aggressive behaviors.* Population Association of America.

Lewis, C. W., Butler, B. R., Bonner, F. A. III, & Joubert, M. (2010). African American Male Discipline Patterns and School District Responses Resulting Impact on Academic Achievement: Implications for Urban Educators and Policy Makers. *Journal of African American Males in Education, 1*(1), 7–25.

Lisbon-Peoples, A. (2014). *Reclaiming our identity: school psychologists' perceptions of their roles in education based on social, political, and economic changes* (Doctoral dissertation). Northeastern University.

Mallett, C. A. (2017). The school-to-prison pipeline: Disproportionate impact on vulnerable children and adolescents. *Education and Urban Society, 49*(6), 563–592. doi:10.1177/0013124516644053

O'Reilly, M., Svirydzenka, N., Adams, S., & Dogra, N. (2018). Review of mental health promotion interventions in schools. *Social Psychiatry and Psychiatric Epidemiology, 53*(7), 647–662. doi:10.100700127-018-1530-1 PMID:29752493

Oelrich, N. (2012). A new "IDEA": Ending racial disparity in the identification of students with emotional disturbance. *South Dakota Law Review, 57*, 9–41.

Owens, C. M., Ford, D. Y., Lisbon, A. J., Jones, S. G., & Owens, M. T. (2016). Too bad to be gifted: Gifts denied for Black males with emotional and behavioral needs. *The Wisconsin English Journal, 58*(2), 121–139.

Peters, T., Margolin, M., Fragnoli, K., & Bloom, D. (2016). What's race got to do with it?: Preservice teachers and white racial identity. *Current Issues in Education (Tempe, Ariz.), 19*(1). https://cie.asu.edu/ojs/index.php/cieatasu/article/view/1661

Simson, D. (2013). Exclusion, punishment, racism, and our schools: A critical race theory perspective on school discipline. *UCLA Law Review. University of California, Los Angeles. School of Law, 61*, 506.

Williams, D., & Williams-Morris, R. (2000). Racism and mental health: The African American experience. *Ethnicity & Health, 5*(3-4), 243–268. doi:10.1080/713667453 PMID:11105267

Wright, B. L., & Ford, D. Y. (2016). This little light of mine: Creating early childhood education classroom experiences for African American boys preK-3. *Journal of African American Males in Education, 7*(1), 5–19.

Wright, B. L., Ford, D. Y., & Young, J. L. (2017). Ignorance or indifference? Seeking excellence and equity for under-represented students of color in gifted education. *Global Education Review*, *4*(1), 45–60.

Zimmerman, M. A., & Arunkumar, R. (1994). Resiliency Research: Implications for Schools and Policy. *Social Policy Report*, *8*(4), 1–20. doi:10.1002/j.2379-3988.1994.tb00032.x

Zimmerman, M. A., Ramírez-Valles, J., & Maton, K. I. (1999). Resilience Among Urban African American Male Adolescents: A Study of the Protective Effects of Sociopolitical Control on Their Mental Health. *American Journal of Community Psychology*, *27*(6), 733–751. doi:10.1023/A:1022205008237 PMID:10723533

This research was previously published in Challenges to Integrating Diversity, Equity, and Inclusion Programs in Organizations; pages 27-40, copyright year 2021 by Information Science Reference (an imprint of IGI Global).

Chapter 49

Action Research, Design Thinking:
Consulting at a Trauma-Informed Community School

William Louis Conwill
University of Illinois at Urbana-Champaign, USA

Ronald William Bailey
University of Illinois at Urbana-Champaign, USA

ABSTRACT

Narratives of unruly Black children in failing schools often normalize hopelessness at the expense of students. Newer, sometimes silenced voices, however, can produce counter-narratives that can lead to ecological solutions for assisting traumatized students. This is a case study of the transformation of a principal who asked, "What's wrong with these children?" to an advocate whose inquiry shifted to "What happened to these children, and what must we do to help them?" With trauma awareness and behavioral management training for her staff, improvements began. The local school board cut her successes short by changing the lock on her office door on the day before teachers returned for the Fall Semester and informed her that her services were no longer needed. What is the lesson for the consultant?

INTRODUCTION

This study demonstrates action research-based consultation (Conwill, 2003) with design thinking (Brown, 2010) during the 2015 Spring Semester at a community school located in a Far South Side Chicago housing project that was built on top of a toxic dump site in 1945. In 2015, as part of its Community Engagement mission, the second author, head of the Department of African American Studies at the University of Illinois at Urbana-Champaign (UIUC) commissioned the first author to provide the principal of An (used for anonymity) Elementary School in Chicago's Far South Side with action research-based

DOI: 10.4018/978-1-6684-4507-5.ch049

Copyright © 2022, IGI Global. Copying or distributing in print or electronic forms without written permission of IGI Global is prohibited.

consultation (Conwill, 2003). Action research is a form of inquiry that allocates participants a research role based on their sharing the vision of committed professionals critically investigating their own practice (Carr & Kemmis, 1986). Action research moves quickly to focus on a specific need; identifies theoretical perspectives and research questions; collects and analyzes data and reports findings; and acts (Conwill, 2003). The purposes for action research in the educational context include developing reflective practitioners, improving school-wide priorities, and building professional cultures. Design thinking is a human-centered innovation method that views challenges and solves problems by meeting people's needs feasibly and efficiently.

AN ELEMENTARY SCHOOL

An Elementary School had a virtually 100% Black student body of 281. In 2013-2014, 98.8% of its students were from low-income households, with 5.6% homeless (http://schools.chicagotribune.com/school/An(usedforanonymity)-elementary-school_chicago). Low-income students are those from families receiving public aid, living in substitute care, or eligible to receive free or reduced-price lunches. High percentages of non-White students and students receiving free and reduced-price meals are two important school climate markers that accompany the delivery of more services and resources at a school (Conwill & Parks, 2007). The segregated housing project had been built atop a toxic dump site for Black veterans returning home from World War II. It is bounded by the Little Calumet River, closed industrial sites, and the freeway. It is virtually a food desert.

The school had performed at consistently low scores on the Illinois Standard Achievement Test (ISAT), a statewide elementary-level assessment in reading, math and science. In 2013, the Illinois State Board of Education raised the standards by which it assesses student performance to match those laid out in the Common Core State Standards Initiative.

The Common Core is a set of academic standards in mathematics and English language arts/literacy (ELA) set forth in 2010. These learning goals outline what a student should know and be able to do at the end of each grade. The standards were created to ensure that all students regardless of where they live, graduate from high school with the skills and necessary knowledge to succeed in college, career, and life. Forty-one states, the District of Columbia, four territories, and the Department of Defense Education Activity (DoDEA) have voluntarily adopted and are moving forward with the Common Core (http://www.corestandards.org/about-the-standards/). As a result, a school's 2013 ISAT composite scores may appear to have dropped considerably even in cases where student achievement has not changed. The Chicago Tribune reported that 23.8% of students at An Elementary met or exceeded Illinois State test standards with a ranking of one, with 10 being the highest. In short, the school appeared to need a great deal of support, regardless of the attempt of the School Board to raise the score standards. The School Board's narrative cast the blame for their performance on the West and South Side schools, with poor scores as an indicator for closure.

Focusing school assessment solely on percentages of students who meet or exceed Illinois State test standards as outcome measures of student academic achievement can be an iatrogenic fix that increases children's risk. The strategy of determining a school's qualifications for closure is fraught with confounds, especially when poverty and race are known to be strong indicators of school performance in the inner-city. In effect, the strategy of closing schools for poor performance is designed to limit the

Action Research, Design Thinking

school system's responses to cosmetic adjustments rather than structural changes in its adaptation to oppressive conditions in the school, legal, and housing systems. Attributing the decision to close schools to unacceptable academic performance levels, while playing down the relationship between poverty and race, is a way of practicing racism without mentioning race.

While poverty may not cause low achievement, many children living in poverty are exposed to certain risk factors that are thought to contribute to their poor performance (Hertert & Teague, 2003, p. 5). Risk factors have a synergistic effect on school performance—children with one risk factor typically do not fare as well as those with none, while children with two or more risk factors lag far behind those with only one. Research also shows that the detrimental effects of poverty are more extreme the earlier it occurs in a child's life, the longer it lasts, and the more severe it is (Hertert & Teague, 2003).

Neoliberal social policies such as extreme educational de-funding of public schools, privatized public services, advances for charter schools, and vouchers for consumer choice mimicking the market in the public sector without significant increases in student performance create structural violence that support these factors, especially in the inner-city. Structural violence exists when institutions and policies are designed so that barriers in society result in lack of food, housing, safe and just working conditions, health, education, economic security, and damaged family relationships (Conwill, 2007; Farmer, 2003; Harrison, 2008, pp. 179-197; 243-245). Structural violence shows up as unequal access to economic resources, political impotence, inadequate education, inaccessible health care, or as discriminatory treatment under the law. In regard to family relationships, structural violence includes demands for dual-income couples and single parents working long hours to meet the increasing cost of living, unsupervised latch-key kids, underfunded day-care, and escalating violence in the schools (Winter & Leighton, 1999).

Within the framework of structural violence, strategies for deflection from system change include school boards battling teacher unions, shifting allegiances away from public schools, and denying equitable resources for education to those who need it most. Instead, ignoring the relationship between poverty and student performance in the classroom, blaming under- and unemployed homeless parents for not participating fully in the life of the school, and attacking teachers for incompetence have emerged as neoliberal responses to reduced support for schools. Closing schools for not raising children's academic performance levels without addressing structural societal impediments to performance brought on by poverty suggests a neoliberal cosmetic trick that appears to be a topical solution to inner-city school crises. Shutting down low-performing urban community schools may appear to decrease risks to the children at such schools, but there are several ways to understand risk (Conwill & Parks, 2007).

Originally, "at-risk" referred to students with sensory deficits and to those who did not achieve their learning objectives due to individual and environmental factors. This is a predictive approach that defines at-risk students as those with certain characteristics that already have been related to poor academic performance and low achievement. Predictive variables may include race, ethnicity, family composition, and socioeconomic status.

The descriptive approach labels students at-risk when they have school-related problems, such as poor grades, truancy, and excessive tardiness. A unilateral approach, on the other hand, considers all students to be at-risk, regardless of descriptive or predictive indicators. Full-service schools, for example, represent universal prevention, to reduce the risks to all students in the school.

The school factors approach understands students to be at-risk because of problems related to the school itself. These include such features as rigid schedules, ineffective instructional methods, inadequate facilities, and inappropriate assessments (Hixson & Tinzmann, 1990; Kronick, 2000).

Action Research, Design Thinking

Finally, we can understand a student to be at-risk when there is a difference or mismatch between the school or school system's expectations and the family or the community's ability to react (Richardson & Colfer, 1990; Natriello, McDill, & Pallas, 1990; Hixson & Tinzmann, 1990; Comer, 1990). In this case, the level of student risk can co-vary with a combination of factors related to the school, the makeup of the student body and their families, and the community's resources (Dappen & Isenhern, 2006).

The student's risk is, then, in practical experimental terms according to an intersectionality paradigm, determined by the interactions of systems of social inequality such as gender, racialized ethnicity and class. These systems intersect to create differences in the way school children experience stress in their lives (Malveaux, 2002; Manson, 1999; Natriello, McDill, & Pallas, 1990; Orland, 1990; Taylor, Tisdell, & Hanley, 2000). In practical experimental terms, this intersectionality paradigm—in contrast to a comparative race paradigm that would attribute group differences to race— examines students' lived experience to understand how systems of social inequality interact to create advantages or disadvantages (Conwill & Parks, 2007; West-Olatunji & Conwill, 2011, p. 46).

The stress that students feel at school can also come from several ecological levels. For example, students who do not have adequate nutrition can experience stress that can affect their performance at school. Likewise, a high-crime neighborhood in a chemically toxic area can induce stress in a school's environment. Drive-by shootings in the neighborhood around An Elementary School were common, and sometimes occurred at the sidewalk in front of the school entrance. A school board's organizational and institutional constraints on certain schools can introduce another level of stressors, to use a bioecological example from a contextual system model (Bronfenbrenner & Morris, 2007).

Action Research

After being assigned to provide services at the school site selected for the department's Community Engagement mission, the first author drove two hours to the Chicago neighborhood surrounding the school to become familiar with the area, and to introduce himself to school personnel. The principal accepted the opportunity to work together with a consultant and discuss her concerns with the school. The author and the principal agreed to a schedule of two days per week that he would be on site to observe and to meet at her convenience.

The principal was anxious about the level of fighting and arguing in the classrooms, especially among her youngest charges. She had a person assigned to oversee detained students who were extremely disruptive in the classroom but revealed that there were many complaints about the harsh tone that person used with the children and parents.

The principal had grown up in this Far South Side Chicago neighborhood and had attended An Elementary School as a child. Years later, she taught at the school. She eventually applied to the school to serve as principal. The school was in the throes of turmoil at a time when many of Chicago's South Side schools were being shut down. The principal threw herself into the task of trying to save the school. She described what she felt was resistance from her staff, parents, and the school system administrators. She had instituted a dress code for teachers and staff that some found imperious. The males, for instance, were not to wear denim jeans to work. The principal herself wore dresses or a skirt, blouse, and suit jacket, with high-heeled shoes.

The principal insisted upon everyone speaking to the children in a kind and pleasant voice at school. She herself maintained exemplary custody over her voice in every exchange at the school and felt that

Action Research, Design Thinking

it was important to model this behavior consistently. She greeted the children in a gentle voice as they entered the building, and throughout the day.

She asked the author to conduct social skills training for the older students to correct their habitual harsh words with each other. The author informed her that he was not available for any direct services with the students, but that he could work with teachers and staff to interact with students around these issues. He directed a social worker intern at the school in the formation of a leadership training group for older students.

The principal informed the consultant about one of the parents who had been trying to have her removed from the school since she arrived as principal because she felt that the principal looked down on her. The parent presented at the entrance virtually every week, unexpected. She had campaigned for, and attained a place on the Local School Council, and then was elected the presiding member. The parent subjected the principal to wave after wave of interruption, accusation, and other forms of intimidation and confrontation over feeling slighted by the principal. The principal asked the consultant after a few weeks of his presence on the site, to attend a meeting with the representatives of the Chicago School Board, parents in the Local School Council, and some community partners, so he could understand the severity of the hostility directed at her and tell her what he thought she could do about the presiding parent.

This request represented one of those tasks that are the bane for consultants. Like the Trials of Odysseus, they are near-impossible feats designed to separate the gods from mere mortals. They present a pass/fail test for the consultant.

The newly-elected president of the Local School Council acted out exactly as the principal had predicted, leaving the other participants aghast. She charged the principal with lack of support for her child's placement in a better school. The Chicago School Board representatives seemed stunned by the anger the Local School Council president and parents showed when accusing the principal of not responding to their needs.

Near the end of the meeting, the principal asked for participants' feedback on the meeting, and fielded comments. After the community partner representatives had their say, the school board representatives took a turn. When they were done, the consultant spoke. He mentioned the high number of disruptions, the jumbled nature of the presentation of complaints, and stated that most of the confusion and hostility generated in the meeting could have been avoided if the meeting had been conducted according to Robert's Rules of Order (Robert, Honemann, & Balch, 2011). At that point, one of the school board members had an "A-Ha!" moment, and looked at the president, having realized she knew nothing about running a meeting. Two of the women in their group volunteered to meet with the new president and teach them to her over lunch. The meeting closed with the president in tears. She was extremely grateful to feel supported in her new position, encouraged with her acceptance by everyone, and less embarrassed by her status as an early drop-out from school. She expressed apologies to the principal, and profusely thanked the assembly. The consultant had passed the test.

Altgeld Gardens

Descriptions of the school environment are readily available in the public domain. The school is situated in a housing project that was built in 1945 with 1,498 units. The housing project is located near numerous former manufacturing plants, former steel mills, waste dumps and landfills. It currently has more than 1,200 units occupied. The development consists primarily of two-story row houses spread over 190 acres. Five hundred units are slated for rehabilitation in this de-industrialized area. In all, a total of

Action Research, Design Thinking

3,400 residents live in a complex of two adjoining projects that includes other public schools within its borders. The Housing Authority's maintenance staff, on-site social services, and medical facilities serve the residents. The residents have long had a growing concern about the number of deaths annually from cancer and other diseases that may be related to environmental hazards within their formerly industrial area. The project was constructed at a time when asbestos was widely used in construction materials at hazardous levels.

In 1980, the residents organized a grassroots campaign to advocate for the removal of asbestos from their flats. Their project is in one of the densest concentrations of potentially hazardous pollution sources in North America. Many of the landfills that surround the project are unregulated, and some are still active. Since most of these landfills as well as many industrial plants are located along the waterways surrounding the area, 11 miles of the 18 miles of rivers and lakes surrounding the project have been assessed as having water quality unfit for human consumption and recreation. However, many local residents continue to fish in these waters, increasing their exposure to hazards by eating local fish.

During the month of March 2015, several crimes in the project were regularly listed in the media. They included assaults with weapons, simple assaults, aggravated assaults, possession of illegal substances, battery, weapons violations, manufacturing and delivery of heroin, harassment by phone, theft, strong-arm robbery, and harboring a runaway. Inside the school, the Chicago Schools office provides a security team to manage violent and aggressive behavior. The housing project also has a private armed security firm on the project grounds. Police were summoned to the school at least two times during the month of March 2015 following shootings in front of the school. All this to say that the neighborhood environment is stressful.

The Chicago Housing Authority (CHA) has worked closely with residents and the larger community over dozens of meetings with residents, community members, sister agencies and organizations, including Business and Professional People for Public Interest (BPI), concerning the revitalization plan. Amenities and improvements include a community center and recreational facilities, and an upgraded library. Additionally, rail service to the development is under construction.

Community Organization

A Consortium was organized across the housing developments to address concerns the parents had. For example, some Consortium members helped provide a measure of safety for the children to travel back and forth from the school.

When the consultant first set up his community engagement with the Far South Side Chicago school and offered consultation to the principal, he presumed that their interactions would be along the lines of a "purchase of expertise" model. Several significant events occurred, however, that indicated the need for expanding the action research-based collaborative consultation model (Conwill, 2003). He included design thinking principles into their engagement model.

The daunting community violence was evident in the school's immediate environment. It afflicted many aspects of the school's daily functioning. Police presence to ensure the safety of the plant was a regular occurrence. It was heightened after shootings along the street in front of the school which was accessible from the freeway and the road into the housing development. The adjustment for school security included a safety officer at the locked entrance to check in visitors, prior to visitors' immediate reporting in the main office. Some parents disrupted meetings, demanding ad hoc attention to their issues. Once inside the building, their interference with school schedules and decorum created dysfunctional conditions.

Action Research, Design Thinking

The resources for problem-solving at the school level were also daunting. The children were not allowed to go outside to play, for fear of gunfire. The school had a gym, but there were no physical education classes because there was no instructor. Whatever tensions that might have been alleviated through exercise had no legitimate release on the school grounds. A CPS counselor that was assigned to the school spent only a few hours a week on site. Angry students could be heard from several hallways away cursing peers or teachers, lending an ominous apprehension at the school.

In this atmosphere of severe economic constraint, signified by lack of necessary personnel and by concerns about school safety, the Chicago mayor had announced the intention to shut down dozens of West Side and South Side schools. The mayor had already engaged in a public feud with the president of the Teachers Union, precipitating a strike that nearly crippled the mayor's hopes for repairing the damage to his prospects for re-election. His political opponents began vigorous campaigning against his school policies throughout the West and South Sides, showing up in caravans with body-guards. With their entourages behind them, they met with interested residents on the sidewalk in front of the school. The Chicago Public School Board's narrative was that it was too expensive to provide services for schools that were not meeting their educational objectives.

Fifty or so schools had been shut down for poor performance already, and at least 50 more were said to be on the chopping block when the consultant from the University of Illinois at Urbana-Champaign offered to provide consultation to the principal. When she lamented one day that the children's behavior was so disordered, she asked, "What's wrong with them?" the consultant answered, "They are traumatized." That response brought order and understanding to the chaos that she saw around her daily. She immediately signed her school staff up for training to recognize and respond to children suffering from trauma.

When she asked, "If we had a school psychologist, what could that person do to help?" she was provided an explanation on the roles and functions of a school psychologist. Casting off her budgetary limitations, she drove to the State Capitol offices in Springfield to plead her case passionately for more funding for her school. She returned with an allotment that would allow her to bring in a school psychologist and funding for more necessary resources for her staff and school.

Her unusual response to a crisis that was created by the Chicago Public School Board's neoliberal approach to school problems in her Far South Side school produced a counter-narrative to the Chicago School Board's that had played strongly in Springfield. Understanding the effects of this counter-narrative is the key to realizing the need for a more extensive analysis that includes design thinking.

The principal was a bright, compliant client committed to the joint action research project of improving her school performance by up-grading her staff's skill level and professionalism, creating a better school climate, lobbying for more resources that would address the needs of the students traumatized on multiple ecological levels, and encouraging more parent and neighborhood alliances to address community violence. Encouraged by her consultant, she had managed much in only a few months. The Local School Council opposition had been checked. Parents had enlisted each other to make sure the children's routes to school were monitored. Teachers had training to recognize and help children with experiences of trauma. A school psychologist would be joining the staff next year. Behavioral health teams trained over the summer months would be ready for implementation during the coming school year. The principal and teachers had regained each other's trust and were functioning as a collegial faculty.

On the day before the school year opened, the principal had entered the school to welcome the teachers, who would be preparing their classrooms for opening. The principal found that the lock on her office door had been changed. A letter awaited her at the secretary's desk. It informed her that her services were no longer required, and that she was to leave the premises immediately. The faculty was devastated by this turn of events. What did it all mean?

Design Thinking

Design thinking is human-centered innovation method that views challenges and solve problems by meeting people's needs feasibly and efficiently (Brown & Wyatt, 2010). Design thinking focuses on the design process, rather than the final product. Design thinking is gaining popularity in fields such as engineering, business, and education, that place a premium on generating creative solutions quickly and integrates expertise from design, social sciences, business and engineering.

Design thinking works well when it brings people from diverse backgrounds together to work to acquire basic knowledge about a situation (Understand), to gain empathy with each other (Observe), to create a typical persona for whom a solution is designed (Define a Point of View), to generate as many ideas as possible (Ideate), to build real prototypes of some of the most promising ideas (Prototype), and to learn from the user's or typical persona's reactions to the various prototypes (Test). The entry of the consultant on the scene, and the principal's successful management of the various salient problems at the school showed that the school was on the way to improvement. So why the school closure at this juncture?

Design thinking often produces counter-narratives and can lead to innovative solutions that demand structural rather than simply cosmetic changes. In some ways, design thinking resembles the general problem-solving approaches introduced through behavioral counseling and consultation theories several decades ago, in contrast to prior, more psychodynamic approaches focused on explanations based on an individual's faulty adjustment to a situation. Throughout this iterative design thinking process, teams gain new insights. Sometimes they may reframe the problem in entirely new ways, as the design thinking framework depicted in Whitter's (2016) model implies. Whitter's framework is presented because of its inclusion of "Storytelling" (Whitter, 2016). In other words, "Storytelling" is the genre of this chapter's recount of the lessons garnered from this engagement in a community school that seemingly operated at cross-purposes with the school board (Conwill, 2018).

SOLUTIONS AND RECOMMENDATIONS

Telling the Rest of the Story of Altgeld Gardens and An Elementary School

According to the Chicago Public School Board narrative, An Elementary School was an abject failure, slated for closure. The Board's decision to remove An's recently assigned principal who spent the summer developing behavioral intervention teams at the school points to a counter-narrative. For the principal, assignment to An Elementary School represented a labor of love, an opportunity to improve children's achievement levels.

After consultation, the principal had sought and obtained Illinois State funding to improve her school's climate through assignment of a school psychologist to An Elementary, teacher and staff training to address trauma, and targeted parent and community agency involvement. Both the school board's and the principal's narratives beg the question of the need for additional historical information to understand why the principal returned to the school at the end of the summer to welcome the faculty and staff, only to find that her key did not fit the principal's office door, and a note that her services were no longer needed.

Action Research, Design Thinking

From its initial planning, Altgeld Gardens suffered a history of decisions made in the context of anti-Black racism and intentional isolation. In 1944, Chicago needed housing for Black veterans who had returned from World War II. Chicago's housing was segregated. The Chicago Housing Authority decided to manage the crisis by creating a housing project location far from downtown, and euphemistically naming it Altgeld Gardens. An all-Black project 130 blocks from the center of the city would satisfy city planners, who placed Altgeld Gardens in a nook of the Little Calumet River that encased it on three sides. In the 1950s, more units and projects—Riverdale and Phillip Murray—were added in the river's nook, obviating the need to build in other nearby locations or push for desegregated public facilities.

Other small Far South Side White ethnic enclaves protested, demanding segregation from Blacks, and were appeased by the containment. It was only a few years ago that train service was extended to Altgeld Gardens. Eventually, nearby jobs that had helped sustain the families of Altgeld Gardens dried up as businesses closed, virtually abandoning the neighborhood. They had produced and processed toxic agricultural and industrial products.

By the 1960s, gang and drug-related violence in Altgeld Gardens surged, as Gangster Disciples, Black P Stones, Vice Lords and Black Disciples groups battled for supremacy in the neighborhood. In the 1970s, chemicals such as asbestos, lead, insecticides and industrial toxins from the closed plants were leaking and heavily polluting the ground and surrounding water with DDT, DDE, DDD and PCB, causing devastating health effects for Altgeld Gardens residents. Now, 50 years later, families are reluctant to move into Altgeld Gardens, even after removal of asbestos and lead from the refurbished project's homes. All this to say that living in Altgeld Gardens is dangerous to its inhabitants' health.

Starting the story of Altgeld Gardens and An Elementary School with the arrival of a consultant from an engaged university offering to provide the principal with consultation gratis and ending the story with a changing of the guard by removing a progressive principal at the school is disingenuous. That story is similar, for instance, to apologizing for government removal of Native American children from their homes to send them to schools that devalued their cultures, but taking no responsibility for the damage to the children and their tribal communities. That story is a distracting absolution of decision-makers reluctant to address social justice and corrective, restorative retribution. More so than other housing projects for African Americans in Chicago, Altgeld Gardens is the worst, given its placement in a polluted environment and its isolation.

Should not present-day admission of past injustices and continuing racist determinants for placement of Altgeld Gardens and An Elementary School on the Far South Side and the collapse of the community's infrastructure for family sustenance in Altgeld Gardens include comprehensive reparation beyond simply shutting down the school and ignoring the ongoing connections between racism and fiscal negligence? Is it possible to repair the damage to lives affected by isolating Altgeld Gardens? Was the School Board attempting to whitewash its decision to close the school by eliminating the counter-narrative of possibility and ridding itself of troublesome parental and neighborhood activists' intrusions?

FUTURE RESEARCH DIRECTIONS

Whitters (2016) model of design thinking suggests the adoption of an expanded version of the story of An Elementary School in Altgeld Gardens that subsumes its former and more immediate past and provides guideposts for determining its future. A starting point for the story of the future of the inhabitants of Altgeld Gardens and children in its schools should be their collective involvement with civil and university-based advisors in developing a plan for closing the projects and re-settling the people who live there. At this point in time, neighborhood coalitions and other organic structures exist for goal setting and community decision-making.

Gautreaux et al. v. Chicago Housing Authority was the nation's first major public housing desegregation lawsuit. In it, Altgeld Gardens resident Dorothy Gautreaux and others charged the Chicago Housing Authority (CHA) and the U.S. Department of Housing and Urban Development (HUD) with violating the U.S. Constitution, which guarantees all citizens equal protection of the laws, and the 1964 Civil Rights Act, which forbids racial discrimination in programs that receive federal funding. District, appellate, and U.S. Supreme Courts found CHA and HUD guilty of discriminatory housing practices for concentrating more than 10,000 public housing units in isolated African-American neighborhoods.

Chicago's original sin of racism in housing will not find expiation without further penitence represented by closure of Altgeld Gardens and assisted re-settlement of its inhabitants. Despite Gautreaux et al. v. Chicago Housing Authority, the city has not taken responsibility for its deed of 70 years ago. Altgeld Gardens still stands, poisoning citizens for generations to come.

CONCLUSION

The story of Altgeld Gardens and An Elementary School as structured here by design thinking is one of narrative, competing counter-narrative, and expansion. When acknowledging the entrenched role of racism in the origins of the decades-old problems in this Chicago Far South Side community, the Chicago Housing Authority, city planners, residents, and university-based advisors can come closer to creating effective models for community development and education. For example, though the principal had been at the school for a couple of years, her understanding of the children's behavior at school was limited. Her frustration level was growing day-by-day as she struggled to maintain her composure with disruptive parents, intransigent staff, and aggressive children. She asked the consultant, "What is wrong with these children?" He answered, "They are traumatized."

That answer was sufficient for her to go into action, and she brought in on-site training for trauma-informed schools. When she asked the consultant to attend a meeting with School Board, parent, and community agency representatives, and sought his reflection at its close, he did so. He informed the group, responding that most of the problems in their meeting were caused by the failure to employ *Robert's Rules of Order* (Robert, Honemann, & Balch, 2011). With this suggestion, the whole tenor of the meeting changed, and appropriate training for the distressed parent-leader began forthwith.

Practical interventions by engaged universities can provide valuable services to community schools. Essential directives include assuring that collectively developed common goals drive the efforts of parents, educators, planners and school boards, and embracing a social justice perspective in examining the kinds of recurrent issues at schools that were uncovered in this study such as persistent violent encounters just outside the school, severe acting out in the classrooms, and lack of personnel trained to provide appropriate services within the school.

Action Research, Design Thinking

REFERENCES

Bronfenbrenner, U., & Morris, A. P. (2007). The Bioecological Model of Human Development. Handbook of Child Psychology Theoretical Models of Human Development. Vol. 1. doi:10.1002/9780470147658. chpsy0114

Brown, T., & Wyatt, J. (2010). *Design thinking for social innovation. Stanford Innovation Review: Winter 2010* (pp. 30–35). Stanford, CA: Stanford Graduate School of Business.

Carr, W., & Kemmis, S. (1986). *Becoming critical: Education, knowledge, and action research.* Philadelphia, PA: Falmer Press.

Comer, J. P. (1990). Home, school, and academic learning. In J. I. Goodlad, & P. Keating (Eds.), *Access to knowledge: An agenda for our nation's schools* (pp. 23–42). New York, NY: College Entrance Examination Board.

Common Core State Standards Initiative. Retrieved from http://www.corestandards.org/about-the-standards/

Conwill, W. L. (2003). Consultation and collaboration: An action research model for the full- service school. *Consulting Psychology Journal: Practice and Research*, 55(4), 239–248. doi:10.1037/1061-4087.55.4.239

Conwill, W. L. (2007). Neoliberal policy as structural violence: Its links to domestic violence in US Black communities. In N. Gunewardena, & A. Kingsolver (Eds.), *The gender of globalization: Women navigating cultural and economic marginalities* (pp. 127–146). Santa Fe, NM: School of Advanced Research.

Conwill, W. L. (2015). Decolonizing Multicultural Counseling and Psychology: Addressing race through intersectionality. In R. D. Goodman, & P. C. Gorski (Eds.), De-Colonizing "Multicultural" Counseling through social justice. Series: International and Cultural Psychology (pp. 117–126). New York, NY: Springer.

Conwill, W. L. (2018). Community engagement: Reflexivity and reciprocal transformation. In R. F. Kronick (Ed.), *Community engagement: Principles, strategies and practices* (pp. 137–158). Hauppauge, NY: Nova Science Publishers.

Conwill, W. L., & Parks, A. (2007). School climate factors in selected full service and traditional elementary school sites in a Southeastern City: Contrasts and comparisons. *The American Association of School Administrators Journal of Scholarship & Practice*, 4(1), 43–51.

Farmer, P. (2003). *Pathologies of power: Health, human rights and the new war on the poor.* Berkeley, CA: University of California Press.

Harrison, F. V. (2008). Outsider within: Reworking Anthropology in the global age. Urbana, IL: University of Illinois Press.

Hertert, L., & Teague, J. (2003). Narrowing the achievement gap: A review of research, policies, and issues. *EdSource*. Retrieved from http://www.edsource.org

Hixson, J., & Tinzmann, M. B. (1990). Who are "at-risk" students of the 1990s? Retrieved from http://www.ncrel.org/sdrs/areas/rpl_esys/equity.htm

Kronick, R. F. (Ed.). (2000). *Human services and the full service school: The need for collaboration.* Springfield, IL: Charles C. Thomas.

Malveaux, J. (2002). Intersectionality--big word for small lives. *Black Issues in Higher Education, 19*(12), 27.

Manson, T. J. (1999). At-risk students: Who are they? In A. Duhon-Ross (Ed.), *Reaching and teaching children who are victims of poverty* , 55, pp. 153–158. Lewiston, NY: Edwin Mellen.

Natriello, G., McDill, E. L., & Pallas, A. M. (1990). *Schooling disadvantaged children: Racing against catastrophe.* New York, NY: Teachers College.

Orland, M. E. (1990). Demographics of disadvantage: Intensity of childhood poverty and its relationship to educational achievement. In J. I. Goodlad, & P. Keating (Eds.), *Access to knowledge: An agenda for our nation's schools* (pp. 43–58). New York, NY: College Entrance Examination Board.

Richardson, V., & Colfer, P. (1990). Being at risk in school. In J. I. Goodlad, & P. Keating (Eds.), *Access to knowledge: An agenda for our nation's schools* (pp. 107–124). New York, NY: College Entrance Examination Board.

Robert, H. M., Honemann, D. H., & Balch, T. J. (2011). Robert's rules of order (Newly revised, 11th ed.). Philadelphia, PA: Da Capo Press.

Taylor, E., Tisdell, E. J., & Hanley, M. S. (2000). The role of positionality in teaching critical consciousness: Implications for adult education. *Adult Education Research Conference*, Vancouver, Canada.

West-Olatunji, C. A., & Conwill, W. L. (2011). *Counseling African Americans. Book in the Supplementary Monograph Series, Multicultural Counseling Primers.* San Francisco, CA: Houghton Mifflin Company/Cengage Press.

Whitter, K. (2016). Design thinking: A success story! Retrieved from https://cohort21.com/katewhitters/2016/04/05/design-thinking-a-success-story/

Winter, D., & Leighton, D. (1999). Introduction. Structural Violence section. Electronic document retrieved from http://www.pych.ubc.ca/~dleighton/svintro.html

This research was previously published in Emerging Perspectives on Community Schools and the Engaged University; pages 145-156, copyright year 2020 by Information Science Reference (an imprint of IGI Global).

xx

Index

A

Ableism 131, 201, 506, 509, 521, 541, 791, 798, 1366

Academia 61, 90, 94, 96-98, 103, 118-119, 142-143, 145-146, 154, 208, 266, 278, 283, 288, 291, 295, 297, 302-303, 377, 407-408, 438, 489, 499, 532, 568, 661, 665, 677, 679, 729-736, 739, 743, 745-746, 750, 812, 820-822, 826, 829-830, 941, 970-975, 1009, 1018, 1025-1027, 1029-1030, 1039, 1041, 1096, 1098-1099, 1102-1103, 1114, 1195, 1222, 1326, 1330, 1337, 1346-1347, 1350, 1353, 1361-1364, 1370

Academic Climate 501, 1090

Academic Engagement 189, 664, 957, 1081-1082, 1084, 1091-1092, 1251, 1334

Acculturation 89, 251, 267, 270, 410, 415-416, 420-422, 427, 429, 958, 968, 1023

ACE 43, 191, 194-195, 367, 659

Achievement Gap 7, 159-160, 162, 166-168, 173, 180, 183-185, 187, 564, 706-707, 764, 862, 931, 1021, 1068-1071, 1073, 1075-1076, 1224, 1226, 1230-1232, 1237, 1243, 1246-1248, 1250, 1281-1283, 1285, 1292-1293, 1295, 1369-1370, 1384

ACPA 191, 194-195, 198, 209, 1090

Action Research 296, 305, 307-308, 509, 533, 632-633, 638, 921-922, 924, 927, 931, 943, 1210, 1300, 1308, 1392, 1399, 1404

Active Learning 353, 358, 370, 655

Activism 23, 41-42, 48, 55-56, 149, 152, 154-155, 207, 209, 213-214, 218, 220, 222-225, 227, 269, 325-327, 334, 341, 345, 347-348, 382, 507, 516, 535-536, 586, 589, 596-597, 604, 606, 610, 613-614, 725, 745, 769-770, 795, 1045, 1067, 1083, 1112, 1334, 1337, 1339-1340

adolescent literacy 1299-1300

adultification 1365-1366, 1370-1371, 1380, 1385

adultism 791

AERA 191, 194-195, 198, 201, 204-205, 208, 1002

Affirmative Action 90, 92, 179, 203, 408, 650, 665, 810, 812, 815, 820, 822, 944, 1028, 1158-1159, 1162, 1169-1170, 1183, 1189, 1203, 1242

African Academics 302, 1025

African American 6, 9, 17-18, 20, 22, 26, 28-29, 34, 36, 38, 48, 105-106, 118-119, 124, 126, 129-130, 158, 161-162, 164, 168-169, 172-174, 177-178, 183-186, 188-189, 252, 257-258, 266-267, 270, 282, 324, 410-411, 413, 458-459, 464-465, 474, 481, 483-484, 493, 559, 580, 601-603, 605-618, 620-621, 647, 658, 660-671, 673-679, 682, 688, 693-694, 697-698, 700, 704-706, 709-714, 716, 718-726, 729-731, 733-734, 736-737, 739-740, 743-744, 746-747, 749, 753-755, 757, 761, 764, 766, 768-770, 785, 788, 790, 810-825, 827, 830, 849, 853-858, 861, 863-867, 870, 872-876, 880, 883-884, 889, 905, 907-921, 953, 956-957, 962, 971-976, 980, 982, 984, 1040, 1043-1045, 1050, 1056, 1059, 1064, 1068-1080, 1090-1095, 1099, 1114-1115, 1122, 1134-1135, 1147, 1149, 1169, 1175, 1180, 1183, 1203, 1209, 1225-1226, 1228, 1231, 1233, 1235-1237, 1241, 1247-1249, 1251, 1311, 1317, 1325-1326, 1340-1344, 1348-1349, 1363, 1365-1386

African American Faculty 706, 731, 971-976, 984, 1043, 1068, 1115, 1349, 1363, 1375-1377

African American Male Theory 907-908

African American PhD success 660

African American Woman 17, 601-603, 606, 611, 621, 661, 665, 678, 719, 730, 819, 1043-1045, 1056

African Diaspora 225, 960, 964, 1041, 1095, 1180, 1206, 1209, 1211, 1220, 1223, 1330, 1332, 1344

Africana existential phenomenology 578-581, 583

Afro-centric 1404

Afrocentric curriculum 572, 581

Afrocentricity 302, 567-568, 572, 578, 581, 583, 1393

agnotology 886-890, 898-903, 905-906

Altruism 1354, 1357, 1360

American Education 185, 187-188, 541, 688, 907, 917, 1005, 1007, 1017-1018, 1029, 1173, 1248,

Volume I: 1-465; Volume II: 466-932; Volume III: 933-1407

Index

1251, 1281, 1285

American Indian 62-63, 65-76, 79, 81-88, 128, 139, 175, 231, 247, 254, 681, 764, 786, 871, 882, 884, 1006-1007, 1012, 1019-1024, 1238, 1325, 1393

Anecdotal 67, 69, 73, 79, 264, 933-944

anecdotal pedagogy 933-939, 941-943

Anti-Bias Education 451, 461, 463, 1375

Antiracism 17, 21, 39, 225, 227, 1281, 1287, 1293, 1385

Antiracist 1, 3, 5, 7, 9, 12, 14, 16, 18-21, 23-24, 382, 396, 617, 1112, 1202, 1218, 1281, 1341, 1361, 1365, 1377-1378, 1382, 1385

Antiracist Educator 3, 9, 1281

Apartheid 5, 103, 186, 283-284, 286-287, 289-290, 292-293, 295, 302-303, 305, 307, 568, 572, 575, 577, 681, 688, 745, 850, 965, 1188-1189, 1191, 1193, 1202, 1205, 1249

ASHE 191-192, 194-195, 201-202, 208, 412, 726, 736, 744, 1093

Asynchronous 265, 352, 358, 361, 370, 372, 645, 1143, 1150, 1152

axiology 1389-1393, 1396, 1399, 1403, 1407

B

Behaviorist Theory 513, 515, 521

Bell Hooks 41, 48, 54-55, 377, 609, 956, 1080

Beloved Community 41, 48, 59-60

Bias 3, 105, 107, 109, 111-113, 116, 120, 123, 160, 171, 179, 184, 186, 188-189, 214-215, 221, 271, 376, 380, 398, 402, 410, 412, 434, 458, 460-462, 465, 506, 531, 549, 563, 577, 649, 690, 709-710, 726, 736, 744, 750, 799, 810-812, 814, 818, 820, 827-828, 830-831, 881-882, 899, 911, 914, 942, 948-949, 958, 1006, 1011, 1014, 1018, 1027-1028, 1033, 1035, 1038, 1088, 1117-1119, 1136, 1211, 1224, 1235, 1243, 1247, 1249-1250, 1252, 1282, 1292, 1339, 1377, 1379, 1398, 1404

Bilingual Education 169, 175, 180-183, 415, 419-423, 429, 482, 634, 636-637, 640-641, 904, 1233, 1239, 1244-1246

Bilingualism 415-418, 424-426, 429, 626, 634, 642

Biliteracy 505-507, 517, 520

Biliterate 507, 521, 636

Binary Thinking 1328

Black African 283-284, 288, 290-292, 294-295, 297-298, 300, 302-303, 306, 720, 1186-1192, 1195-1196, 1205

Black Church 617, 676, 694, 700-701, 705-706, 708, 836, 1131

Black Families 5, 453, 683, 689-696, 698-700, 702, 708, 918

Black feminisms 601-602, 607, 609-615, 618, 621, 642

Black feminist standpoint theory 660, 663, 674-676

Black Feminist Thought 215, 217, 225, 560, 609, 616, 661, 663, 678, 1043-1044, 1067, 1112, 1202, 1327, 1361

Black Panther Party 768-772, 774, 778, 782, 786-790

Black Women PhD 660

black women professors 1043

Black/African American 29, 666, 1079, 1095

Blackness 99, 197, 209, 291, 325-326, 328, 332-333, 335, 340, 342-344, 542, 567, 569, 577, 581, 583, 589, 667, 774, 957, 1332

Black-Panther-Politics-Conflict-Urban-Guerrilla-US-Movement 768

Blood Memories 1005, 1007, 1024

broaden participation in CS 751

Broadening Participation 754, 825

Broederbond 283-284

Burnout 396, 546-547, 558, 560-561, 847-848, 850, 852-854, 858, 862, 864-865, 1117, 1120-1122, 1130, 1357-1358, 1360

buzz words 1173

C

Campus Climate 111-112, 115, 192, 405, 412, 867-868, 870-872, 876, 878, 880-881, 883-885, 979-980, 1160, 1166, 1260-1261, 1269, 1272, 1279-1280

capstone course 212-213, 218-224

Career Readiness 212, 271-272, 278, 282, 945

caring respect 538-540, 545, 548-551, 554-558, 565

Carlisle Indian Boarding School 1013, 1024

Carol Dweck 1079, 1083, 1089, 1095

Catholic social teaching 41-42, 46-48, 57, 60-61

Challenges Intersectionality 729

Change Agents 212, 222, 291, 758, 762, 988

chemical dependency 63

Cheryl Matias 886

child-centric analysis 430, 432

Child-Led Research Methodology 432, 450

Children at Risk 921

Christine Sleeter 377

cis-gender 540, 543, 565

Civic Virtue 1354, 1356, 1360

Classism 261, 267, 274, 376-377, 382, 384, 389, 614, 620, 664-665, 680, 683, 687, 689-691, 695, 697-699, 701-703, 908, 1366

Cognitive Dissonance 19, 21-22, 383, 896, 899

collaborative activities 1135, 1141, 1145, 1376

Collaborative Theory 513-514, 521

college climate 1254, 1262-1263, 1266-1268, 1272,

xxi

1274, 1279

Colonial Violence 152, 585-588, 590-591, 594-595

Coloniality 283-284, 287, 289, 291, 293-294, 296, 303, 305-309, 509, 570, 580-583

Coloniality Of Knowledge 287, 583

Color Caste 1327-1328

Colorism 261, 536, 704, 970, 974, 984, 1327, 1329

Community Cultural Wealth 276, 521, 636, 642, 689-691, 698-699, 701, 703, 707-708, 1362

community engaged learning 41-42, 46-48, 52, 54, 58

community mapping 631, 636-637, 642

community-based learning 56, 221, 227

Community-Building 41-42, 586-587, 589, 591, 594, 1102

Community-Engaged Learning 60

Confianza 633, 642

Connectivism 271, 278, 282, 367-368

Conscientiousness 1117, 1354, 1357, 1360

Constructionism 709, 1328-1329

Constructivism 354, 356, 358, 375, 380, 471, 727, 1374, 1388

Constructivist Theory 138, 215, 513-514, 521, 712, 1392

content-led research 522-523, 528, 530, 533-534, 536

context-aware learning 350, 355

Contingent 473, 491-492, 577, 736, 1096, 1098-1103, 1110-1111, 1353

Cooperative learning 375, 390, 469, 482

Counter-Storytelling 91-92, 104, 898, 1043-1044, 1068, 1297

Courageous Conversations 97, 229-230, 236, 238, 240, 1365, 1373-1374, 1377, 1381, 1384-1385

covert racism 1043-1044, 1056-1057, 1061, 1067, 1349

Critical Disability Studies 907

critical librarianship 1096, 1113

Critical Literacy 8, 1220, 1222, 1299-1300, 1303-1307, 1309-1310, 1313-1320, 1331, 1335

Critical Pedagogy 24, 238, 380-383, 387, 392-394, 396, 505-506, 508-509, 517, 521, 1113, 1152, 1223, 1317

Critical Race Theory (CRT) 90, 92, 102-104, 118, 120, 122, 127, 138, 140, 173-174, 187, 205, 209-211, 241, 245, 253-254, 256, 274, 314, 323, 343, 345, 392, 395-396, 415-416, 426, 434, 449, 451, 455, 463-464, 505-506, 520-521, 531, 538-541, 559-560, 562-563, 565, 587, 641-642, 690-691, 696, 704-707, 709, 712, 726-727, 792-793, 807, 887-888, 898, 900, 902-903, 905-906, 919, 944, 946, 949, 963, 965, 970, 972, 974-975, 978-979, 982-984, 1025, 1029, 1035, 1038, 1040, 1044, 1068-1070, 1076-1078, 1096, 1113-1114, 1116,

1129-1130, 1206-1207, 1218-1223, 1237, 1250, 1260, 1275-1276, 1281, 1289-1290, 1292, 1295-1296, 1298, 1330-1332, 1337, 1340-1344, 1365-1366, 1377, 1379-1380, 1385, 1392

Critical Race Theory In Education (Crte) 253-254, 520, 705, 793, 807, 903, 1068, 1130, 1206-1207, 1222, 1295, 1298, 1331, 1340-1341, 1344

Critical Theory 105, 120, 195, 280, 522-536, 609, 707, 727, 887-888, 1174-1175, 1184-1185, 1208, 1388, 1391

Critique 54-55, 85, 91, 103, 203, 209-210, 217, 239, 293, 311, 475-476, 485, 522-524, 526, 531, 534-536, 584-585, 587-589, 597, 606-607, 609, 614, 617, 639, 704, 760, 803-804, 900, 907, 915, 988, 996, 1005-1006, 1010, 1112, 1128-1129, 1136, 1185, 1202, 1207-1208, 1218, 1299, 1303, 1308, 1313, 1342, 1361, 1392

cross cultural counseling 25

Cultural Capital 193, 312-313, 315, 471, 477-478, 648, 671, 675, 689-691, 696, 698-699, 703, 706, 708, 1033, 1338

Cultural Competence 25-26, 30-31, 40, 72, 143, 367, 460, 467, 548, 559, 758, 847, 851, 865, 1136, 1138, 1373, 1375, 1377-1378

Cultural Diversity 11, 40, 87, 104, 116, 119, 123, 125, 127, 130-133, 135, 138, 140-141, 258, 268, 274, 278, 306, 313, 323, 351, 406, 408, 410, 413, 468-469, 472, 475-479, 482, 563, 629, 658, 672, 721, 725-726, 728, 763, 836, 1003, 1019-1020, 1039, 1132-1135, 1137-1148, 1151, 1341, 1343, 1384

Cultural Humility 25-26, 31-34, 39-40, 88, 128, 141, 988-989, 1001-1002

Cultural Identity 26, 30, 67, 122-126, 135-136, 258, 415, 422, 425, 428, 471, 626, 757, 761-762, 847-851, 854, 858, 860, 865, 1023, 1201, 1219, 1306

Cultural Psychology 62, 66-67, 69, 83, 85-86, 931

Cultural Relevancy 1005, 1024

Cultural Responsiveness 243, 251-252, 473, 847, 865, 913, 1136

cultural taxation 1120, 1346, 1353, 1359-1360

cultural tradition 1005-1006, 1015-1016, 1018, 1024, 1179

Culturally Relevant Pedagogy 23, 350, 467-469, 475, 481, 483-484, 503, 705, 757, 764, 807, 1136, 1144, 1149, 1220, 1283, 1297

culturally responsive caring 1069, 1074

Culturally Responsive Pedagogy 175-176, 180, 259, 312, 314-315, 350-351, 368, 370, 377, 466-467, 469-474, 481-482, 484-486, 507, 629, 647, 654, 658-659, 759, 764, 766, 855, 861, 1089, 1135-1136, 1153, 1239-1240, 1243

xxii

Index

Culturally Responsive Practice 557, 631, 1320

Culturally Responsive Teaching (CRT) 22, 175-176, 184-185, 257-258, 261-262, 267-270, 310, 315-316, 322-324, 365, 367-369, 424-426, 467, 469, 471, 474, 480-483, 486, 559, 561, 565, 644, 647-649, 657-659, 725, 751-752, 756-758, 763-764, 766, 806, 865, 1132, 1135, 1143-1144, 1147-1148, 1152, 1239-1240, 1247-1248, 1305, 1313, 1315-1316, 1318, 1342-1343

Culturally Sustaining Pedagogy 210, 238-239, 395, 468, 470, 485, 505-507, 509, 517, 520-521, 637, 727

Culture Theory 970, 974, 984

Cyber-Race 325, 327, 342, 346, 348

cyber-space 341-342, 348

D

DACA 1254-1263, 1266, 1268-1275, 1277-1280

DACA students 1255, 1257, 1259-1261, 1266, 1269-1274, 1279-1280

DACA-Mexico Origin (D-MO) Students 1255, 1279

Dataisation 327, 348

Decolonial 287, 291, 304-305, 308, 509, 567, 576-581, 583, 588, 594

Decolonial Curriculum 567

Decoloniality 287, 304, 567, 572, 576, 578, 581, 583

decolonizing research 1387-1389, 1395, 1405

Decolonizing Theory 505-506, 509-510, 517, 521

Design thinking 921-922, 926-932

dialogic education 1337-1338, 1344

Diaspora Experiences 1025

Dichotomy 159, 188, 217, 893, 1326, 1328-1329, 1332

Differentiation 246, 313, 319, 323, 357, 456, 644, 651-652, 654, 658, 683, 855, 904, 1015, 1028, 1210

Digitization 325

Disability Critical Race Theory 521

Disciplinary Literacy 486, 1299-1304, 1306-1307, 1309-1311, 1313-1320

Discrimination 71-73, 79, 87, 107-109, 112-114, 117-118, 131, 139, 157-158, 164, 174, 177-178, 180, 229, 236, 270, 274, 276-277, 289, 294, 302, 336, 382, 404, 406, 415, 431-435, 437-441, 444-446, 449, 460, 470, 478, 492, 506, 530-531, 607, 610, 664-665, 689-690, 693, 695, 697-700, 706, 708, 710, 712, 714, 723, 738, 750, 770, 795, 810, 813, 816, 829, 840, 845, 867-885, 887, 894, 911, 918, 930, 933, 945, 949, 954, 958-959, 965, 970-979, 982-984, 1006, 1010, 1014-1015, 1019, 1021-1022, 1028-1029, 1033, 1043-1044, 1055-1056, 1059-1064, 1066, 1070, 1075, 1098, 1110, 1116-1117, 1120, 1125, 1129, 1156, 1158, 1160,

1170, 1184, 1188-1189, 1196, 1202, 1211, 1219, 1228, 1237, 1241-1242, 1244, 1259-1260, 1279, 1326-1327, 1329-1333, 1336, 1350-1351, 1367, 1371-1372, 1378, 1380, 1382, 1385-1386, 1392

Discrimination Attribution 867

Discrit 505-507, 517, 520, 791, 793, 795, 807, 1295

Diverse Learners 254, 322, 365, 456, 462, 647, 651, 756, 916, 989, 1132, 1134, 1140, 1143, 1145-1146, 1384

Diverse Students 143, 175, 244-245, 262, 269, 316, 318, 322, 351, 396, 399, 467, 470, 484, 644-645, 649-650, 652-656, 674, 757-759, 762, 867, 870, 875, 1002, 1133-1136, 1138, 1140-1141, 1144-1146, 1206-1208, 1217, 1219, 1239, 1303, 1306, 1308, 1369, 1375

Diverse Teaching 758, 850, 854, 915, 1142, 1206-1208, 1210, 1212, 1216, 1218

Diversity Consultant 970, 977-980, 984

Diversity Gaps in CS 751

Double Discrimination 1326, 1329

Double Loop Approach 970, 974, 984

E

economic refugee 969

Eco-Systems 444-445, 450

Educational Technology 210, 365-370, 656, 658, 764, 1149-1151, 1320

emerging bilinguals 623-627, 636-639, 642

emerging technologies 1149, 1151

emotional disability 802, 907, 911-912

emotionally responsive pedagogy 228

empire 567-578, 581-584, 773, 787

employer expectations 271, 278, 282

English Language Learners 163, 175, 180-182, 188, 317, 415-416, 419-424, 427, 481, 483, 641, 758, 987, 995, 1152, 1226, 1238-1239, 1243-1245, 1251

Epistemology 210, 477, 509, 521, 663, 667, 1039, 1102, 1109, 1186-1187, 1191-1192, 1195-1196, 1200-1201, 1203, 1223, 1290, 1387-1394, 1396-1407

Equality 35, 91, 115, 118, 123, 126, 128-133, 157-158, 160-164, 166-169, 177, 182-183, 276-277, 319, 326, 345, 349, 388, 439, 443, 460, 463, 470, 473, 475-476, 486, 489, 494, 524, 526, 573, 597, 614, 620, 682, 686, 711, 713-714, 716, 723, 760, 781, 803, 830, 896, 933, 961, 965-966, 968, 971-972, 975-977, 984, 1037, 1126, 1170, 1189, 1202, 1224-1228, 1230, 1232-1233, 1240, 1245-1246, 1252, 1331-1332, 1342, 1344, 1368

Equity 6-7, 23, 32, 50, 61, 91, 103, 111, 115, 147-148,

xxiii

157, 159-162, 167-170, 173-174, 176-177, 179,
182-183, 185, 188, 193-194, 196, 198, 201-202,
205-206, 213, 215, 218-219, 221, 224, 226-227,
240, 254-256, 262, 319, 377, 383, 388, 393-394,
399-400, 405, 409, 411-412, 420, 443, 450, 464,
470, 481, 484, 486, 503, 566, 642, 650, 660, 678-
679, 690, 703, 707, 710, 713, 758, 760-761, 765,
767, 793, 805-806, 810-811, 825, 828-831, 859-
860, 862, 881, 887, 899, 901-904, 906-907, 914,
917, 920, 932, 968, 978-979, 1001-1002, 1020,
1034, 1064, 1068, 1092, 1094, 1101, 1113, 1140,
1149, 1152, 1159-1160, 1169-1170, 1179, 1182,
1188-1190, 1201-1202, 1204, 1224-1226, 1230,
1232, 1234, 1237, 1239-1240, 1242, 1245-1246,
1248, 1251-1252, 1270-1271, 1273, 1276, 1281-
1285, 1287-1288, 1292-1294, 1296-1298, 1316,
1342, 1356, 1373-1375, 1377-1385
Equity In Education 159, 168, 183, 188, 758, 907, 914,
1092, 1094, 1232, 1246
Essentialism 970, 972-973, 984
ethical clearance 283, 291-293, 295-296, 300, 302-
303, 309
ethical decision 222, 387, 394
Ethnicity 1, 7, 12, 22-23, 29, 39, 84, 94-95, 102, 116,
122, 125-127, 136, 154, 166, 169, 172-174, 177,
193, 209, 216, 244, 249, 258-259, 267, 273-274,
281, 307, 315, 318, 346, 377, 383, 392, 398-399,
402, 410, 431, 454, 462, 472, 501, 506, 521,
541-543, 545, 547-549, 553, 563, 565, 610, 616,
618, 642, 647, 649, 657, 686, 704-705, 707, 713,
727, 730, 734, 738, 749, 766, 827, 857, 866, 887-
888, 892, 904-905, 911, 918-919, 923-924, 945,
955, 960, 963, 966, 969, 983, 1028, 1039, 1092,
1114, 1126, 1130-1131, 1135, 1146-1148, 1152,
1158, 1170, 1172, 1185, 1191, 1193-1194, 1200,
1207, 1210-1211, 1216, 1219, 1224, 1230, 1233,
1235, 1237-1238, 1240, 1260, 1262, 1267, 1276,
1280, 1296, 1305-1306, 1324-1328, 1331-1332,
1335, 1340, 1350, 1359, 1362-1364, 1380, 1382,
1384, 1389
Ethnography 103, 344, 533, 547, 568, 596, 657, 688,
808, 1039, 1111, 1223, 1399, 1401
Eurocentric 12, 128, 134, 173, 284-286, 289, 292-293,
295, 298, 302, 403, 440, 567, 569-570, 572, 574-
575, 578, 580-581, 583, 861, 874, 886, 891-892,
906, 1124, 1179-1181, 1201, 1236
evaluative respect 538, 548-550
Exclusion 43, 106, 123, 158, 291-292, 295, 300, 303,
314, 404, 431, 439-440, 446-448, 450, 528, 544,
562, 569, 577, 695, 701, 703, 706, 710, 734, 805,
807, 833, 837-839, 844, 866, 919, 1028, 1126,

1161, 1174, 1187, 1211, 1216, 1254-1256, 1259-
1260, 1274, 1278, 1280, 1324
Expectancy Theory 973, 983-984
Experiential Learning 60, 212, 225, 227, 611, 656
Exploring Computer Science (ECS) 755

F

Faculty Of Color 90, 92, 94, 96-99, 102-104, 110-
111, 116, 119, 398-399, 401-402, 405-411, 413,
489-491, 496, 502-503, 665, 675, 744-745, 747,
842, 983, 1028, 1038, 1040, 1064, 1113, 1160,
1170-1171, 1173, 1176-1177, 1182-1183, 1346-
1347, 1351-1353, 1359-1361, 1364
Fanon 287, 293, 295, 304, 567-572, 577, 580, 582,
584-586, 588, 594, 596, 773, 1113, 1326-1327
Fees Must Fall 303, 571
female managers 1187, 1191-1193, 1196
feminist classroom 488, 494-495, 503
First Nations 62, 83, 1006, 1013-1015, 1024
first-generation PhD 660
fixed mindset 1079, 1083-1085
Florence Country Museum 709, 712, 714, 722
Florence County Museum 709-710, 712, 715, 728
Forced Migrants 949, 969
foreignness 1025-1027, 1030-1032, 1034-1035, 1039,
1041-1042
Framing 14, 46, 278, 312, 325-326, 328, 332-334,
342-343, 345-348, 382, 391, 447, 594, 898, 944,
996, 1006, 1015, 1017, 1174, 1178, 1185, 1208,
1210, 1290, 1294-1295, 1406
Frantz Fanon 567, 584, 1113
funds of identity 623-624, 626-627, 629, 634, 638-
639, 643
Funds Of Knowledge 420, 423, 427, 623-624, 626,
628, 630, 641

G

Gaslighting 847, 849-850, 853, 864, 866
Gender Microaggressions 104, 108, 116-117, 732, 750
Genocide 62-63, 66, 68, 70-71, 73-75, 77, 79-80, 88-89,
130, 151-152, 772, 804, 1007, 1012, 1024, 1174
Grit 828, 893, 904-905, 1083, 1090, 1117-1118, 1124,
1127-1130
Grounded Theory 81, 411, 532, 679, 951, 990, 1038,
1186, 1190, 1279
growth mindset 1079, 1084-1085, 1089-1090, 1092,
1094

Index

H

Habitus 292, 806

Han 43-44, 60, 370, 883, 1332, 1343

Han-puri 44, 60

hashtags 196-197, 199-201, 205-208, 211, 325-326, 329, 332-333, 337-338, 340-341, 343, 348-349

Hashtivism 325-326, 349

HBCU 90, 99, 101-102, 257-259, 261, 267-268, 452-453, 459, 729-730, 739-741, 743, 753, 756, 821, 827, 1077, 1093, 1118, 1122

Hegemony 19, 92, 418-420, 428-429, 435, 466, 470, 477, 607, 696, 708, 908, 1178, 1208, 1210, 1216, 1223, 1289, 1396

Heritage Language 415, 418-419, 481, 883

heterocentric-patriarchy 601-603, 606-608, 610-611, 613-615, 621

Hidden Curriculum 88, 219, 680, 686-687, 689, 694-696, 698, 703, 708

high impact instruction 375-376, 389-391

Higher Education 2, 23, 31, 39, 51, 54, 59, 88, 90, 92, 94, 102, 104, 110-111, 115-116, 119-121, 131, 143, 148, 164, 186, 191-195, 197, 206-210, 213, 217, 221, 258, 267, 269-272, 277, 280, 284-286, 296-298, 302-306, 308, 310, 312, 323, 350-351, 361, 364, 366-367, 369, 398-405, 409-414, 419, 424, 428, 451-452, 464-465, 484, 489, 501-503, 511, 541, 562, 582, 596, 629, 644-647, 649, 651, 654, 657-662, 664-665, 672, 676-680, 682, 685-686, 688, 726, 729, 731-732, 734-736, 738-739, 744-749, 765, 801, 808, 814, 831, 858, 867, 880, 882-885, 902, 932-933, 935-936, 941-945, 963, 966, 971-972, 974-977, 979, 981-983, 1001, 1008-1009, 1017, 1020, 1022-1023, 1025-1030, 1033-1041, 1044, 1046, 1067-1073, 1075-1077, 1079-1080, 1082, 1085, 1091-1096, 1098-1099, 1101, 1111-1124, 1126-1131, 1133, 1138, 1147, 1149-1150, 1155-1162, 1166-1173, 1176-1177, 1179, 1183, 1185, 1203, 1210-1211, 1218-1219, 1221-1222, 1227-1228, 1249, 1254-1257, 1259-1262, 1264, 1269-1274, 1276-1280, 1327, 1329, 1349-1351, 1353, 1358-1364, 1405

Higher Institutions Of Learning 283, 285-286, 289-291, 294-296, 301-302, 1026, 1029, 1034-1035, 1037

Historical Consciousness 63, 69, 84, 88, 1020

Historical Trauma 62-78, 80-83, 85, 87, 89, 1005-1006, 1014-1015, 1018-1020

historical traumatic response 63-64, 66, 70, 72, 74, 76-77

Historically Black Colleges And Universities (HBCU) 90, 257, 268, 452, 465, 676, 739, 744, 747, 750, 753, 767, 972, 1070, 1080, 1082, 1088, 1093, 1157, 1168

horizontal assimilation 950-951, 969

Human Dignity 47, 50, 287-288, 522-523, 527-528, 1357

I

Ida B. Wells 617, 682, 886, 889-890, 905

Idea 1, 33, 68, 139, 148, 150, 157, 169, 173, 204, 206, 208, 221, 251-252, 259-260, 272-273, 312-314, 318, 326-327, 336, 341, 359, 389, 417, 420, 422, 429, 480, 489-492, 503-504, 526, 529, 540, 544-545, 549, 552, 555, 557, 565, 571, 574, 577, 589-590, 632, 645, 648, 650-651, 657, 665, 680, 685, 696, 714, 720-721, 733, 737, 762, 772-773, 782, 785, 801, 834-835, 914, 919, 935, 941, 959-960, 1000, 1011, 1017, 1026, 1028, 1049, 1055, 1059, 1089, 1092, 1094, 1099, 1104, 1107-1108, 1126, 1174-1176, 1178-1181, 1184, 1195, 1233, 1237, 1272, 1301, 1322, 1335, 1373, 1377, 1385

ideological clarity 623-624, 639, 643

Ideology 90-91, 101, 127-128, 133, 163, 176, 301, 308, 314, 392, 395, 420, 435, 506, 531, 548, 563, 588, 602, 608, 614, 648, 687, 689, 703, 705, 772-774, 776, 778, 785-787, 790, 806, 868, 874, 883, 886-888, 891-902, 904-906, 919, 965, 988, 1066, 1070, 1075-1076, 1098, 1107-1109, 1111, 1125-1127, 1133, 1173-1174, 1176-1179, 1183-1184, 1223, 1227, 1239, 1373

Immigrant 7, 132, 315, 377, 399, 401, 418, 422-424, 426-428, 440, 473-474, 624, 626, 637-638, 641-642, 648-649, 681, 686, 693-694, 700, 878-879, 946-964, 966-969, 1206, 1209, 1211, 1256, 1268, 1275, 1277, 1279, 1325, 1328, 1340

Immigration 8, 56, 136, 274, 328, 332, 344, 346, 419, 423, 426, 429, 443, 448, 680, 691, 705, 903, 947-949, 954-955, 964, 966, 995, 1047, 1210, 1254-1255, 1257-1260, 1263, 1266, 1268, 1271-1274, 1276-1279, 1303, 1325, 1327, 1335

Implicit Bias 3, 105, 111, 113, 116, 120, 398, 402, 549, 810, 827, 899, 914, 1136, 1292

Incarceration 27, 41-43, 46, 48, 51-52, 55-56, 59, 140, 169, 172-173, 319, 1080, 1233, 1236

Inclusive Campuses 1155, 1160, 1172

Indentured Laborers 1188, 1205

indigenous epistemology 1387-1390, 1393-1394, 1397-1407

Indigenous Knowledge 142, 283-284, 293, 296, 299, 304, 308-309, 567-569, 574, 578, 581, 583-584, 1387, 1390, 1392-1393, 1395-1400, 1402-1403,

xxv

1405-1406

Indigenous Knowledge Systems 296, 299, 304, 308, 567-568, 574, 578, 581, 583-584, 1393, 1395

Individual Ideology 893, 897-898, 906

Informal and Lifelong Theory 513, 516, 519, 521

Institution Of Higher Education 94, 465, 729, 867, 880, 981, 1009

Institutional Racism 143, 147-148, 153, 162, 176, 201, 376, 408, 541, 549, 558, 689-691, 702-703, 772, 820, 911, 915-916, 973, 1044, 1056-1058, 1116, 1119, 1126, 1156, 1226, 1240

Instructional Leader 644

InTASC Standard 9 375, 379

Intentional Design 350

Intercultural Communication 428, 466, 468, 470-475, 477, 479, 482, 484, 486, 1139

Intercultural Education 369, 469-472, 474-475, 481-482, 484-486, 1170

Interculturalism 469-470, 472-473, 486

interculturality 466, 468-474, 476-479, 481, 486

interculturally relevant pedagogy 466, 468, 472, 474-476, 479-480, 486

Interest Convergence 91, 102, 507, 1281, 1289

intergenerational historical trauma 62-63

intergenerational trauma 1005, 1007, 1013-1015, 1019, 1022, 1024

interpersonal theory 25

Interpretivist approach 1186

Intersectionality 3, 103, 122, 127, 138, 229, 332-333, 335, 340, 381, 388, 488, 501, 503-505, 508-509, 540-542, 555, 560, 565-566, 601, 607, 614, 621, 662, 664-665, 729, 733-734, 738, 745, 750, 762, 795, 807, 924, 931, 946, 975, 1069-1070, 1075, 1102, 1112, 1186-1188, 1190-1192, 1194-1196, 1200, 1202-1205, 1208, 1276, 1331, 1346, 1349-1350, 1361, 1363, 1366

Islamophobia 328, 384, 430-439, 441-450, 948

J

James Banks 377

Jennifer Logue 886

K

Kanter 973-974, 983-984, 1346-1349, 1351-1352, 1359, 1362

kinship 41-42, 45, 47-49, 52, 55, 59-60, 149, 152, 281

L

language as resource 623, 628, 636, 638, 643

language as right 623, 634, 636, 638, 643

language loss 415, 419

Language Privilege 422, 427

language shift 421-422, 426-427, 429

Latinidad 635, 643

Latinx 16, 20, 123, 126, 140, 244, 415-416, 420, 423-425, 427, 488, 492, 517, 554, 623-626, 629, 634, 638-639, 643, 791, 798, 867, 870, 878, 880, 892, 1097, 1182, 1208, 1211, 1261, 1276, 1283, 1286, 1290-1291, 1331

Learning and Teaching Support Theory 513, 516, 519, 521

learning diverse 644-646, 650, 652-653, 655

Learning Experiences 4, 7, 12, 19, 46, 212-213, 215, 224, 314, 351-352, 354, 356, 364, 369-370, 379, 476, 639, 656, 709-714, 721, 723-724, 752, 761, 902, 1133-1134, 1144-1145, 1149, 1162, 1305, 1307

Life Story Interviews 1205

linguistic disadvantage 949, 958-959, 969

living energy 69-70, 89

Lori Patton 191-192

Loteria 637, 640, 643

Low Income 412, 680-681, 693, 700, 958

low socioeconomic status 689-690, 694

M

Machitia 505-507, 510, 513-519, 521

Macro Environment 1190, 1205

Macroaggressions 101, 105, 112, 116, 120, 1036, 1081

Majority-Minority Area 969

Marginalization 31, 246, 251, 296, 389, 404, 410, 422, 435, 440, 445-446, 485, 536, 658, 734, 819, 822, 824-825, 833, 840, 842, 844, 848, 857, 886-887, 906, 949, 972, 975, 1048, 1119-1120, 1128, 1294, 1307, 1350, 1352, 1371-1372, 1388-1389, 1392

Marginalized Groups 22, 91, 106, 110, 112-113, 174, 402, 474, 490, 497, 732, 738, 750, 860, 894, 900, 989, 998, 1017, 1047, 1105, 1110, 1238, 1388

Meaningful Learning 350-351, 358-359, 365-366, 368-370, 566, 712, 723, 1341

Medicine Wheel 62, 77-78, 88

Meso Environment 1190, 1205

method-led and content-led research 522-523, 528

method-led research 528, 530, 536

Mexican Citizens and Mexican Immigrants 1279

Micro Environment 1190, 1205

Index

Microaffirmations 105, 120

Microaggressions 26, 31, 34, 40, 92, 94-95, 99, 104-110, 112-121, 127, 140, 209, 211, 391, 398-399, 401-405, 408, 412-413, 437, 448, 612, 619-621, 672, 674, 677, 732, 738, 750, 835, 839, 884-885, 888, 982, 1020, 1029, 1040, 1068, 1071, 1075, 1078, 1093-1094, 1119-1120, 1127, 1130, 1185, 1321, 1326, 1347-1348, 1351, 1367, 1369-1370, 1372, 1378, 1385

Microassaults 26, 108, 120, 127, 1367, 1385

Microinequities 114, 121

Microinsults 121, 127, 975, 1367, 1385

Microinvalidations 121, 127, 1367, 1385

Minority Male Teachers 451

Minority Students 115, 170, 177, 182, 188, 246, 258, 267, 317, 322, 413, 420, 424, 439, 459-461, 463, 489, 549, 647-648, 650, 680, 746, 751-758, 760-762, 766, 807, 863, 867-868, 870, 880-881, 885, 1092, 1132, 1134-1135, 1138, 1140-1141, 1144-1146, 1149, 1155-1167, 1169, 1172, 1219, 1234, 1241, 1245, 1250, 1294, 1352

Minority Teacher Shortage 458, 464-465, 904

Mobile Pedagogy 350

Model Minority 138, 948, 951, 963, 967-969

monoculturalism 122, 126

moral reasoning 375, 379, 393, 395

morale 971, 976, 1116, 1120, 1126-1127

Mother Tongue 298, 415-416, 418-425, 955

multicultural contents 1132, 1139, 1142

Multicultural Education 21-23, 39-40, 139, 176, 183, 219, 269, 304-305, 314, 318, 322, 376-377, 380-383, 387-388, 393, 395-396, 428, 456, 464, 468-469, 475-476, 480-486, 490, 641, 648-650, 656-657, 765, 839, 963-966, 985-986, 988, 994-997, 1000-1003, 1111, 1141, 1151-1152, 1185, 1221, 1239, 1246, 1328, 1339-1344

Multicultural Instruction 466, 468, 470, 1149

Multicultural Literature 214, 1317, 1330-1331, 1335-1342, 1344

Multiculturalism 66, 122, 125, 132, 138, 140, 176, 213-214, 226, 286, 289, 400, 406, 414, 417, 439, 445, 469, 473, 479, 481, 485, 642, 658, 949, 1034, 1101, 1152, 1155, 1161-1162, 1166, 1171-1172, 1219, 1239, 1284, 1338, 1343, 1383

multilingualism 429, 469

Muslim children 430-433, 436-441, 444-445

N

narrative pedagogy 257, 259-260

Narratives and Counter-narratives 757, 921

NASPA 191, 194-195, 199, 201, 203-205, 211, 502, 1093

Native American 62-83, 85, 87-88, 110, 126, 128, 173, 228-231, 233-235, 237-238, 266, 453, 465, 474, 488, 761, 814, 867, 870-871, 874, 876, 881-882, 885, 929, 1005-1024, 1237, 1326, 1350

Naturalistic Inquiry 81, 678, 1223

Neoliberalism 288, 1112

neurotypical 791, 794, 800-801

Non-Voluntary Migrants 969

novice teachers 538-539, 545-547, 556, 558-559, 847

O

online imagery 585-586, 593

online learning program 1153

Online Learning Resources 1153

Oppression 3, 22, 27, 32-33, 37, 46, 53, 57, 60, 68, 72, 77, 80, 86, 90-91, 99, 101-102, 112, 127, 133, 148, 158, 192-193, 200-201, 203, 205-206, 216, 243, 246, 251, 267, 273-274, 290, 326, 333-334, 347-348, 376-377, 380-382, 384, 388-389, 399-400, 403, 417, 425, 443, 488-489, 491-492, 500-502, 504, 508, 521, 530-532, 540-543, 545, 565, 572, 580-581, 588, 597, 601-603, 606-607, 609-611, 613-615, 621, 649, 664, 690, 695, 701, 712, 721, 729, 732, 738, 750, 772-774, 782, 791, 795-796, 799, 803, 807, 833, 840, 842, 845, 866, 886-887, 906-908, 915-916, 972-973, 984, 1010, 1014-1015, 1045, 1058, 1065, 1089-1090, 1096-1097, 1102, 1108-1109, 1112, 1119, 1123, 1156-1157, 1177, 1187-1189, 1191-1192, 1194, 1196, 1200, 1285, 1306, 1325, 1331-1333, 1349-1350, 1361, 1366-1369, 1371, 1376-1378, 1385, 1392

Organizational Culture 110, 731, 736, 739-740, 744, 750, 847, 862, 975, 1347

Othering 7, 847-850, 852, 863, 866, 1059, 1394-1395, 1401

P

Paolo Freire 392

Parental Involvement 689-692, 694-695, 698, 701-703, 705, 1169

Parker Palmer 54

Paul Gorski 377, 886

peace circle 54

Perceived Discrimination 72, 87, 884, 970-974, 976, 979, 982-984, 1260, 1279

Political Refugee 969

Popular Culture 33, 344, 349, 466-468, 471, 473-474,

476-482, 484-486, 826, 1299, 1304, 1306-1308, 1310, 1313-1315, 1317, 1320

Positionality 3, 13-14, 19, 34-35, 122, 126, 140, 194, 381, 388, 400, 455, 508, 580, 765, 932, 1045, 1086-1087, 1210, 1281

Positivism 85, 523, 526, 530, 537, 1175, 1388

Post-Racial 4, 204, 325-327, 341, 343, 349, 675, 810, 812, 1097, 1111, 1115, 1118, 1126, 1131

Postsecondary Education 157, 210, 488, 858, 884, 1023, 1069-1073, 1075-1076, 1087-1088, 1120-1121, 1156, 1167

Praxis 42, 45-46, 57, 86, 116, 191-194, 252, 313, 381-382, 391-392, 482-483, 503, 561, 563, 644, 650, 655, 661, 705, 778, 1115, 1130, 1204, 1315, 1319

Predominantly White Institution 26, 96, 452, 465, 493, 498, 666, 867, 880, 883-884, 1043, 1077, 1079, 1085, 1107, 1177

Professional Development 1-3, 5, 7, 12, 20-21, 23-24, 113-114, 176, 186, 194-195, 267, 367-368, 377-379, 393, 407, 460, 462-463, 511, 539, 623-625, 627-628, 633, 636-639, 642, 647, 662, 675, 724, 726-727, 732-733, 735-736, 740-742, 755-756, 762-763, 799, 842, 847, 850, 855, 860, 899, 1101, 1240, 1249, 1287, 1289, 1373

Proficiency-Based Learning 505, 521

Public Education 157-158, 160, 162, 167, 174, 179, 182, 184, 188-189, 310, 321, 420, 426, 439, 645, 680, 684-688, 699, 701, 757, 812, 849, 1080, 1093, 1221, 1224, 1226, 1231, 1237, 1242, 1245, 1247, 1251-1252, 1256, 1286, 1370, 1382

Public Schools 5, 9, 11, 110, 159-162, 169, 176, 179, 181, 183, 188, 231, 238, 310-311, 437-438, 447, 457-458, 462, 541, 582, 680-687, 689-704, 710, 722, 763, 791-792, 795, 847-848, 857, 907, 923, 926, 946, 962, 1216, 1224-1225, 1233, 1240, 1242-1244, 1256, 1284, 1287, 1379, 1381, 1383, 1385

PWI 90, 95-97, 99, 101-102, 266, 452-453, 665-666, 676, 730, 867, 1083-1084, 1088-1089, 1116, 1118, 1123, 1126-1127

Q

Qualitative Meta-Synthesis 432, 450

QuantCrit 1282, 1292

Queer Theory 505-506, 508, 517, 521, 1178, 1392

R

R Proctor 886

Race And Class 118-119, 173, 185, 412, 677, 679, 682, 694, 772-773, 830, 903, 1102, 1114, 1202, 1237, 1248, 1283, 1326, 1361-1364

Race And Gender 3, 115, 257, 406, 500, 502, 540, 609, 672, 732, 739, 1194-1195, 1203, 1346, 1350, 1352, 1360

Racial Discrimination 433, 690, 693, 695, 706, 708, 770, 840, 872, 884, 918, 930, 958, 971, 976, 1014, 1019, 1021-1022, 1044, 1055-1056, 1059-1064, 1066, 1116-1117, 1125, 1196, 1211, 1333, 1351, 1367, 1382, 1385-1386

Racial Identity 13-14, 16, 19, 23, 26, 30-31, 38-39, 123, 229, 234, 237, 240, 258, 273, 402, 474, 490, 565, 609, 709, 713-714, 720-722, 725-726, 728, 747, 785, 842, 903, 913, 918-919, 967, 1082-1083, 1090, 1092, 1125, 1183, 1328, 1331-1332, 1341-1342

racial trauma 1104, 1106, 1117, 1129, 1367, 1371, 1382, 1386

racially integrated 5

Racially Responsive Teaching 709, 721-722, 728

Racism 3, 6-9, 17, 20-22, 26, 30-35, 38-39, 42-43, 46, 48, 53, 55, 60, 71-73, 76-77, 79-80, 90-92, 98, 101-103, 106-107, 109, 116-118, 138, 141, 143, 147-148, 150-151, 153-156, 158, 160, 162, 173, 176, 186-187, 192, 201, 204, 206, 209-211, 217, 221, 223, 227, 229-230, 235-237, 239-241, 245, 247, 251, 253, 267, 274, 280, 292, 294, 303, 307, 321, 326-328, 332, 334-335, 337, 343, 348, 376-377, 382, 384, 389-391, 395, 400-401, 403, 408, 410, 412, 417-418, 426, 431, 434, 438-439, 445, 447-449, 455, 489, 506, 531, 539, 541, 545, 549, 558-559, 580, 582-584, 587, 597, 601, 607, 609, 611, 614, 617, 620, 622, 640, 664-665, 672, 674-675, 677, 680, 683-684, 687-691, 695-699, 701-705, 708, 710, 712, 714, 716-717, 720-725, 727, 732-733, 738-739, 768-769, 772-774, 776, 785-786, 789, 798, 810-811, 813, 815, 819-823, 825-826, 828-831, 840-841, 843, 846, 848, 860, 864, 867, 871-874, 879-880, 883, 888, 891, 894, 899-900, 903-905, 908, 911, 914-919, 923, 929-930, 935-937, 944-945, 949, 958, 967, 971-975, 977, 982-984, 994, 1015-1016, 1019, 1022-1023, 1028-1029, 1033, 1035, 1043-1044, 1054, 1056-1058, 1061, 1065-1072, 1075, 1077, 1080, 1089-1092, 1098, 1102, 1104-1106, 1108-1109, 1111-1112, 1115-1120, 1122-1127, 1129-1130, 1156-1159, 1167, 1169, 1177, 1180, 1182-1184, 1187, 1194, 1202, 1210, 1216, 1219, 1223-1224, 1226, 1237, 1240, 1249, 1261, 1281, 1284, 1286-1290, 1294, 1306, 1328-1329, 1331-1332, 1334, 1342, 1344, 1349, 1352, 1363, 1366-1368, 1370-

Index

1371, 1373, 1375-1383, 1385

racist based self-actualisation 291-292

Radical Healing 505-509, 517-518, 521, 606, 1123, 1128

Ranciere 585, 587, 589-594, 597

Reification 525, 527, 537

relational-cultural theory 25, 33, 38-39

religious bullying 430, 432, 437-438, 441-442, 444, 450

Religious Stereotype 450

Research Ethics Committee 288, 304, 308-309

Research Paradigm 526, 1203, 1290, 1387-1395, 1400, 1402, 1405-1407

restorative justice 45, 49, 56, 60

Rhetoric of Color-Blindness 1329

Ritual 41-42, 45, 49, 52-55, 61, 579

Rural Farming 8-9, 630

S

Scatted 601, 622

school race culture 1281-1282, 1293-1294

school to prison pipeline 680, 913

School-Based Social Work 450

seamless learning 350-351, 354, 356, 358-359, 361, 364-371

segmented assimilation 946, 949-950, 956, 967-969

Segregation 129, 157-159, 161-167, 174, 177, 180-181, 183, 186-188, 230, 290, 292, 322, 376, 435, 541, 562, 681, 684, 695, 714, 720, 723, 770, 834, 841, 909, 929, 1115, 1157, 1159, 1161, 1167, 1225-1231, 1238, 1240, 1243-1244, 1250-1251, 1284, 1288, 1296-1297, 1329, 1366-1367, 1384

Self-Efficacy 222, 241-242, 248, 252, 254, 261, 319, 323, 354, 651, 671, 751, 753, 755, 758, 762, 764, 854, 861, 864, 1081-1083, 1090-1091, 1093-1094

Self-Study 409, 1299-1300, 1306, 1308, 1316-1318, 1320

Sense Of Belonging 111, 244, 267, 416, 424-425, 428, 435, 461, 521, 698, 735, 751, 754, 765-766, 851, 871, 883, 1009, 1015, 1018, 1020, 1081, 1093-1094, 1126, 1254, 1260-1269, 1273-1274, 1279-1280, 1333-1335, 1355, 1372, 1375

Service-Learning 212, 214-218, 221-223, 227, 279, 456, 985-1003

seven generations 1005-1006, 1024

Sexual Orientation 40, 106, 115, 119, 140, 216, 258, 315, 377, 382-384, 389, 399, 413, 443, 491, 500, 503-504, 541-544, 607, 610, 620, 646, 649, 877, 888, 908, 1152, 1172, 1185, 1284, 1334-1335

Shaun Harper 191

Social And Emotional Learning 241, 243, 253-256,

365, 520

Social Capital 193, 276, 541, 596-597, 655, 664, 693, 698-699, 735, 746, 966, 1082, 1089, 1093, 1209, 1330-1331, 1333, 1337-1339, 1355, 1359-1360

Social Connectedness 508, 513-515, 519-521, 1216

Social Constructionism 1328-1329

Social Emotional Learning 252, 254-255, 507, 1345

Social Exclusion 439-440, 447-448, 450, 1254-1256, 1259-1260, 1274, 1278, 1280

Social Isolation 407, 480, 1347, 1352, 1364

Social Justice 21-23, 25, 30, 32, 37-39, 52, 56, 87, 91, 101, 114, 119, 145, 149, 158, 187, 192-193, 196, 200-201, 205-207, 214, 218, 220-222, 224, 226-227, 274, 304, 375-377, 380-384, 387-397, 400, 408, 411, 424, 455, 466, 469-470, 472-477, 481-482, 484-486, 489, 503, 506, 508-509, 520-521, 525, 540, 555, 566, 603, 605, 609, 705, 712, 714, 717, 720-724, 726-728, 759-760, 788, 793, 797-800, 804, 806, 808, 812, 854, 883, 887-888, 894, 901, 908, 929-931, 933, 942, 983, 997, 1001-1002, 1069-1070, 1075, 1114, 1136, 1159-1160, 1168, 1221, 1295, 1302-1306, 1313, 1316, 1319, 1341, 1350, 1361, 1363, 1365-1366, 1373, 1375-1377, 1382-1386, 1388, 1391-1392, 1397, 1406

Social Justice Advocacy 387, 1365, 1377, 1386

social location 539-544, 551-553, 556-558, 566, 660, 663

Social Media 14, 19, 147-151, 153-155, 191-197, 199, 201, 204, 206-211, 223, 264-265, 326-331, 340-342, 344-346, 457, 485, 514, 544, 586-587, 590-591, 593, 596, 598, 602, 614, 655, 716, 812, 1080, 1096, 1099, 1102-1103, 1106-1108, 1110-1112, 1287, 1325

social media mining 191-192, 195, 211

social networking sites 197, 211, 341

social reproduction 964, 1206-1208, 1210-1211, 1216, 1223

Social Stigma 882, 1256, 1259-1260, 1280

social work response model 432

Sociology 32, 115, 145-147, 154, 209, 345-346, 448-449, 456, 489, 491-493, 498, 500-502, 504, 523, 525-526, 533, 535, 559, 568, 705-706, 708, 883, 963-964, 966-968, 1091, 1096-1098, 1100, 1111, 1131, 1201, 1204, 1221, 1283, 1297, 1363, 1388

Soft Skills 212-213, 243, 1034

Solidarity 38, 47-48, 54, 56-57, 59, 61, 95, 192, 326, 333, 336, 435, 439, 573, 590, 597, 607, 614, 738, 776, 779, 790, 833-834, 836, 841, 843, 846

Sonia Nieto 377, 382, 424

Special Education 93, 169-172, 179, 184, 186, 188, 252, 310-324, 358, 366, 384, 423, 451, 453, 462,

xxix

560, 645, 649-651, 658, 757, 791-803, 805-807, 910, 912, 914-916, 1080, 1136, 1139, 1212, 1233-1235, 1243, 1247, 1249, 1251, 1366, 1369

Sportsmanship 1354, 1356, 1360

Stereotype Threat 112, 402, 404-405, 410-413, 618, 737, 739, 748, 750, 853, 857, 864, 866, 1081, 1084, 1090, 1093-1094, 1363

Stereotypes 6, 8, 17, 21, 43, 49, 91, 103, 107-108, 119-120, 123, 216, 243, 272, 276-277, 282, 328, 335, 343, 345-346, 348, 352, 376, 404-405, 411-413, 433, 435, 438, 441, 443, 445, 470, 475, 478, 493, 502, 542, 549, 561, 604-605, 608, 611-612, 710, 712-713, 725, 729-731, 737, 739, 743-745, 750, 754, 765, 813-814, 816-817, 853, 864, 869, 876, 880-881, 987-988, 994-996, 1026-1027, 1029, 1031, 1033, 1037-1038, 1071-1072, 1080-1082, 1084, 1130, 1336, 1340, 1347, 1352, 1369, 1400

Storytelling 13, 23, 48, 53-54, 91, 141, 246, 252, 259-260, 269, 498, 531, 661, 677, 898, 928, 933, 936, 943-945, 1108, 1394, 1401

Strategic Planning 46, 119, 276, 850-851, 863, 866, 1161, 1169, 1377

Structural Empowerment 973, 984

Structural Ideology 894, 904-906

structural inequality 540-541, 566

Structural Racism 539, 545, 768, 848, 936, 1043, 1156, 1281

Student Affairs 110, 116, 194-195, 209-210, 274, 277, 282, 385, 412, 677, 884, 1091, 1107, 1114-1115, 1169-1170, 1256, 1269, 1275-1276

Student Success 169, 209, 221, 243, 269, 278, 280, 321, 353, 558, 657, 730, 746, 847, 933, 935-936, 939, 941-943, 945, 1069-1070, 1074, 1081-1083, 1089-1090, 1092, 1094, 1160, 1168, 1210, 1216, 1232, 1293, 1366

Student Voice 18, 22, 220, 799, 1288

Students Of Color 18, 22, 38, 103, 193, 210, 228, 237, 242-246, 258, 266, 315, 317, 321, 380, 391, 401-406, 408-410, 412, 458, 460, 493, 498, 538, 541, 548, 551, 647-648, 664, 676, 680, 692, 698, 707, 709-710, 713, 722, 757, 763, 798-799, 805, 833, 836, 840, 842-843, 847, 850, 854, 857-862, 872, 881, 884-885, 891-892, 901, 920, 933-934, 936, 941-943, 945, 997, 1043-1046, 1049-1050, 1056-1058, 1060, 1067, 1100, 1119, 1160, 1183, 1208, 1210, 1217, 1219, 1221, 1306, 1330, 1332, 1334-1335, 1339-1340, 1350, 1359-1360, 1377, 1384-1385

student-teacher relationships 538-539, 545-548, 554-555, 564

Substance Use 28-29, 37, 72, 82, 84-85, 88, 918

Synchronous Learning 1153

systemic advocacy 1365-1366, 1386

Systemic Racism 26, 30-31, 43, 221, 326, 403, 677, 691, 695-696, 720, 738, 810, 823, 825-826, 828-829, 860, 911, 914, 916, 972, 1069, 1075, 1109, 1216, 1286, 1288, 1366-1367, 1378, 1385

T

Teacher Education 12-13, 22-23, 176, 183, 189, 239, 256, 268-269, 313, 317, 321-324, 375-376, 378-380, 382, 385, 390-397, 411, 427, 449, 451, 453-454, 459, 462, 464-465, 469, 482-486, 502, 539, 559, 561-565, 640-642, 657, 706, 759, 764, 766, 808, 837, 864, 882, 904-906, 918, 985-986, 990, 998, 1000-1003, 1114, 1147, 1151-1152, 1206-1208, 1210, 1212, 1215, 1217-1218, 1221, 1240, 1246, 1252, 1317, 1343, 1384

Teacher Education Partnerships 465

Teacher Preparation 176, 183, 232, 310-311, 313-314, 316, 318-323, 375, 379-382, 387, 391, 397, 423-424, 452, 454, 460, 724, 793, 857-858, 861, 892, 916, 964, 1002, 1206, 1210-1212, 1215-1216, 1218, 1240, 1246

Teacher Retention 310, 465, 858

Teacher Shortage 451, 458-459, 462, 464-465, 904, 1216, 1220

Teacher Turnover 168, 231, 233, 454, 465, 848, 854, 856, 1231

teaching method 651, 752, 933-936, 942, 945

Tenure 92, 94-95, 100-101, 111, 114, 116, 198, 398, 406-408, 410-411, 488-490, 499, 502, 729-733, 735-737, 739, 741, 745-748, 750, 860, 942, 982, 1027-1028, 1033-1035, 1040-1042, 1045, 1098, 1102, 1112-1113, 1177, 1321-1322, 1346, 1351-1353, 1358-1359, 1364

Theory of Structural Empowerment 973, 984

Thobani 585-586, 588, 597

transferable skills 212, 272, 278

Transformation 9, 12, 45-47, 52, 57, 102, 159, 176, 203, 209, 253-254, 283-285, 290-292, 303, 306, 359-360, 364, 411, 470, 474-475, 489, 505-506, 508, 513, 521, 524, 530, 534, 556, 571, 588, 593, 609, 625, 679, 771, 805, 830, 840, 883, 921, 931, 1003, 1114, 1130, 1157, 1161, 1166, 1169, 1175, 1184, 1202-1203, 1221, 1239, 1290, 1304, 1339, 1341, 1375, 1391, 1397, 1399, 1405

U

ubiquitous learning 350-351, 357-358, 365, 367-371

Index

Ubuntu 284, 287-289, 298, 300, 302, 306, 573, 1393, 1402
underrepresented communities 277
underrepresented student leader 271, 277
Undocumented 399-401, 1254-1261, 1266, 1269-1280
Universal Design For Learning 220, 225-227, 313, 350-351, 353, 364-367, 369-371, 658
Upward Assimilation 969
Upward Mobility 130, 407, 736, 854, 866, 1186, 1190-1191
Urban Education 209-210, 241, 271, 278, 311, 463, 485, 520, 559-561, 641, 658, 703, 707, 764-766, 905-906, 966, 1077, 1112, 1114, 1149, 1170, 1219, 1221, 1342-1343, 1384

V

Visual Culture 341, 585, 587, 724-725, 1219

W

Way Of Being 62, 67, 74, 76, 79-80, 577
White Fragility 20, 22, 25-26, 30, 32, 34, 38, 138, 239, 891, 899-900, 903, 1370, 1380

White Gaze 193, 585-586, 590, 593, 595, 1107
White Privilege 6, 20, 30, 38-39, 91-92, 139, 219, 226, 237, 243, 246, 274, 391, 418, 422, 490, 542, 736, 750, 840-842, 994, 1129, 1157, 1342
white savior industrial complex 241, 245, 252-253
Whiteness As Property 91, 103, 1289
Whiteness Ideology 886-888, 891-893, 896, 899-902, 905-906
Whole-Learner Education 1331, 1345
Woke 11, 191-192, 202, 206, 208, 211, 261, 1111, 1365-1367, 1372, 1378
Womanism 48-49, 61, 607, 609-610, 621
Workplace 92, 103, 114-115, 118, 130, 213, 272, 275-277, 306, 410, 562, 737, 815-816, 818, 820-823, 825, 828-830, 850, 858, 865, 883, 950, 976, 979, 982, 984, 1026-1028, 1030, 1033-1038, 1104, 1119, 1123, 1171, 1173, 1175, 1180, 1185-1187, 1189-1191, 1194, 1205, 1347, 1364

Y

Yoder 242, 254, 1346, 1348-1349, 1351, 1364

Recommended Reference Books

IGI Global's reference books are available in three unique pricing formats:
Print Only, E-Book Only, or Print + E-Book.

Shipping fees may apply.

www.igi-global.com

ISBN: 978-1-7998-0018-7
EISBN: 978-1-7998-0019-4
© 2020; 317 pp.
List Price: US$ **195**

ISBN: 978-1-5225-9412-3
EISBN: 978-1-5225-9414-7
© 2020; 477 pp.
List Price: US$ **195**

ISBN: 978-1-5225-9195-5
EISBN: 978-1-5225-9197-9
© 2020; 341 pp.
List Price: US$ **195**

ISBN: 978-1-5225-5996-2
EISBN: 978-1-5225-5997-9
© 2018; 398 pp.
List Price: US$ **195**

ISBN: 978-1-7998-0128-3
EISBN: 978-1-7998-0130-6
© 2020; 338 pp.
List Price: US$ **195**

ISBN: 978-1-7998-1702-4
EISBN: 978-1-7998-1704-8
© 2020; 301 pp.
List Price: US$ **195**

Do you want to stay current on the latest research trends, product announcements, news, and special offers?
Join IGI Global's mailing list to receive customized recommendations, exclusive discounts, and more.
Sign up at: www.igi-global.com/newsletters.

Publisher of Peer-Reviewed, Timely, and Innovative Academic Research

www.igi-global.com ✉ Sign up at www.igi-global.com/newsletters   f facebook.com/igiglobal   t twitter.com/igiglobal   in linkedin.com/igiglobal

Ensure Quality Research is Introduced to the Academic Community

Become an Evaluator for IGI Global Authored Book Projects

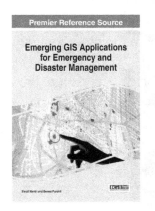   

The overall success of an authored book project is dependent on quality and timely manuscript evaluations.

Applications and Inquiries may be sent to:
development@igi-global.com

Applicants must have a doctorate (or equivalent degree) as well as publishing, research, and reviewing experience. Authored Book Evaluators are appointed for one-year terms and are expected to complete at least three evaluations per term. Upon successful completion of this term, evaluators can be considered for an additional term.

If you have a colleague that may be interested in this opportunity, we encourage you to share this information with them.

IGI Global Author Services

Providing a high-quality, affordable, and expeditious service, IGI Global's Author Services enable authors to streamline their publishing process, increase chance of acceptance, and adhere to IGI Global's publication standards.

Benefits of Author Services:

- **Professional Service:** All our editors, designers, and translators are experts in their field with years of experience and professional certifications.
- **Quality Guarantee & Certificate:** Each order is returned with a quality guarantee and certificate of professional completion.
- **Timeliness:** All editorial orders have a guaranteed return timeframe of 3-5 business days and translation orders are guaranteed in 7-10 business days.
- **Affordable Pricing:** IGI Global Author Services are competitively priced compared to other industry service providers.
- **APC Reimbursement:** IGI Global authors publishing Open Access (OA) will be able to deduct the cost of editing and other IGI Global author services from their OA APC publishing fee.

Author Services Offered:

English Language Copy Editing
Professional, native English language copy editors improve your manuscript's grammar, spelling, punctuation, terminology, semantics, consistency, flow, formatting, and more.

Scientific & Scholarly Editing
A Ph.D. level review for qualities such as originality and significance, interest to researchers, level of methodology and analysis, coverage of literature, organization, quality of writing, and strengths and weaknesses.

Figure, Table, Chart & Equation Conversions
Work with IGI Global's graphic designers before submission to enhance and design all figures and charts to IGI Global's specific standards for clarity.

Translation
Providing 70 language options, including Simplified and Traditional Chinese, Spanish, Arabic, German, French, and more.

Hear What the Experts Are Saying About IGI Global's Author Services

"Publishing with IGI Global has been **an amazing experience** for me for sharing my research. The **strong academic production** support ensures quality and timely completion." – Prof. Margaret Niess, Oregon State University, USA

"The service was **very fast, very thorough, and very helpful** in ensuring our chapter meets the criteria and requirements of the book's editors. I was **quite impressed and happy** with your service." – Prof. Tom Brinthaupt, Middle Tennessee State University, USA

Learn More or Get Started Here:

For Questions, Contact IGI Global's Customer Service Team at cust@igi-global.com or 717-533-8845

IGI Global
PUBLISHER of TIMELY KNOWLEDGE
www.igi-global.com

Celebrating Over 30 Years of Scholarly Knowledge Creation & Dissemination

www.igi-global.com

InfoSci-Books

A Database of Nearly 6,000 Reference Books Containing Over 105,000+ Chapters Focusing on Emerging Research

GAIN ACCESS TO **THOUSANDS** OF REFERENCE BOOKS AT **A FRACTION** OF THEIR INDIVIDUAL LIST **PRICE**.

InfoSci®-Books Database

The **InfoSci®-Books** is a database of nearly 6,000 IGI Global single and multi-volume reference books, handbooks of research, and encyclopedias, encompassing groundbreaking research from prominent experts worldwide that spans over 350+ topics in 11 core subject areas including business, computer science, education, science and engineering, social sciences, and more.

Open Access Fee Waiver (Read & Publish) Initiative

For any library that invests in IGI Global's InfoSci-Books and/or InfoSci-Journals (175+ scholarly journals) databases, IGI Global will match the library's investment with a fund of equal value to go toward **subsidizing the OA article processing charges (APCs) for their students, faculty, and staff** at that institution when their work is submitted and accepted under OA into an IGI Global journal.*

INFOSCI® PLATFORM FEATURES

- Unlimited Simultaneous Access
- No DRM
- No Set-Up or Maintenance Fees
- A Guarantee of No More Than a 5% Annual Increase for Subscriptions
- Full-Text HTML and PDF Viewing Options
- Downloadable MARC Records
- COUNTER 5 Compliant Reports
- Formatted Citations With Ability to Export to RefWorks and EasyBib
- No Embargo of Content (Research is Available Months in Advance of the Print Release)

*The fund will be offered on an annual basis and expire at the end of the subscription period. The fund would renew as the subscription is renewed for each year thereafter. The open access fees will be waived after the student, faculty, or staff's paper has been vetted and accepted into an IGI Global journal and the fund can only be used toward publishing OA in an IGI Global journal. Libraries in developing countries will have the match on their investment doubled.

To Recommend or Request a Free Trial:
www.igi-global.com/infosci-books

eresources@igi-global.com • Toll Free: 1-866-342-6657 ext. 100 • Phone: 717-533-8845 x100

www.igi-global.com

CPSIA information can be obtained
at www.ICGtesting.com
Printed in the USA
LVHW060446300122
709439LV00050B/247

9 781668 450178